AND
T0402279

LANDSCAPE

King Island (*Ugiuvak*). This small island in the Bering Sea, located off the southwest coast of the Seward Peninsula, is known for the unusual style of the wooden dwellings on stilts that were built along the steep slopes of the island's now abandoned village, but its interior landscape is equally striking. The group of tors in the distance is called *Navatat*, while the cluster in the background on the right is called *Kiŋikmiut*. View to the north, June 2006. Photograph by Matt Ganley.

Strong winds and choppy waters herald the beginning of winter near the Inuit village of Kangiqsujuaq, in Nunavik, 2008. The waters around Kangiqsujuaq are home to polar bears, seals, and beluga whales. A bowhead whale hunt has been revitalized in the nearby Hudson Strait—an activity that involves the entire community. Photograph by Scott A. Heyes.

Grand Central Pass, in the Kigluaik Mountains of the Seward Peninsula. At the summit of this broad pass lies *Kuuŋmiut* (Bear Rock Monument), a site commemorating the slaying of a brown bear by *Tudliq*, an ancestral hero of the Qawiaramiut, who lived in the area. View to the north along the Kougarok Road from Nome, 2012. Photograph by Matt Ganley.

EDITED BY KENNETH L. PRATT AND SCOTT A. HEYES

MEMORY AND LANDSCAPE

AU PRESS

Published by AU Press, Athabasca University
1 University Drive, Athabasca, AB T9S 3A3

https://doi.org/10.15215/aupress/9781771993159.01

Cover image by Felix St-Aubin
Cover design by Marvin Harder
Interior design by Natalie Olsen
Maps on pages 29, 63, 130, 159, 240, 303, 304, 306, 308, 311 by
Eric Leinberger
Printed and bound in Canada

Library and Archives Canada Cataloguing in Publication
Title: Memory and landscape : Indigenous responses to a changing North / edited by Kenneth L. Pratt and Scott A. Heyes.
Names: Pratt, Kenneth L., editor. | Heyes, Scott A., editor.
Description: Includes bibliographical references and index.
Identifiers: Canadiana (print) 20220399328 | Canadiana (ebook) 20220400768 | ISBN 9781771993159 (softcover) | ISBN 9781771993166 (PDF) | ISBN 9781771993173 (EPUB)
Subjects: LCSH: Human ecology—Arctic regions. | LCSH: Arctic peoples—Social life and customs. | LCSH: Indigenous peoples—Arctic regions—Social life and customs. | LCSH: Economic development—Arctic regions. | LCSH: Climatic changes—Arctic regions.
Classification: LCC GF891 .M46 2022 | DDC 304.20911/3—dc23

We acknowledge the assistance provided by the Government of Alberta through the Alberta Media Fund.

Fields of cottongrass blanket the gently rolling tundra landscape in the Kougarok area of the central Seward Peninsula, 2009. Photograph by Matt Ganley.

Contents

Part One
Indigenous History and Identity

Part Two
Forces of Change

Part Three
Knowing the Land

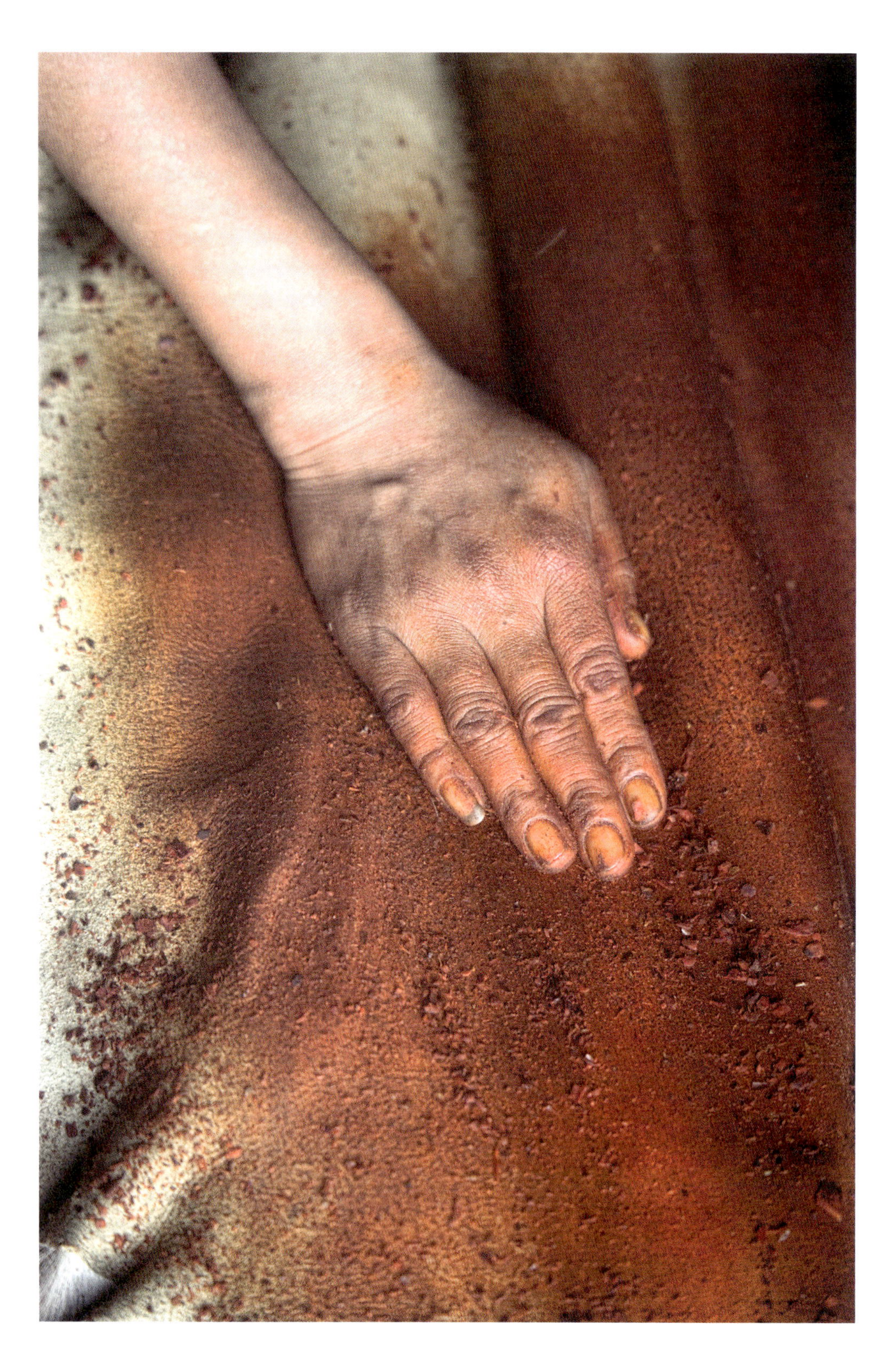

FIGURE F.1 A Chukchi woman rubs boiled alder bark into a reindeer skin to dye it. The skin will be used for making clothes. Iultinsky District, Chukotka Autonomous Okrug, Russia, 2013. Photograph by Bryan Alexander.

Foreword

Each society builds over many centuries its encyclopedia of information and insights. These are what create the very possibility of finding and harvesting the resources of the land. For the Indigenous peoples of the Arctic and Subarctic, as for all who live by hunting and gathering, this expertise, with its detailed understanding of so much of the world in which they live and move, can be a matter of life and death.

Great compendia of knowledge have been passed on from generation to generation in stories and myths—oral culture that is held and shared in the language of each society. A way of speaking is also the intellectual zone where memory and territory converge. The meaning of a place can be said to be inseparable from the language used to describe, understand, and name it. I remember an elder in the North Baffin Island settlement of Mittimatalik saying, in an interview I was filming with him, “The land cannot be known, except by our knowledge.” And when I put together a place-name map for the area around his village, he looked at the myriad of names, which appeared to cover every possible topographical feature, and said, “You can see now how it is that we Inuit never get lost.”

This is a book that explores the many implications of this profound connection between language and land, revealing, in a set of remarkable essays, the detailed links between the way Northern intellectual heritage and language work and the relationships implied between people and their ways of living in their world. At the heart of the significance of each language is, of course, an issue of identity: every Northern culture has seen itself as a distinct people in significant measure because of a way of life and a territory they regard as theirs and a distinctive web of myth, stories, and histories. And of course, they have established and sustained their identity with, and in, their own language. Many Northern peoples have a word for themselves that can be translated as “the human beings” or “real people.” Inuit, Inupiaq, Yupik, Dene, Innu—all these peoples refer to themselves in this way. For them, as for so many hunter-gatherer societies around the world, the idea or even the possibility of being fully human centres on who they are. Other peoples, other ways of speaking and of knowing the land, are, by implication, different in some aspect of their humanity. The force and validity of this view lies in the way each language is tied, and each hunting system ties every member of its community, to a particular physical and intellectual landscape.

The colonial project—or set of projects—that has shaped the North also has to be part of Northern scholarship. Every person who lives with the challenges and transformations that have come to their communities and lands will speak to this aspect of history. From the arrival of whaling ships

to the establishment of trading posts and missions, to the imposition of boarding school programs to climate change—Northerners' lives speak again and again to this complex nexus of events and experience. As the essays here by William E. Simeone, Kenneth L. Pratt, and others reveal, analysis of Arctic and Subarctic heritage must include a deep understanding of how a "Native" land came to be claimed and remade as part of powerful newcomers' territorial and economic domination and domains. Just as these colonists sought to make every part of the world their own by mapping it in their way, and mapping it into their imperial and dominating mindsets, Indigenous peoples have been taking on the task of making their own maps, and of asserting their own expertise, to restate, and where necessary reclaim, their world and their ways of knowing it.

So what happens if Indigenous languages are displaced by the language of the colonists and subsequent newcomers? Do the people now find that they do, after all, "get lost"? Non-speakers of the native language have come to be a majority in many Northern communities. But they still hunt, fish, trap, and tell their stories. Knowledge can be held and passed on in English, French, or Russian. Identity as Yupik, Inupiaq, Inuit, Dene, or Innu does not dissolve if, for instance, Inuktitut, Athabascan, or Inuaimun are no longer spoken by a person, a family, or even a whole society. The loss of a language can seem like the burning to the ground of an entire and

irreplaceable library. But questions about what this loss means to those whose parents or grandparents were unable to pass on their language are of great importance. The colonial suppression of Indigenous languages is a central feature of the history of the North. These and related issues, as discussed in this book, lead us to what both language and language loss mean to an Indigenous person or community of the North at the beginning of the twenty-first century.

There are risks—intellectual and political—that come with a single-minded focus on what is lost. As Mark Nuttall indicates in his chapter here, there is a long tradition in the Arctic of lamenting all that has passed away, often accompanied by fatalistic predictions of cultural and social doom. The North can become a region defined by all that is deemed to be disappearing. Yet analysis of Indigenous societies in the Arctic must include complex understandings of how change is also adaptive, and resilience a feature of Indigenous peoples' history—both modern and ancient. Much scholarship has led to new understandings of both continuity and loss. Compelling research to this effect has come from a range of disciplines—from linguistics to ethnobiology to landscape archaeology to cultural mapping. Each of these, as the reader will discover, can make fascinating contributions to our understanding of Northern peoples, languages, and landscapes by paying the closest possible attention

FIGURE F.2 View of the Imuruk lava field looking north from a volcanic dome known as Gosling Cone, August 2010. Located along the northern coast of the Seward Peninsula, the lava field is a remnant of the now largely submerged Bering Land Bridge that once connected Russia with North America. Volcanic rock features in the area, such as Gosling Cone, traditionally served as the calving ground for the Seward Peninsula caribou herd. Photograph by Matt Ganley.

to what Northern peoples say, know, and do. This is not salvage ethnography so much as the continuing and compelling application of academic discourse to Indigenous knowledge.

Understanding place names—dependent at their foundations on Indigenous peoples' links to their territories—has long been an important element in research on the North. To talk about the land is to use the names for places that are of local and regional significance. For Northern hunting peoples, there are many kinds of significance. The features of the landscape itself—headlands, bays, and hills, as well as lakes, rivers, and shorelines; sites where people have often wanted to live—the spring hunting site, the place where there are many ringed seals, the sheltered area; the location of a piece of ancient history—the spot where a group once starved, where a landslide happened; or of modern history—where a ship was wrecked or a *qallunaaq* (an outsider from the South) is buried; and places of mythic significance. As I learned when living in the Arctic, there are wonderful riches to these place names: the island that is like a pisspot, the red cliffs, the place for quarrying green soapstone. To know these names is to know the territory, to feel linked to the landscape. The essays here show that to document such places, as a matter of scholarship and cultural preservation, is to find and celebrate and sustain a huge, almost infinite treasury of Northern heritage. Michael Chlenov, Robert Drozda, and Murielle Nagy, among others in this volume, take us deep into this fascinating intellectual domain. Gary Holton makes the vital point: "Landscape is a semantic domain."

Indigenous peoples face both the old, all-too-familiar difficulties, and the many new challenges, including modern forms of poverty, self-harming, and socio-political marginalization. Language loss sits among these as both an example and a symbol. Yet the defiance of difficulty, and the refusal to accept losses, are also at the heart of Northern cultural life. Identity is bound up with history and territory, with memory and landscape, as well as with language. It is also linked to the present, and to what is called "modernity." Understanding and appreciating the ancient markers of heritage is one part of understanding the nature of, and risks to, identity. A generation of Arctic leaders and spokespersons testifies to the multifaceted nature of Yupik, Inupiaq, or Athabascan identity. Meaning in life, the meaning of a heritage, cannot be reduced to language or a particular form of activity. Language, memory, and landscape are given their sounds, contents, and significances in a multiplicity of ways. Scholarship explores and discovers the nature of a part of the whole, often by revealing the features of one particular facet. Only with the help of compendia of scholarship does meaning as a whole—of culture as it is and languages as they are spoken—begin to be revealed.

Recovery of history, defending and reclaiming of territory, claiming and augmenting memory—these are part of what it means to be a Northern Indigenous person. Identity turns on what we are, and, with crucial and life-giving relevance, on what we fight to sustain. Scholarship is a vital and enduring part of this battle. Hence the significance of the research and analysis, the data and the reflections on data, set out in this fascinating and invaluable book.

Hugh Brody

Note on Orthography and Terminology

In this book, "Indigenous" is used in its standard sense, to refer to all autochthonous peoples worldwide or to a subset of them resident in a particular area. The term "Native" is no longer current in Canada, nor is "Aboriginal" except with reference to constitutional definitions. The Indigenous peoples of northern Canada are correctly termed "Inuit," while those living in the southern provinces are known as "First Nations." In contrast, the Yup'ik, Inuit, and Dene peoples of Alaska are collectively termed "Alaska Natives," both by the government and the people themselves. Recognizing that such generic terms inevitably erase cultural, linguistic, and geographical differences, however, contributors to this book prefer whenever possible to use the name of the specific group, clan, tribe, nation, or linguistic community under discussion.

Most (although not all) of the Indigenous peoples who appear in this volume speak languages that belong to one of two overarching language families: Yupik and Inuit. Historically, the two families have been grouped into a category called "Eskimo," a term still in use among linguists, although many now prefer the hyphenated term "Inuit-Yupik" (or "Yupik-Inuit"). The Inuit family divides into four main branches, each of which consists of a number of closely related dialects. Moving west to east, the four are Inupiaq, Inuvialuktun, Inuktitut, and Kalaallisut. The first, Inupiaq, is spoken in western coastal areas ranging from Norton Sound and the Seward Peninsula north to Kotzebue and the Kobuk River and then all across Alaska's North Slope. (When the reference is to the dialects spoken north of the Seward Peninsula, "Inupiaq" is spelled "Iñupiaq" to reflect a characteristic shift in pronunciation.) Dialects of Inuvialuktun and Inuktitut are principally spoken in the Canadian North, the former chiefly in the Inuvialuit Settlement Region and the latter in Nunavut, Nunavik, and Nunatsiavut. Kalaallisut is the prevailing dialect of the Inuit language spoken in Greenland. Note that, both culturally and linguistically, it is inaccurate to apply the term "Inuit" to speakers of Yupik languages and dialects.

The Yupik family comprises four languages (or groups of dialects): Naukan, Central Siberian Yupik, Central Alaskan Yup'ik, and Alutiiq. Of these, the Naukan language is critically endangered: its speakers, all of whom reside in far northeastern Russia, on the northernmost tip of the Chukotka Peninsula, now number well under a hundred. The Chukotka Peninsula is also home to one of the two dialects of Central Siberian Yupik, most commonly called the Chaplinski dialect, while the other is spoken on St. Lawrence Island—a large island in the Bering Sea that is officially part of the United States but geographically closer to Russia. Dialects of Central Alaskan Yup'ik—

the apostrophe signals a slight elongation of the *p* sound not present in Central Siberian Yupik—are spoken in western Alaska south of the Seward Peninsula and on nearby Nunivak Island. Finally, Alutiiq (also called Sugpiaq) is spoken in southern coastal areas of Alaska, specifically along the Kenai Peninsula in the vicinity of Prince William Sound and to the southwest, on Kodiak Island and in the upper portion of the Alaska Peninsula.

In addition to Inuit and Yupik languages, many of the Indigenous peoples in Alaska and the Canadian North speak languages that belong to an entirely different family, which linguists have traditionally called Athabaskan (also spelled Athabascan—the standard spelling in Alaska—or Athapaskan). Especially in Canada, however, speakers of these languages increasingly prefer "Dene" to "Athabaskan," as the former is an autonym while the latter is not. Dene/Athabaskan languages are spoken throughout the vast region of the Alaska Interior, as well as in Canada's Yukon, the Northwest Territories, and the northern areas of the western provinces all the way to Manitoba.

It was only well into the post-contact era that these languages began to be written down in the roman alphabet (or, in Alaska, initially in the Cyrillic alphabet). Unsurprisingly, early Euro–North American explorers and missionaries transcribed words and names phonetically, without reference to any consistent orthographic conventions, given that none existed. The predictable result was multiple variations in the spelling of the same name or term. This was the situation faced in the mid-1970s by researchers in Alaska who were responsible for documenting historical places and cemetery sites identified in claims filed under the Alaska Native Claims Settlement Act (ANCSA). In this case, linguists associated with the Alaska Native Language Center, at the University of Alaska Fairbanks, were able to assist ANCSA researchers by providing the correct spellings of Indigenous site names. These spellings were then typically highlighted in some way (by italic, boldface, or underlining) in final reports on the sites.

The practice endures with ANCSA researchers and has since been adopted by some other researchers in Alaska: Indigenous place and personal names are italicized when their spellings are known to conform to the standard orthographic system now used for the language in question. Not only does the italic serve to indicate that a given spelling is correct, but it also focuses attention on the importance of both accuracy and consistency in the representation of Indigenous names and terms. Fortunately, we have moved beyond the era in which Indigenous languages were actively suppressed, with Indigenous individuals assigned new, Christian names, and points on the landscape routinely rechristened. Vigorous and dedicated efforts are now underway to resuscitate and reclaim Indigenous languages that were (and in too many cases still are) hovering on the brink of extinction. We further hold that, if researchers who study Indigenous cultures seek to honour Indigenous languages, they must be willing to learn how to spell the words in them and, with the aid of a guide to the orthographic system in use, at least to approximate their pronunciation. As we embark on the United Nations International Decade of Indigenous Languages (2022–32), making such a commitment seems more than merely appropriate: it is a matter of solidarity.

MEMORY AND LANDSCAPE

FIGURE I.1 In the depth of winter, the forested bottomlands of Alaska, dominated by spindly, stunted black spruce, exhibit an otherworldly quality—a feeling exaggerated by an atmosphere of dim light and frigid temperatures. Under such conditions, it is not unusual to glimpse things in the shadows that may or may not be there. Attempting to capture this ethereal world at −30°C (−22°F), the photographer used a vintage Polaroid SX-70 camera loaded with film not intended for use at temperatures below 10°C (50°F). This photograph was taken in February 2018 near the confluence of the Chena and Little Chena Rivers, upstream from Fairbanks, Alaska. Photograph by Robert Drozda.

Introduction

We pay respect to the Indigenous peoples whose homelands are represented in this book and to their elders, past and present, for sharing their wisdom and for making their knowledge available for future generations.

This is fundamentally a book about cycles of life, both natural and cultural. It concerns changes in nature, in people, in language, culture, lifestyles, and ways of thinking—changes that can ultimately be understood only through the context of the past. But it also is a book about loss, dispossession, hope, resilience, regeneration, and the difficulties involved in trying to interpret and comprehend the complex relationships between Indigenous peoples and Northern landscapes. More concisely, it explores how relationships among language, memory, and landscape shape Indigenous identity but remain fluid and may be reworked in response to environmental changes and external cultural pressures.

The book presents multifaceted perspectives on belonging and knowing in Northern landscapes, with identity, representation, land-based connections, heritage, oral history, place names, linguistics, and culture change as cross-cutting themes. The essential and inextricable connections between the land and Indigenous self-identity have been explored in anthropological studies that focus primarily on the ethnographic dimensions of Indigenous landscapes (see, for example, Basso 1996; Feld and Basso 1996; Collignon 2006; Johnson and Hunn 2010; Krupnik, Mason, and Horton 2004). Although this book does the same, our approach differs in emphasizing the *diachronic* dimension of Indigenous languages and family or group histories on the land, as preserved and interpreted through memory. This diachronic orientation underscores our conviction that an awareness of the historical contexts of Indigenous peoples' relationships with their homelands is essential to interpreting Indigenous identity. Indeed, it would be inaccurate to portray *any* Indigenous group in a manner that denies them a history, as if the connection its members feel to the land—and their basic cultural identity—has remained unchanged over time. In more pragmatic terms, situating the place-based maps and personal testimonials on which Indigenous land claims are often founded (see, for example, Freeman 1976; Goldschmidt and Haas 1998; Tobias 2009) within their historical contexts can significantly increase their value and authority in the legal arena (see Miraglia 2009; Pratt 2009b).

In this book, Indigenous and non-Indigenous occupants and researchers of the North share their voices, stories, and experiences of Northern landscapes. Across twelve chapters that explore Indigenous perspectives on language, memory, and landscape—taking in the geographic regions of

Alaska, Arctic Canada, Greenland, and Siberia—the contributors delve into the intricacies of place, attempting to understand how Arctic settings are perceived by those who have long inhabited them. In so doing, they shed light on hitherto unfamiliar associations embedded in these landscapes and on the sense of belonging and sustained connection that Northern peoples feel in relation to specific places (see Brody 1976, 1998; Cruikshank 2005; Nelson 1983).

The individual chapters in this book consider the issue of Indigenous identity from different yet complementary disciplinary perspectives—anthropology, archaeology, architecture, cartography, ethnography, ethnohistory, geography, history, linguistics, and oral history. Some chapters rely heavily on the oral testimony of elders who constituted the last generation of their people to grow up in an essentially traditional lifestyle, rooted in their Indigenous languages, ceremonialism, subsistence practices, and ancestral homelands (Chlenov, Nagy, Pratt, Rank). Other chapters concern themselves more with contemporary Indigenous life in the North and associated tensions created by cultural, economic, environmental, and technological changes over the past century (Dowsley et al., Heyes and Jacobs, Nuttall). Still other chapters focus mainly on interpretive matters related to prehistory, colonialism, and language (Crowell, Dawson et al., Drozda, Holton, Simeone). As a whole, the contributions to this volume reveal both direct and subtle ways in which memories inextricably tied to the land continue to define and express Indigenous identity.

Collectively, the essays gathered here also showcase the richness of Indigenous knowledge and illustrate the ways in which it is continually updated and expanded. It is our hope that researchers and students working in the North, along with those interested in Indigenous knowledge more broadly, will take away from the book a sense of how Indigenous identities are formed through land-based interactions, as well as by working to keep languages alive and remembering the past through tangible forms and intangible practices.

With continuing declines in Indigenous-language speakers and the reduced amount of time members of many Indigenous groups now spend on the land, the study and documentation of place names has become increasingly important as a means for understanding Indigenous histories in Northern landscapes. Place names are records of collective memory that provide information about a broad range of topics, including Indigenous cultural history, subsistence practices, and perceptions of local landscapes (see Collignon 2006; Holton and Thornton 2019; Kari and Fall 2003; Pratt 2009a; Schreyer 2019)—as well as associated changes over time. They testify to the deep connections between Indigenous peoples and the land and to the traditional importance of learning and remembering the names of local places, which cannot be overemphasized. Knowledge of place names and the stories attached to them gave Indigenous peoples rich mental maps of the landscapes they inhabited, enabling them not only to navigate those lands but also to survive in them (see Aporta 2016; Burch 1971). Place names are also particularly valuable evidence for interpreting Indigenous peoples' use and occupancy of the landscapes that constitute their homelands and for reconstructing population movements and the sometimes shifting boundaries between the territories in which specific groups

FIGURE I.2 Elijah (*Kakiññaaq*) Kakinya (1895–1986), seen here wearing a *sigguktaak*, or loon-skin headdress, was the last surviving Nunamiut hunter to have wielded a spear in a *tuttsiuvaqtuat* hunt, in which herds of caribou were driven into a lake and then speared from *qayaqs*. Once commonplace among his people, the Inland Iñupiat (Nunamiut) of the Brooks Range in north-central Alaska, these hunts rapidly fell out of use in the early 1890s with the widespread availability of reliable repeating rifles. The hunt in which Kakinya participated took place during the late summer of 1944 at *Narvaqłuqtaq*, better known today as Little Chandler Lake. This photograph was taken in the summer of 1985. when Kakinya returned to the site of the 1944 hunt to recount his memories of the event. Photograph by Grant Spearman.

lived (Burch et al. 1999; Pratt 2012). Collections of Indigenous place names can also contribute substantially to the documentation and preservation of Indigenous languages.[1] For all of these reasons, it is no surprise that half of the contributors to this volume focus on one aspect or another of Indigenous place names.

Indigenous voices and oral history are at the core of this volume. Elevating Indigenous voices and recognizing Indigenous people as experts in their own history are crucial steps toward a better understanding of how Northern settings are known and conceptualized. With the support and guidance of our Indigenous friends, collaborators, and colleagues, we have thus consistently sought in this book to place Indigenous knowledge first, while at the same time approaching it thoughtfully and critically (as one should any piece of information or knowledge), thereby upholding its status as evidence (for examples, see Burch 1991, 1998, esp. 12–19, 2010; Pratt 2010, 2021; Trigger 1987), rather than accepting it at face value, which seems to us to

FIGURE I.3 Despite the changes wrought by modern Western culture, hunting, fishing, trapping, processing wild game, sharing, and getting out on the land continue to provide not merely sustenance but also a vital opportunity to pass down cultural traditions from one generation to the next. Here, a Yup'ik woman named Sophie Phillip processes muskrat and spring waterfowl in the kitchen of her family's home in Tuluksak, Alaska, May 1988. Photograph by Robert Drozda.

diminish its legitimacy. We have also ensured that, as far as is possible, Indigenous names and terms are spelled in accordance with the standard systems of orthography that have been developed for specific languages. This underscores our conviction that if one wishes to demonstrate respect for Indigenous languages, then one needs to transcribe them accurately and in a systematic manner. We consider this practice especially important relative to Indigenous place and personal names, many of which colonial parties willfully replaced with new names to further their efforts to dispossess Indigenous peoples of their homelands and to erase all traces of their former presence. Those actions also undermined Indigenous identities and languages and contributed to the loss of cultural histories.

The book comprises three thematic parts, each of which begins with a brief reflection that approaches the theme from an Indigenous perspective. The first section, "Indigenous History and Identity," opens with a poetic celebration of the land written by two Inuk hunters from Kangiqsualujjuaq, a village located off the southeastern shore of Ungava Bay, in the territory of Nunavik, in northern Québec: Vinnie Baron, who works as a teacher, and her husband, Felix St-Aubin, who is a photographer. Together, they set the scene and tone of the book, reminding us that the land is beautiful in so many ways. It provides nourishment, it serves as a tonic, and it has the capacity to bring families together. The land heals. The photographs that accompany their words were taken on family hunting and fishing excursions. Overall, the contribution underscores how enduring subsistence practices and living on the land continue to define Indigenous identity in the North for men and women alike.

In the first chapter, Aron Crowell discusses creation stories held in oral traditions by the Yakutat Tlingit of Southeast Alaska and reports on the findings of a research project that sought to better understand the migration route their ancestors used to reach their present-day homeland. Crowell develops a picture of the timing and probable shape of this route by drawing on three sources: migration stories recounted by elders, geological information about the deglaciated period, and archaeological data obtained from the excavation of historical settlements, including housing forms, tools, ornamentation, and faunal remains. Although archaeologists have long tended to ignore Indigenous oral history as a potential source of information, Crowell does the opposite by emphasizing oral history accounts about Tlingit history in the Yakutat Bay area in his interpretations of related archaeological and other evidence. As such, the essay helps to bridge the divide between oral traditions and Western scientific methods and highlights the inherent value of the knowledge embedded in oral traditions.

In the following chapter, Murielle Nagy focuses on the Inuvialiut people of the western Canadian Arctic and explores the conventions they use to name and remember places on the land. Drawing on separate toponomy studies held decades apart, she discusses why knowledge of Inuvialuit place names has decreased in recent times and considers the impact this loss may be having on Inuvialuit constructions of identity. Her case study illustrates changes in the way that Indigenous languages are used to recall specific points on the landscape and environmental features—changes that are relevant to other Indigenous communities around the globe

FIGURE I.4 Setting up camp near favoured fishing grounds in the Koroc River valley, in northern Nunavik, not far from the Labrador border. A propane gas lamp illuminates an Inuit campsite, casting enough light to chop wood and prepare bedding for a warm night outdoors. A wood stove, crafted from an outboard motor gas tank, keeps the occupants warm throughout an autumn night in 2008. Photograph by Scott A. Heyes.

in which identity is especially strongly bound up with land-based activities, resources, and mobility.

The interplay between toponomy and identity continues in chapter 3 with Robert Drozda's intricate effort to trace the origins of two place names on Nunivak Island, located in the Bering Sea off the southwestern coast of Alaska. Informed by his deep personal knowledge of the island and its people—and a long-standing interest in the Cup'ig language, which is unique to Nunivak Island—Drozda's systematic and comprehensive research journey yields tantalizing clues but no clear answers. In the course of his quest, however, intriguing details about the Cup'ig language are revealed that raise many stimulating questions, none of which will be easily resolved. His analysis touches on complex aspects of the island's Indigenous history (including regional intergroup relations), and reveals strong and enduring ties between place names and local oral traditions. It also highlights the urgent need for further linguistic research on the endangered Nunivak Cup'ig language and the abundance of existing resources available to support such work.

In the fourth and final chapter in part 1, Martha Dowsley, Scott Heyes, Anna Bunce, and Williams Stolz explore Inuit women's identity and the land in the eastern Canadian Arctic region through the activities associated with berry picking. The essay highlights how berry picking is more than a peripheral activity carried out by Inuit women and children while Inuit men are out hunting. Rather, it serves as an opportunity to recall memories and stories related to specific places on the land, for observing and accumulating knowledge about climatic conditions, and for maintaining physical health and mental well-being. From an ethnoecological perspective, berry picking is one of many examples of human-plant relationships among Northern peoples that have arguably been undervalued and warrant in-depth research.

Part 2, "Forces of Change," is introduced by Apay'u Moore, an accomplished artist from the Bristol Bay region of Alaska whose deeply felt connections to the land and to her Yup'ik roots infuse her artistic creations. She speaks openly and honestly of her struggles as a person of mixed ancestry—to earn ownership of the Yup'ik identity she proudly embraces. In this quest to internalize her heritage, she has worked to become fluent in the Yup'ik language, to learn and practice traditional subsistence skills, and to live simply and economically, without wasting what has been given to her. Moore also reflects on her upbringing, on the extremely close bond she enjoyed with her namesake uncle, on her love of family and fishing, and on the awakening and growth of her Yup'ik spirit. In so doing, she tacitly reveals what it means to be Indigenous in a modern setting.

In chapter 5, Mark Nuttall offers an intriguing and thoughtful discussion of human-environment relations among the Inuit of West Greenland. In his analysis, he pays special attention to the concept of "absence" to highlight the people's strong attachment to place and sense of community, as well as their mobility, flexibility, and resilience. Nuttall reasons that the Inuit people's long history of adaptations to and perseverance in the face of past social, economic and environmental changes have prepared them well for contending with the impacts of rapid climate change today. He makes the important point that Indigenous peoples of the North are far better equipped—practically and philosophically—to respond successfully to the threats posed by modern climate change than others might believe. His discussion provides a much-needed counterpoint to ill-informed but widely held assumptions that position Indigenous peoples as powerless victims when confronted with situations of rapid change.

In the following chapter, Kenneth Pratt marshals an array of documentary evidence—including Indigenous oral histories, archaeological survey data, archival documents, and historical accounts—to describe and interpret landscape changes in Alaska's Yukon Delta over the past century or so, as well as to illustrate people's enduring connections to place. He emphasizes the fact that landscapes and environments are dynamic and that Yup'ik people in the Yukon Delta have often been able to meet the demands that changes bring. In the relatively recent past, Indigenous residents of the region were able to relocate their villages in response to major transformations in the landscape and environmental disasters such as floods. Yet the infrastructure of modern communities undermines such flexibility and mobility, and rapid climate change challenges peoples' anticipatory capacity. Finally, Pratt offers a cautionary warning to researchers that major ecosystem changes in a specific region during a period of indisputable climate change may not be explainable solely in terms of that process.

In chapter 7, William Simeone focuses on the Ahtna people of the Copper River region of Alaska and, in particular, on how the doctrine of *terra nullius* allowed colonial cartographers to obliterate Ahtna history and their traditional custodianship of the land. The Copper River's important associations with trade and transportation, the mining industry, and salmon fishing draw attention to the power wielded by colonial cartographers in their production of maps. While early maps included details and locations of Ahtna territorial boundaries and place names, these were progressively erased from subsequent maps as Euro-American presence within the Ahtna homeland expanded. Simeone presents and discusses a series of maps of the region to illustrate their significance to non-Ahtna outsiders (such as explorers, miners, speculators, and developers) and to demonstrate how those maps supported a campaign of sovereignty that, on paper, dispossessed the Ahtna of their Copper River homeland. Simeone also reminds us, however, that maps are only one way of looking at place and that Ahtna culture, identity, and knowledge of place names has remained steadfast.

In chapter 8, Scott Heyes and Peter Jacobs discuss the built environment in Nunavik, the Inuit region that spans roughly the northernmost third of Québec, and explore the ways in which the Inuit sense of identity with the land might be amplified through the creation of a more culturally appropriate approach to planning, architecture, and design. The authors present examples of how Inuit have created and shaped their built environment in historic and contemporary times and argue that the environment of Arctic communities and village settings would be enriched by attention to Inuit perceptions of the environment and the skills and talents they possess with regard to placemaking and design. As they strongly suggest, architectural forms across the Arctic should be less formulaic and more representative of the particular physical and social settings that distinguish Inuit communities from each other.

Part 3, "Knowing the Land," is introduced by Evon Peter, who grew up in a Gwich'in village in far northeastern Alaska. Recalling the time he spent as a child with his grandfather, Peter writes of the urgent need for efforts to preserve the Gwich'in language and cultural identity. It was from his grandfather that he learned to appreciate how the land was perceived and understood by his elders and came to realize that the knowledge they hold—the entire Gwich'in cultural heritage—is inextricably bound up with the Gwich'in language itself, a Dene (or Athabascan) language that has for some time hovered on the brink of extinction. As Peter recognizes, he and other members of his community have both cultural and moral obligations to rescue and revitalize their language. His commitment to preserving the heritage on which Gwich'in cultural identity rests illustrates the ongoing application of the knowledge and values instilled by elders.

In chapter 9, Gary Holton provides an insightful, comparative discussion of the important role of landscape in the languages and ontologies of Indigenous Arctic peoples. His focus falls on how the language of the land is constructed and spatially conceptualized in Inuit-Yupik (Eskimo) and Dene (Athabascan) languages. Holton approaches his topic by unpacking the structure of both languages, with an emphasis on orientation systems and ways of conveying nearness, motion, and position in each language. As his analysis suggests, understanding the structural elements of Indigenous language and the influence these linguistic structures have on how people conceptualize their position in space and place provides valuable insights into how Indigenous people mentally map the environment and their homelands. Holton's comparison of these two language families demonstrates that even though Indigenous groups may share knowledge of the same physical settings, their language usage is likely to privilege particular ways of parsing the landscape that in turn give rise to different place-naming strategies.

In the following chapter, Louann Rank examines conventions for naming settlements and waterways in an inland area of Alaska's Yukon-Kuskokwim Delta located along an upstream section of the Kuskokwim River. Drawing extensively on Yup'ik oral histories, she discusses how place names reflect an extensive knowledge of fish species and their life-cycle activities, as well as of the routes along which they migrate. In particular, she identifies an intriguing pattern in which a base name, often that of a particular stream, is also incorporated into the name of the stream's source lake and the name of a seasonal fish camp, often located at the mouth of the stream where it joins a larger river. As attested in interviews conducted in the 1980s with elders whose families have lived in the area for many generations, fish were, and remain, the single most important source of subsistence for Yup'ik communities, including those situated at some distance from the coast. Unsurprisingly, then, not only have fishing practices long shaped the relationship of local groups to the land and waterways around them: they have become inseparable from Yup'ik identity itself.

In chapter 11, Peter Dawson, Colleen Hughes, Donald Butler, and Kenneth Buck explore the capacity of local place names to serve as a guide to the emotional attachments that Indigenous people have to the landscapes they inhabit. Seeking to respond to critics of the "phenomenological turn" in landscape archaeology, the authors set out to develop a systematic methodology for assessing the subjective dimensions of language. Drawing on an electronic database of Inuit place names from the Kivalliq Region of Nunavut, they apply an algorithmic natural language processing technique known as sentiment analysis to assess the emotional valence of place names in the area. The authors contend that landscapes are more than the sum of topographical and geological features—that terrain is as much affective as physical. They accordingly argue that attention to the subjective content of place names is essential to understanding the experience of landscape and can provide archaeologists with a more complete picture of sites under study. Their analysis suggests that sentiment analysis can be a valuable methodological tool for capturing the intangible qualities of place.

The final chapter, by Michael A. Chlenov (translated from the Russian by Katerina Wessels), focuses on Siberian Yupik and Chukchi place names in the Senyavin Strait area of the Chukotka Peninsula, in far northeastern Russia. His discussion is introduced by Igor Krupnik, who provides background information about the Senyavin Strait region, an area whose Indigenous residents underwent a process of relocation by Soviet authorities in the 1950s that saw them removed from their traditional villages. Krupnik also calls attention to the progressive loss of both language and cultural heritage, notably in Yupik communities. Chlenov then turns to the linguistic history of the Chukotka Peninsula, where Yupik languages have long coexisted with Chukchi, a language that belongs to an entirely different family. Drawing on irreplaceable research undertaken in the 1970s and 1980s, Chlenov analyzes a corpus of Indigenous place names collected in the Senyavin Strait region. Details are provided about the etymology, definition, and context of each place name, and the location of the site or feature to which the name refers is marked on one in a series of maps. Chlenov's work is especially invaluable at a time when Russian geographical names have gained primacy in the region, while those who can remember the traditional names have all but vanished. More than any other, this closing chapter starkly underscores the fact that once someone dies that person's knowledge is truly lost.

Together, the chapters in this book highlight both the robustness and the fragility of Indigenous knowledge in a variety of cultural and geographic contexts. They also illustrate the inextricable relationship between memory, in which knowledge resides, and place. Perhaps above all, though, they demonstrate that knowing the land itself—walking upon it and feeling its pulse—remains critically important to Indigenous peoples, just as it was for their ancestors. One cannot ultimately appreciate, much less understand, a landscape without standing in it. Nonetheless, we hope this book will convey something of the experience of place and the meanings and memories embedded in landscape. We also hope that the book will illustrate the capacity of Northern Indigenous peoples not only to adapt to but to absorb change.

FIGURE 1.5 On the sea-ice trail at –40°C (–40°F), in the winter of 2005. Here, Inuit hunters from the Nunavik village of Kangiqsualujjuaq make their way north along the Ungava Bay coastline to *Alluviaq* (Abloviak Fiord), a popular winter hunting ground where seals and polar bears abound. Supplies to accommodate three days of travel are carried on a wooden sled known as a *qamutik*. Photograph by Scott A. Heyes.

Acknowledgements

We are sincerely grateful to our Indigenous teachers, friends, and colleagues. Their expertise, insights, and breadth and depth of memory are the bedrock on which this book rests. We thank Francis Broderick, of Arch Graphics, for his initial advice regarding aspects of design and layout; Matt Ganley for permitting us to use his photographs; Emily Kearney-Williams for her illustrations; Dale C. Slaughter for the various maps he produced; Bob Sattler, of the Tanana Chiefs Conference, and the Bureau of Indian Affairs, Branch of Environmental and Cultural Resources Management, for assorted support and assistance. We also thank Pamela Holway, and Megan Hall at Athabasca University Press, for their advice and professional acumen, Erica Hill for producing the index, and the three anonymous reviewers of the original manuscript for helpful comments and suggestions that improved this book.

Ken Pratt thanks all of the contributors for their patience and understanding throughout the compilation and production process, including delays tied to the COVID-19 pandemic. He also greatly appreciates the support and encouragement received from his friends and colleagues Robert Drozda, Matt Ganley, Annie Pardo, Kristin K'eit, Bill Simeone, Margaret Willson, Viktoria Chilcote, and Georgia Blue over the course of this project. A special note of thanks is extended to Robert Drozda for input offered on orthographic considerations and selected parts of the introduction.

Scott Heyes thanks his wife, Christine Heyes LaBond, for her enduring faith and support of this book project and dedicates his work on the book to his sons, Jacob and Henley. . He also wishes to pay special thanks to his Inuit friends in Nunavik, Canada, and particularly to Daniel Annanack and his family in Kangiqsualujjuaq, who have always made him feel welcome and connected to their village and ancestral lands on the Ungava-Labrador Peninsula. Thank you for sharing your knowledge and understandings of the land and the sea with me.

Note

1 One excellent example is the Koyukon Athabaskan dictionary (Jetté and Jones 2000) compiled by native speaker and linguist Eliza Jones, who drew on a lengthy collection of geographical names left behind by Father Jules Jetté (see Jetté 1910), a Jesuit missionary who travelled and lived along the Yukon River for twenty-six years between 1898 and 1927.

References

Aporta, Claudio

2016 Markers in Space and Time: Reflections on the Nature of Place Names as Events in the Inuit Approach to the Territory. In *Marking the Land: Hunter-Gatherer Creation of Meaning in Their Environment*, edited by William Lovis and Robert Whallon, pp. 67–88. Routledge Studies in Archaeology. Routledge, New York.

Basso, Keith H.

1996 *Wisdom Sits in Places: Landscape and Language Among the Western Apache*. University of New Mexico Press, Albuquerque.

Brody, Hugh

1976 Land Occupancy: Inuit Perceptions. In *Inuit Land Use and Occupancy Project: A Report. Volume One: Land Use and Occupancy*, edited by Milton M. R Freeman, pp. 185–242. Department of Indian and Northern Affairs, Ottawa.

1998 *Maps and Dreams*. Douglas and McIntyre, Vancouver.

Burch, Ernest S., Jr.

1971 The Nonempirical Environment of the Arctic Alaskan Eskimos. *Southwestern Journal of Anthropology* 27(1): 148–165.

1991 From Skeptic to Believer: The Making of an Oral Historian. *Alaska History* 6(1): 1–16.

1998 *The Iñupiaq Eskimo Nations of Northwest Alaska*. University of Alaska Press, Fairbanks.

2010 The Method of Ethnographic Reconstruction. *Alaska Journal of Anthropology* 8(2): 123–140.

Burch, Ernest S., Jr., Eliza Jones, Hannah P. Loon, and Lawrence D. Kaplan

1999 The Ethnogenesis of the Kuuvaum Kaŋiaġmiut. *Ethnohistory* 46(2): 291–327.

Collignon, Béatrice

2006 *Knowing Places: The Inuinnait, Landscapes, and the Environment*. Circumpolar Research Series No. 10. Canadian Circumpolar Institute, Edmonton.

Cruikshank, Julie

2005 *Do Glaciers Listen? Local Knowledge, Colonial Encounters and Social Imagination*. University of British Columbia Press, Vancouver.

Feld, Steven, and Keith H. Basso (editors)

1996 *Senses of Place*. School of American Research Press, Santa Fe.

Freeman, Milton M. R. (editor)

1976 *Inuit Land Use and Occupancy Project*. Department of Indian and Northern Affairs, Ottawa.

Goldschmidt, Walter R., and Theodore Haas

1998 *Haa Aani / Our Land: Tlingit and Haida Land Rights and Use*. With an Introduction by Thomas F. Thornton. Sealaska Heritage Foundation, Juneau, and University of Washington Press, Seattle.

Heyes, Scott A., and Kristofer Helgen

2014 *Mammals of Ungava and Labrador: The 1882–1884 Fieldnotes of Lucien M. Turner, Together with Inuit and Innu Knowledge*. Smithsonian Scholarly Press, Washington, DC.

Holton, Gary, and Thomas F. Thornton (editors)

2019 *Language and Toponymy in Alaska and Beyond: Papers in Honor of James Kari*. Language Documentation and Conservation Special Publication No. 17. University of Hawai'i Press, Honolulu, and Alaska Native Language Center, Fairbanks.

Jetté, Jules, S.J.

1910 On the Geographical Names of the Ten'a. "Jottings of a Missionary." Unpublished manuscripts, Alaska Mission Collection, M/F 96, roll 34, Rasmuson Library Archives, University of Alaska Fairbanks.

Jetté, Jules, S.J., and Eliza Jones

2000 *Koyukon Athabaskan Dictionary*. Alaska Native Language Center, University of Alaska Fairbanks.

Johnson, Leslie Main, and Eugene S. Hunn (editors)

2010 *Landscape Ethnoecology: Concepts of Biotic and Physical Space*. Berghahn Books, New York.

Kari, James, and James A. Fall

2003 *Shem Pete's Alaska: The Territory of the Upper Cook Inlet Dena'ina*, 2nd ed. University of Alaska Press, Fairbanks.

Krupnik, Igor, Rachel Mason, and Tonia Horton (editors)

2004 *Northern Ethnographic Landscapes: Perspectives from Circumpolar Nations*. Arctic Studies Center, Smithsonian Institution, Washington, DC.

Miraglia, Rita A.

2009 The Chugach Smokehouse: A Case of Mistaken Identity. In *Chasing the Dark: Perspectives on Place, History and Alaska Native Land Claims*, edited by Kenneth L. Pratt, pp. 250–259. U.S. Department of the Interior, Bureau of Indian Affairs, ANCSA Office, Anchorage.

Nelson, Richard K.

1983 *Make Prayers to the Raven: A Koyukon View of the Northern Forest*. University of Chicago Press, Chicago.

Pratt, Kenneth L.

2009a Interpreting the Record: Kulukak Bay Area Place Names and Cultural Geography. In *Chasing the Dark: Perspectives on Place, History and Alaska Native Land Claims*, edited by Kenneth L. Pratt, pp. 186–201. Bureau of Indian Affairs, ANCSA Office, Anchorage.

2009b Reflections on Russian River. In *Chasing the Dark: Perspectives on Place, History and Alaska Native Land Claims*, edited by Kenneth L. Pratt, pp. 278–297. Bureau of Indian Affairs, ANCSA Office, Anchorage.

2010 The 1855 Attack on Andreevskaia Odinochka: A Review of Russian, American, and Yup'ik Eskimo Accounts. *Alaska Journal of Anthropology* 8(1): 61–72.

2012 Reconstructing 19th-Century Eskimo-Athabascan Boundaries in the Unalakleet River Drainage. *Arctic Anthropology* 49(2):94–112.

2021 A 1925 Epidemic in the Lower Yukon, Alaska. *Arctic Studies Center Newsletter* 28: 7–11. Smithsonian Institution, Washington, DC.

Schreyer, Christine

2019 T'aaḵú Téix̱'i / The Heart of the Taku: A Multifaceted Place Name from the Taku River Tlingit First Nation. In *Language and Toponymy in Alaska and Beyond: Papers in Honor of James Kari*, edited by Gary Holton and Thomas F. Thornton, pp. 57–73. Language Documentation and Conservation Special Publication No. 17. University of Hawai'i Press, Honolulu, and Alaska Native Language Center, Fairbanks.

Tobias, Terry N.

2009 *Living Proof: The Essential Data-Collection Guide for Indigenous Use-and-Occupancy Map Surveys*. Ecotrust Canada and Union of British Columbia Indian Chiefs, Vancouver.

Trigger, Bruce G.

1987 *The Children of Aataentsic: A History of the Huron People to 1660*. McGill-Queen's University Press, Montréal and Kingston.

PART ONE

INDIGENOUS HISTORY AND IDENTITY

VINNIE BARON AND FELIX ST-AUBIN

PERSPECTIVE

Well, here goes our take on our land. Not so eloquent, but to the truth.
As we are.

We try and go out on the land as much as we can. When we can. When we are able to relieve ourselves
from our day-to-day responsibilities.

We go camping with our children,
even when they are still in the *amauti*.
And our children grow up learning to love the land.

When we spend too much time in our community, then we start getting restless and moody.
Being out on the land is therapy. It soothes our souls. It makes us happy. We feel connected.
Being in nature is a natural high. You can't beat it.
It makes you healthy in body and soul.
Even though you have been physically moving, you feel rested.
The work week is much more bearable after we have been out on the land.

We hunt for subsistence. We do not hunt to kill. We do not hunt for trophy.
Or to boast.
We hunt for our food. The most healthy diet.

The land is ours. It is beautiful. It gives us nourishment.
It teaches us that we need to take care of it.
To respect it. And in return, it will respect us.
And nourish us.

We are happy when winter is here. Because everything freezes over and
we are able to go everywhere we want to go.
The land is much more accessible. We can go caribou hunting.
Ptarmigan hunting.

We are happy when spring is here. It is not too cold and not too warm.
We as family go geese hunting. And ice fishing.
The fish are much more alive and go for our hooks!

We are happy when it's summer. We are able to go on our boats and go
camping. Go seal hunting. Go pick mussels and *ammuumajuq*
when low tide is at its lowest.

FACING PAGE A site not far from the Inuit village of Kangiqsualujjuaq, the home of Vinnie Baron and Felis St-Aubin. "This is during Easter when we as a family have a chance to go for a long trip. It is near *Ikirasakittuq*. It is down the bay. The lake is called *Inuksulik*. Meaning there are rock markers. People build rock markers to indicate different things, and they are fixed in different forms. The marker for the lake indicates there are fish. Many, many *big* char there." Photograph by Felix St-Aubin, July 2015.

We are happy when it's fall. The mosquitoes are less. The berries are ripe.
The fishing is good. The fish climb upstream to go to lakes where they
will spend their winter and we are able to hook them with our *nitsik*.
We start collecting fish eggs to make *suvalik*. A great dessert!
The seals are abundant.
We go caribou hunting and their *tunnuq* is thick and delicious!

I can go on and on. But we are essentially a part of our land.
And we strive to practice our ways.
And to speak our language.
We are proud to be an Inuk.
Wouldn't want to be anything else.

NOTE In the Inuktitut language, an *amauti* is the hood of a woman's parka, in which babies are often carried; *ammuumajuq* are clams; a *nitsik* is a hook or lure used in jigging; *suvalik* is a mix of local berries, fish eggs, and oil; and *tunnuq* is fat.

TOP "This is a picture of our daughter, Brenda, fishing at a place called *Kuururjuaq*. This river is located inland and north of our village of Kangiqsualujjuaq. *Kuururjuaq* is a great place to fish all summer long. Brenda loves to go outdoors, and here she is taking out a char. The best fishing at this place is when the ice is gone at the beginning of the summer." Photograph by Felix St-Aubin, April 2017.

BOTTOM "This photograph was taken at *Qamanikallak*, which is some distance up the George River (*Kangirsualujjuap Kuunga*) from our community of Kangiqsualujjuaq. We have to paddle the creek to reach our fishing spots. We start going upriver during fall when the fish are spawning. We had a lunch of fresh fish and tea." Photograph by Felix St-Aubin, August 2015.

FIGURE 1.1 The pyramidal 18,000 ft. (5500 m) peak of Mount Saint Elias (Was'ei Tashaa) rises above the St. Elias Range to the north of Yakutat Bay. Beyond the peak lie the glaciers of the vast Bagley Icefield, which Ahtna migrants crossed on foot during their perilous trek to Yakutat from the Copper River. The mountain's summit on the horizon guided the travelers across the ice and is represented by a totemic crest of the Gineix Kwáan clan. Courtesy Smithsonian Institution, photograph by Aron Crowell, 2014.

ARON L. CROWELL

1 What "Really Happened"

A Migration Narrative from Southeast Alaska Compared to Archaeological and Geological Data

We came from Copper River, like Moses going out of Egypt.
MAGGIE HARRY, 1952 (IN DE LAGUNA 1972, 236)

The Athapascans did not know about the sea, and they called one another together. They said, "What is that so very blue?" They said, "Let us go down to it."
K'ÁADASTEEN, 1904 (IN SWANTON 1909, 349)

When they came down there it was a foreign country. They didn't know what to eat, they didn't know how to live. And the spirits of that place adopted the humans.
CHEWSAA (ELAINE ABRAHAM), 2011

Two categories of oral tradition are recognized by the Yakutat Tlingit of Southeast Alaska. The first is *tlaagú* (myth), ancient narratives with themes that include encounters with *at.óow* beings (animal and nature spirits associated with the genesis of clans) and Raven's acts of cosmological creation. The second is *shkalneek* (story or history), concerning the lives of ancestors, migrations, wars, cataclysms, and other memorable events that occurred closer to the present and "really happened" (de Laguna 1972, 210–211; Edwards 2009). Similar distinctions are maintained by other Northwest Coast groups (Hymes 1990; Thom 2003). Both kinds of narrative are a foundation for cultural heritage and identity (Tlingit *shagóon*) and together with indigenous place names construe a sacred geography of the landscapes where ancestors lived and current generations abide (Thornton 2012). Northwest Coast oral traditions are perpetuated in multiple cultural frames, including songs and recitations at *k̲u.éex'* (Tlingit, memorial services or potlatches) and through depictions of *at.óow* on crest objects and ceremonial regalia.

The two categories of oral tradition may intersect, as when Raven and other *at.óow* beings (like the glacier spirit above) factor in otherwise realist narratives, but recent research suggests that *shkalneek* are substantially endowed with "historicity"—a foundation in knowable and demonstrable fact (Whitely 2002). The historicity of Tlingit, Tsimshian, and other Northwest Coast and interior oral traditions—in particular narratives that are recognized by descendant communities as having this quality—has been probed through comparisons with data from archaeology and geology. Orally recorded events of human and natural history (including earthquakes, glacial advances, and volcanic eruptions) have been correlated with confirmatory evidence and radiocarbon chronologies that extend back up to two millennia (Connor et al. 2009; Crowell and Howell 2013; Crowell et al. 2013; Cruikshank 1981, 2005; de Laguna 1972; Marsden 2001; Martindale 2006; McMillan and Hutchinson 2002; Monteith et al. 2007; Moodie, Catchpole, and Abel 1992; Sterritt 1998).

The aim of this conjunctive approach, carried out in co-operation with Indigenous scholars and communities, is not to prove or disprove the truth of oral traditions. It is, rather, to enjoin two independent sources of information about the past, taking into account their very different modes of production and transmission. Oral narrative is a linguistic medium, one uniquely capable of rendering and conveying through time the rich particularities of past action, personalities, and cultural perspective. Yet spoken stories are inevitably modified as they are told and retold through the generations, no matter how strict the social control over their reproduction (Henige 1974; Mason 2000; Vansina 1965). This inherent plasticity leads to the coexistence of multiple versions of a narrative, the loss or addition of story elements, attributions of events to varied actors or settings, and the comingling of occurrences from different periods. Untethered by calendrical dates, oral narratives tend to have uncertain chronologies and internal ordering.

In contrast, archaeology, geology, and allied sciences utilize quantitative techniques for correlating history and time such as stratigraphic excavation and radiocarbon dating. Given favourable preservation conditions, the buried remains studied by field scientists are far more durable and fixed than verbal accounts. In particular, the archaeological record of dwellings, artifacts, faunal remains, and other traces of human behaviour reveals cultural patterns and progressions that may have been imperceptible to historical participants.

The epistemological characteristics—and limitations—of this type of scientific evidence must also be considered. Excavations uncover only a tiny fraction of the actual physical record, introducing potentially significant sampling biases. Radiocarbon analysis and other dating techniques, while useful, entail error ranges measured in decades or longer, a level of temporal resolution that allows historical periods to be discerned (for example, an era of warfare or cultural change), but which seldom permits single events of lesser duration to come into distinct focus. In contrast to the vivid spoken testimony of oral tradition, archaeology is a strictly forensic record of collective human activity in which any particular individual, however prominent in historical memory, is rarely traceable. With certain exceptions (such as recovered texts, art, and ceremonial facilities), archaeology offers only limited and inferential access to intangible culture and the life of the mind. The contrasting interpretive potentials of oral tradition and scientific data about the human and environmental past thus give rise to both opportunities and challenges for synthesis.

Integrating Oral Tradition, Archaeology, and Geology Related to a Yakutat Migration Narrative

A multi-source methodology is used here to elucidate an important *shkalneek* narrative, about five centuries old, describing the migration of an Athabascan Ahtna clan known as the Gineix̲ K̲wáan from their village at Chitina, on the Copper River, to Yakutat Bay, on the Gulf of Alaska coast. This breakaway group belonged to the Lower Ahtna, who controlled native copper sources in the Chitina River basin and traded extensively in this valuable resource both before and after Western contact with the Tlingit, Eyak, Sugpiat, Dena'ina, Tutchone, and other Indigenous peoples of southern Alaska and the Yukon Territory (de Laguna and McClellan 1981; Pratt 1998).

The migration of the Gineix̲ K̲wáan was a perilous trek of over three hundred kilometres up the Chitina River drainage, south over the Bagley Icefield to the slopes of Mount Saint Elias (North America's second-highest peak) and on to Icy Bay, then over Malaspina Glacier to Yakutat Bay (figure 1.2). On the coast, they encountered and married into an Eyak clan called the G̲alyáx̲ Kaagwaantaan. The narrative concludes with the group's purchase of Yakutat Bay using copper brought from their homeland; the adoption of a new name, Kwáashk'i K̲wáan, referring to a salmon stream in the acquired territory; and the beginning of a new lifeway as coastal hunters (Cruikshank 2001, 382–384; de Laguna 1972, 231–247; Harrington 1940; Swanton 1909, 347–368). The subsequent arrival of Tlingit and Tlingit-Athabascan

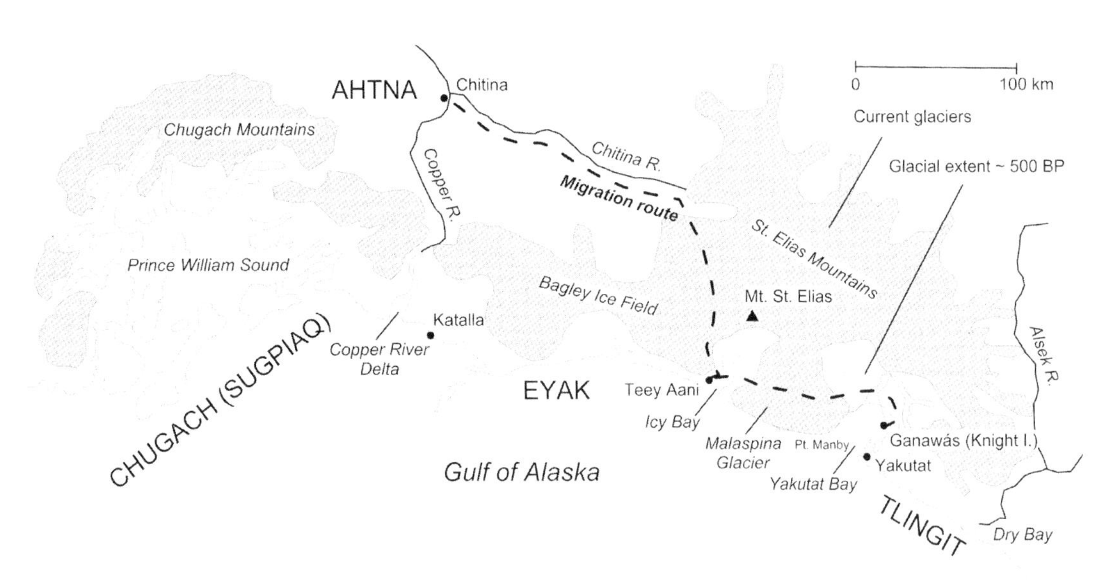

FIGURE 1.2 The Gineix̲ K̲wáan migration route.

immigrants from Dry Bay and further south during the eighteenth century contributed to cultural fusion at Yakutat Bay, and the Kwáashk'i K̲wáan became Tlingit speakers while maintaining aspects of their Ahtna-Eyak cultural identity.

The migration narrative continues to be told by Kwáashk'i K̲wáan elders and is symbolized by an *at.óow* crest design depicting Mount Saint Elias, which guided the migrants across the glaciers. Surviving place names of Eyak, Tlingit, and Ahtna origin commemorate locations on the migration route and at Yakutat Bay (de Laguna 1972; de Laguna et al. 1964; Thornton 2012).

Archaeological sites in the Copper River basin (Hanson 2008; Ketz 1983; Pratt 1998; Shinkwin 1979; Workman 1977) provide a baseline for the group's Ahtna culture in its original setting, but the most specific evidence for dating the Gineix̲ K̲wáan migration comes from Yakutat Bay itself. According to the migration narrative, the clan's first settlement in their new territory was on Ganawás (Knight Island), a village that came to be known as Tlákw.aan (Tlingit, Old Town). Frederica de Laguna, who pioneered efforts to combine ethnology, archaeology, and oral history in the Tlingit region, excavated extensively at Tlákw.aan in 1951 (de Laguna 1972; de Laguna et al. 1964). Her work suggested that Eyak and perhaps Ahtna elements were represented in the culture of the inhabitants and that the site might have been founded as early as the mid-sixteenth century. There was no evidence of occupation into the period of Russian, Spanish, British, and American contact, which started in the late 1780s.

In 2014, the Smithsonian Institution's Arctic Studies Center investigated Tlákw.aan (State of Alaska archaeological site designation YAK-00007) as part of an historical landscape study of Yakutat Bay in collaboration with the Yakutat Tlingit Tribe, the Sealaska Corporation (an Alaska Native regional entity), the US Forest Service, the National Park Service, the State of Alaska, and the National Science Foundation (Crowell 2012). The site was selected as an historical place (site AA-10532) by the Sealaska Corporation (1975) under section 14(h)(1) of the Alaska Native Claims Settlement Act (ANCSA) and certified eligible by the Bureau of Indian Affairs in 1983 (see Pratt [2009] for a discussion of the ANCSA 14(h)(1) Program). Data recovery was conducted through a memorandum of agreement signed by all of the co-operating parties and authorized by the National Historic Preservation Act (16 USC 470f, s. 106).

Fieldwork authorized by the agreement was limited to surface surveys and controlled excavation of a 4 × 1 metre test trench in the shell- and bone-rich midden adjacent to de Laguna's excavations. The objectives of subsurface testing included reinterpretation of the cultural sequence and stratigraphy; recovery of faunal remains for identification; and precise radiocarbon dating of the occupation. De Laguna's Tlákw.aan artifact collection, curated at the University of Pennsylvania Museum in Philadelphia, was subsequently re-examined and photographed. Kwáashk'i K̲wáan elders Elaine Abraham and Lena Farkas retold and helped to interpret the migration story and provided Knight Island and Yakutat Bay place names, assisted by Kwáashk'i K̲wáan Indigenous studies researcher Judith Ramos (University of Alaska Fairbanks) and linguist Gary Holton (University of Hawai'i).

Glaciological data are also relevant to dating the Gineix̲ K̲wáan migration and the reconstruction of its environmental context. During the late Neoglacial period, Yakutat Bay was completely filled with ice—comprised of the combined masses of Hubbard and Malaspina Glaciers—until recession began around AD 1200 during the warming climate of the Medieval Optimum (Barclay, Calkin, and Wiles 2001; Calkin, Wiles, and Barclay 2001). Oral narratives indicate that when the Gineix̲ K̲wáan first arrived, Hubbard Glacier—which today is located some sixty kilometres from the bay's entrance—was

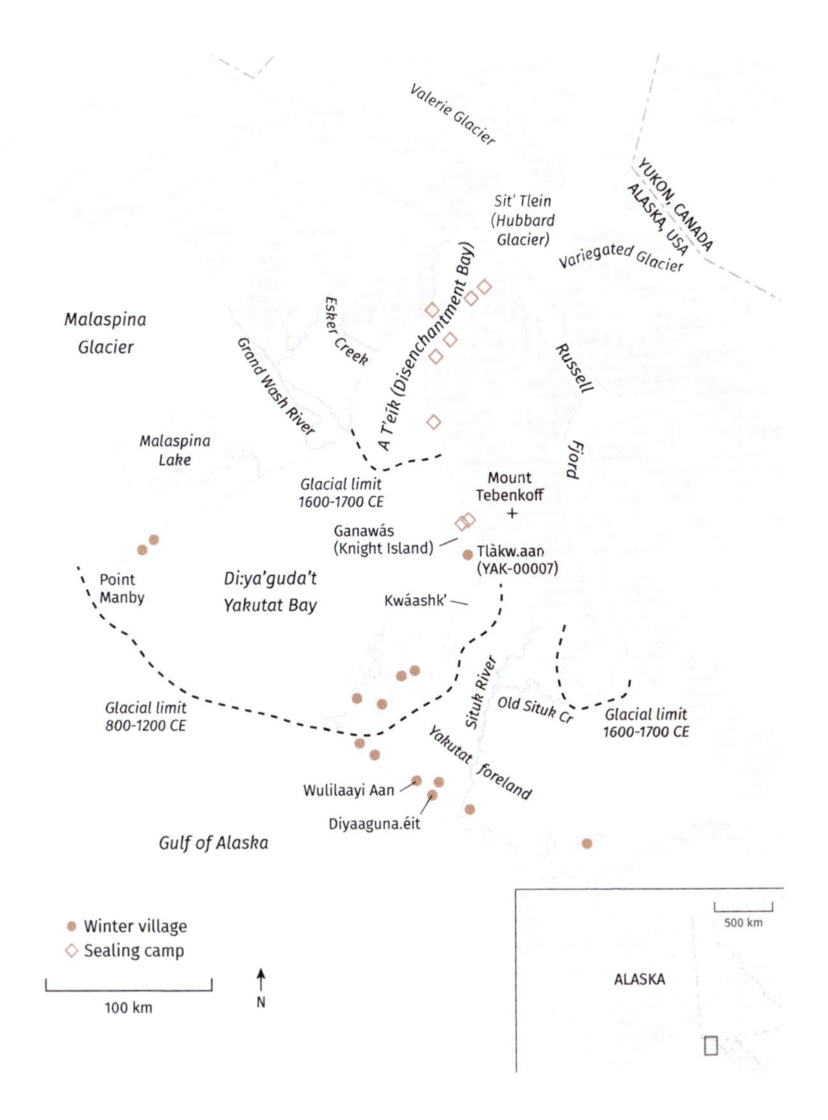

FIGURE 1.3 Glacial limits and archaeological sites, Yakutat Bay and Disenchantment Bay.

still in mid-retreat, a fact to which the Eyak place name for Yakutat Bay (Di:ya'guda't, meaning "mouth of body of salt water") refers (Thornton 2012, 18). Knight Island is said to have then been treeless, indicating recent deglaciation. Geological studies place the glacier's front north of the island near Blizhni Point by about the mid-fifteenth century, suggesting that occupation as early as AD 1400 might have been possible (Barclay et al. 2001). Eyak clans whom the Gineix̱ K̲wáan immigrants found already living at Yakutat Bay, and from whom they purchased the territory, resided by AD 800 at Diyaaguna.éit, Wulilaayi Aan, and other sites on the Yakutat foreland, which remained ice-free during the Neoglacial period (Davis 1996). Yakutat Bay archaeological sites and glacial limits are shown in figure 1.3.

Proximity to the glacier may have been especially significant to the people of Old Town because harbour seals concentrate among the ice floes near its face during the spring birthing and mating season. Hunting at the ice floe rookery, now much farther from Knight Island than in past centuries because of glacial retreat, was traditionally a central focus of the Yakutat subsistence economy and remains important today (Burroughs, Muir, and Grinnell 1901; Crowell 2016; de Laguna 1972; Goldschmidt and Haas 1998; Kruse and Springer 2007; Springer, Iverson, and Bodkin 2007; Wolfe and Mishler 1994).

The Gineix̲ K̲wáan Migration in Oral Tradition

The Gineix̲ K̲wáan migration narrative has been transcribed in multiple versions, which are collated here to demonstrate the core features of the story, illustrate the range of variation, and identify aspects that are potentially verifiable by archaeological or geological data. The earliest documented recounting was given in Tlingit to linguist John Swanton at Sitka in 1904 by K'áadasteen, a Kwáashk'i K̲wáan elder (Swanton 1909, 347–368; see also Jones 2017). This was already several centuries after the original event, so K'áadasteen's was not the "original" version but rather the first to be fixed in writing. A summary of his account is presented below in ten episodes, interposed with variants and additions provided by later narrators. In the collation the speakers are identified by their initials and clan affiliations, and author's notes are in square brackets.

In addition to K'áadasteen (K., Kwáashk'i K̲wáan), the narrators include Maggie Harry (MH, Kwáashk'i K̲wáan), who told the migration story to linguist John Harrington in 1939 (Harrington 1940) and later to Frederica de Laguna (de Laguna 1972, 235–236). In 1949, Harry Bremner (HB, Kwáashk'i K̲wáan) provided the longest and what de Laguna considered to be the most authoritative recent version (de Laguna 1972, 231–233). She heard other retellings and comments between 1949 and 1954 from Sarah Williams (SW, Kwáashk'i K̲wáan); Susie Abraham (SA, Kwáashk'i K̲wáan); Katy Dickson Isaac (KDI, Kwáashk'i K̲wáan); Helen Bremner (HB, G̲alyáx̲ Kaagwaantaan); John Bremner (JB, Kwáashk'i K̲wáan); Olaf Abraham (OA, Teikweidí); Jack Ellis (JE, L'uknax.adí); and Jenny Kardeetoo (JK, Kwáashk'i K̲wáan) (de Laguna 1972, 236–241). George Johnson (GJ, Tcicqédi), an Eyak man born in Cordova, commented on the story to Harrington (Harrington 1940). Elaine Abraham (EA, Kwáashk'i K̲wáan) and Lena Farkas (LF, Kwáashk'i K̲wáan) recounted the story to us at Yakutat in 2011 (figure 1.4). De Laguna transcribed Ahtna songs dating to the migration (de Laguna 1972, 1155–1157, 1226–1227), and these are still performed at contemporary Yakutat potlatches.

FIGURE 1.4 Lena Farkas and Elaine Abraham recording Yakutat place names, 2011 (Courtesy Judith Ramos).

SUMMARY NARRATION

1. K'áadasteen's account begins with the death of a chief named Łtaxda'x who owned a valuable feast dish [an *at.óow* object symbolizing clan identity] and a *tináa* [copper shield, an *at.óow* wealth item]. The name of the clan was Ca'dadūx (K).

   a. Łtaxda'x was the leader of a Raven moiety Copper River [Ahtna] clan that lived at Chitina. This clan was called the Gineix̱ K̲wáan [rather than or in addition to Ca'dadūx], a name that comes from the Gineix̱ (Big Bremner) River, which joins the Copper River below Chitina (HB).

   b. The clan's name was Gineix̱ K̲wáan but the leader's name was GuditŁa (SW, KDI).

   c. The dish was made of horn from a giant moose (HB, KDI, EA); the moose horn was decorated with abalone shell (SW, KDI); the dish was made of walrus ivory inset with beautiful stones (MH); it was made of wood with dentalium shells around the edge (KDI). [The bowl combines products of the interior and coast and may be a symbol of trade or migration.]

2. There was a dispute over inheritance of the feast dish, leading to a schism in the chief's house [*hít*, "house" and the matrilineal kin group residing there]. A faction of about forty people led by four brothers decided to leave and "go straight for that mountain" [Mount Saint Elias] (K).

   a. One brother kept the dish at Chitina and the other three left with their families, one going down the Copper River and settling at its mouth; one travelling south on the ocean to Yakutat in a skin boat; and the fourth setting out across the glacier. The migration across the ice took a hundred years; the people travelling by boat arrived at Yakutat before them (MH).

   b. "They [women of the clan] moved in a body to the side of the younger brother, which meant they were voting for the younger brother to be their chief. So he leaned over and got that bowl. That signified that he's chief. And then that migration started." The brother who was not chosen as leader led the migration to Yakutat (EA).

   c. The migration took place ten generations ago, and ancestors from each generation can be named (MH).

3. The travellers crossing the glacier wore hats, coats made of weasel and marten skins, and nose pins. As they approached the mountain they found a place with many ground squirrels. They clubbed the squirrels, which caused fog to appear. The group became lost in the fog, and some were separated and disappeared (K).

   a. The group that split off in the fog turned back and came out at the mouth of the Copper River, later moving to Katalla up the coast; they were given the name Ganaxtedi (HB).

   b. The people crossing the glacier were starving. In the distance they saw a little hill with trees [a pinnacle projecting above the ice] and mistook it for a wolverine. They later saw what they thought was a rabbit, but it turned out to be the distant peak of Mount Saint Elias. "It was a compass for the people so they wouldn't get lost" (HB).

c. The brother and his family who were travelling by sea saw the snowy peak of Mount Saint Elias in the distance and thought it was a seagull on the water (MH).

4. The migrating group climbed toward Mount Saint Elias [across Bagley Icefield], and then found a way around its west side [descending through a pass to Yahtse Glacier]. As they struggled on the ice they sang a song from their Copper River homeland and mourned loved ones who had been left behind or lost in the fog (K).

   a. The people composed songs in the Ahtna language that they sang on the migration. One was a mourning song about a man who accidentally shot his brother with an arrow (MH). Some say he was shot with a gun (KDI), but there were no guns at that time (HB).

5. From the heights they saw the ocean [Gulf of Alaska] for the first time, saying, "What is that so very blue?" They went down to the ocean to save themselves [following Yahtse Glacier to Icy Bay]. At the bottom they crossed a [meltwater] river that was boiling out from under the ice. They claimed Mount Saint Elias as an *at.óow* crest because they were the first to pass by it (K).

   a. They came upon Mount Saint Elias and adopted it as a crest. "They danced down from that mountain. They were happy when they are coming on this side. Lots of things happen there and there are songs" (SW).

   b. "The glacier was formed so there were steps all the way down to the water, and there was gravel on top of the ice. And every step or platform that was there, they made songs and danced" (KDI).

6. They built a house beside the river to shelter for the winter, naming it Mountain House [Shaa Hít, Swanton 1909, 350] in memory of how close they came to dying on the trek. They resided at Icy Bay for ten years, building a whole town (K).

   a. At Icy Bay "the glacier was all over the bay, way out" [at its maximum extent, larger than today]. The settlement at Icy Bay (Was'ei*)* was a temporary camp called Teey Aaní ("Yellow Cedar Bark Town," Thornton 2012, 17), named for bark they brought with them to cover their dwellings. The place was just west of what is now the bay, at Was'ei Dak ("Outside of Was'ei," Thornton 2012, 17) (HB).

7. At Icy Bay a woman adopted a seagull that grew to a giant size. Young men were sent from Icy Bay in a skin boat to explore along the coast to the south. They got to Yakutat Bay and crossed it to a town where Koskedi and Łuẋedi residents [probably Eyak clans living at Lost River] turned them away. They returned to Icy Bay. Some months later, a group of [G̲alyáx̲] Kaagwaantaan came to Icy Bay in a skin canoe from the mouth of Copper River and they were welcomed (K).

   a. The leader of the Gineix̲ K̲wáan at Icy Bay was concerned that they would become a "lost tribe" because they were Ravens and had no Eagle moiety partners to marry. The arrival of the G̲alyáx̲ Kaagwaantaan, an Eagle Eyak clan, saved the Gineix̲ K̲wáan men from having to marry their "sisters" of the same clan (HB).

   b. The leader of the G̲alyáx̲ Kaagwaantaan was a Teikweidí [Tlingit Eagle] man named Xatgawet. He married two beautiful Gineix̲ K̲wáan sisters, 'Àndúł and Dúhàn, and became rich because of the copper they owned (SA, EA, LF; see de Laguna 1972, 242–245).

c. The Gineix̲ K̲wáan encountered the G̲alyáx̲ Kaagwaantaan after finding blood on the ice where hunters had been skinning seals (HB). [Icy Bay is a major harbour seal rookery.]

d. While they were living at Icy Bay a boy fell into a glacial crevasse and could not be rescued; his mother adopted a seagull in his memory (SW, SA, HB). [A mourning song for the child is still performed at Yakutat in the Ahtna language; see de Laguna 1972, 1157]. According to Harry Bremner, this was the origin of the giant seagull story, which he described as myth (*tlaagú*) (HB).

e. The people whom the bothers met living at the town in Yakutat Bay were Łuẋedi, an Eagle clan (KDI) or "Aleuts" [Chugach Sugpiaq people from Prince William Sound] (MH, SW).

8. Six Gineix̲ K̲wáan brothers returned to the Copper River to retrieve a *tináa* [copper shield or plate] whose "real owner" [possibly the clan leader Łtaxda'x from episode 1 above] had died. Bringing the *tináa* with them, the group [Gineix̲ K̲wáan and G̲alyáx̲ Kaagwaantaan, now intermarried] went to Yakutat Bay by boat. They crossed Yakutat Bay and came ashore on the other side in an area occupied by the Koskedi [an Eyak clan] (K).

a. [Instead of by sea] the group went on foot "across the ice" all the way from Icy Bay to the east side of Yakutat Bay near Mount Tebenkoff [a route that implies that, at the time, the conjoined Malaspina and Hubbard glaciers extended across Yakutat Bay at a point north of Knight Island; see figure 1.3]. The travellers saw a "beautiful beach" below [possibly Logan Beach] and went down to it, meeting the Hmyedi in the vicinity of Knight Island (HB).

b. "They came walking overland from Icy Bay and found Yakutat" (GJ). Some boys from Icy Bay ran across the [Malaspina] glacier to Yakutat Bay and discovered that people were there from signs of seal hunting (SW).

c. A solid glacier covered all of Yakutat Bay and extended north to Icy Bay and beyond; it began receding when the Gineix̲ K̲wáan immigrants killed a dog as they approached Icy Bay and threw it into a crevasse (KDI).

d. "When the people first came to this area, the glacier extended from Point Latouche [see figure 1.3] across to the Manby side [west side of the bay]. The Manby side was apparently then all ice. Knight Island was bare of trees, just as it is now around . . . those areas from which the glaciers have recently retreated." The sandy places on Knight Island around Old Town were covered with strawberry plants, and there was no forest on Krutoi Island (JB).

e. The whole of Knight Island was a strawberry patch; there were no trees (OA).

9. The Koskedi were hostile to the new arrivals, and when they discovered a man from the immigrant group fishing at a stream called Kwáashk' (Eyak, "humpback salmon") they broke his salmon spear. To settle the dispute the six brothers bought Yakutat Bay with the *tináa*, which was worth ten slaves. All of the Koskedi and Łuẋedi then left the bay (K).

a. The original owners of Kwáashk' creek [variously the Koskedi (K), Hmyedi (HB), Yinyeidi (EA, LF), or Aleuts (SW)] sold the creek, and the new owners [the Gineix̲ K̲wáan] thus acquired the name Kwáashk'i K̲wáan [people of Kwáashk'] (HB, KDI, EA).

b. The same group that owned Kwáashk' creek caught the Kwáashk'i K̲wáan daughter of a G̲alyáx̲ Kaagwaantaan clan leader as she was picking strawberries on Ganawás [Knight Island] and cut the berry basket from her back. Her father then bought Knight Island for her clan (HB). Alternatively, the girl's brother, Dux, bought the island (JK); or it was Xatgawet who paid with copper for Kwáashk' creek and Knight Island (EA, LF, SA, KDI).

c. The purchase of territories in Yakutat Bay was made with the *tináa* brought from Copper River (worth eight enslaved people) and also sea otter furs (HB), or with a canoe that had fourteen *tináa* tied to its thwarts, each worth ten enslaved people (SW). "Because they lived up the Copper River the Kwáashk'i K̲wáan had *tináa* then. They used copper for everything—for knives, whenever they had a war" (SW).

d. The immigrants built a big town on Ganawás; it had only Kwáashk'i K̲wáan houses (SW). Dux, a Kwáashk'i K̲wáan clan leader, built the first house there, called Noow Hít (Fort House) and a man married to his sister built Xóots Hít (Bear House) (JK). The village on Knight Island was the oldest one around Yakutat Bay (OA). Its real name was Yéil Áa Daak Wudzigidi Yé (Place Where Raven Fell Down) because "there were so many big houses there, and when it's calm weather, the smoke goes straight up. So the raven that tries to fly over never gets to the end. It falls down" (OA, SA, EA). The people lived there before the Russians ever came to Yakutat (figure 1.5). [The earliest contact was in 1788, with the Izmailov-Bocharoff expedition.]

e. It was Xatgawet, a Teikweidí rich man who owned many slaves, who built the village on Knight Island (EA, LF, JE, SA, KDI). He named it Tlákw.aan (Old Town) after Tlákw.aan (Klukwan) on the Chilkat River in Southeast Alaska, in order "to pretend it was a high-class people's place" [provided by various Yakutat commentators; however, others believe Xatgawet lived during Russian times and had nothing to do with the Gineix̲ K̲wáan migration; see de Laguna 1972, 245–247].

f. Another name for Knight Island was K'ootsinadi.aan (Shaken Land), "because there were so many of them, the land shook when they walked" (EA, LF).

10. A mountain spirit granted the youngest of the six brothers great hunting powers and showed him that the animals of Yakutat Bay, including grizzly bears, black bears, and mountain sheep, lived inside a mountain. Later the brothers all went together in a canoe to hunt for seals in front of the glacier, which was "the seals' home" and where the animals were abundant [the ice floe harbour seal rookery at Hubbard Glacier]. The position of the glacier at that time was "just at the head of Kwáashk'" [that is, at the head of the creek's drainage, also suggesting a mid-bay position similar to that described above in commentaries to episode 8]. Before crossing that glacier [or in front of it], people listened inside a hollow cottonwood tree for sounds of approaching storms that might make the crossing dangerous (K).

a. "When they came down there it was a foreign country. They didn't know what to eat; they didn't know how to live. And the spirits of that place adopted the humans. [. . .] They showed them how to hunt seal, and they became friends of the spirit of the glacier. That is why they have a special connection with the glaciers and the mountains in all that area." (EA).

The remainder of K'áadasteen's narrative diverges from the Gineix̲ K̲wáan migration story and is not relevant to the present analysis (Swanton 1909, 361–368).

FIGURE 1.5 *Raven's Flight over* Tlákw.aan by Emily Kearney-Williams, 2017. Tlákw.aan, the first village built by people of the Gineix̱ Ḵwáan clan after their migration to Yakutat Bay, is depicted on the basis of archaeological evidence. In oral tradition, Raven once tried to fly over the settlement but was overcome by smoke from its many hearth fires, an incident commemorated by the place name Yéil Áa Daak Wudzigidi Yé (Place Where Raven Fell Down). The large wooden plank structures are lineage houses; the smaller are food storage caches and other outbuildings. The scene depicts young spruce trees growing on a recently deglaciated landscape.

THE ORAL TRADITION

Variations in the Gineix Kwáan migration narrative, including the differing names recalled for places, individuals, and clans, are noted in the synopsis above. Given the continual process of change inherent in oral tradition and the multiplicity of narrators in each generation, it is possible that some of these variants already existed at the time of K'áadasteen's recounting in 1904, while others may have arisen more recently.

Despite such differences in detail, the same basic sequence of events occurs in all versions, suggesting that long-term fidelity to what "really happened" resides in the main plot elements of the narrative. Among these core elements is the migration itself from the Copper River up the Chitina River basin and over montane icefields to Icy Bay and Yakutat Bay (episodes 2 through 5 above), although a coastal route for part of the group was recalled by one narrator (episode 2a). All versions agree that an interim settlement was built at Icy Bay (episode 6); that the immigrants found Yakutat fjord still filled with glacial ice to a point north of Knight Island (episodes 8, 10); that the immigrants came into conflict with Yakutat residents over access to food resources (episode 9); and that one of their leaders bought territory, including Knight Island and Kwáashk' stream, using one or more *tináa* brought from the Copper River homeland (episode 9). The Kwáashk'i Kwáan then built the town known as Yéil Áa Daak Wudzigidi Yé or Tlákw.aan on Knight Island and lived there until abandoning the settlement prior to Western contact (episode 9). They fished for salmon (episode 9), hunted seals along the glacial edge, and harvested land animals, including bears and mountain sheep (episode 10).

The temporal uncertainty of oral tradition is reflected in the difficulty of deriving a secure date for the migration from narrative evidence alone. Maggie Harry (episode 2c) believed that it took place ten generations prior to her own and was able to list ancestors from each cohort (de Laguna 1972, 240). This suggests a date of about AD 1690, although generations are often under-counted in oral tradition (Henige 1974, 27–38; Vansina 1965, 153–154). In connection with the Kwáashk'i Kwáan purchase of Knight Island, the same narrator in the 1950s commented that "three hundred years ago there were no trees at Yakutat—just strawberries" (de Laguna 1972, 236). However, Maggie Harry's belief that the migration across the montane ice took an entire century is unsupportable given the hostility of that environment to human occupation. Katy Dickson Isaac's reference to the use of a firearm during or before the migration (episode 4a) is clearly an anachronism, since all other information places the migration in pre-Russian times. Similarly, the Tlingit leader Xatgawet is ambiguously associated with both the migration and post-contact times (episodes 7b, 9e), possibly an example of temporal compression (mixing of eras) in oral narrative (Crowell and Howell 2013) or due to two individuals possessing the same name.

Observations about environmental change are embedded in the narrative and in associated place names, a regional cultural-linguistic pattern (Connor et al. 2009; Cruikshank 2001; Monteith et al. 2007; Thornton 1997, 2008; 2012, xi–xxiii). The extent of Yahtse Glacier in Icy Bay (episode 6a) and of the Hubbard/Malaspina ice mass in Yakutat Bay (episodes 8, 10) are noted in addition to glacial retreat (episode 8c), the exposure of new land (episodes 8d, 8e), and post-glacial plant succession (episodes 8d, 8e). Katy Isaac Dickson's explanation for the glaciers' retreat—that a dead dog was thrown into a crevasse (episode 8c)—is based in the belief that glaciers are sentient beings who respond to an invitation "to eat" by advancing and to pollution or human disrespect by pulling back (Connor et al. 2009; Cruikshank 2001, 2005; de Laguna 1972, 286–287).

A guiding cultural theme of the story is reciprocity between Raven and Eagle moieties (Raven and Seagull among the Athna), the complementary "halves" of matrilineal Tlingit, Eyak, and Athabascan societies that intermarry, exchange resources, and support each other during times of loss and grief (de Laguna 1972, 1990a, 1990b; Worl 2010). In the Gineix̲ K̲wáan migration story, the shared moiety structure supports intermarriage and the exchange of wealth and knowledge across cultural-linguistic boundaries. Thus, an Eyak Eagle clan (the G̲alyáx̲ Kaagwaantaan) shares its skin boats, weapons, and sea mammal hunting skills with its Ahtna Raven marriage partners, the Gineix̲ K̲wáan (episode 7a), enabling them to learn "how to live" in the coastal environment of Yakutat Bay where they become seal hunters (episode 10), aided by protective mountain and glacier spirits (episode 10a). In turn, the Gineix̲ K̲wáan use *tináa* made of native copper from the riverine interior to buy land at Yakutat and to fund their social partnership with the G̲alyáx̲ Kaagwaantaan. It is also said that Xatgawet, a Tlingit Eagle of the Teikweidí clan and leader (in some versions) of the G̲alyáx̲ Kaagwaantaan, "became rich" in copper through his marriage to two Gineix̲ K̲wáan sisters (episode 7b).

Comparison of the Oral Accounts to Archaeological Evidence from Tlákw.aan

To identify aspects of consilience between oral tradition and archaeology and to integrate both views of the past, key narrative points of the Gineix̲ K̲wáan migration epic are now considered in the light of archaeological evidence from Tlákw.aan, the village that the migrants founded in Yakutat Bay. Other settlements along the migration route, including the Icy Bay village named Teey Aaní, have potentially been preserved as archaeological sites but remain undiscovered. The Tlákw.aan of oral record, however, may be securely identified as the YAK-00007 site on the south shore of Knight Island, both on the basis of strong local attribution and the absence of other candidate sites (Crowell field notes 2011–2014; de Laguna et al. 1964, 20–23; Sealaska Corporation 1975). One other pre-contact settlement is known to exist on Knight Island, a hunting camp discovered in 2012 (YAK-00205); but this site, with only three small house pits, is too limited in scale to correspond with the ancient village.

SETTLEMENT SIZE AND POPULATION

In oral tradition, Tlákw.aan is described as the first and most important Yakutat Bay settlement of the Gineix̲ K̲wáan and is given the name Yéil Áa Daak Wudzigidi Yé because of its "many big houses" with smoking hearths. The Tlákw.aan site should therefore be extensive, containing the remains of numerous multi-family houses.

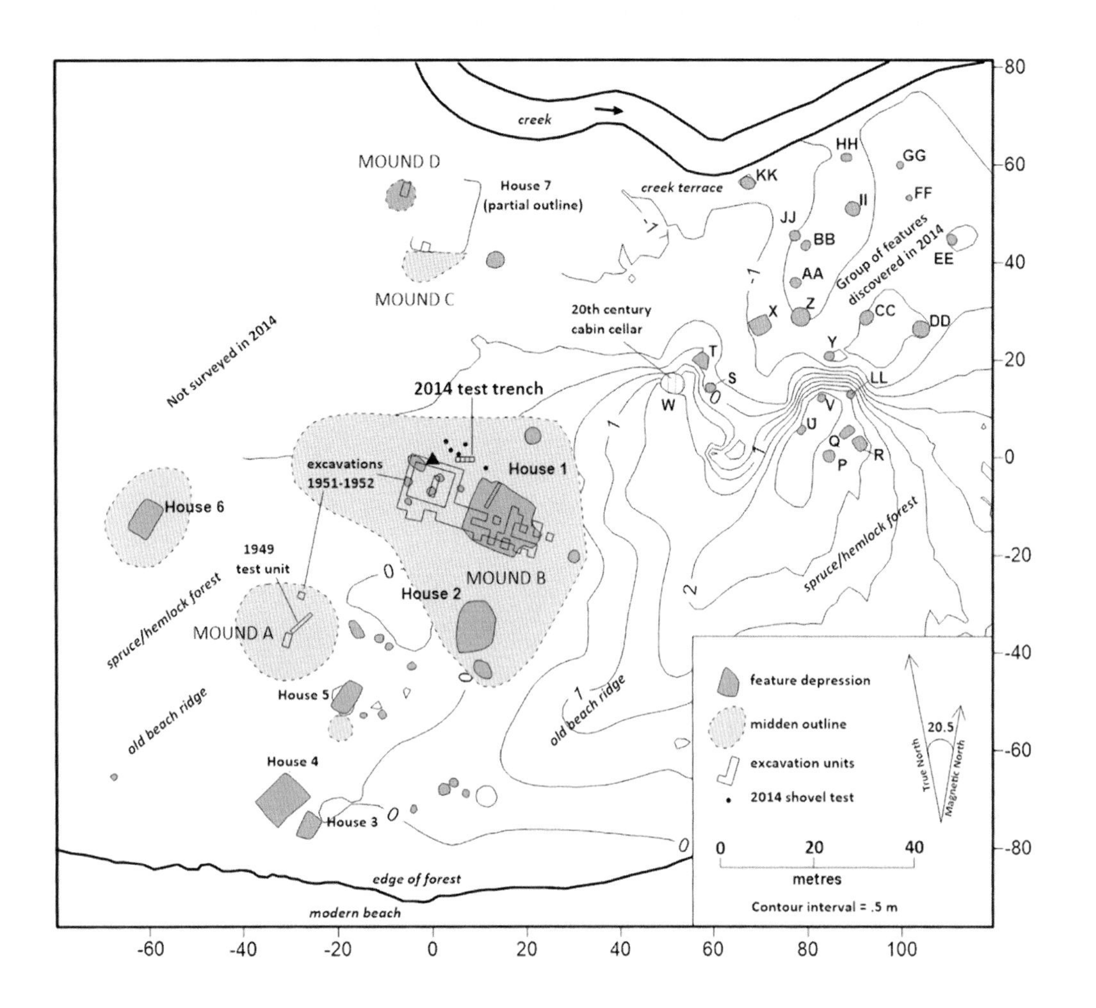

FIGURE 1.6 The Tlákw.aan/ Old Town archaeological site (YAK-00007). The same terrain and cultural features are depicted in figure 1.5. Mapped in 2014 by author, combined with de Laguna et al. 1964.

The YAK-00007 site (figure 1.6) occupies a forest clearing of about 200 × 100 metres (2.0 hectares, or 4.94 acres) bordered by a mature spruce and hemlock forest with trees up to 1.5 metres in girth. Ages of the largest trees have not been determined but are in the range of two to three centuries. Younger trees have encroached on the clearing over the last century or more, and vegetation in open areas includes rye grass, wild celery, and salmonberry bushes.

De Laguna mapped seven square or rectangular house pits at the site (Houses 1–7) as well as smaller surface depressions left by underground storage caches. Four areas of midden were found containing animal bones, shell, charcoal, and fire-cracked rock (Mounds A–D). Average midden depth was less than 75 centimetres (30 inches), but some pits extended up to 230 centimetres (90 inches) below the surface. Over forty subsurface pits and buried structures were uncovered, representing earlier phases of occupation. The two largest dwellings at the site were House 1 and House 7, both about 15.6 metres (50 feet) long. The other houses were 5.9 metres to 9.1 metres (18 to 30 feet) long.

A second group of cultural depressions was discovered in 2014 to the northeast of the main occupation area (see figure 1.6, Features P–KK). These are circular to rectangular and range in size from 2.0 metres to 4.4 metres in maximum dimension. While some of the larger pits could represent small semi-subterranean houses, most or all were probably winter storage caches for meat, dried fish, berries, and other foods utilized by the inhabitants of Tlákw.aan.

The areal extent and number of houses at the YAK-00007 site confirm that Tlákw.aan was at least a moderately sized village, although not as vast as oral tradition suggests. It is more extensive than most other Yakutat sites, although Diyaaguna.éit on the Lost River is far larger, with twenty-six house pits (Davis 1996, 192–200).

An approximation of the population of Tlákw.aan may be derived from comparative ethnohistoric information. The largest traditional houses in the Tlingit region were 15 metres to 18 metres square (49 to 59 feet square) and sheltered forty to fifty people (de Laguna 1972, 294–299, 1990a, 207–208; Emmons 1991, 59–68). This suggests an average of about 6 square metres of interior space per person. If one extrapolates from the total floor area of the houses at Tlákw.aan (707 square metres, without including any of the northeastern pits), the resident population would have been around 118 persons. This assumes that all the surface houses were occupied at the same time, although some evidence (discussed below) indicates that this was probably not the case. Also, because it is based on surface features, the estimate would apply only to the final period of site occupancy rather than to deeper, older layers. K'áadasteen (episode 2) stated that the original group of Ahtna migrants included 40 people, who were joined by an unknown number of Eyaks at Icy Bay (episode 7). The descendants of this relatively small founding group might have increased in number over time, expanding the village.

ARCHITECTURE OF THE HOUSES

The primary line of oral tradition holds that a Copper River Ahtna Raven clan (the Gineix̲ K̲wáan) joined an Eyak Eagle clan (the G̲alyáx̲ Kaagwaantaan) during the migration, and that members of both groups built the village of Tlákw.aan (episode 7). In an alternative version, Xatgawet, a Tlingit Teikweidí clan leader, constructed the settlement (episode 9e). House remains at YAK-00007 should permit identification of the cultural origins of the site's founders, to the extent that Ahtna, Eyak, and Tlingit houses differed from each other in style and construction.

The traditional residential structures of the Ahtna, Eyak, and Tlingit—variously known in English as lineage, chiefs', or winter houses—shared basic features of design as well as variations that can be archaeologically distinguished. All were plank buildings with wooden frames and housed multiple families related by matrilineal descent and marriage. The Ahtna chief's house of the nineteenth century was reported to be rectangular (5–10 metres long) with a floor excavated up to 1 metre below ground level (Allen 1887, 130; de Laguna and McClellan 1981, 645; Ketz 1983, 145–149; Shinkwin 1979, 40–50). Wooden sleeping platforms lined the walls and were partitioned into family compartments. The house had a central cooking hearth, overhead smoke vent, vertical and/or horizontal wall planks, and a bark roof supported by single or double ridge poles. A rectangular annex for steam bathing was often connected to the main house.

Eyak multi-family dwellings were similar in size and construction to their Ahtna counterparts but had only a single ridge pole (Birket-Smith and de Laguna 1938, 32–43; de Laguna 1990b, 181). Birket-Smith and de Laguna described historic Eyak house floors as level with the ground, but Davis (1996, 210–309) interpreted pit houses at Diyaaguna.éit and Wulilaayi Aan on the Yakutat foreland as Eyak because they antedated Tlingit migration into the area. These were associated with calibrated radiocarbon dates as early as the tenth century AD and were built inside pits up to 2 metres deep with vertical plank walls that extended to the bottom; several had earthen benches and sleeping platforms around the central hearth. The Eyak practice of using grooved base frames to secure the lower ends of vertical wall planks (de Laguna et al. 1964, 73) was not observed at these sites.

Tlingit lineage houses of the eighteenth and nineteenth centuries varied in size (6–18 metres long) but were typically larger than Ahtna or Eyak dwellings of the same period (de Laguna 1972, 294–299, 1990a, 207–208; Emmons 1991, 59–68; Russell 1891, 79–80; Seton Karr 1887, 156–157). The house had vertical plank walls based at ground level without a bottom frame. Entry was through a circular opening in the front wall. The interior pit was up to 4 metres deep and surrounded by stepped residential platforms that were divided into family apartments. A wood-burning hearth occupied the centre of the floor with a smoke hole above. The roof was covered with spruce planks and supported by two heavy beams. Posts that held up the ridge beams were often carved and painted with clan crests, as was the house front. In some houses a screen with crest emblems divided the house leader's apartment from the rest of the interior space.

De Laguna interpreted all the houses at YAK-00007 as Tlingit in design, apparently because they had excavated floors and lacked the basal wall frames she believed were indicative of Eyak construction (de Laguna et al. 1964, 43–76). Nonetheless, all had Eyak- or Ahtna-like aspects and did not conform entirely to the Tlingit ethnohistoric model. House 8, found buried under Mound B deposits and built early in the history of the site, had vertical wall planks inside a pit as at Diyaaguna.éit, a bark-covered roof, and a single ridge pole. House 9, which dated to a later period based on its superposition over House 1, was similarly constructed with a single ridge pole and no side benches. House 1 had a side bench along its north wall and a double-beam gabled roof "as on the large Tlingit houses of historic times" but lacked a stepped pit and central hearth. House 7, also interpreted as a Tlingit-style lineage house, had a deeply excavated floor but no side benches.

Given these variations, and taking into account the architecture of Eyak houses built at Diyaaguna.éit and Wulilaayi Aan, de Laguna's identification of the Tlákw.aan structures as Tlingit is questionable. The structures instead seem to reflect the mixed Ahtna-Eyak heritage that the oral tradition would project, although most of the houses were larger than either of those groups built during the post-contact period after they had suffered severe population decline. It is notable that House 7, one of the largest dwellings at Tlákw.aan, was interpreted by de Laguna as one of the oldest because of the mature spruce trees that have overgrown it, making it unlikely to have been a product of late Tlingit influence.

FIGURE 1.7 South wall profile of 2014 test trench at the Tlákw.aan site, including locations of paleobotanical samples.

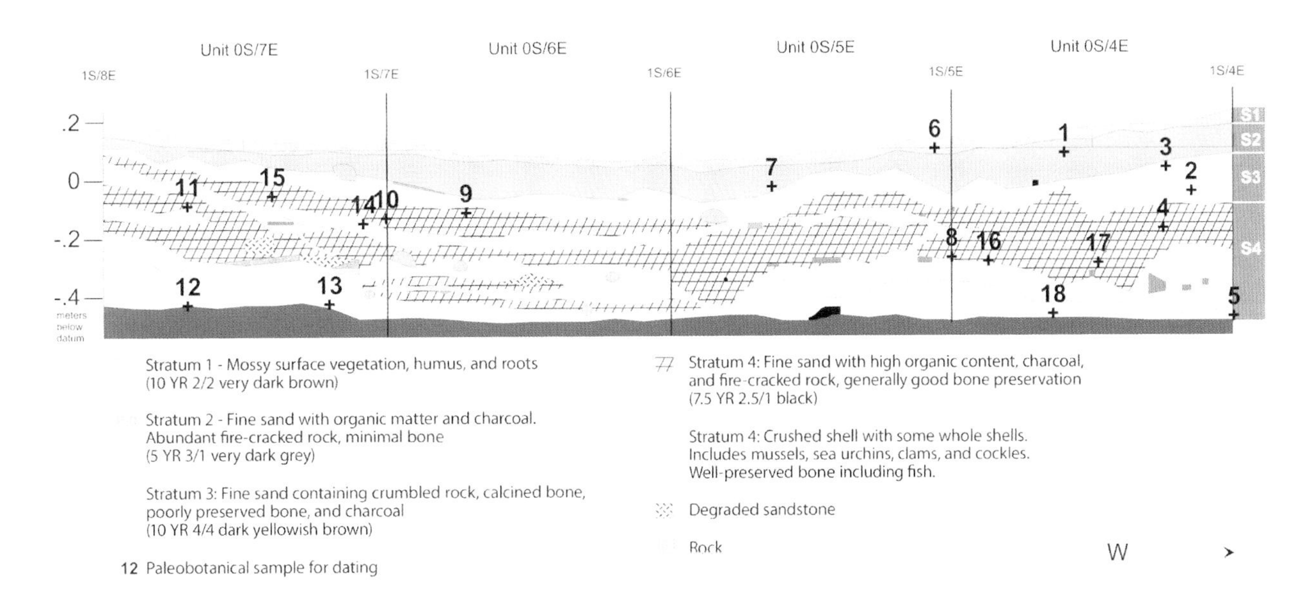

AGE AND DURATION OF OCCUPATION

Maggie Harry believed that Tlákw.aan was founded ten generations, or about 200 years, before her own birth in 1892, and that people lived there until shortly before Russian or Spanish contact (episodes 2c and 9d). The implied span of occupation is thus about a century, approximately AD 1690–1780. Archaeologically, multiple layers of cultural debris would be expected for a site that was inhabited for this period of time or longer, and the exact chronology of occupation should be determinable from calibrated radiocarbon dates on samples of plant material (charcoal or wood, for example) from different levels of the midden.

De Laguna reported two uncalibrated dates on charred wood from the lower levels of Mound B: 136 ± 62 radiocarbon years before "present" (or RCYBP; this would mean 1950) and 328 ± 78 RCYBP (de Laguna et al. 1964, 206). The older of these dates falls in the early seventeenth century AD, about as expected from Maggie Harry's oral information. However, the two dates are quite different and do not adequately define the occupation period.

One purpose of the 2014 test trench was to record midden stratigraphy and collect a vertically controlled series of radiocarbon samples for more precise dating. The trench deposits (figure 1.7) were 60 to 65 centimetres deep and corresponded to the general site stratigraphy reported by de Laguna (de Laguna et al. 1964, 36–41). Stratum 1 consisted of brown humus accumulated from vegetal growth over the centuries since the site was last inhabited. Stratum 2 was the uppermost cultural layer, composed of sand mixed with large amounts of charcoal and fire-cracked rock generated by cooking fires and steam bathing. Stratum 3 was sand mixed with lesser amounts of fire-cracked rock, charcoal, and fragments of burnt animal bone. Stratum 4 at the base of the midden (the earliest period of occupation) was the thickest and most complex deposit, composed of beach sand interlayered with charcoal, fire-cracked rock, and well-preserved fish and animal bones, as well as small piles of marine shell (littleneck clams, cockles, mussels, sea urchins, and snails). De Laguna reported that bone, stone, and copper artifacts occurred throughout the midden but at a somewhat higher frequency in the upper cultural strata (de Laguna et al. 1964, 85–86).

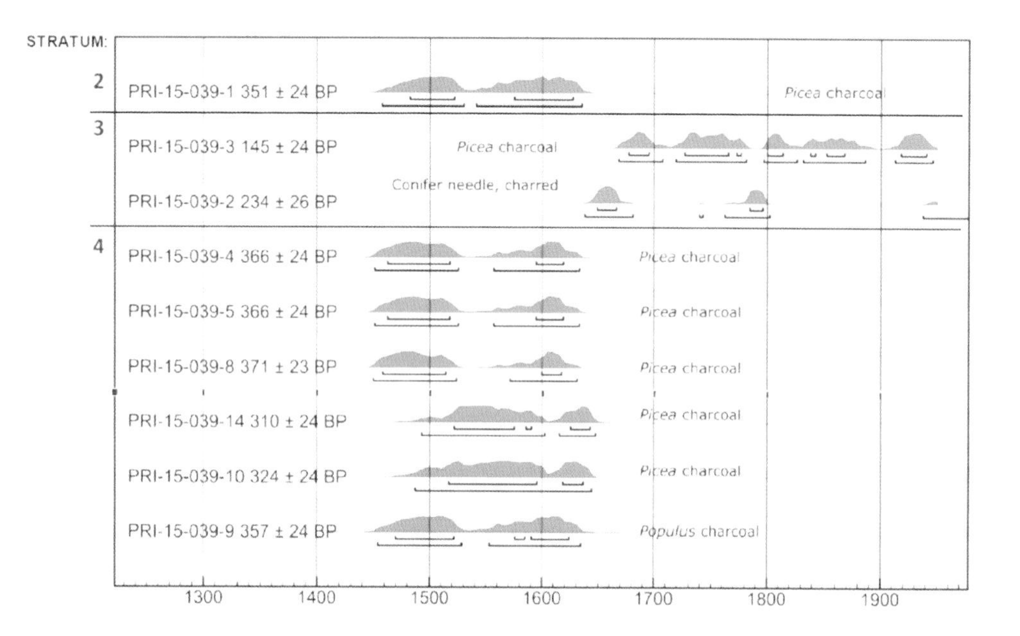

FIGURE 1.8 Multiplot of AMS results (CAL AD) from Tlákw.aan/ Old Town, YAK-00007, 2014 test trench, PaleoResearch Institute. Source: Kováčik and Cummings 2015.

Seventeen samples of wood charcoal, wood, bark, and conifer needles were collected from Strata 2, 3, and 4 of the trench, as indicated in figure 1.7, and submitted for species identification and AMS (accelerator mass spectrometer) dating to the PaleoResearch Institute (in Boulder, Colorado). All samples, including those from the base of the deposit, were identified as *Picea* (spruce) except for one fragment of *Populus* (aspen or cottonwood) (Kováčik and Cummings 2015).

AMS dates were run on nine of these samples and fell into two groups, with the oldest seven ranging between 371 ± 23 RCYBP and 310 ± 24 RCYBP (table 1.1; figure 1.8). Six of the samples in this group were from Stratum 4 and one was anomalously from Stratum 2. These estimates intersect a plateau in the dendrochronological calibration curve and so have bimodal calendrical distributions. The earlier ranges start in the mid- to late 1400s and the later ranges in the early 1500s to early 1600s (figure 1.8). The early peaks are close to the deglaciation of Knight Island about six hundred years ago and older than the local availability of spruce, so are implausible on that basis. The younger peaks are quite similar to each other without the variability that random growth ring sampling of centuries-old trees (the "old wood problem") would produce, so it is likely that the source trees were young, first-growth spruce that germinated around AD 1500 or later. Overall, this set of seven dates identifies the mid-1500s to mid-1600s as the most likely span of deposition represented by Stratum 4.

The second group includes two dates from Stratum 3: 234 ± 26 RCYBP on a conifer needle and 145 ± 24 RCYBP on spruce charcoal. The former is the most reliable because needles stop growing and absorbing atmospheric carbon after only five to seven years,

TABLE 1.1 AMS Radiocarbon Results for Samples from the Tlákw.aan Site YAK-00007, PaleoResearch Institute

Sample No.	Sample identification	AMS ^{14}C date	1-sigma calibrated date (68.2%)	2-sigma calibrated date (95.4%)	$\delta^{13}C$ (0/00)	Stratum
PRI-15-039-1	*Picea* charcoal	351 ± 24 RCYBP	AD 1480–1530 AD 1570–1630	AD 1450–1530 AD 1540–1640	−28.14	S2
PRI-15-039-3	*Picea* charcoal	145 ± 24 RCYBP	AD 1670–1700 AD 1720–1780 AD 1790–1820 AD 1830–1870 AD 1910–1940	AD 1660–1890 AD 1910–1950	−24.75	S3
PRI-15-039-2	Conifer needle, charred	234 ± 26 RCYBP	AD 1640–1670 AD 1780–1800	AD 1630–1690 AD 1730–1750 AD 1760–1810 AD 1930–	−25.92	S3
PRI-15-039-4	*Picea* charcoal	366 ± 24 RCYBP	AD 1460–1520 AD 1590–1620	AD 1450–1530 AD 1550–1640	−26.35	S4
PRI-15-039-5	*Picea* charcoal	366 ± 24 RCYBP	AD 1460–1520 AD 1590–1620	AD 1450–1530 AD 1550–1640	−24.23	S4
PRI-15-039-8	*Picea* charcoal	371 ± 23 RCYBP	AD 1450–1520 AD 1590–1620	AD 1440–1530 AD 1570–1640	−25.63	S4
PRI-15-039-9	*Populus* charcoal	357 ± 24 RCYBP	AD 1460–1530 AD 1570–1630	AD 1450–1530 AD 1550–1640	−26.48	S4
PRI-15-039-10	*Picea* charcoal	324 ± 24 RCYBP	AD 1510–1600 AD 1610–1640	AD 1480–1650	−26.35	S4
PRI-15-039-14	*Picea* charcoal	310 ± 24 RCYBP	AD 1520–1590 AD 1620–1650	AD 1490–1650	−25.60	S4

SOURCE KOVÁČIK AND CUMMINGS 2015.

avoiding the old wood problem. The earliest two calibrated date ranges for the needle (AD 1630–1690 and AD 1730–1750) are the most reliable, since there is no evidence at Tlákw.aan of Spanish or Russian contact. Therefore, the most likely dates for accumulation of Stratum 3 are the late 1600s to early 1700s, with no indication of a temporal gap between Stratum 3 and Stratum 4 below.

In sum, radiocarbon dates from the 2014 test trench in Mound B near House 1 suggest that Tlákw.aan was inhabited by the mid-1500s and that people lived there through the 1600s and into the early 1700s. These results would push the beginning of occupation back more than a century before the AD 1690 estimate inferred from Maggie Harry's genealogical account.

Another time marker embedded in the migration story suggests an even earlier date for the founding of the settlement. In episode 8d, Knight Island is described as having been so recently deglaciated that it lacked trees and was covered with strawberries, a stage of plant succession that would probably have obtained no later than the early to mid-1400s (Barclay, Calkin, and Wiles 2001). This oral evidence does not appear to be consistent with paleobotanical data from the 2014 test trench, where spruce—a species that does not take hold for at least a century after deglaciation—occurs from top to bottom and where no early succession tree species such as willow and alder were found. The likely explanation is that Mound B was not formed during the earliest phase of occupation at the site, as also supposed by de Laguna, who thought that House 7 and associated Mounds C and D might be older (de Laguna et al. 1964, 85). Thus, while the exact date for the founding of Tlákw.aan remains unresolved, a date somewhere in the mid-fifteenth century seems possible.

ARTIFACTS

Projectiles. Copper arrow points from Tlákw.aan (n = 5) have leaf-shaped blades, sloping shoulders, and narrow, pointed tangs (figure 1.9A–C). They are closely comparable to leaf-shaped points from Ahtna sites, including GUL-00077, which dates from approximately AD 925 to 1485 (Hanson 2008, Figure 9; Workman 1977) and the early nineteenth-century Dakah De'Nin's Village (Shinkwin 1979, Figure 10). Trace element analyses of two of the Tlákw.aan points (Cooper et al. 2008; Veakis 1979) indicated that the metal probably came from a Chitina River source.

Large ground slate endblades for lances (n = 3; figure 1.9D) and smaller slate endblades for arrows (n = 6; figure 1.9E) are relatively uncommon at Tlákw.aan in comparison to late prehistoric Eyak (Davis 1996, 466–471, and Figures 95 and 96) and Sugpiaq sites (e.g., de Laguna 1956, 1975; Clark 1974; Crowell and Mann 1998; Knecht 1995). Workman (1977) noted that among the Ahtna, copper replaced stone and bone as the material used for many types of tools.

Unilaterally barbed arrow points with conical tangs made of bone or antler (n = 19; figure 1.9H–J; de Laguna et al. 1964, Figure 17) are an archaeologically documented Ahtna type (Hanson 2008, Figure 16; Shinkwin 1979, Figures 13D and 14D; VanStone 1955), although also widespread during the past millennium among most Alaskan Athabascan and Inuit groups as well as the Tlingit. Unilaterally barbed bone harpoon heads with tapered tangs and line holes, used for taking seals, dolphins, and sea lions

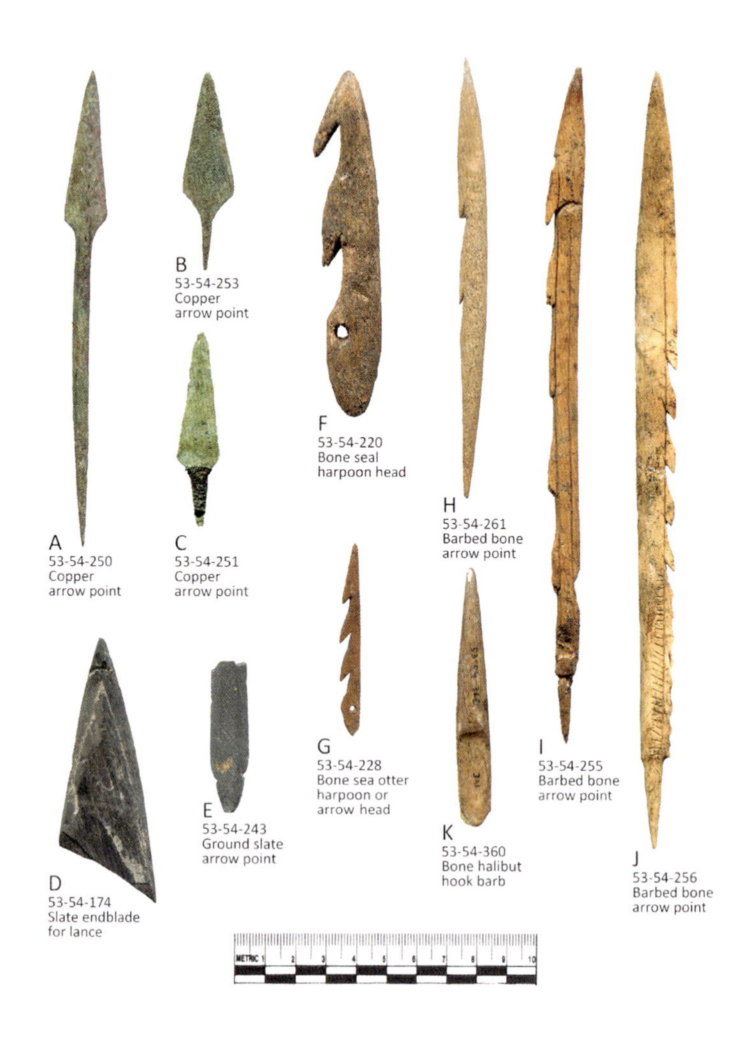

FIGURE 1.9 Projectile points and harpoon heads from the Tlákw.aan site YAK-00007

(n = 12, figure 1.9F), reflect the maritime focus of the Tlákw.aan subsistence economy and were used by all southern Alaskan coastal groups including the Tlingit (de Laguna 1960), Eyak (Birket-Smith and de Laguna 1938), and Chugach (de Laguna 1956), but not by the Ahtna in their original inland territory. Small, barbed harpoon arrowheads for sea otters (n = 9; figure 1.9G) had a similar cultural distribution. Pointed bone pieces with flattened sides, identified by de Laguna as gaff hook points but which actually served as barbs for halibut hooks (n = 5, figure 1.9K), represent another facet of coastal adaptation.

Woodworking tools. Splitting adzes (n = 14, figure 1.10A and B) made of pecked and ground greenstone or schist with hafting knobs or grooves were broadly distributed after 1000 BP across southeastern and southern Alaska as far west as Kodiak Island, but have not been reported for the Copper River Ahtna. Other Tlákw.aan woodworking tools include stone planing adzes (n = 13, figure 1.10C), stone chisels (n = 76, figure 1.10D and E), and beaver or porcupine teeth (n = 13, figure 1.10G and H) used as carving knives. These types have been found at Ahtna sites (Rainey 1939; Shinkwin 1979; Workman 1977), Eyak sites on the Yakutat foreland (Davis 1996), and in Prince William Sound (de Laguna 1956). Nails and small fragments of iron, almost certainly derived from driftwood or wreckage (n = 19; not illustrated), were probably used as bits for wood and bone-working tools (de Laguna et al. 1964, 88–90).

FIGURE 1.10 Woodworking, cutting, and scraping tools from the Tlákw.aan site YAK-00007

FIGURE 1.11 Copper semi-lunar knives from the Tlákw.aan site YAK-00007

FIGURE 1.12 Stone lamps from the Tlákw.aan site YAK-00007

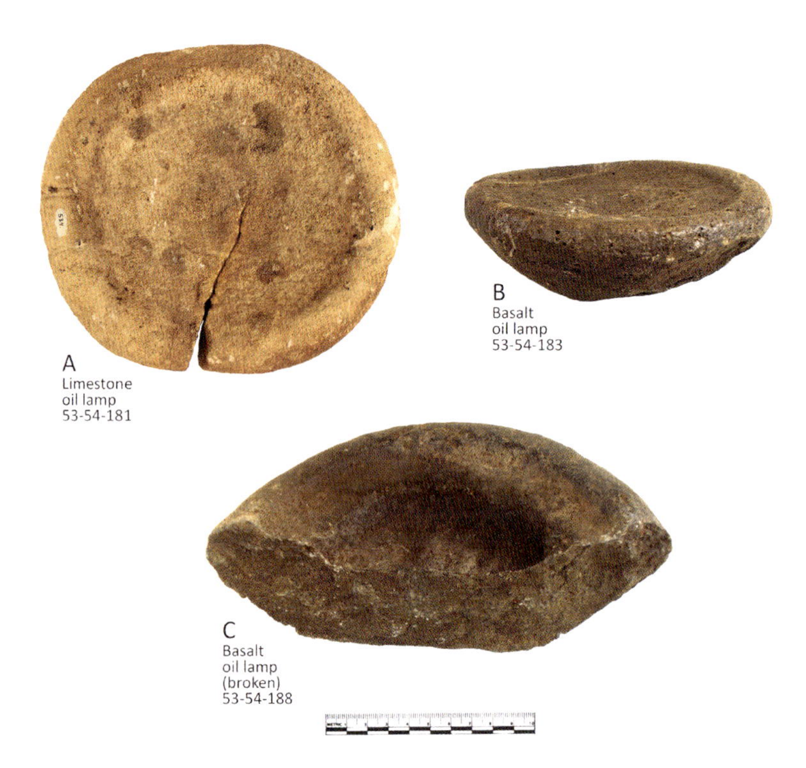

Cutting and scraping implements for skin and meat. The Tlákw.aan assemblage includes paddle-shaped scrapers made of flaked slate or schist (n = 5, figure 1.10F) as well as semi-lunar slate scrapers (n = 7, figure 1.10I), both comparable to Chugach types (de Laguna 1956, 131–135) and used for hide preparation. Boulder spall scrapers (n = 6, figure 1.10J) used for preparing skins are a predominant artifact in the Ahtna region (Hanson 2008, 122–123; Ketz 1983, 174–175, 187–188; Shinkwin 1979, 61–62; Workman 1977) and occur in other Athabascan, Eyak, and Sugpiaq areas.

The most distinctively Ahtna cutting tools from Tlákw.aan are semi-lunar knives with wooden handles and crescentic copper blades (n = 9, figure 1.11A and B) used for slicing salmon and other fish, a type that is duplicated at the pre-contact GUL-00077 site (Hanson 2008, Figure 11). There is also a unique Tlákw.aan copper semi-lunar knife with a grass-wrapped tang (figure 1.11C).

Lamps. Undecorated oil lamps (n = 51, figure 1.12A–C) hollowed from limestone, basalt, and other rocks are abundant in the Tlákw.aan collection and were used to light house interiors. Stone lamps for burning sea mammal oil are a coastal trait unknown in Ahtna territory. Stone lamps are rare in Tlingit collections, although a few were found at the Daax Haat Kanadaa site near Angoon (de Laguna 1960). They were universally used by other Alaskan coastal peoples, including the Eyak (Davis 1996, 490–496), Chugach (de Laguna 1956, 143–146), and Kodiak Island Sugpiaq (Clark 1984).

Ornaments. Tlákw.aan ornaments made of native copper included bracelets (n = 6, figure 1.13A), rings (n = 4, figure 1.13B), coiled wire beads (n = 2, figure 1.13C), tinkler cones (n = 4, figure 1.13D), and pins (n = 4, figure 1.13E). The rings and cones have close parallels among the pre-contact Ahtna copper jewelry from GUL-00077 (Hanson 2008, Figures

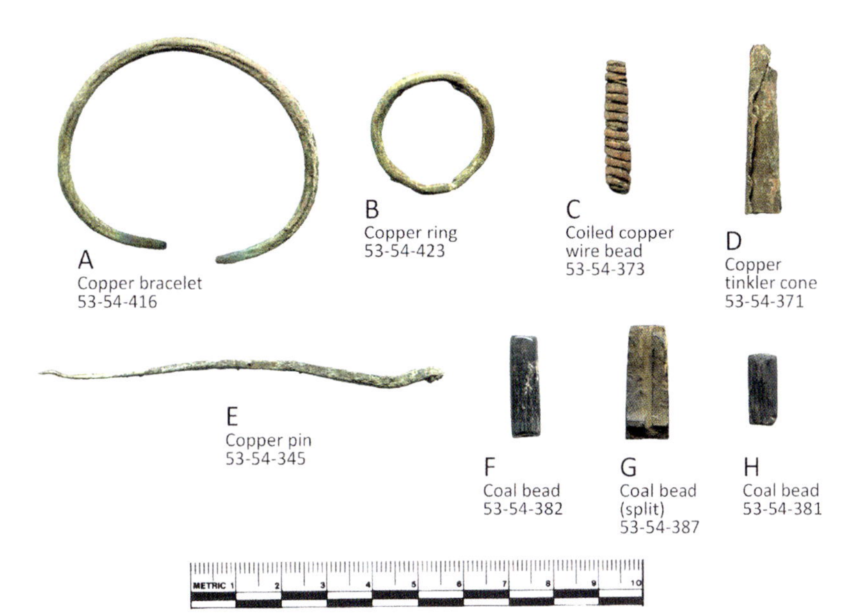

FIGURE 1.13 Personal ornaments from the Tlákw.aan site YAK-00007

12 and 13). The Eyak and Sugpiaq also wore copper ornaments and examples have been discovered at archaeological sites, including a bracelet from Kachemak Bay (de Laguna 1975, Plate 49-10). These pieces may have represented the wealth and high status of Tlákw.aan's inhabitants, as recalled in oral tradition. They also wore coal beads (n = 36, figure 1.13F–H), possibly made from coal collected at seams along Esker Creek on the west side of Yakutat Bay. Unfinished beads and coal fragments suggest on-site manufacture. Holes through the beads are straight (figure 1.13G), suggesting possession of metal drill bits. Coal beads were common in Prince William Sound, Cook Inlet, and elsewhere on Alaska's southern coast.

Overall, artifacts from the site appear to be a combination of Ahtna implements and Eyak, Sugpiaq, or Tlingit types, the latter primarily related to maritime hunting and fishing. This result, while not definitive, is consistent with the combined Ahtna-Eyak origin of the migrants as described in oral tradition and with indications (episode 10) that the Ahtna adjusted to coastal life by adopting maritime technologies (such as sea mammal harpoons, ground slate knives, stone lance points, halibut hooks, and seal oil lamps) from their Eyak affines.

Distinctive Ahtna identity at Tlákw.aan is most strikingly represented by diverse native copper items (arrow points, knives, earrings, bracelets, rings), which have only rare Eyak, Tlingit, or Sugpiaq counterparts. Copper artifacts at Tlákw.aan link the site's inhabitants to their Copper River homeland, and the relatively high frequency of these items in the upper levels of the site (de Laguna et al. 1964, 87–88) indicates that a trade connection must have been maintained long after the original migration (Pratt 1998). No direct references to post-migration contact with the Copper River region appear in the oral narratives except the incident in which six Gineix̲ K̲wáan brothers return home to retrieve a copper *tináa* for the purchase of Knight Island (episode 9). Perhaps this element of the story has a larger meaning, signifying an enduring connection between Yakutat Bay and Lower Ahtna territory on the Copper River. Sarah William's statement that the Gineix̲ K̲wáan "used copper for everything—for knives, whenever they had a war" (episode 9c) might refer not just to copper items the migrants were able to bring with them on their original journey but to continuing importation and use. Finally, it is notable that YAK-00007 is the only site in Yakutat Bay where pre-contact copper artifacts have been found, supporting its identification as Tlákw.aan village.

FAUNAL REMAINS

According to the migration narrative, the residents of Tlákw.aan fished for salmon (episode 9), hunted harbour seals at their glacial rookery (episodes 10 and 10a), and took terrestrial game including bears and Dall sheep (episode 10). At YAK-00007, where animal bones are well-preserved due to the buffering of soil acidity by calcium carbonate from marine shells, these and other species should be represented.

Species identifications of faunal remains from the 2014 trench (Etnier 2017) are generally consistent with earlier findings from the site (de Laguna et al. 1964, 77–84). The total number of identified specimens (NISP) from all strata was 10,632 (table 1.2). Fish remains (NISP = 6,669, or 63% of the total assemblage) were dominated by salmon, with the addition of a few cod and dogfish. Mammals (NISP = 3,255, or 30%) were predominantly marine species, including harbour seals, fur seals, dolphins, sea lions, and sea otters. Harbour seals (NISP = 1,044) were by far the most numerous. There was a minor representation of terrestrial animals (deer, artiodactyl [possible mountain goat], black bear, beaver, or porcupine, NISP = 40, or 0.4%) and of birds (NISP = 18, or 0.2%).

The age distribution of the harbour seal remains gives a strong indication of rookery harvesting, with a concentration on the hunting of pups or a practice of bringing these smaller animals back to the village site as whole carcasses. Harbour seal specimens of determinable age (n = 173) included 28 newborn pups (16%), 27 transitional pups up to 2 months old (16%), 27 weaned pups up to 7 months old (16%), 52 subadults (30%), and 39 adults (22.5%) (Etnier 2017).

The faunal assemblage verifies oral accounts of subsistence practices at Tlákw.aan and indicates that hunting and fishing extended from spring (harbour seal, shellfish, sea otter, and fur seal) through summer (salmon, sea mammals) and into fall (mountain sheep or goat, black bear).

TABLE 1.2 Number of Identified Faunal Specimens (NISP) by Taxon from the 2014 Test Trench at Tlákw.aan (YAK-00007)

Stratum level	4.5	4.4	4.3	4.2	4.1	3.1	2.1	No provenance	TOTAL
Invertebrates									
Tube worm	–	–	–	–	–	1	–	–	1
Urchin	–	–	1	–	–	0	–	–	1
Barnacle	–	–	–	9	17	2	–	–	28
Limpet	–	–	–	2	6	–	–	–	8
Littorina spp.	–	1	–	14	5	2	–	–	22
Nucella spp.	–	–	–	–	1	–	–	–	1
Terrestrial snail	–	–	–	1	–	–	–	–	1
Mytilus spp.	–	6	3	4	99	24	–	1	137
Leukoma staminea	–	3	–	17	128	4	1	–	153
Saxidomus gigantea	–	–	–	–	2	–	–	–	2
Scallop	–	–	–	1	1	–	–	–	2
Unidentified bivalve	–	–	–	79	52	9	–	5	145
Unidentified invertebrate	–	1	–	–	8	–	–	–	8
Invertebrates subtotal	0	11	4	127	319	42	1	6	509

Stratum level	4.5	4.4	4.3	4.2	4.1	3.1	2.1	No Prov	TOTAL
Fish									
Dogfish	–	3	5	1	–	–	–	–	9
Salmon	–	656	1,250	512	517	496	5	4	3,440
Cod	–	–	–	–	–	1	1	–	2
Unidentified fish	0	259	471	906	1,441	128	12	1	3,218
Fish subtotal	0	918	1,726	1,419	1,958	625	18	5	6,669
Birds									
Unidentified bird	–	7	3	5	4	3	–	–	18
Birds subtotal	0	7	3	5	4	3	0	0	18
Mammals									
Beaver	–	–	–	1	–	–	–	–	1
Probable porcupine	–	–	–	–	1	–	–	–	1
Beaver/Porcupine	–	1	4	2	–	–	–	–	7
Rodent	–	–	1	1	1	–	–	–	3
Deer	–	–	–	3	–	1	–	–	4
Cervidae	–	–	–	1	–	1	–	–	2
Artiodactyla	–	–	6	2	–	–	1	–	9
Probable artiodactyla	–	1	1	2	–	–	–	–	4
Dog	–	–	1	–	–	–	–	–	1
Sea otter	–	–	–	–	–	1	–	–	1
Bear	–	–	–	2	–	–	–	–	2
Probable bear	–	–	–	–	–	–	–	1	1
Unidentified carnivore	–	–	4	–	–	–	1	–	5
Harbour seal	–	77	165	220	199	208	9	35	913
Probable harbour seal	–	8	18	35	29	38	2	1	131
Fur seal	–	4	2	2	1	–	–	–	9
Probable Fur seal	–	–	–	–	1	1	–	–	2
Sea lion	–	–	–	1	–	–	–	–	1
Unidentified pinniped	–	1	–	2	1	7	–	–	11
Phocoena phocoena	–	1	–	2	5	–	–	–	8
Probable *phocoena phocoena*	–	–	–	2	1	–	–	1	4
Phocoenidae	1	2	8	18	14	6	–	2	51
Probable phocoenidae	–	–	–	3	–	–	–	–	3
Probable cetacea	–	1	–	–	–	–	–	–	1
Unidentified mammal	3	124	253	437	461	578	146	79	2,080
Mammals subtotal	4	220	463	736	714	841	159	119	3,255
Unidentified vertebrates									
Unidentified vertebrate	–	100	15	11	36	20	–	–	181
Unidentified vertebrates subtotal	0	100	15	11	36	20	0	0	181
GRAND TOTAL	4	1,256	2,211	2,298	3,031	1,531	178	130	10,632

SOURCE: ETNIER 2017.

Conclusions

The archaeological record of the Tlákw.aan/ YAK-00007 site—including its size, architecture, age, artifact assemblage, and faunal remains—is remarkably consistent with oral narratives that describe the Gineix Kwáan migration from Copper River, the clan's co-founding with the Galyáx Kaagwaantaan of a village on Knight Island, and residence there until shortly before Western contact. Archaeological data confirm that the migration occurred, provide a chronological framework for the event and its aftermath, and demonstrate the cultural transformation of an inland riverine people to hunters and fishers on the Gulf of Alaska coast. Maritime adaptation, an explicit theme of the migration narrative itself, is verified by the tangible evidence of animal bones and implements used for hunting, fishing, skin processing, and food preparation.

In evaluating the debate between skeptics and advocates of integrating oral tradition with archaeology (see, for example, Anyon et al. 1997; Echo-Hawk 2000; Mason 2000), Whiteley concluded that "oral traditions and other forms of encoded cultural representations, like ritual dramas and place-names, contain genuinely historical components that are readily usable in interpreting the past, as well as more strictly mythological elements" (Whiteley 2002, 412–413). The strong historicity inherent in *shkalneek* oral traditions—as opposed to essentially mythical *tlaagú*—is recognized by Tlingit oral scholars, and despite the epistemological contrasts between oral and materialist knowledge systems (Dods 2004) there are significant areas of intersection in which "scientific history and oral tradition may be mutually informative and verifiable" (Crowell and Howell 2013, 19).

This proposition is demonstrated by the methodology of heuristic tacking between both kinds of evidence. For example, oral narratives describe the position of Hubbard Glacier and the early stage of vegetational succession on Knight Island at the time of the immigrants' arrival, generating archaeological hypotheses that were tested by means of stratigraphic excavation, radiocarbon dating, and paleobotanical analysis. The scientific evidence yielded an earlier estimate of when the migration occurred than implied by generational counting. And yet, the predominance of spruce in the midden test trench is incompatible with oral descriptions of a treeless island at the time of settlement, suggesting that part of the Tlákw.aan site must be older than the area excavated.

Similarly, the affiliation of Ahtna and Eyak clans during the migration implies that artifacts and houses at Tlákw.aan should materially express both cultures, a prediction that is borne out by archaeological findings. On the opposite tack, archaeological data indicate that trade in copper with the Ahtna homeland continued long after the original migration, a dynamic that is not portrayed in the oral accounts, although copper and its social value are otherwise important themes. While the practice of ice floe rookery hunting for harbour seals is only implied by K'áadasteen's mention of the legendary brothers' hunting trip to the "seals' home" at the glacier's edge (see figure 1.14), faunal data highlight the dietary importance of this annual spring harvest. In these and other instances, archaeology's broad frame of reference for the interpretation of cultural patterns and processes complements oral tradition's specificity of person, place, and action. When brought together, the two systems of knowledge provide a way of "reading the past" that is powerfully enriched in cultural meaning and historical understanding (Hodder and Hutson 2003).

Demonstrating the productivity of this type of evidentiary dialogue has been one purpose of the present chapter; it is hoped that this may provide a methodological contribution to ethnohistorical archaeology. For younger generations at Yakutat, including those who helped us in the field in 2014, this work underlines the importance and validity of the history that elders teach.

FIGURE 1.14 Yakutat Tlingit elder George Ramos Sr. (Woochji'xoo eesh) looks out across the head of Yakutat Bay toward Sit' Tlein (Hubbard Glacier). Ramos grew up hunting among the ice floes discharged by the glacier, where thousands of harbour seals gather each spring to give birth and nurse their pups. Courtesy Smithsonian Institution, photograph by Aron Crowell, 2011.

Acknowledgements

The guiding principle for undertaking this type of bridging research is that oral tradition, perpetuated through many generations by careful retelling and respectful listening, will be recognized for its true historical and cultural value. My sincere gratitude is extended to Elaine Abraham, Lena Farkas, George Ramos Sr., Ted Valle, Raymond Sensemeier, and Judith Ramos for helping to maintain this knowledge and for so generously sharing it. The Yakutat Tlingit Tribe, Sealaska Corporation, and Sealaska Heritage Institute (SHI) provided essential co-operation and support that allowed work at the Tlákw.aan site, with special thanks to Victoria Demmert (President, YTT), Rosita Worl (Director, SHI), and Chuck Smythe (Director, Culture and History Department, SHI). The US Forest Service through Myra Gilliam, archaeologist at the Tongass National Forest, and the National Park Service through Greg Biddle, cultural resource manager for Wrangell–St. Elias National Park, permitted and supported research at sites around Yakutat Bay from 2011 through 2014. I also want to thank the archaeological team that conducted research in 2014 on Knight Island, including Mark Luttrell, Tim Johnson, Darian LaTocha, and Avery Underwood; University of Alaska Anchorage field school students Lorena Medina-Dirkson, Ray Dummar, Hillary Hogue, Daniel Thom, Alexandra Painter, Penelope Baggs, Pierce Batemen, Emalie Thern, and Kaitlyn McGlamery; and Yakutat high school students Kayla Drumm, Hayley Lekanof, and Devlin Anderstrom, supervised by Maka Monture. Funding was generously provided by the National Science Foundation through Arctic Social Sciences Program EAGER grant 1132295 in 2011 and Research Grant 1203417 in 2012, with the advice and support of Anna Kerttula, NSF-ASSP Program Director. William Wierzbowski (Keeper, American Section) generously assisted with access and photography of de Laguna's Tlákw.aan artifact collection at the University of Pennsylvania Museum of Archaeology and Anthropology in Philadelphia.

This chapter is dedicated to Frederica de Laguna for her incalculable contribution to documenting the history and culture of the Yakutat people.

References

Abraham, Elaine

2011 Oral interview in Yakutat on June 10, 2011, for the research project "Glacial Retreat and the Cultural Landscape of Ice Floe Sealing in Yakutat Bay, Alaska." Arctic Studies Center, Smithsonian Institution, Anchorage.

Allen, Henry T.

1887 *Report of an Expedition to the Copper, Tananá and Kóyukuk Rivers, in the Territory of Alaska, in the Year 1885, for the Purpose of Obtaining All Information Which Will Be Valuable and Important, Especially to the Military Branch of the Government.* Government Printing Office, Washington, DC.

Anyon, Roger, T. J. Ferguson, Loretta Jackson, Lillie Lane, and Philip Vicenti

1997 Native American Oral Tradition and Archaeology: Issues of Structure, Relevance, and Respect. In *Native Americans and Archaeologists, Stepping Stones to Common Ground*, edited by Nina Swidler, Kurt E. Dongoske, Roger Anyon, and Alan S. Downer, pp. 77–87. AltaMira Press, Walnut Creek, CA.

Barclay, David J., Parker E. Calkin, and Gregory C. Wiles

2001 Holocene History of Hubbard Glacier in Yakutat Bay and Russell Fiord, Alaska. *Geological Society of America Bulletin* 113(3): 388–402.

Birket-Smith, Kaj, and Frederica de Laguna

1938 *The Eyak Indians of the Copper River Delta, Alaska.* Levin and Munksgaard, Copenhagen.

Burroughs, John, John Muir, and George Bird Grinnell

1901 *Alaska.* Vol. 1, *Narrative, Glaciers, Natives.* Harriman Alaska Expedition with cooperation of Washington Academy of Sciences. Doubleday, Page and Company, New York.

Calkin, Parker E., Gregory C. Wiles, and David J. Barclay

2001 Holocene Coastal Glaciation in Alaska. *Quaternary Science Reviews* 20: 449–461.

Clark, Donald W.

1974 *Contributions to the Later Prehistory of Kodiak Island.* Mercury Series No. 20, Archaeological Survey of Canada. National Museum of Man, Ottawa.

1984 Prehistory of the Pacific Eskimo Region. In *Handbook of North American Indians*, vol. 5, *Arctic*, edited by David Damas, pp. 136–148. Smithsonian Institution Press, Washington, DC.

Connor, Cathy, Greg Streveler, Austin Post, Daniel Monteith, and Wayne Howell

2009 The Neoglacial Landscape and Human History of Glacier Bay, Glacier Bay National Park and Preserve, Southeast Alaska, USA. *The Holocene* 19(3): 381–393.

Cooper, H. Kory, M. John M. Duke, Antonio Simonetti, and GuangCheng Chen

2008 Trace Element and Pb Isotope Provenance Analysis of Native Copper in Northwestern North America: Results of a Recent Pilot Study Using INAA, ICP-MS, and LA-MC-ICP-MS. *Journal of Archaeological Science* 35: 1732–1747.

Crowell, Aron L.

2011–2014 Project field notes, "Glacial Retreat and the Cultural Landscape of Ice Floe Sealing in Yakutat Bay, Alaska." Arctic Studies Center, Smithsonian Institution, Anchorage.

2012 Collaborative Research: Glacial Retreat and the Cultural Landscape of Ice Floe Sealing at Yakutat Bay, Alaska. Proposal to the National Science Foundation, Arctic Social Sciences Program, ARC-1203417.

2016 Ice, Seals, and Guns: Late Nineteenth-Century Alaska Native Commercial Sealing in Southeast Alaska. *Arctic Anthropology* 52(2): 11–32.

Crowell, Aron L., and Wayne K. Howell

2013 Time, Oral Tradition, and Archaeology at Xakwnoowú, a Little Ice Age Fort in Southeastern Alaska. *American Antiquity* 78(1): 2–23.

Crowell, Aron L., Wayne K, Howell, Daniel H. Mann, and Greg Streveler

2013 *The Hoonah Tlingit Cultural Landscape in Glacier Bay National Park and Preserve: An Archaeological and Geological Study.* National Park Service, Glacier Bay National Park and Preserve, Gustavus, Alaska.

Crowell, Aron L., and Daniel H. Mann

1998 *Archaeology and Coastal Dynamics of Kenai Fjords National Park, Alaska.* National Park Service, Alaska Region, Anchorage.

Cruikshank, Julie

1981 Legend and Landscape: Convergence of Oral and Scientific Traditions in the Yukon Territory. *Arctic Anthropology* 18(2): 67–93.

2001 Glaciers and Climate Change: Perspectives from Oral Tradition. *Arctic* 54(4): 377–393.

2005 *Do Glaciers Listen? Local Knowledge, Colonial Encounters, and Social Imagination.* University of British Columbia Press, Vancouver.

Davis, Stanley D.

1996 *The Archaeology of the Yakutat Foreland: A Socioecological View.* PhD dissertation, Department of Anthropology, Texas A&M University, College Station.

de Laguna, Frederica

1956 *Chugach Prehistory: The Archaeology of Prince William Sound, Alaska.* University of Washington Press, Seattle.

1960 *The Story of a Tlingit Community: A Problem in the Relationship Between Archeological, Ethnological and Historical Methods.* Bureau of American Ethnology Bulletin No. 172. Washington, DC.

1972 *Under Mount Saint Elias: The History and Culture of the Yakutat Tlingit.* Smithsonian Contributions to Anthropology Vol. 7. Smithsonian Institution Press, Washington, DC.

1975 *The Archaeology of Cook Inlet, Alaska.* 2nd ed. Alaska Historical Society, Anchorage.

1990a Tlingit. In *Handbook of North American Indians*, vol. 7, *Northwest Coast*, edited by Wayne Suttles, pp. 203–228. Smithsonian Institution Press, Washington, DC.

1990b Eyak. In *Handbook of North American Indians*, vol. 7, *Northwest Coast*, edited by Wayne Suttles, pp. 189–196. Smithsonian Institution Press, Washington, DC.

de Laguna, Frederica, and Catharine McClellan

1981 Ahtna. In *Handbook of North American Indians*, vol. 5, *Subarctic*, edited by June Helm, pp. 641–663. Smithsonian Institution Press, Washington, DC.

de Laguna, F., F. A. Riddell, D. F. McGeein, K. S. Lane, J. A. Freed, and C. Osborne

1964 *Archaeology of the Yakutat Bay Area, Alaska.* Smithsonian Institution Bureau of Ethnology Bulletin No. 192. Government Printing Office, Washington, DC.

Dods, Robert R.
2004 Knowing Ways/Ways of Knowing: Reconciling Science and Tradition. *World Archaeology* 36: 547–557.

Echo-Hawk, Roger C.
2000 Ancient History in the New World: Integrating Oral Traditions and the Archaeological Record in Deep Time. *American Antiquity* 65(2): 267–290.

Edwards, Keri
2009 *Dictionary of Tlingit*. Sealaska Heritage Institute, Juneau.

Emmons, George Thornton
1991 *The Tlingit Indians*. Edited with additions by Frederica de Laguna. University of Washington Press, Seattle.

Etnier, Michael A.
2017 Faunal Analysis of the Tlākw.aan (Knight Island) Site (YAK-00007), Yakutat, Alaska. Unpublished paper in possession of author. Anthropology Department, Western Washington University, Bellingham, Washington.

Goldschmidt, Walter R., and Theodore H. Haas
1998 *Haa Aaní / Our Land: Tlingit and Haida Land Rights and Use*. Edited and with an introduction by Thomas F. Thornton. University of Washington Press, Juneau, and Sealaska Heritage Foundation, Juneau. Originally published in 1946 as *Possessory Rights of the Natives of Southeastern Alaska*.

Hanson, Diane K.
2008 Archaeological Investigations in the 1990s at the Ringling Site, GUL-077, near Gulkana, Alaska. *Alaska Journal of Anthropology* 6(1–2): 109–130.

Harrington, John P.
1940 Yakutat notes. Files EY940H11940a and EY940H1940c. Alaska Native Language Archive, University of Alaska, Fairbanks.

Henige, David P.
1974 *The Chronology of Oral Tradition, Quest for a Chimera*. Clarendon Press, Oxford.

Hodder, Ian, and Scott Hutson
2003 *Reading the Past: Current Approaches to Interpretation in Archaeology*. 3rd ed. Cambridge University Press, Cambridge.

Hymes, Dell
1990 Mythology. In *Handbook of North American Indians*, vol. 7, *Northwest Coast*, edited by Wayne Suttles, pp. 593–601. Smithsonian Institution Press, Washington, DC.

Jones, Zachary R.
2017 Haa Daat Akawshixit / "He Wrote About Us": Contextualizing Anthropologist John R. Swanton's Fieldwork and Writings on the Tlingit Indians, 1904–1909. *Alaska Journal of Anthropology* 15(1–2): 126–140.

Ketz, James A.
1983 *Paxson Lake: Two Nineteenth Century Ahtna Sites in the Copper River Basin, Alaska*. Anthropology and Historic Preservation, Cooperative Park Studies Unit, Occasional Paper No. 33. University of Alaska, Fairbanks.

Knecht, Richard A.
1995 The Late Prehistory of the Alutiiq People: Culture Change on the Kodiak Archipelago from 1200–1750 A.D. PhD dissertation, Department of Anthropology, Bryn Mawr College, Bryn Mawr, Pennsylvania.

Kováčik, Peter, and Linda Scott Cummings
2015 Charcoal Identification and AMS Radiocarbon Age Determination, Site YAK-00007, Yakutat Bay, Alaska. With assistance from R. A. Varney. PaleoResearch Institute, Golden, Colorado.

Kruse, Gordon H., and Alan M. Springer
2007 Marine Mammal Harvest and Fishing. In *Long-Term Ecological Change in the Northern Gulf of Alaska*, edited by Robert B. Spies, pp. 192–219. Elsevier, Amsterdam.

Marsden, Susan
2001 Defending the Mouth of the Skeena: Perspectives on Tsimshian Tlingit Relations. In *Perspectives on Northern Northwest Coast Prehistory*, edited by Jerome S. Cybulski, pp. 61–106. Mercury Series No. 160, Archaeological Survey of Canada. Canadian Museum of Civilization, Hull, Québec.

Martindale, Andrew
2006 Methodological Issues in the Use of Tsimshian Oral Traditions (*Adawx*) in Archaeology. *Canadian Journal of Archaeology* 30(2): 158–192.

Mason, Ronald J.
2000 Archaeology and Native North American Oral Traditions. *American Antiquity* 65(2): 239–266.

McMillan, Alan D., and Ian Hutchinson
2002 When the Mountain Dwarfs Danced: Aboriginal Traditions of Paleoseismic Events Along the Cascadia Subduction Zone of Western North America. *Ethnohistory* 49(1): 41–68.

Monteith, Daniel, Cathy Connor, Gregory P. Streveler, and Wayne Howell
2007 Geology and Oral History—Complementary Views of a Former Glacier Bay Landscape. In *Proceedings of the Fourth Glacier Bay Science Symposium, October 26–28, 2004, Juneau, Alaska*, edited by John F. Piatt and Scott M. Gende, pp. 50–53. Scientific Investigations Report 2007-5047. US Geological Survey, Reston, Virginia.

Moodie, D. Wayne, A. J. W. Catchpole, and Kerry Abel
1992 Northern Athapaskan Oral Traditions and the White River Volcano. *Ethnohistory* 39(2): 148–170.

Pratt, Kenneth L.
1998 Copper, Trade, and Tradition Among the Lower Ahtna of the Chitina River Basin: The Nicolai Era, 1884–1900. *Arctic Anthropology* 35(2): 77–98.
2009 A History of the ANCSA 14(h)(1) Program and Significant Reckoning Points, 1975–2008. In *Chasing the Dark: Perspectives on Place, History and Alaska Native Land Claims*, edited by Kenneth L. Pratt, pp. 3–43. Bureau of Indian Affairs, ANCSA Office, Anchorage.

Rainey, Froelich G.
1939 Archaeology in Central Alaska. *Anthropological Papers of the American Museum of Natural History* 36(55): 351–405.

Russell, Israel C.
1891 An Expedition to Mount St. Elias, Alaska. *National Geographic Magazine* 3: 53–204.

Sealaska Corporation
1975 *Native Cemetery and Historic Sites of Southeast Alaska (Preliminary Report).* Wilsey and Ham, Inc., Consultants, Seattle.

Seton Karr, Haywood W.
1887 *Shores and Alps of Alaska.* Sampson, Low, Marston, Searle, and Rivington, London.

Shinkwin, Anne D.
1979 *Dakah De'nin's Village and the Dixthada Site: A Contribution to Northern Athapaskan Prehistory.* Mercury Series No. 91, Archaeological Survey of Canada, National Museum of Man, Ottawa.

Springer, Alan M., Sara J. Iverson, and James L. Bodkin
2007 Marine Mammal Harvest and Fishing. In *Long-Term Ecological Change in the Northern Gulf of Alaska*, edited by Robert B. Spies, pp. 352–378. Elsevier, Amsterdam.

Sterritt, Neil J.
1998 *Tribal Boundaries in the Nass Watershed.* University of British Columbia Press, Vancouver.

Swanton, John R.
1909 *Tlingit Myths and Texts.* US Government Printing Office, Washington, DC.

Thom, Brian
2003 The Anthropology of Northwest Coast Oral Traditions. *Arctic Anthropology* 40(1): 1–28.

Thornton, Thomas F.
1997 Know Your Place: The Organization of Tlingit Geographic Knowledge. *Ethnology* 36(4): 295–307.
2008 *Being and Place Among the Tlingit.* University of Washington Press, Seattle, and Sealaska Heritage Institute, Juneau.

Thornton, Thomas F. (editor)
2012 *Haa Léelk'w Hás Aaní Saax'ú: Our Grandparents' Names on the Land.* Sealaska Heritage Institute, Juneau, and University of Washington Press, Seattle.

Vansina, Jan
1965 *Oral Tradition: A Study in Historical Methodology.* Clarendon Press, Oxford.

VanStone, James W.
1955 Exploring the Copper River Country. *Pacific Northwest Quarterly* 46(4): 115–123.

Veakis, Emil
1979 *Archaeometric Study of Native Copper in Prehistoric North America.* PhD dissertation, Department of Anthropology, State University of New York at Stony Brook, Ann Arbor.

Whitely, Peter M.
2002 Archaeology and Oral Tradition: The Scientific Importance of Dialogue. *American Antiquity* 67(3): 405–415.

Wolfe, Robert J., and Craig Mischler
1994 *The Subsistence Harvest of Harbor Seal and Sea Lion by Alaska Natives in 1993.* Technical Paper No. 233. Alaska Department of Fish and Game, Division of Subsistence, Juneau.

Workman, William B.
1977 Ahtna Archaeology: A Preliminary Statement. In *Prehistory of the North American Arctic: The Athapaskan Question. Proceedings of the 9th Annual Conference of the University of Calgary Archaeological Association*, edited by J. W. Helmer, S. Van Dyke, and F. J. Kense, pp. 22–39. University of Calgary, Calgary, Alberta.

Worl, Rosita
2010 Tlingit. In *Living Our Cultures, Sharing Our Heritage: The First Peoples of Alaska*, edited by Aron L. Crowell, Rosita Worl, Paul C. Ongtooguk, and Dawn D. Biddison, pp. 200–225. Smithsonian Books, Washington, DC.

FIGURE 2.1 Inuvialuit elders interviewed in 1990 at Herschel Island, situated in the Beaufort Sea off the coast of the Yukon North Slope. Left to right: Dora Malegana, Jean Tardiff, Sarah Meyook, and Kathleen Hansen. Photograph by John Tousignant for the Heritage Branch, Government of Yukon.

MURIELLE NAGY

2 Inuvialuit Ethnonyms and Toponyms as a Reflection of Identity, Language, and Memory

Alarmed by the threat that the rapid expansion of oil and gas exploration in the 1970s presented to their culture and territory in a changing northern society, the Inuvialuit of the western Canadian Arctic mandated the Committee for Original Peoples Entitlement (COPE) to negotiate a land claim with the Government of Canada (Ho et al. 2009). When the final agreement was reached in 1984, the Inuvialuit had exchanged exclusive ownership and control of their traditional territory for specific rights over land, wildlife management, and financial compensation. The Inuvialuit Settlement Region spans about twenty percent of the Canadian Arctic and includes six communities: Aklavik, Inuvik, Paulatuk, Sachs Harbour, Tuktoyaktuk, and Ulukhaktok.

The Inuvialuit, who number roughly five thousand, consider themselves a distinct sociopolitical entity (Dahl 1988; Dorais 1994, 258). Although they are generally said to speak an Inuit language known as Inuvialuktun, they in fact belong to three linguistic groups, which in turn reflect differences in cultural origins (figure 2.2). Very few fluent speakers of any of the dialects remain, but most Inuvialuit know some words, phrases, and songs in their dialect. Language loss was accelerated from the 1930s onward by the growing prevalence of residential schools in Arctic communities, where children were forced to speak only English, and by a process of diglossia that resulted in English becoming the dominant language. By 1950, most Inuvialuit parents were teaching only English to their children (Dorais 1989, 201).

When it became clear that Inuvialuktun was endangered, COPE formed an Inuvialuktun Language Commission in 1980. The Commission undertook the Inuvialuktun Language Project in 1981 to produce dictionaries and grammars for the three dialects (Osgood 1984). The fieldwork was undertaken by linguist Ronald Lowe, who published a grammar and a dictionary for each dialect (Lowe 1983, 1984a, 1984b, 2001; Kudlak and Compton 2018). Despite these efforts, English is the dominant language of the area and Inuvialuktun spoken mainly by elders and understood only passively by Inuvialuit youth. Language revitalization efforts continue through programs at local schools, cultural activities, and the production of educational material by the Inuvialuit Cultural Centre Pitquhiit-Pitqusiit, which was established in 1998.

Despite this language diversity, however, the Inuvialuit have built a common identity around the sharing of a vast territory and the oral traditions associated with it (see, for example, Alunik, Kolausok, and Morrison 2003; Lyons 2009; Oehler 2012).[1] Through traditional knowledge, oral history, and toponyms (place names), the Inuvialuit are keeping a record for future generations of the ways their ancestors lived on that land. Since parts of their territory are no longer actively used, some of that heritage could have been lost, but oral history projects undertaken either by or with the Inuvialuit have kept it alive (see Arnold et al. 2011; Gray 2003; Hart 2001, 2011; Inuvialuit Elders with Bandringa 2010; Lyons 2010; Nagy 1994, 1999, 2006; Parks Canada 2004).

In this chapter, I will first discuss the Inuvialuit's three linguistic groups with a focus on the origin and meaning of their ethnonyms.[2] Then I will compare toponyms mentioned by Inuvialuit of all linguistic groups during oral history projects. Although fewer toponyms were documented than expected, a close look at their location and meaning reveals that Inuvialuit from different cultural origins had, and probably still have, specific ways of naming their territory and shared similar ways of remembering their toponyms.

The data that will be discussed come from three Inuvialuit oral history projects about Herschel Island (1989–1991), the Yukon North Slope (1991–1994), and Banks Island (1995–1999) (Nagy 1994, 1999). These projects, which were funded through the Inuvialuit Social Development Program, collected oral history on the use and knowledge of the areas. They were undertaken by the Inuvialuit Regional Corporation to fulfill the obligation of the Government of Canada and the Government of Yukon to conduct oral history studies as a part of the designation of parks on Inuvialuit territory. The three parks related to these projects are Herschel Island-Qikiqtaruk Territorial Park (designated in 1987), the Ivvavik National Park on the Yukon coast (1984), and the Aulavik National Park on northern Banks Island (1992). Most of the 134 interviews conducted were with Inuvialuit elders born between the 1900s and 1930s. Over one hundred archival tapes were translated into English. The majority of the participants spoke at least one of the three Inuvialuit dialects and interviews were conducted in their mother tongue for both methodological and archival reasons. Indeed, Inuvialuktun transcriptions and English translations of the interviews and archival tapes were not only necessary to complete final reports, articles, and a video, but they also provided material that could be used for future research, educational, and interpretive purposes.

Inuvialuit Linguistic Groups: Siglit, Uummarmiut, and Kangiryuarmiut

When the Inuit of the western Canadian Arctic were preparing their land claim, they chose Inuvialuit as their collective name. After the Inuvialuktun Language Commission was created, they selected Siglit, Uummarmiut, and Kangiryuarmiut to name their three linguistic groups (Osgood 1984, viii). In the latter two ethnonyms, the suffix –miut means "inhabitants of" (Lowe 1984a, 133, although the term is not specific to humans, it is often translated as "people of/from." Their dialects are named by adding the suffix –un to the end of the ethnonym, Inuvialuktun being the term used to encompass all three. The Inuvialuktun dialects are part of the Inuit language family, which is divided into the following groups from west to east: Alaskan Iñupiatun (also called Iñupiaq), western Canadian Inuktun, eastern Canadian Inuktitut, and Greenlandic Kalaallisut. Uummarmiutun is a dialect of the Northern Alaska Iñupiatun subgroup, Siglitun and Inuinnaqtun are dialects of the western Canadian Inuktun, and Kangiryuarmiutun is a subdialect of Inuinnaqtun (Dorais 2010, 28–29).

The term Inuvialuit means "real people," (singular, Inuvialuk "real person") (Lowe 2001, 358). According to linguist Louis-Jacques Dorais, after contact with Europeans, the Indigenous peoples of the North American Arctic attributed themselves names encompassing all their local groups to be distinguished from the newcomers. In Canada and Alaska, this was done by either using Inuit as an ethnic name including all regional groups, or creating names with the wordbase *inu-* (as in *inuk*, "person" and its plural *inuit*, "people" which originally applied to all humans) followed by morphemes meaning "real" or "genuine" to indicate that the Inuit are the prototype of Arctic humanity (for example, Iñupiat, Inuvialuit, and Inuinnait) (Dorais 2020, 77–78). Thus, it was likely after contact with foreigners other than their Dene neighbours that the Siglitun speakers used the ethnonym Inuvialuit "to refer to themselves, no matter where they lived" (Osgood 1984, viii).

Indeed, the Siglit are the original Inuvialuit, who traditionally occupied a vast area that extended from Barter Island, off the northern coast of Alaska not far west of the Yukon boundary, as far east as Cape Lyon (figure 2.2). Archaeologists trace their origins to the Thule people, whose culture developed in coastal western Alaska sometime around AD 1000 and quickly populated the Canadian Arctic and Greenland eight hundred years ago (Friesen and Arnold 2008). At least until the first half of the nineteenth century, the Inuvialuit comprised eight main territorial groups. From west to east, these were the Tuyurmiat of the Yukon coast (including the Qikiqtaryungmiut of Herschel Island); the Kuukpangmiut and the Kitigaaryungmiut of the Mackenzie Delta; the Imaryungmiut of Eskimo Lakes, along the south-western side of the Tuktoyaktuk Peninsula; on its northern part, the Nuvugarmiut of Atkinson Point; the Kuungmiut of the Anderson River; the Avvarmiut of Cape Bathurst; and southeast of it, the Igluyuaryungmiut of the Franklin Bay area (Betts 2009, 7; Hart 2011, 117; Morrison 2003a, 14–17; Nagy 1994, 25–28, 2012a, 153).[3]

The term Siglit (singular, Sigliq) was first recorded by Oblate missionary Émile Petitot as "Tchiglit" during one of his five travels to the Mackenzie Delta region between 1865 and 1870. It is also possible that Petitot was given the term by the young Siglit couple that stayed at Fort Good Hope Catholic mission in the summer of 1868 or by Arviuna ("bowhead whaler"), a teenager who spent two months with Petitot in the summer of 1870 helping him to complete his French-Inuit dictionary (Petitot 1876, i; 1887, 226–227, 279).

Published in 1876, Petitot's dictionary includes a monograph of the Siglit and a short grammar of their language. Without defining the word Tchiglit explicitly, Petitot indicated that the Inuit living along the shores of the Arctic sea, between Colville River (Alaska) in the west and as far east as Cape Bathurst, used it to identify themselves (Petitot 1876, i, x). Later, he specified that their western limit was Point Barrow (Petitot 1886, 3). However, his monograph is restricted to the Tchiglit of the Mackenzie and the Anderson Rivers because they were the only groups he had visited. Although Petitot wrote *innok* (Inuk) and its plural *innoït* (Inuit) as translations of the word *Esquimau*, he stipulated that those at the mouths of the Anderson and Mackenzie Rivers were called Tçiglit and that its singular was Tçigleꝑk (Petitot 1876, 29).[4] Those two last terms are now pronounced Siglit and Sigliq.[5]

Petitot's 1887 book, *Les Grands Esquimaux,* has a copy of his 1875 map attached, which includes the three territorial groups he mentioned in his 1876 dictionary: the Taréorméut of the Mackenzie Delta (Tariurmiut, "coast dwellers," Lowe 2001, 147), the Kragmalit of the Tuktoyaktuk Peninsula and the Anderson River (Qangmalit, "people of the east," Lowe 2001, 104), and the Kragmalivit of Cape Bathurst ("places of the Qangmalit").[6] These terms are too generic to have been the endonyms of local Siglit groups, but were used by people of the Mackenzie Delta to designate their eastern neighbours (see Stefansson 2001, 115). On his map, Petitot added, in parentheses, the term Tchizaré for the people at the mouth of the Anderson River. He did not translate Tchizaré but described it as equivalent to Tchiglit (Petitot 1887, 2). In his dictionary, he specified that Tchizaꝑéni was the corrupted form of an Inuit term meaning "on the shore" that the Dene used to designate people of the Anderson River (Petitot 1876, x).

Despite calling "chief of the Tchiglit" the leader of the Anderson River people, Petitot did not restrict that ethnonym to this group (1887, 3). He referred to three peoples—from the west, the centre, and the east of the Mackenzie River—as part of the Inuit he was describing (Petitot 1887, 298). To complicate the matter, Petitot cited a story told by Arviuna about the origins of the Tchiglit, which he translated this time as meaning "humans" (1876, xxiv, 1886, 3). If Arviuna provided this translation, it must have reinforced Petitot's understanding that Tchiglit was an endonym used to designate an entire nation made of territorial groups. However, Petitot also translated the singular form Tchiglerk to mean "fellow" and "man" when twice quoting Arviuna (1887, 283–284).

Petitot also stated that Arviuna belonged specifically to the Taréorméout (Tariurmiut), a term he translated as "people of the high sea." However, he also wrote that they lived west of the Mackenzie Delta (where he had placed them on his map), a discrepancy that suggests they lived along the Yukon North Slope (1887, 279). During our interviews, Ishmael Alunik insisted that the people of the Yukon coast called themselves Tuyurmiat but since the Kitigaaryungmiut called them Siglit, they started to use that name (Nagy 1994b, IA91-14A, 2). Alunik then corroborates Arviuna's use of Tchiglit (Siglit) to talk about his people. Petitot mentioned the "Tuyormiyat" (Tuyurmiat) as one of the Inuit "tribes" known to the Siglit, but he placed them in the Bering Strait.

Tuyurmiat (singular, Tuyurmiaq) means "guests" in Siglitun and Uummarmiutun (Lowe 1984a, 224; 2001, 159). Stefansson mentioned that the Kitigaaryungmiut called the people west of the Mackenzie River up to Herschel Island and a little beyond it the Tuyormiut (Tuyurmiat) (1919, 23). The Inuvialuit we interviewed also called those people Tuyurmiat and indicated that they spoke Siglitun but with a dialect slightly different from that of the Kitigaaryungmiut (Nagy 1994, 26). Linguistic informants from Tuktoyaktuk also identified them as Tuyurmiat but specified that they spoke an Alaskan dialect (Lowe 1991, 185n4). In 1991, Emmanuel Felix explained that Tuyurmiat was the name the Kitigaaryungmiut used for the people from Qitiqtaryuk (Herschel Island) and Tapqaq (Shingle Point), but Lily Lipscomb said that her grandmother, who was originally from inland Alaska, used it only in reference to the people of Pattuktuq (Demarcation Point), Alaska, close to the Yukon border (Nagy 1994b, EF91-5A, 1 and LL91-25A, 3).[7]

Although the term Siglit had been used for a long time, its meaning was no longer known by the 1980s and most speakers of Siglitun agreed that it was given to them by others. Only the inhabitants of Paulatuk unhesitatingly called themselves by that name (Osgood 1984, viii). In 1991, Emmanuel Felix suggested that the term Siglit might refer to one of the two places called Siglialuk north of Tuktoyaktuk and that it may have originated from an older version of the Siglit language (Nagy 1994a, EF90-5A, 1–2). Asked about the meaning of the toponym Siglialuk located at the bottom of Hutchison Bay, David Nasogaluak explained that some people called the inhabitants of the Tuktoyaktuk area Siglit to differentiate them from those who lived more inland, thus implying that both Siglialuk and Siglit are derived from the wordbase *sigyaq* (Hart 2011, 70).[8]

Although Hart described *sigyaq* as the word for "shore" in Siglitun, which could apply to rivers, lakes, or the sea, its meaning is in fact "seashore" (Hart 2011, 70; Lowe 2001, 525, 529). As Siglit comprises the beginning of *sigyaq* and –lit, which seems an assimilation of –lliit, the plural of the suffix –lliq ("the one located at the most X") (Lowe 2001, 128, 245), it probably means "those more toward the seashore" and hence corroborates Duncan Pryde's translation of this ethnonym (Fortescue, Jacobson, and Kaplan 2010, 87). Furthermore, this definition explains why Siglitun was previously called the "coastal dialect" (Lowe 1991, 142). Convinced that Siglit is a mispronounciation or misspelling of

Sallit, the Inuvialuit Regional Corporation has recently replaced Siglit with Sallirmiut (translated as "coastal people" on their website) and Siglitun with Sallirmiutun.[9] If one follows this interpretation, rather than originating with the word *sigyaq*, Siglit is closer to *sallit*, the plural of *salliq* ("the one located closest to shore") (Lowe 2001, 121). However, this new name might be confused with the extinct Sallirmuit (formerly spelled Sadlermiut) of Southampton Island in Hudson Bay. Since I will be discussing historical sources and data collected in the 1990s and for the purposes of avoiding anachronisms, I will use the terms Siglit and Siglitun in this text.

British explorer Captain John Franklin visited the Siglit in the nineteenth century, roughly forty years prior to Petitot. Both estimated the Siglit population to have been around 2,000 although it may have been close to 2,500, according to geographer Peter Usher's reconstruction from various sources (Franklin [1828] 1971, 86–228; Petitot 1876, x; Usher 1971a, 169–171). Robert McGhee (1974, xi) and Derek Smith (1984, 349) argued that because of their ability to hunt down large numbers of beluga whales in the Mackenzie Delta during the summer months, the Siglit were able to sustain one of the largest Inuit populations in the Arctic before contact with whalers, traders, and missionaries at the end of the nineteenth century. Sadly, these interactions resulted in major epidemics during the first two decades of the twentieth century that drastically reduced the Siglit population.

The largest village of the Siglit was Kitigaaryuit (McGhee 1974). From 1911 to 1917, it had an Anglican mission and, from 1912 to 1933, a Hudson's Bay Company trading post which was moved to Tuktoyaktuk in 1934 where most Kitigaaryungmiut relocated (Hart 2011, 31, 50). During the 1930s, fox trapping attracted some Siglit to Banks Island, while others moved east of Cape Bathurst to the Cape Parry area to trap and hunt. Southeast of Bathurst, a new community was formed in Paulatuk after a Catholic mission with a small trading post opened in 1935 (Parks Canada 2004). When the last trading post of Herschel Island closed in 1937, most Siglit living there and along the Yukon North Slope moved to Tuktoyaktuk. Now, the Siglit live in Inuvik, the mainland coastal communities of Tuktoyaktuk and Paulatuk, as well as in Sachs Harbour, on Banks Island (figure 2.2).

Uummarmiut means "inhabitants of the evergreens or green willows" and refers to the vegetation of the Mackenzie Delta. Linguistic evidence indicates that the Uummarmiut are the descendants of Iñupiatun speakers from northern Alaska, many of whom were originally from the Anaktuvuk Pass area (Lowe 1984a, xv, 47, 63). During our interviews, the terms Iñupiat, Nunataarmiut, and sometimes Nunamiut, were terms used by Siglit to refer to the Uummarmiut and by the Uummarmiut to refer to themselves. Both Iñupiatun and Uummarmiutun were names given to their language (Nagy 1994a, 1994b). Iñupiat ("real people," singular, Iñupiaq "real person") is an endonym that represents the Iñupiatun speakers of northwest and northern Alaska and their descendants. Although both terms contain the wordbase *nuna* ("land"), Nunamiut and Nunataarmiut originally had different meanings. Nunamiut ("inland inhabitants") is used in contrast to Tariurmiut ("coastal inhabitants"), both being generic terms depicting different ways of life (Burch 1998, 3). After the creation of the village of Anaktuvuk Pass in 1949, its inland inhabitants were often called Nunamiut in the anthropological literature, but they now call themselves Naqsragmiut.

Nunataarmiut refers to the inhabitants of the Nunatak or Noatak River (Hall 1984, 345).

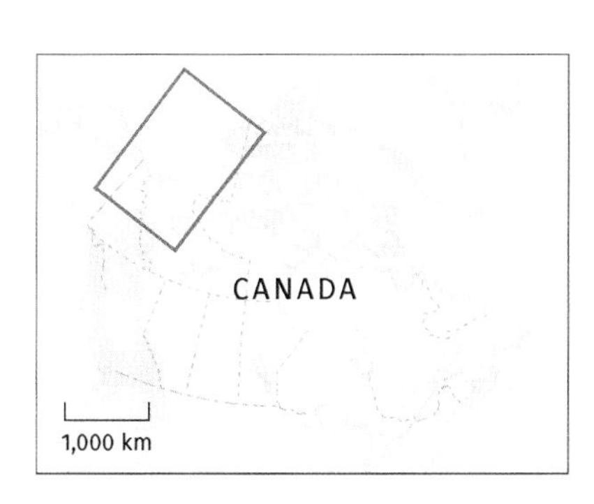

FIGURE 2.2 Territory of the Inuvialuit in the western Canadian Arctic and their three linguistic groups and six communities (adapted from Lowe 1984a and Nagy 1994, 3).

According to Ernest ("Tiger") Burch (1984, 318–319), Nunataarmiut originally designated the inhabitants of the entire Noatak River drainage, although Iñupiatun speakers of the Alaska North Slope used it for those of the drainage's upper part. Maps in his latest books depict the Nunataarmiut north of the Nuataarmiut, thus including the Anaktuvuk Pass area in the Brooks Range (Burch 2005, 37, 2006, 8). In the mid-1880s, Nunataarmiut referred to people who came to the Alaskan Arctic coast, east of Colville River, but it soon became a general term for all former inland inhabitants regardless of their origins (Burch 1984, 319). Indeed, Stefansson (1919, 23) mentioned that the Kitigaaryungmiut called most of the people from western Alaska Nunataarmiut.

Toward the end of the nineteenth century, some Nunataarmiut began to migrate inland to the northern Yukon and the Mackenzie Delta region in response to a decrease in Alaska caribou populations in the Brooks Range, a decline which had begun in the 1860s (Burch 2012, 119; Nagy 1994, 1–2). During our interviews, Uummarmiut mentioned that the caribou decline also led their grandparents and parents to move to Old Crow Flats (Yukon), the inland territory of the Vuntut Gwitchin (Nagy 1994, 2).[10]

Although Petitot located the Nuna-tag-méut (Nunataarmiut) toward the Bering Strait, he listed them as another Inuit "tribe" known to the Siglit (1876, x). Petitot may have met Nunataarmiut coming to trade at Fort McPherson (south of the Mackenzie Delta) in the summer. In fact, evidence of the presence of Nunataarmiut appears in Petitot's dictionary, which includes the word *innopiap* (Iñupiaq) as the translation of "human," when the Siglitun version of that word is *inuk* (1876, 38). If Siglit is neither an exonym of the Tuyurmiat of the Yukon North Slope nor an endonym of the Mackenzie Delta and Anderson River inhabitants, it might have been used by the Nunataarmiut to distinguish themselves from the Inuvialuit coming from inland.

Starting in 1889, Nunataarmiut and other Iñupiat from coastal villages of northwest Alaska worked as hunters and seamstresses for American whalers, who often hired entire families for two years or more (Bockstoce 2018, 86). The whalers were hunting bowhead whales, mainly for their baleen, around Herschel Island and later expanded to the area around Baillie Islands, west of Cape Bathurst, as well (Bockstoce 1986; Morrison 2003b).[11] In 1894 and 1895, caribou hunters were so essential to whalers that most Iñupiat from Point Barrow were at Herschel Island along with another one hundred from Point Hope (Bockstoce 1986, 274). From 1906 to 1918, a dozen Nunataarmiut were employed by Canadian anthropologist and explorer Vilhjalmur Stefansson and his colleagues (Gray 2003; Jenness 1991; Stefansson 1919, 1921, 1922, 2001).

After the 1908 collapse of the whaling industry, some whalers stayed in the Inuvialuit territory and became trappers or traders. Many Nunataarmiut families did not return to Alaska, preferring to trap for furs along the Yukon North Slope and in the Mackenzie Delta and remain near the important trading centres of Herschel Island and the Hudson's Bay Company trading post Aklavik, which opened in 1912 (Morrison and Kolausok 2003). More Nunataarmiut came in the 1920s, as muskrat trapping developed in the Mackenzie Delta area. A final migration of Nunataarmiut occurred in the mid-1930s and 1940s, as local trading posts near the Alaska-Yukon border closed down (Nagy 1994, 1–2).

While they worked on their dictionary in the early 1980s, the Iñupiatun speakers of the Mackenzie Delta decided to be called Uummarmiut since Nunataarmiut had become a misnomer and could have a pejorative connotation (Lowe 1991, 185n6). Most Uummarmiut now live in Aklavik and Inuvik, although some are in Sachs Harbour.

Kangiryuarmiut means "people of the large bay," referring to Prince Albert Sound (Kangiryuaq), on the western coast of Victoria Island (Kudlak and

Compton 2018, 85). They now live primarily in the village of Ulukhaktok (formerly Holman), at the entrance to the sound, although a few families have been residing in Sachs Harbour on Banks Island since the mid-1950s. Both culturally and linguistically, the Kangiryuarmiut are closely connected to the Inuinnait (once known as the Copper Inuit) of the Kitikmeot Region of Nunavut, particularly those of Kugluktuk (formerly Coppermine), at the mouth of the Coppermine River, and Cambridge Bay on the southeastern shore of Victoria Island (see, for example, Collignon 1996, 2006; Condon 1996; Kudlak and Compton 2018).

Inuinnait, which means "genuine people" and designates all the Inuinnaqtun speakers regardless of local identity (Dorais 2020, 78), has been used as a regional name since at least the 1990s (Collignon 2006, 21). Ten years after the creation of Nunavut in 1999, Inuinnaqtun became one of its two official languages, along with Inuktitut. In recognition of their origins, Kangiryuarmiut might refer to themselves as both Inuinnait and Inuvialuit, and most prefer to call their language Inuinnaqtun rather than Kangiryuarmiutun (Dorais 2010, 33; Lowe 1983, xv). For example, in contrast to the title of the first Kangiryuarmiutun dictionary, which did not mention Inuinnaqtun (Lowe 1983), the latest version of the dictionary indicates that its subject is the Kangiryuarmiut dialect of the Inuinnaqtun language (Kudlak and Compton 2018). The Kangiryuarmiut remain proud of their Inuinnait ancestry while also being Inuvialuit, a double identity reflected in the definition of Kangiryuarmiut provided in the dictionary: "Inuinnait and Inuvialuit of the Prince Albert Sound" (Kudlak and Compton 2018, 85). Since the Aulavik Oral History Project captured stories about the past, the Kangiryuamiut we interviewed about Banks Island often called themselves Inuinnait and referred to their language as Inuinnaqtun (see also Kelvin 2016, 37).[12]

In his analysis of the ethnogenesis of the Inuvialuit, Jens Dahl (1988) pointed out that before the turn of the twentieth century, there was no single ethnic territory encompassing the Siglit of the Mackenzie Delta and the Kangiryuarmiut of western Victoria Island and Banks Island. Indeed, early accounts suggest that the two groups lived in different areas and rarely, if ever, interacted before the visits of fur traders and explorers in the early 1900s, who arrived in the company of Siglit, as well as a number of Iñupiat from Alaska (for example, Franklin [1828] 1971; Stefansson 1919, 1922). However, once contacts were made in the first part of the twentieth century, relationships and intermarriages took place with the Kangiryuarmiut as it had happened before between Siglit, Iñupiat, whalers, Métis, non-Indigenous trappers, and Gwich'in neighbours (Lyons 2009).[13]

Before the three linguistic groups that now form the Inuvialuit decided to work together on the land claim that would result in the 1984 Inuvialuit Final Agreement, their sense of identity, as that of Inuit in general, was at the local level (Collignon 2006; Dorais 1994). In her study of the Inuinnait, Béatrice Collignon (2006, 21) remarked that "the territory is dotted with their temporary camps, and it is this territory that gives them their sense of identity, and their name." She further noted that even years after Inuinnait groups had moved into permanent settlements, "their social life still revolves around the original sub-groups, around their traditional territorial identity" (Collignon 2006, 57). I had the same impression while interviewing Inuvialuit from each of the linguistic groups. Often those from multiple origins felt they belonged primarily to one specific group. At the same time, when Kangiryuarmiut, Siglit, and Uummarmiut, including those with diverse ancestry, collectively call themselves "Inuvialuit," it is to reflect a new identity founded on their shared occupation, use, and management of a vast territory stretching from the Yukon North Slope to the western part of Victoria Island.

Toponyms as Guardians of the Inuvialuit Territory

Toponyms form part of what Mark Nuttall (1992, 39) has called "memoryscape" which is constructed with people's mental image of remembered places. During his fieldwork with Northwest Greenland Inuit, they used memoryscape to recall local and mythical narratives about past events or experiences (Nuttall 2001, 63). As Collignon (1996, 2006) demonstrated, toponyms are essential to the integration of Inuinnait in their milieu, which then becomes humanized and allows cultures to blossom. She also noted, "The history and beliefs of the people are rooted in the territory, so that the territory becomes the keeper of the community's memory and values" (Collignon 2006, 42). This echoes the observation made by Keith Basso (1984, 44) that "geographical features have served the Apache people for centuries as indispensable mnemonic pegs on which to hang the moral teachings of their history." Similarly, in an account of the life stories told by three women of Tagish, southern Tutchone, and Tlingit ancestry from the Yukon, Julie Cruikshank (1990, 354) remarked that toponyms do more than simply identify particular places: by allowing people to "use points in space to talk about time," they provide an entryway into the past.

Although the Inuvialuit oral history projects we worked on had a broader scope, place names were an important aspect of the data we hoped to collect. We interviewed thirty-two Inuvialuit in 1990 and 1991 and fifty in 1996. Using maps and archival photographs, we asked people to tell us about their life along the Yukon North Slope and on Banks Island (figures 2.3 and 2.4). We also enquired about toponyms and stories associated with those names. We brought people back to old camps, by boat in 1990 and by helicopter in 1991 and 1996, hoping that being physically in specific places would ignite memories, which indeed proved to be the case. The meanings of the place names mentioned reflected geographical features (including analogies with human anatomy), specific animals, plants, and rocks, or activities that were held there. Because the people interviewed used their own dialect to identify places, some of them had more than one toponym, although they often shared the same meaning.

During the projects on Herschel Island and the Yukon North Slope, we visited 20 sites and documented 90 toponyms in Inuvialuktun (specifically, Siglitun and Uumarmiutun).[14] Although Inuvialuktun place names are now used in maps of the Yukon coast (for example, Burn and Hattendorf 2012, 22; Irrgang et al. 2019, 109), official maps published by the Government of Canada had mainly English names. Indeed, many originated from Captain John Franklin's 1826 expedition and a survey of Herschel Island made in 1889 by Charles H. Stockton (Burn and Hattendorf 2012; Government of Yukon 2015). During our research, it was impossible to translate some Inuvialuktun names, they either have no meaning or, more likely, include vocabulary no longer used. Most of the toponyms referred to places located on the Yukon coast and those mentioned repeatedly designated large camps where families had lived. Noticeably, the major camp sites along the Yukon coast were located at regular intervals of about 10 to 20 kilometres.

For the project on Banks Island, we visited twenty-two sites and documented 74 toponyms, including 49 in Inuvialuktun (specifically, Kangiryuarmiutun, Siglitun, and possibly some Uummarmiutun). In comparison, the Government of the Northwest Territories (2015) lists 175 toponyms for Banks Island including 29 in Inuvialuktun. Most of the foreign names were given by outsiders; first by British Captain Robert McClure who spent four winters between 1850 and 1853 with his crew on Banks Island when the HMS *Investigator* got stuck in ice while searching for the lost Frankin expedition, and then by anthropologist and explorer Vilhjalmur Stefansson who led the Canadian Arctic Expedition between 1913 and 1918 (Gray 2003; McClure 1865; Stefansson 1922). During our interviews, the majority of toponyms that were mentioned designated camps of various sizes.

FIGURE 2.3 Richardson Mountains, Yukon North Slope, 1985. Courtesy Murielle Nagy.

Collignon (2006, 84–90) lists three types of narratives associated with Inuinnait toponyms: the first is about the origin of a land feature, the second about how to use the land in the wisest way, and the third are local stories of anecdotal nature. People we interviewed had life stories associated with specific places but rarely information regarding how the places got their names. Furthermore, in contrast to the 1,007 toponyms collected among the Inuinnait of Victoria Island by Collignon (1996, 2006) in the 1990s, and the 314 among the Siglit of the Tuktoyaktuk Peninsula by Hart (2011) during the same period, the smaller numbers recorded for the Yukon North Slope and Banks Island are surprising, especially given the size of the areas in question (roughly 18,000 square kilometres and 70,000 square kilometres, respectively). Various factors may have contributed to this outcome.

FIGURE 2.4 Beaufort Sea coast as seen from the Yukon North Slope, 1985. Courtesy Murielle Nagy.

First, our methodological approach had certain limitations. We started by interviewing all Inuvialuit participants in their homes to find those who were particularly knowledgeable about their territory and its place names. Then, we brought as many elders as possible back to old camps. We had only a short period of time at these sites, which might not have been sufficient to document toponyms. Indeed, with the exception of two occasions on which we travelled by boat and camped with elders along the Yukon North Slope and at Herschel Island in 1990, most of our visits were made by helicopter within the space of a single day. Given the time it took to travel, we never stayed for more than a few hours at each site. Although we might have met with greater success had we been able to spend longer periods of time travelling and camping with just a few elders, this would have been more complicated logistically, as well as possibly hazardous for the health of some elders, in view of the tremendous distances between camps. Moreover, we would have had to try to judge in advance who might have the best memories, given that elders had often not returned to these sites for somewhere between forty and sixty years. With the exception of the summer camp at Tapqaq (Shingle Point), this temporal gap was especially pronounced for sites on the Yukon coast, which had been almost completely abandoned by the 1940s, when most people moved to and around the hamlets of Aklavik and Tuktoyaktuk.

Another methodological issue was the use of maps. Even if elders remembered toponyms, some had difficulty locating them on a map. Indeed, most participants in the Herschel Island and Yukon North Slope projects were not comfortable with maps of that area, possibly because they had not been back there for a long time or because they "knew" the land from a different perspective—by travelling on the water, for example, or on the ice.[15] This, however, was not a problem with elders of Banks Island because they were used to maps of their island, some having taken part during the 1960s and 1970s in studies of their trapping activities, which included the identification of trap lines on maps (Usher 1966, 1971b, 1976). Thus, they were familiar with maps of the island and place names attributed by explorers since 1820, including those by explorer and anthropologist Vilhjalmur Stefansson a century later (Stefansson 1919).

Second, fewer toponyms might reflect the nature and intensity of territorial occupation, and the absence of transmission. The Tuyurmiat of the Yukon coast were described by the Inuvialuit we interviewed as distinct from the rest of the Siglit, with a dialect slightly different, rather isolated, and not too numerous (Nagy 1994, 27). Thus, they probably did not occupy the Yukon North Slope in an intense manner. Furthermore, many of those people died during the big epidemics of the early 1900s and of 1928, and since oral history is normally passed on by elders, all their knowledge of place names might not have survived them.

In the case of Banks Island, the toponyms that we recorded were associated with the different groups who have lived there: the Kangiryuarmiut, on the one hand, and the Siglit and Uummarmiut, on the other. The Kangiryuarmiut had been going to Banks Island seasonally for hundreds of years, mainly to hunt muskox, caribou, seals, and geese. Their intermittent use of the island is reflected in its name, Ikaahuk, which means "the crossing place," in reference to traversing from their main camps in Kangiryuaq (Prince Albert Sound) on western Victoria Island.

FIGURE 2.5 Frank Carpenter's fox skins being aired out, July 1958, Sachs Harbour. NWT Archives/Robert C. Knights fonds/N-1993-002-0265. Photograph by Robert C Knights.

Accordingly, the Kangiryuarmiutun toponyms we collected are located mainly on the eastern and southern coasts of Banks Island. Although from 1853 to possibly the late 1890s, the Kangiryuarmiut also went north of the island to Mercy Bay to salvage wood and metal from the shipwrecked HMS *Investigator* (Hickey 1986), only a few place names were mentioned for that area.

In contrast, Banks Island was an unknown territory for the Siglit and Uummarmiut families who started to come there from the mainland in the late 1920s and 1930s, to trap white fox during the fall and the winter, before travelling back to the Mackenzie Delta and Herschel Island in the summer to sell their furs and get supplies (figure 2.5). Such journeys were possible because the high prices of furs allowed them to buy motor schooners from trading companies (Bockstoce 2018, 229; Usher 1971b). They established a dozen camps mainly in the western and southern coasts of Banks Island and identified them, and nearby rivers, by the names of schooners (for example, Blue Fox Harbour) and trappers or used previous toponyms given by explorers. By 1960, most families had moved from these camps to Sachs Harbour, the only community on Banks Island (Usher 1971b, 1:58).

A common practice by Banks Island's Inuvialuit of all origins is to call lakes and creeks by the name of a person, in either Inuvialuktun or English. Although it might be too soon to talk of a language shift (see, for example, Marino 2006), there are presently at least sixteen toponyms bearing the English first names of Inuvialuit individuals, including a few new ones recorded in 2016 by Kelvin (232–240). Some locations might have been renamed since because we recorded four that did not appear on Kelvin's list. Even if these place names are not in Inuvialuktun, they are nonetheless Inuvialuit since they have been chosen by people of Banks Island.

Third, although it would be unrealistic to expect that each toponym has a story associated with it, the fact that we gathered only a few stories about how some places were named might have to do with the different types of names that were recorded. In her study of Inuinnait toponyms, Collignon (2006, 137–138) found that specific geographic terms represented 21 percent and spatially referenced terms (that is, those with meanings such as "on the other side" or "across from each other" that imply a known reference point) accounted for 12 percent. In the case of the Yukon North Slope toponyms that were collected, 28 percent were specific geographic terms and 15 percent were spatially referenced terms. As for those recorded for Banks Island, 33 percent were specific geographic terms and 4 percent were spatially referenced terms. Although our samples are much smaller than Collignon's, the presence of geographic terms (with or without spatial references) explains why those places had no stories related to their name. As for the other toponyms without associated stories, they may have become "only names." Indeed, as explained by Moscovitch (2012, 108), most memories do not retain perceptually rich information, but instead become more schematic with time.

Fourth, perhaps the people being interviewed did not spend their formative years along the Yukon North Slope and Banks Island and therefore did not become familiar with toponyms and their stories. Indeed, one's early years spent at specific places seems to influence one's toponymic knowledge and memory.[16] Hence, the example of Lily Lipscomb, who was born in 1948 and was adopted by her maternal grandparents, themselves born in the late 1870s. She lived with them mostly around Arvagvik (Roland Bay), along the Yukon coast, until the early 1960s.[17] While we spent about three hours in Arvagvik with Lily Lipscomb, she shared life stories about herself and her grandparents but also mentioned 34 place names and specifically 16 within that area. She told us that her grandmother was originally from the Kuvuk (Kobuk River) area in Alaska and called her a Nunataarmiuq, which she defined as an inland person, while her Siglit grandfather was from Tikiraq (Kay Point), along the Yukon coast, and she called him a Tariurmiuq or coastal person (Nagy 1994b, LL91-25A, 1–2, 9). Because of their different backgrounds, she sometimes had two different toponyms for the same place, one used by her grandmother and the other by her grandfather, as they each taught her their own language and traditions.

Another case in point is that of Edith Haogak, who was born in the early 1930s and raised in Kangiryuaqtihuk (Minto Inlet) and Kangiryuaq (Prince Albert Sound), both on the western side of Victoria Island, but who also travelled to Banks Island with her parents to hunt (figure 2.6). In the late 1950s, she moved to Sachs Harbour, the newly built community on the island. Having been widowed early in her adult life, she had to support her family by hunting and trapping for furs. When we interviewed her, she had been living on Banks Island for almost forty years. Although she was one of the few people who knew most of the Kangiryuarmiutun toponyms for the eastern coast of Banks Island, these numbered only about ten. Yet she had an extensive knowledge of more than 120 toponyms from the west coast of Victoria Island, where she was raised, and all of which she could locate on a map (Nagy 2006, 77). Of the 58 toponyms she listed for Kangiryuaqtihuk and the area north of it, I found all but four in Collignon (2006, 235–257). Collignon (2006, 106) had a similar experience with a seventy-one-year-old man from Ulukhaktok who only knew the place names of the lower part of Kangiryuaq, "where he had grown up but had hardly ever returned as an adult."

Thus, it seems that individuals are more likely to form lasting memories of specific places while they are still fairly young, with their experiences as children and adolescents making an especially strong imprint. This observation is supported by research on autobiographical memory that has identified the "reminiscence bump" (Rubin, Wetzler, and Nebes 1986), a cross-cultural tendency of adults over forty years old to have more recollection of memories from adolescence and early adulthood (Zaragoza Scherman, Shao, and Bernsten 2015).[18] However, there are divergent opinions regarding the range of the bump, particularly its onset. Initial research associated it with ages between 10 and 30 (Rubin, Wetzler, and Nebes 1986), but later studies placed it between 6 and 15 (Jansari and Parkin 1996, 88); 5 and 30 (Rubin and Schulkind 1997, 529); 6 and 20 (Janssen, Rubin, and St. Jacques 2011, 1); 5 and 20 (Corning and Schuman 2015, 164); and 15 and 30 (Zaragoza Scherman, Shao, and Bernsten 2015). These various ranges open the possibility for an earlier onset of the reminiscence bump after childhood amnesia, which usually ends between 3 and 7 (see Rubin 2000).

First memories represent the beginning of consciousness (Cohen-Mansfield et al. 2010, 571) and

FIGURE 2.6 Aerial photograph of polygonal patterned ground located by the Thomsen River near Castel Bay on Banks Island, Yukon Territory, 2014. Courtesy Gregory Lehn.

indeed, when recalling them, Inuvialuit interviewed used expressions related to "becoming aware" or "coming to their senses" while vividly describing their surroundings (see Nagy 2006). Cohen-Mansfield et al. (2010, 565, 571) explain that memories of formative events or those reflecting formative processes shape the identity of the individual and give a strong sense of group belonging. Among the Inuvialuit, not only were various places visited seasonally, but their names were included in discussions and storytelling with parents, the extended family, and one's group as part of what Halbwachs (1950) called *mémoire collective* ("collective memory"). The encoding of those toponyms in the memory was likely reinforced by peer interactions as exemplified by Paatlirmiut children playing a contest listing place names (Correll 1976, 178).

As noted by Bernsten (2012, 294), the importance of emotion in relation to encoding and maintenance of memory is well established. Thus, the emotional link to the first places an individual remembers might be the key to which toponyms are better known and recalled. Indeed, as Basso (1996, 76) wrote about the Western Apache, "Because of their inseparable connection to specific localities, place names may be used to summon forth an enormous range of mental and emotional associations—association of time and space, of history and events, of persons and social activities, of oneself and stages in one's life." Furthermore, when referring to Inuinnait toponyms associated with local stories that are shared only within an extended family or hunting group, Collignon (2006, 90) emphasized that "their geographic dimension is that of the intimate scale of family, individuals, and emotions." This intimate link to the land and its temporal connotations was very well expressed by Mark Emerak, who lived on Victoria Island: "I should send [that story] somewhere to the land where I first got my memory" (quoted in Nagy 2006, 76).

When trying to understand why fewer toponyms than expected were recorded, one last point to consider is the conclusion that Collignon (2006, 106) drew from her own interviews—namely, that the skills of the travellers are not related to the number of place names that they know. She emphasized that toponyms are mainly landmarks of history rather than travel and survival aids. A traveller who knows the names of places in a particular area will use them not for purposes of orientation but rather to feel connected to the land in a familiar way (Collignon 1996, 117). Her hypothesis was confirmed by the fact that specific geographic terms and those spatially referenced represented only 33 percent of the toponyms she collected. Similarly, such terms accounted for 43 percent of the toponyms we gathered on the Yukon North Slope and 37 precent of those from Banks Island. Furthermore, even though the elders we interviewed on Banks Island mentioned fewer toponyms than we had anticipated, they had extensive knowledge of particular areas and showed us on a map where they hunted and trapped (Nagy 1999, 2004).

Conclusions

Inuvialuit ethnonyms and toponyms are an entryway to language, identity, and memory issues. Most of the toponyms recorded during oral history projects about Herschel Island, the Yukon North Slope, and Banks Island indicated geographical features, specific resources, and activities that were held at particular places. They also reflected the diverse origins of the Inuvialuit involved in naming their territory. Hence, along the Yukon North Slope, the toponyms were mostly in Siglitun and in Uummarmiutun, the dialects of the two different groups that lived there up to the 1940s. In contrast, a linguistic and temporal dichotomy was apparent between the place names on the eastern and western coasts of Banks Island. On the eastern coast, toponyms reflected centuries of seasonal occupations by the Kangiryuarmiut of western Victoria Island, while those of the western coast demonstrated the more recent occupation of the island, which started in the late 1920s, by people of Siglit and Uummarmiut origins. The English toponyms created by the Inuvialuit of Banks Island do not represent a language shift, as many bear the names of either people or schooners. Despite the fact that English is now the dominant language among the Inuvialuit, it seems unlikely that they will use it to create all their new toponyms, given that Inuvialuktun place names are such a powerful symbol of the Inuvialuit presence throughout their traditional territory.

Depending on their experience of living on the land, the elders we interviewed demonstrated various degrees of knowledge and memory regarding place names and the stories associated with them.

Knowledge of toponyms seems linked to the emotional connection to the first places an individual remembers, with memories established during formative years (childhood and adolescence) lasting longer. All these factors are tied to family origins and are thus grounded in the various identities of the Inuvialuit.

Acknowledgements

A preliminary version of this chapter was presented at the session "Language, Memory, and Landscape" at the 18th Inuit Studies Conference (see Nagy 2012b). I am grateful to Kenneth Pratt for organizing that session and for inviting me to participate. I offer most sincere thanks to all the Inuvialuit elders who participated in the oral history projects on Herschel Island, the Yukon North Slope, and Banks Island as well as to Inuvialuit research assistants Renie Arey, Elizabeth Banksland, Shirley Elias, Jean Harry, and Agnes White. Translations and transcriptions were done by Barbra Allen, Beverly Amos, Helen Kitekudlak, Agnes Kuptana, and Agnes White. The projects were administered by the Inuvialuit Social Development Program of the Inuvialuit Regional Corporation. Funding and logistical support were provided by Parks Canada; the Government of Yukon's Heritage Branch; the Government of Northwest Territories' Language Enhancement Program; the Government of Canada's Polar Continental Shelf Program and Northern Oil and Gas Action Plan; and the Inuvik Research Centre. Finally, I want to thank two anonymous reviewers, Kenneth Pratt, Shirleen Smith, as well as the Athabasca University Press copyeditor Ryan Perks, senior editor Pamela Holway, and director Megan Hall for their comments, suggested revisions, and editing of the text.

Notes

1. This said, I agree with Lyons (2009, 63) that "like individual identities, collective Inuvialuit identity is subject to multiple definitions and understandings, depending on context."
2. Ethnonym is used here to represent the name(s) a group of people calls itself or is called by others. Ethnonyms can be divided into endonyms or autonyms (self-given) and exonyms (given by others).
3. Although the official Inuvialuktun name of Herschel Island is Qikiqtaruk, it was transcribed "Qikiqtqruk" by the transcribers of our Uummarmiutun interviews and "Qikiqtaryuk" by the transcriber of our Siglitun interviews (Nagy 1994).
4. Contrary to Petitot, I do not use italics for ethnomyms in this text. As can be seen with the use of "ç" rather than "ch," Petitot's spelling system was not only very complex, but also inconsistent (Lowe 1991, 144).
5. The sound changes from "c" (like in chair) to "ts" and "s" are explained in Fortescue, Jacobson, and Kaplan (2010, xvi).
6. Petitot (1876, xi) had previously called Kragmalit the Anderson River people. Betts (2009, 6–7) did the same without taking into account that Petitot (1887) used Kragmalit to encompass people of a wider area than stricly the Anderson River.
7. In previous texts, Lily Lipscomb's last name was incorrectly spelled with an "e" at the end.
8. Hart also mentioned the possibility that Siglialuk is the name of a person. Indeed, the suffix -aluk means "old, pitiful, from a long time ago" and can be used as a term of endearment (Hart 2011, 70; Lowe 2001, 189).
9. Regarding the terminological change, see "Inuvialuit History," Inuvialuit Regional Corporation, accessed 12 February 2022, https://irc.inuvialuit.com/about-irc/culture/inuvialuit-history.
10. Regarding this Dene-speaking people, see Vuntut Gwitchin First Nation and Smith (2009).
11. Concerning the different origins of the Uummarmiut other than Nunataarmiut, Ishamel Alunik specified families from Kuvuk (Kobuk River), Kotzebue, Point Hope, and Point Borrow (Nagy 1994a, IA90-35B, 8).
12. In previous publications, I also called their language Inuinnaqtun but will designate it as Kangiryuarmiutun here.
13. On relationships with the Gwich'in, see McCartney and Gwich'in Tribal Council (2020).
14. Although Nagy (1993) lists 122 Inuvialuktun toponyms, some were pronunciation variations and thus spelled differently while others were not located in the Yukon North Slope.
15. I thank Kenneth Pratt for this suggestion.
16. Although I am not dealing here with cultural change but with memory of toponyms, I thank Kenneth Pratt for bringing to my attention the "early learning hypothesis" of Bruner (1956, 194): "That which was traditionally learned and internalized in infancy and early childhood tends to be most resistant to change in contact situations." In the case of toponyms, the resistance would be against forgetting them.
17. Previously transcribed as Arvakvik ("place of bowhead whale"), the proper spelling is Arvagvik (see Irrgang et al, 2019, 109).
18. I am grateful to Shirleen Smith for making me aware of the reminiscence bump.

References

Alunik, Ishmael, Eddie D. Kolausok, and David Morrison

2003 *Across Time and Tundra: The Inuvialuit of the Western Arctic.* Raincoast Books, Vancouver; University of Washington Press, Seattle; and Canadian Museum of Civilization, Gatineau, Québec.

Arnold, Charles, Wendy Stephenson, Bob Simpson, and Zoe Ho (editors)

2011 *Taimani—At That Time: Inuvialuit Timeline Visual Guide.* Inuvialuit Regional Corporation, Inuvik.

Basso, Keith H.

1984 Stalking with Stories: Names, Places, and Moral Narratives Among the Western Apache. In *Text, Play, and Story: The Construction and Reconstruction of Self and Society*, edited by Edward M. Bruner, pp. 19–55. American Ethnological Society, Washington, DC, and Waveland Press, Prospect Heights, Illinois.

1996 *Wisdom Sits in Places: Landscape and Language Among the Western Apache.* University of New Mexico Press, Albuquerque.

Bernsten, Dorthe

2012 Spontaneous Recollections: Involuntary Autobiographical Memories as a Basic Mode of Remembering. In *Understanding Autobiographical Memory: Theories and Approaches*, edited by Dorthe Bernsten and David C. Rubin, pp. 290–310. Cambridge University Press, Cambridge.

Betts, Matthew W.

2009 Chronicling Siglit Identities: Economy, Practices, and Ethnicity in the Western Canadian Arctic. *Alaska Journal of Anthropology* 7(2): 1–28.

Bockstoce, John R.

1986 *Whales, Ice and Men: The History of Whaling in the Western Arctic.* University of Washington Press, Seattle.

2018 *White Fox and Icy Seas in the Western Arctic: The Fur Trade, Transportation, and Change in the Early Twentieth Century.* Yale University Press, New Haven and London.

Bruner, Edward M.

1956 Cultural Transmission and Cultural Change. *Southwestern Journal of Anthropology* 12(2): 191–199.

Burch, Ernest S., Jr.
1984 Kotzebue Sound Eskimo. In *Handbook of North American Indians*, vol. 5, *Arctic*, edited by David Damas, pp. 303–319. Smithsonian Institution Press, Washington, DC.
1998 *The Iñupiaq Eskimo Nations of Northwest Alaska*. University of Alaska Press, Fairbanks.
2005 *Alliance and Conflict: The World System of the Iñupiaq Eskimos*. University of Nebraska Press, Lincoln and London.
2006 *Social Life in Northwest Alaska: The Structure of the Iñupiaq Eskimo Nations*. University of Alaska Press, Fairbanks.
2012 *Caribou Herds of Northwest Alaska, 1850–2000*, edited by Igor Krupnik and Jim Dau. University of Alaska Press, Fairbanks.

Burn, Christopher, and John B. Hattendorf
2012 Place Names. In *Herschel Island Qikiqtaryuk: A Natural and Cultural History of Yukon's Arctic Island*, edited by Christopher Burn, pp. 20–27. University of Calgary Press, Calgary.

Cohen-Mansfield, Jiska, Dov Shmotkin, Nitza Eyal, Yael Reichental, and Haim Hazan
2010 A Comparison of Three Types of Autobiographical Memories in Old-Old Age: First Memories, Pivotal Memories and Traumatic Memories. *Gerontology* 56(6): 564–573.

Collignon, Béatrice
1996 *Les Inuit: Ce qu'ils savent du territoire*. L'Harmattan, Paris.
2006 *Knowing Places: The Inuinnait, Landscapes, and the Environment*. Canadian Circumpolar Institute Press, Edmonton.

Condon, Richard G.
1996 *The Northern Copper Inuit: A History*. University of Toronto Press, Toronto.

Corning, Amy, and Howard Schuman
2015 *Generations and Collective Memory*. University of Chicago Press, Chicago.

Correll, Thomas C.
1976 Language and Location in Traditional Inuit Societies. In *Inuit Land Use and Occupancy Project*, vol. 2, *Supporting Studies*, edited by Milton M. R. Freeman, pp. 173–179. Indian and Northern Affairs, Ottawa.

Cruikshank, Julie
1990 *Life Lived Like a Story: Life Stories of Three Yukon Native Elders*. University of Nebraska Press, Lincoln.

Dahl, Jens
1988 Self-Government, Land Claims and Imagined Inuit Communities. *Folk* 30: 73–84.

Dorais, Louis-Jacques
1989 Bilingualism and Diglossia in the Canadian Eastern Arctic. *Arctic* 42(3): 199–207.
1994 À propos d'identité inuit. *Études/Inuit/Studies* 18(1–2): 253–260.
2010 *The Language of the Inuit: Syntax, Semantics, and Society in the Arctic*. McGill-Queen's University Press, Montréal and Kingston.
2020 *Words of the Inuit: A Semantic Stroll Through a Northern Culture*. University of Manitoba Press, Winnipeg.

Fortescue, Michael, Steven Jacobson, and Lawrence Kaplan
2010 Comparative Eskimo Dictionary, with Aleut Cognates. 2nd. ed. Research Paper No. 9. Alaska Native Language Center, University of Alaska Fairbanks.

Franklin, John
[1828] 1971 *Narrative of a Second Expedition to the Shores of the Polar Sea in the Years 1825, 1826 and 1827*. Hurtig, Edmonton.

Friesen, T. Max, and Charles D. Arnold
2008 The Timing of the Thule Migration: New Dates from the Western Canadian Arctic. *American Antiquity* 73(3): 527–538.

Government of Northwest Territories
2015 *Gazetteer of the Northwest Territories*. Northwest Territories Cultural Places Program, Prince of Wales Northern Heritage Centre, Yellowknife.

Government of Yukon
2015 *Gazetteer of Yukon*. Geographical Names Program, Department of Tourism and Culture, Whitehorse.

Gray, David
2003 Northern People, Northern Knowledge: The Story of the Canadian Arctic Expedition, 1913–1918. Canadian Museum of Civilization, Gatineau, Québec. Virtual exhibition, https://www.historymuseum.ca/cmc/exhibitions/hist/cae/indexe.html.

Hall, Edwin S. Jr.
1984 Interior North Alaska Eskimo. In *Handbook of North American Indians*, vol. 5, *Arctic*, edited by David Damas, pp. 338–346. Smithsonian Institution Press, Washington, DC.

Halbwachs, Maurice
1950 *La mémoire collective*. Presses universitaires de France, Paris.

Hart, Elisa J.
2001 *Reindeer Days Remembered*. Inuvialuit Cultural Resource Centre, Inuvik.
2011 *Nuna Aliannaittuq / Beautiful Land: Learning About Traditional Place Names and the Land from Tuktoyaktuk Elders*. Inuvialuit Cultural Resource Centre, Inuvik, and Prince of Wales Northern Heritage Centre, Yellowknife.

Hickey, Clifford G.
1986 An Examination of Processes of Culture Change Among Nineteenth Century Copper Inuit. *Études/Inuit/Studies* 8(1): 13–35.

Ho, Zoe, Peggy Jay, Gerry Roy, and Roger Connelly (editors)
2009 *Inuvialuit Final Agreement: Celebrating 25 years*. Inuvialuit Regional Corporation, Inuvik.

Inuvialuit elders, with Robert W. Bandringa
2010 *Inuvialuit Nautchiangit: Relationships Between People and Plants*. Inuvialuit Cultural Resource Centre, Aurora Research Institute, and Parks Canada, Inuvik.

Irrgang, Anna M., Hugues Lantuit, Richard R. Gordon, Ashley Piskor, and Gavin K. Manson
2019 Impacts of Past and Future Coastal Changes on the Yukon Coast—Threats for Cultural Sites, Infrastructure, and Travel Routes. *Arctic Science* 5: 107–126.

Jansari, Ashok, and Alan J. Parkin
1996 Things That Go Bump in Your Life: Explaining the Reminiscence Bump in Autobiographical Memory. *Psychology and Aging* 11(1): 85–91.

Janssen, Steve M. J., David C. Rubin, and Peggy L. St. Jacques
2011 The Temporal Distribution of Autobiographic Memory: Changes in Reliving and Vividness Over the Life Span Do Not Explain the Reminiscence Bump. *Memory and Cognition* 39(1): 1–11.

Jenness, Diamond
1991 *Arctic Odyssey: The Diary of Diamond Jenness, Ethnologist with the Canadian Arctic Expedition in Northern Alaska and Canada, 1913–1916*, edited by Stuart E. Jenness, Canadian Museum of Civilization, Gatineau, Québec.

Kelvin, Laura Elena
2016 *There Is More Than One Way to Do Something Right: Applying Community-Based Approaches to an Archaeology of Banks Island, NWT.* PhD dissertation, University of Western Ontario, London.

Kudlak, Emily, and Richard Compton
2018 *Kangiryuarmiut Inuinnaqtun Uqauhiitaa Numiktitirutait—Kangiryuarmiut Inuinnaqtun Dictionary.* Nunavut Arctic College Media, Iqaluit.

Lowe, Ronald
1983 *Kangiryuarmiut Uqauhingita Numiktittitdjutingit: Basic Kangiryuarmiut Eskimo Dictionary.* Committee for Original Peoples Entitlement, Inuvik.
1984a *Uummarmiut Uqalungiha Mumikhitchirutingit: Basic Uummarmiut Eskimo Dictionary.* Committee for Original Peoples Entitlement, Inuvik.
1984b *Siglit Inuvialuit Uqausiita Kipuktirutait: Basic Siglit Inuvialuit Eskimo Dictionary.* Committee for Original Peoples Entitlement, Inuvik.
1991 *Les trois dialectes inuit de l'Arctique canadien de l'Ouest: Analyse descriptive et étude comparative.* Groupe d'études inuit et circumpolaires, Travaux de recherche no. 11. Université Laval, Sainte-Foy, Québec City.
2001 *Siglit Inuvialuit Uqautchiita Nutaat Kipuktirutait Aglipkaqtat: Siglit Inuvialuit Eskimo Dictionary.* 2nd ed., revised and expanded. Éditions Nota bene, Québec City.

Lyons, Natasha
2009 Inuvialuit Rising: The Evolution of Inuvialuit Identity in the Modern Era. *Alaska Journal of Anthropology* 7(2): 63–79.
2010 The Wisdom of Elders: Inuvialuit Social Memories of Continuity and Change in the Twentieth Century. *Arctic Anthropology* 47(1): 22–38.

Marino, Elizabeth K.
2006 *Negotiating the Languages of the Landscape: Place Naming and Language Shift in an Inupiaq Community.* Master's thesis, Department of Anthropology, University of Alaska Fairbanks, Fairbanks.

McCartney, Leslie, and Gwich'in Tribal Council
2020 *Our Whole Gwich'in Way of Life Has Changed: Stories from the People of the Land/Gwich'in K'yuu Gwiidandài' Tthak Ejuk Goonlih.* University of Alberta Press, Edmonton.

McClure, Robert
1865 *The Discovery of a North-West Passage*, edited by Sherard Osborn. Fourth edition. William Blackwood and Sons, Edinburg and London.

McGhee, Robert
1974 *Beluga Hunters: An Archaeological Reconstruction of the History and Culture of the Mackenzie Delta Kittegaryumiut.* Newfoundland Social and Economic Studies No. 13. Memorial University of Newfoundland, St. John's.

Morrison, David
2003a Ingilraqpaaluk (A Very Long Time Ago). In *Across Time and Tundra: The Inuvialuit of the Western Arctic*, by Ishmael Alunik, Eddie D. Kolausok, and David Morrison, pp. 1–45. Raincoast Books, Vancouver; University of Washington Press, Seattle; and Canadian Museum of Civilization, Gatineau, Québec.
2003b The Winds of Change Blow Hard: The Whaling Era, 1890–1910. In *Across Time and Tundra: The Inuvialuit of the Western Arctic*, by Ishmael Alunik, Eddie D. Kolausok, and David Morrison, pp. 79–112. Raincoast Books, Vancouver; University of Washington Press, Seattle; and Canadian Museum of Civilization, Gatineau, Québec.

Morrison, David, and Eddie D. Kolausok
2003 Trappers, Traders and Herders, 1906–. In *Across Time and Tundra: The Inuvialuit of the Western Arctic*, by Ishmael Alunik, Eddie D. Kolausok, and David Morrison, pp. 113–144. Raincoast Books, Vancouver; University of Washington Press, Seattle; and Canadian Museum of Civilization, Gatineau, Québec.

Moscovitch, Morris
2012 The Contribution of Research on Autobiographical Memory to Past and Present Theories of Memory Consolidation. In *Understanding Autobiographical Memory: Theories and Approaches*, edited by Dorthe Bernsten and David C. Rubin, pp. 91–113. Cambridge University Press, Cambridge.

Nagy, Murielle
1993 *Herschel Island and Yukon North Slope Inuvialuit Oral History Project: Gazetteer of Inuvialuit Place Names.* Inuvialuit Social Development Program, Inuvik.
1994 *Yukon North Slope Inuvialuit Oral History.* Hudç Hudän Series, Occasional Paper in Yukon History no. 1. Government of the Yukon, Department of Tourism, Heritage Branch, Whitehorse.

1999 Aulavik Oral History Project on Banks Island, NWT: Final Report. Inuvialuit Social Development Program, Inuvik.

2004 "We Did Not Want the Muskox to Increase": Inuvialuit Knowledge About Muskox and Caribou Populations on Banks Island, Canada. In *Cultivating Arctic Landscapes: Knowing and Managing Animals in the Circumpolar North*, edited by David Anderson and Mark Nuttall, pp. 93–109. Berghahn Books, New York.

2006 Time, Space, and Memory. In *Critical Inuit Studies: An Anthology of Contemporary Arctic Ethnography*, edited by Pamela Stern and Lisa Stevenson, pp. 71–88. University of Nebraska Press, Lincoln.

2012a Inuvialuit Ancestors. In *Herschel Island Qikiqtaryuk: A Natural and Cultural History of Yukon's Arctic Island*, edited by Christopher Burn, pp. 153–157. University of Calgary Press, Calgary.

2012b Inuvialuit Identity as Reflected Through the Use and Memory of a Common Territory. Paper presented at the 18th Inuit Studies Conference, Washington, DC, October 27.

Nagy, Murielle (editor)

1994a Qikiqtaruk (Herschel Island) Cultural Study: English Translations and Transcriptions of Interviews 1 to 35. Inuvialuit Social Development Program, Inuvik.

1994b Yukon North Slope Cultural Resources Survey: English Translations and Transcriptions of Interviews 1 to 29. Inuvialuit Social Development Program, Inuvik.

Nuttall, Mark

1992 *Arctic Homeland: Kinship, Community and Development in Northwest Greenland*. University of Toronto Press, Toronto.

2001 Locality, Identity and Memory in South Greenland. *Études/Inuit/Studies* 25(1–2): 53–72.

Oehler, Alexander C.

2012 *Inuvialuit Language and Identity: Perspectives on the Symbolic Meaning of Inuvialuktun in the Canadian Western Arctic*. Master's thesis, Interdisciplinary Studies Graduate Program, University of Northern British Columbia, Prince George.

Osgood, Lawrence

1984 Foreword. In *Siglit Inuvialuit Uqausiita Kipuktirutait: Basic Siglit Inuvialuit Eskimo Dictionary*, by Ronald Lowe, pp. vii–xv. Committee for Original Peoples Entitlement, Inuvik.

Parks Canada

2004 *Paulatuuq Oral History Project: Inuvialuit Elders Share Their Stories*. Parks Canada Western Arctic Field Unit, Inuvik.

Petitot, Émile

1876 *Vocabulaire Français-Esquimau: Dialecte des Tchiglit des bouches du Mackenzie et de l'Anderson, précédé d'une monographie de cette tribu et de notes grammaticales*. Bibliothèque Linguistique et d'Ethnographie Américaines, vol. 3. Ernest Leroux, Paris.

1886 *Traditions indiennes du Canada Nord-Ouest*. Les littératures populaires de toutes les nations, tome 23. Maisonneuve Frères et Ch. Leclerc, Paris.

1887 *Les Grands Esquimaux*. E. Plon, Nourrit et Cie, Paris.

Rubin, David C.

2000 The Distribution of Early Childhood Memories. *Memory* 8(4): 265–269.

Rubin, David C., and Matthew D. Schulkind

1997 Distribution of Important and Word-Cue Autobiographical Memories in 20-, 35-, and 70-Year-Old Adults. *Psychology and Aging* 12(3): 524–535.

Rubin, David C., Scott E. Wetzler, and Robert D. Nebes

1986 Autobiographical Memory Across the Adult Lifespan. In *Autobiographical Memory*, edited by David C. Rubin, pp. 202–221, Cambridge University Press, Cambridge.

Smith, Derek G.

1984 Mackenzie Delta Eskimo. In *Handbook of North American Indians*, vol. 5, *Arctic*, edited by David Damas, pp. 347–358. Smithsonian Institution Press, Washington, DC.

Stefansson, Vilhjalmur

1919 *The Stefansson-Anderson Arctic Expedition of American Museum: Preliminary Ethnological Report*. Anthropological Papers of the American Museum of Natural History Vol. 14(1). American Museum of Natural History, New York.

1921 *The Friendly Arctic*. MacMillan Company, New York.

1922 *Hunters of the Great North*. Harcourt, Brace and Company, New York.

2001 *Writing on Ice: The Ethnographic Notebooks of Vilhjalmur Stefansson*, edited and introduced by Gísli Pálsson. Darthmouth College and University Press of New England, Hanover.

Usher, Peter J.

1966 *Banks Island: An Area Economic Survey, 1965*. Department of Indian Affairs and Northern Development, Ottawa.

1971a The Canadian Western Arctic: A Century of Change. *Anthropologica*, new ser., 13(1–2): 169–183.

1971b *The Bankslanders: Economy and Ecology of a Frontier Trapping Community*. 3 vols. Northern Science Research Group, Department of Indian Affairs and Northern Development, Ottawa.

1976 The Inuk as Trapper: A Case Study. In *Inuit Land Use and Occupancy Project*, vol. 2, *Supporting Studies*, edited by Milton M. R. Freeman, pp. 207–216. Department of Indian Affairs and Northern Affairs, Ottawa.

Vuntut Gwitchin First Nation, and Shirleen Smith

2009 *People of the Lakes: Stories of Our Van Tat Gwich'in Elders / Googwandak Nakhwach'ànjoo Van Tat Gwich'in*. University of Alberta Press, Edmonton.

Washington, John

1850 *Eskimaux and English Vocabulary, for the use of the Arctic Expeditions*. John Murray, London.

Zaragoza Scherman, Alejandra, Zhifang Shao, and Dorthe Bernsten

2015 Life Span Distribution and Content of Positive and Negative Autobiographical Memories Across Cultures. *Psychology of Consciousness: Theory, Research, and Practices* 2(4): 475–490.

FIGURE 3.1 *Nuratar*, Andrew Noatak (b. ca. 1900), and *Ukayir*, Helen Noatak (b. ca. 1929), aboard a Lomen Reindeer Corporation boat at Nash Harbor, Nunivak Island, Alaska, 1941. Photograph by Amos Burg. Courtesy of the Oregon Historical Society, Portland.

ROBERT DROZDA

3 Wandering in Place

A Close Examination of Two Names at Nunivak Island

Of the Arctic regions of the world, the Chukotka and Bering Sea area can be considered the most complex from a linguistic point of view. In this area, the Eskimo languages, those spoken in the past and those in the present, are more diverse than anywhere else.
WILLEM DE REUSE (1994, 295)

Nunivak was perhaps not so isolated in the old times.
LOUIS L. HAMMERICH (1954, 420)

The inaccessibility of the Bering Sea island of Nunivak is frequently cited as a key factor contributing to the cultural and linguistic distinctiveness of its residents. The island lies not far off the southwestern coast of mainland Alaska, separated from it by the Etolin Strait. At their closest points Nunivak is only about 30 kilometres from the mainland, but shallow waters and strong, shifting currents make this relatively short distance particularly treacherous for the sea traveller. All the same, Nunivak Islanders

FIGURE 3.2 Indigenous languages and selected dialects spoken in the study area. Boundaries, marked with broken lines, are fluid and particularly complex in the region around Norton Sound and the southern Seward Peninsula, where dialects of Yup'ik and Inupiaq overlap. Adapted from Jacobson (1998) and Krauss (1986); see also Fortescue, Jacobson, and Kaplan (2010, viii–ix).

reportedly covered long distances by kayak and open boat prior to the introduction of motorized travel (Hammerich 1954, 420; Lantis 1946, 170; VanStone 1984a, 207; 1989, 5). Conversely, Nunivak was a destination for other Indigenous residents of the greater Bering Sea region, some of whom came for trade and for the island's rich and easily exploitable natural resources (Lantis 1960, 5, 16–17; Pratt 2001, 37–42; Pratt 2009a, 252–253). In this chapter, I discuss how former Nunivak settlements and the language spoken on the island may have been affected by interactions resulting from these back-and-forth travels. My point of departure is a comparative look at two enduring and presumably ancient place names. The names are derived from a single word that is no longer present in the island lexicon, yet they persist, and the meanings applied to them over time at the local level and by anthropologists and linguists vary significantly.

The Indigenous people of Nunivak Island (*Nuniwar*) call themselves Nuniwarmiut or Cup'it, the singular form of which, Cup'ig, is also the name of their language.[1] Linguists generally present Cup'ig as a dialect of mainland Central Alaskan Yup'ik. However, historically there are conflicting views regarding the degree of mutual intelligibility between Cup'ig and Yup'ik and whether or not Cup'ig is, or was, a unique language. My research revealed complex linguistic and cultural associations between the Nuniwarmiut and other Bering Sea peoples and languages. While such associations with mainland Yup'ik peoples were expected, those linking Nuniwarmiut to groups and languages of northwest Alaska (Inupiaq), St. Lawrence Island (Central Siberian Yupik), and possibly the Chukotka Peninsula (Chukchi) were also present and compelling (see figure 3.2). Several difficulties related to Nunivak language documentation and place-name research emerged, and discussions of these challenges comprise a major part of this chapter.

Geographic and Linguistic Background

Nunivak Island is the second largest island in the Bering Sea, after St. Lawrence Island. Today it is home to a relatively stable population of about two hundred individuals, all of whom reside in the island's sole village of Mekoryuk (*Mikuryarmiut*). Spanning 60° north latitude, the island is approximately equidistant, south to north, between the western tip of the Alaska Peninsula and the Bering Strait. It lies to the west of Nelson Island, which is, for all practical purposes, part of the mainland. Nunivak is volcanic in origin and, along with the central uplands of Nelson Island, stands in sharp contrast to the vast semi-saturated lowlands and riverine environs of the adjacent Yukon-Kuskokwim Delta. The island's "geographic advantages" (Lantis 1984, 209) and rich terrestrial and marine environment provide an ideal setting for a thriving northern culture (Pratt 2009a, 146; USBIA 1995, 1:3–8; VanStone 1989, 2). Archaeologists believe that the island has been inhabited for at least 2,500 years (Griffin 2004, 33; Pratt 2009a, 105–108; VanStone 1989, 1; USBIA 1995, 1:87–89, Table 1:3). The population is thought to have been considerably larger in precontact and historical times than it is today (Pratt 1997; 2009a, 126–132), as evidenced by the many documented village and camp sites situated in all parts of the island, most now abandoned but some still in use seasonally (Drozda 1994; Hammerich 1954, 420; Lantis 1946, 162–163; 1984, 212–213; Pratt 2001, 41; 2009a, 126, 129, 154–182; USBIA 1995, 1:22).

The isolation and inaccessibility frequently associated with Nunivak is a perception based largely on the fact that, until about 1946, when regular air service began to operate, the island was physically cut off from the mainland for much of the year by the lack of solid ice formation in the Etolin Strait (*Akularer*) (Drozda 2010, 6; Griffin 2004, 29, 116; Lantis 1984, 209; Pratt 2009a, 214, 252; USBIA 1995, 1:6; VanStone 1989, 2, 42). The island is certainly remote, but not in the sense of its distance from the mainland, especially in comparison to other Bering Sea islands, such as St. Lawrence, St. Matthew, the Pribilofs, and much of the Aleutian chain. The Etolin Strait and the seaward (north, south, and west) margins of the island were purposely avoided by nineteenth- and early twentieth-century explorers and passing whaling ships (Griffin 2004, 82–86; Hammerich 1954, 404; Jarvis 1900, 34; Lantis 1984, 209; VanStone 1973, 33), but Indigenous travellers with their kayaks and umiaks were less deterred by hazards affecting larger ships (Hammerich 1954, 420) (Figure 3.3).

The exceptional stability and seaworthiness of the Nunivak kayak is well documented. VanStone (1989, 15, 41) noted that the Nunivak kayaks were the largest in southwest Alaska and their makers possessed such skills "that their boats could easily be sold or traded to mainland Eskimos." Lantis (1946, 170) reported that in 1940 Nuniwarmiut still made summer trading trips by umiak to the Kuskokwim, although similar trips to the Yukon River had evidently stopped about twenty years earlier. She noted that a crew of four or five men "cooperated in manning the boat," which "had no oarlocks or else rope oarlocks, had a rectangular sail made of matting or strips of walrus gut sewed together, and a paddle for a rudder." Hammerich (1954, 420) observed in the early 1950s Nuniwarmiut were still making regular summer trips up the Kuskokwim, remarking that "it is a much greater risk to cross the twenty-two miles [35.4 km] of Etolin Strait in a modern motor-boat than it was in an old-fashioned skin-boat."

Travel to and from the island was not easy, but obstacles to travel that are frequently cited as having insulated the Nuniwarmiut from outside contact might also have led to prolonged interactions with "strangers." Early Indigenous travellers in search of

FIGURE 3.3 Fractured and shifting ice with open leads in the shallow waters of Etolin Strait. Aerial view from the vicinity of Nunivak Island looking east toward Cape Vancouver, on Nelson Island. Courtesy U.S. Fish and Wildlife Service, Yukon Delta National Wildlife Refuge, Bethel. n.d.

resources or trade, others escaping overcrowding or warfare or simply exploring "new" territory, and/or those who had drifted and arrived by accident may have "discovered" Nunivak. Finding favorable living conditions, they might choose to stay or become marooned for extended periods of time. These possibilities, coupled with its central location on Alaska's west coast, would allow a dynamic amalgam of Bering Sea languages and dialects to develop at a linguistic "crossroads" of sorts (Pratt 2001, 42). Such a view contrasts to portrayals of Nunivak as an isolated backwater and the minimizing of its language as "just a subdivision of Central [Alaskan] Yupik" (Krauss 1986, 3).

The Cup'ig language has, at least since the early 1970s, been presented primarily as a single uniform dialect, while subdialects have received little or no attention at all. As such, it is described either as a remnant of an earlier Eskimo language or dialect chain, or as an aberrant form of Central Alaskan Yup'ik that diverged from the language spoken on the mainland as a result of Nunivak's geographic isolation (Hensel et al. n.d., i; Jacobson 1984, 627–628; Krauss 1973, 822; Lantis 1984, 209–210; VanStone 1989, 42). Expanding on these views, Anthony Woodbury (2001) added,

> [Cup'ig] probably represents the endpoint of a relatively longer period of independent development [relative to mainland Yup'ik dialects]. It also may represent a relic of earlier linguistic diversity in southwestern Alaska which may have disappeared when Yup'ik spread over the large region that it now occupies. Thus, to preserve Cup'ig is to preserve a very ancient and unique piece of linguistic and cultural heritage.[2]

Dialect mixing naturally occurred on the mainland among Yup'ik speakers (see, for example, Miyaoka 1985, 62*n*12). But among the Nuniwarmiut the land also supported numerous local groups, each occupying a specific watershed-based area (see Pratt 2009a, 220–228; USBIA 1995). Some western Nunivak settlements were in fact quite isolated and the speech of their residents could have developed quite differently than that typically described as a homogeneous dialect of the Yup'ik language.

Published remarks regarding historic travel and prehistoric migration of Bering Sea peoples to and from Nunivak largely refer only to the region in which Central Alaskan Yup'ik is now spoken—an area stretching from Norton Sound, in the north, all the way south to Bristol Bay, including inland along the major rivers, as shown in figure 3.2 (Griffin 2001, 78; 2004, 71–74; Jacobson 1998, xv–xix; Lantis 1946, 164; Pratt 2009a, 252–256). Margaret Lantis (1946, 170), who conducted field research on the island in 1939–1940, noted that "mainlanders rarely came to the island to trade." However, she also reported that the oldest man on the island, whose memories stretched back as far as the 1860s, recalled that, in his youth, many men came to southern Nunivak from the Kuskokwim River area for purposes of trade. "They stayed a while and went back," he said. "They came often, by kayak" (quoted in Lantis 1960, 5).

Other reported travels to Nunivak were associated with late nineteenth-century caribou hunting. These visits mostly involved Yup'ik-speaking groups living in adjacent coastal areas on the mainland, and largely Inupiaq-speaking groups from the southern Seward Peninsula (Pratt 2001, 37; VanStone 1989, 10). Of the period from 1890 to 1940, Lantis wrote, "The details of Nunivak life have been changed . . .

more by contact with Eskimos from the Norton Sound region than by direct contact with [non-Indigenous] outsiders" (Lantis 1946, 161).

Few published accounts exist of travel to or from Nunivak involving areas beyond those just mentioned. Presumably referring to unrecorded comments he had heard from St. Lawrence Island elders, Willem de Reuse (1994, 298–299) wrote, "It is said on SLI that there have been contacts with Nunivak." Louis Hammerich (1954, 420) had earlier reported that "Nunivakers have tales of crews, surprised by the breaking of ice in the spring, drifting as far as St. Lawrence Island or Asia, and coming back in the fall—at least some of them." Hammerich (1954, 420) also noted a relatively large number of Russian loan words at Nunivak (recorded in 1950 and 1953). It seems likely that these borrowings reflect interactions between residents of the island and speakers of Yupik (from St. Lawrence Island), Inupiaq (from the Seward Peninsula and the northern Norton Sound area), or Sugpiaq (from the Alaska Peninsula), all of whom would have had more frequent contact with Russians than did the Nuniwarmiut. But Hammerich did not dismiss the possibility that some words were adopted via direct relations with Russian speakers.[3] Interestingly, writing in 1950, Frank Waskey—a prospector and businessman from Minnesota who spent considerable time in western Alaska and whose Yup'ik was described by a fluent speaker of the language as "fairly competent" (Pratt 2012, 38)—noted, "Among the Yut [Yup'ik], the one people whose vocabulary includes distinctively St. Lawrence Island words are the Nunivaks" (Waskey [1950] 2012, 48).

Language Documentation

In the nearly two hundred years since the Russian explorers A. K. Etolin and V. S. Khromchenko first recorded Cup'ig words at Nunivak Island (Jacobson 2012, 943; VanStone 1973, 72–75), the language has undergone much change. The first dedicated linguistic analysis, that of Hammerich, occurred after 1950 (Krauss 1986, 5, 13; Woodbury 1981, 14), at a time when major cultural changes had been taking place on the island for several decades, brought about by the arrival of Western education, Christian missionaries, commercial activities, and government institutions (Griffin 2004, 107–132; Pratt 2009a, 227–228; USBIA 1995, 1:16–17). These outside forces resulted in the consolidation of the island's population from thirty or more villages in the late nineteenth century (figure 3.4) to just two by about 1950 and to a single village, Mekoryuk, by 1960 (see Pratt 2009a, 156–182, for a description of the original villages). In addition to the widespread adoption of English, this process of centralization led to a loss of linguistic variety. Given that dialectic differences can develop over relatively short distances, it is quite possible that residents of each of the earlier villages spoke their own subdialect of Cup'ig.[4] At the very least, there were surely subdialects corresponding to clusters of villages or groups associated with specific geographic areas.

Although modern linguistic descriptions of Cup'ig—or NUN, as the Nunivak language is often abbreviated—portray it as the most divergent of Central Alaskan Yup'ik (CAY) dialects, perceptions of the scope of mutual intelligibility of the NUN and CAY dialects has varied significantly over the past decades. Hammerich (1970, 6; see also Hamp 1976) initially pronounced the Nunivak dialect and mainland Yup'ik dialects to be "mutually incomprehensible." Since then, assessments of mutual intelligibility have ranged from "easy" (Krauss 1980, 102) to "generally mutually intelligible, though not always easily" (Jacobson 2003, vii–viii). Yet credible statements from others, including vigorous and unambiguous assertions from elders on the mainland whose first language is Yup'ik (specifically, the Yukon River dialect), contradict claims of cross-region mutual intelligibility (Polty et al. 1982; see also Pratt 2009a, 132–137).

Nearly thirty years elapsed between Hammerich's work on the Nunivak language, in the early 1950s, and the early work of Steven Jacobson, of the Alaska Native Language Center (ANLC) (see Jacobson 1979a, b). Considering the rapid disintegration of Cup'ig that was occurring during the period, they were probably describing two considerably different language scenarios.

In 1984, the ANLC published Jacobson's *Yup'ik Eskimo Dictionary* (*YED*). It was a groundbreaking work, the first of its kind for an Alaska Native language. In the *YED*, Jacobson summarized the main Yup'ik dialects, including NUN, and subsequently speculated that "two or more subdialects" existed on Nunivak Island (Jacobson 1985, 38*n*18). However, to achieve a goal of a unified writing system for the Yup'ik language region, specific and cumbersome rules for spelling and pronunciation were necessary for Nunivak forms included in the dictionary (Jacobson 1984, 37; 2012, 44). These rules, it would turn out, were unworkable for the Nuniwarmiut.

The most recent period of Nunivak linguistic research, which began in the mid-1980s, has been characterized by increased local interest in language preservation and documentation by the Nuniwarmiut themselves. From 1986 to 1991, under the auspices of the Alaska Native Claims Settlement Act (ANCSA) program of the US Bureau of Indian Affairs, major fieldwork was undertaken on Nunivak Island, with a view to documenting historical places and cemetery sites (see Pratt 2009b, 2–43; USBIA 1995). The BIA research generated an enormous body of historical,

FIGURE 3.4 Villages on Nunivak Island in the period from 1880 to 1960. Adapted from Pratt 2009a, 161.

archaeological, and linguistic data. The linguistic material, which includes over 175 tape recordings of interviews conducted primarily with monolingual (or limited bilingual) Nunivak elders, ultimately led to the identification of at least one remaining subdialect of Cup'ig, which I call "western Nunivak."

In 1986, the BIA contracted with Yup'ik language experts at the ANLC to produce full bilingual transcripts of ANCSA project tapes (Pratt 2009b, 42), including those from Nunivak. Irene Reed coordinated the effort for ANLC and began working with the Nunivak recordings later the same year. The recordings are not strictly narratives or monologues but also preserve dialogues, including cross-generational discussions. In this sense, as common discourse, their linguistic value is increased. The Nunivak recordings are, however, sometimes fragmented and difficult to follow, and they proved difficult for Reed and her staff, most of whom had little or no previous experience working with the Cup'ig language. The largest challenge was presented in the recordings of Andrew Noatak (pictured in the image at the opening of this chapter), one of the last fluent speakers of the Western Nunivak dialect (Drozda 2007, 102–105; see also Jacobson 2006 and Woodbury 1999).

To illustrate, the Noatak translations and transcriptions prepared by ANLC staff frequently credit a cadre of Yup'ik (and sometimes Cup'ig) collaborators working together on individual recordings. Despite this group effort, these works contain blank lines for words and phrases that were beyond even their combined knowledge and abilities. Transcribers sometimes added notes in the text to acknowledge the challenges they encountered, such as, "The translation of the previous paragraph and many other parts of this piece of narration is guess work" (Noatak 1986a, 36).

Other notes made by Reed, concerning somewhat less problematic Nunivak recordings, provide valuable information about particular narrators and their speaking style. For instance, she informed future readers that elders Kay Hendrickson (b. 1909) and his wife, Mattie (b. 1926), had been living in Bethel for some years and often spoke "using mainland pronunciation styles" (Hendrickson and Hendrickson 1986). Another elder, Jack Williams Sr., it was noted, commonly used Yup'ik endings on Cup'ig words, including place names, when he spoke in English (Williams 1986a). Reed's comments provide a window into how the language of Cup'ig speakers varied in the 1980s and the ways in which speech was affected under different circumstances (see Fienup-Riordan 2000, 190; Hammerich 1952, 113; Hensel et al. n.d., i).

The Nunivak tapes exposed ANLC linguists and others to some of the limitations of previous work with the language (see Fienup-Riordan 2000, 190*n*176). Jacobson's Nunivak research was secondary to that concerning the most widely spoken dialect, General Central Yup'ik; he later acknowledged that limitation (Jacobson 2006, 137). His Nunivak work did not involve elder speakers of the language and relied exclusively on a younger person living in the mainland community of Bethel. In 1990, he replied to a detailed inquiry from a linguistics graduate student who had expressed an interest in Nunivak: "I must confess that all my [Nunivak] research was based on one person, and I suspect that I didn't get a very complete picture of everything that is going on in that amazing dialect" (Jacobson 1990b). Interestingly, in the same letter, he refers to a large (but unspecified) number of reel-to-reel tape recordings that Hammerich made while at Nunivak—tapes that have unfortunately been lost.

At about the same time (late 1980s), leaders and educators in the village of Mekoryuk began efforts to preserve and revitalize their Native language. In addition to Howard Amos and Muriel Amos, active in these efforts were Dorothy Kiokun, Ike Kiokun, Prudy Olrun, and Marianne Williams, no doubt along with others unknown to me. Eventually, with much effort, they convinced Lower Kuskokwim School District administrators in Bethel (headquartered 250 kilometres away) of the need for educational materials printed in the Cup'ig language (see Jacobson 2003, vii–viii; Nuniwarmiut Piciryarata Tamaryalkuti 2001). Previously, Native language educators at the Nuniwarmiut School spent countless hours modifying the district's Yup'ik materials. For example, they changed orthography, vocabulary and translations to reflect the Cup'ig language; physically pasting these revisions over the existing Yup'ik texts.

This period also saw a major accomplishment with the publication by the ANLC of the *Cup'ig Eskimo Dictionary* [*CED*] (Amos and Amos 2003). The *CED* increased manifold the documentation of the lexicon of Nunivak language, which has "many words found nowhere else in Eskimo [languages]" (Jacobson 2012, 42). Still, the *CED* is a preliminary work. Much of the BIA material remains unexamined and, without accurate transcription and translation, largely inaccessible. These materials certainly include previously undocumented lexical items and could provide further insight into the structure and history of the Nunivak language and its dialects.

Place Name Documentation

The corpus of documented Nunivak Island place names is relatively large, numbering about a thousand (Drozda 1994; Pratt 2009a, 154–156), yet few of them are included in either the *CED* or the *YED*.[5] The names and associated narratives comprise a large geographical vocabulary, reflecting in part a relatively stable and ancient subset of the language. Treating the names as such and studying their components comparatively with those of other Bering Sea regions might provide further insight into past relationships between the various regional languages and groups.

By definition toponyms are rooted in landscape, as such they may be thought of as relatively stable or more persistent than other aspects of language (Hammerich 1952, 113; Schreyer 2005). But also, several Nunivak examples—including those on which the chapter focuses—reveal evolving names and/or meanings over time. The malleability is partly explained by dynamics such as language shift, dialect, memory, folk etymology, and changing land use patterns. Loss of names, their meanings, and the dilution of traditional knowledge associated with them are accelerated in contemporary times not only by the passing of elder culture bearers, but also by changing land use patterns and, in the case of Nunivak, by the endangered status of the language.

The intensive documentation of Nunivak Island place names relied primarily on elders of two generations, born between 1900 and the early 1920s. Some members of the older group were occasionally critical of the younger generations and spoke directly about the erosion of traditional knowledge. In some cases, same-generation elders also criticized one another for reasons that might reflect village social tensions rather than any lack of specific knowledge. In any case, place names elicited and re-elicited by researchers from multiple elders were overwhelmingly consistent, while place-based narratives (memories of place) showed more variation. Place names can serve as mnemonic devices (Drozda 1994, ix), but their capacity to summon to mind complex life events and learned stories requires an acute memory that often fades with time.

Asweryag and *Asweryagmiut*

The remainder of this chapter focuses on two principal but geographically separate Nunivak Island place names, *Asweryag* and *Asweryagmiut*.[6] Linguists may recognize their common base *aswer-* as a cognate of the word for "walrus" in other Eskimo languages, but in Cup'ig determining the correct gloss is not as straightforward. Apart from the two place names, *aswer* is not part of the modern Cup'ig lexicon. Translations by bilingual Cup'ig-English speakers differ from those of Yup'ik linguists, and these do not correlate with historical references, which are inconsistent and imprecise in their own right. Statements by elders regarding the antiquity and origins of the names, associations to other place names, and traditional stories suggest off-island origins and connections to places, languages, and cultural groups from further north, including those on the Seward Peninsula, on St. Lawrence Island, and on Russia's Chukotka Peninsula.

Like all Eskimo languages, Cup'ig is polysynthetic. That is, words consist of an initial noun or verb base (or stem) often followed by a number of modifying suffixes called postbases, and an ending which indicates case, mood, person, and number. Such words can function as complete sentences.[7] The Cup'ig name *Asweryagmiut* is analyzed as follows: *aswer-* (walrus) +*yag-* (many) +*miut* (village/residents of).[8]

The literal translations of *Asweryag* as "many walrus" (Jacobson 1998, 44; 2006, 148; 2012, 146; Reed in Noatak and Kolerok 1987, 18) and as "an abundance of walrus" (Woodbury, pers. comm., 16 January 2016) may reflect a historical meaning still preserved in some parts of mainland CAY. However, as we will see, these translations, while etymologically correct, no longer accurately represent the colloquial meaning of the name as understood by the Nuniwarmiut.

While the CED has no entry for *Asweryag*, it does list *Asweryagmiut* as a place name, with the base translated as "beached walrus." It does not, however, have an entry for *aswer*; rather, the standard term for "walrus" among Cup'ig speakers is *kaugpag* (Amos and Amos 2003, 156–157, 532; Jacobson 1998, 144; 2006, 148; 2012, 146). In a review of dozens of Cup'ig-English bilingual transcripts that include some discussion of walrus in various contexts, "walrus" is always *kaugpag*, except, as noted, when associated with the translation of the *Aswer-* place names. In that context, some elders considered *Aswer-* to refer to a "dead walrus," often presented in contemporary translations as a "beached walrus" (here, assumed dead). Relatively recent translations provided by Nunivakers vary, however, reflecting a lack of familiarity with the word. Translations include "sea mammals," "walrus or whale" (Amos and Amos 2012; Drozda 1994, 83–84), "whales" (Amos and Amos 2013), and simply "walrus" (Amos and Amos 2003, 49; Howard Amos, pers. comm., 22 November 2016). Despite the inconsistency regarding the type of sea mammal, all of the translations from Nunivak Island include the modifier "beached." By contrast, contemporary mainland meanings offer no evidence of the "beached" or "dead" qualifiers, which seem to have originated on Nunivak.

An example of the gap in understanding is illustrated in the transcript of an interview with Andrew Noatak and Robert Kolerok (1987), during which Howard Amos provided an oral interpretation in English. In the transcript, prepared by Yup'ik linguists at the ANLC, Amos's use of the adjective "dead" was called into question: "she came to *Asweryagmiut* and found a lot of dead walrus in that place. That's why it's called *Asweryagmiut*. *Aswer* is dead [*sic*] walrus." Hoping to identify the "correct" interpretation, I later put the question of the meaning of *aswer* to Howard Amos himself. He replied that his father, Walter Amos (a monolingual Cup'ig speaker born 1920) "always said *aswer* referred to dead walrus" (Howard Amos, pers. comm., 22 November 2016).

Commenting on an early draft of this chapter, Anthony Woodbury (pers. comm., 16 January 2016) noted that, for modern Cup'ig speakers (who may or may not be familiar with the CAY term *asveq*), the derivation of *Aswer-* place names presents a "bit of a puzzle." He suggests that the Nunivak interpretation of *aswer-* as referring to a "dead/beached walrus" or, as I suggest, something "walrus-like" may provide clues as to how the meanings of the term have evolved on the island. The multiple interpretations reflected in the various translations and apparently shifting definitions do not necessarily constitute inconsistencies but are rather the result of contemporary speakers trying to make sense of an older, seemingly foreign name.

Aswer in the Historical Literature

The few translations of NUN *aswer* found in the published literature offer a different interpretation than those presented above. The earliest word list for Nunivak was recorded in 1822 by Etolin and Khromchenko (VanStone 1973, 56, 74). Their list, comparing languages (and dialects) of the Bering Sea region, includes the following terms for "walrus":

azibok: Nunivak Islanders
azyuk: Konyag
ayv-gyt: Stuart Islanders
kchikhpak: Aglegmiut

As linguistic evidence, early word lists such as this one are far from wholly reliable, in part owing to orthographic idiosyncrasies. Yet the term *kchikhpak*—recorded among the Aglegmiut (or Aglurmiut, as they are known today) may possibly be related to the Nunivak word *kaugpag*.

A century later, in his notes accompanying drawings of masks made by Nuniwarmiut in 1925, Knud Rasmussen referred to an "âsvarpaq," which he described as

> a kind of giant walrus which does not appear to breathe when it comes up out of the sea . . . while one hears ordinary walruses gasping for breath, one never hears this walrus gasp . . . It is as if it just sticks its gigantic head up – – it eats seals – – in contrast to other sea animals . . . when they catch a seal – – they first suck out the flesh – – and then afterwards eat the skin – – so strong – – – that they just suck it out. (Quoted in Sonne 1988, 162*n*27; punctuation as in the original)

Rasmussen's notes were made from interpretations by Paul Ivanoff (Sonne 1985), who translated *âsvarpaq* as "giant walrus."[9] By way of contrast, Sonne (1988, 149) offers descriptions, again based on Rasmussen's notes, of walrus masks using the term *kaugpag* (written "kauxpax" and "kowggpuk" by Hammerich and Ivanoff, respectively). This demonstrates that at least as early as the 1920s Nunivakers made a distinction between *kaugpag* (an ordinary walrus) and *aswer*, which even then appeared difficult to define.

What appear to be older forms of *aswer* are also preserved in song lyrics recorded by Lantis (1946, 277), which include "ayuwi'a ma / ayu'wi'ama" and "ayuwi'aka," both translated as "my young walrus." In addition, Lantis (1946, 154, 162; see also 154 [map]) provided the first record of the place name "a'z·uwa'γăyă'γamiut" (*Asweryagmiut*), which she described as "formerly a year-round village, now abandoned." The name was one of thirty she recorded in 1939 and 1940, and, while she was not always able to determine their precise meaning, she offered the following interpretation of "a'z·uwa'γăyă'γamiut": "[from] a'z·uwax, walrus, specifically a mean old walrus bull; exact meaning of whole name not clear, formerly a year-round village, now abandoned." Again, this is not a typical walrus. It is possible that the "dead walrus" in contemporary *aswer* translations may be a recreated meaning, the closest English term for a concept that does not easily translate, possibly representing an entity for which there is no recognized Western equivalent.

Dictionary Interpretations and Cognates

According to the *Yup'ik Eskimo Dictionary*, *asveq* (Cup'ig *aswer*) is "walrus"—but (again) not in Cup'ig, where "*kaugpak* (Cup'ig *kaugpag*) rather than *asveq* is used for walrus." The entry further notes that, in the Nunivak dialect (NUN, that is, Cup'ig) *asverpak*—literally, "big walrus" (*-rpak* = big, large)—is a "'rogue' walrus, a dangerous walrus that attacks seals and boats, and *asverrluk* is 'beached walrus carcass,'" with the postbase *-rrluk* signifying something that "has departed from its natural state" (Jacobson 2012, 146, 861).[10] The first description is similar to and may be derived from Rasmussen's *âsvarpaq*, while the second corresponds more closely to *asweryag* as defined by the Amoses.

Jacobson (1998, 144) identifies *asveq* ("walrus") as "otherwise" (that is, other than in NUN) pan-Eskimo, but he includes *kaugpak* (NUN *kaugpag*) as an alternate term, suggesting that it is "a central coast innovation based on an obsolete [Yup'ik] word *kauk*, which is cognate to the Iñupiaq word for "edible walrus skin" (see MacLean 2014, 143). Jacobson also records the term *kaugpak* in environments beyond walrus habitat, such as upstream on the Kuskokwim River, where the meaning shifts to "thick edible layer of walrus skin" (Jacobson 1998, 144). This meaning, according to Jacobson, derives from "Nunivak people who took walrus skin upriver to sell."[11]

As Jacobson (1998, 144) notes, the distribution and frequency of the use of the term *kaugpak* on the mainland also vary. An example of this fluid situation is nicely captured in an intergenerational bilingual recording (Kelly 1985) made in the Yukon Delta village of Emmonak. While Jacobson had only recorded *asveq* for "walrus" at Emmonak, the interview tape shows the use of both terms. More importantly, it shows that *asveq* is not recognized by at least one fluent Yup'ik speaker of the younger generation. The exchange between a father (the interviewee) and his son (interpreter) revolves around a mainland Yup'ik place name, *Asvertuli*:

> *Andrew* (son): Augna-mi Asvertuli cauga?
> (What is *Asvertuli*?)
>
> *Anthony* (father): Tua-w' tamana kuiga.
> (That's the name of that creek.)
>
> *Andrew*: I mean camek atengqengqerta?
> (I meant what [does the] name [mean]?)
>
> *Anthony*: Imarpigtaat-w' tua-i. Asveret.
> (Those [that] live in the ocean. The walruses.)
>
> *Andrew*: Asveq. Caulria-ll' im' asveq?
> (*Asveq*. What is an *asveq*?)
>
> *Anthony*: Qaurpak.
> (A walrus.)
>
> *Andrew*: Oh! Okay!
>
> *Anthony*: Walrus-aanek-w' pilaqait. Tauna tua-i taumek atengqertuq. (They call them walruses [in English]. That place has that name.)
>
> *Andrew* [to interviewer]: This village is named after a walrus.
>
> (Kelly 1985, 21)

Recordings such as this may provide insight into shifts in the standard lexicon and could be useful in augmenting Jacobson's dialect study.

The *Dictionary of Alaska Place Names* (Orth 1967, 54) includes an entry "Ahzwiryuk Bluff," listing as a variant "Azwiryak Bluff," for a site on Nunivak Island located about a mile east of the village of Nash Harbor. The dictionary offers no etymological information, however, describing the term only as an "Eskimo name" obtained in 1949 by United States Coast and Geodetic Survey. The name appears on United States Geological Survey (USGS) maps as "Ahzirwuk" and clearly refers to the place known locally as *Asweryag* (about which more will be said below). Neither *Asweryag* nor *Asweryagmiut* (including variant forms) appear in the dictionary or on USGS maps. Orth (1967, 729) and USGS maps include a separate but relevant anglicized CAY term, "Osviak," for a mainland settlement, now abandoned, that was situated on the north shore of Bristol Bay. The site, which was investigated by the BIA in 1986, is well known in the region as an ancestral village of present-day Togiak (*Tuyuryaq*). In the modern Yup'ik orthography "Osviak" is written *Asvigyaq*. Wright and Chythlook (1985, 14) offer the spelling "Asviryaq," while ANCSA records identify the site as *Asvigyarmiut*. Orth (1967, 97) lists another variant spelling, "Azeviuk," and includes a 1919 definition provided by G. L. Harrington, of the USGS, according to which the name means "walrus."

Like the *Asweryag* names at Nunivak, the original meaning of *Asvigyaq* is also apparently lost among contemporary speakers of the Bristol Bay dialect. Evidently, the base *asvig-* exists there today only in the place name. BIA transcripts and associated place name lists (Reed 1984, 1989) contain statements such as "etymology unknown," "analysis uncertain," and a speculative "from *asveq* 'walrus'??" An interactive map produced by the Bristol Bay Native Corporation suggests that the name *Asvigyaq* is "possibly related to stabilize; to be solid." This seems to me a questionable interpretation, no doubt based on *asvaite-*, "to be solid, to be stable; to be immovable" (Jacobson 2012, 146).[12] Assuming that Harrington's 1919 definition is correct, it seems likely that the name originally referred to "walrus," but the meaning as well as the pronunciation has changed over time. In language surveys at Togiak and Twin Hills, the two contemporary villages closest to Osviak, Jacobson (1998, 144) recorded the Yup'ik word *asveq* for "walrus."

Possible Central Siberian Yupik and Chukchi Cognates

The *St. Lawrence Island / Siberian Yupik Eskimo Dictionary* (Badten et al. 2008, 100, 762–763) lists the name of an old village site, located on the northwestern tip of St. Lawrence Island just east of Gambell as *Ayveghyaget* literally, "many walrus," (Walunga 1987, 16). The residents of this village were called Azveghyagmiut; the CAY and NUN equivalents are Asveryagmiut and Asweryagmiut, respectively.[13]

Jacobson (2006, 148; 2012, 146) and other Yup'ik scholars note that the CAY name for St. Lawrence Island is *Asveryak*; its residents are accordingly Asveryagmiut ("Asviryagmiut" in John 2003, 510–511; and in Mather 1985, 41). Yup'ik elder Andrew Tsikoyak (*Ciquyaq*, b. ca. 1901), of the lower

FIGURE 3.5 *Kalirmiu*, Peter Smith (1912–1995) at the village of Nash Harbor. The bluff, *Asweryag*, is seen in the background.

Kuskokwim region tundra village of Nunapitchuk (*Nunapicuaq*) stated:

> *Nunivaam neglirnera qikertartangqellinilria. Asvigyamek aipaa-wa Ukiivik.*
>
> We have discovered there are other islands north of *Nunivaaq* [*Nuniwar*, Nunivak Island]. One is called *Asvigyaq* [St. Lawrence Island] and the other *Ukiivik* [*Ugiuvak*, King Island]. (Tsikoyak 1988)

Note that Tsikoyak's pronunciation *Asvigyaq* matches that recorded for Osviak in the contemporary Bristol Bay dialect at Togiak. The other spellings cited above (*Asveryag-*, *Asviryag-*, *Asvigya*(*g*)-) probably reflect minor dialectical differences or individual idiosyncrasies.

One St. Lawrence Islander wrote: "The *Ayveghyagmiit* . . . had a village [on St. Lawrence Island]. Some mainland Alaskan Eskimos still refer to us as 'Ayveghyags'" (Apassingok, Walunga, and Tennant 1985, 5; English plural *s* in "Ayveghyags"). Evidently such references were not restricted to Alaska Native peoples. The Russian biologist Lyudmila Bogoslovskaya remarked that "18th and 19th century Europeans referred to the [Siberian/ St. Lawrence Island] Yupiks as 'the walrus people'" (Bogoslovskaya et al. 2016, 80).

In the entry for *Asveryak*, Jacobson (2012, 146) also refers to the St. Lawrence Island village:

> There is a particular site on St. Lawrence Is. called Ayvəʀyaɣət [*Asveryaget*], '(place with) lots of walrus,' by the people there, and this may be the actual source of the Central Yup'ik word [*Asveryak*], indicating that Central Yup'ik familiarity with St. Lawrence Islanders was through people of that particular place.

If Jacobson's statement is accepted, it opens the possibility that the cognate Nunivak place names also originated with people from St. Lawrence Island. Speaking in English, Nunivak elder Peter Smith (b. 1912) (figure 3.5) stated:

> You know the same name [is] down in the St. Lawrence Island [. . .] Gambell is called *Asweryagmiut*, the same name. It means 'lots of walrus.' [. . .] I don't know [why they called the Nunivak site *Asweryagmiut*], that's how I heard the name, I never heard the meanings. [. . .] must be one man he found the walrus, a live one. (Smith 1986a)

Smith's evident uncertainty about the meaning of the name underscores the general lack of familiarity with the term *Asweryag* at Nunivak.

Viewed from the other side of the Bering Strait, Orth (1967, 826) quotes Joseph Billings (commander of a 1790–1792 Russian expedition to Alaska) as reporting that "the Chukchi natives of Siberia call this island [St. Lawrence Island] E-oo-vogen," which Billings also spells Eivoogiena. Other variants include Eivugen (from G. A. Sarichev, a member of the same expedition); Eiwugi-en (Krauss 2005, 165); and Eiwugi-nu (Merck 1980, 194). Hughes (1984, 276) reports that the Chukchi name for the island's people is Eiwhue'lit (generally written in English as Eiwhuelit) and goes on to note: "There is evidence that this term traditionally designated only one of the groups living in Gambell, the (now small) *u γá·li·t* clan whose ancestors founded and therefore 'own' the village" (Hughes 1984, 277, citing Collins 1937, 18; Hughes 1960; Moore 1923). Hughes (1960, 252) also glosses *u γá·li·t* as "Ualeit ('people living at the north end'—of Gambell)."

According to de Reuse (1994, 410), the Chukchi name *Eywelət* (his spelling of Eiwhuelit, he notes) means "SLI [St. Lawrence Island] Eskimos" and is "probably related to Ch. Aywan." He links the term *Aywan*, "Eskimo," to the Chukchi word *eygəsqən*, "north," through CSY *aywaa-* and *aygugh-*, both meaning "north, to go north." (For further discussion, see Fortescue 2005, 18–19). Although the resemblance may be coincidental, it seems probable that *Eywelət* is also related to CSY *ayveq* (walrus), as seen in St. Lawrence Island place names with the stems *Ayvegh-* and *Ayvigh-*. One might see a relationship between the Chukchi sound written "ei," as in eivug, eiwug, eivoog, and eiwhue, with those of CSY, CAY, and NUN written in the current orthography of those languages as "ay" as in *ayveq*, "as" as in *asveq* and *aswer*. It should be noted that the phoneme "z" as represented by the letter "s" in CAY often alternates with the "y" sound (de Reuse 1994, 355n5; Jacobson 1990a, 278).

Similar names or cognates alone do not necessarily indicate a direct connection between the places. Linking comparable place names (or vocabulary) across languages or dialects is problematic, especially when names were recorded by individuals whose language skills were limited. De Reuse (1994, 321) makes this point with respect to eighteenth-century word lists: "As with all such early lists," he writes, "the translation of many words is inaccurate, the spelling is inconsistent and difficult to interpret, and typos are very common."

Analyses and comparison of the above names yield intriguing associations relevant to Nunivak in light of other reported links between the two islands. Connections include additional place names and abandoned Nunivak historic sites attributed to "northerners" in general and, according to one elder, to St. Lawrence Islanders specifically. In any case, Nuniwarmiut refer to these people and two of their documented settlements at Nunivak not as *Asweryagmiut*, as might be expected on the basis of the CAY ethnonym, but instead as *Qaviayarmiut*.

Asweryag, a Qaviayarmiut Burial Site?

Asweryag (USGS Ahzwiryuk Bluff) is a steep bluff situated on the northwest coast of Nunivak Island immediately east of the historic village of *Ellikarrmiut* (Nash Harbor) (figure 3.6). The area on top of the bluff was identified by elder Jack Williams (b. 1911) (figure 3.7) as a burial site consisting of one or more mass graves. According to Williams (1986b), the grave(s) contain the remains of a group of Qaviayarmiut—for now, let us just consider them "northerners"—who had previously settled at two eastern Nunivak sites which will be discussed later on (Williams 1991a, 1991b). The exact location of the reported mass burial(s) is unknown, and the oral accounts presented by Williams sometimes appear confusing or contradictory. Williams was the only elder to describe mass graves at the site and to associate them with the Qaviayarmiut. Andrew Noatak (b. ca. 1900) simply described the area of *Asweryag* as "the one with a lot of graves" (Noatak 1986b, 25; USBIA 1995, 3:97–99). Two large rock features that could be interpreted as burials were located in the vicinity of *Asweryag* (see USBIA 1995, 3: 95–120) (figures 3.8 and 3.9).

(FACING) FIGURE 3.6 The abandoned village of Nash Harbor, July 1965, consisting of *Qimugglugpagmiut* (foreground) and *Ellikarrmiut* (middle). Clearly visible in the distance is the bluff, *Asweryag*. Courtesy of the US Fish and Wildlife Service, Yukon Delta National Wildlife Refuge, Bethel.

(ABOVE) FIGURE 3.7 *Qussauyar* (Herman Humpy) and *Uyuruciar* (Jack Williams), ca. 1920s. Photograph by L. J. Palmer. Palmer Collection, Alaska and Polar Regions Collections, Archives, University of Alaska Fairbanks.

To the east of *Ellikarrmiut,* in the vicinity of *Asweryag* (USGS Ahzwiryuk Bluff), are two rock features that could be interpreted as large burials. The features were identified and described in two separate BIA ANCSA surveys (USBIA 1995, 3: 95–120). The Cup'ig name of the bluff was applied to the report covering the further east of the features, which consists of a solitary mound of rocks about 1 meter high and measuring 3.5 metres in diameter at the base (USBIA 1995, 4:135) (figures 3.8 and 3.9).

Citing the testimony of Williams, the BIA report on Nunivak Island implies that the Qaviayarmiut were killed by the Nunivakers in apparent "retribution for [their] wasteful and disrespectful treatment of the island's caribou" (USBIA 1995, 3:97). It is true that Williams and other Nunivak elders spoke about the mistreatment of animals on Nunivak and elsewhere at the hands of the Qaviayarmiut. Olie Olrun (1991) reported, for example, that his grandfather used to talk about the Qaviayarmiut destroying caribou and that they "apparently severed many of their heads." Yet Williams (1986b) also provides another explanation for the massacre of those buried near *Asweryag* (Griffin 2004, 74). According to Williams, after the Qaviayarmiut established their Nunivak settlements (or camps), a pair of Nelson Island men arrived one spring to hunt caribou. The Nunivak people considered the Nelson Islanders allies and welcomed them as friends.

(FACING) FIGURE 3.8 An aerial view of *Asweryag* looking toward the village of Nash Harbor, August 1986. A large mound of piled rocks in the center of the photo is one of at least two features in the vicinity of the bluff that fit descriptions of a reported mass burial of the Qaviayarmiut. Photograph by Susan Wilson, Bureau of Indian Affairs, ANCSA 14(h)(1) Collection (case file AA-9306), Anchorage.

(ABOVE) FIGURE 3.9 Large rock mound at *Asweryag*. Possible mass burial of Qaviayarmiut. Illustration by Emily Kearney-Williams based on photographs in case file AA-9306 of the Bureau of Indian Affairs, ANCSA 14(h)(1) Collection, Anchorage.

FIGURE 3.10 *Nuratar*, Andrew Noatak (ca. 1900–1990) and *Qungutur*, Robert Kolerok (ca. 1901–1998) at Mekoryuk, November 1987. Photograph by Robert Drozda.

But the Qaviayarmiut killed both men at Triangle Island (*Qikertar*), just off the northeastern coast of Nunivak. When the Ellikarrmiut heard about the killing, they feared that they would be next and took action to circumvent that possibility.

Other elders recounted the story of a dual homicide at Triangle Island differently. Walter Amos (1991) said that it was Nunivakers who were responsible for killing two "mainlanders" as the latter prepared to escape with stolen goods (Pratt 2001, 39*n*18). Kay Hendrickson (Hendrickson and Williams 1991) recalled that two successful hunters from the Kuskokwim River were camping overnight at the island prior to crossing back to the mainland with their caribou meat. They were discovered and killed not by Nuniwarmiut but by two men from the Yukon River (who may or may not have been considered Qaviayarmiut). As it stands, it is difficult to reconcile the differences in these versions of the story. The events occurred before any of the elders who recounted them were born, so it is possible they remembered or heard elements of the story differently. It is also possible that inadequacies in the existing translations contribute to some of the discrepancies.

In a published account based on the Williams (1986b) transcript, Ann Fienup-Riordan (Fienup-Riordan and Rearden 2016, 69) further complicates the issue by reporting that Williams identified the people who killed the men from Nelson Island as "Qaviayaarmiut (Iñupiat) from the Seward Peninsula." Actually, despite his limited command of English, he clearly describes them as St. Lawrence Islanders: "People was killed down there at the Nash Harbor by some kind of against each other [*sic*] from Saint Lawrence Island people. The long time ago they coming and they call them Qaviayarmiut" (Williams 1986b).

Williams (1991a) retold the story five years later, at which point he was eighty years old. This time he did not mention why the two Nelson Islanders were killed, but he recounted the circumstances of their death in the same way and again specifically mentioned the burial site of *Asweryag*. This later narrative was primarily in Cup'ig interspersed with some English (I have edited the translation slightly for the sake of clarity):

> These Qaviayarmiut, I don't know the real reason as to why they were killed. I have heard from sources that they were taken to *Ellikarrmiut* [Nash Harbor]. They were trapped in a huge net [seal net]. They died from hypothermia. Some elderly person may know something about that. I'm not from west Nunivak Island, so I don't know. Messengers went to go get them [from their eastern settlements] in winter as far as I know. They let them enter the hot *qasgir* [men's community house at *Ellikarrmiut*] and plugged up the porch with lots of, a pile of wood; nobody can go out. Then they placed the net over the skylight, using a huge net. That is how it is. Some made an attempt to exit, but when snared in the net they re-entered.
>
> When they all died, they were buried below a high place and covered with large flat stones, a big pile of rocks. That is where they're buried, below a place called *Asweryag*. It looks like there is something there in pairs, next to one another, flat rocks piled up there, if erosion hasn't taken them down. I reckon those are Qaviayarmiut people. (Williams 1991a)

Asweryagmiut and a Woman Who Named Places

Asweryarmiut is a former habitation site located on the southwest coast of Nunivak Island. Like many of the island's settlements, it was established at the mouth of a stream associated with a sheltered estuary. The BIA report (1995, 2:286) noted a general "lack of knowledge about *Asweryagmiut* among Nunivak elders," suggesting the abandonment of the site before the end of the nineteenth century (Pratt 2009, 175). Despite the lack of specific site information, the name is remembered, together with fragments of stories regarding its origin. Two Nunivak elders, Andrew Noatak and Robert Kolerok (figure 3.10), identified *Asweryagmiut* as one of at least ten prominent former habitation sites on the western and southern coast of the island that were originally named by an ancestral woman. Both men believed that she named the sites in the distant past, "during the time there weren't that many people" (Noatak and Kolerok 1987, 29) or "before people came to the land" (Kolerok and Kolerok 1991a, 26). Interpreting for Noatak, Howard Amos explained: "He thinks that woman was one of the first people on Nunivak Island, because when people were not very many she started going on the coast and started naming the inlets and bays and so forth" (Noatak and Kolerok 1987, 29).

The names that the ancestral woman gave to particular places are descriptive and are based, it is said, on her experiences or observations at each place. The most thorough tally of the sites she named was provided by Robert Kolerok (Kolerok and Kolerok 1991a). Dorothy Kiokun, a fluent speaker of both Cup'ig and English, provided an oral interpretation of part of his narrative[14]:

> That lady named those places. First she came to *Talungmiut* and the reason why she named *Talungmiut* is because the river was going crooked, going that way, and that's when they start calling the place *Talungmiut*, because that river was all curled up, I guess, or something like that.[15] Then she went to *Qayigyalegmiut*. She saw spotted seals. Then they used to call those spotted seals *qayigyat*.[16] So that's when she named that place *Qayigyalegmiut*. Then she went to *Carwarmiut* and she couldn't cross the river, so she put two driftwoods together. She got onto those and she was trying to go across, but she floated all the way down and landed across, way far down, and that's when she called it *Carwarmiut*. That's how she named that place *Carwarmiut*, because the current was so strong. So that woman named those three places. (Kolerok and Kolerok 1991a)

Kolerok continued and sequentially identified seven more places (west to east) originally named by the woman. These names, along with those mentioned below by Noatak, are listed in table 3.1, moving counter-clockwise from *Iqugmiut*, the westernmost site on the island. Together, the sites span a range of 120 kilometres, and their locations are marked on figure 3.12 (below).

Noatak (Noatak and Kolerok 1987, 28) was less specific, stating: "I don't know exactly where she started from. Probably from *Iqug* ('the end' of Nunivak). She named them all on one side (of the island) on down to *Iqugmiut* down there." Howard Amos then interpreted: "He does not have a definite location of where that woman started naming the spots in this coast, but he thinks she started off from Cape Mohican (*Iqug*) all the way probably to Cape Mendenhall (*Cingigglag*)" (Noatak and Kolerok 1987, 28). Noatak's list begins at a point further west and does not extend as far east as does Kolerok's list.

TABLE 3.1 Nunivak Places Named by Ancestral Woman

Name	Translation
Iqugmiut	village of *Iq'ug* (the end) [westernmost point of Nunivak Island]
Talungmiut	village of *Talung* (natural projection that blocks view of village from the sea)
Qayigyalegmiut	village of *Qayigyal'eg* (spotted seals)
Carwarmiut	village of *Carwar* (stream with strong currents)
Asweryagmiut	village of *Asweryag* (many beached [dead] walrus)
Penacuarmiut	village of *Penacuar* (bluff, small cliff)
Mecagmiut	village of *Mec'ag* (wet, swampy)
Tevcarmiut	village of *Tevcar* (portage)
Kangirtulirmiut	village of *Kangirtul'ir* (one with a deep bay)
Kuigaaremiut	village of *Kuigaar* (small river)
Tacirmiut	village of *Tac'ir* (bay)
Paamiut	village of *Paa/Paanga* (river mouth)

Noatak (Noatak and Kolerok 1987, 30) provided brief biographical information about the woman: "They tell stories (*univkangssi*) about that one," he noted.[17] He said her parents resided at *Kangi'irerrlagmiut* (also known as *Kangiirlagmiut*), a site on the northeastern coast of Nunivak Island located well outside the range of the places she reportedly named. It may be significant that other elders, as well as place name records, indicate that one of the two Qaviayarmiut settlements is located in very close proximity to *Kangi'irerrlagmiut*. A field map (Hansen n.d.) also includes a faded annotation, "where couple lived," attributed to Nunivak elder Lily Jones (b. 1898).[18] The note is placed precisely at the Qaviayarmiut settlement located by several elders a short distance upstream of *Kangi'irerrlagmiut*. The "couple" might refer to the parents of the woman who named places, although the reference could be to some other couple associated with a different traditional Nunivak story.

Lantis's oldest informant offers what is probably among the earliest recorded memories of a Nunivaker. "Once when people came from the mainland," he recalled, "a Nunivak woman fell down a cliff on the west side and was killed. The mainland people helped Nunivak people bury her on top of the cliff" (translated and quoted in Lantis 1960, 5–6). A recently uncovered narrative, which has yet to be fully investigated, provides another interesting twist to the story. In an interview conducted in 1987, both Andrew Noatak and interpreter Howard Amos (Noatak and Kolerok 1987, 21–22, 29–30) referred to the murder of the daughter of the couple living at *Kangi'irerrlagmiut*, who was evidently pushed off a cliff near *Asweryagmiut* by her husband (USBIA 1995, 2:293). Noatak (Noatak and Kolerok 1987, 22; see also

FIGURE 3.11 *Penat* ("cliffs"). In 1986, BIA ANCSA researchers documented a number of stone features atop these cliffs, two of which are visible in the lower part of the image (see arrows). A caribou antler was found inside the feature on the left. Photograph by Karl Reinhard, August 1986. ANCSA 14(h)(1) Collection, case file AA-9284, Bureau of Indian Affairs, Anchorage.

Noatak 1986c, 22) described the aftermath of the woman's death:

> I don't know about it because it happened so long ago. But her parents lived over there at *Kangi'irerrlagmiut*. When they heard that she [her body] hadn't been brought back up [to the top of the cliff], they went traveling through back there and went to bring her up. When they brought her up, they placed her on top of it [the cliff] and placed an antler on top of her grave.

The murder reportedly happened at a coastal cliff known by the generic name *Penat* ("cliffs"), at the base of which is a small beach named *Qaugyit* ("sands," "their sandy area") (Amos and Amos 2012; Drozda 1994, 84). As described in the BIA's Nunivak report (USBIA 1995, 5:113), the cliff—"nearly vertical" and about 30 metres in height—rises above a terrace adjacent to the beach, which consists of "a band of boulders below which is a broad expanse of sand." The site is located only 3.6 kilometres west of *Asweryagmiut* (see figure 3.4). Pratt identified the site as a spring and summer camp used by residents of *Asweryagmiut* for bird hunting and egg gathering by a technique known as "cliff-hanging" (Pratt 2009a, 140, 175). In 1986, BIA archaeologists found what was apparently a grave containing an antler, at the top of *Penat* very near the cliff edge (figure 3.11) (USBIA 1995, 2:294, 4:152).[19]

An intriguing bit of lore from St. Lawrence Island reveals a possible link to the Nunivak story of the woman who named places and her origins. Elder Bobby Kava (b. ca. 1910), of Gambell, had a relative named *Aghnangiighaq*—the older sister of Kava's great-grandfather. In the mid-nineteenth century, her family came to Southwest Cape, on St. Lawrence Island, from a village on the southern coast of the Chukotka Peninsula not far from Avan (figure 3.13). As Kava recalled, "We heard tell of a person by the name of *Aghnangiighaq* who lived on Nunivak Island a long, long time ago. We have that very same name in our clan" (Apassingok, Walunga, and Tennant, 1985, 7, quoting Kava).

Nunivakers do not recall the name of the person who named the sites, referring to her simply as *arnar* ("woman"). When Howard and Muriel Amos questioned Nunivak elder Ida Wesley (b. 1929) about the woman's name, however, she told them that she had heard it in the past but that it was not a Nunivak name. In Cup'ig, *Aghnangiighaq* is pronounced (and spelled) *Arnangiar*. According to Howard Amos, "Ida Wesley made a statement that *Arnangiar* departed from Nunivak Island to somewhere up north, she doesn't know where she relocated. She only heard of her in stories, therefore we are assuming that *Arnangiar* departed before she [Ida] became aware" (Howard Amos, pers. comm., 15 November 2016). Amos also said that Wesley did not know of or mention *Arnangiar*'s association with a particular site or area on Nunivak. As he pointed out, though, the information that *Arnangiar* moved from Nunivak to a place further north made them realize that she "may very well have been the same person [mentioned] by the St. Lawrence people" (Howard Amos, pers. comm., 15 November 2016).

Finally, a St. Lawrence Island elder from the village of Gambell, Willis Walunga (b. 1924), said in an interview that his parents, who came to St. Lawrence Island in 1922 from Siberia, had told him stories about a group of people who had arrived at *Pughilek* (Southwest Cape) many years earlier (figure 3.13).[20] Walunga did not know how long ago it was, but he thought it might have been the 1600s or 1700s (Drozda 1999). Eventually some of them returned to Siberia, while others stayed at St. Lawrence Island. A third group went south, but how far south or precisely to where his parents did not know. Listening to what Walunga said, elder Melvin Seppilu, of Savoonga, added that he also heard stories that Nunivakers were from St. Lawrence Island (Drozda 1999).[21]

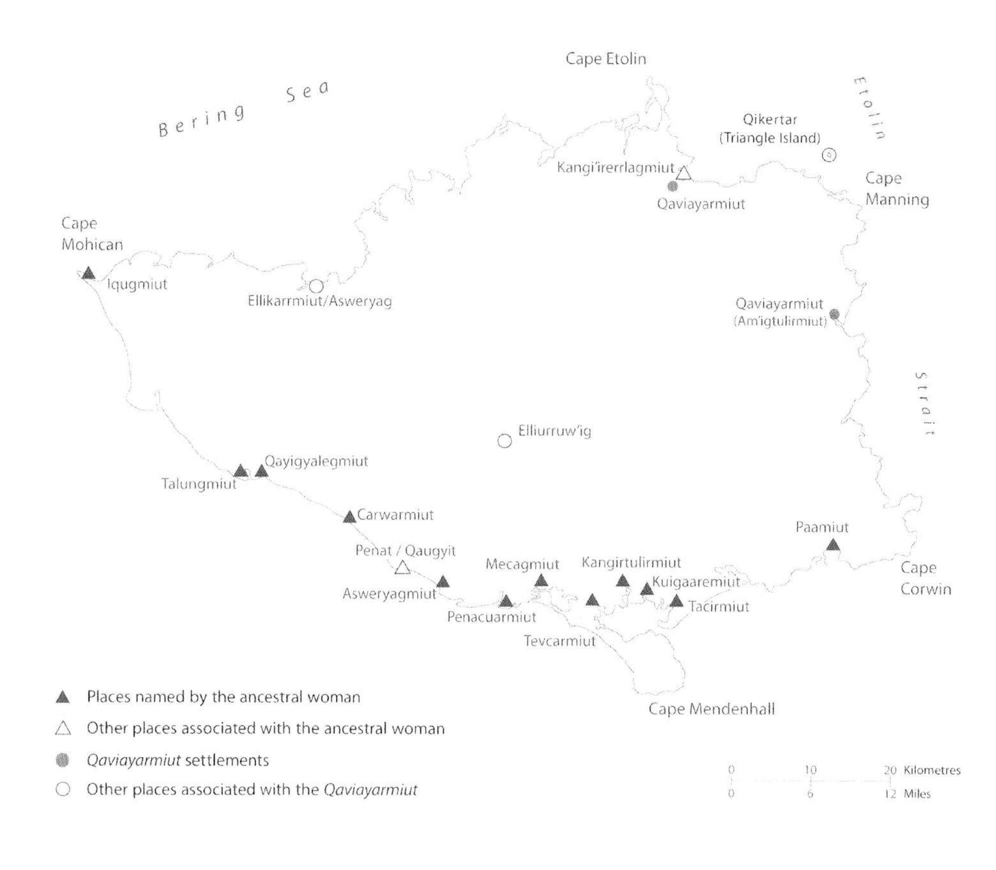

(TOP) FIGURE 3.12
Places associated with the ancestral woman and/or the Qaviayarmiut.

(BOTTOM) FIGURE 3.13
Possible Chukotkan, St. Lawrence Island, and Nunivak Island connections

Qaviayarmiut Migration to Nunivak Island

The 1821 journal of V. S. Khromchenko includes a curious statement according to which the residents of Golovnin Bay, on the southern coast of the Seward Peninsula, were related to three tribes descended from "three women and three stallions of various colors. They multiplied and are the Ukivokmut [*Ugiuvak,* King Islanders], Aziagmut [Sledge Islanders], and Nunivokmut [Nuniwarmiut, Nunivak Island people]" (Pierce 1994, 320–325).[22] King Island and Sledge Island are located in the Bering Sea, off the southwest coast of the Seward Peninsula.

Aside from the above legend, a nineteenth-century southward migration of Inupiaq peoples from the Bering Strait region is well documented in the literature. Loss of or severe decline in the Seward Peninsula caribou population is considered the main impetus for this migration, which began in the 1860s (Pratt 2001, 37; Pratt et al. 2013, 43–44; see Ganley 1995). Lantis (1946, 173) reported that hunters came to Nunivak from Norton Sound or southern Seward Peninsula communities to hunt the thriving Nunivak herds but that caribou "disappeared from the island" in the 1880s. Pratt (2001, 42) cites census records from 1900 that show that Inupiaq families occupied Nunivak "for relatively significant amounts of time in the second half of the 19th century" and that at least four individuals identified as "Kavaigmiut" Inupiat were reportedly born on the island between 1874 and 1881.

From the linguistic and geographic perspective, it seems logical to associate or even equate the Nunivak Qaviayarmiut with the Seward Peninsula "Kavaigmiut" (Qaviaraġmiut, in the Inupiaq orthography). The similarity of the names is unmistakable, and the ethnographic evidence that Pratt and Griffin cite seems persuasive. All the same, we cannot be certain that those referred to by Nuniwarmiut as Qaviayarmiut are the same as those identified by others as Qaviaraġmiut.

Both the *CED* (Amos and Amos 2003, 274) and *YED* (Jacobson 2012, 546) refer to a site on Nunivak called *Qaviayarmiut* and identify its former inhabitants in general terms as "native people from northern Alaska." The *YED* also includes the Yup'ik names "Qaviayarmiu[t]" and "Qaviayak" (attested in the Yukon and Bristol Bay dialects of CAY, respectively), peoples defined more specifically as "Inupiaq Eskimo."[23] Jacobson does not associate the two terms with a specific Inupiaq group or place, but an association is implied by his derivation of the Yup'ik terms from Inupiaq "Qawiažak" (written "Qawiaraq" in MacLean 2014, viii). In the opinion of Woodbury (pers. comm., 10 August 2017), it is "very possible that the SP [Seward Peninsula] Iñupiat who now call themselves 'Qaviarmiut' were Yupik speakers [of some sort] a century or more ago" (see also Ray 1984, 285).

Pratt (2001, 38) suggests that the use of the term among the Nuniwarmiut probably refers to people, primarily caribou hunters, from Seward Peninsula, but he also allows that St. Lawrence Islanders may have been included among them (USBIA 1995, 1:20–21). Griffin (2004, 74) states simply of the Qaviayarmiut that their "true origin is unknown."

Some Nuniwarmiut Perceptions of Qaviayarmiut

At least eight Nunivak elders interviewed from 1986 to 1991 spoke about the Qaviayarmiut at Nunivak Island. In addition to St. Lawrence Island (Williams 1986a, 1986b, 1991a, 1991b), other locations mentioned, if very speculatively, as the group's homeland included Kotzebue (Hendrickson and Williams 1991, 8) and the southern Seward Peninsula "near Nome" (Noatak 1990, 15). Contrary to Williams, Edna Kolerok said they were from the mainland, somewhere "above Nome," and specifically not from St. Lawrence Island (Kolerok and Kolerok 1991b, 7–8).

Elders agreed that the Qaviayarmiut arrived and left sometime before they themselves were born. Robert Kolerok said that perhaps it was when their "fathers were little boys" (Kolerok and Kolerok 1991c). Kay Hendrickson described the time as "way in the past," saying they came to hunt caribou and used the same areas and hunting shelters in the island's interior as the Nuniwarmiut (Hendrickson and Williams 1991, 7). Indeed, Nuniwarmiut blame the Qaviayarmiut for the disappearance of caribou on Nunivak Island (Griffin 2004, 80; Pratt 2001, 37–39; USBIA 1995, 1:21).

Peter Smith (1986b) did not use the name Qaviayarmiut, but he said that, before his father was born, caribou became scarce on the mainland and many people came from far away to hunt at Nunivak. Smith reported that people came from the adjacent mainland areas of the Kuskokwim River, Hooper Bay, Goodnews Bay, and Nelson Island, but also from further north—Unalakleet, St. Michael, the Yukon River—and included five families from the village of Teller, on west edge of the Seward Peninsula.[24] Pratt (2001, 37) notes that, at the time these events apparently took place, the village of Teller did not yet exist and that the reference is probably to the general area of Port Clarence.

It bears repeating that Williams alone identified the Qaviayarmiut as St. Lawrence Islanders. In particular, he recalled his conversation with a St. Lawrence Island elder in which they discussed the Qaviayarmiut:

> Old man-*am-ggur taum* Savoonga-*neg* Gambell-*am-llu kangirrluagneg egkuani kiani wiitania.*
>
> The old man said that their settlement was located in the estuary for Savoonga and Gambell bay. (Williams 1991b, 11)

As Pratt (2001, 38) points out, no settlement with a name equivalent to Qaviayarmiut has been identified on St. Lawrence Island. In the quotation above, Williams states that the settlement was "in" the estuary, presumably situated between the modern villages of Savoonga and Gambell. He uses the common Cup'ig geographic term *kangir*, meaning "estuary" or "bay." Not surprisingly, several place names on Nunivak Island contain this base, including *Kangi'irerrlagmiut*—reported by Nunivakers to be the location of a Qaviayarmiut settlement and also the place that Noatak identified as the village of the parents of the woman who named places. In addition, one of the places she named is *Kangirtulirmiut.*

Maps of St. Lawrence Island (Crowell and Oozevaseuk 2006, 6; Krupnik and Chlenov 2013,

22) show a settlement named *Kangii* (var. Kangi, Kangee) located between the villages of Savoonga and Gambell. In this connection, it is perhaps worth noting that St. Lawrence Island elder Willis Walunga gave *Kangii* or *Kangighmitt* as other names for the Gambell-based *Amigtuughet* clan, also known as the *Qelughileq* or *Qelughileghmiit* clan (see Krupnik and Krutak 2002, 222–224). The *Kangii* site is identified as both a permanent settlement and a "seasonal and herding camp" (Krupnik and Chlenov 2013, 112, 120*n*18), with a population of six according to the 1910 census. It is tempting to suggest that some of the Nunivak Qaviayarmiut originated from this St. Lawrence Island village.

Qaviayarmiut Settlements at *Kangi'irerrlagmiut* and *Am'igtulirmiut*

The Qaviayarmiut are associated with two sites on Nunivak Island, each bearing the name of the group. One is situated on the northeast coast in the vicinity of *Kangi'irerrlagmiut* and the other further south on the coast near the village of *Am'igtulirmiut* (see figure 3.13). Notably, of the nearly one hundred recorded settlement names on Nunivak with -miut endings, *Qaviayarmiut* is the only one that repeats. Elders referred to the Qaviayarmiut sites and their residents in different ways. Some spoke of the settlements without naming them but instead located them in relation to other places and by means of a complex system of demonstratives (see Charles 2011, 209–212; Jacobson 2012, 965–966). Others named the sites but did not use the ethnonym Qaviayarmiut when referring to the inhabitants, describing them in other ways (such as Robert Kolerok's "hunters from far away," in the quotation below). Yet, despite their different ways of speaking about and remembering the Qaviayarmiut, elders were characteristically able to locate the group's settlements with relative geographic precision. A few examples:

> There is an old village there further in the bay . . . further in from *Am'igtulirmiut* at the cove's point. It does not bear the name from this island. People from Nunivak did not establish the place. Those hunters from far away established the village. (Kolerok and Kolerok 1991d, 30)

> So he [my grandfather, *Qiawigar*] has talked about the people who arrived from out there, the Qaviayarmiut. There's a little old site above *Am'igtulirmiut* in a little cove. They say they stayed there in the winter and hunted. (Olrun 1991)

> Those Qaviayarmiut cannot stay in one place since they left their own area [up north]. This story is true, I saw the cabin on the other side of Mekoryuk [in the *Kangi'irerrlagmiut* area] and down in that *Am'igtulirmiut* area. I reckon those people were living down there, divided by two. (Williams 1986b, 1; see also Williams 1991b, 3)

Noatak (1990, 14–16) reported that the Qaviayarmiut spent two winters on Nunivak Island and were led by a *nukalpiar* (a great hunter) named *Qengaciar.* He confirmed Williams's statement that the newcomers divided into two groups and settled in the vicinities of *Am'igtulirmiut* and *Kangi'irerrlagmiut.* At *Am'igtulirmiut,* Noatak said, they settled upstream on a point of land called *Taklir* (the "cove's point" mentioned by Kolerok), where they built a house and "were recognized as Takliaremiut" by Nuniwarmiut. Williams (1986b, 5) also referred to a site upstream from *Am'igtulirmiut* on a point of land named *Taklir* where Qaviayarmiut lived a "long time ago." He said (speaking in English) that "old Qaviayaq people coming from St. Lawrence Island, they [were] living right there." In this instance Williams did not specifically name the place *Qaviayarmiut*, referring to it instead as part of a general area associated with *Am'igtulirmiut*.

Regarding those who settled at *Kangi'irerrlagmiut*, Noatak (1990, 16) said, "I don't know the exact location of their settlement." Here again other elders described the location relative to a fixed point, such as "upriver from *Taprarmiut* is the old village of *Qaviayarmiut*" (Shavings and Shavings 1986, 20). *Taprarmiut* is located directly across a small outlet stream from *Kangi'irerrlagmiut*. In some contexts, all three sites—*Taprarmiut*, *Qaviayarmiut*, and *Kangi'irerrlagmiut*—may be referred to collectively by the latter name.

Curiously, one elder—Peter Smith (b. 1912)—did not mention *Qaviayarmiut* (village or people) by name. It seems unlikely that he did not know the ethnonym.[25] He offered the following account (which I have edited slightly for clarity):

> Five families from Teller lived down there at *Am'igtulirmiut*. They got another village there in the inner bay at *Am'igtulirmiut*. The Teller people lived there for five years. A daughter of one of the families who lived there, when she was an old lady I met her in Kwethluk, a village [on the Kuskokwim River] above Bethel. She told me her family lived down in that place in five years. She's kind of an old lady, and I was pretty young when I saw her. Her parents hunt for caribou, five years, from Teller. She said there were five families. Our people never mentioned how many families were there, but this lady she told me five families live there, from Teller, for caribou hunting. And after five years they move from island back to some other place. (Smith 1986b; see also Smith 1991)

In another interview Smith (1988, 17) identified a mountain in the Nunivak interior as the location of "Teller caribou hunter's camp." The mountain was later identified by the name *Elliurruw'ig* (Drozda 1994, 82). Smith said the name meant "put it right there." The place name itself does not appear in the CED, but it evidently relates to the word *elliwig,* glossed "shelf" in the dictionary (Amos and Amos 2003, 108). The CED also includes the base *elli-*, "to put, to set down," which would seem to conform more closely to the meaning put forward by Smith.

Elliurruw'ig shares a common base with *llivelghaq,* in the St. Lawrence Island dialect of CSY (Badten et al. 2008, 231) and, in the Qawiaraq dialect of Inupiaq, with *illwik*, both of which are glossed "shelf." In CAY, *ellivik* is also "shelf," but, according to Jacobson (2012, 253), in NUN it refers specifically to an elevated cache. Some of the residents of the village of Teller are speakers of the Qawiaraq dialect (Fortescue, Jacobson, and Kaplan 2010, ix; MacLean 2014, viii). Given the field map notation "Teller caribou hunters camp," as well as Smith's definition, it seems likely, or at least possible, that the name *Elliurruw'ig* was introduced by Qawiaraq-speaking people from the vicinity of present-day Teller.

Conclusions

Oral accounts concerning *Asweryag*, *Asweryagmiut*, and the Qaviayarmiut probably relate to more than one historical episode of peoples from northern areas migrating to Nunivak Island, probably most often in search of abundant and reliably obtained subsistence resources. These new arrivals might have established settlements and certainly would have interacted with existing populations. No doubt some would remain longer than others, and presumably some would remain permanently. Many, if not most, would have spoken different languages or dialects. Perhaps this linguistic intermixing contributed to the development of specific local dialects of Cup'ig.

With respect to Yup'ik dialects, Jacobson (1998, xi) suggests that it would be "interesting to endeavor to reconstruct the general situation as it was at various times in the past." The challenges involved with investigating just two Nunivak place names leads me to the related conclusion that it would be interesting and worthwhile as well to begin a comprehensive comparative study focused strictly on Indigenous place names in the region of the Bering Sea. The BIA ANCSA records—including site reports, oral histories, and field maps—include thousands of place names. These documents are indispensable for further study, yet they remain virtually untapped in terms of the analysis of dialects, and the toponyms embedded in them have not been surveyed in a systematic or comprehensive way.

This chapter contains much that is speculative. Some of my statements are provisional, and the evidence I cite is open to other interpretations. To some degree, this uncertainty reflects the difficulty of working with material originally in Cup'ig that has been transcribed and translated by linguists and others who are not fluent speakers of the language. I have deliberately resisted the impulse to attempt to reconcile what appear to be conflicting statements in the oral histories, in large part because I am conscious of the need for more complete transcriptions and more careful interpretations of many of the recordings.

This chapter does not pretend to offer a comprehensive report on the two *Asweryag* place names or a new theory regarding the Qaviayarmiut. Rather, in the course of my research into these two Nunivak place names (and I feel I have just scratched the surface), I was drawn down many interesting paths. Some led to discoveries that surprised me, others proved to be more like reaching a cul-de-sac precisely where I had hoped there would be more, and some were left unexplored, at least for the present. The further along I travelled, the more connections I discovered to other places and peoples, connections that were not apparent on the surface or simply in the literal translations of names. Many of the links are speculative and/or only vaguely defined, pending further research. Nonetheless, they can serve to remind us of the interconnectedness of language, memory, and landscape and the dynamic relationships among them.

Acknowledgements

Thanks to the elders of the village of Mekoryuk, past and present, whom I have had the privilege to know. Thanks also to Steven Jacobson for deepening my understanding of the Nunivak language and to Howard and Muriel Amos for sharing their knowledge and so much more with me. Finally, I thank Tony Woodbury and Ken Pratt for constructive comments and criticisms on earlier drafts of this chapter.

Notes

1 Cup'ig names and words set in italic conform to an orthography developed for the language by Muriel Amos and Howard Amos, with the support of Irene Reed and Steven Jacobson of the Alaska Native Language Center (ANLC). The co-compilers of the *Cup'ig Eskimo Dictionary* (2003), the Amoses were raised with Cup'ig as their first language but also experienced the impacts of its rapid decline. Their consequent dedication to the preservation of the language and the reconstruction of older components of it has added immeasurably to the study of the language (see Jacobson 2003, vii–x). The Nunivak elders quoted in this chapter were in fact among the last generation of monolingual Cup'ig speakers.

2 Woodbury is the author of the definitive study of Cup'ik (Woodbury 1981), one of the two subdialects of the Hooper Bay–Chevak dialect of Central Alaskan Yup'ik (CAY), which is spoken in the mainland village of Chevak, situated on the west coast of Alaska some 150 kilometres north of Nunivak Island. Despite the similarity of name, Cup'ik is closer to CAY than it is to Cup'ig. Speakers of both Cup'ik and Cup'ig typically substitute an initial *c* (pronounced like the English "ch") for the initial *y* of CAY. In connection with the preparation of the *Cup'ig Eskimo Dictionary*, Woodbury (2001) commented that "reading through it convinced me of how highly distinct Cup'ig was from Cup'ik or Yup'ik."

3 Hammerich (1954, 420) relates a tale he heard of a failed attempt by Russians to establish a herd of wild horses on Nunivak, although this is something that I have never heard from Nunivakers. The Russian and Cup'ig words for horse are, respectively, *loshad* (Hammerich 1954, 410) and *luussitar* (Amos and Amos 2003, 186). There are no horses on Nunivak today.

4 Woodbury (1981, 3, 8) determined, for example, that what is now known as the Hooper Bay–Chevak dialect of Central Alaskan Yup'ik consists of two subdialects, spoken in two villages (Hooper Bay and Chevak) that are separated by only 27 kilometres. On Nunivak Island, Mekoryuk (*Mikuryarmiut*) and the second-longest surviving village, Nash Harbor (*Ellikarrmiut*), are separated by about 46 kilometres, and their residents, or former residents in the case of *Ellikarrmiut,* report two distinct subdialects of Cup'ig. Other pre-1960 villages were considerably farther apart or less accessible, especially given that travel between them would probably have been most often by kayak, along coastal routes.

5 Ken Pratt and I began working with the community of Mekoryuk in 1986 to document traditional and contemporary geography as part of the BIA ANCSA historical places and cemetery sites project. The work resulted in the mapping of about a thousand Cup'ig-language place names, many of them verified in the field with Nunivak elders, along with a draft manuscript, "Qikertamteni Nunat Atrit Nuniwarmiuni: The Names of Places on Our Island Nunivak," initially compiled in 1994, with major revisions in progress.

6 Both sites were investigated in 1986 by archaeologists associated with the BIA ANCSA 14(h)(1) historical places and cemetery sites project (USBIA 1995). As the crow flies, the sites are approximately 40 kilometres apart, but the distance is about 100 kilometres by the coastal route. The degree of geographic separation is significant because, given the similarities of the names, it would be logical to assume a closer geographical relationship, based on known patterns of naming seen in some Cup'ig and Yup'ik place names, especially those including habitation sites with *-miut* endings (see Pete 1984, 51).

7 Woodbury states that there are polysynthetic languages that have little or no suffixation. But he describes Cup'ig, Cup'ik, and Yup'ik, in which words are formed almost entirely through suffixation, as "exuberantly polysynthetic" (Woodbury 2017b, 536; see also Fienup-Riordan and Rearden 2016, 115; Reed et al. 1977, 8).

8 The postbase *-miu* means "inhabitant of," the plural form, *-miut* is found in all Eskimo languages and refers, variably, to the residents of a place or region or to members of a group (Jacobson 2012, 808; Fortescue, Jacobson and Kaplan 2010, 455). At Nunivak Island the people identify themselves as Nuniwarmiut (residents of, or people of *Nuniwar*). In the Central Alaskan Yup'ik language, as well as in Cup'ig, *-miut*, when used to form a place name, has come to mean "village." At Nunivak Island virtually all settlements include the suffix *-miut* and this is understood to refer not only to the inhabited (or formerly so) place, but also to its residents. In this way the addition of *-miut* tells us that it is not only a place, but also that it is, or was, a place where people congregated or settled. Fienup-Riordan (in Fienup-Riordan and Rearden 2011, xliii) implies that the inclusion of *-miut* in Central Alaskan Yup'ik place names is more or less at the discretion of the speaker, this is certainly not the case among the Nuniwarmiut. The inconsistency that Fienup-Riordan identifies with respect to CAY may be a more recent innovation, and in part reflect changes in the language stemming from the longer separation of mainland Yup'ik from their respective historical settlements. It may also reflect the adoption of abbreviated anglicized forms in use among "English speakers" (Ray 1971, 20), as well as the influence of geographers and cartographers who found the *-miut* ending repetitive and unnecessary (Baker 1902, 16–17; Ganley 1995, 106; O'Leary 2009, 209).

At Nunivak I have found that the naming of settlements and associated geographic features (most notably streams and estuary/bay systems) is formulaic and predictable, precisely as reported by Dorothy Jean Ray (1971, 1) for the Seward Peninsula region, where she referred to "constellations of place-names." Both Ray (1971, 29) and Mary Pete (1984, 51) contend that, once settlements were abandoned, the *-miut* ending would be dropped, leaving in most cases just the name of a geographic feature, although this is clearly not the case at Nunivak today. In this chapter, I use *-miut* to refer to both settlements and inhabitants of places, depending on the context.

9 Ivanoff's spelling of Cup'ig words (adopted, in turn, by Rasmussen) appears in some respects to reflect the Yup'ik that Ivanoff spoke more than the Cup'ig spoken on Nunivak—as, for instance, in the use of Yup'ik velar stops (final *k* or *q*) as compared to Hammerich's Cup'ig endings (voiced fricatives, such as *g* or *r*). Thus the spelling of the postbase as *+paq*, rather than as the Cup'ig *+pag*. Ivanoff, who was of mixed Russian-Inupiaq descent, came from the Norton Sound area, and his endings reflect the mainland influence, be it Inupiaq or Yup'ik. Further, he was just twenty years old when he interpreted for Rasmussen and had not spent much time at Nunivak Island. Ken Pratt (pers. comm., n.d.) points out that "outsiders essentially treated Ivanoff (an outsider himself) as the islanders' spokesperson in many instances." Those evaluating Rasmussen's Nunivak vocabulary should thus be skeptical of the spellings that Ivanoff provided and likewise of his translations (see also Himmelheber 1993, 3, 7; Jenness 1928, 3).

10 The spelling *asverpak* corresponds to the CAY pronunciation. Jacobson's notes (1979), however, include the spelling *asverpag* and also imply that this walrus had "dark tusks." I want to reiterate that no form of *asver-* occurs in the *Cup'ig Eskimo Dictionary.*

11 Jacobson's survey data (responses to questionnaires) appear limited with respect to "walrus." See Jacobson's discussion of the methodology and limitations of his study in his introduction to the *Yup'ik Dialect Atlas* (Jacobson 1998, viii–xxii).

12 BBNC Web Map, Bristol Bay Online! Native Place Names Project, accessed 28 June 2022, https://bbonline.bbnc.net/placenames/. Woodbury (pers. comm., 10 August 2017) raised another possibility related to the postbase "*-vig-*" meaning, "place to" or "place for" or "place where." When combined with the base *at'e-* ("to put on clothing; to don"), it becomes *ayvik* or *asvik* ("place to put on clothing").

13 Note that contemporary orthographies used for Central Siberian Yupik (CSY), for Central Alaskan Yup'ik, and for Cup'ig differ slightly. Also, here the *y/z* spelling discrepancy may be a typographical error with both spellings occurring in the same work, but also *y/z* commonly shift in both CSY and CAY.

14 Kiokun was, at the time of the interview, a bilingual teacher at the Nuniwarmiut School. She was also an advisor to Irene Reed of the ANLC on matters relating to the Cup'ig language. She had direct knowledge of the Western Nunivak dialect or perhaps an intermediary dialect spoken at Nash Harbor (see Pratt 2009a, 282). The Native language portions of the Koleroks' recording have not been fully translated or transcribed. The existing transcript is riddled with blank lines and question marks where the highly fluent and experienced Yup'ik translator lacked the knowledge to adequately translate the Cup'ig language. Although Kiokun did not interpret all of Kolerok's narrative at the time of interview, her English renderings are much more useful than the patchy ANLC draft translation.

15 The meaning of the name *Talungmiut* has yet to be firmly established; its base, *talung-*, appears to be unique to Cup'ig. Lantis (1946, 162) derived the name from *talu'q*, a word meaning "windbreak," While linguists relate the name to Proto-Eskimo **talu-*, "partition" or "screen" (Fortescue, Jacobson, and Kaplan 2010, 356; Jacobson 1984, 355, 592). The *Cup'ig Eskimo Dictionary* (Amos and Amos 2003, 307) includes the term *talung*, "a natural projection that blocks view of village from the sea," and the related *talurte-*, "to disappear over a hill." The immediate physical geography of the site itself includes a prominent boulder-strewn spit that separates the habitation area (*Talungmiut)* from the sea. Therefore, each of these interpretations, including Kiokun's reference to the river "going crooked," seems plausible, but the exact meaning is unknown.

16 Kiokun's statement reflects the fact that spotted seals are now called *suuri* in Cup'ig, probably a fairly recent change adopted from CAY *issuri*, itself said to be borrowed from Aleut. *Qayigyar* ("spotted seal") is otherwise a virtually pan-Eskimo term and may remain in the place name as a remnant of a proto-Eskimo language (see Fortescue, Jacobson, and Kaplan 2010, 301).

17 Noatak's statements about the woman who named places were not made in a storytelling context but rather as asides while recording place names. It is unfortunate that the stories were not elaborated on further, as now they are mere fragments of what must have been a rich oral narrative.

18 Lily Jones (*Elluwagar*) was interviewed by Susan Hansen on September 11, 1975 (Jones 1975). The interview tape has not been fully transcribed or translated, in part due to poor sound quality. Apparently, the bulk of the narrative is a Nunivak traditional tale referred to by Hansen (1979) as "The Deceitful Husband."

19 The BIA report (USBIA 1995, 2:293, 2:318, 5:113) does not identify the woman who was pushed from the cliff and also cites a separate account (Noatak 1986e, 23) of a man who fell at or near the same location and was subsequently revived by a shaman.

20 Krupnik and Krutak (2002) report, "The dialect of the Southwest Cape people is supposed to be quite pronounced and the people are very much for themselves, (and) are not in favor of bringing into their homes Eskimos who do not belong to their particular tribe." [See also Otto Geist Collection, box 4, folder 94, Alaska and Polar Regions Collections and Archives, Elmer E. Rasmuson Library, University of Alaska Fairbanks].

21 Woodbury (pers. comm., 10 August 2017) reports that he also used to hear this in Chevak.

22 Much thanks to Matt O'Leary for bringing Khromchenko's remark to my attention.

23 Here Qaviayarmiu (singular) and Qaviayak are not toponyms but rather ethnonyms. The Yukon and Nunivak dialects use the same term. The author is unaware of any mainland Yup'ik sites that have a similarly derived place name. Also, like speakers of CAY, Nunivakers use the term Qagkumiut to refer to "northerners" in general.

24 Similar accounts have been recorded on the mainland. For instance, Hooper Bay elder Dick Bunyan (1984) recalled that, before the "kass'aqs" (Caucasians) arrived in the area, many people "from all over" travelled to Nunivak to hunt caribou. Bunyan did not identify any specific places, however, other than his own village of Hooper Bay.

25 Elder Peter Smith was a principal contributor to the documentation of Nunivak Island historical places and Cup'ig place names (Drozda 1994). He was bilingual: the BIA ANCSA collection includes forty-four tape recordings of interviews with him, only two of which involved an interpreter. He preferred to be interviewed in English, but his narratives are not always easy to follow and require careful interpretation.

References

Amos, Muriel M., and Howard T. Amos (compilers)

2003 *Cup'ig Eskimo Dictionary.* Alaska Native Language Center, University of Alaska Fairbanks.

2012 Place name revisions Area 06. Nunivak Island Place Names Project. 29 October. Mekoryuk, Alaska. Unpublished typescript in possession of author.

2013 Place name revisions Area 09. Nunivak Island Place Names Project. 14 January. Mekoryuk, Alaska. Unpublished typescript in possession of author.

Amos, Walter

1991 Taped interview and transcript. Ken Pratt and Robert Drozda, interviewers. Abraham David, interpreter. Mekoryuk, Alaska. 6 August. Tape 91NUN021. Bureau of Indian Affairs, ANCSA Office, Anchorage.

Apassingok, Anders, Willis Walunga, and Edward Tennant (editors)

1985 *Sivuqam Nangaghnegha: Siivanllemta Ungipaqellghat / Lore of St. Lawrence Island: Echoes of Our Eskimo Elders*, vol. 1, *Gambell.* Bering Strait School District, Unalakleet, Alaska.

Badten, Linda Womkon, Vera Oovi Kaneshiro, Marie Oovi, and Christopher Koonooka (compilers)

2008 *St. Lawrence Island / Siberian Yupik Eskimo Dictionary.* Edited by Steven A. Jacobson. Alaska Native Language Center, University of Alaska Fairbanks.

Baker, Marcus

1902 *Geographic Dictionary of Alaska.* US Government Printing Office, Washington, DC.

Bogoslovskaya, Lyudmila S., Ivan V. Slugin, Igor A. Zagrebin, and Igor Krupnik

2016 *Maritime Hunting Culture of Chukotka: Traditions and Modern Practices.* Translated by Marina Bell. Edited by Igor Krupnik and Rachel Mason. National Park Service Shared Beringian Heritage Program, Anchorage. First published, in Russian, 2007.

Bunyan, Dick

1984 Taped interview and transcript. Robert Waterworth, interviewer. Lillian Pingayak, interpreter. Hooper Bay, Alaska. 8 August. Transcription/translation by Lillian Pingayak. Tape 84VAK085. Bureau of Indian Affairs, ANCSA Office, Anchorage.

Charles, Stephen "Walkie"

2011 Dynamic Assessment in a Yugtun Second Language Intermediate Adult Classroom. PhD dissertation, University of Alaska Fairbanks.

Collins, Henry B.

1937 Archeology of St. Lawrence Island, Alaska. *Smithsonian Miscellaneous Collections*, vol. 96, no. 1: 1–431. Smithsonian, Washington, DC.

Crowell, Aron, and Estelle Oozevaseuk

2006 The St. Lawrence Island Famine and Epidemic, 1878–80: A Yupik Narrative in Cultural and Historical Context. *Arctic Anthropology* 43(1): 1–19.

de Reuse, Willem J.

1994 *Siberian Yupik Eskimo: The Language and Its Contacts with Chukchi.* University of Utah Press, Salt Lake City.

Drozda, Robert M.

1994 *Qikertamteni Nunat Atrit Nuniwarmiuni* / The Names of Places on Our Island Nunivak. Draft manuscript on file at IRA Council of Mekoryuk and in Alaska Native Language Archive, Identifier no. CY987D1994, University of Alaska Fairbanks.

1999 Interview with Willis Walunga and Melvin Seppilu. Fairbanks. 15 April. Notes in possession of author.

2007 Introduction to *Uraquralzrig* / Sibling Brothers, Told by *Nuratar* Andrew Noatak. Transcribed and translated by Howard *Nakaar* Amos. In *Words of the Real People: Alaska Native Literature in Translation*, edited by Ann Fienup-Riordan and Lawrence D. Kaplan, pp. 102–105. University of Alaska Press, Fairbanks.

2010 *Nunivak Island Subsistence Cod, Red Salmon and Grayling Fisheries: Past and Present.* Final Report for Study 05-353. US Fish and Wildlife Service, Office of Subsistence Management, Fisheries Resource Monitoring Program, Anchorage.

Fienup-Riordan, Ann

2000 Yup'ik and Cup'ig Oral Traditions. In *Where the Echo Began and Other Oral Traditions from Southwest Alaska Recorded by Hans Himmelheber*, edited by Ann Fienup-Riordan, pp. 187–200. Translated by Kurt Vitt and Ester Vitt. University of Alaska Press, Fairbanks.

Fienup-Riordan, Ann (editor), and Alice Rearden (transcriber and translator)

2011 *Qaluyaarmiuni nunamtenek qanemciput / Our Nelson Island Stories: Meanings of Place on the Bering Sea Coast.* Calista Elders Council, Anchorage, and University of Washington Press, Seattle.

2016 *Anguyiim Nalliini / Time of Warring: The History of Bow-and Arrow Warfare in Southwest Alaska.* University of Alaska Press, Fairbanks.

Fortescue, Michael

2005 *Comparative Chukotko-Kamchatkan Dictionary.* Mouton de Gruyter, Berlin.

Fortescue, Michael, Steven Jacobson, and Lawrence Kaplan

2010 *Comparative Eskimo Dictionary, with Aleut Cognates*. 2nd ed. Research Paper No. 9. Alaska Native Language Center, University of Alaska Fairbanks.

Ganley, Matthew

1995 The Malimiut of Northwest Alaska: A Study in Ethnonymy. *Études/Inuit/Studies* 19(1): 103–118.

Griffin, Dennis

2001 Nunivak Island, Alaska: A History of Contact and Trade. *Alaska Journal of Anthropology* 1(1): 77–99.

2004 *Ellikarrmiut: Changing Lifeways in an Alaskan Community*. Aurora Monograph Series No. 7. Alaska Anthropological Association, Anchorage.

Hammerich, Louis L.

1952 The Dialect of Nunivak. In *Proceedings of the Thirtieth International Congress of Americanists, Held in Cambridge, 18–23 August 1952*, pp. 110–113. Royal Anthropological Institute, London.

1954 The Russian Stratum in Alaskan Eskimo. *Word* 10(4): 401–428.

1970 The Eskimo Language. Nansen Memorial Lecture, 10 October 1969. Norwegian Academy of Science and Letters, Oslo.

Hamp, Eric P.

1976 *Papers on Eskimo and Aleut Linguistics*. Chicago Linguistic Society, Chicago.

Hansen, Susan

1979 Letter to Solomon Williams. ANCSA Museum Collection, Susan Hansen Records, box 53: Village Notes, folder 24. Bureau of Indian Affairs, ANCSA Office, Anchorage.

n.d. *Nunivak Island and Cape Mendenhall*. USGS composite quadrangle map, 1:250,000 scale, with annotations. Compiled by Susan Hansen, ca. 1975–1976. ANCSA Museum Collection, Maps, folder 7. Bureau of Indian Affairs, ANCSA Office, Anchorage.

Hendrickson, Kay, and Mattie Hendrickson

1986 Taped interview and transcript. Dennis Griffin and Brian Hoffman, interviewers. Mattie Hendrickson, interpreter. Bethel, Alaska. 7 September. Transcription/translation by David Chanar, Vernon Chimegalrea, and Irene Reed. Tape 86NUN073. Bureau of Indian Affairs, ANCSA Office, Anchorage.

Hendrickson, Kay, and Jack U. Williams Sr.

1991 Taped interview and transcript. Robert Drozda and Ken Pratt, interviewers. Ike Kiokun, interpreter. Mekoryuk, Alaska. 22 July. Transcription/translation by Marie Meade and Irene Reed (incorporating field notes and translations provided by Dorothy Kiokun). Tape 91NUN001. Bureau of Indian Affairs, ANCSA Office, Anchorage.

Hensel, Chase, Marie Blanchett, Ida Alexie, and Phyllis Morrow

n.d. *Qaneryaurci Yup'igtun: An Introductory Course in Yup'ik Eskimo for Non-speakers*. Prepublication copy, ca. 1980. Yup'ik Language Center, Bethel, AK.

Himmelheber, Hans

1993 *Eskimo Artists (Fieldwork in Alaska, June 1936 until April 1937)*. University of Alaska Press, Fairbanks.

Hughes, Charles C.

1960 *An Eskimo Village in the Modern World*. Cornell University Press, Ithaca, NY.

1984 Saint Lawrence Island Eskimo. In *Handbook of North American Indians*, vol. 5: *Arctic*, edited by David Damas, pp. 262–277. Smithsonian Institution Press, Washington, DC.

Jacobson, Steven

1979a Nunivak lexical and grammatical notes. From work with Margie McDonald of Mekoryuk, Nunivak Island. Typescript. 96 pp. (unpaginated). Identifier no. CY972J1979a. Alaska Native Language Archive, Elmer E. Rasmuson Library, University of Alaska Fairbanks. https://www.uaf.edu/anla/record.php?identifier=CY972J1979a.

1979b Report on Nunivak dialect and orthography problems. From work with Margie McDonald of Mekoryuk, Nunivak Island. Typescript. 7 pp. Identifier no. CY972J1979b. Alaska Native Language Archive, Elmer E. Rasmuson Library, University of Alaska Fairbanks. https://www.uaf.edu/anla/record.php?identifier=CY972J1979b.

1984 *Yup'ik Eskimo Dictionary*. Alaska Native Language Center, University of Alaska Fairbanks.

1985 Siberian Yupik and Central Yupik Prosody. In *Yupik Eskimo Prosodic Systems: Descriptive and Comparative Studies*, edited by Michael E. Krauss, pp. 25–45. Research Paper No. 7. Alaska Native Language Center, University of Alaska Fairbanks.

1990a Comparison of Central Alaskan Yup'ik Eskimo and Central Siberian Yupik Eskimo. *International Journal of American Linguistics* 56(2): 264–286.

1990b Correspondence, reply to 30 January letter from Don Weeda, graduate student in linguistics at University of Texas at Austin. 9 March. Identifier no. CY986W1990. Alaska Native Language Archive, Rasmuson Library, University of Alaska Fairbanks. https://www.uaf.edu/anla/record.php?identifier=CY986W1990.

1998 *Yup'ik Dialect Atlas and Study*. Alaska Native Language Center, University of Alaska Fairbanks.

2003 Introduction. In *Cup'ig Eskimo Dictionary*, compiled by Muriel M. Amos and Howard T. Amos, pp. vii–xvi, Alaska Native Language Center, University of Alaska Fairbanks.

2006 The Participial Oblique, a Verb Mood Found Only in Nunivak Central Alaskan Yup'ik and in Siberian Yupik. *Études/Inuit/Studies* 30(1): 135–156.

2012 *Yup'ik Eskimo Dictionary*. 2nd. ed. Alaska Native Language Center, University of Alaska Fairbanks.

Jarvis, D. H.

1900 *Alaska: Coast Pilot Notes on the Fox Islands Passes, Unalaska Bay, Bering Sea, and Arctic Ocean as Far as Point Barrow*. US Coast and Geodetic Survey Bulletin No. 40. US Government Printing Office, Washington, DC.

Jenness, Diamond
1928 *Comparative Vocabulary of the Western Eskimo Dialects.* Part A of *Report of the Canadian Arctic Expedition, 1913–18,* vol. 15, *Eskimo Language and Technology.* F. A. Acland, Ottawa.

John, Paul
2003 *Qulirat Qanemcit-llu Kinguvarcimalriit / Stories for Future Generations: The Oratory of Yup'ik Eskimo Elder Paul John.* Translated by Sophie Shield. Edited by Ann Fienup-Riordan. Calista Elders Council, Bethel, in association with University of Washington Press, Seattle.

Jones, Lily
1975 Taped interview and transcript. Susan Hansen, interviewer. Solomon Williams, interpreter. Mekoryuk, Alaska. 12 September. Tape 75NUN004. Bureau of Indian Affairs, ANCSA Office, Anchorage.

Kelly, Anthony
1985 Taped interview and transcript. Harley Cochran, interviewer. Andrew Kelly, interpreter. Emmonak, Alaska. 12 June. Transcription/translation by Monica Shelden, August 2012. Tape 85ALA006. Bureau of Indian Affairs, ANCSA Office, Anchorage.

Kolerok, Edna, and Robert Kolerok
1991a Taped interview and draft transcript. Robert Drozda, interviewer. Dorothy Kiokun, interpreter. Mekoryuk, Alaska. 31 July. Partially transcribed and translated by Marie Meade. Tape 91NUN016. Bureau of Indian Affairs, ANCSA Office, Anchorage.
1991b Taped interview and draft transcript. Robert Drozda, interviewer. Dorothy Kiokun, interpreter. Mekoryuk, Alaska. 31 July. Partially transcribed and translated by Marie Meade. Tape 91NUN015. Bureau of Indian Affairs, ANCSA Office, Anchorage.
1991c Taped interview and draft transcript. Robert Drozda, interviewer. Dorothy Kiokun, interpreter. Mekoryuk, Alaska. 31 July. Partially transcribed and translated by Marie Meade. Tape 91NUN014. Bureau of Indian Affairs, ANCSA Office, Anchorage.
1991d Taped interview and transcript. Ken Pratt, interviewer. Abraham David, interpreter. Mekoryuk, Alaska. 5 August. Transcribed and translated by Howard Amos. 14 August 2008. Tape 91NUN035KP. Bureau of Indian Affairs, ANCSA Office, Anchorage.

Krauss Michael E.
1973 Eskimo-Aleut. In *Linguistics in North America*, edited by Thomas A. Sebeok, 2:796–902. Current Trends in Linguistics Vol. 10. Mouton, The Hague.
1980 *Alaska Native Languages: Past, Present, and Future.* Research Paper No. 4. Alaska Native Language Center, University of Alaska Fairbanks.
1982 *Native Peoples and Languages of Alaska.* Map. Alaska Native Language Center, University of Alaska Fairbanks.
1986 Central Yupik. Chapter 5 in Eskimo and Aleut Languages, reading materials for the survey course "Alaska Native Languages" (ANL215), University of Alaska Fairbanks. Unpublished manuscript in possession of author.
2005 Eskimo Languages in Asia, 1791 on, and the Wrangel Island–Point Hope Connection. *Études/Inuit/Studies* 29(1–2): 163–185.

Krupnik, Igor, and Michael Chlenov
2013 *Yupik Transitions: Change and Survival at Bering Strait, 1900–1960.* University of Alaska Press, Fairbanks.

Krupnik, Igor, and Lars Krutak
2002 *Alcuzilleput Igacjullghet / Our Words Put to Paper: Sourcebook in St. Lawrence Island Heritage and History.* Compiled by Igor Krupnik and Lars Krutak. Edited by Igor Krupnik, Willis Walunga (Kepelgu), and Vera Metcalf (Qaakaghlleq). Contributions to Circumpolar Anthropology Vol. 3. Arctic Studies Center, National Museum of Natural History, Smithsonian Institution, Washington, DC.

Lantis, Margaret
1946 The Social Culture of the Nunivak Eskimo. *Transactions of the American Philosophical Society*, n.s., 35(3): 153–323.
1960 *Eskimo Childhood and Interpersonal Relationships: Nunivak Biographies and Genealogies.* University of Washington Press, Seattle.
1984 Nunivak Eskimo. In *Handbook of North American Indians*, vol. 5, *Arctic*, edited by David Damas, pp. 209–223. Smithsonian Institution Press, Washington, DC.

MacLean, Edna Ahgeak (compiler)
2014 *Iñupiatun Uqaluit Taniktun Sivunniuġutiŋit / North Slope Iñupiaq to English Dictionary.* Alaska Native Language Center, University of Alaska Fairbanks.

Mather, Elsie P.
1985 *Cauyarnariuq.* Alaska Historical Commission Studies in History No. 184. Lower Kuskokwim School District, Bethel.

Merck, Carl H.
1980 *Siberia and Northwestern America, 1788–1792: The Journal of Carl Heinrich Merck, Naturalist with the Russian Scientific Expedition Led by Captains Joseph Billings and Gavriil Sarychev.* Translated by Fritz Jaensch. Edited and with an introduction by Richard A. Pierce. Limestone Press, Kingston, Ontario.

Miyaoka, Osahito
1985 Accentuation in Central Alaskan Yupik. In *Yupik Eskimo Prosodic Systems: Descriptive and Comparative Studies*, edited by Michael E. Krauss, pp. 51–76. Research Paper No. 7. Alaska Native Language Center, University of Alaska Fairbanks.

Moore, Riley D.
1923 Social Life of the Eskimo of St. Lawrence Island. *American Anthropologist* 25(3): 339–375.

Noatak, Andrew
1986a Taped interview and transcript. Ken Pratt, interviewer; Howard Amos, interpreter. Mekoryuk, Alaska. 25 June. Transcription/translation by Dora David, Irene Reed, and Sophie Shield, with in-text modifications by Margie David. Tape 86NUN004. Bureau of Indian Affairs, ANCSA Office, Anchorage.

1986b Taped interview and transcript. Ken Pratt, interviewer; Howard Amos, interpreter. Mekoryuk, Alaska. 4 September. Transcription/translation by Sophie Shield, Margie David, Marie Meade, and Irene Reed. Tape 86NUN067. Bureau of Indian Affairs, ANCSA Office, Anchorage.

1986c Taped interview and transcript. Bill Sheppard and Brian Hoffman, interviewers; Howard Amos, interpreter. Mekoryuk, Alaska. 18 July. Transcription/translation by Dora David, Sophie Shield, Margie David, and Irene Reed. Tape 86NUN021. Bureau of Indian Affairs, ANCSA Office, Anchorage.

1986d Taped interview and transcript. Ken Pratt and Miriam Stark, interviewers; Howard Amos, interpreter. Mekoryuk, Alaska. 25 August. Transcription/translation by Dora David, Sophie Shield, and Irene Reed. Tape 86NUN061. Bureau of Indian Affairs, ANCSA Office, Anchorage.

1986e Taped interview and transcript. Ken Pratt, interviewer; Howard Amos, interpreter. Mekoryuk, Alaska. 12 July. Transcription/translation by Sophie Shield and Irene Reed. Tape 86NUN015. Bureau of Indian Affairs, ANCSA Office, Anchorage.

1990 Taped interview and transcript. Ken Pratt, interviewer; Howard Amos, interpreter. Mekoryuk, Alaska. 3 April. Transcription/translation by Howard Amos and Muriel Amos. Tape 90NUN002KP. Bureau of Indian Affairs, ANCSA Office, Anchorage.

Noatak, Andrew, and Robert Kolerok

1987 Taped interview and transcript. Robert Drozda, interviewer; Howard Amos, interpreter. Mekoryuk, Alaska. 5 November. Transcription/translation by Irene Reed, Sophie Shield, and Margie David, incorporating English notes by Robert Drozda. Tape 87NUN005. Bureau of Indian Affairs, ANCSA Office, Anchorage.

Nuniwarmiut Piciryarata Tamaryalkuti

2001 Cup'ig Language Materials and Curriculum Development. Grant proposal prepared by Robert Drozda and Howard Amos for submission to Administration for Native Americans, US Department of Health and Human Services. Award No. 90NL0216/01. 16 March. Copy in possession of author.

O'Leary, Matthew B.

2009 Edward W. Nelson's Winter Sledge Journey, 1878–1879. In *Chasing the Dark: Perspectives on Place, History and Alaska Native Land Claims*, edited by Kenneth L. Pratt, pp. 204–221. Bureau of Indian Affairs, ANCSA Office, Anchorage.

Olrun, Olie

1991 Taped interview and transcript. Ken Pratt, interviewer; Hultman Kiokun, interpreter. Mekoryuk, Alaska. 27 July. Transcription/translation by Marie Meade and Irene Reed. Tape 91NUN010. Bureau of Indian Affairs, ANCSA Office, Anchorage.

Orth, Donald J.

1967 *Dictionary of Alaska Place Names*. Geological Survey Professional Paper No. 567. US Government Printing Office, Washington, DC.

Pete, Mary C.

1984 Yup'ik Place-Names: Tapraq, a Case Study. Department of Anthropology, University of Alaska Fairbanks. Manuscript in possession of author.

Pierce, Richard (editor)

1994 *Notes on Russian America Parts II–V: Kad'iak, Unalashka, Atkha, The Pribylovs, by Kiril Timofeevich Khlebnikov*. Compiled and with an introduction and commentaries by R. G. Liapunova and S. G. Fedorova. Translated by Marina Ramsay. Limestone Press, Kingston, Ontario.

Polty, Noel, Ben Fitka, Dan Greene, and Wassilie Evan

1982 Taped interview and transcript. Ken Pratt, interviewer; Ben Fitka, interpreter. Pilot Station, Alaska. 9 July. Transcription/translation by Monica Shelden. Tape 82RSM062. Bureau of Indian Affairs, ANCSA Office, Anchorage.

Pratt, Kenneth L.

1997 Historical Fact or Historical Fiction? Ivan Petroff's 1891 Census of Nunivak Island, Southwestern Alaska. *Arctic Anthropology* 34(2): 12–27.

2001 The Ethnohistory of Caribou Hunting and Interior Land Use on Nunivak Island. *Alaska Journal of Anthropology* 1(1): 28–55.

2009a Nuniwarmiut Land Use, Settlement History and Socio-Territorial Organization, 1880–1960. PhD dissertation, Department of Anthropology, University of Alaska Fairbanks.

2009b A History of the ANCSA 14(h)(1) Program and Significant Reckoning Points, 1975–2008. In *Chasing the Dark: Perspectives on Place, History and Alaska Native Land Claims*, edited by Kenneth L. Pratt, pp. 2–43. Bureau of Indian Affairs, ANCSA Office, Anchorage.

2012 Introduction to "Tribal Divisions of the Eskimo of Western Alaska" by Frank H. Waskey (1950). *Alaska Journal of Anthropology* 10(1–2): 37–41.

2013 Deconstructing the Aglurmiut Migration: An Analysis of Accounts from the Russian-America Period to the Present. *Alaska Journal of Anthropology* 11(1–2): 17–36.

Pratt, Kenneth L., Joan C. Stevenson, and Phillip M. Everson

2013 Demographic Adversities and Indigenous Resilience in Western Alaska. *Études/Inuit/Studies* 37(1): 35–56.

Ray, Dorothy Jean

1971 Eskimo Place Names in Bering Strait and Vicinity. *Names* 19(1): 1–33.

1984 Bering Strait Eskimo. In *Handbook of North American Indians*, vol. 5, *Arctic*, edited by David Damas, pp. 285–302. Smithsonian Institution Press, Washington, DC.

Reed, Irene

1984 Name lists for BIA ANCSA tapes 84TOG002, 84TOG003, 84TOG006, 84TOG010, 84TOG012, 84TOG014, 84TOG015 and 84TOG016. Bureau of Indian Affairs, ANCSA Office, Anchorage.

1989 Name lists for BIA ANCSA tape 89BBN006. Bureau of Indian Affairs, ANCSA Office, Anchorage.

Reed, Irene, Osahito Miyaoka, Steven Jacobson, Paschal Afcan, and Michael Krauss

1977 *Yup'ik Eskimo Grammar*. Alaska Native Language Center and the Yup'ik Language Workshop, University of Alaska Fairbanks.

Schreyer, Christine

2005 The Persistence of Place Names and Language Revitalization. In *Resilience in Arctic Societies: Papers from the Third IPSSAS Seminar, Fairbanks, Alaska, 23 May–3 June 2005*, edited by Lawrence Kaplan and Michelle Daveluy, pp. 43–50. International PhD School for Studies of Arctic Societies, Fairbanks.

Shavings, Harry, and Susie Shavings
1986 Taped interview and transcript. Dennis Griffin and Bill Sheppard, interviewers; Gertrude Russie and Lillian Lindgren, interpreters. Anchorage, Alaska. 21 May. Transcription/translation by Sophie Manutoli Shield and Irene Reed. Tape 86NUN001. Bureau of Indian Affairs, ANCSA Office, Anchorage.

Smith, Peter
1986a Taped interview. Bill Sheppard and Karl Reinhard, interviewers. Mekoryuk, Alaska. 4 July. Partial transcription by Karl Reinhard. Tape 86NUN011. Bureau of Indian Affairs, ANCSA Office, Anchorage.
1986b Taped interview and transcript. Ken Pratt and Robert Drozda, interviewers. Mekoryuk, Alaska. 29 July. Transcription by Robert Drozda. Tape 86NUN037. Bureau of Indian Affairs, ANCSA Office, Anchorage.
1988 Taped interview and transcript. Robert Drozda, interviewer. Anchorage, Alaska. 31 December. Transcription by Robert Drozda. Tape 88NUN010. Bureau of Indian Affairs, ANCSA Office, Anchorage.
1991 Untaped interview notes. Ken Pratt, interviewer. Mekoryuk, Alaska. 9 September. Accession no. 91NUN-IN02. Bureau of Indian Affairs, ANCSA Office, Anchorage.

Sonne, Birgitte
1985 Nunivak word lists. Nunivak words taken down by Knud Rasmussen in Nome, 1924. Paul Ivanoff, interpreter. Identifier no. CY921RHH1921. Alaska Native Language Archive, University of Alaska Fairbanks. https://www.uaf.edu/anla/record.php?identifier=CY921RHH1921 [scan 03].
1988 *Agayut: Nunivak Eskimo Masks and Drawings from the 5th Thule Expedition, 1921–24, Collected by Knud Rasmussen. Report of the Fifth Thule Expedition*, Vol. 10, Part 4. Glydendal, Copenhagen.

Tsikoyak, Andrew
1988 Taped interview and transcript. Matt O'Leary, interviewer; Marie Meade, interpreter. Nunapitchuk, Alaska. 14 September. Transcribed and translated by Alice Fredson and Monica Shelden, September 2008. Tape 88CAL206. Bureau of Indian Affairs, ANCSA Office, Anchorage.

United States, Bureau of Indian Affairs (USBIA)
1995 *Nunivak Overview: Report of Investigation for BLM AA-9238 et al. (Calista Corporation)*. 6 vols. Compiled and edited by Kenneth L. Pratt. Bureau of Indian Affairs, ANCSA Office, Anchorage.

VanStone, James W.
1984a Southwest Alaska Eskimo: Introduction. In *Handbook of North American Indians*, vol. 5, *Arctic*, edited by David Damas, pp. 205–208. Smithsonian Institution Press, Washington, DC.
1984b Mainland Southwest Alaska Eskimo. In *Handbook of North American Indians*, vol. 5, *Arctic*, edited by David Damas, pp. 224–242. Smithsonian Institution Press, Washington, DC.
1989 *Nunivak Island Eskimo (Yuit) Technology and Material Culture.* Fieldiana Anthropology, new ser., No. 12. Field Museum of Natural History, Chicago.

VanStone, James W. (editor)
1973 *V. S. Khromchenko's Coastal Explorations in Southwest Alaska, 1822.* Edited and with an introduction by James W. VanStone. Translated by David H. Krauss. Fieldiana Anthropology Vol. 64. Field Museum of Natural History, Chicago.

Walunga, Willis (compiler)
1987 *St. Lawrence Island Curriculum Resource Manual*. Title VII Bilingual/Bicultural Program, St. Lawrence Island Bilingual Education Center, Gambell, Alaska.

Waskey, Frank H.
[1950] 2012 Tribal Divisions of the Eskimo of Western Alaska. Edited and annotated by Kenneth L. Pratt. *Alaska Journal of Anthropology* 10(1–2): 42–52.

Williams, Jack U., Sr.
1986a Taped interview, transcript, and place-name list. Robert Drozda, interviewer. Mekoryuk, Alaska. 4 August. Tape 86NUN-PN2. Transcription and translation by Sophie Manutoli Shield and Irene Reed. Bureau of Indian Affairs, ANCSA Office, Anchorage.
1986b Taped interview and transcript. Robert Drozda, interviewer. Mekoryuk, Alaska. 12 August. Transcribed by Robert Drozda. Tape 86NUN058. Bureau of Indian Affairs, ANCSA Office, Anchorage.
1991a Taped interview and transcript. Robert Drozda, interviewer; Hultman (Ike) Kiokun, interpreter. Mekoryuk, Alaska. 24 July. Transcribed and translated by Howard Amos, March 2009. Tape 91NUN005. Bureau of Indian Affairs, ANCSA Office, Anchorage.
1991b Taped interview and transcript. Robert Drozda, interviewer; Hultman (Ike) Kiokun and Dorothy Kiokun, interpreters. Mekoryuk, Alaska. 24 July. Transcribed and translated by Howard Amos, February 2009. Tape 91NUN004. Bureau of Indian Affairs, ANCSA Office, Anchorage.

Woodbury, Anthony C.
1981 Study of the Chevak Dialect of Central Yup'ik Eskimo. PhD dissertation, Department of Linguistics, University of California, Berkeley.
1999 Utterance-Final Phonology and the Prosodic Hierarchy: A Case from Cup'ig (Nunivak Central Alaskan Yup'ik). In *Proceedings of the Fourth Linguistics and Phonetics Conference*; edited by Osama Fujimura, Brian D. Joseph, and Bohumil Palek, pp. 47–63. Karolinum Press, Prague.
2001 Email exchange with author and letter supporting Cup'ig Language Materials and Curriculum Development grant proposal submitted by Nuniwarmiut Piciryarata Tamaryalkuti to Administration for Native Americans, US Department of Health and Human Services. Copies in possession of author.
2017b Central Alaskan Yupik (Eskimo-Aleut): A Sketch of Morphologically Orthodox Polysynthesis. In *The Oxford Handbook of Polysynthesis*, edited by Michael Fortescue, Marianne Mithun, and Nicholas Evans, pp. 536–59. Oxford University Press, Oxford, UK.

Wright, John M., and Molly B. Chythlook
1985 *Subsistence Harvests of Herring Spawn-on-Kelp in the Togiak District of Bristol Bay*. Technical Paper No. 116. Alaska Department of Fish and Game, Division of Subsistence, Juneau.

FIGURE 4.1 The hillsides of the Ungava Peninsula, in northern Nunavik, come alive with berries in the summertime. Pictured here, not far from the village of Kangiqsualujjuaq, are *kimminaqutik*, or mountain cranberries, which the Inuit use to cure sore throats, ulcers of the mouth, snow blindness, and thrush among children. Photograph by Scott A. Heyes, 2010.

MARTHA DOWSLEY, SCOTT A. HEYES, ANNA BUNCE, AND WILLIAMS STOLZ

4 Berry Harvesting in the Eastern Arctic

An Enduring Expression of Inuit Women's Identity

For many decades, berry harvesting was eclipsed by hunting in studies of Inuit subsistence activities. Hunting was (and still is) perceived as a quintessentially male pursuit (see, for example, Condon, Collings, and Wenzel 1995; Lee and Devore 1969), one in which women's role was confined to the domestic sphere. In the context of Arctic subsistence economies, moreover, hunting was essential to survival and, with the arrival of the fur trade, also provided a source of income. In contrast, berry picking was principally a female activity and, as such, may have been relatively invisible to, and possibly also of less interest to, early ethnographers, who were for the most part male. Berry picking was accordingly relegated to the status of a secondary activity and was even assumed to be an idle pursuit—a pleasant way to spend a summer afternoon. Such attitudes were not swift to disappear, even by the late twentieth century. Witness the opinion of a Sierra Club member who, writing in 1985 in defence of Alaska's public lands, dismissed berry picking as a "trivial activity" (quoted in Pratt 1994, 355–356).

This history notwithstanding, berry harvesting remains a central and highly respected cultural practice among the Inuit, one that has survived a century of economic and social change. As a characteristically female activity, berry harvesting reveals much about the connections that Inuit women have with the land—about how they conceive of their natural and social environments and their place in them. Its study not only offers insight into the persistence of Indigenous subsistence practices in tandem with the encroachment of capitalism but also contributes to a more nuanced understanding of how land-based activities are integrated into the complex economic, geographic, and social situations of modern times. In addition, the ensuing discussion of berry picking suggests the potential value of further research into other women's activities, such as seaweed harvesting and clam collecting, not as idle pursuits but as Inuit cultural practices in their own right.

Land, Identity, and Plants

The land is an inextricable part of Indigenous peoples' identity and well-being. More than merely a physical space, the land holds a spiritual meaning integral to the very nature of Indigenous cultures, a truth recognized in the United Nations Declaration on the Rights of Indigenous Peoples (see United Nations 2007, esp. article 25). Speaking to the Northern context, Nuttall (2001) has observed that land is fundamental to the expression of identity and feelings of belonging for Greenlandic Inuit. We might apply this insight to how Arctic peoples more broadly connect to the land:

> The expression of locality appeals to the sense of a bounded nature of a specific territory or area in which people live and to which they belong . . . [and] implies a sense of belonging or coming from those places, of being born in a particular place and having kinship relations there—in short, having roots. (Nuttall 2001, 54)

This observation suggests that a sense of continuity and tradition holds localities together through stories, place names, and individual experiences, and that memories cannot be separated from the places in which they are formed. Discussing significant sites, returning to them time after time, and harvesting the land's bounty are important activities and interactions necessary for Inuit to remain close and connected to the land and to their history. This land-based connection is fundamental to the continuation and preservation of identities (Jacobs 1986).

Inuit maintain a land-based identity that is a product of their travels, food-procurement activities, and social interactions (Dowsley 2015; Gombay 2005). They historically named local bands and places after landscape features (Boas 1888; Briggs 1970), and they keep memories alive and transmit their knowledge of the land to younger generations by frequently visiting old occupation and resource-use sites (Dowsley 2015; Nuttall 2001).

Their interactions with the land often take into account the non-human occupation of the land too. Many places are understood by Inuit to be associated with the behaviour and actions of spirits and legendary beings (Burch 1971; Hill 2012; Pratt 1993). This non-empirical element of the landscape, with roots in the pre-Christian, shamanistic past, persists as a belief among many Inuit even though Christian missionaries encouraged them to abandon such world views. Likewise, long-held beliefs about reciprocity, sharing, and obligation have also persisted into modern times in the face of increasingly capitalistic economic relations (Dowsley 2010, 2015). The Inuit world view holds that animals are sentient beings who offer their bodies to people in return for respectful treatment (see Stairs and Wenzel 1992). Productive hunts will only follow on the basis that hunters share their quarry with other

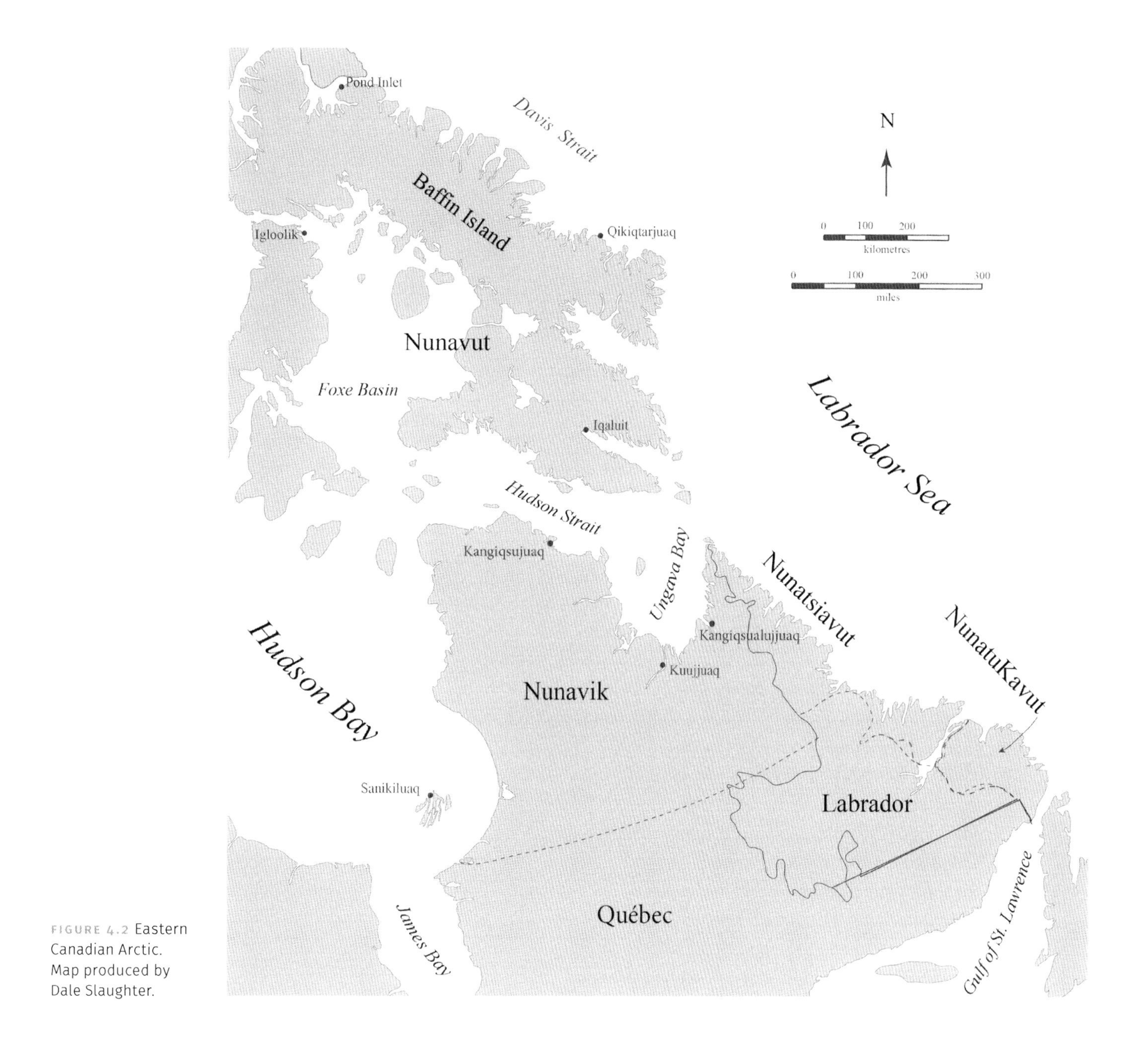

FIGURE 4.2 Eastern Canadian Arctic. Map produced by Dale Slaughter.

Inuit, and that they treat the land and its animals with respect. Inuit have long maintained that a departure from this mutual understanding and obligation will likely result in a poor hunt and a lack of game.

Given the meat-based diet of the Inuit, their lack of agriculture, and the arctic biomes they inhabit, early ethnographers tended to infer that their interactions with the botanical realm were insignificant. Accounts and reports of early explorers and naturalists generally lack descriptions of Inuit knowledge and conceptions of the plant world. Of course, Inuit have maintained a deep understanding of plants for generations, with a rich knowledge passed on through oral means concerning their medical qualities, nutritional value, properties, flavour, seasonal characteristics, and their use by birds and animals (Hantzsch 1928).

The Historical Context of Berries Within the Plant, Spirit, and Pragmatic Worlds

Inuit maintain a system for knowing and naming plants, a taxonomy that is only now being understood and appreciated by non-Inuit ethnobotanists (see Pigford and Zutter 2014; Whitecloud and Grenoble 2014). A detailed classification system is presented in a study of the botanical knowledge held by Inuit elders in Kangiqsujuaq, a village located in Nunavik, on the northeastern tip of the Ungava Peninsula (see Cuerrier et al. 2011, 72) (figure 4.2). The study reports that plants (*pirurtuq*) are conceptually connected to *nuna*—the Inuit word for "land," although *nuna* can also mean "everything that grows in the earth, vegetation," as well as "country that is inhabited" (Cuerrier et al. 2011, 72; Schneider 1985, 223). While berries (*paurngaq*) are not explicitly assigned to a particular category of plant in the study (presumably they would be classified under *pirursiaq*, "small plants with flowers"), a significant part of the study nonetheless contains descriptions, names, and information about activities associated specifically with berries, including berry picking (Cuerrier et al. 2011, 72; Schneider 1985, 259).

To some degree, land-use studies across the Canadian Arctic have identified, but not necessarily placed emphasis on, the cultural significance of berries through the mapping and identification of berry-picking locations, berry camps, and associated travel routes. One example is the *Inuit Land Use and Occupancy Project* (Freeman 1976). This study used ethnographic techniques to depict and describe the extent and type of land, ice, and sea use engaged in by Canadian Inuit. The resulting maps were based on details provided through interviews with Inuit men; the perspectives of Inuit women and their interactions with the land were not captured in this project. Hugh Brody was the only regional director of research, out of seven in the study, that mentioned berries. He recognized that a more complete understanding of berry picking would probably have been gained if Inuit women had been canvassed for the study.

> There are reasons for supposing that the range is understated. As well as restriction to the best or core areas, there is a tendency for men to disavow berry picking as a subject of importance. Even the core areas marked are likely to be fewer in number or less detailed than that that women could have marked. (Brody 1976, 171)

Regrettably, the maps to which Brody refers did not make their way into the study's published findings. The omission of information on berry- and other plant-harvesting activities makes it impossible to study longitudinal shifts in the importance of berries to the Inuit of those regions, especially in the face of the increasing availability of store-bought foods, alterations to the physical landscape, and changes in Inuit cultural practices of land use. In the absence of information on plants, the report unfortunately conveys the sense that the harvesting of caribou, fish, geese, and whales is of greater significance than the gathering of plants to the Inuit cultural landscape in general.

The lack of mention of berries in most historical documentation on the Canadian Inuit is a remarkable oversight given that both Inuit and non-Inuit people have always harvested berries, especially since some accounts in the historical record suggest berries were more than just sources of food. Evidence suggests that berries were associated with spiritual understandings of landscape. This is apparent in Rasmussen's account, in *Intellectual Culture of the Hudson Bay Eskimos* (1929), of a shamanistic séance in which a woman is healed for breaking a whole range of taboos, among them "eating of the earth" (berries and sorrel) when she is in an unclean state:

> *Shaman*: Even for so hardened a conscience there is release. But she is not yet freed. Before her I see green flowers of sorrel and the fruits of sorrel.
>
> *Listeners*: Before the spring was come, and the snow melted and the earth grew living, she once, wearing unclean garments, shovelled the snow away and ate of the earth, ate sorrel and berries, but let her be released from that, let her get well, tauva! (Rasmussen 1929, 139)

Similarly, the naturalist Edward Nelson recorded a Yup'ik story from Alaska in the late 1800s that possibly connected berries to shamanistic practice. This appears in an account relating to Yup'ik beliefs on moon travel:

> On the lower Yukon [River] and southward they say that there are other ways of getting to the moon, one of which is for a man to put a slip noose around his neck and have the people drag him about the interior of the kashim [men's house] until he is dead. At one time two noted shamans on the Yukon did this, telling the people to watch for them as they would come back during the next berry season. When the season designated had passed, the people of the village said that one of the shamans came back, coming a little out of the ground, looking like a doll, but he was very small and weak and there was no one outside the houses at the time to feed and care for him, except some children, so that he was overlooked and went away again. (Nelson 1899, 430–431)

The majority of descriptions relating to berries in the written record, however, pertain to abundance and crops. The accounts relating to the names Inuit ascribed to berries, and remarks on the distribution of berries, provide a sense of how important berries have always been to Inuit as a food source. The Hudson's Bay Company trading post records and missionary reports contain some mention of the quality and quantity of berry harvests. Sutton (1912, 285), a missionary doctor in Labrador, noted that the berry crop of that region failed in 1904 because "a plague of mice had eaten the young shoots in springtime." Reporting on Labrador Inuit lifeways in the early 1900s, Hawkes (1916, 34) observed: "The abundance of various kinds of berries compensates for the absence of large fruit. Nearly twenty varieties of edible berries are distinguished and named by the natives." On naming and knowing berries, Hawkes (1916, 35) also reported that Inuit "distinguish several varieties of blueberries and blackberries as to colour and shape," adding that "these distinctions may be due only to seasonal changes, but go to show what sharp observers of natural phenomena the Eskimo are." Writing on the Inuit living in what was then the District of Ungava (northern Québec), Hantzsch (1928, 172), an ornithologist who visited Labrador in 1906, observed: "If September is warm in the vicinity of Killinek [Killiniq], large quantities of berries ripen. I found such especially in *Arctostaphylos alpina* [mountain bearberry]." He went on to note that "it only pays to gather them in exceptional years" and that "much of this is done by the Eskimos in districts of Labrador situated farther south."

Hantzsch (1928, 226) further noted Inuit use of this berry as a prophylactic for rash—hence the Inuktitut name for the berry, *kallaqutik*, from *kalaq*, a scabrous sore (Schneider 1985, 118). The closely

FIGURE 4.3 "Eskimo Berry Pickers, Nome, Alaska." Alaska State Archives, Lomen Bros. Photo Collection, 1903–1920 (ASL-P28-032).

related Iñupiaq of Alaska also used several berries for medicine (Burch 2006, 188–189). Common juniper (*Juniperus communis* or *tulukkam asriaq*) berries, along with the leaves and stems, were brewed as medicinal tea. "Blackberry (*Empetrum nigrum*, or *paunġaq*) juice was squeezed into the eye to relieve the symptoms of cataracts and snow blindness" (Burch 2006, 278). Burch also noted that lowbush cranberries (*Vaccinium vitis-ideae*) "were used, along with seal or fish oil, to cure loss of appetite; they were mashed into a paste and placed around the neck to cure a sore throat; and they were similarly wrapped around a person's abdomen to cure a potentially fatal affliction known as *siksisaq*" (Burch 2006, 189).

Burch (2006, 188) also provides a description of berry-harvesting methods among the Iñupiat:

> Salmonberries [*Rubus chamaemorus*] and blackberries [*Empetrum nigrum*] were carefully picked by hand, but the others were picked quickly and in a seemingly chaotic manner. Women placed small baskets or buckets beneath the shrubs. The shrubs were then stroked with a special instrument resembling a short-handled pitchfork . . . or whacked with a spoon or a dipperlike implement known as a *qalutaq*. This knocked the berries off the stems and into the container without damaging them. A considerable quantity of leaves and twigs inevitably fell into the container as well. The berries were periodically separated from the leaves and twigs by pouring them slowly from the small container, held two or three feet (60–100 cm) high, into a larger container resting on the ground. If there was even a light breeze, the detritus was blown away, leaving the container full of nothing but berries.

Berries were consumed raw across the Arctic, but their use in more processed dishes is also sometimes mentioned. Mixing berries with caribou fat, fish eggs, and other summer foods like eggs and sorrel leaves was common among the Iñupiaq (see Burch 2006, 213), who, it should be noted, had access to more species of berry shrubs as well as other plant foods compared to the more eastern Inuit. The Iñupiat preserved their berry harvests both through immersion in seal oil and through storage in food caches dug into the ground (Burch 2006, 222).

The Persistence of Berry Harvesting in Northern Cultures

Over the past few generations there has been a decline in berry harvesting across the northern hemisphere in both Indigenous and non-Indigenous communities (see Berkes et al. 1994; Pouta, Sievänen, and Neuvonen 2006), which is attributed to the wider selection of imported food and increasingly urban lifestyles (Dowsley 2015; Pouta, Sievänen, and Neuvonen 2006). For example, in Finland the national participation in berry picking declined from 69 percent in 1981 to 55 percent in 2000 (Pouta, Sievänen, and Neuvonen 2006). A similar trend has been observed among the Attawapiskat Cree in the Canadian Subarctic near James Bay (Cummins 1992). What is intriguing, however, is how, in the face of the rapidly changing socio-economic landscape, the practice of berry picking has persisted while the harvesting of many other wild plants has declined precipitously. The reasons for this persistence are

apparently not related directly to material benefit, because of the availability of alternate foods in most areas. Instead, we find much evidence that the value of berry harvesting relates more to its facilitation of social and cultural practices.

Norrgard (2009) found that around Lake Superior in Minnesota, Wisconsin, and Michigan, berry harvesting allowed Ojibwe (Anishinaabe) to continue to practice traditional activities and embody cultural values, like sharing and mutual support, during periods of historical change. From the mid-nineteenth century to the post–World War II period, which was marked by the growing induction of Indigenous peoples into the wage economy, commercial sales of berries provided a significant amount of cash income for the Ojibwe of the region. Berries were picked both by individuals (usually women) and also in larger groups of both women and men, especially during periods when fewer opportunities were available for employment in traditionally male occupations such as lumbering. People travelled long distances to participate in berry-harvesting expeditions, and some berry patches were large enough to support pickers from the neighbouring Ho-Chunk (Winnegabo) people in an amicable intertribal harvest and celebration.

FIGURE 4.4 Women picking cranberries, Ford Harbour, Labrador, 1929. L. T. Burwash/Library and Archives Canada. MIKAN No. 3376359.

The harvest itself represented both an enactment of harvesting traditions rights and an expression and confirmation of Indigenous identity and relationships with the environment. The decline, after World War II, in the market value of berries, and thus of the quantities harvested, has not diminished their cultural value. Thomas Peacock, from the Ojibwe Fond du Lac community in Wisconsin, stated, "Our ancestors saw bears eating blueberries. Our grandchildren will do the same. We are part of a story that goes on forever" (quoted in Norrgard 2009, 54–55). Being on the land and harvesting berries as part of the endless cycle of life remain integral parts of Indigenous identity, despite changing economic circumstances.

As part of the traditional subsistence economy, berry picking has historically been a major seasonal activity for many Indigenous groups (see, for example, McDonald, Arragutainaq, and Novalinga 1997; Parlee, Berkes, and Teetl'it Gwich'in Renewable Resources Council 2005; Pigford and Zutter 2014; see also figure 4.5 below). Norrgard (2009) reported that the Ojibwe around Lake Superior spent much of the summer season in berry camps. Among the Iñupiaq nations of northwest Alaska, the men left on hunting forays in the fall while the women focused on harvesting fish and on collecting berries and other plants (Burch 1998, 73). Even now, the Nunivak Islanders in Alaska often spend up to a month on the land in activities that include harvesting berries (Pratt 1994, 336–337). Such dedication of time to the activity clearly situates berry harvesting as a major opportunity for nurturing the human-land relationship in many Indigenous cultures.

Michell describes this experience for Cree people (in central and northern Ontario) as follows:

> Gathering berries brings family together. Any sense of alienation and isolation quickly dissipates as people actively engage in simple talk. Getting in touch with the earth fosters an overall sense of interconnectedness. The fresh air, the sun, the wind, and the sounds and smells of nature refresh the mental, spiritual, emotional, and physical dimensions of our being. Gathering berries helps people communicate with that quiet stillness where peace and wisdom dwell. It is through berry picking and prolonged periods of time out on the land that we bond with the natural world. (Michell 2009, 66)

Further north, Parlee, Berkes, and the Teetl'it Gwich'in Renewable Resources Council (2005) worked with the Gwich'in in the Canadian Northwest Territories to identify nine values derived from berry picking that strengthen women's connection to the land: individual preference; individual well-being; family well-being; social connectivity; cultural continuity; land and resource use; stewardship; self-government; and spirituality. It is interesting to note that the research participants did not list among these values the commercial sale of berries, which is legal and commonly occurs at the roadside or in some instances to companies for jam or other foodstuff production. These numerous examples of berry harvesting from different North American Indigenous groups illustrate the devotion of time, opportunities for nurturing human-environment and social relationships, as well as the key role of women in berry harvesting across cultures.

Inuit Women and Berries: Context and Change

In many Northern cultures, including the eastern Canadian Inuit, berry picking (figure 4.4) is the major land-based activity organized by women (Giffen 1930; Pouta, Sievänen, and Neuvonen 2006; Whitecloud and Grenoble 2014). Giffen (1930, 10), writing on Inuit gender roles, states that, "in the autumn, abundant stores of berries are gathered by the women, who seem to have this department of the economic life entirely to themselves." In our work with Inuit in the eastern Canadian Arctic over fifteen years, we have often learned about berry harvesting. In exploring some of these lessons below, we include comments made by our Nunavut research participants.[1] The general information was collected from Nunavik (northern Québec), Nunatsiavut and NunatuKavut (Inuit homelands in northern and southern Labrador, respectively), and across Baffin Island (Nunavut).

Inuit women's involvement in berry harvesting is noted in early reports (see, for example, Birket-Smith 1924; Dall 1870; Hall 1865; Langsdorff 1814; Nelson 1899; Porter 1893; Thalbitzer 1914). Recent decades have seen a decline in many Inuit land-based activities for a variety of economic, social, and environmental reasons (Collings 2014; Dowsley 2015).

However, Inuit women have often indicated to us that berry picking is their most important food-procurement activity, and it draws the greatest number of participants among women in their communities. As Rachel Qaqqaq (Dowsley interview, 2012), a resident of Qikiqtarjuaq, an island community off the eastern coast of Baffin Island, emphatically stated, "Berry picking is the number one priority for ladies in September!" It is also apparent that women's berry-picking activities are important for recalling and transmitting values and traditions about land, people, places, place names, and related phenomena. Berry harvesting thus sustains and reproduces Inuit identities, particularly for women. As the primary means through which Inuit women independently articulate their relationship with the natural environment, an examination of berry harvesting provides us with a forum for addressing the gender gap that several authors observe in environmental and Indigenous geography (Kermoal and Altamirano-Jiménez 2016; Reed and Christie 2009).

CONTEXT

In the eastern Canadian Arctic (central and southern Baffin Island and Nunavik), berry harvesting is generally conducted during the open-water season starting in late July and extending into October or November, depending on local conditions. While warm summer and early fall days are the most pleasant for picking, "some berries are at their best only after the first frosts of early fall" (Brody 1976, 171). The diversity of berry species generally declines with increasing latitude, as do the length of the growing season and size of the plants and berries. For example, the Inuit of Sanikiluaq—a community situated on the Belcher Islands in the southeastern portion of Hudson Bay, at a latitude of approximately 56°N—reported that they consume five local species of berries: blueberries (*Vaccinium uliginosum*), crowberries (*Empetrum nigrum*), bog cranberries (*Vaccinium oxycoccus*), cloudberries (*Rubus chamaemorus*), and, more rarely, red bearberries (*Arctostaphylos uva-ursi*) (Wein, Freeman, and Makus 1996). Roughly 1,400 kilometres due north, Inuit living on northwestern Baffin Island in the vicinity of Foxe Basin reportedly distinguished four different types of berry (Brody 1976, 171). Surveys undertaken in Qikiqtarjuaq, situated slightly to the south but on the east coast of Baffin Island, indicate that the resident Inuit harvest three species: alpine bearberries/*kallait* (*Arctostaphylos alpina*), blueberries/*kigutangirnait*, and crowberries/*paurngait* (Inuktitut spellings from Ziegler, Joamie, and Hainnu 2009). Approximately 1,300 kilometres due east, the Inuit of southern Greenland also harvest three species: crowberries and blueberries, as well as lingonberries (*Vaccinium vitis-ideaea*) (Whitecloud and Grenoble 2014).

Rather than attempt a nutritional and/or quantitative analysis of berries, which is available elsewhere (see, for example, Boulanger-Lapointe 2017; Jones 2010; Kuhnlein and Turner 2009; Pouta, Sievänen, and Neuvonen 2006; Whymper 1869), we focus here on the social and cultural aspects of berry picking. We agree with Parlee, Berkes, and the Teetl'it Gwich'in Renewable Resources Council (2005) that a quantitative approach would be too reductionist to ascertain the cultural nuances that inform our focus on identity, gender, and environment. In any case, the Inuit we spoke to did not describe their harvest in terms of quantity, but rather in terms of time needed for the harvest or length of time they had berries in their larders (consumption time). We observed that a weekend of berry picking can fill from one to three 5-kilogram buckets. Berries last for various lengths of time, depending on the household. There are some houses that only eat the berries fresh, while many others freeze their harvest. Some families run out of berries before winter, while others can make their harvest last until near Christmas, and in a good year, some are able to make theirs last into February. Berries are sometimes turned into jam as well, but some people indicated that they do not know how to make anything out of the berries. Consuming berries fresh was the most common method of eating them, and a few women add berries to muffins. Considered a delicacy by some community members, berries mixed with seal brains, melted blubber, and blood are readily consumed when available. Berries can also be added to caribou, seal, or narwhal fat, or mixed with char fish eggs as well. Interviewed in 1999 as part of the Igloolik Oral History Project, Rachael Uyarasuk described popular ways to utilize berries:

> *Q:* When you are mixing caribou back fat for pudding, what would you add in the mixture?
>
> *RU:* Caribou stomach content, when it was still frozen, having shaved it into small pieces, this could be supplemented with caribou back fat, the one that is mixed when it is not frozen, even in the winter. Berries would be added, or meat would be minced while it is frozen. These were the things that were used to supplement the caribou back fat. Or adding rancid blubber, where you would find it in the abandoned tent rings, if a [piece of] blubber had been left behind. The rendered oil from the blubber would get rancid, [and] by adding arctic willow, you would chew it as you would with a [piece of chewing] gum. And if there were berries, then you would collect them, the rancid blubber that we had made into gum, then by adding rendered oil, the colour would turn white like the colour of a caribou back fat. Then adding berries, you would make a pudding and eat it.
>
> *Q:* Even using a rancid blubber?
>
> *RU:* Yes.
>
> *Q:* What would you use to hold the rancid oil?
>
> *RU:* In the abandoned tent sites, or abandoned winter dwelling, once it thaws out, then it would [be] exposed where there might have been some blubber, so you can tell easily where the rancid oil is—so the arctic willows would be gathered, and you would chew these by adding rancid oil, then you would make gum so that it became quite large, then you would use that for mix.
>
> *Q:* The rancid oil must be sticky?
>
> *RU:* If you add Arctic willow, it no longer becomes sticky, that is, when you are chewing it. It is sticky when the rancid oil is not mixed with anything. That way you would make gum, after you had it for gum, as we would be berry picking, then the one that we were chewing would be mixed with oil, the dish would get large after you had added berries. That was the way we did it. They may not be appealing; nevertheless, we used to eat them.

These various reports on harvesting and using berries give an idea of how berries were utilized by the women in various ways as food, and they also give some hint of the large amount of time spent picking.

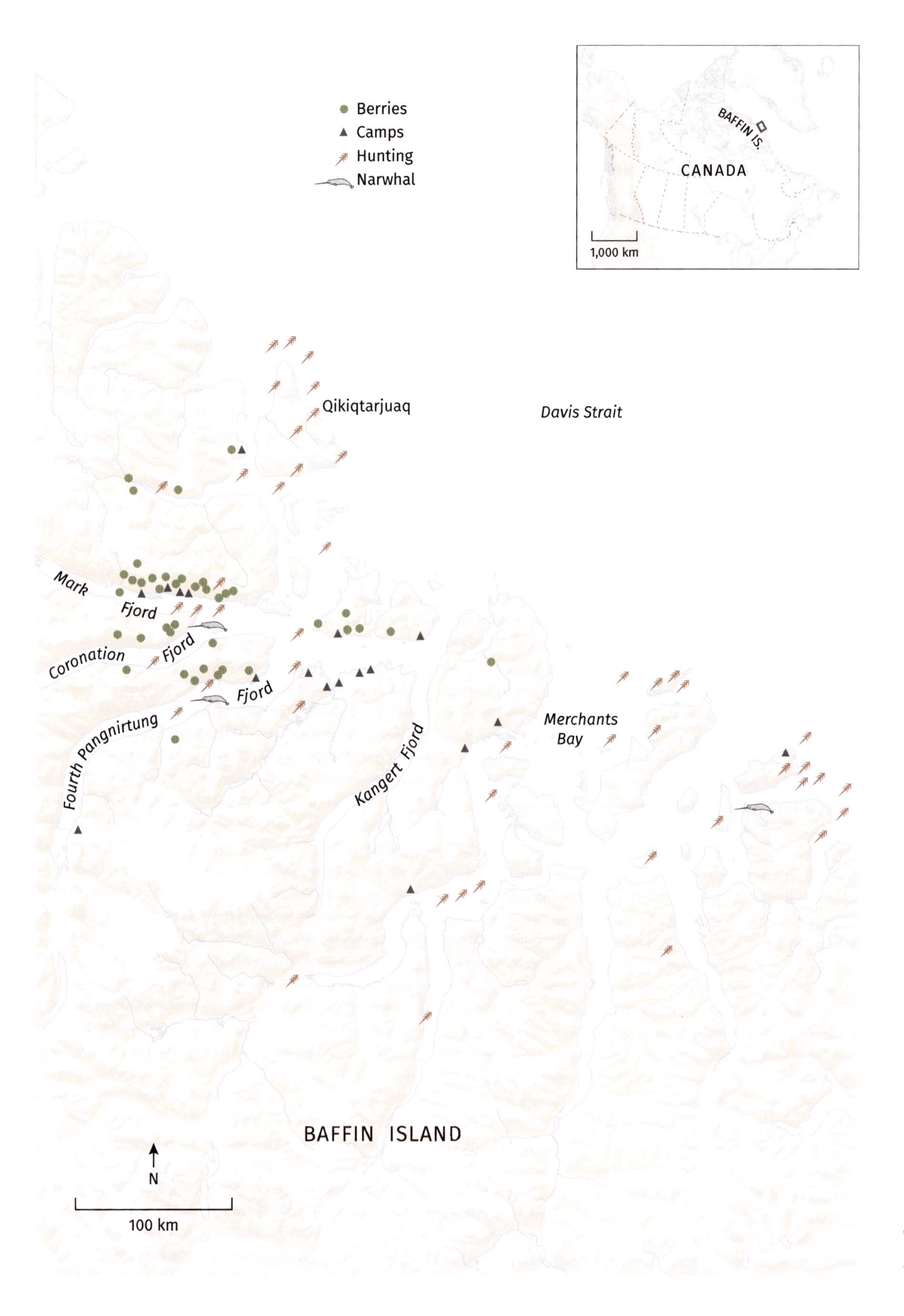

FIGURE 4.5 Campsites and locations of subsistence resources identified by local Inuit in the area around the island of Qikiqtarjuaq, on the eastern coast of Baffin Island, Nunavut. Map created by Williams Stolz, 2017.

CHANGE

The natural environment has always exhibited change that humans found noteworthy. At the same time human behaviour, land use patterns, and populations have changed as well. Both of these types of change affect the relationship between people and berries. With regard to the natural environment, Burch (1998, 176) reported vegetation change in Alaska's Kobuk River Delta, an area on which local Iñupiat rely:

> The delta had unusually lush growths of sourdock, rhubarb, and salmonberries. The use of the past tense here is deliberate, because oral sources say that the supply of berries particularly has declined since the first decade of the twentieth century. Daniel Foster told me that, when he was young, the whole outer delta was colored red in late summer and fall, a virtual field of salmonberries. Now they are gone. No one has been able to explain this change to me, but it could be that reindeer herds devastated the berry bushes here, as they are said to have done in the Kivalina district.

Interviewed in 1991 in connection with the Igloolik Oral History Project, Zachariasie Uqalik, an elder living near Pond Inlet, discussed how changing weather conditions in recent decades are affecting berries:

> The earth and the natural environment are so much different now from what it was in the past. In those days, plants grew very healthy and the weather conditions used to be good for a prolonged period of time, which resulted with good plant growth. But now the plants hardly ever grow; as a matter of fact, the plants do not even get a chance to grow as they did in the past. This is not just this past summer, but it had been noticeable in the summers past. In those days, they used to grow, but in recent times the plant growth is almost non-existent. As a matter of fact, they seem to be dying off even in the middle of the summer. Indeed, there are hardly any more berries around. In the years past, in the autumn we used to collect berries under the snow because they had grown very well in the preceding summer.

Another activity central to Inuit subsistence was caribou hunting. Caribou were hunted year-round, but especially during the summer and fall, which is also the time when berries ripen. Up to the middle of the twentieth century, Inuit living on central Baffin Island hunted caribou during the summer and fall by setting up camps in coastal areas and then hiking inland (see Brody 1976, 160, for a detailed description). Elderly and infirm people were not able to walk long distances, so some family members, including children, remained at camps near the coast, and the caribou hunters returned there late in the fall. Regardless of whether they travelled inland as part of a caribou-hunting party or stayed near the coast, women took the opportunity to harvest berries.

Rachel Qaqqaq (Dowsley interview, 2012), who was born in the 1940s, remembered this harvesting pattern from the time she was a young girl:

> Our summer camp was Ukkusiksaq. In the winter we stayed in Paallavvik [south of Qikiqtarjuaq]. At that time, my dad and uncle went caribou hunting, [as] there were caribou in the area.

> Ukkusiksaq is a small island. I remember berry picking. In those days people walked inland to hunt, [but] my generation stopped doing that. Now we go berry picking only in fall and summer. Most women go berry picking as their main activity on the land. Maybe one reason women go less today is the danger of polar bears. We are scared to death of them: there are too many. Our ancestors saw really nice scenery walking inland. It's so peaceful on the land; we are missing out.

As Qaqqaq explains, berry harvesting was the work of women and children, which they conducted while the men hunted caribou. These two subsistence activities are linked elsewhere in the Arctic as well (see, for example, Todd 2016, 206), given that they occur during the same seasons of the year.

Since the late 1970s, following the wide adoption of boats, a decline in caribou in central Baffin Island, and a renewed focus on autumn narwhal hunting, late summer and fall camps (and therefore berry-picking locations) have been more frequently located on the coast, in particular in fjords, which are good places to catch narwhal. Figure 4.5 shows the close proximity of contemporary berry-harvesting sites to camps and hunting sites in the central Baffin region.

Rachel Qaqqaq also indicated that the most concerning change for women on Baffin Island today is the increase in polar bears (see Dowsley and Wenzel 2008 for broader comments on this issue). This increase is not attributed to climate change, but instead to a bear population that is hunted under a strict quota system and has shown natural growth over the past few decades. The threat posed by polar bears is of grave concern for women berry pickers. As Qaqqaq explained, "While berry picking you must be aware of bears. This summer a lady was approached by an adult bear and two cubs. They stood on their back legs and looked at her, not more than ten feet away from her. They were showing they were bigger, and then they left. No attack."

The threat of bear attacks is common to women picking berries throughout many parts of Canada, and men are often tasked with protecting the women and children from bears (Anderson 2011):

> My parents were outpost campers. I liked berry picking better than hunting. My mother used to go—I learned from her and started to like it. This autumn, in September I went on an overnight [trip] to Mattatujana with my husband and two grandkids. Almost the whole town goes [on this sort of trip]. We go by boat. We don't usually just go with women because there are polar bears and we have to be aware of that. Growing up, our parents used to tell us to be advised of polar bears. I think there are more polar bears today—lots this autumn. (Hannah Audlakiak, Dowsley interview, 2012)

During a community consultation in Clyde River on Baffin Island regarding polar bear-human interactions, one participant stated,

> We always need a "watch person" while berry picking. We always hear [from media and government that] polar bears are decreasing, but that's not true. We like berry picking and walking in summer, but we need rifles to protect ourselves. If you are going to talk about the past, there were fewer then than there are today. This is the time of the most polar bears. (quoted in Dowsley and Taylor 2006, 71)

These statements describing concerns about bears also mention some of the pleasures associated with berry picking, such as walking, enjoying the scenery, and how peaceful it is to be out on the land. The comradery associated with the berry harvest is also alluded to in Hannah Audlakiak's comment about her mother teaching her to pick berries and growing to like that activity more than hunting. Polar bears were always a threat, but the increase in bear sightings in recent years have caused an adjustment to how berry picking is organized. Now, ironically, in order to enjoy the peacefulness of the land, Baffin Island women need armed guards.

On Baffin Island, the decline in caribou (Ferguson, Williamson, and Messier 1998) and the increase in polar bears (York et al. 2016) are two of the most obvious changes associated with the Inuit-land relationship. The changes in both are attributed to natural factors: caribou follow a cyclical population pattern, while polar bear numbers have simply increased due to restrictions on hunting. Climate change is a more subtle transformation. Many women have been going to the same place to pick berries for years, and Dowsley queried some on their observations in Qikiqtarjuaq. Oolootie Cormier (Dowsley interview, 2009) had been going to the same locations for ten to fifteen years and reported seeing no changes. Blueberry patches seem to persist on the Arctic islands indefinitely once established, with Elizapee Kopalie (Dowsley interview, 2009) saying, "Blueberry plants stay there forever, no succession of plants." Tina Alookie (Dowsley interview, 2009) had seen no difference in the location of plants or quality of berries since she was young, which is in agreement with elder Mary Onga Audlakiak (Dowsley interview, 2009), who had picked in the same patch for her whole life and has seen no changes to berries in size or location over more than sixty years.

When asked about climate change affecting berries near Qikiqtarjuaq (Nunavut), there were many different views. Some women did not notice any change to the berries, while Daisy Arnaquq (Dowsley interview, 2009) observed that berries are ripening at the beginning of August instead of the end of that month, and Olasie Kooneelusie (Dowsley interview, 2009) observed the berries are still around past the end of October and into November, and can even be dug out of the snow. Softer, larger blueberries have been observed by community members along with a gradual shift in the colour of the ground during summer, from brown toward green around Qikiqtarjuaq. As the Arctic warms, new plants are being found around Qikiqtarjuaq, including blueberries, which never used to grow in the vicinity of the community. Previously, the Qikiqtarjuarmiut could only find them in the fjords to the south of the community. It was also noted that berry plants are healthier in the protected habitat of deep fjords compared to plants on the coast and islands exposed to the open ocean.

In Iqaluit, located some 470 kilometres south of Qikiqtarjuaq, women noted that berries had changed over time, describing them as "smaller and seedier" now and more difficult to find close to town. "Good" berries, described as large and juicy, were often said to be located across Frobisher Bay, necessitating access to a boat. One community elder recalled that, when she was growing up at an outpost camp, the berries "were always big and nice and juicy and very good to the taste and over the years I've noticed they're getting smaller" (Bunce, interview no. 4, 2015). Women frequently attributed these changes to shifting climate regimes and noted the specific conditions berries need to grow. Women discussed a balance of moisture as being important for growing conditions. One woman recalled, "We had a lot of rain and not enough sun so the berries bloomed later and then when they did bloom they weren't as plump" (Bunce, interview no. 1, 2015). The timing of rain, sun, and snow were also consistently mentioned as crucial factors in the growth of berries. As another woman noted,

> Berries, they don't grow as much because of no sun. Not enough sun for the past few years. Too much rain in July. July, August—too much rain or too cold. Because it has to have sun and rain for berries. My mom said, "Oh no, there's not enough snow on the land. There's not going to be as much berries or no berries." (Bunce interview no. 6, 2015)

Many women described reaching out to family members in other communities to send them berries during years in which berries around Iqaluit were of poor quality or were not accessible. As is becoming increasingly common with many forms of country food, family members in communities with an abundance of a particular type of food will ship it to relatives in communities that lack access to that same item. This often results in berries being sent as carry-on luggage with someone flying between communities. One woman in Iqaluit commented,

> I called Pang [Pangnirtung] and said, "Hey my mum's craving for berries. Do you got some?" "Yep, I'll send some over." Nice and huge. I asked a couple times for them to bring some because I have family there, aunts, uncles, cousins. I called up my cousin because she's always saying on Facebook she went berry picking. [. . .] I said, "You went berry picking every day, spare us some berries. We're craving for berries." So she sent us berries and [ptarmigan] eggs. (Bunce interview no. 13, 2015)

In Alaska, the desire to harvest berries draws women back home to rural communities from urban centres (Kenneth Pratt, pers. comm., 2017). The official purpose of the trips is to harvest berries, but they also allow for re-engaging with the land, friends, and family in the home community. These urban migrant women are sometimes stigmatized by rural peers as being removed from their cultural roots. Thus, berry picking can become a way to prove one's Indigenous identity is still strong, and urban women may work hard to gather sufficient berries to impress their worth upon others. In such cases, berry picking can become competitive, with the volumes of berries harvested being carefully noted.

Further related to the increasing urbanization of some Arctic communities, many Inuit women in the eastern Arctic expressed dismay to us at the loss of good berry-picking areas due to the expanding infrastructural development of some communities. Since becoming the capital of Nunavut, Iqaluit has grown and now houses almost eight thousand residents; it is the only settlement in Nunavut large enough to be considered a city. The large population puts greater demands on the berry patches near town, as described by one woman: "I mean it's been hard. Because every year we're all berry picking. And we're all picking berries at almost the same spot as the year before, so we're not giving them enough time to grow. [. . .] I haven't had big picked berries in so many years" (Bunce interview no. 6, 2015).

Many women in Iqaluit said that their favourite berry-picking spots are now occupied by houses or other buildings (Bunce et al. 2016). There was also a preference for obtaining berries away from town due to the sand and dust blown around by cars on the unpaved roads, which settles on the berries and leads to concerns about pollution. "I know it's much nicer out on the land," a grandmother said, "but when you're close to Iqaluit it's much different from the sand and stuff. The dust. The [berries] taste weird maybe. I don't berry pick close to here. Only away from town. As far as much as I can go" (Bunce interview no. 9, 2015).

Women living in Iqaluit expressed great disappointment in the changes occurring, as berries are a country food for which women mentioned feeling strong cravings. Unlike other land-based activities such as hunting, berry picking does not require access to a costly snowmobile or boat (or, as is often the case, a man to operate them); nor does berry picking necessitate taking time off work or cause conflict with child-care duties. Anyone with some spare time, a bucket, and access to a nearby berry patch can go berry picking. The egalitarian nature of berries as a resource is one of the most appealing aspects of the harvest. We hope that calling attention to this resource might encourage urban planners in the North to accommodate this activity in the future by planning for berry "parks" that are managed for berry bushes as settlement expansion occurs. Such attention to berries as a resource would help Inuit women adapt to some of the changes they have experienced that affect berry harvesting, and serve to support the next generation in carrying on this traditional activity.

The Modern Organization of Berry Harvesting and the Creation of Female Space

Berry bushes are quite common across the Arctic, but berries are not available everywhere, nor are the bushes equally productive across all areas. Berry picking does not occur homogeneously across the landscape, nor is it restricted to the best berry patches in terms of productivity, size, or other features of the berries. It is instead directed by social decisions in addition to ecology. Trusler and Johnson (2008) examined the factors that determine the location of berry-harvesting patches in the traditional territories of the Gitksan (Gitxsan) and Wet'suwet'en in British Columbia. They found that the locations were not strongly based on natural ecological characteristics. Instead, multiple factors such as proximity to human settlements, scheduling of other seasonal activities, resource management, and social and political structures, were also important. They labelled berry patches as cultural ecotopes, or a particular kind of place. Similarly, Inuit selection of berry-harvesting sites involves several factors unrelated to ecology of the berries. For example, the land in central Baffin Island is quite mountainous and many slopes are covered in berry bushes—but these are too steep to allow the berries to be gathered safely. Furthermore, if the harvesters wish to stay overnight, they will need an area with fresh water and flat, dry ground for camping. Cabins thus often become the headquarters for berry picking, regardless of whether they happen to be situated in the vicinity of the best berry patches.

FIGURE 4.6 "The Berry Pickers." Siberian Inuit (Yuit) women and children picking berries, Siberia, Russia, ca. 1903–1915. Photographer: Lomen Brothers, Nome, Alaska. Glenbow Museum Archives/ NC1 488.

Transportation to berry patches is another important factor. Women may walk or drive all-terrain vehicles to areas where berries grow. However, in the community of Qikiqtarjuaq, which is on an island, boat transportation is considered essential for a serious expedition. Boats are nearly universally operated by men. Usually, women travel with close male relatives, but occasionally they hitch a ride with other groups. Ulusi Rosie Koksiak (Dowsley interview, 2009) reported that she has to find someone to give her a lift. Another woman who lacks transportation has been known to berate the men on the community radio, telling them to take her berry picking. She always gets an invitation. Culturally, the human-land relationship is of central importance, and, out of respect, a woman who indicates her desire to get out on the land is usually obliged. However, Sheila Kopalie (Dowsley interview, 2009) explained that berry pickers who lack transportation usually have little choice but to use whatever berry patch the boat is already heading toward. Lacking close male relatives with whom to coordinate picking as a family event, she focuses instead on maximizing her harvest:

> Every year I pick them. I find a way to go. I pick one bucket Friday to Sunday. It's from my elbow to the tip of my fingers deep. The berries are mixed together in the bucket because the patches of berries are scattered so there are a lot of small patches. I systematically cover an area each day and take all of them. There are blue and blackberries. I don't pick any other kinds. I go out alone, tagging along with another family, so [I] don't bring my daughter.

Other women in Iqaluit likewise struggle to gain access to the land. Opportunities to go out in boats are in high demand in the community, and women with limited social networks are often at a disadvantage. Some women, particularly young women, described feeling shy about asking to go berry picking, preferring to be invited.

For many people, the geographic location of a summer/fall trip on the land is based on a site from which to harvest the more patchy hunting resources, and the fairly ubiquitous berries are collected in that locality as well. Thus, for both women travelling with their families and women hitching a ride, women's berry picking is often tied closely to men's hunting activities. This does not mean that berries are considered a less valuable resource than the products of men's hunting. Both are valued in their own way: meat is the staple food, but berries are only seasonally available and are considered somewhat tedious to collect—and for these reasons berries are a delicacy. The privileging of geographic orientation toward hunting merely indicates the efficient spatial organization of Inuit harvesting. Berry bushes are abundant while animals are quite uneven in their distribution across the landscape. It is logical to travel to a good hunting area and harvest berries there rather than vice versa, which would reduce hunting success and only marginally (if at all) increase berry harvests.

The composition of a berry-harvesting party thus often includes men serving as pilots, providers of fresh meat to the camp, and bear guards. Children help out, but males are a major source of other forms of support. As Anore Jones (2010, 74) observes, "Although women pick most of the berries, children of all ages are highly praised for what they contribute.

Many men pick berries, too. Those who don't pick show their appreciation in other ways by tending camp, cooking, washing dishes, babysitting, and whatever will allow the women to pick more berries."

The involvement of Alaska Native men in berry picking is an individual choice and results in some very committed male berry harvesters (Kenneth Pratt, pers. comm., 2017). The partial reversal of gender roles, where men become caregivers and keepers of the camp, as well as continuing their traditional masculine roles of pilots, hunters, and protectors, illustrates the flexibility of Inuit social structure (Giffen 1930). It also serves to strengthen the respect between spouses as they appreciate the contribution each makes to the household. The joy of being out on the land, combined with the shift in gender roles, makes berry season a time for family bonding, as everyone is involved in the fun and the family functions under slightly different norms (figure 4.6).

Berry-picking expeditions also often involve children, as Inuit women are generally the primary caretakers. Much berry picking is done close to camps or communities so that children might accompany their mothers or other relatives. Berry harvesting further from permanent dwellings is often accomplished through travelling to a base camp with the whole family. In the case of berry harvesting during a longer expedition, when the men are not occupied in hunting or fishing, they will watch the youngest children while the women pick berries. As Hannah Audlakiak (Dowsley interview, 2012) says of berry picking, "It is a long tradition, mainly upheld by the women, but with men as important support. Children are taught it at a young age and it is very popular with people of all ages." In fact, as elders reduce their involvement with more rigorous harvesting activities, they often continue to participate in berry picking. Kenneth Pratt (pers. comm. 2017) suggests that berry picking is probably the first and last subsistence activity engaged in by individual members of Indigenous groups in Alaska; and we suspect that this is generally true for Indigenous peoples across the Arctic. Tutoring children in how to pick often involves encouraging them not to eat berries during picking or using other motivational games to increase the likelihood that they will not return to camp empty-handed. It is seen as important to introduce children to a subsistence lifestyle in which their contributions to feeding the group are recognized, and their identities as providers, group members, and descendants of their ancestors are built.

It is, of course, often difficult to keep children focused on harvesting, and berry picking with children can devolve into an amusing day on the land, with memories of exploration, adventure, and teachings about other aspects of the environment as the main product, rather than berries. As a multifaceted event, going berry picking entails many other activities that serve as training for children in interacting with the environment. Picnics often occur; children explore rocks, vegetation, water bodies, capture and examine small animals, or hunt birds and small mammals. Women and children often climb hills to take in the view and perhaps build an inukshuk. For some women, including Sheila Kopalie, maximizing the volume of berries collected is one goal; but for many women, interacting with the land and enjoying each other's company is the major benefit of berry picking.

During the rest of the year, the female domain is the household and the workplace, in addition to the social aspects of the community. Women participate in community life as volunteers sitting on various governance committees (particularly those focused on education, health, and families), as unpaid caregivers for the elderly and children, and, increasingly, as heads of household (Dowsley et al. 2010). In the workplace, women tend to hold more white-collar and full-time jobs than men do, and a hunter needs a wife who earns a good income to finance his hunting (Kuokkanen 2011; Quintal-Marineau 2017; Todd 2016). This is because purchasing and maintaining hunting equipment, including boats and snowmobiles, is expensive. Before the mid-1980s, when fur trade bans were activated in Europe and the Inuit seal skin trade collapsed, women used to process the skins of seals and sell them to support their husbands' hunting (Wenzel 1991). Thus, subsistence was a closed economic cycle, with men hunting for food, women preparing the meat and seal skins, and the proceeds from the fur trade in seal skins being used to support all the subsistence activities of the family, including subsistence hunting and berry harvesting. Today skins have little economic value, so the family needs another source of income. If men are to spend significant amounts of time hunting, their wives need to supply the money to do so. Women whose male partners are involved in hunting tend to be more involved in subsistence or land-based activities themselves because the family owns the equipment and the husband possesses the skills necessary to support her and the rest of the family in excursions (Inksetter 2012). Ironically, then, a woman needs to participate in the market economy in order to participate in the subsistence economy under these conditions. Her participation, however, requires her to spend most of her time working, thus contributing to the development of a gendered division of space, in which the land is a place for male hunters and the village becomes feminine.

The exception to this division is most strongly seen in berry picking. Berry harvesting is both a feminine time and a feminine place that extends out from the normal female domain of the household and community and into the masculine-dominated landscape. When not constrained by their transportation providers, women make the decisions about when and where to pick berries, as well as which species and the quantity they will harvest. Unlike most discussions of gendered divisions of labour in contexts where the feminine is said to lack any essential qualities, and is instead defined as the complement or support of masculine activities, in berry season, we see women as the leaders of the activity and the men as supporters or minor actors (Simard-Gagnon 2013). Indeed, the hillsides and berry patches, places offering few hunting opportunities for men, are female spaces. To sit on such a hillside on a warm late-summer afternoon and watch the men on the shore of the fjord far below fetching water, fishing, or chasing after toddlers, and to be only in the company of other women, is at the core of how Inuit women relate to their landscape. People enjoy picking berries together, but they do not necessarily position themselves close enough for conversation with anyone. The space is simultaneously social and solitary. This peaceful, relaxed cultural space is shared by the related Iñupiat of Alaska:

> Berries are by far the most popular plant food harvested from the land. Groups of women and whole families go out for days and weeks at a time to camp where the berries grow. They put up tents, set a fish net if possible, and hunt for meat to supplement whatever store food they have brought. These camps capture much of the beautiful aspects of the old Iñupiat. Long hours are spent picking berries and packing them back to camp. This is a happy time of living outside on the land and enjoying the friendship of partners and family. It is also a lovely time to be alone with your thoughts as you pick. (Jones 2010, 75)

Berry picking is the primary time for women to interact with the environment, and it is also their major vacation from the demands of work and village life. But in addition to that, it is a time and space in which they can enjoy a reprieve from their social responsibilities as caretakers and are in charge of a materially productive activity. It is where they are most free to relate to their environment, reflect on their lives, and nurture their spirits.

Ownership, Sharing, and Inuit Identity

Although berry picking is often located within the context of male hunting excursions, we have learned about some cultural norms governing rights to berries and berry patches. Exclusive ownership of either the berry patch or the berries themselves is a delicate matter in Inuit culture. Sharing and respecting the gifts of the earth are paramount concepts (Dowsley 2015; Stairs and Wenzel 1992), and people are obliged to share country foods including meat, fish, and berries. However, in other Indigenous cultures, use and ownership rules are well-known and transgressions are socially proscribed (see, for example, Parlee, Berkes, and Teetl'it Gwich'in Renewable Resources Council 2006; Trusler and Johnson 2008). To prevent the overuse of common resources—otherwise known as a "tragedy of the commons" (Hardin 1968)—Indigenous communities have often developed institutions or rules-in-use that govern common resources such as berries (Parlee, Berkes, and Teetl'it Gwich'in Renewable Resources Council 2006). Similarly, women engaged in berry picking in the eastern Canadian Arctic have also developed their own loose rules, though they have not reported any serious pressure on the resource that might cause overuse or create the conditions in which stricter rules might become necessary.

In many communities, there is a family-based territorial system for berries. Berry patches are passed down from generation to generation. These may be located around current camps or cabins, which are often built on ancestral family lands. The traditional areas of past generations are also recognized, and people may have social sanction to pick at these old sites even without owning a modern cabin nearby. As Elizapee Kopalie (Dowsley interview, 2009) explained, "It's not strict who can go there; a friend might come, or they might tell a friend and the friend decides to go or not." A woman given a lift by another family is de facto invited to pick in their area for that trip. Parlee, Berkes, and the Teetl'it Gwich'in Renewable Resources Council (2006) noted that among the Gwich'in of the Northwest Territories, rules of access became stricter during times of berry scarcity. In our discussions with Inuit women, we found that in response to "bad" (unproductive) berry seasons, women commonly reported going berry picking earlier the following year because they were craving berries (Hannah Audlakiak, Dowsley interview, 2012). They also reported going to other areas in search of berries, although this choice depended on the accessibility of those areas and pickers' social licence to harvest there.

There are also cultural norms around distribution of the berries. Traditional sharing networks are at the core of the subsistence economy (Gombay 2009). It is in the distribution of products from the land where Inuit social identity is most strongly enacted (Dowsley 2015; Kuokkanen 2011). It is therefore common for harvesters to ensure that non-pickers have berries, especially the elderly or others who cannot pick themselves. Eva Nookiguak (Dowsley interview, 2009), of Qikiqtarjuaq, explained that she gets berries from four different family members because she is too scared to cross the ocean in a small boat from her island community and harvest herself. Sheila Kopalie (Dowsley interview, 2009), whose description of her methodical picking procedures we read above, provides berries for the elders that she looks after as an in-home care worker, even though she has to find a spot on a boat in order to gather berries. She only consumes berries fresh, so after she supplies the elders, she will put her excess berries out in front of her house for everyone to share so that the berries do not go to waste. The pleasure Sheila derives from sharing her berries is consistent with the observations of Nicole Gombay (2009) and Martha Dowsley (2015), who emphasize that sharing is an integral part of being an Inuk.

Berries and Inuit Health

The integration of the physical, social, psychological, and nourishing features of berry harvesting is one aspect of the way that Inuit conceptualize health (figure 4.7). Rather than the mere absence of disease, health is understood holistically, to include a person's connection to the environment and all living things, both human and non-human (see, for example, Richmond et al. 2005). This holistic view of the person in the environment extends to plants, whether they are consumed as food or are used in the preparation of medicines.

Elisapee Ishutak (Dowsley interview, 2012) remembered a time when food came from the land, and there were hardly any grocery stores. People were healthier than they are today, partly because they had not yet developed a taste for foods high in fat, salt, and sugar. Her view of health extended beyond non-Indigenous conceptions of physical health. Rather, she was referring to the deeper feelings of harmony and well-being engendered by the experience of both picking berries and sharing them with other people. Much as being on the land nurtures Inuit identity, the berries harvested there are part of that larger social fabric of Inuit communities. They feed people, but they also nurture relationships and reciprocity, engender good feelings toward others, and thus make everyone feel better.

FIGURE 4.7 Berries are a crucial component of the traditional Inuit diet. Pictured are the black crowberries locally known as *paurngaqutik*, growing in a thicket of *tingaujaq* (reindeer lichen) and *mamaittuqutik* (Labrador tea)—two other plants of medicinal importance to Inuit. Photograph taken near Kangiqsualujjuaq by Scott A. Heyes, 2012.

Conclusions

What comes through unmistakably when one listens to the voices of Inuit women in the eastern Canadian Arctic is that berry picking holds a value beyond the need for subsistence, which may explain why the act of berry picking has persisted in the face of capitalism and the constraints imposed by modern living conditions. Rauna Kuokkanen (2011) agrees, citing the intrinsic cultural values of land-based activities as the reason why a reticence exists in Indigenous communities about relying on money for anything other than securing supplies for a subsistence lifestyle:

> Indigenous economies such as household production and subsistence activities extend far beyond the economic sphere: they are at the heart of who people are culturally and socially. These economies, including the practices of sharing, manifest indigenous worldviews characterized by interdependence and reciprocity that extend to all living beings and to the land. In short, besides an economic occupation, subsistence activities are an expression of one's identity, culture, and values. They are also a means by which social networks are maintained and reinforced. (Kuokkanen 2011, 217)

As Kuokkanen points out, the Western development paradigm that emerged following World War II brought with it a sustained discursive assault on subsistence economies. Drawing on Rosa Luxemburg's analysis of imperialism in *The Accumulation of Capital* ([1913] 1951), Kuokkanen notes that the expansion of capitalism into new markets requires the ongoing, and typically coercive, destruction of the economic autonomy of subsistence producers so as to render them dependent on wage labour. Once wage labour comes to be viewed as the only productive form of work, however, women's unpaid contributions to household economies cease to hold value (Kuokkanen 2011, xx). At the same time, in Indigenous communities characterized by mixed economies, cash income is often valued primarily as a means to purchase the materials and equipment now required for the pursuit of subsistence activities (Kuokkanen 2011, xx; Quintal-Marineau 2017, xx). Despite limited job opportunities in the Arctic, Indigenous communities have retained their resilience and have managed to adapt to the market economy in ways that allow them to continue their subsistence lifestyle, which is the basis of their culture.

While berries provide sustenance to Inuit communities in the eastern Canadian Arctic, berry picking has become increasingly difficult. In particular, because of the capitalist system, the monetary cost of supplies, such as boats or snowmobiles and gasoline to go out on the land, has been increasing. However, as we have demonstrated, Inuit women stand to incur a far greater social and cultural cost if they stop berry picking. For these women, berry picking provides a way to maintain and strengthen cultural and ecological values, as well as community relationships and relationships with the land.

Berry and other plant harvesting is often classified as women's work, and it has not been explored extensively by researchers (but see Simard-Gagnon 2013 and Boulanger-Lapointe 2017). This omission underscores the continued neglect of women in research on human-environment relations. We see a similar neglect in the study of other human-plant interactions (Head and Atchison 2009). Although plants and their potential pharmaceutical uses have been examined in scientific studies, more research needs to be conducted from a social and cultural perspective. Indeed, in order to appreciate the complex relationships between humans and their environment, we need to bridge the divide between science and humanities by combining quantitative and qualitative studies (Ryan 2011). We look forward to seeing more attention paid in the future to the human-plant relationship, and the gendered nature of that relationship, as part of an increasing focus on Indigenous women and the environment.

Acknowledgements

We thank our Inuit colleagues and friends for passing on their knowledge of the land to us, and for welcoming us into their homes. Thank you to John MacDonald and Carolyn MacDonald for providing constructive feedback and comments on an earlier draft of this chapter.

Notes

1 Unless otherwise indicated, interviews were conducted on eastern Baffin Island, by Martha Dowsley, or in Iqaluit, by Anna Bunce, and are identified in the text accordingly. (For further details, see Dowsley 2015 and Bunce 2015.) When research participants gave permission to use their real names, we have done so.

Interviews

Interviews conducted by Anna Bunce in connection with Gender and the Human Dimensions of Climate Change: Global Discourse and Local Perspectives from the Canadian Arctic. Department of Geography, McGill University, Montréal. Interviews were conducted in English, unless otherwise indicated. Transcripts in possession of Bunce.

Iqaluit mother. Interview no. 1. June 2015.

Iqaluit elder (female). Interview no. 4. June 2015. Inuktitut, translated into English by Naomi Tatty

Iqaluit mother. Interview no. 6. June 2015.

Iqaluit grandmother. Interview no. 9. June 2015.

Iqaluit mother. Interview no. 13. June 2015.

Interviews conducted by Martha Dowsley in connection with Inuit Women and Subsistence: Social and Environmental Change. Department of Geography and the Environment, Lakehead University, Thunder Bay, Ontario. Interviews were conducted in Qikiqtarjuaq, NU unless otherwise noted. Transcripts in possession of Dowsley.

Tina Alookie. Interview #B250609-1. 25 June 2009.

Daisy Arnaquq. Interview #B080609-2. 2009. 8 June 2009. Interview conducted by Jocelyn Inksetter

Hannah Audlakiak. Interview #20121215-Q2. 15 December 2012.

Mary Onga Audlakiak. Interview #B090609-1. 9 June 2009. Interpreter: Lavinia Curley

Oolootie Cormier. Interview #B060609-1. 6 June 2009. Interpreter: Lavinia Curley

Elisapee Ishutak. Interview #20121212-P2. 12 December 2012, Pangnirtung, NU. Interpreter: William Kilabuk

Ulusi Rosie Koksiak. Interview #B-070609-1. 7 June 2009.

Olasie Kooneelusie. Interview #B200609. 20 June 2009.

Elizapee Kopalie. Interview #B080609-1. 8 June 2009.

Sheila Kopalie. Interview #B210609-1. 21 June 2009.

Eva Nookiguak. Interview #B270609-1. 27 June 2009.

Rachel Qaqqaq. Interview #20121215-Q1. 15 December 2012. Interpreter: Martha Nookiguak

Igloolik Oral History Project. Igloolik Oral History Centre, Nunavut Arctic College, Igloolik.

Zachariasie Uqalik. Interview #IE-209. 1991.

Rachael Uyarasuk. Interview #IE-436. 1999.

References

Anderson, Kim
2011 *Life Stages and Native Women: Memory, Teachings, and Story Medicine.* University of Manitoba Press, Winnipeg.

Berkes, Fikret, Peter J. George, Richare J. Preston, Alan Hughes, John Turner, and Brian D. Cummins
1994 Wildlife Harvesting and Sustainable Regional Native Economy in the Hudson and James Bay Lowland, Ontario. *Arctic* 47(4): 350–360.

Birket-Smith, Kaj
1924 *Ethnography of the Egedesminde District with Aspects of the General Culture of West Greenland.* Meddelelser om Grønland No. 66. C. A. Reitzel, Copenhagen.

Boas, Franz
1888 *The Central Eskimo.* Annual Report No. 6. Bureau of American Ethnology, Washington, DC.

Boulanger-Lapointe, Noémie
2017 *Importance of Berries in the Inuit Biocultural System: A Multi-disciplinary Investigation in the Canadian North.* PhD dissertation, Department of Geography, University of British Columbia, Vancouver.

Briggs, Jean
1970 *Never in Anger: Portrait of an Eskimo Family.* Harvard University Press, Cambridge, Massachusetts.

Brody, Hugh
1976 Inuit Land Use in North Baffin Island and Foxe Basin. In *Inuit Land Use and Occupancy Project*, vol. 1, *Land Use and Occupancy*, edited by Milton M. R. Freeman, pp. 153–171. Department of Indian and Northern Affairs, Ottawa.

Bunce, Anna
2015 Gender and the Human Dimensions of Climate Change: Global Discourse and Local Perspectives from the Canadian Arctic. Master's thesis, Department of Geography, McGill University, Montréal.

Bunce, Anna, James Ford, Sherilee Harper, Victoria Edge, and Indigenous Health Adaptation to Climate Change Research Team
2016 Vulnerability and Adaptive Capacity of Inuit Women to Climate Change: A Case Study from Iqaluit, Nunavut. *Natural Hazards* 83(3): 1419–1441.

Burch, Ernest S., Jr.
1971 The Nonempirical Environment of the Arctic Alaskan Eskimos. *Southwestern Journal of Anthropology* 27(2): 148–165.
1998 *The Iñupiaq Eskimo Nations of Northwest Alaska.* University of Alaska Press, Fairbanks.
2006 *Social Life in Northwest Alaska: The Structure of Iñupiaq Eskimo Nations.* University of Alaska Press, Fairbanks.

Collings, Peter
2014 *Becoming Inummarik: Men's Lives in an Inuit Community.* McGill-Queen's University Press, Montréal.

Condon, Richard G., Peter Collings, and George W. Wenzel
1995 The Best Part of Life: Subsistence Hunting, Ethnicity, and Economic Adaptation Among Young Adult Inuit Males. *Arctic* 48(1): 31–46.

Cuerrier, Alain, and Elders of Kangiqsujuaq
2011 *The Botanical Knowledge of the Inuit of Kangiqsujuaq, Nunavik.* Nunavik Publications, Avataq Cultural Institute, Montréal.

Cummins, Bryan D.
1992 *Attawapiskat Cree Land Tenure and Use, 1901–1989.* PhD dissertation, Department of Anthropology, McMaster University, Hamilton, Ontario.

Dall, William H.
1870 *Alaska and Its Resources.* Lee and Shepard, Boston.

Dowsley, Martha
2010 The Value of a Polar Bear: Evaluating the Role of a Multiple Use Resource in the Nunavut Mixed Economy. *Arctic Anthropology* 47(1): 39–56.
2015 Identity and the Evolving Relationship Between Inuit Women and the Land in the Eastern Canadian Arctic. *Polar Record* 51(260): 536–549.

Dowsley, Martha, Shari Gearheard, Noor Johnson, and Jocelyn Inksetter
2010 Should We Turn the Tent? Inuit Women and Climate Change. *Études/Inuit/Studies* 34(1): 151–165.

Dowsley, Martha, and Mitchell K. Taylor
2006 *Community Consultations with Qikiqtarjuaq, Clyde River and Pond Inlet on Management Concerns for the Baffin Bay Polar Bear Population: A Summary of Inuit Knowledge and Community Consultations.* Final Wildlife Report No. 2. Department of Environment, Government of Nunavut, Iqaluit.

Dowsley, Martha, and George W. Wenzel
2008 "The Time of the Most Polar Bears": A Co-management Conflict in Nunavut. *Arctic* 61(2): 77–89.

Ferguson, Michael A. D., Robert G. Williamson, and François Messier
1998 Inuit Knowledge of Long-Term Changes in a Population of Arctic Tundra Caribou. *Arctic* 51(3): 201–219.

Freeman, Milton M. R. (editor)
1976 *Inuit Land Use and Occupancy Project*, vol. 1, *Land Use and Occupancy.* Department of Indian and Northern Affairs, Ottawa.

Giffen, Naomi M.
1930 *The Roles of Men and Women in Eskimo Culture.* University of Chicago Publications in Anthropology, Chicago.

Gombay, Nicole
2005 Shifting Identities in a Shifting World: Food, Place, Community and the Politics of Scale in an Inuit Settlement. *Environment and Planning D: Society and Space* 23: 415–533.

2009 Sharing or Commoditising? A Discussion of Some of the Socio-Economic Implications of Nunavik's Hunter Support Program. *Polar Record* 45(233): 119–132.

Hall, Charles F.
1865 *Arctic Researches and Life Among the Eskimaux: Being a Narrative of an Expedition in Search of Sir John Franklin, in the Years of 1860, 1861, and 1862.* Harper and Bros., New York.

Hantzsch, Bernhard
1928 Contribution to the Knowledge of the Avifauna of North-Eastern Labrador. Translated by M. B. A. Anderson and R. M. Anderson. *Canadian Field-Naturalist* 42: 221–227. Originally published in German, 1908.

Hardin, Garrett
1968 The Tragedy of the Commons. *Science* 162(3859): 1243–1248.

Hawkes, Ernest W.
1916 *The Labrador Eskimo.* Government Printing Bureau, Ottawa.

Head, Lesley, and Jennifer Atchison
2009 Cultural Ecology: Emerging Human-Plant Geographies. *Progress in Human Geography* 32(2): 236–245.

Hill, Erica
2012 The Nonempirical Past: Enculturated Landscapes and Other-than-Human Persons in Southwest Alaska. *Arctic Anthropology* 49(2): 41–57.

Inksetter, Jocelyn B.
2012 *Women and Work: Analyzing the Mixed Economy in Qikiqtarjuaq, Nunavut.* Master's thesis, Department of Geography, Lakehead University, Thunder Bay, Ontario.

Jacobs, Peter
1986 Sustaining Landscapes: Sustaining Societies. *Landscape and Urban Planning* 13: 349–358.

Jones, Anore
2010 *Plants That We Eat: Nauriat Niginaqtuat.* University of Alaska Press, Fairbanks.

Kermoal, Nathalie, and Isabel Altamirano-Jiménez (editors)
2016 *Living on the Land: Indigenous Women's Understanding of Place.* Athabasca University Press, Edmonton.

Kuhnlein, Harriet V., and Nancy J. Turner
2009 *Traditional Plant Foods of Canadian Indigenous Peoples: Nutrition, Botany and Use.* Food and Nutrition in History and Anthropology Vol. 8. Gordon and Breach Publishers, Philadelphia.

Kuokkanen, Rauna
2011 Indigenous Economies, Theories of Subsistence, and Women: Exploring the Social Economy Model for Indigenous Governance. *American Indian Quarterly* 35(2): 215–240.

Langsdorff, Grigory H.
1814 *Voyages and Travels in Various Parts of the World During the Years 1803, 04, 05, 06, and 07,* Vol. 2. Henry Colburn, London.

Lee, Richard B., and Irven Devore (editors)
1969 *Man the Hunter.* Aldine, Chicago.

Luxemburg, Rosa
[1913] 1951 *The Accumulation of Capital.* Edited by W. Stark; translated by Agnes Schwarzschild. Routledge and Kegan Paul, London. Originally published as *Die Akkumulation des Kapitals: Ein Beitrag zur ökonomischen Erklärung des Imperialismus*

McDonald, Miriam, Lucassie Arragutainaq, and Zack Novalinga (editors)
1997 *Voices from the Bay: Traditional Ecological Knowledge of Inuit and Cree in the Hudson Bay Bioregion.* Canadian Arctic Resources Committee and the Environmental Committee of the Municipality of Sanikiluaq, Ottawa.

Michell, Herman J.
2009 Gathering Berries in Northern Contexts: A Woodlands Cree Metaphor for Community-Based Research. *Pimatisiwin: A Journal of Aboriginal and Indigenous Community Health* 7(1): 65–73.

Nelson, Edward W.
1899 *The Eskimo About Bering Strait.* Bureau of American Ethnology, 18th Annual Report, Part 1, 1896–1897. Government Printing Office, Washington, DC.

Norrgard, Chantel
2009 From Berries to Orchards: Tracing the History of Berry Picking and Economic Transformation Among Lake Superior Ojibwe. *American Indian Quarterly* 33(1): 33–61.

Nuttall, Mark
2001 Locality, Identity and Memory in South Greenland. *Études/Inuit/Studies* 25(1–2): 53–72.

Parlee, Brenda, Fikret Berkes, and Teetl'it Gwich'in Renewable Resources Council
2005 Health of the Land, Health of the People: A Case Study on Gwich'in Berry Harvesting in Northern Canada. *EcoHealth* 2(2): 127–137.
2006 Aboriginal Knowledge of Ecological Variability and Commons Management: A Case Study on Berry Harvesting from Northern Canada. *Human Ecology* 34(4): 515–528.

Pigford, Ashley-Ann, and Cynthia Zutter
2014 Reconstructing Historic Inuit Plant Use: An Exploratory Phytolith Analysis of Soapstone Vessel Residues. *Arctic Anthropology* 51(2): 81–96.

Porter, Robert P.
1893 *Report on the Population and Resources of Alaska at the Eleventh Census, 1890.* Government Printing Office, Washington, DC.

Pouta, Eija, Tuija Sievänen, and Marjo Neuvonen
2006 Recreational Wild Berry Picking in Finland: Reflection of a Rural Lifestyle. *Society and Natural Resources* 19: 285–304.

Pratt, Kenneth L.
1993 Legendary Birds in the Physical Landscape of the Yup'ik Eskimos. *Anthropology and Humanism* 18(1): 13–20.

1994 "They Never Ask the People": Native Views About the Nunivak Wilderness. In *Key Issues in Hunter-Gatherer Research*, edited by Ernest S. Burch Jr. and Linda J. Ellanna, pp. 333–356. Berg, Providence, Rhode Island.

Quintal-Marineau, Magalie
2017 The New Work Regime in Nunavut: A Gender Perspective. *Canadian Geographer* 61(3): 334–345.

Rasmussen, Knud
1929 *Intellectual Culture of the Hudson Bay Eskimos*. Gyldendal, Copenhagen.

Reed, Maureen G., and Shannon Christie
2009 Environmental Geography: We're Not Quite Home—Reviewing the Gender Gap. *Progress in Human Geography* 33(2): 246–255.

Richmond, Chantelle, Susan Jean Elliott, Ralph Matthews, and Brian Elliott
2005 The Political Ecology of Health: Perceptions of Environment, Economy, Health and Well-Being Among Namgis First Nation. *Health and Place* 11(4): 349–365.

Ryan, John C.
2011 Cultural Botany: Toward a Model of Transdisciplinary, Embodied and Poetic Research into Plants. *Nature and Culture* 6(2): 123–148.

Schneider, Lucien
1985 *Ulirnaisigutiit: An Inuktitut-English Dictionary of Northern Quebec, Labrador and Eastern Arctic Dialects*. Translated by Dermot Ronan F. Collis. Les Presses de l'Université Laval, Québec City.

Simard-Gagnon, Laurence
2013 *Vivre et manger le territoire: La gestion des petits fruits par les femmes inuites en context contemporain*. Master's thesis, Department of Geography, Laval University, Québec City.

Spalding, Alex, with Thomas Kusugaq
1998 *Inuktitut Dictionary: A Multi-dialectal Outline (with an Aivilingmiutaq Base)*. Nunavut Arctic College, Iqaluit.

Stairs, Arlene and George W. Wenzel
1992 "I am I and the Environment": Inuit Hunting, Community and Identity. *Journal of Indigenous Studies* 3(1): 1–12.

Sutton, Samuel K.
1912 *Among the Eskimos of Labrador*. J. B. Lippincott, Philadelphia.

Thalbitzer, William
1914 *Ethnographical Collections from East Greenland*. Meddelelser om Grønland No. 39. C. A. Reitzel, Copenhagen.

Todd, Zoe
2016 "This Is the Life": Women's Role in Food Provisioning in Paulatuuq, Northwest Territories. In *Living on the Land: Indigenous Women's Understanding of Place*, edited by Nathalie Kermoal and Isabel Altamirano-Jiménez, pp. 191–212. Athabasca University Press, Edmonton.

Trusler, Scott, and Leslie M. Johnson
2008 "Berry Patch" as a Kind of Place—the Ethnoecology of Black Huckleberry in Northwestern Canada. *Human Ecology* 36: 553–568.

United Nations
2007 *United Nations Declaration on the Rights of Indigenous Peoples*. UN Document A/RES/61/295. United Nations, New York. https://www.un.org/development/desa/indigenouspeoples/wp-content/uploads/sites/19/2018/11/UNDRIP_E_web.pdf.

Wein, Eleanor E., Milton M. R. Freeman, and Jeanette C. Makus
1996 Use of and Preference for Traditional Foods Among the Belcher Island Inuit. *Arctic* 49(3): 256–264.

Wenzel, George W.
1991 *Animal Rights, Human Rights: Ecology, Economy and Ideology in the Canadian Arctic*. University of Toronto Press, Toronto.

Whitecloud, Simone S., and Lenore A. Grenoble
2014 An Interdisciplinary Approach to Documenting Knowledge: Plants and Their Uses in Southern Greenland. *Arctic* 67(1): 57–70.

Whymper, Frederick
1869 *Russian America or "Alaska": The Natives of the Youkon River and Adjacent Country*. Transactions of the Ethnological Society of London Vol 7. John Murray, London.

York, Jordan, Martha Dowsley, Adam Cornwell, Miroslaw Kuc, and Mitchell Taylor
2016 Demographic and Traditional Knowledge Perspectives on the Current Status of Canadian Polar Bear Subpopulations. *Ecology and Evolution* 6(9): 2897–2924.

Ziegler, Anna, Aalasi Joamie, and Rebecca Hainnu
2009 *Walking with Aalasi: An Introduction to Edible and Medicinal Arctic Plants*. Inhabit Media, Iqaluit.

PART TWO
FORCES OF CHANGE

APAY'U MOORE

PERSPECTIVE

But who am I? This question has been a part of me since I have known how to feel. In so many ways, society has given the burden of anxiety to many, like myself, who look one way but only know another. The twists of fate and random acts of life bringing new generations into the world. The impacts of colonialism and damning of identity. From people who knew the land as an extension of themselves, my living spirit was transformed by death from being a connected part of the world to being reborn and watching it and feeling from a distance, knowing that the wilderness is a part of me, but not knowing how to fully connect myself again to the land.

FACING PAGE *Our Way of Life*, acrylic on canvas, by Yup'ik artist Apay'u Moore of Aleknagik, Alaska, 2015. Courtesy of Apay'u Moore.

As a mother, I'd relate it to the feeling of having my first child. She came from my body, I felt her in me as a part of me, I knew she existed through me, but when she emerged from my body, I felt like I needed to ask someone if I could touch her. The emotions that swarm around that injustice, understanding that it shouldn't be like that, but it is, and for reasons that don't present themselves without strenuous and dedicated periods of thought that eventually lead to the realization of how history brings us to our present-day realities. I felt like I needed to ask authority figures in the hospital if I, the lesser being, was worthy enough to touch a newborn in their society.

Fortunately, my ancestral spirit lives hungry inside of me and my heart hears the voice within telling me to do the right thing. To be Yup'ik. My birth certificate lacks the name of a father. My mother is a beautiful Yup'ik woman. She brought me home—stamped with the physical appearance of a *kass'aq*, a white person—to a village with under a hundred residents, predominantly Yup'ik. I was given a Yup'ik name, and I heard the language of our people. It planted foundational seeds in my infant ears, and my heart spread out roots that grew into every soul that said my Yup'ik name, reminding me that, despite my looks, I was *Apay'uq*, my grandpa's fishing partner and my grandma's uncle, a Yup'ik man with a sense of humour and charisma who won the hearts of all he teased. I got his teasing back tenfold as a child! Some might call it karma. But that karma was of the best kind.

Eventually, I won the heart of a commercial fisherman, whom I call dad. I think it was a partnership that was planned out by *Apay'uq*. My dad couldn't stay away from the water and had me back out on the boat by the time I was four. Along with a dad came five older sisters and, after that, two younger brothers. This family has tested me and loved me, and it has encouraged in me even more dedication to be true to *Apay'uq*.

When I would return to Twin Hills in the summers with my mom's family, I'd embrace the constant reminders that I was a person of the land. That I had years of fishing experience and hunting stories. My humour was the most memorable part of me, and to this day everyone who knew *Apay'uq* gives me a huge familial smile, like they know a good story and a part of me that I have yet to learn about. My grandma reminds me that I tease her, just like he did. Those smiles and reminders are enough to push me forward in my search to know more about me and what I'm capable of giving to our future generations.

In a way, it's like the lifetime of teasing that *Apay'uq* dished out was preparing his white-looking, female self to be ready for all the comments and comebacks. This new world has not always been kind, but I know for a fact that because our Yup'ik people always treated me like him, I was better prepared for my new role in our society as a white-looking Yup'ik woman. Joke's on you now, male *Apay'uq!* We have the craziest minority stereotypes: bastard, white-looking female who is actually a Native person. In this irony, humour is all we've got.

Today, I am navigating and finding my way as I learn to reattach to our ancestral ways. I purposely make my life less convenient by Western standards, with the understanding that well-being isn't about having to do as little movement as possible in a day through the conveniences of power buttons. *Apay'uq* wasn't a cheerful man because he did less—he was full of character because he did more. I planted myself in Aleknagik, a village on the shores of Aleknagik Lake that feeds into the Wood River. Salmon fill the river and the surrounding lakes and creeks in the summer, and each season I thrive, experiencing a little bit more out there in the wilderness, connecting my soul to where it belongs and creating a pathway to ease my children into where they belong.

With the aspiration to live more in the Yup'ik way of life, and being right here, where each year I'm doing a little bit more, I feel all those times that *Apay'uq* made people feel vulnerable through teasing when I reach out to ask something that would be common sense to other Yup'ik people. As I learn how to do the simplest subsistence tasks and need to ask, "Where do I tie this string?" or "How do I cut this fish?" or "How long do I boil this meat?" I get those funny looks that say, "How do you not know this?" and feel a little embarrassed and need to chuckle and tease my inner self: "See this? Look, you should have teased less, *Apay'uq!*"

Despite the occasional embarrassment, my heart relishes the triumphs of facing these moments through the insecurity of being Yup'ik but looking like a white woman, wanting to bring out the Yup'ik namesake who is bursting to do what he loved again. I want to go fishing and share my catch; I want to go hunting and share my catch; I want to go hunting and fail because we had some disaster that ended in laughter and a good story; I want to be at the side of the river, listening to the bugs and the swift push of water trickling over rocks in small creeks; I want to breathe in the sweet smell of tundra tea as I fill my berry bucket. My list of things that I know that I miss without quite knowing how that is even possible goes on and on. Commercial fishing—this is perhaps one of the things I miss the most, along with drinking a hot cup of cowboy coffee and speaking my own language, cackling while sharing stories. I miss my grandpa, who in my early years called me his "pard'na." My tongue waits in anticipation to sing out phrases fluently, and prematurely my heart sputters in this moment with the knowledge of how great that will be, and what weight will be lifted from my chest when I burst out phrases with full confidence that I am Yup'ik.

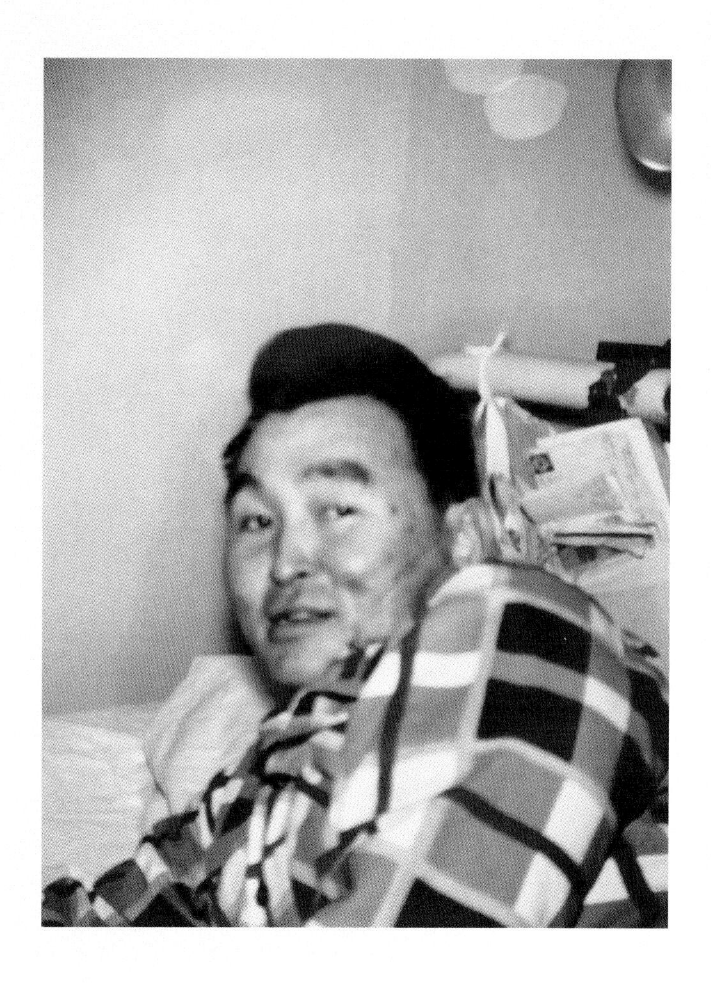

FACING View of the Peace River where it flows into Lake Beverley. Wood-Tikchik State Park, Alaska, 2012. Photograph by Tim Troll.

ABOVE *Apay'uq* (Adolph Bavilla), ca. 1975. Photographer unknown. Courtesy of Mary Bavilla.

FIGURE 5.1 Kangersuatsiaq, in the Upernavik district of northwest Greenland, May 2017. Photograph by Mark Nuttall.

MARK NUTTALL

5 Places of Memory, Anticipation, and Agitation in Northwest Greenland

Climate change, contaminants, and globalization pose significant threats to the resilience of circumpolar ecosystems, landscapes, waters, icescapes, animal habitat, societies, and cultures. The melting geographies of the Arctic are apparent through retreating glacial ice, the thinning and loss of sea ice, thawing permafrost, and changes to the migration routes and population sizes of animals and fish. Extractive industries are also increasingly active in exploration and production across the Arctic, while the disappearance of sea ice allows for the possibility for new shipping lanes in northern waters previously thought inaccessible.

The Arctic is also being made and remade through narratives animated by a scientific and environmental vernacular expressing the fragility, the precariousness, and the instability of an exceptional region and the loss of its wildlife and ecosystems. This vernacular has a long use in ecological research (see, for example, Dunbar 1973), but there is a greater urgency expressed by scientists, conservationists, and environmentalists today in how the sense of precarity, and the warnings stemming from the research on tipping points, must inform the shaping of regional and global approaches to protecting the Arctic (see Wadhams 2017). Animals such as polar bears, narwhals, and caribou, along with such phenomena as sea ice, glaciers, warming waters, coastal erosion, and permafrost, enter into international discourses that position them as indicators of biodiversity loss, environmental change, and the future health of the cryosphere.

Politically, economically, and in a cultural sense, a new global Arctic is said to be emerging. New geographies and new forms of society are taking shape, alongside disappearing icescapes, topographic transformations, and rapidly changing Indigenous and local communities. However, discussion about economic opportunities is tinged with recognition of the possibility that things that define the high latitudes of the planet (such as snow, ice, iconic polar wildlife) may be absent from the region in the near future. This recognition becomes a vital aspect of how ice, animals, and landscapes are represented as threatened and disappearing in global imaginaries about melt in the North, and how those places may look when ice, polar bears, and other charismatic species—sentinels of the global climate crisis—are no longer there (Dodds and Nuttall 2016).

Little of this concern with disappearance and transformation, or over the future of a region that would be characterized by the absence of the things that have until now seemed to have defined it, is attentive, however, to the particularities of place (and what constitutes places) or to what the absence of ice, animals, or the loss of livelihoods means for people who live in small, often remote Arctic communities, or even to how absence is a central aspect of how people think of human-environment relations, rather than something with which they are suddenly confronted as a result of rapid change. Nor is it sufficiently interrogative of the nature of social and economic change and the impacts and legacies of colonialism on Indigenous lives, bodies, and places that predate current observed trends in climate change and global processes.

In this chapter, I draw from recent research in the Upernavik and Melville Bay area of northwest Greenland (see figure 5.2) concerned with the effects of shifting and thinning ice, the nature of changing social worlds, oil exploration, and seismic surveys on people's lives. I consider some of the ways local people often think of and talk about their surroundings and how they relate to them, their encounters with the non-human things that fill these surroundings, the nature of anticipatory experience, and how absence figures in everyday life. In doing so, I point to the need for greater awareness and understanding of Indigenous ontologies that challenge scientific categorizations of the changing physical states of the Arctic and how those changes are usually framed in the language of melt, tipping points, and disappearance (Nuttall 2019).

As Mikkel Bille, Frida Hastrup, and Tim Sørensen (2010, 4) argue, "absences are cultural, physical and social phenomena that powerfully influence people's conceptualizations of themselves and the world they engage with." People in the Upernavik area are certainly not unconcerned about climate change and its effects, or about disappearing ice, and they have worries about economic conditions and circumstances now and in the future. But they do not necessarily talk about their surroundings in terms that convey a sense of fragility or vulnerability in the same way as the dominant "melting ice" narrative. Rather, a vernacular concerned with hunting, fishing,

FIGURE 5.2 Upernavik and northwest Greenland. Source: Data from Howat, Negrete, and Smith 2014.

and travel in the ever-changing surroundings that people experience expresses an awareness of fluidity, flexibility, and anticipation. This orientates people to living in a world of intentionality, action, agency, twists and turns, imagination, possibility, and choice; but it is also about being doubtful, unsure, uncertain, fearful, anxious, and apprehensive (Nuttall 2010). However, memories of lifestyles seemingly now gone, of family and friends who have died or moved away from the district, of places no longer visited or used, or of animals that are harder to find and hunt, coupled with a sense of both absence and loss, also run through the conversations I have with many people about the kinds of social, economic, and environmental changes they observe and experience, how they feel about seasonal, temporary, or permanent movement from their communities, and how they live in a world of movement and surprise.

Place, Agitation, and the Making of Resource Spaces

About 2,800 people live in several small communities along a 450-kilometre stretch of the northwest coast of Kalaallit Nunaat, or Greenland, from the area close to the northern edges of Sigguup Nunaa (Svartenhuk) in the south to Qimusseriarsuaq (Melville Bay) in the northern part of Baffin Bay. This is an archipelago of headlands, fjords, channels, and islands that constituted the municipality of Upernavik until January 2009, when a new regional governance structure realigned and reduced the number of Greenland's municipalities from eighteen to four. The municipality of Upernavik became part of the larger (indeed, the world's largest) administrative region of Qaasuitsup Kommunia, which also included the northernmost settlements in the Qaanaaq area and extended into Greenland's coastal stretches along Nares Strait. Ilulissat, in Disko Bay, became its administrative centre. In January 2018, Qaasuitsup was itself reorganized. Most of it, now known as Avannaata Kommunia, comprises the northern parts, including Upernavik, while the southern region became Qeqertalik Kommunia. Avannaata's administrative headquarters remain located at Ilulissat. Despite this restructuring, and a centralization of decision making away from Upernavik, the area retains a distinct identity as a separate district, a place local people often feel is far removed from Ilulissat and even further from Nuuk, Greenland's ever-growing capital. Indeed, I often hear talk of how the region and people's daily lives appear peripheral and distant to politicians and decision makers in these more southerly centres. Many people feel frustrated by bureaucratic procedures and by the fact that it often takes considerable time for local interests and concerns to be dealt with—if they are addressed at all—by the municipal authorities in Ilulissat.

Identity is not always contingent on or constituted by location, of course, but place matters to people in the Upernavik area, as it does in other parts of Greenland (see Nuttall 2001), with many exhibiting a powerful attachment to their localities. Livelihoods and household economies are based mainly on fishing and hunting, primarily for seals, narwhals, beluga, walrus, polar bears, and several species of whale, and the significance of this is reflected in the fact that Upernavik retains a status as its own resource-management district (called *aqutsiverqarfik* in Greenlandic), with hunting and fishing quotas allocated according to the boundaries of the old Upernavik municipality. Most of the decisions about quotas, however, are made in government departments in Nuuk, and are based on scientific stock assessments. Much of what is caught is used for household consumption, but fish such as Greenland halibut and cod, as well as some marine mammal products, find their way into and around local, regional, and national distribution channels.

As Tim Ingold (2000, 42) remarks, people become immersed in places and landscapes in an "active, practical and perceptual engagement with the constituents of the dwelt-in world." In the Upernavik region, local knowledge of the places in which hunting and fishing activities occur is rich and deep. Those places are suffused with memories of events, activities, and actions that occur and unfold through the entanglements and trajectories of the human and non-human. There are strong networks of kinship and close social relatedness throughout the district, expressed most markedly in the practice of naming people after the deceased and the use of namesake and kin terms. A distinctive regional dialect of Greenlandic—which can often confuse visitors from southern Greenland—adds to the sense that Upernavik is a place apart. The town of Upernavik has a population of around 1,100, and some 1,700 people inhabit nine smaller villages, ranging in size from about fifty people, in Naajaat, to 450, in Kullorsuaq. Upernavik town remains an administrative and supply centre for the villages, and a number of public sector services and private businesses provide some employment. I have come to know the area through anthropological fieldwork, beginning with my first sojourn there in the late 1980s (see Nuttall 1992). I maintain friendships in the district; have followed the transitions in the local economy from marine mammal hunting to fishing for Greenland halibut; have been kept informed of people's movements in and around, as well as from, the district (often to Nuuk); and have worked in recent years with local people and scientists to understand the effects of the changes that are happening to sea ice as well as their perspectives on oil exploration in Baffin Bay and mineral prospecting elsewhere in northern Greenland.

The construction of an airport at Upernavik town in the early 2000s has meant a regular Air Greenland Dash-8 flight from Ilulissat, if weather permits, allows easier access to places further south—yet "regular" means once or twice a week, depending on the season (the flight takes around seventy minutes and the aircraft often continues to Qaanaaq before returning to Ilulissat via Upernavik). Air Greenland also connects most of the settlements to the town with a weekly Bell 212 helicopter service (although winter darkness halts it for a few weeks and the service is cancelled when there is poor visibility or strong winds), while a Royal Arctic Line ship brings supplies in containers from Denmark via Nuuk during summer and autumn, when the coastal waters are ice-free.

Sea ice is present for several months of the year but is forming later in the winter and, in many places along the coast, is not always as firm and fast as it should be to allow for travel on it. Over the past twenty years or so, the spring sea ice breakup has also been happening progressively earlier in the season, a trend that makes hunting and fishing

by dog sled precarious when the ice is not solid and yet still covers large stretches of water; by the same token, travel between communities by open boat is tenuous during this time, as the ice that lingers during the early weeks of open water hinders mobility. Less ice, though, means the ship can arrive with much-needed freight a few weeks earlier than in previous years (by late winter and early spring, supplies run low in the stores in the town and surrounding villages). The open-water season around the town is now from around early/mid-May to early November, although sea ice can remain in the bays, channels and fjords, often blocking access to and from the villages until mid-June. The rest of Greenland—and the wider world—may seem somewhat closer than was the case twenty or thirty years ago, but weather and ice still disrupt and upset air schedules and delay coastal travel by boat or ship. Upernavik is situated on a small island, with the airport constructed on its highest point (which required the levelling of the mountaintop). Flights are frequently cancelled because of winter storms, late spring or early summer snowfall, or the seemingly persistent low cloud cover and fog

FIGURE 5.3 Hunters and fishers rely on sea ice during winter and spring, but the ice is changing quickly. Melville Bay, near Savissivik, March 2015. Photograph by Mark Nuttall.

that obscures the runway during summer and autumn. Travellers taking the Dash-8 service to and from Upernavik must be prepared to wait in either Ilulissat or Upernavik for several days.

In northwest Greenland, flexibility in settlement patterns, resource use practices, and in the ways people organize their social lives has enabled hunting societies to live from coastal resources (as well as hunting and gathering some terrestrial resources) for the past 4,500 years. When I first went to the Upernavik district in spring 1987, hunting—for different species of seals throughout the year and for other marine mammals seasonally—was the mainstay of the economy of the town and the settlements, as it had been for generations. Community life, kinship and close social association, patterns of sharing meat and fish, and human-environment relations were all bound up with an annual seasonal round of hunting and fishing activities, of travel on the sea ice by dog sled in winter and spring (figure 5.3) and by boat though the inner fjords and around the dense pattern of islands in summer and autumn (Nuttall 1992).

But the area was beginning to undergo a transition to small-scale fishing for Greenland halibut in a more intensive and commercial way, an activity that would gradually erode the importance of hunting for some households or replace it altogether. Anti-sealing campaigns by Europe- and North American–based animal-rights groups and environmentalist organizations had done considerable damage to markets for seal skins and other products from the hunt, denying households much of their income. A small-scale commercial fishery was viewed by many people as a way to earn money instead, but the municipal authorities also saw fishing as a way of improving living conditions and raising people's economic prospects. The coastal halibut fishery was highlighted as central to the district's development strategy, and fishing today takes place mainly within the area around the Upernavik Icefjord and the Giesecke Icefjord (known locally as Gulteqarffik, "the Place of Gold," on account of its richness as a fishing ground), as well as around the northern settlements of Nuussuaq and Kullorsuaq.

Oil exploration has also taken place in recent years, and around a decade ago there was some excitement in the town (mainly on the part of municipal authorities and some local entrepreneurs) at the prospect that Upernavik would transition into a base for the oil industry on northern Greenland's new resource frontier. With no trace of oil found, companies then focused their attention instead on exploration in the waters off northeast Greenland. Local perspectives varied about the prospects of the seismic survey vessels or exploration ships returning to northern Baffin Bay. As one local entrepreneur (who provides survey, construction, logistical, and lodging services) put it to me in the spring of 2017, "I really had hopes that oil development would happen here in Upernavik. It would have been good for the town and the district, and the exploration had already been good for my business when the ships and the companies were here. But oil prices are so low now that I don't think there will ever be any development happening out at sea." In July 2021, Greenland's new coalition government (formed after a snap election three months' earlier) suspended the award of new offshore exploration licences.

Hydrocarbon exploration may be on hold at the moment, but the development of mining projects remains a key part of the economic policies of Greenland's self-rule government. A ruby mine opened near Qerqertarsuatsiaat in southwest Greenland in May 2017 and the government's minerals agencies and regulatory authorities for extractive industries expect more mining projects to proceed to the development phase in the next few years. In Greenland's most northerly regions, mining companies are also engaged in prospecting and are developing plans for a number of projects (a large zinc-lead mine in Citronen Fjord near the northern coast edging the Arctic Ocean and situated in the vast Northeast Greenland National Park, the world's largest national park) has been given approval by the mineral licensing authorities in Nuuk, and an impact benefit agreement aims to ensure employment opportunities for Greenlanders in the project.

Yet, while exploratory activity related to mining seems to offer some people hope for economic benefits, it makes many others in the Upernavik and Melville Bay area anxious. Their concerns are informed by what they remember about extensive seismic surveys carried out in 2012, when several companies combined efforts for the most intensive exploration for oil ever seen in Greenland, and in 2013, when Shell conducted a series of seismic site surveys, some of which overlapped with a narwhal protection zone in Melville Bay. There are two populations of narwhals that spend the summer in northwest Greenland: one in Kangerlussuaq (Inglefield Bredning), in the Qaanaaq area (estimated at over 8,000 narwhals), the other in Melville Bay (estimated at around 6,000 narwhals). There is a hunting quota of around 80 narwhals per year in Melville Bay, most of which are hunted during the open-water season from August to September. This is the same period when seismic activities were operating in the area. Following the surveys in 2012 and 2013, hunters from communities in the Upernavik district, as well as from Savissivik, in the northwestern corner of Melville Bay, reported that narwhal behaviour was different, with some feeling that the hunt had been influenced negatively by the seismic activities in the area (Nuttall 2016).

Narwhals are acutely sensitive to anthropogenic activities, and especially to the noise generated by them, so the high-energy air gun pulses used in marine seismic surveys are of concern to marine biologists, hunters, and environmentalists (Greenpeace, for instance, has been especially active in campaigning against seismic activities in the Arctic). They argue that long-term monitoring is necessary to determine the potential impacts, not just from resource exploration but from increased shipping. For a couple of years, starting in 2014, together with colleagues from the Greenland Climate Research Centre in Nuuk and community partners in northwest Greenland, I was concerned with identifying and understanding some of these effects and worked to contribute to a process of community-based monitoring.

Environmental impact assessments that were carried out in advance of the exploratory campaigns suggested there would be little disturbance from the seismic surveys. The reports from marine mammal observers onboard the vessels concluded that this was so during the sailings. However, local observations from hunters throughout Upernavik and the Melville Bay area indicated soon after that narwhals were increasingly restless and disturbed, moved closer to the coast, and swam deeper into ice-choked fjords and inlets (which increases the risk of ice entrapment for narwhals when the sea eventually freezes in autumn or early winter). While environmental changes in the marine ecosystem, such as thinning and declining sea ice, changing water temperatures, and changes in the migration and distribution of fish, also play their part and likely affect and influence narwhal movement, hunters felt that narwhals were not *agitated* by such changes alone. They did say, though, that the seismic surveys *pikitsippaa* the narwhals (*pikitsisivoq* means something makes someone or an animal alarmed, restless, or agitated). There are other words for different kinds of restlessness and agitation, and hunters used these to describe narwhal behaviour and movement since the seismic surveys were conducted. *Katsungaarpoq*, for instance, refers to narwhals being restless, agitated, and in a hurry (the opposite, *katsorpoq*, is to feel an inner calm and peace). Some narwhals, by contrast, have been described as *eqqissinngilaq*, which refers to an absence of inner peace. And hunters also observe that narwhals are sometimes confused or perplexed because they are frightened of something (*uisanguserpoq*).

For hunters, northern waters have become—in the way Anderson and Wylie (2009) describe in their discussion of turbulent materialities—places of agitation and disruption. This seems to have coincided not just with seismic surveys and increased marine traffic, but with recent warming trends. Places on land and sea can themselves be agitated, just as marine mammals and fish are. Sea ice, for example, can break off and suddenly go adrift because it is agitated and surprised (*siku uippoq*; *uippoq* has the meaning of surprise or fright). Hunters say that following the seismic activities, they also noticed this happening more in areas close to the coast, where there was still fast shore ice, but that the ice was breaking off and going adrift in winter more often. The Greenlandic name for the North Water Polynya between northwest Greenland and Arctic Canada is Pikialasorsuaq, "the Great Upwelling." This refers, in a sense, to a different kind of agitation, to how the mixing of water currents results in the upwelling of nutrients and so producing the attractive conditions and feeding opportunities favourable to marine mammals, fish, and birds (*pikialavoq* and *pikialaarpoq* mean "to well out," *pikippoq* means to be restless or to jump up, *pikiarpoq* means a bird "dives out of the water," while *pikiarsaarpoq* means a seal "dives out of the water"). In areas in northern Upernavik district and in Melville Bay, though, birds and seals were observed by hunters as "diving out of the water" with greater restlessness for three or four years since the seismic activities took place.

The kinds of concerns people in the coastal Northwest express over what they see as agitated waters, sea ice that is surprised, and marine mammals that are anxious in relation to seismic surveys are consistent with how mining activities and oil exploration, involving intensive seismic surveys and subsurface mappings, and large-scale industrial development plans such as hydropower and aluminum smelter projects, have provoked considerable, and often fraught, political and social debates throughout Greenland. At the same time, these debates have revealed a diverse array of political, economic, and cultural perspectives describing what the environment and resources mean to the country and its economic, political, and cultural future at a time of increased assertions of Indigenous sovereignty and processes of state formation. Concerns are routinely expressed by local people, grassroots organizations, and environmental groups anxious and agitated about threats to community viability and human health, as well as to wildlife and indeed entire ecosystems, from oil development and the extraction of iron, gold, rare earths, and, in the case of possible uranium mining in South Greenland, about an imagined future of biohazards, contaminated landscapes and coastal waters, and generalized environmental ruin.

These different ideas concerning places and resources are common features of discourses about resource frontiers in other parts of the world, and they are consistent with what Anthony Bebbington, Nicholas Cuba, and John Rohan (2014) see as a phenomenon of "overlapping geographies" associated with the expansion and intensive development of extractive industries. They point to this notion of overlapping geographies as involving different ideas about who should access, use, and occupy particular spaces, who should govern and control what goes on in those spaces, how resources should be extracted, and who should benefit from such development. In recent writing, I have argued that assumptions about landscapes and waters as empty spaces devoid of any kind of social and cultural significance, as well as their economic importance for local communities—to be marked off and defined as resource spaces and sacrifice zones important for economic development and state formation—are apparent in the ways extractive industries approach working in Greenland, as well as in the fact that government authorities are ready to grant exploration and development licences without a deep appreciation of the meaning of place (Nuttall 2017). The planning for extractive industries involves a range of very specific economic, volumetric, and stratigraphic procedures and practices concerning landscapes, coastal waters, and the Greenlandic underlands that are used to define, demarcate, lay claim to, and regulate and govern particular places as resource spaces—remote hinterlands viewed as being at the edge of human society—rather than recognize them as lively worlds of past and present Inuit societies in which astonishing encounters between the human and more-than-human occur.

Anticipation and Becoming

I have also written previously about how people in the Upernavik area see their surroundings as places of becoming and movement (Nuttall 2009, 2017). Hunting and fishing not only require skill, technique, know-how, resourcefulness, equipment and technology, as well as a little bit of luck at times; such occupations also demand of the hunter and fisher a willingness to be ready at all times in this world of constant surprise and continual shifts and turns (Nuttall 2010). Taking nothing for granted—especially the weather, the sea, and the ice—daily life needs to be attuned to the vagaries of the weather, to the seasonal migrations and local availability of marine mammals and fish, or to the power of the sea and the formation, permutations, and fickleness of sea ice, and to the possibilities of animals being anxious or disturbed by something unsettling (animals can also be unsettled by the wrong kind of hunter, one who lacks knowledge and skill). But it is also informed by the ways people relate to one another, how they encounter and anticipate change, and how they think about the possibilities of engagement with their surroundings and the non-human (including not just the animals that people hunt and the fish they entice from the water, but the sled dogs they rely on for transportation and hunting partnerships). Hunting and fishing require an ability to sense and imagine what may be there, but also what may be absent. Being ready means anticipating what the weather could be like and the prospects for a successful hunt, for instance, or the likelihood of experiencing ice that is suddenly cut up by the current (*aakarneq*), but also being prepared for the absence of things and for places to no longer contain the essence of animals. Seals, perhaps, may not be in places one might expect, or muskox and reindeer may have moved to other parts of the landscape, or, as I have described, narwhals may be found closer to the coast in agitated and restless states.

Recent anthropological approaches to anticipation seek to understand it in terms of lived experience (for examples, see Bryant and Knight 2019; Stephan and Flaherty 2019), privileging its experiential nature rather than seeing it only in terms of speculation, prediction, or forecast. Similarly, I think of anticipation in Greenlandic hunting communities less as being bound up with future-making and adaptation, and more as a way of moving within the world, experiencing, encountering, and engaging with one's surroundings, and thinking through and experimenting with the possibilities of social relatedness, not just with other people, but with the more-than-human too. Anticipation is as much about the lived moment as it is about an immediate, near, or distant future. In Greenlandic, anticipation may be rendered as either *isumalluarneq* or *ilimasunneq*, which have "thought"/"reason" (*isuma*) and "expect" (*ilima*) as their roots. *Ilimasunneq* conveys a sense of not only "anticipation" and "expectation" for things (especially animals and fish), which may be there, but also "feeling" and "clue." Hunters express this in a number of other ways as well. For example, *ilimagaa* means "to expect something," while *neriugaa* means "to hope for, or be hopeful of something." Anticipation also, but not always, involves a measure of uncertainty, anxiety, nervousness, fear, and disappointment, as well as agitation; *ilimasuppoq*, for instance, can mean that one expects something fearful, does not feel safe, or senses or feels danger (*ilimatsappoq* is to be in a constant state of anxious expectation; for example, if a hunter is on the lookout for polar bears, but it also means an awareness of danger—of headland cracks suddenly opening up when travelling on sea ice, or of the possibility of a walrus rising up from the water and capsizing a boat). Hunters set out on the ice in winter with their sled dogs or go out to sea in summer in small boats with the hope, expectation even, of returning home with seals (they may say they are expecting something good to come from the hunt when they set out from home—*ilimasuarnarpoq*), while anticipating that they may not catch anything at all. One can be hopeful (*neriugaa*) or anxious and fearful, especially of bad weather (*aarleraa*).

When I first went out hunting with people from Kangersuatsiaq in the late 1980s, I was taught the importance of being prepared for the surprise of seeing the unexpected, the real, the imagined, or the spectral (*aliortorpoq*) when at sea, on the ice, or walking on the land. There is a word—*puisaarpoq*—for something that appears to be present but that can turn out to be nothing at all; something, a shape, a moving figure, or an animal itself may appear to be there, ahead in the water, or on land, but suddenly disappear. (As an aside, and related to *puisaarpoq*, the generic word for seal is *puisi*, which means, in one sense, "raises its head out of the water.") A hunter may see what he thinks is a seal or narwhal—quite clearly—but it may turn out to be nothing. Stories are frequently told of hunters seeing a kayak, a boat, or a dog sled, or people moving in the landscape, or of campsites ahead in a valley or close to the shore, only for these images to disappear suddenly when the hunter approaches (*puisaartitsivoq*). They may be residual memories—or traces and glimmers of the essence—of the people and animals that inhabited the landscape and moved through the coastal waters in previous times, or they may be ghosts, other non-human entities such as beings and creatures that live underground, or visions, or they may occur because of a playful light or a trick of the eye. When one is certain a seal, narwhal, or whale has been spotted, but it disappears below the surface of the water or behind waves so that it is no longer visible, then one would describe this as *qapangippoq* rather than *puisaarpoq*. *Qappivoq* means to disappear below the water, or for the sea to close above and over something; *qapivaa* means to lose sight of something because it has disappeared below a wave or below the horizon (*qapittarpoq* means something disappears frequently from view because of waves in a rough sea). This is quite different from the experience of *puisaartitsivoq*, when something you think you can see in front of you—in the water, up on a ridge, in a dip between the mountains—suddenly disappears. Indeed, being prepared for uncertainty, disappointment, and failure (in other words, anticipating this possibility and expecting to be anxious, in terms, say, of not feeling safe—*ilimasuppoq*), or for not finding what you may think is there, or that you think you see, and to recognize and acknowledge that animals are elusive, and being aware of the unseen and that things may not be what they seem or appear, is a hallmark of successful adaptation to one's surroundings and engagement with a more-than-human world in which the spatial and temporal converge and blur (Nuttall 2010, 25–26).

People in northwest Greenland have met with and responded to environmental, economic, and social change at many times in the past, but they have also anticipated possibilities and economic opportunities, seeking out, discovering, and exploring places to hunt and fish, and creating new seasonal camps and more permanent settlements in which to live and raise families (Nuttall 2010; Petersen 2003). In the mid- to late twentieth century, many places were established, abandoned, resettled, and abandoned again for various reasons, although some are still used seasonally, and place names indicate and are suggestive of what is at those places, or what one may expect to find there, such as good hunting and fishing opportunities; occasionally they also hint at what—and who—was once there and trigger memories of people, genealogies, occasions, and events, as well as spectral figures and shadows that haunt the landscape. Even the traces of the things one may have thought were there, but which suddenly disappeared, remain present in the stories told about these happenings.

Throughout the year, people move between their home settlements and spring, summer, and autumn camps, or move to other communities for the winter to take advantage of the Greenland halibut fishery. People travel regularly and extensively, whether to hunt and fish, to visit relatives, to shop in Upernavik, or to spend time living seasonally in other villages or in camps. As fishing for Greenland halibut is the mainstay of the household and the regional economy, people often travel between specific places and points. Fishers must locate themselves near the best fishing grounds, often spending several months of the year away from their home communities. Movement between places is also a matter of capacity in the fishing industry. Most villages have fish landing and freezing facilities owned by Royal Greenland, a Greenland government–owned company focused on fishing and fish processing, but communities such as Naajaat and Kangersuatsiaq do not (the facility in Kangersuatsiaq closed in 2011, which I discuss in more detail below), meaning fishers must travel to places such as Kullorsuaq, Nuussuaq, Nutaarmiut, Innaarsuit, and Tasiusaq in the more northerly parts of the district to fish and land their catch. Some even make a more or less permanent move to those communities, settling there because of the better possibilities for fishing and selling the Greenland halibut they pull out of the water on longlines. Much fishing is also done for the household and for wider community sharing. From May onward, fishing camps (which become centres of family activity, as well as places of procurement for household consumption and sale) are established in the southern and central parts of the district. Arctic char and Greenland halibut are caught, then prepared, dried, or smoked at the camps; cod are boiled and eaten as soon as they are caught, or dried for later, Atlantic wolfish are consumed with relish, while fjord cod are caught for dog food (plentiful supplies are needed for autumn and winter).

Sea ice (*siku*) remains central to how people arrange and configure their lives for several months of the year, yet even before climate change became a local concern, people have always had to be attentive to how *siku*'s apparently solid nature, its thickness, fixity, and fastness, cannot and should not be taken for granted. Today, however, anticipatory knowledge is challenged by changes to sea ice cover. The flexibility that has been characteristic of life along the coast is reduced—yet a hunter's openness to uncertainty, to movement, to presence and absence, and knowing and appreciating that the world is full of surprise, means a life characterized by anticipation goes a considerable way to helping meet this challenge (see also Hastrup 2016). People are increasingly encountering difficulties in gaining access to hunting and fishing places (as well as in travelling between communities) because of quite rapid and dramatic changes in sea ice cover and extreme weather conditions (figure 5.4). The sea still freezes (*sikornepoq*) in the Upernavik area during winter, but people say the cover of ice that forms on the sea is no longer all that solid (*sikorluppoq*), and *sikuaq* (thin ice), rather than *siku*, is a more common way of describing what now does form in many places, while *sikunnaq*, weather that promises a cover of ice, seems an increasingly rare occurrence in some months. Travel by dog sledge between some communities is also now almost impossible in winter, especially from the settlements to the town of Upernavik (Nuttall 2017).

FIGURE 5.4 Changing ice conditions mean that hunters have to venture further out into the swell during summer. Near Kangersuatsiaq, June 2015. Photograph by Mark Nuttall.

The consequences of a changing climate are noticeable throughout the district. Fjords and bays are filled with the detritus of ice from tidewater glaciers, and land is being revealed as those glaciers recede (often providing opportunities to establish new campsites and places for hunting and fishing—even as glacial ice disappears, places emerge, and local topographies are reshaped). Increased meltwater runoff from glacial fronts is affecting water temperature and circulation patterns as well as the formation of sea ice (Briner, Håkansson, and Bennike 2013). This has an influence on the distribution and availability of the marine mammals—the seals, walrus, narwhals, beluga, and whales—and the fish that hunters seek out. In summer and autumn, some seals have been moving further away from coastal waters with the shifting pack (and some hunters in the southern part of the district say that they noticed the absence of seals following the seismic activities that were carried out in Baffin Bay). The pack ice that remains also acts as a barrier for getting to and from the settlements. This makes it necessary for hunting forays and journeys between some communities to be made some distance from the coast, to get around the ice, into what hunters call *iluakkooq* (the swell) and even further out to sea where the swell is heavier (*iluakkoorpoq*). This adds a greater element of risk and danger to hunting and to travel at sea. The world around them may not be seen as fragile or vulnerable, as scientists and environmentalists might have it, but while people in the Upernavik district increasingly reflect upon it as a world that is changing, moving, turbulent, and precarious in ways it may not usually have been experienced, it is also one of absence.

Absence, Loss, and Memory

When they talk about changes in the weather and their surroundings, people will generally give the same accounts of thinning, patchy ice, or brittle ice (*sikulaaq*), and areas of open water where the surface of the sea no longer freezes (*sikujuippoq*). Certainly, this has been the trend recently, yet I was able to experience how the winter of 2015 brought good, solid ice throughout much of the district. Some hunters made journeys by dog sled from the central part of the district south to Upernavik town and to Kangersuatsiaq. Stories were told to young people that these trips lasting several days were like those both people and dogs were able to make "in the old days," invoking memories (and recalling photographs) of travel on sea ice in places many are no longer able to visit and experience in winter. But when people talk of "the old days" or "times in the past" (*qangarsuaq*), or situate their memories "in former times" or "in times gone by" (*itsaq*), this sense of temporality encompasses the 1980s and early 1990s as much as it does decades before, a relatively recent time before observations and experiences of the recent changes in climate and a transforming icescape indicated what was to become more usual.

In mid-February that winter, I experienced temperatures of around −35°C and saw a wide extent of ice cover throughout the district—extensive even around the town of Upernavik—during a helicopter flight from Upernavik to Kullorsuaq. Yet during the following winter, the ice was not so good again, and people were reminded that climate change was perhaps the new norm. People did not feel that the winter of 2015 had intimated a possible return to how the ice used to be. A friend from Kangersuatsiaq (which is located to the south of Upernavik town) told me he was fishing near the district's most southerly community of Upernavik Kujalleq on 21 December 2016; it was very cold, he said, and he was fishing and moving around the area in his boat in the mid-winter darkness, but there was no sea ice and he was able to take his catch by boat back to Upernavik. When the ice did form a few weeks later, it was almost gone by early March 2017, although when I travelled between Upernavik and Kangersuatsiaq by boat with him in May that year some of the fjords were still frozen and the ice extended a few kilometres from the coast. This was not good ice, though, people in the community said. They could not, for the most part, get out to the fjords during winter to fish by dog sled or snowmobile as the ice was not solid enough or had not formed at all in parts, while the hunting of seals by open boat was hindered by the moving pack. Places such as Salleq, an island to the north of Kangersuatsiaq, can no longer be reached in winter by dog sled, and the ice pack often makes it difficult even to get there by boat. For example, when I first lived in Kangersuatsiaq, in the late 1980s, Salleq was a key place for seal hunting in winter and spring, and Itilleq, a dip on the western point of the island, was an important crossing place for those travelling by dog sled. Yet the winter route across Itilleq has hardly been used since the early 2000s. In May 2017, I travelled out to Salleq by boat with friends, and we told stories of setting seal nets under the ice around the island, reminiscing about spending cold January days huddled around the stove in the hunters' hut on the island. People from Kangersuatsiaq now seldom come to Salleq in winter, they said, and they often pass it by during summer as well.

My first period of fieldwork in the Upernavik district was focused mainly on the social world of Kangersuatsiaq (see figure 5.1) and what people there thought about place and landscape and how they experienced human-environment relations. At that time, Kangersuatsiaq had a reputation in northern Greenland as a place with a young, hard-working, ambitious population. Like many other hunting communities in Greenland, though, as well as in the eastern Canadian Arctic, Kangersuatsiaq had been hit hard by the European ban on most seal skin products, following the successful campaigns run by anti-sealing and anti-trapping environmentalist and animal-rights groups. The sale of seal skins had provided the main source of income for most families. The experimental fishery for Greenland halibut was beginning and local people saw an opportunity to earn an income. The village prospered throughout the 1990s and early 2000s. Today, however, around one-third of the houses in Kangersuatsiaq are now empty as people have moved to Upernavik or to other communities over the past decade or so. One reason for this is that Royal Greenland closed the fish processing plant in 2011 because of the difficulties and expense of providing it with a supply of fresh water. This has nothing to do with climate change; the village is on a small island with no source of fresh water other than from the icebergs that surround it.

The closure of the fish plant has meant that fishing has declined in importance and the village is no longer considered a centre for the Greenland halibut fishery as there are no longer landing and processing facilities in the village and, as a result, no opportunity to sell the catch there. Many of those who still live in Kangersuatsiaq, and who were spending most of their time in recent years on fishing, have returned to being full-time hunters. Difficulties remain in selling seal skins or other products from the hunting of marine mammals, but this return to hunting has brought to the act of procurement a greater focus on the provision of meat and fish for the household and the wider community. Patterns of sharing and distributing meat and fish also remain strong, a fact that local people say also accounts for what makes it possible for those who remain in Kangersuatsiaq to sustain their livelihoods in the community. "People here share, we help each other out," they say.

Movement away from Kangersuatsiaq began earlier than the closure of the fish processing facility, though. Some Kangersuatsiarmiit (people from Kangersuatsiaq) have always left, as people from other places have done, for purposes of education or work, or marriage, and they are to be found in many parts of Greenland as well as living in Denmark. But there had for some decades been a stability to the population, and it even increased in the mid-1990s and early 2000s as people from other parts of Upernavik district moved there because of the good fishing prospects. Movement today amounts to a process of steady depopulation, and it seems to be lamented. People in Upernavik and other parts of the district say "Kangersuatsiarmiit ikillipput" ("The Kangersuatsiarmiit have become fewer") and this is something people from the village say of themselves too. Local explanatory accounts say that the closure of the fish processing plant, or the changing weather, or the lack of sea ice has "made them fewer" (*ikillivai*). But older people in the village say that those who turned full-time to fishing gave up their dogs in favour of snowmobiles and forgot their skills as hunters—those who did not anticipate the necessity of retaining hunting skills and knowledge or, in the face of a changing climate, those unable to read the signs and cues of how their surroundings take on different forms in a world of becoming (those who seemed to lack *ilimasunneq*)—could not make a living as hunters when the fish factory closed. A return to full-time hunting was necessary, but many chose to leave the village to be able to live as fishers in Upernavik town and other villages.

As the population declines, it is old people who are mainly left in the village today (as well as a few active hunters in their forties and fifties and their families), but their number is dwindling. When I returned to Upernavik in May 2017, the first news I was given was that four old people I knew in Kangersuatsiaq—I was on my way there—had died during the winter. On my recent visits to Kangersuatsiaq, conversations tend to begin with an account of those who have passed away or who have moved elsewhere since the last time I was there. These conversations with friends in their homes are almost always accompanied by photographs of people and places. They aid the stories that are told about the places in which people have hunted, about how traces of past lives are woven through the landscape and infuse the coastal waters. Memories of people who are long deceased remain alive in stories of hunting, fishing, and community events, as well as through their names. Places are saturated with memories of travel, hunting, fishing, and individual and family action and events. These stories express powerful feelings about what and who is no longer present, whether it is a person, sea ice, or a way of life, or winter dog sled routes that can no longer be traced on maps, and about who is being lost—whether through death, suicide, or movement away. People may be fewer in terms of their actual physical presence in the village, but naming practices and the stories that are told about them mean Kangersuatsiarmiit retain their social presence after death.

Naming and memory are ways of making absence felt, but also of retaining the presence and the essence of people, things, and events that have passed, and the places that are no longer visited or used. Children are named after deceased relatives and close friends, and place names and stories about places recall the intermingling of people and events with those places, so that some (for example, campsites, an island where a polar bear was caught, a sea cave where hunters would wait in their kayaks for passing seals, a mountain slope where ghosts ooze from cracks in the rocks, or a headland that emerged as a glacier receded) assume a reputation for being inextricably connected to people and their actions and with the things people see and experience. As Meyer (2012) points out, absences have traces, but absences are themselves also traces. While this hints at the spectral aspects of place (Maddern and Adey 2008), and of the traces of the things that may still linger and possibly haunt landscapes and people's lives, absence and loss are not necessarily expressed in memories of things past that are unduly nostalgic or that can be considered mere reminiscence, but rather in practices of remembering people, places, and activities that are rooted in the present (Degnen 2005; Meier, Frers, and Sigvardsdotter 2013). By this I mean that memories are not merely traces of things that were once present and are now absent—they retain a vitality and are essential to the contemporary meanings and everyday conversations about places. Indeed, memories, traces, ghosts, the ethereal, and the more-than-human inhabit and "people" the landscape (*innersorpaa*), expanding the world and bringing it into being. As Meyer (2012) also argues, absence has a materiality and it exists within and has considerable effects on the spaces and places people inhabit and use, as well as on their everyday experiences and practices.

I argue that this sense of absence—memories of people and things that are seemingly absent or of places that are seldom or no longer visited or used, as well as an awareness of things, non-human entities and substances such as ice, that are materially absent or that could be absent in the near future (see, for example, Bille, Hastrup, and Sørensen 2010)—is essential to the continuity of life, with memories of people and events, or of winters with thick, solid ice, brought into the present. This rich, social vitality contributes to the very making of a sense of community and a sense of place and it goes some considerable way toward explaining the nature of resilience in communities in the Upernavik district in the face of the social, economic, and environmental changes that are so often abrupt. As one woman put it to me in the summer of 2017, in response to my question about how she and her husband saw themselves in the future in Kangersuatsiaq: "We will stay. Yes, people are leaving and life can be a little hard here, but one gets peace (*eqqissivoq*) in Kangersuatsiaq."

Conclusions

The rapidly changing Arctic demands the convergence of diverse ways of knowing and understanding in a dialogue on being and becoming in the world. This might then point the way toward new directions for interdisciplinary, collaborative research to inform thinking about sustainability, resilience, and adaptation. But it also demands greater understanding of people's relationships with place, the nature of place, how the livelihoods and trajectories of human and more-than-human selves are entangled and bring places into being, and how these livelihoods shape and are also shaped by political, economic, and cultural forces and processes (for example, see Kirksey and Helmreich 2010, 545; Kohn 2007). Such an approach is attentive to the concerns raised by some recent multi-species scholarship in anthropology about the ways in which, as Anna Tsing (2013) has it, worlds are made and come into being through the intersecting trajectories of many species. In northern Greenland, these trajectories include those of humans, whether they are hunters, marine biologists, or oil and mineral exploration crews, other species such as narwhals, whales, seals, and polar bears, and other non-human entities such as sea ice and icebergs, as well as seismic lines from exploration vessels that leave no visible trace on the surface of the water but that have lingering effects in the darkest depths of the sea (Nuttall 2017).

To this I would add the importance of understanding anticipation, absence, and loss, as well as the memories, traces, and trajectories of the lives of people who have died but who continue on through their names, and how the significance of the places associated with them continue to have a lively presence. People who have passed on or who have left their home communities for somewhere else may be physically absent, but they retain a social presence not just in stories and in ways of remembering, but through names and naming relationships that inform the everyday enactment, continuation, and reproduction of social relationships (Nuttall 1992). So, too, does ice, which may have disappeared from parts of the coast, or which may not be forming as people say it should. The traces of sea ice linger in stories, experiences, community memories, and in the photographs that fill family albums. However, while people, when talking about the future, have hope that the sea ice may return to how it used to be, feelings of agitation and anxiety also play some part in how they articulate concerns over what they worry the long-term effects of oil and other resource exploration bring. These phenomena haunt northern seascapes, particularly those resulting from the seismic surveys that have been carried out in recent years in Baffin and Melville Bays.

Rapid and quite abrupt change is nothing new for the Arctic and its peoples, of course. The legacies of colonialism, resettlement by the state, and economic transitions, or international environmentalist opposition to marine mammal hunting or fur trapping, for example, continue to have their effects in many Indigenous communities in Alaska, Canada, Greenland, northern Fennoscandia, and northern Russia today, while seasonal variations have always posed challenges to hunters, fishers, and herders. Yet the kinds of changes people are witness to and now experience in weather and climate, in the sea ice and coastal waters, and in the behaviour and habits of animals, bring a quite different range of challenges to life in northern places. Current interest in the Arctic as a global space that is either open for business or that demands protection is rarely attentive, though, to the nature of place and human-environment relations, or to the relations between humans and animals, and how people are affected by resource development or conservation practices. Nor is it sufficiently attentive to anticipation and anticipatory experience, or the need to be prepared to find that something is not there, or is no longer there—something that could be absent rather than present—and to acknowledge that deep engagement with one's surroundings means that one has to be prepared for uncertainty and astonishment in a world of constant surprise, disappearance, and emergence.

Acknowledgements

This chapter draws from research carried out in northwest Greenland under the auspices of the Climate and Society research program at the Greenland Climate Research Centre (GCRC Project 6400), as well as the EU-funded ICE-ARC FP7 project (grant number 603887) and the ArcticChallenge project funded by the Norwegian Research Council.

References

Anderson, Ben, and John Wylie
2009 On Geography and Materiality. *Environment and Planning A* 41(2): 318–335.

Bebbington, Anthony, Nicholas Cuba, and John Rohan
2014 The Overlapping Geographies of Resource Extraction. *ReVista: Harvard Review of Latin America* 13(2): 20–23.

Bille, Mikkel, Frida Hastrup, and Tim Flohr Sørensen (editors)
2010 *An Anthropology of Absence and Loss: Materializations of Transcendence and Loss.* Springer, New York.

Briner, Jason P., Lena Håkansson, and Ole Bennike
2013 The Glaciation and Neoglaciation of Upernavik Isstrøm, Greenland. *Quaternary Research* 80: 459–467.

Bryant, Rebecca, and David M. Knight
2019 *The Anthropology of the Future.* Cambridge University Press, Cambridge.

Degnen, Cathrine
2005 Relationality, Place, and Absence: A Three-Dimensional Perspective on Social Memory. *Sociological Review* 53(4): 729–744.

Dodds, Klaus, and Mark Nuttall
2016 *The Scramble for the Poles: The Geopolitics of the Arctic and Antarctic.* Polity, Cambridge.

Dunbar, M. J.
1973 Stability and Fragility in Arctic Ecosystems. *Arctic* 26(3): 179–185.

Hastrup, Kirsten
2016 Climate Knowledge: Assemblage, Anticipation, Action. In *Anthropology and Climate Change: From Actions to Transformations*, edited by Susan A. Crate and Mark Nuttall, pp. 35–57. Routledge, London.

Howat, I. M., A. Negrete, and B. E. Smith
2014 The Greenland Ice Mapping Project (GIMP) Land Classification and Surface Elevation Datasets. *Cryosphere* 8: 1509–1518. doi:10.5194/tc-8-1509-2014.

Ingold, Tim
2000 *The Perception of the Environment: Essays on Livelihood, Dwelling and Skill.* Routledge, London.

Kirksey, S. Eben, and Stefan Helmreich
2010 The Emergence of Multispecies Ethnography. *Cultural Anthropology* 25(4): 545–576.

Kohn, Eduardo
2007 How Dogs Dream: Amazonian Natures and the Politics of Transpecies Engagement. *American Ethnologist* 34(1): 3–24.

Maddern, Jo Frances, and Peter Adey
2008 Editorial: Spectro-Geographies. *Cultural Geographies* 15(3): 291–295.

Meier, Lars, Lars Frers, and Erika Sigvardsdotter
2013 The Importance of Absence in the Present: Practices of Remembrance and the Contestation of Absences. *Cultural Geographies* 20(4): 423–430.

Meyer, Morgan
2012 Placing and Tracing Absence: A Material Culture of the Immaterial. *Journal of Material Culture* 17(1): 103–110.

Nuttall, Mark
1992 *Arctic Homeland: Kinship, Community and Development in Northwest Greenland.* University of Toronto Press, Toronto.
2001 Locality, Identity and Memory in South Greenland. *Études/Inuit/Studies* 25(12): 53–72.
2009 Living in a World of Movement: Human Resilience to Environmental Instability in Greenland. In *Anthropology and Climate Change: From Encounters to Actions*, edited by Susan A. Crate and Mark Nuttall, pp. 292–310. Left Coast Press, Walnut Creek, California.
2010 Anticipation, Climate Change, and Movement in Greenland. *Études/Inuit/Studies* 34(1): 21–37.
2016 Narwhal Hunters, Seismic Surveys and the Middle Ice: Monitoring Environmental Change in Greenland's Melville Bay. In *Anthropology and Climate Change: From Actions to Transformations*, edited by Susan A. Crate and Mark Nuttall, pp. 354–372. Routledge, London.
2017 *Climate, Society and Subsurface Politics in Greenland: Under the Great Ice.* Routledge, London.
2019 Icy, Watery, Liquescent: Sensing and Feeling Climate Change on Northwest Greenland's Coast. *Journal of Northern Studies* 14(2): 71–91.

Petersen, Robert
2003 *Settlements, Kinship and Hunting Grounds in Traditional Greenland: A Comparative Study of Local Experiences from Upernavik and Ammassalik.* Meddelelser om Grønland, Man and Society No. 27. Danish Polar Center, Copenhagen.

Stephan, Christopher, and Devin Flaherty
2019 Introduction: Experiencing Anticipation. *Cambridge Journal of Anthropology* 37(1): 1–16.

Tsing, Anna
2013 More-than-Human Sociality: A Call for Critical Description. In *Anthropology and Nature*, edited by Kirsten Hastrup, pp. 27–42. Routledge, London.

Wadhams, Peter
2017 *A Farewell to Ice: A Report from the Arctic.* Oxford University Press, Oxford.

FIGURE 6.1 Morning scene with the southern foothills of *Askinaq* (Askinuk Mountains), one of only a few highland areas in the Yukon Delta region, floating on the horizon. The numerous lakes, ponds, and watercourses visible in the nearer distance are far more typical of the regional landscape. View to the east-northeast, July 1981. Photograph by Kenneth Pratt.

KENNETH L. PRATT

6 "The Country Keeps Changing"

Cultural and Historical Contexts of Ecosystem Changes in the Yukon Delta

It seemed that we had said farewell to the ice, but from midnight on the fog closed in, and when I came on deck at eight o'clock in the morning of the 29th, I found that the brig was becalmed in the midst of heavy ice. Great numbers of walrus with their young, deafening us with their roar, were now clawing at the boat, now turning somersaults or climbing out on the nearby floes to stare with apparent surprise at their strange neighbor. We had no time to busy ourselves with them or we might have shot or harpooned up to a hundred head. By six in the evening, with the help of oars and a light wind from the south, the brig escaped to open waters.

LAVRENTIY ZAGOSKIN, 29 JUNE 1842

The event described above by Russian naval lieutenant Lavrentiy Zagoskin (1967, 89) occurred near Sledge Island in northern Norton Sound, just north of the Yukon Delta. It is distant not only in time but also in relation to modern climatic conditions in the region, where progressively warmer waters and attenuated winters have rendered the prospect of encountering solid pack ice teeming with walrus *in late June* a virtual impossibility.

Climate change in the Arctic is a real and growing problem, and related issues in the region are justifiably receiving intensive scientific attention, especially given irrefutable evidence—from science

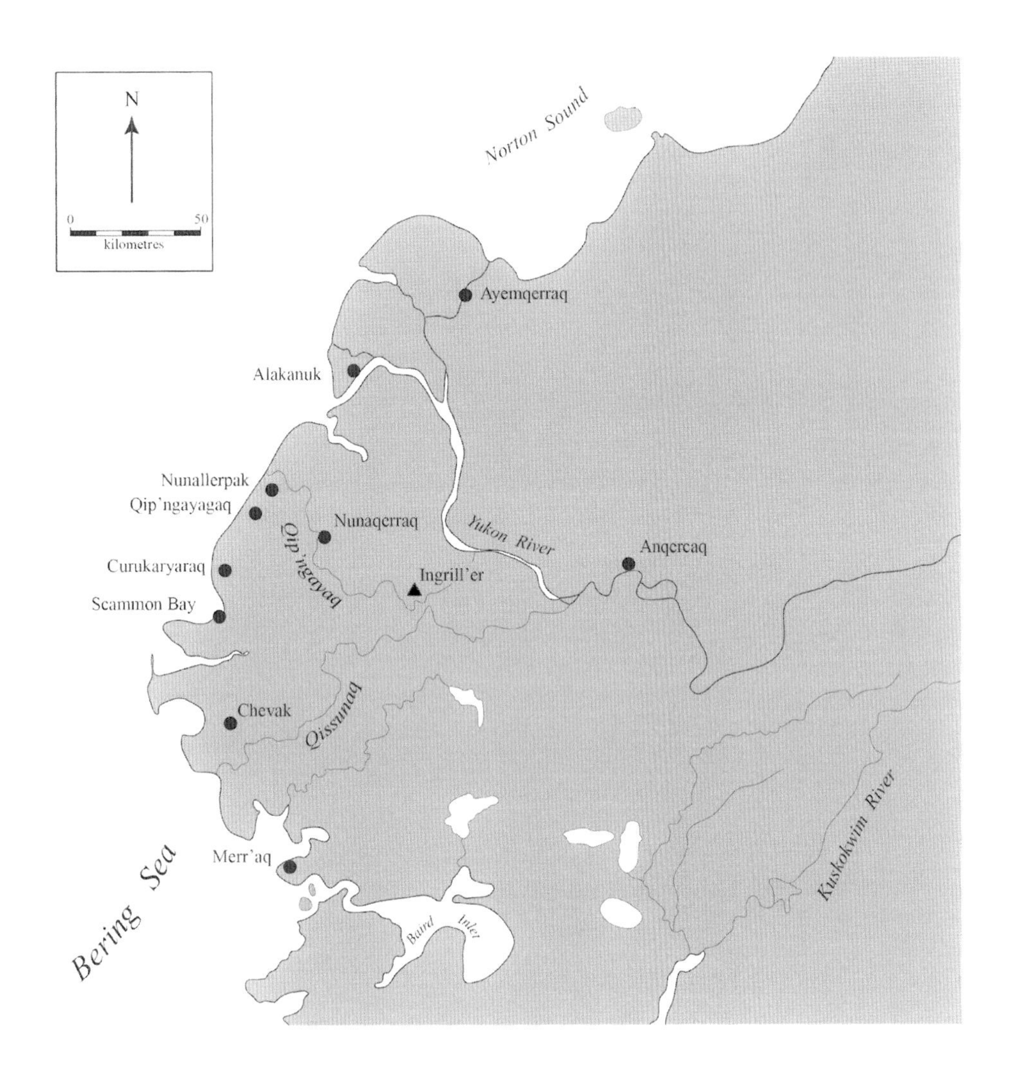

FIGURE 6.2 Study area.
Map produced by Dale Slaughter.

and Indigenous observations—for altered weather patterns and dramatic declines in the extent and thickness of winter sea ice. Obviously, any long-term continuation of these trends will have increasingly negative impacts on resident human communities and the fish and wildlife populations on which their livelihoods depend. When it comes to Arctic lands, however, researchers must be cautious about interpreting evidence of landscape changes occurring today as the sole result of recent climate change. This is particularly true in highly dynamic landscapes like the Yukon Delta in Southwest Alaska (figure 6.2).

In this chapter, documentary and ethnographic data are used to examine aspects of recent and historic landscape changes in the region. Related information about the cultural history of the delta's Indigenous peoples is presented to help broaden the context and emphasize the fact that these people are, and long have been, an important part of this ecosystem. My primary focus is on a number of former Yup'ik village and cemetery sites recorded in the 1980s pursuant to section 14(h)(1) of the 1971 Alaska Native Claims Settlement Act (ANCSA). This effort included archaeological surveys, oral history research with Indigenous knowledge holders, site mapping, and photography (see Pratt 2009a). Comparing these earlier findings with observations made at the same sites since 2004 has yielded interesting results, some of which are highlighted in examples discussed below.

The ANCSA 14(h)(1) Program

The ANCSA legislation aimed to resolve long-standing disputes regarding land rights. In addition to a cash settlement, the legislation granted Alaska's Indigenous people title to approximately 40 million acres of land, while also extinguishing all prior claims to Aboriginal title (Arnold 1978, 146). Section 14(h)(1) of the act allowed twelve newly created Alaska Native Regional Corporations to receive a portion of their acreage entitlement in the form of Native historical places and cemetery sites (see Pratt 2009b). This is the only part of the act that affords Alaska Natives the right to claim lands based specifically on their significance in cultural history and traditions. The term "cemetery sites" is self-explanatory; whereas "historical places" encompass former villages, camps, trails, legendary/spiritual sites, and the like.

While untold thousands of locales in Alaska could legitimately be called Native historical places or cemetery sites, only sites determined to be located on available federal lands at the time of application are potentially eligible for conveyance under ANCSA section 14(h)(1). Thus, of the nearly 4,000 applications originally filed by the regional corporations (39 percent of which were filed by Calista Corporation for sites in the Yukon-Kuskokwim region of Southwest Alaska), fewer than 2,300 were forwarded for investigation to the Bureau of Indian Affairs (BIA), the agency charged with implementing the program (see Pratt 2009b, 9).[1] The BIA is required to verify the existence, physical location, and extent of each site; determine its significance in local Indigenous history; and produce a written report of the findings. On-ground work at each site included a reconnaissance-level archaeological survey, wherein identified cultural features are numbered, measured, and described. Detailed maps are then produced that show the location of all features relative to one another, as well as characteristics of the site environment (for example, vegetation, physical terrain, bodies of water) and the site boundaries. Photographs are taken of cultural features and the overall site, usually from both the ground and the air.

Site excavations are not performed on this program, and most sites also are not subjected to subsurface testing—since testing usually is not necessary to establish site significance under the ANCSA eligibility criteria. When it does occur, however, testing is often limited to a single shovel probe. While this practice may yield a radiometric date, chronological information about most sites is generally reliant on oral history (and written historical accounts, if available).

Each report of investigation includes a sketch of the given site's history (Indigenous name, site type, seasonality of use, approximate dates of occupation and abandonment, affiliated families or settlements, etc.), the details of which are the basis for certifying whether or not the site satisfies the eligibility requirements for title conveyance to Alaska Natives. Barring selected land status conflicts (or legal appeals), sites certified eligible by the BIA are ultimately scheduled for US surveys and then conveyed to the applicant regional corporations.[2] Although it was originally anticipated to be completed within a period of just six years, the ANCSA 14(h)(1) Program has now been in operation for forty years, and indeed is ongoing (for context regarding this situation, see Pratt 2009b, 3–4).

The program has generated a massive, irreplaceable collection of data about Alaska Native history and culture (see O'Leary, Drozda, and Pratt 2009; Pratt 2009a). Its components include reports that describe and interpret the research findings on all 2,300 or so investigated sites. There are also about 2,000 tape recorded oral history interviews with Alaska Native elders, and notes on another 600 or so interviews that were not tape recorded. Other key components of the collection include roughly 50,000 photographs, 15,000 artifacts, 4,500 field notebooks, and 130 composite field maps.[3] If one were to name a topic in Alaska Native cultural history, information about it would almost certainly be found in the ANCSA 14(h)(1) Collection—the question is where in the collection or within which component. In other words, a large amount of records processing still must be done in order to create finding aids to facilitate access to and use of the data in this collection.

FIGURE 6.3 Sandra Kozevnikoff assisted a 1982 ANCSA crew based in her home village of Russian Mission, Alaska, by serving as an interpreter in oral history interviews with local elders, and also by providing translations of recorded Yup'ik place names. Attired in a yellow flight suit, here Sandra displays a pot of berries she opportunistically picked during a lunch stop between helicopter flights. Photograph by Robert Drozda.

For instance, oral history research with Alaska Native elders was essential to properly locate and document many of the sites described in ANCSA 14(h)(1) applications (see Drozda 1995; Pratt 2004).[4] Since most of the elders interviewed spoke little or no English, however, the vast majority of oral history tape recordings are bilingual (see figure 6.3). It is very difficult and expensive to produce complete and accurate bilingual translations and transcriptions of such recordings. But even if money were no object, the main problem on this front is finding qualified people who can do the work, namely, fluent speakers of an Indigenous language who can also write in it. Such individuals are few and far between; most are either employed and too busy to commit the necessary time to the task, or are burned out from prior experiences doing this type of tedious and highly challenging work. Consequently, much of the oral history preserved on ANCSA tape recordings remains untranslated.

Traditional Yup'ik Land Use and Settlement Patterns

Named for the language they speak, the Yup'ik peoples in Alaska were traditionally organized in economically self-sufficient local groups, composed of one or more nuclear or extended families whose annual round revolved around a winter village and associated seasonal camps. Each group followed a subsistence lifestyle that, depending on resource availability, involved moving between two to five different residence localities over the course of the year (Pratt 2009c, 76). For about half of every calendar year the people affiliated with a given winter village were dispersed across the landscape in individual (nuclear or extended) family units. Virtually every family had camps to which it claimed ancestral use rights, often dating back for generations (see Andrews 1989; Fienup-Riordan 1982; Pratt 2009c; Wolfe 1979).

Traditionally, houses were semi-subterranean in design: pits were excavated then wall and roof framings of wood were put in place and covered on the exterior with sod. Most villages contained larger structures called *qasgit* (sing. *qasgiq*) that were constructed in the same manner and served as a men's community house (among the Yup'ik, men were residentially divided from women and children). This sexual division of communities was not found in other Alaskan Native societies. Some of these other societies did not have "men's houses," and among those that did, the structures were functionally different from those of the Yup'ik—as they did not serve as residences for men (Pratt 2009c, 67).

Since the majority of the region is underlain by shallow permafrost, burials were above ground. Cemeteries were typically located adjacent to but outside the habitation areas of the camps or villages with which they were affiliated.

Subsistence and settlement patterns in the region remained essentially as described above through at least 1930 or so. By 1950, virtually every local Yup'ik group had been compelled to occupy centralized, year-round villages to accommodate the Western educational system. Churches and missionaries associated with such villages were also a factor in this coalescence of what had previously been scattered Indigenous populations. This process of centralization led to significant changes in population distribution and customary patterns of land use, including a decrease in mobility on the family level (for example, see Oswalt 1963, 130–131). It also resulted in the permanent abandonment of many otherwise viable villages and camps due to logistical constraints imposed by the sometimes great distance between these settlements and the modern villages. Accordingly, many areas that formerly were heavily utilized for subsistence purposes began to be used infrequently.

Site-Specific Examples of Landscape Change

I now provide some site-specific examples to illustrate some of the dramatic but common landscape changes occurring in the Yukon Delta. Historical and ethnographic accounts about each site are supplemented by recent field observations to show that most of the processes of landscape change documented in these examples are not new.

EXAMPLE 1: CURUKARYARAQ

When ANCSA researchers surveyed the site of *Curukaryaraq* (AA-10361) in June 1981 (figure 6.4), they found three depressions in a setting that suggested they could be of natural origin.[5] However, Alaska Native elders unanimously (and independently) described them as the remains of semi-subterranean structures. Radiometric data suggest the site was probably established by the mid-1700s, which is consistent with oral history accounts asserting that the site existed prior to European contact (ca. 1833 in the study region). Before its abandonment following a smallpox epidemic around 1900 (USBIA 1984a), the site was occupied as a spring and fall camp for harvesting blackfish, whitefish, and mink.

Scammon Bay elder Dan Akerelrea (1981a) was interviewed on the site and indicated it had been "higher" the last time he had seen it, decades earlier. He also said that *Ciutnguilleq,* the river along which the site is situated, used to be wide enough for large boats to navigate.[6] By 1981, however, the river was less than 3 metres wide in the site area and essentially unnavigable. The interpreter for this interview, Xavier Simon (also from Scammon Bay), assisted with another interview with Dan Akerelrea a few days later—the circumstances of which led to an exchange in which he spoke briefly about landscape changes in the region:

> ***Xavier Simon:*** *Curukaryaraq*. That's the first spot we hit. *Curukaryaraq*.
>
> ***Interviewer:*** There were a couple of houses there, and maybe one [*qasgiq*]?
>
> ***Xavier Simon:*** Mm-hm.
>
> ***Interviewer:*** They seem to be built into the bank where they couldn't be seen.
>
> ***Xavier Simon:*** Well, they were. . . . You know, they were high places. [The people] won't build on the low places [. . .] the whole site just sunk. . . . There are a lot of changes Dan said. Some creeks [got] narrower. Some creeks [got] wider; and [there] used to be lakes. Now they're all [dry] lake beds. You know, the country keeps changing. There's lot of changes. That's why no matter even [if a site is] lost, you know, the whole thing might be lost. The whole [site] might just be disappearing. [But what we are doing now] is the [important] thing: [showing] where they are and [giving] the correct name. It'll be the same site [even if it disappears]. . . . Maybe ten years from now you won't see anything [at *Curukaryaraq*].
>
> (Akerelrea 1981b, 24)

Xavier's words were somewhat prophetic, because by 2012 the site was completely underwater (figure 6.5).[7] The current lack of surface indications of past cultural use means the prior work by ANCSA researchers is now the only evidence that a site exists at this locale.[8] There is little question that the site's surface disappearance is due to thermokarst melting, but that event did not happen over the course of a few years. As indicated in Native oral history accounts, it was instead part of a process the region's Indigenous people have witnessed before, which in this instance spanned a minimum period of about seventy years. Finally, in addition to the site's submergence, since 1981 the river has become even narrower and willows that were then present at *Curukaryaraq* have completely disappeared—no doubt because they cannot grow in water.

FIGURE 6.4 *Curukayaraq*, June 1981. Dwelling remains are in the light-coloured grassy area (encircled) at lower left-centre, near base of high-ground area and partially surrounded by willow thickets; *Ciutnguilleq* (river) in foreground and upper right. View to northwest. Photograph by Robert Drozda. ANCSA 14(h)(1) Collection, case file AA-10361, Bureau of Indian Affairs, Anchorage.

FIGURE 6.5 *Curukayaraq*, September 2012. Note that the dwelling area (encircled) has been replaced by a pond and marsh, and the willow thickets have disappeared. View to northwest. Photograph by Matthew O'Leary. ANCSA 14(h)(1) Collection, case file AA-10361, Bureau of Indian Affairs, Anchorage.

FIGURE 6.6 *Anqercaq* ("Razbinsky") in January 1879 (originally published as Plate LXXXII in Nelson 1899). Courtesy of Smithsonian Institution.

EXAMPLE 2: *ANQERCAQ*

In 1982, Native elders described *Anqercaq* (AA-9774 [USGS Ankachak]) as the "grand-daddy village" of the lower Yukon River—a reference to the settlement's antiquity, regional significance, and large size (see figure 6.6). Established in prehistoric times, the village was linked to a number of noteworthy historical events—including an 1855 attack on the Russian trade post of Andreevskaia Odinochka that resulted in the deaths of several employees and the looting of the post (Pratt 2010). The attackers were residents of *Anqercaq*, a settlement Russians and later American visitors to the region thereafter referred to as Razboiniskaia (or "Robbers Village") (see Zagoskin 1967, 278) (see figure 6.7).

The site had an estimated population of 122 in 1844 (Zagoskin 1967, 306) and 151 in 1880 (Petroff 1884, 12), at which time it evidently contained 25 houses and about 30 graves (Nelson 1899, 247–248). An epidemic of smallpox around 1900 led to the deaths of many residents. *Anqercaq* remained occupied for several more decades, but by 1935 it had been destroyed by erosion (USBIA 1984c, 46).

FIGURE 6.7 Map of the lower Yukon River (1916) by R. H. Sargent (in Harrington 1918) showing location of *Anqercaq* ("Razboinski"), near upper centre of image.

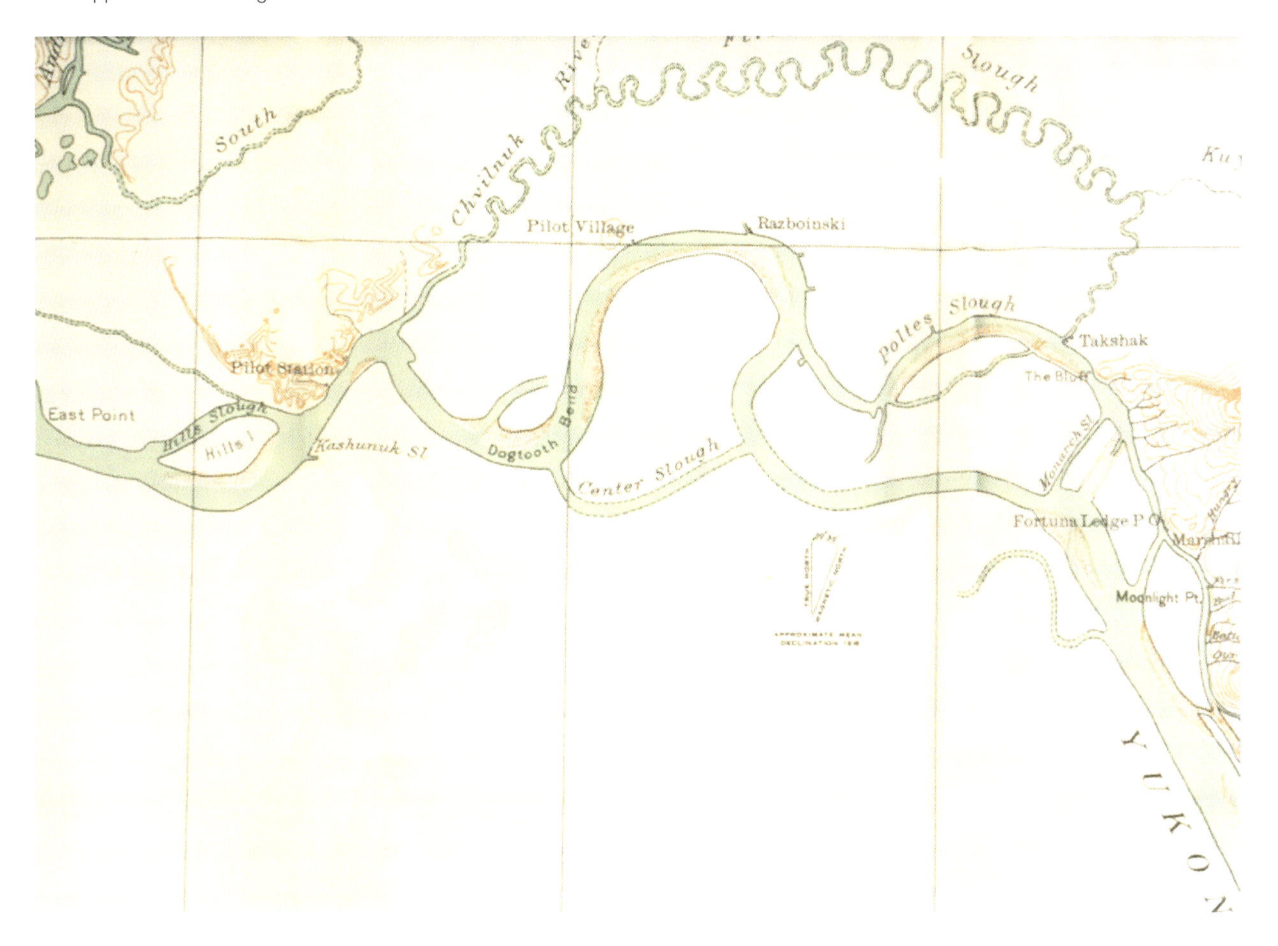

Based on a comparison of aerial photos taken in 1982 (figure 6.8) and 2004 with published topographic maps, about 700 meters of the Yukon's north bank in this area has been lost to erosion since 1951 (USBIA 2008, 19–20).

But channel migration and bank erosion has not affected all areas of the Yukon River in the same way. Thus, *Ayemqerraq* (AA-10067)—a small village contemporary with *Anqercaq* but located more than 100 kilometres downstream on the river's north mouth, *Apun* (USGS Apoon Pass)—is still intact today.[9] *Ayemqerraq* also occupies the Yukon's north bank; however, channel migration and associated erosion has led to bank accretion in its vicinity. In fact, comparisons of aerial photographs and published topographic maps reveal that *Ayemqerraq* (figure 6.9) was some 270 metres inland from the river by 1951—and that distance had increased to about 360 metres by 2012 (USBIA n.d.). The site's abandonment around 1920 (USBIA 1989) may have been tied to this process of accretion, which was effectively making the river less and less accessible from the site.

FIGURE 6.8 Erosion in the former area of *Anqercaq* village, August 1982. Yukon River in foreground, *Anqercaq* (slough) at upper left. View to north-northwest. Photograph by Kenneth Pratt. ANCSA 14(h)(1) Collection, case file AA-9774, Bureau of Indian Affairs, Anchorage.

FIGURE 6.9 Remains of the small village of *Ayemqerraq* (see arrow) appear as a small grassy area in the centre of this image. The low ground to its left marks the former channel (see dashed line) of *Apun*—the north mouth of the Yukon River. The modern channel of *Apun* flows across the upper third of the image. View to northwest, June 2009. Photograph by Kenneth Pratt. ANCSA 14(h)(1) Collection, case file AA-10067, Bureau of Indian Affairs, Anchorage.

EXAMPLE 3: *MERR'AQ*

Once an important spring camp for sea mammal hunting, when ANCSA researchers surveyed *Merr'aq* (AA-11430) in July 1983 they found a cemetery containing the graves of at least ten people (figure 6.10)—all of whom apparently died during a 1940 diptheria epidemic (USBIA 1985, 7). No evidence was found of other surface cultural features, but a large *qasgiq* reportedly once stood just north of the cemetery area: it was destroyed by erosion sometime before 1983 (Inakak 1983). The existence of such a structure (in combination with the cemetery remains) indicates that a substantial settlement may have been associated with *Merr'aq*; and radiometric data suggest cultural use of the area as early as the mid- to late 1600s. An unusually large accumulation of sea mammal and other faunal remains along the shoreline fronting the cemetery testifies to obvious long-term use of the area (figure 6.11). It also raises the possibility that a pond or small lake may once have separated the cemetery from the presumptive habitation area; if so, some of the faunal accumulations are likely tied to traditional disposal practices that required people to place the bones of certain animals in water (for examples, see Nelson 1899, 437; Fienup-Riordan 1994, 107–118).

FIGURE 6.10 Overgrown graves at *Merr'aq*. View to northwest, July 1983. Photograph by Dan Joyce. ANCSA 14(h)(1) Collection, case file AA-11430, Bureau of Indian Affairs, Anchorage.

FIGURE 6.11 Example of exposed faunal remains on beach at *Merr'aq*; notebook for scale. View to south-southeast, September 2011. Photograph by Matthew O'Leary. ANCSA 14(h)(1) Collection, case file AA-11430, Bureau of Indian Affairs, Anchorage.

FIGURE 6.12 Shoreline erosion at *Merr'aq*. The cemetery area (encircled) is located at the approximate centre of the photo, between the river *Merr'aq* and the Bering Sea (foreground). View to south-southwest, September 2011. Photograph by Matthew O'Leary. ANCSA 14(h)(1) Collection, case file AA-11430, Bureau of Indian Affairs, Anchorage.

But whatever the case, the lack of dwelling remains at the site was understandably attributed to shoreline erosion, the extent and ongoing process of which led the 1983 researchers to predict that "the whole site area . . . in the near future, will probably erode into the Bering Sea" (USBIA 1985, 11). In September 2011, ANCSA researchers revisited *Merr'aq* expecting to find it destroyed by erosion.[10] Instead, the cemetery was intact—despite the loss of an estimated 5–10 meters of shoreline across the site area between 1983 and 2011. Erosion in this area (see figure 6.12) is ongoing and will no doubt continue, but the cemetery might remain essentially as is for another decade or more.

EXAMPLE 4: *QAVINAQ*, *QISSUNAQ*, AND *CEV'ALLRAQ*

In June 2015, it was reported that artifacts were eroding out of a cutbank at the site of *Qavinaq* (AA-9389), a former settlement that evidence suggests was established by the early eighteenth century if not earlier. Native oral history indicates the site was abandoned in prehistoric times after an attack by Yup'ik warriors from the Yukon River who burned the village and killed its male residents.

The 2015 report generated a flurry of activity among Alaska Native and federal government parties concerned about the site's preservation: much of the concern was, to be blunt, based on a lack of understanding about certain "natural" realities of the regional landscape. In other words, this is just one of literally hundreds of sites in the Yukon Delta that are being steadily consumed by erosion,

FIGURE 6.13 Bank erosion at the western dwelling cluster of *Qavinaq*. View to southwest, September 2012. Photograph by Matthew O'Leary. ANCSA 14(h)(1) Collection, case file AA-9389, Bureau of Indian Affairs, Anchorage.

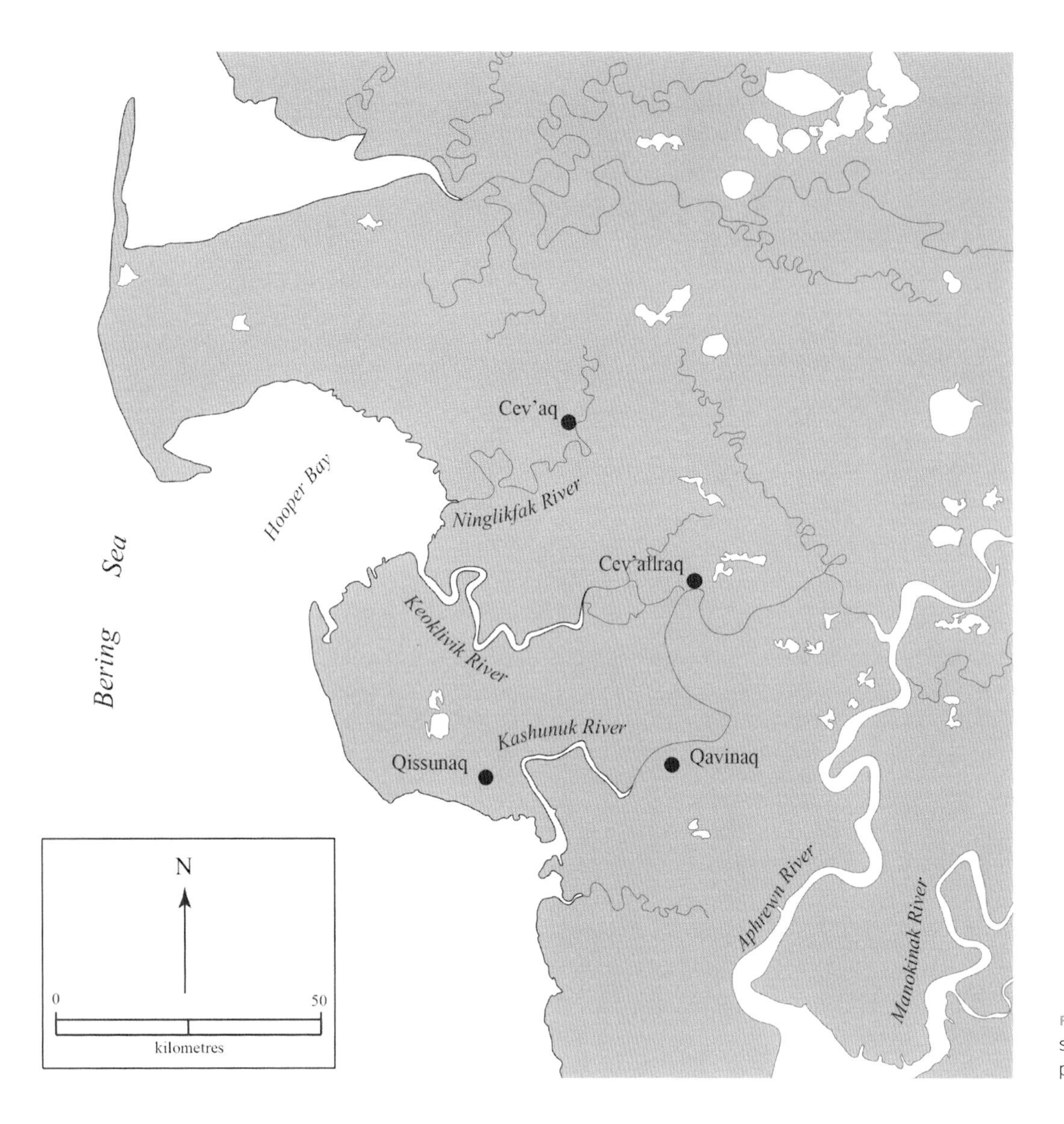

FIGURE 6.14 Chevak area sites discussed in text. Map produced by Dale Slaughter.

a process that was well underway at *Qavinaq* when ANCSA researchers first visited the site in 1981 (USBIA 1984d, 7, 34–36; see also figure 6.13 in this chapter). The main purpose of discussing *Qavinaq* here is that it is the first in a multi-village sequence that illuminates the linked processes of erosion, village abandonment, and resettlement in this region.

Located along a river of the same name, *Qavinaq* lies about 19 kilometres inland from the Bering Sea coast (see figure 6.14).[11] Despite its inland setting, however, the probable causes of past and ongoing erosion at the site are tidal surges that significantly alter the river's water level and flow. This point is clarified by an observation made by Edward Nelson in January 1879:

> From the mouth of the Yukon to that of the Kuskokwim, excepting merely the small part covered by mountains[. . .], the country is so low that the tide flows up the river[s] from 10 to 50 miles, and we were frequently unable to find a fresh-water stream or lake from which to obtain drinking water, even 20 to 30 miles from the coast. (Nelson 1882, 669)

FIGURE 6.15 Main occupation mound at *Qissunaq*. This large mound contained the remains of two large *qasgit* (men's community houses) and an estimated thirty-five dwellings. View to southeast, August 1981. Photograph by Robert Drozda. ANCSA 14(h)(1) Collection, case file AA-9391, Bureau of Indian Affairs, Anchorage.

Although the event was not instigated by erosion, when *Qavinaq* was abandoned many of its residents relocated to *Qissunaq* (AA-9391 [USGS Kashunuk])—a large village some 13 kilometres to the west and situated adjacent to a major river bearing the same name (i.e., *Qissunaq* [USGS Kashunuk River]). In about 1880, the village contained an estimated 125 people and 20 houses (Petroff 1884, 54), and the settlement is well-documented in the historical literature on the region (for examples, see Nelson 1899, 382–391; USBIA 1981). Among other distinctions, *Qissunaq* was the site of the region's first church (built ca. 1925) and the headquarters of its full-time missionary, a testament to the settlement's size and importance. Situated atop an approximately twelve-metre-high mound (figure 6.15) and surrounded by a seemingly endless expanse of low, marshy ground, the site was a prominent feature of the physical landscape, and is literally visible for miles on a clear day. *Qissunaq* had been established by the mid-seventeenth century (Frink 1999, 4)—sometime prior to the abandonment of *Qavinaq*—and was occupied through the mid- to late 1940s, when it was abandoned due primarily to a series of major fall

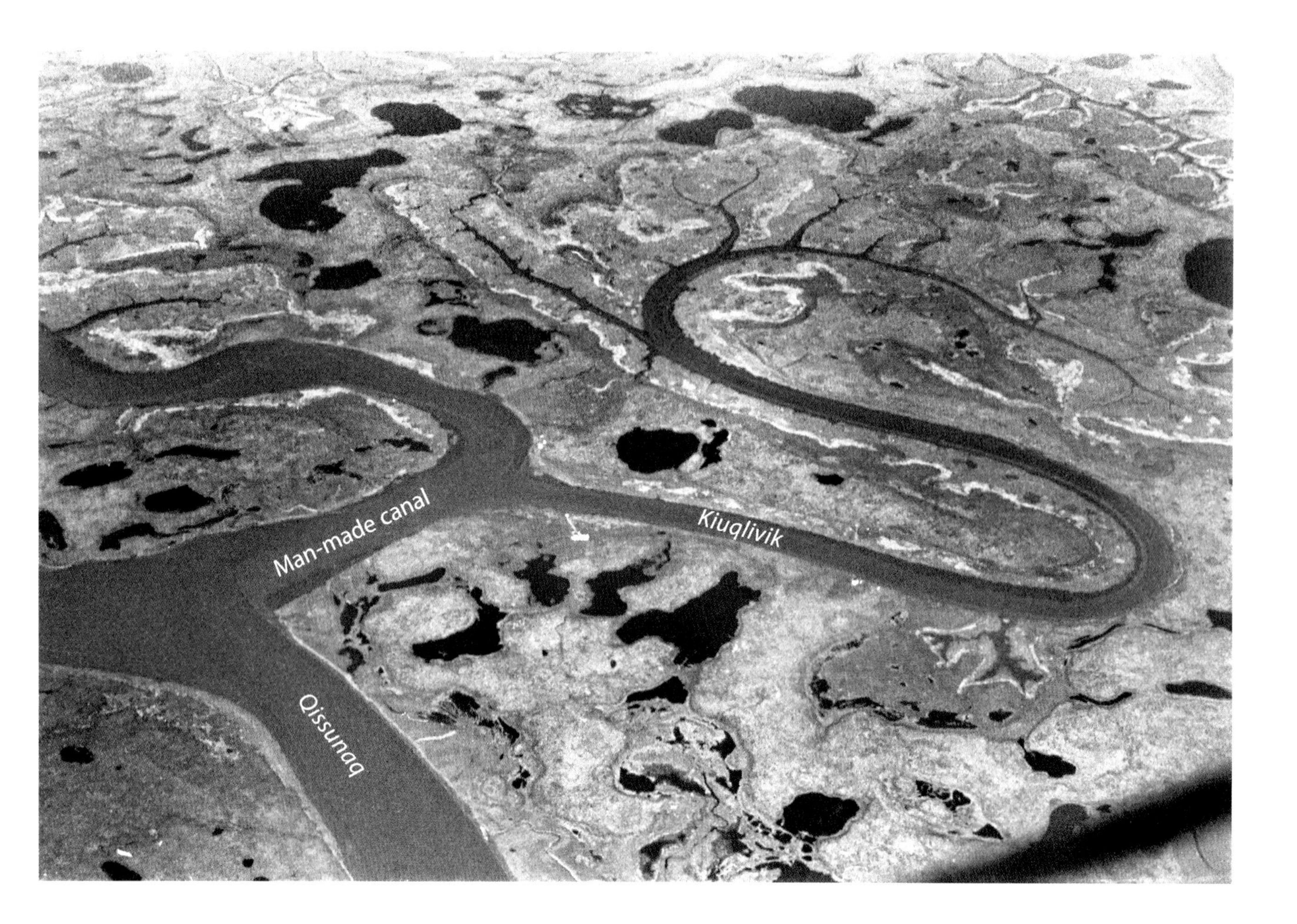

and winter floods (see Barker 1979; USBIA 1981, 67; Woodbury 1984, 10; see also Fienup-Riordan 1986, 23–27). Generated by a combination of high tides and strong winds, the floods repeatedly inundated much of the village with salt water and ice.

Many of the former *Qissunaq* residents moved to *Cev'allraq* (AA-11257 [USGS Old Chevak]), about 19 kilometres to the northeast. Notably, they disassembled the church at *Qissunaq* and moved it to *Cev'allraq*. *Cev'allraq* was a small village in its own right at that time but some *Qissunaq* people had also used it as a summer fish camp (USBIA 1984e, 6–7). The site's population had grown to an estimated 150 people by the early 1950s, at which it, too, was abandoned in response to frequent flooding (USBIA 1984e, 7–8; Woodbury 1984, 11). The residents next moved to *Cev'aq* (Chevak), that is, "New Chevak," a site situated on comparatively high and dry ground approximately 13 kilometres to the northwest.

Human-caused landscape change was also the genesis for the place names *Cev'allraq* ("former *cev'aq*") and *Cev'aq* ("cut-through place where the river has carved a channel; man-made channel") (Jacobson 2012, 199). At *Cev'allraq*, someone once cut a channel in the marshy tundra extending between *Qissunaq* (USGS Kashunuk River) and *Kiuqlivik* (USGS Keoklivik River) to connect the two watercourses (Nayamin 1981; USBIA 1984e, 9, 53)—evidently for the purpose of simplifying boat travel. The channel grew wider over time, probably thanks largely to the erosional action of tidal surges, and by 1981 looked like a natural feature of the landscape (figure 6.16).

FIGURE 6.16 This aerial view of *Cev'allraq* shows the man-made canal (left-centre) that now connects the *Qissunaq* (lower left) and *Kiuqlivik* (right) rivers. View to west, August 1981. Photograph by Kenneth Pratt. ANCSA 14(h)(1) Collection, case file AA-11257, Bureau of Indian Affairs, Anchorage.

Three other such channels are known to have been cut in the area between *Cev'allraq* and the modern village of *Cev'aq* (Matthew O'Leary, pers. comm., 2015). The cutting of these channels clearly express Indigenous knowledge of local hydrological and erosion processes.

In short, the "village ancestry" of today's residents of Chevak can be traced sequentially backward in time to *Cev'allraq*, *Qissunaq*, and *Qavinaq*; and "coastal" flooding was the driving force behind two of the three associated village-abandonment events. These examples illustrate the resiliency and adaptability of the region's Indigenous population in the aftermath of natural disasters like floods (see also Griffin 1996; Pratt, Stevenson, and Everson 2013). It also begs comparison with certain high-profile situations in present-day Alaska involving the proposed relocations of rural/Alaska Native villages now threatened by coastal erosion (for example, Shishmaref, Kivalina, Shaktoolik, Newtok, etc.). Village relocations in rural Alaska that occurred prior to 1950 or so certainly had their own complications, but most of the related work could nevertheless be accomplished by the villagers themselves. Mobility and flexibility were still hallmarks of their ways of life; and villages were smaller and far more self-sufficient in those days, largely because they lacked the major infrastructure of modern communities (electrical lines, fuel tanks, generators, water/sewer systems, and so on). Thus, when natural processes forced people to acknowledge that their community was situated in a bad location and therefore must be relocated, they were capable of resolving the problem on their own. That is no longer the case today. In essence, flexibility has been lost as a key element of northern Indigenous societies.

Changes Related to Reduced Human Use of the Landscape

The above examples show that the Yukon Delta ecosystem is not static, and that changes can be highly localized. Traditionally, Indigenous residents of the region were sufficiently attuned to the ecosystem to have anticipated and prepared for many of its changes (see for example, Nuttall 2010). But while natural processes account for the ecosystem changes just described, others may arguably be associated with declining human use of the landscape.

A logical starting point here is the centralization, as in other parts of the circumpolar North, of populations in response to legal mandates requiring Indigenous children to become students in the Western educational system, the end result of which was fewer and larger "centralized" villages in the region, and permanent changes to traditional patterns of land use and settlement. The annual round of subsistence life in the region had previously been an extended family affair, involving children and adults alike; but in order to care for and avoid having to separate from school-age children, many adult females could no longer participate in subsistence activities in some seasons of the year (see Polty 1982, 13–14). Seasonal camps that remained in use were therefore occupied for shorter durations of time and by fewer people, typically adult males (figure 6.17). Associated losses in traditional learning from life on the land occurred, in concert with a decline in multi-generational contacts and interactions (Oswalt 1990, 153).[12]

FIGURE 6.17 Muskrats were a very important subsistence and material resource for traditional Indigenous residents of the Yukon Delta. "Muskrat hunting across the Yukon River on one of many lakes." Coloured pencil on paper by Yup'ik artist Patrick Minock of Pilot Station, Alaska, March 2015. Courtesy of Patrick Minock.

Nevertheless, through at least the 1980s many Indigenous residents of the Yukon Delta continued to occupy family subsistence camps in a customary manner. For example, families left their home villages to live and harvest fish, berries, and other resources at remote camps for weeks at a time. In so doing, they travelled extensively on the delta's rivers, lakes, and sloughs, as well as upon the terrestrial landscape. Their direct links to and presence on the land were plainly evident, especially in summer, when boats constantly plied the waterways and fish racks, cabins, and canvas tents dotted the adjacent uplands. In the space of the last generation, however, people have generally become far more sedentary. One indicator of this is that family-occupied fish camps are becoming a thing of the past in some parts of the Yukon Delta. For many people, summer fishing now commonly occurs in the form of day trips.

There are numerous reasons for this changing pattern of land use, of course, including the high costs of gasoline, equipment, and other materials, and harvest restrictions due to a persistent cycle of poor salmon runs (often blamed on commercial fishing bycatch practices but increasingly also linked to climate change [for example, see Biela et al. 2022]). Families with one or more adults with steady, wage-earning jobs may also find it difficult to schedule sufficient time away from their villages to engage in subsistence camping. But another pervasive factor is that many Alaska Native youths today—like their non-Native, urban counterparts—cannot tolerate long periods of separation from the technology and media, like television and the Internet, that is inaccessible from remote sites. As such, a reasonable argument could be made that advances in electronic and digital technology over the past generation constitute one of the most serious threats yet to the preservation (through first-person experiences) of customary and traditional practices of Yup'ik life on the land. That being said, technologies like the Global Positioning System [GPS]) can also contribute to the preservation of certain customary practices.

That new technology can lead to cultural and land-use change is a well-known fact. For instance, the arrival of snow machines to the Yukon Delta effectively marked the end of travel by dog team and the associated abandonment of many cold-season camps. Pilot Station elder Noel Polty (1982, 4–5) explained this using winter trapping as an example. A trapper on snow machine could travel longer distances from his village in shorter periods of time than was possible with a dog team; indeed, he could potentially go from his home all the way to the end of his trapline and back again all in the space of a single day (see also Wolfe 1979, 76–77). With a dog team, the same trip would take two or more days, requiring at least one overnight camp. Once travel by snow machine became the norm, the cold-season camps that were abandoned were typically those located *nearest* to permanent villages. Noel observed that younger generations consequently knew nothing about many of the old sites situated closest to their villages; those sites had essentially become indistinct from the larger landscape that travellers on snow machines glimpse only in passing, if at all.

In stark contrast to the cultural impacts associated with snow machines and other technological changes, however, recent and ongoing advances in communication technology threaten to disconnect Indigenous youths from their ancestral cultural and physical landscapes—neither of which can

be learned in detail from books, films, YouTube, Wikipedia, and the like. Such learning requires extensive personal time on the land and active engagement with elderly culture bearers, whose collective knowledge constitutes a non-renewable resource. These learning tools are easily lost to Indigenous youths obsessed with being constantly connected to a virtual world.

Perhaps the most apparent landscape change in the Yukon Delta that can be linked to reduced human use of the country is the choking off of watercourses due to beaver dams. Although no formal surveys have been conducted to estimate beaver populations in the delta (Doolittle 2013), all parties agree that their numbers have increased exponentially in recent decades. At the time of Russian contact, the delta's Indigenous peoples reportedly hunted beavers specifically for their meat and had little interest in their hides (Zagoskin 1967, 269). The value placed on their furs by Euro-American traders eventually led Indigenous hunters to increase their focus on the harvesting of beavers, a factor that contributed to a decline in their numbers in the region by 1900 (see, for example, Nelson 1887, 279–280; Wolfe 1979, 65–66).[13] Beaver hunting and trapping continued in the delta (albeit at reduced levels) through the 1960s; but it has declined significantly since the 1970s because of major reductions in the commercial value of animal furs.

FIGURE 6.18 Beaver-killed watercourse near left/south bank of the Yukon River, west of Mountain Village, Alaska; September 2012. Photograph by Kenneth Pratt. ANCSA 14(h)(1) Collection, Calista region digital photographs, Bureau of Indian Affairs, Anchorage.

Today, trapping of these animals still occurs and some people continue to use beavers as food; but there is no question that fewer beavers are being harvested now than at any time in the past—despite the fact that today there are no closed seasons, licence requirements, or bag limits on beavers.[14] Reduced harvesting of beavers (together with increased shrubification, which has allowed them to expand their range) has made the animals ubiquitous throughout the delta. The most obvious indicators of their proliferation are dams that have caused the deaths of many rivers and streams once heavily used by Indigenous people (figure 6.18). As the late Teddy Sundown, of Scammon Bay, stated in 1985, "[The beavers have] destroyed our hunting areas. They've destroyed the streams and lakes we used to hunt and fish in" (Sundown 1985, 3).

Indigenous residents of the region have registered complaints about the animals to the US Fish and Wildlife Service (Doolittle 2013), the federal agency with management jurisdiction over most of the Yukon Delta; but there are no harvest restrictions to prevent people from dealing with specific beaver problems on their own. The complaints usually concern inconveniences beavers cause in connection with travel on local rivers. If significant numbers of the area's Indigenous residents still used the country as extensively for boat travel as occurred in the 1980s, however, there is little doubt they would also be harvesting beavers in greater numbers, if only to preserve access to important waterways. Instead, boat travel is increasingly restricted to the main channels of the Yukon and selected portions of major tributaries.

But very little in nature is simply black or white. Thus, from a biological standpoint there are also known "positives" associated with beavers and their lodges. Studies have shown that the presence of these animals can not only increase the productivity of many waterfowl species, but also the productivity of sockeye, coho, and chinook salmon (Doolittle 2013). Beaver ponds provide excellent habitat for juvenile salmon, and fluctuating water levels in the ponds (especially in the spring and fall) enable the fish to easily move into adjacent river systems (Rearden 2013). Beavers therefore contribute to the health and viability of several key subsistence resource species.[15]

In some areas of the delta, another ecosystem change in which decreased human use of the land is implicated is the in-filling of rivers by vegetation. Thus, travel by powerboat has become highly problematic on one major tributary of the Yukon, the *Qip'ngayaq* (USGS Black River). As recently as the 1980s, summer fish camps were common along this river—hence boat travel on its waters was comparatively heavy. But, in 2011, researchers travelling downstream on the *Qip'ngayaq* in powerboats from the Yukon River were unable to reach the vicinity of *Ingrill'er* (USGS Kusilvak Mountain) owing to the repeated fouling of boat propellers by submerged aquatic vegetation. Although not documented, a mix of environmental factors (warmer weather and shallower water allowing more sunlight to reach underwater plants, for example) has likely accelerated the growth of such vegetation in the area in recent decades; however, navigability problems of this sort had already developed on the *Qip'ngayaq* by the 1950s. In fact, the site of *Nunaqerraq* (USGS New Knockhock [AA-9365])—situated about 56 kilometres downriver from where the 2011 research team had to turn back—was abandoned as a village by 1960 due to increasing "shallowness" (that is, in-filling) of the

Qip'ngayaq even further downstream (USBIA 1986, 25). In other words, boat travel between *Nunaqerraq* and the river's outlet on the Bering Sea had become impracticable. Regardless of environmental factors, vastly reduced boat travel on the river has arguably contributed to its in-filling by vegetation in some areas. If human use of the *Qip'ngayaq* had not decreased so dramatically, the river's main channel might still be navigable today—partly because boat propellers would regularly "trim" submerged vegetation. But people might even be "caring" for the river in accordance with ancestral traditions. As Joshua Phillip, of Tuluksak, explained to ANCSA researchers in 1988:

> The people in the past watched over the land with respect and honor. [The] rivers and sloughs we just looked at with much marsh and mire, when [people travelled] through these places they would clean them. They would remove all the bog and overhaul the [mouths and outlets]. This is done since the rivers are food sources. They paid great attention to the land. We were instructed to clean and groom the rivers and sloughs when we travel through them. (Phillip 1988, 5)

This "cleaning" of waterways served both to facilitate boat travel and to prevent barriers to the migrations of blackfish, whitefish, and salmon (see, for example, Moses 1988, 24–27)—subsistence resources of critical importance to the delta's Indigenous people. Thus, regularly travelled rivers and sloughs were cared for in a manner analogous to basic road maintenance in today's "built environment." But, not surprisingly, decreased travel on such waterways is correlated with decreased maintenance of them.[16]

"New" Burials at Long-Abandoned Sites

In spite of declining human use of the country, enduring personal connections to place have been documented not only in stories but also physical evidence discovered in recent visits to some sites. This is illustrated by examples from the *Qip'ngayagaq* (USGS Kipniyagok) drainage, where "new" burials have been noted at two long-abandoned sites—a testament to the deceased individuals' deep connections to place. Since neither site is easily accessible from modern communities, the existence of these burials also reflects the commitment of surviving family members/friends to honour the deceased's wishes relative to burial locations (even if doing so may violate state laws).

EXAMPLE 1: *NUNALLERPAK*

Radiometric evidence indicates that *Nunallerpak* (AA-9373 [also known as *Qip'ngayagaq*]) was occupied as early as the mid-1300s (USBIA 2011). It was a major year-round village starting sometime before 1900 through to about 1920, when mortalities linked to an epidemic (most likely the 1918–1919 influenza) may have caused its virtual abandonment (Akerelrea 1981c, 16–17; Henry 1981, 17–20). But its subsequent reoccupation as a winter village is evidenced by the fact that it was home to 43 people in January 1940 (US Bureau of the Census 1940 ["Nunalakpuk"]).[17] The site was also used as a spring camp for sealing, fishing, and beluga whale hunting (Tunutmoak 1981), probably until about 1960. When ANCSA researchers investigated *Nunallerpak* in 1981, they found the remains of more than 40 dwellings in the habitation area and 45 graves in an adjacent cemetery (USBIA 1984f) (figure 6.19).

FIGURE 6.19 Cemetery area at *Nunallerpak*, June 1981. Grassy "burial knoll" in approximate centre of image to right of pond near intact plywood grave boxes (graves 10 and 11) on adjacent rise; *Qip'ngayagaq* (river) in background. View to southeast. Photograph by Robert Drozda. ANCSA 14(h)(1) Collection, case file AA-9373, Bureau of Indian Affairs, Anchorage.

FIGURE 6.20 Cemetery area at *Nunallerpak*, September 2011. Note tundra-covered "burial knoll" in lower centre of image and "new" (1996) burial at left-centre. View to southwest. Photo by Matthew O'Leary. ANCSA 14(h)(1) Collection, case file AA-9373, Bureau of Indian Affairs, Anchorage.

Nine of the graves were situated on a small mound ("burial knoll"); during an on-site interview, Scammon Bay elder Dan Akerelrea (1981c, 12) said they appeared to be the oldest burials at the site.

Nunallerpak was revisited in 2011 with the objectives of testing the habitation area and re-inspecting the cemetery (figure 6.20). The survey located no trace of graves on the "burial knoll" (those features having been completely overgrown with tundra vegetation) but did record a new burial at the site dating to 1996 (figure 6.21). The interred person ("A. Canoe [Died 04-13-96]") is believed to be Alice Canoe, who probably lived in the modern village of Alakanuk (60 kilometres to the northeast) at the time of her death. She was living at *Nunallerpak* with her husband and three children in January 1940 (US Bureau of the Census 1940), so it is reasonable to think this place had special meaning to her. It is unknown how long she was a resident of *Nunallerpak*, but other members of her family may also be buried there.

EXAMPLE 2: *QIP'NGAYAGAQ*

The former year-round village of *Qip'ngayagaq* (AA-9883) was remembered as a particularly good site for fox trapping and harvesting whitefish. Site usage probably began by the mid- to late 1700s and its occupation as a village reportedly ended about 1930. But for four or five decades thereafter several individuals regularly used the site as a spring and summer subsistence camp for the harvesting of blackfish, geese, and berries (USBLM 1983). When *Qip'ngayagaq* was investigated by ANCSA researchers in 1981, it consisted of three areas that collectively contained thirty-one houses and twenty-five graves (USBIA 1984g). The smallest of these areas ("Area A") included the remains of nine houses, a collapsed cabin, and one grave. This particular burial differed from all others at the site because the coffin was intact and a sewing machine was attached to its cover (figure 6.22).

(FACING) FIGURE 6.21 Close-up of "new" burial at *Nunallerpak*, September 2011. View to east-southeast. Photograph by Kenneth Pratt. ANCSA 14(h)(1) Collection, case file AA-9373, Bureau of Indian Affairs, Anchorage.

(RIGHT) FIGURE 6.22 "Sewing-machine grave" at *Qip'ngayagaq*, June 1981. Sewing machine is a vibrating shuttle type; possibly Singer brand, Model 26 or 27. View to east; Alouette Gazelle helicopter in background. Photograph by Steve Deschermeier. ANCSA 14(h)(1) Collection, case file AA-9883, Bureau of Indian Affairs, Anchorage.

(TOP) FIGURE 6.23 "Sewing-machine grave" at *Qip'ngayagaq*, September 2011. View to west-southwest. Photograph by Kenneth Pratt. ANCSA 14(h)(1) Collection, case file AA-9883, Bureau of Indian Affairs, Anchorage.

(MIDDLE) FIGURE 6.24 "New" burials at *Qip'ngayagaq*, September 2011. From front to back: 1989 burial; 1982 burial; "sewing-machine grave." View to south. Photograph by Kenneth Pratt. ANCSA 14(h)(1) Collection, case file AA-9883, Bureau of Indian Affairs, Anchorage.

(BOTTOM) FIGURE 6.25 Grave at *Nunaqerraq*, with *Qip'ngayaq* (river) in background. Note that the grave box was made of plywood, bound with nylon rope, and placed on a sled. View to northwest, June 1985. Photograph by Harley Cochran. ANCSA 14(h)(1) Collection, case file AA-9365, Bureau of Indian Affairs, Anchorage.

(FACING) FIGURE 6.26 Close-up view of 1982 grave at *Qip'ngayagaq*, September 2011. View to west. Photograph by Kenneth Pratt. ANCSA 14(h)(1) Collection, case file AA-9883, Bureau of Indian Affairs, Anchorage.

A 2011 revisit to "Area A" of the site unexpectedly revealed two additional burials next to the "sewing-machine grave" (figures 6.23 and 6.24). Later research determined the individuals interred in the "new" graves were half-brothers: Tom and Fred Augustine. Both men formerly lived at the site (Xavier Simon, in Akerelrea 1981c, 36). Tom died in April 1982 and his funeral was held in Alakanuk (see Fienup-Riordan 1986, 210); afterwards, his body was transported some 70 kilometres southwest for burial at *Qip'ngayagaq*.[18] Fred (who also was born at this site) was buried in 1989. Another brother, Willie Augustine, is also buried here (Augustine 1985; Yupanik 1985), but the date and precise location of his burial on the site is unknown. Circumstantial evidence suggests the "sewing-machine grave" is likely that of a female relative of the Augustine brothers. Thus, the three graves constitute a family grouping.

Interestingly, the grave dating to 1982 is today the least visible of the three, being almost completely overgrown by tundra (figure 6.26). If not for the prior work by ANCSA researchers, it would be easy to conclude from surface appearances that this is the oldest burial in this part of the site.

FIGURE 6.27 Grave 29 at *Pastuliq*, August 1985; notebook for scale. The grave box sides and top crosspieces (associated with the now collapsed cover) are plainly visible; but the entire interior of the burial had sunken below ground and the grave box cavity was completely filled with water. There is no chance any surface evidence of this burial would be visible today. View to southwest. Photograph by Kenneth Pratt. ANCSA 14(h)(1) Collection, case file AA-10071/AA-10391, Bureau of Indian Affairs, Anchorage.

Conclusions

It is no surprise that landscape changes are a constant in the Yukon Delta because natural environments are never static. But even in this highly dynamic ecosystem there is little doubt that landscape changes are occurring more rapidly today—with the undeniably warming climate being the key factor. My earlier claim that climate change should not be treated as a default explanation for landscape changes being observed in the region today is supported by contextual information about historical processes of ecosystem change found in Indigenous oral history accounts, and indeed in other documentary records. Such records show, for instance, that although erosion is continuous along the Yukon River (see, for example, Petroff 1884, 6, 10; Pratt 2018, 67–69), sites of similar antiquity that occupied its banks have not been impacted consistently. In other words, the same process of erosion that destroys sites along one part of the river may help preserve them in another. Erosion affecting sites along the Bering Sea coastline may be more predictably destructive, but, again, it often is not reasonable or accurate to characterize the negative impacts noted at coastal sites today as entirely the result of recent climate change.[19]

Existing USGS topographic maps of the region (most dating to the early 1950s) depict scores of hydrological features that do not accurately represent the contemporary physical landscape. Some rivers have carved new channels while others have disappeared; and coastlines have been dramatically altered. What was yesterday a large lake may today be a dry lake bed; and two adjacent lakes may now have merged into one. Navigating this country by map is thus a daunting and potentially highly confusing undertaking. The fact that Indigenous place names often remain for settlements and natural features that have vanished (see, for example, Drozda 2009) adds another layer of challenges to the situation.[20] Overall, the comparatively fine-grained data contained in the ANCSA 14(h)(1) Collection provide an invaluable tool for assessing ecosystem changes through time in many areas of Alaska.

The merit of the preceding observation is reinforced by a recent article about cemeteries at Kongiganak and Kwiggilingok, Yup'ik villages on the western shore of Kuskokwim Bay. The article (Cotsirilos 2017) describes the serious impacts of thawing permafrost, including grave crosses sticking "out of the sunken ground at odd angles" and some burials completely submerged in water. The villagers' inability to prevent these problems is an unfortunate reality, one to which they are for the most part reluctantly resigned. The article succeeds as a human-interest story, but it also attributes the problems in these two cemeteries to recent climate change, which, as I have argued, is only part of the explanation. The ANCSA 14(h)(1) Collection contains hundreds of photographs from the 1980s documenting similar conditions in cemeteries throughout the Yukon-Kuskokwim region (see figure 6.27 for an example). Simple explanations for change—either cultural or ecological—should always be suspect, because history is layered and often opaque.

As demonstrated above, revisiting sites recorded and photographed thirty or more years ago to compare their "then and now" appearances can bring certain processes of landscape change into much sharper focus. It can also be a powerful reminder that, in some ecosystems, surface evidence of past cultural use of an area can be entirely eliminated or obscured by natural processes in comparatively short spans of time. Thus, land that today appears wholly natural and free of human traces may actually have been heavily used by people in the past. Another important result of the site revisits described in this chapter is the *physical evidence* they revealed of strong feelings about and associations with certain "abandoned" landscapes among contemporary Indigenous residents of the region (see figure 6.28). This is especially true with regard to abandoned sites where "new burials" have been observed. Site revisits have recently taken place in many areas of the Yup'ik region, but new burials at long-abandoned sites seem to be restricted to a relatively small portion of the region. The individuals interred in those burials were residents of the lower Yukon River—the first part of the Yup'ik region to experience widespread Indigenous language loss. The new burials thus represent an interesting nexus of memory and landscape relative to matters of identity. Most of the individual sites discussed above have a long history of cultural use, and many of them contained abundant surface remains testifying to that fact. But some of the landscape changes noted at those sites during recent revisits should be taken as cautionary lessons to archaeologists (and not just those with research interests in the Yukon Delta). Perhaps the main lesson is that surface cultural remains alone are an insufficient basis for definitive statements about a site's physical extent or the intensity of its past use. For example, consider the case of *Nunallerpak* (discussed above). In 1981, archaeologists recorded 45 graves at the site's associated cemetery; however, by 2011, surface evidence of at least 15 of the graves had disappeared, none by erosional processes likely to have destroyed them (they had instead sunk beneath the surface or been completely overgrown with vegetation). Given the site's long history of use, this finding strongly suggests that the *Nunallerpak* cemetery contains *more than* the 45 graves seen in 1981. This reinforces the idea that the results that flow from most archaeological site investigations are best understood as "snapshots in time."

FIGURE 6.28 Cairn on a southern ridge of *Ingrill'er* (USGS Kusilvak Mountain), with *Qip'ngayaq* (USGS Black River) and the delta flats in the background. The lack of lichen growth on the stones used in the cairn's construction is clear evidence that the feature is not old, which, in turn, is another indication of recent, continuing use of the area. View to south, September 2011. Photograph by Kenneth Pratt. ANCSA 14(h)(1) Collection, Calista region digital photographs, Bureau of Indian Affairs, Anchorage.

My main objective in this chapter has been to point out that knowledge of how a given ecosystem looked and operated in the past is an essential tool for assessing how directly that ecosystem is being affected by contemporary climate change. In processual terms, reliable evaluations of the latter require reasonably deep perspectives—which, in the view of this author, should be based on minimal temporal periods of at least fifty years. We know that active human use of an ecosystem can trigger or contribute to landscape changes, many of which involve ongoing natural processes. But in some ecosystems such changes may also be linked to reduced human use of the land. By devoting greater attention to this largely unexplored topic, researchers have the potential to expand our understanding of Indigenous patterns of land use and environmental stewardship in the Arctic. This could help generate more complete, balanced, and defensible interpretations of climate change impacts. Critically examining how people confronted, thought about, and responded to landscape change in the past would also contribute to discussions about how anticipatory knowledge can help people meet the challenges of current and projected climate change.

Acknowledgements

The author has been fortunate to work with many outstanding Yup'ik elders and interpreters from communities across the Yukon Delta, and also with some excellent colleagues on early ANCSA 14(h)(1) field crews that worked in the region: I thank all of these individuals for their contributions to the collection of data on which this chapter rests. Frequent discussions about landscape changes in the Yukon Delta with my long-time colleague Matthew O'Leary were especially valuable and appreciated; his insights have strongly influenced my thinking on the topic. I am particularly grateful to Mark Nuttall for his thoughtful observations on and questions about my topic. I also thank Robert Drozda for assistance in obtaining certain photographs included in the chapter; Dale Slaughter for producing the maps; Kristin K'eit for information concerning federal and state environmental laws; and Scott Heyes for comments offered on an earlier draft of this chapter.

Notes

1 Land status issues in Southeast Alaska prevented Sealaska Corporation from filing claims for its total ANCSA land entitlement prior to the various deadlines for doing so. More than three decades later, that problem was rectified when the US Congress passed the 2014 National Defense Reauthorization Act (Public Law No, 113-291). Section 3002 ("Sealaska land entitlement finalization") of that act authorized Sealaska Corporation to make additional land selections, including 76 new ANCSA 14(h)(1) site applications. As a result, the total number of ANCSA 14(h)(1) claims filed by the regional corporations is now 4,047.

2 US surveys are typically performed by surveyors under contract with the Bureau of Land Management (BLM). The US surveys correct and refine the draft survey information ANCSA researchers compiled on each ANCSA 14(h)(1) site; they constitute the government's final, official land descriptions on which land patents for the sites are based. In accordance with an existing agreement between the BIA and BLM, if the surveyors encounter problems with the boundaries reported for a given site, they are authorized to seek resolution by contacting BIA from the field. Sometimes the identified problems can be resolved only by further BIA fieldwork; in such cases, the BLM places the US survey on hold and reschedules it at a later date. Since virtually every other type of land claim authorized by the ANCSA legislation was prioritized above the ANCSA 14(h)(1) claims, US surveys of these sites often do not occur until several decades after the associated ANCSA field investigations were conducted. Thus, when opportunities to do so arise, BIA staff revisit previously investigated sites to obtain new aerial photography and improved locational coordinates. The results are shared with the BLM so they can be incorporated into future US survey contracts.

3 Every "composite field map" consists of two or more United States Geological Survey (USGS) topographical maps that were either glued or taped together. Some of these composites served as project area/reference maps for ANCSA field crews, but the majority were used in oral history interviews with Alaska Native elders. As a result, many composite field maps are heavily annotated with place names and other cultural information (for example, cabin and camp sites, grave locations, trails, and so on).

4 The primary objective of oral history research on the project was to obtain site-specific information that would help us evaluate the local and/or regional significance of the applied-for sites. But ANCSA 14(h)(1) oral history tape recordings are extremely rich in data concerning a wide range of other cultural history and heritage topics (for example, subsistence practices, settlement patterns, religious/ceremonial life, warfare, technology, human-animal relationships, and culture change).

5 Every ANCSA 14(h)(1) claim was assigned a discrete case file number by the BLM, the federal agency to which site applications had to be submitted. The relevant case file numbers (AA-10361, for example) are listed for all ANCSA 14(h)(1) sites discussed in this chapter. It was not uncommon for ANCSA researchers to determine that two or more applications had been filed for the same site. In such cases, BIA combined the applications and issued a single report, with the lowest numbered case file given precedence (AA-10071 over AA-10391, for example).

6 The watercourse is identified on USGS maps as the "Ear River." The river's Yup'ik name is *Ciutnguilleq* ("former thing that was like an ear"[?]) (Henry 1981; see also Jacobson 2012, 218, 227). According to Orth (1967, 294), Ear River is "an abbreviated translation of an Eskimo name 'Tsut-muilk,' reported by USC&GS [United States Coast and Geodetic Survey] in 1949." (Note that when Yup'ik place names presented in this chapter are not correlated with USGS names, it means the landscape features in question are unnamed on official maps.)

7 The purpose of the 2012 visit to *Curukaryaraq* was to obtain new aerial photographs and improved locational coordinates and to conduct archaeological testing at the site in hopes of obtaining an organic sample that could be dated to provide further information about the site's chronology. Fortunately, a shovel probe in sod that was slumping into the pond which now covers the main site area produced sufficient charcoal flecks to generate a radiocarbon date.

8 The scheduled 1982 investigation of a former spring and fall camp named *Naruyat Paingat* (AA-11481) had to be cancelled after ANCSA researchers found the site was entirely submerged beneath the waters of *Elaayiq* (USGS Israthorak Creek) (USBIA 1984b). At least one semi-subterranean house pit could be seen through the water; but there was no way the site could be recorded. Its location was confirmed by Yup'ik elder John Wassillie of Akiachak, the Kuskokwim River village with which *Naruyat Paingat* is affiliated. Oral history accounts suggest the site may have remained in use through about 1930; it is not known how long it had been submerged as of 1982. In fact, since notable high-water conditions were present across the region in the summer of 1982 it is possible the site's submergence may have been only temporary. When ANCSA researchers revisited the area in 2004, however, the site was still underwater (USBIA 2004).

9 Radiometric data from *Ayemqerraq* indicate its initial occupation occurred as early as the mid-1600s; and, like *Anqercaq*, this site also holds a significant place in regional history concerning internecine warfare—which probably ended in the Yukon Delta prior to 1800 (see Pratt n.d.).

10 In August 2011, surveyors performing a US survey at the site contacted the BIA and reported that erosion had exposed "hundreds" of bones along and beyond the shoreline margin of the site and suggested the site boundaries should be expanded accordingly. Revised boundaries were tentatively agreed upon, but final completion of the survey was delayed until BIA staff could assess the situation first-hand, in part to determine if any of the eroding bones might be human. This was the impetus for the September 2011 BIA site visit.

11 ANCSA composite field map number 84VAK02 contains an annotation indicating that the river is also named *Qavinaq*.

12 Because it was inextricably linked to the Western educational system, the population-centralization process also had significant negative impacts on the vitality of Indigenous languages in the region.

13 Data limitations preclude estimating the number of beaver hides Indigenous hunters and trappers in this region may have traded to Euro-Americans annually from about 1840 through the early 1900s (see Arndt 1996; Wolfe 1979, 54–79).

14 By comparison, in the 1970s licences were required to harvest these animals and a limit of ten beavers per licence was enforced (Wolfe 1979, 77).

15 In some areas of the larger Yukon-Kuskokwim region, however, Indigenous residents have directly blamed major reductions in local fish populations on increased beaver populations and the animals' dam-building activities (see, for example, Williams and Nook 1988, 4–5).

16 Ironically, today such traditional river "maintenance" practices might even be punishable under state or federal environmental laws. This would be the case if, for example, the plants being removed were considered sensitive aquatic species, sensitive habitat contributors, or species of importance with respect to bird habitat and nesting.

17 The obvious correlation of the site name reported in the census ("Nunalakpuk") with *Nunallerpak* supports oral history accounts that suggest the site was abandoned for some amount of time and then later reoccupied as a winter village. That is, *Nunallerpak* essentially means "big old village"—and in traditional Yup'ik place-naming practices, the base *nuna-* was usually only applied to abandoned villages (see also Pratt 2013, 32n21).

18 Given the month of death, the body (contained in a wooden coffin) was most likely loaded on a sled and pulled behind a snow machine all the way from Alakanuk to *Qip'ngayagaq*. This is probably also how the body of "A. Canoe" was transported from Alakanuk to *Nunallerpak* in 1996. Clear evidence for this method of transporting coffins to burial locations during winter months is seen in figure 6.25. The grave pictured therein was recorded by ANCSA researchers at the site of *Nunaqerraq*, located in close proximity to the *Qip'ngayagaq* drainage.

19 This point is reinforced by a consideration of erosion occurring at a former Yup'ik village site on Kuskokwim Bay excavated by researchers with the University of Aberdeen. The site, *Agalik* (Pratt 2013 ["Nunalleq" (Knecht 2014)]), has received considerable press in the past decade—partly because its excavation has been portrayed as

a race to save the village from certain destruction by the impacts of climate change (Knecht 2014). One publication about the excavation suggests—with no supporting evidence cited—that the 1964 Alaska earthquake initiated erosion of the site (Knecht 2014, 43); it also asserts the rate of erosion has increased dramatically since 2009 (Knecht 2014, 44–45), clearly implying climate change caused that increase. As in the Yukon Delta, coastal erosion is no doubt negatively impacting sites all along Kuskokwim Bay, and global warming is almost certainly accelerating that process. For instance, decreases in the extent and thickness of sea ice can significantly exacerbate rates of coastal erosion during fall and winter storms. But the operative word here is "process"—that is, coastal erosion is continuous in this region. Returning to the village of *Agalik*, notable erosion of that site was actually occurring by the early 1930s—such that Clark Garber (n.d., 3) speculated at the time that the entire site might soon be lost to the ocean. Assigning climate change sole responsibility for the increased rate of erosion observed at *Agalik* since 2009 also does not take into account possible impacts of the archaeological excavation itself on that process. It was reported that 232 square metres of excavation blocks were opened at the site between 2009 and 2013 (Knecht 2014, 44–45). Stated another way, by 2013 excavators had removed 232 square metres of insulating sod from the surface of the site. That action must have increased thermokarst melting to some degree, and hence may have contributed to accelerated erosion at the site.

20 The voluminous place names data contained in the ANCSA 14(h)(1) Collection constitutes an outstanding resource for exploring topics like the suggestion of Mary Pete (1984, 51–52, 70n91]) that a form of "name taboo" is practiced among the Yup'ik in connection with former habitation sites that have been lost to erosion. This author is dubious about that finding for several reasons (for example, see discussion above on *Anqercaq*), but it is certainly possible that not all Yup'ik groups had identical practices relative to place name usage.

References

Akerelrea, Dan

1981a Tape-recorded oral history account. Gene Smerchek and Steve Christy, interviewers; Xavier Simon, interpreter. On-site interview, *Curukaryaraq* (AA-10361), Alaska. 15 June. Transcribed (English only) by Robert Drozda. Tape 81ROMO29. Bureau of Indian Affairs, ANCSA Office, Anchorage.

1981b Tape-recorded oral history account. Alan Ziff, Kenneth Pratt, and Ted Maitland, interviewers; Xavier Simon, interpreter. 22 June. Scammon Bay, Alaska. Translated and transcribed by Monica Shelden. Tape 81ROMO03. Bureau of Indian Affairs, ANCSA Office, Anchorage.

1981c Tape-recorded oral history account. Alan Ziff and Ted Maitland, interviewers; Xavier Simon, interpreter. 23 June. On-site interviews, *Nunallerpak* (AA-9373) and *Qip'ngayagaq* (AA-9883), Alaska. Translated and transcribed by Monica Shelden. Tape 81ROMO05. Bureau of Indian Affairs, ANCSA Office, Anchorage.

Andrews, Elizabeth F.

1989 *The Akulmiut: Territorial Dimensions of a Yup'ik Eskimo Society.* Technical Paper No. 177, Alaska Department of Fish and Game, Division of Subsistence, Juneau.

Arndt, Katherine L.

1996 Dynamics of the Fur Trade on the Middle Yukon River, Alaska, 1839 to 1868. PhD dissertation, Department of Anthropology, University of Alaska Fairbanks.

Arnold, Robert D.

1978 *Alaska Native Land Claims.* Alaska Native Foundation, Anchorage.

Augustine, Fred

1985 Tape-recorded oral history account. Phyllis Gilbert and John Peterkin, interviewers; Monica Murphy, interpreter. 28 June. Alakanuk, Alaska. Transcribed (English only) by Sylvia Damian. Tape 85ALA028. Bureau of Indian Affairs, ANCSA Office, Anchorage.

Barker, James H.

1979 From Mud Houses to Wood: Kashunuk to Chevak. *Alaska Journal* (Summer): 24–31.

Biela, Vanessa R. von, Christopher J. Sergeant, Michael P. Carey, Zachary Liller, Charles Russell, Stephanie Quinn-Davidson, Peter S. Rand, Peter A. H. Westley, and Christian E. Zimmerman

2022 Premature Mortality Observations Among Alaska's Pacific Salmon During Record Heat in 2019. *Fisheries* 47(4): 157–168.

Cotsirilos, Teresa

2017 "As Permafrost Thaws, Western Alaska Cemeteries Sink into Swampland." *Anchorage Daily News*, 19 December.

Doolittle, Tom

2013 Written communication with the author. Email messages dated 2 May.

Drozda, Robert M.

1995 "They Talked of the Land with Respect": Interethnic Communication in the Documentation of Historical Places and Cemetery Sites. In *When Our Words Return: Writing, Hearing, and Remembering Oral Traditions of Alaska and the Yukon*, edited by Phyllis Morrow and William Schneider, pp. 98–122. Utah State University Press, Logan.

2009 ANCSA Field Maps and Native Knowledge—GIS in the Raw. In *Chasing the Dark: Perspectives on Place, History and Alaska Native Land Claims*, edited by Kenneth L. Pratt, pp. 458–461. Bureau of Indian Affairs, ANCSA Office, Anchorage.

Fienup-Riordan, Ann

1982 *Navarin Basin Sociocultural Baseline Analysis.* Technical Report No. 70. Alaska Outer Continental Shelf Socioeconomic Studies Program, Bureau of Land Management, Anchorage.

1986 *When Our Bad Season Comes: A Cultural Account of Subsistence Harvesting and Harvest Disruption on the Yukon Delta.* Aurora Monograph Series No. 1. Alaska Anthropological Association, Anchorage.

1994 *Boundaries and Passages: Rule and Ritual in Yup'ik Eskimo Oral Tradition.* University of Oklahoma Press, Norman.

Frink, Lisa

1999 Preliminary Report of the 1999 Chevak Traditional Council Archaeology Project. Report No. 3. Unpublished manuscript. Department of Anthropology, University of Wisconsin–Madison.

Garber, Clark M.

n.d. The Quinhagak-Tununak War and the Founding of Ahlahlich. Unpublished manuscript in possession of author.

Griffin, Dennis

1996 A Culture in Transition: A History of Acculturation and Settlement near the Mouth of the Yukon River, Alaska. *Arctic Anthropology* 33(1): 98–115.

Harrington, George L.

1918 *The Anvik-Andreakski Region, Alaska.* US Geological Survey Bulletin 683. Government Printing Office, Washington, DC.

Henry, John

1981 Tape-recorded oral history account. Alan Ziff, Kenneth Pratt, and Steve Deschermeier, interviewers; Xavier Simon, interpreter. Translated and transcribed by Monica Shelden; reviewed by Alice Fredson. 11 July. Scammon Bay, Alaska. Tape 81ROMO09. Bureau of Indian Affairs, ANCSA Office, Anchorage.

Inakak, Henry

1983 Tape-recorded oral history account. Donna Fesselmeyer and Patricia McCoy, interviewers; Eliza Lincoln, interpreter. 29 July. Tununak, Alaska. Transcribed (English only) by Patricia McCoy. Tape 83TUN031. Bureau of Indian Affairs, ANCSA Office, Anchorage.

Jacobson, Steven A.

2012 *Yup'ik Eskimo Dictionary.* 2nd ed. Alaska Native Language Center, University of Alaska Fairbanks.

Knecht, Rick

2014 Nunalleq: Rescuing an Eskimo Village from the Sea. *British Archaeology* 136: 42–49.

Moses, George, Sr.

1988 Tape-recorded oral history account. Robert Drozda, interviewer; Vernon Chimegalrea, interpreter. 23 August. Akiachak, Alaska. Translated and transcribed by Lucy Coolidge Daniel; with reviews and editing by Sophie Manutuli Shield and Irene Reed. Tape 88CAL162. Bureau of Indian Affairs, ANCSA Office, Anchorage.

Nayamin, Ulrich

1981 Tape-recorded oral history account. Robert Drozda and Kris Andre, interviewers; Leo Moses, interpreter. 25 July. Chevak, Alaska. Transcribed (English only) by Robert Drozda. Tape 81ROM022. Bureau of Indian Affairs, ANCSA Office, Anchorage.

Nelson, Edward W.

1882 A Sledge Journey in the Delta of the Yukon, Northern Alaska. *Proceedings of the Royal Geographical Society* 6: 660–670, 712. Edward Stanford, London.

1887 *Report upon Natural History Collections Made in Alaska Between the Years 1877 and 1881.* Arctic Series of Publications Issued in Connection with the Signal Service, US Army, No. 3. Government Printing Office, Washington, DC.

1899 *The Eskimo About Bering Strait.* Bureau of American Ethnology, 18th Annual Report, Part 1, 1896–1897. Government Printing Office, Washington, DC.

Nuttall, Mark

2010 Anticipation, Climate Change, and Movement in Greenland. *Études/Inuit/Studies* 34(1): 21–37.

O'Leary, Matthew B., Robert M. Drozda, and Kenneth L. Pratt

2009 ANCSA Section 14(h)(1) Records. In *Chasing the Dark: Perspectives on Place, History and Alaska Native Land Claims*, edited by Kenneth L. Pratt, pp. 452–457. Bureau of Indian Affairs, ANCSA Office, Anchorage.

Orth, Donald J.

1967 *Dictionary of Alaska Place Names.* US Geological Survey Professional Paper 567. Government Printing Office, Washington, DC.

Oswalt, Wendell H.

1963 *Mission of Change in Alaska: Eskimos and Moravians on the Kuskokwim.* Huntington Library, San Marino, California.

1990 *Bashful No Longer: An Alaskan Eskimo Ethnohistory, 1778–1988.* University of Oklahoma Press, Norman.

Pete, Mary C.

1984 Yup'ik Place-Names: Tapraq, a Case Study. Master's thesis, Department of Anthropology, University of Alaska Fairbanks.

Petroff, Ivan

1884 *Report on the Population, Industries, and Resources of Alaska: Tenth Census of the U.S.A., 1880.* Government Printing Office, Washington, DC.

Phillip, Joshua

1988 Tape-recorded oral history account. Robert Drozda, interviewer; Vernon Chimegalrea, interpreter. 29 June. Tuluksak, Alaska. Translated and transcribed by Marie Meade; reviewed and edited by Irene Reed. Tape 88CAL046. Bureau of Indian Affairs, ANCSA Office, Anchorage.

Polty, Noel

1982 Tape-recorded oral history account. Kenneth Pratt and Steve Banks, interviewers; Ben Fitka, interpreter. 13 August. Pilot Station, Alaska. Partial transcription (English only) by Matthew O'Leary. Tape 82RSM036. Bureau of Indian Affairs, ANCSA Office, Anchorage.

Pratt, Kenneth L.

2004 Observations on Researching and Managing Alaska Native Oral History: A Case Study. *Alaska Journal of Anthropology* 2(1–2): 138–153.

2009b A History of the ANCSA 14(h)(1) Program and Significant Reckoning Points, 1975–2008. In *Chasing the Dark: Perspectives on Place, History and Alaska Native Land Claims*, edited by Kenneth L. Pratt, pp. 2–43. Bureau of Indian Affairs, ANCSA Office, Anchorage.

2009c Nuniwarmiut Land Use, Settlement History and Socio-Territorial Organization, 1880–1960. PhD dissertation, Department of Anthropology, University of Alaska Fairbanks.

2010 The 1855 Attack on Andreevskaia Odinochka: A Review of Russian, American, and Yup'ik Eskimo Accounts. *Alaska Journal of Anthropology* 8(1): 61–72.

2013 Deconstructing the Aglurmiut Migration: An Analysis of Accounts from the Russian-America Period to the Present. *Alaska Journal of Anthropology* 11(1–2): 17–36.

2018 Two Oral History Narratives by *Uicimaalleq* (Walter Kelly): Pilot Station, Alaska. Translated by Monica Shelden; edited and annotated by Kenneth L. Pratt. *Alaska Journal of Anthropology* 16(2): 67–74.

n.d. Thoughts on the "Killing Bank" and Yup'ik Eskimo Warfare. Manuscript in possession of the author.

Pratt, Kenneth L. (editor)

2009a *Chasing the Dark: Perspectives on Place, History and Alaska Native Land Claims*. Bureau of Indian Affairs, ANCSA Office, Anchorage.

Pratt, Kenneth L., Joan C. Stevenson, and Phillip M. Everson

2013 Demographic Adversities and Indigenous Resilience in Western Alaska. *Études/Inuit/Studies* 37(1): 35–56.

Rearden, Spencer

2013 Written communication with the author. Email message dated 2 May.

Sundown, Teddy

1985 Tape-recorded oral history account. Harley Cochran, interviewer; Ledwina Jones, interpreter. 25 July. Scammon Bay, Alaska. Transcribed (English only) by Monica Murphy. Tape 85ALA056. Bureau of Indian Affairs, ANCSA Office, Anchorage.

Tunutmoak, Tom

1981 Tape-recorded oral history account. Steve Christy, Kris Andre, and Marcy Farrell, interviewers; Xavier Simon, interpreter. 12 June. Scammon Bay, Alaska. Partial transcription (English) by Beth Shide. Tape 81ROM028. Bureau of Indian Affairs, ANCSA Office, Anchorage.

United States, Bureau of the Census

1940 Sixteenth Census of the United States: 1940. Second Judicial District, Wade Hampton Recording District, Sheet No. 22B, 14 January. Department of Commerce, Washington, DC.

United States, Bureau of Indian Affairs (USBIA)

1981 *Report of Investigation for Kashunuk Village and Burials, BLM AA-9391 (Calista Corporation).* Bureau of Indian Affairs, ANCSA Office, Anchorage.

1984a *Report of Investigation for* Curukaryaraq, *BLM AA-10361 (Calista Corporation).* Bureau of Indian Affairs, ANCSA Office, Anchorage.

1984b *Report of Investigation for* Naruyat Paingat, *BLM AA-11481 (Calista Corporation).* Bureau of Indian Affairs, ANCSA Office, Anchorage.

1984c *Report of Investigation for* Anqercaq, *BLM AA-9774 (Calista Corporation).* Bureau of Indian Affairs, ANCSA Office, Anchorage.

1984d *Report of Investigation for* Qavinarmiut, *BLM AA-9389 (Calista Corporation).* Bureau of Indian Affairs, ANCSA Office, Anchorage.

1984e *Report of Investigation for Old Chevak, BLM AA-11257 (Calista Corporation).* Bureau of Indian Affairs, ANCSA Office, Anchorage.

1984f *Report of Investigation for* Nunallerpak, *BLM AA-9373 (Calista Corporation).* Bureau of Indian Affairs, ANCSA Office, Anchorage.

1984g *Report of Investigation for* Kepnagyurarmiut, *BLM AA-9883 (Calista Corporation).* Bureau of Indian Affairs, ANCSA Office, Anchorage.

1985 *Report of Investigation for* Merr'aq *Cemetery, BLM AA-11430 (Calista Corporation).* Bureau of Indian Affairs, ANCSA Office, Anchorage.

1986 *Report of Investigation for* Nunaqerraq, *BLM AA-9365 (Calista Corporation).* Compiled by Harley Cochran. Bureau of Indian Affairs, ANCSA Office, Anchorage.

1989 *Report of Investigation for* Ayemqerraq, *BLM AA-10067 (Calista Corporation).* Compiled by Marjorie Connolly and Kenneth L. Pratt. Bureau of Indian Affairs, ANCSA Office, Anchorage.

2004 Memorandum on August 2004 Site Visit (AA-11481). Written by Matthew O'Leary. Bureau of Indian Affairs, ANCSA Office, Anchorage.

2008 *Supplemental Report for Anqercaq, BLM AA-9774 (Calista Corporation).* Written by Matthew O'Leary. Bureau of Indian Affairs, ANCSA Office, Anchorage.

2011 Notes in administrative case file for *Nunallerpak*, AA-9373. Bureau of Indian Affairs, ANCSA Office, Anchorage.

n.d. Administrative case file for *Ayemqerraq*, AA-10067. Bureau of Indian Affairs, ANCSA Office, Anchorage.

United States, Bureau of Land Management (USBLM)

1983 *Native Allotment Field Report, Serial Number F-18708A.* Bureau of Land Management, Alaska State Office, Anchorage.

Williams, Sinka, and Stanley Nook

1988 Tape-recorded oral history account. Philippa Coiley, interviewer. 20 July. Lower Kalskag, Alaska. Translated and transcribed by Monica Shelden. Tape 88CAL081. Bureau of Indian Affairs, ANCSA Office, Anchorage.

Wolfe, Robert J.

1979 Food Production in a Western Eskimo Population. PhD dissertation, Department of Anthropology, University of California, Los Angeles.

Woodbury, Anthony C.

1984 *Cev'armiut Qanemciit Qulirat-llu: Eskimo Narratives and Tales from Chevak, Alaska.* Alaska Native Language Center, University of Alaska Fairbanks.

Yupanik, Jimmy

1985 Tape-recorded oral history account. Harley Cochran and John Peterkin, interviewers; Andrew Kelly, interpreter. 17 June. Emmonak, Alaska. Partial transcription (English only) by Matthew O'Leary. Tape 85ALA020. Bureau of Indian Affairs, ANCSA Office, Anchorage.

Zagoskin, Lavrentiy A.

1967 *Lieutenant Zagoskin's Travels in Russian America, 1842–1844.* Translated by Penelope Rainey; edited by Henry N. Michael. University of Toronto Press, Toronto.

FIGURE 7.1 The confluence of the Copper and Tonsina Rivers. In the Ahtna language, the Copper River is *Atna* ("beyond river"), and the Tonsina River is *Kentsii Na'* ("spruce bark canoe river"). View to the east from the Edgerton Highway at *Kentsii Cae'e*, the mouth of Tonsina River. Photograph by William E. Simeone, 2006.

WILLIAM E. SIMEONE

7 Inventing the Copper River

Maps and the Colonization of Ahtna Lands

Ever since Euro-Americans arrived in Alaska, they have made maps. These maps reveal the accumulation of geographical knowledge and chart the history of exploration. Explorers, prospectors, geologists, anthropologists, developers, and biologists created maps for their own purposes, adding layers of knowledge. At the same time, maps have served as tools of colonization (Boelhower 1988; Hämäläinen 2008). They reveal how Indigenous lands were transformed into Euro-American territory through a process of "cartographic dispossession," whereby Indigenous territorial claims were delimited and delegitimized (Hämäläinen 2008, 195).

The maps described and analyzed in this chapter were selected as representative of different periods in the post-contact history of Alaska. The earliest map in the series dates from 1834, while the most recent dates from 2015. The maps represent a section of east-central Alaska that is the homeland of the Ahtna, an Athabascan-speaking people whose traditional territory encompasses approximately 40,000 square miles in the area of the upper Copper and upper Susitna Rivers (figure 7.2).[1] Archaeological evidence indicates that prior to contact with Euro-Americans, the Ahtna had inhabited this area of Alaska for more than a millennium (see, for example, Workman 1977).

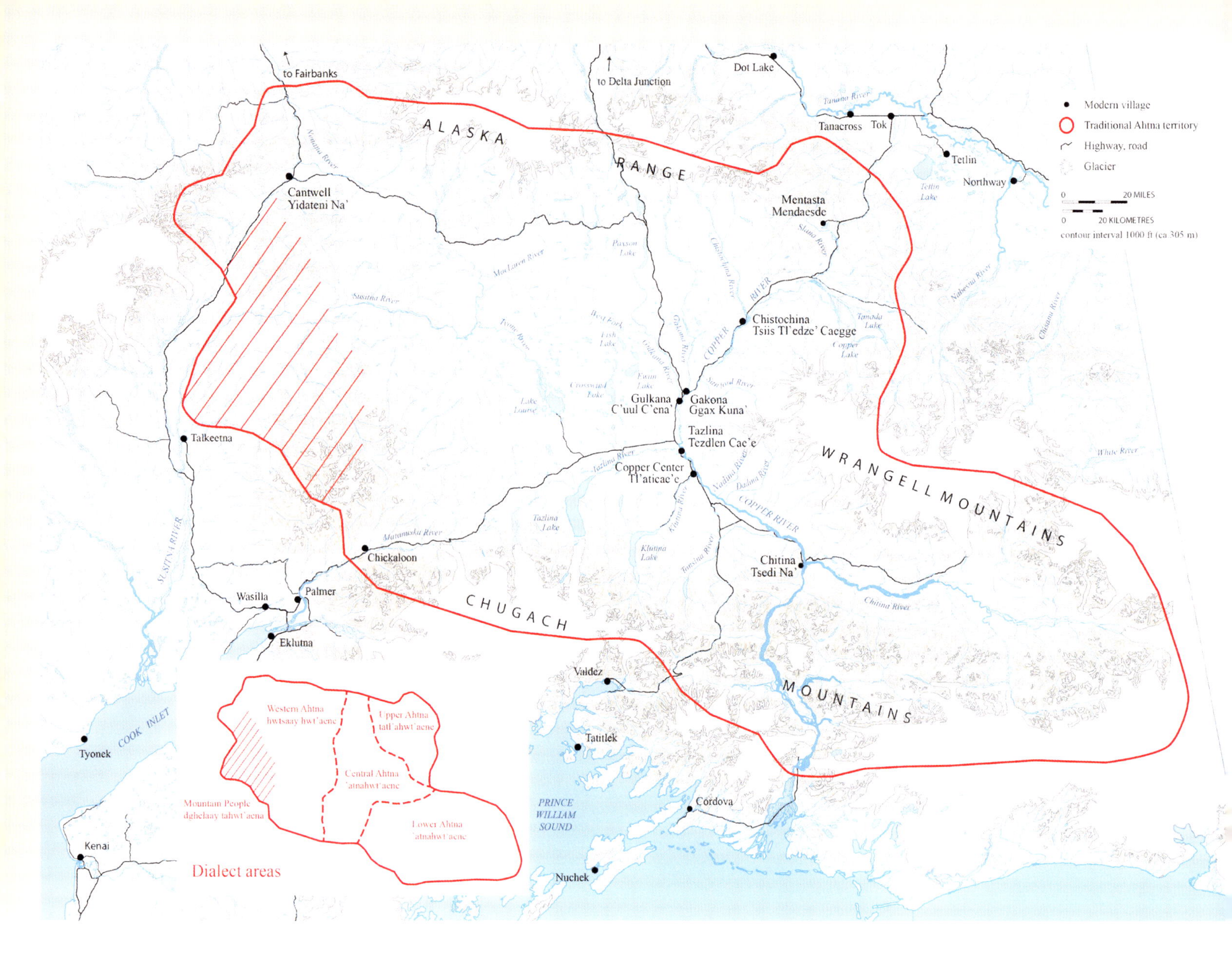

In the nineteenth century, the Ahtna comprised four regional groups, the Lower, Central, Upper, and Western Ahtna, each corresponding to a distinct geographical area and speaking one of four dialects of the Ahtna language (de Laguna and McClellan 1981, 642–643). Ahtna bands were composed of people who belonged to one of several matrilineal clans, but one clan often asserted its inherent right over a specific territory (J. Justin 1991). The Chitina River, for example, was considered *Udzisyu* country, while the upper Copper River belonged to the *'Alts'e'tnaey* clan. Over time, rights to a territory could shift from one clan to another. For instance, Tyone Lake was originally home to the *Tsisyu* clan but was later claimed by the *Taltsiine* clan, as *Tsisyu* men married *Taltsiine* women.

The significance of place is embedded in the Ahtna language. The word for a person or people is *koht'aene*, literally translated as "those who have a territory." Regional band names are a combination

FIGURE 7.2 Traditional Ahtna territory, showing the areas occupied by the four regional bands. *Sources*: Frederica de Laguna and Catharine McClellan (1981, 642); James Kari (2010). Map produced by Matthew O'Leary.

of a place name with the word *hwt'aene*, indicating "people of a place" or "people who possess an area." Lower and Central Ahtna are thus *'Atnahwt'aene*, "people of the Copper River," Upper Ahtna are *Tatl'ahwt'aene*, or "headwaters people," and Western Ahtna are *Hwtsaay hwt'aene*, or "small timber people" (Simeone et al. 2019, 127).

Certain Ahtna leaders, called *denae*, were known as *nen'k'e hwdenae'*, or "on the land person," and described by Ahtna elder Annie Ewan as "men who lived and died in a particular place," signifying their close association with a specific place. *Denae* held titles composed of a place name and either the word *ghaxen* or *denen*. The *denae* of Mentasta was known, for example, as *Mendaes Ghaxen*, "person of shallow lakes." The Ahtna recognized at least seventeen chiefs' titles: eight located in Lower Ahtna territory, six in Central Ahtna territory, one in Western Ahtna territory, and two in Upper Ahtna territory. This suggests that the titles were associated with sources of copper, important salmon fishing sites, and major trails leading into and out of Ahtna territory (Kari 1986, 15).

Ahtna recognized territorial rights based on continual use and occupation. Territorial boundaries were enforced, but obligations based on kinship and clan affiliation meant that food resources had to be shared, especially in times of shortage. As a result, many people had some recognized right to resources in another band's territory (Reckord 1983, 76–78). Uninvited interlopers, however, risked being killed on sight (de Laguna and McClellan 1981, 644; McClellan 1975, 227). American explorers observed several instances where non-local Indigenous people were reluctant to enter a "foreign" or "alien" territory (Abercrombie 1900, 598; Rice 1900, 786).

Ahtna regional territories can be thought of as multi-dimensional spaces consisting of people, animals, plants, earth, water, and air; a terrain lived in and lived with. Wilson Justin put it this way when he talked about his home territory to the east of the upper Copper River:

> So when I say "Nabesna," I'm not talking about where I was born, I'm talking about the idea that my family and my clan lived, hunted, died, and spent their time in the area called Nabesna. Not just where I was born, but the whole area.
>
> When I say Nabesna, I'm not talking about a specific plot of ground, 20 or 30 acres that I was born in. I'm talking about the trails that led through to Nabesna, the trails that lead up and down the river, the hunting trails that go to the sheep [hunting] sites—the camps that we [. . .] have used for hunting areas for centuries.
>
> So you don't say "I'm from Nabesna" in a street sense. You say, "I'm from the area where my clan has obtained exclusive use and jurisdiction over many, many, many thousands of years." (Quoted in Ainsworth 1999, 43)

Justin later provided a detailed description of the boundaries of Upper Ahtna territory in which he mentions that the area around the Nabesna and Chisana Rivers and the White River (see figure 11.2) is "well known to my family since that's where we are from" (W. Justin 2014, 77).

The cartographic colonization of Ahtna territory took place in stages. Initially, explorers and cartographers relied on Ahtna knowledge to produce the first maps of Ahtna territory, and they frequently retained Alaska Native toponyms to fill

FIGURE 7.3 "Hunting camp of Upper Copper River Indians, head of Delta River, Alaska." Gulkins district, Copper River region. 1898. Photograph by Walter Mendenhall. United States Geological Survey, USGS Denver Library Photographic Collection, mwc00027.

in the "blank" spaces. Ahtna geographic knowledge was essential in developing both the local fur trade and the regional mining industry. As colonialism matured and administration became the priority, the Ahtna presence was reduced and eventually eliminated, their culture erased under an overlay of alien place names. Alaska was not only an alien landscape to Euro-Americans; it was land never before subject to the sovereignty of a state and therefore considered *terra nullius*, or "vacant land." Because it was no person's property and unencumbered by legal title, the land was deemed to be part of the public domain and was thus open for settlement and development.

Nation-states acquire power by creating physical boundaries through the process of mapping, measuring, and surveying, a classificatory exercise that enhances control over a profitable hinterland, such as interior Alaska (Cruikshank 2005; Innis 1950). These efforts are rationalized both as a production of knowledge and as serving the interests of state administration, but they undermine local traditions, so, for example, Indigenous land claims are diminished as people's presence is erased (figure 7.3).

In the colonizing process, maps serve as ideological tools in making claims about a particular territory. Maps precede settlers and developers and then assume a normative role in pre-establishing a spatial order for hegemonic claims. Place names are one tool used both in establishing and securing those claims. Through place names, the landscape is symbolically transformed as new toponyms reflect a foreign, imposed history and culture. Toponyms can be read as the inscribed body of the nation, as glosses on a somewhat magical unit called the "the United States of America" (Boelhower 1988).

Maps are powerful tools because we assume they reflect reality, but they are only an explanation or interpretation of reality, and their production is influenced by the political and cultural views of their makers (Harley 1989; Medzini 2012, 24). Euro-Americans assume that maps mirror reality, in part because they are produced through scientific means and use conventions such as the cardinal points of north, south, east, and west, which are assumed to exist in nature. But not all cultures make textual maps nor use the same geographical conventions. For example, the Ahtna have no tradition of making or using textual maps. Instead, they have developed and used a shared, memorized, verbally transmitted geographic system based on a set of principles different from those used by Western cartographers (Kari 2008). For one thing, the Ahtna did not use the four cardinal directions, or left and right, for spatial orientation or in geographic terminology (Berez 2011; Kari 2008). All directions refer to the major river drainage. For Ahtna living in the Copper River basin, this is the Copper River, while for the Western Ahtna it is the Susitna River. In addition, Ahtna geographic terms often contain information not included in standard United States Geological Survey (USGS) feature types. For example, the Ahtna have words describing not only the flow *into* a lake (*'ediłeni*), but the flow *from* a lake (*'edadiniłeni*) and the flow from a *hillside* (*ts'idiniłeni*).

Over the past thirty years, linguist James Kari has documented over 2,500 Ahtna place names through interviews with Ahtna elders and archival research (Kari 2008). Figure 7.4 shows the density of Ahtna place names just associated with salmon fishing on the Copper River and its tributaries. The author created this map using archival sources and data from Kari's (2008) *Ahtna Place Name Lists*. Today, there are 2,206 officially recognized toponyms for the Copper River region, but only about 237, or 10 percent, derive from an Ahtna place name (Kari 2008). Approximately 125 of those names were mapped or written down prior to 1910, primarily by Henry Tureman Allen, of the US military, and geologists of the USGS, while another one hundred names were added later (Kari 2008). The dearth of Ahtna place names in the official record is a reflection, in part, of the colonial process in which the use of Alaska Native languages has been systematically undermined by the state. The Ahtna place names that do exist only dimly reflect peoples' presence in the Copper River basin or the fact that the basin is the Ahtna homeland.

Probably the earliest map of the upper Copper and Susitna Rivers was produced under the direction of Ferdinand von Wrangell (or, in German, Wrangel), chief manager of the Russian-American Company from 1830 to 1835. A German in Russian service, Wrangell was also a founder of the Russian Geographic Society and a member of the Saint Petersburg Academy of Sciences (Pierce 1990).

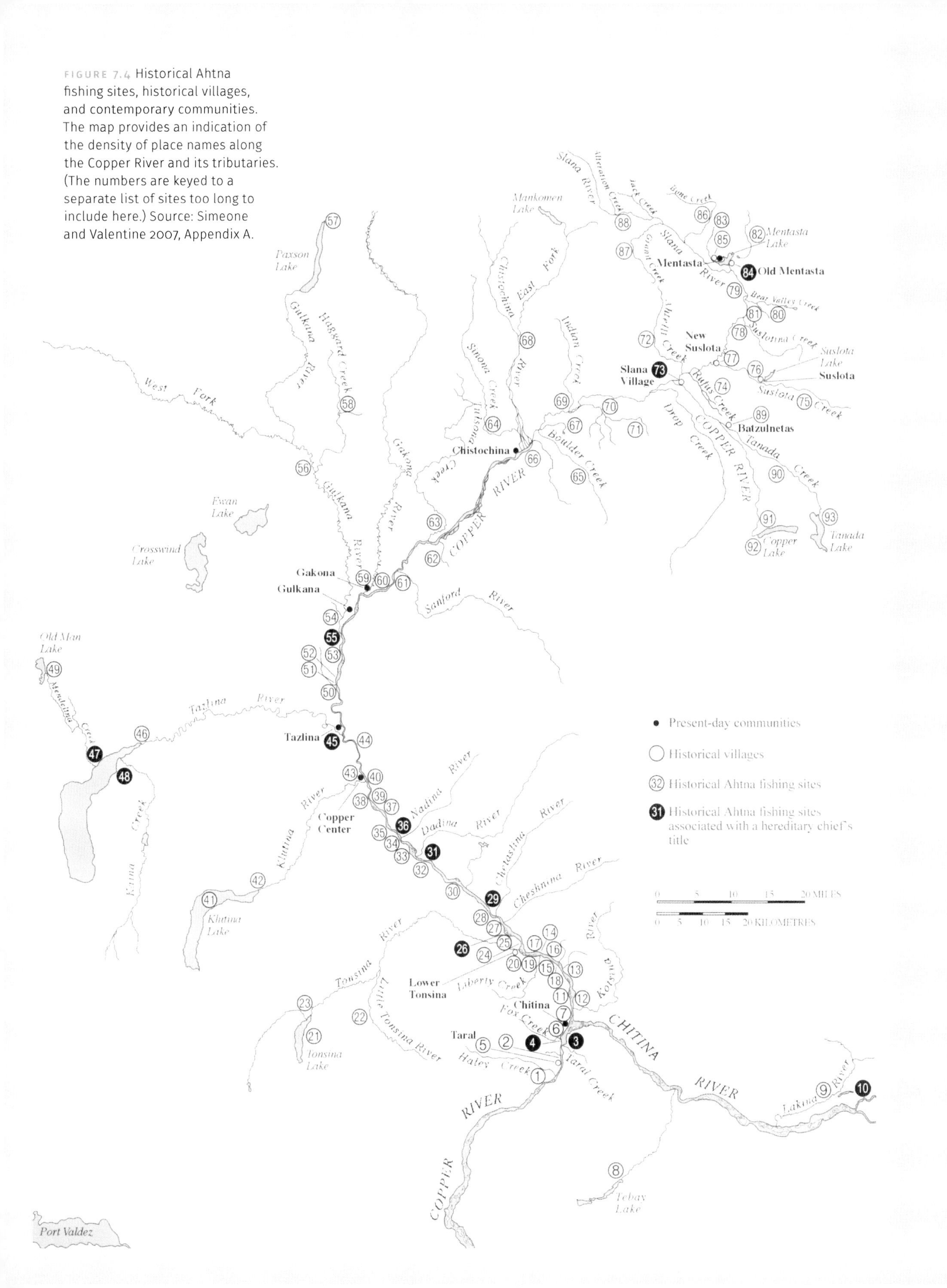

FIGURE 7.4 Historical Ahtna fishing sites, historical villages, and contemporary communities. The map provides an indication of the density of place names along the Copper River and its tributaries. (The numbers are keyed to a separate list of sites too long to include here.) Source: Simeone and Valentine 2007, Appendix A.

FIGURE 7.5 Detail of the Wrangell map of 1839. The map shows the Copper and Susitna River drainages as well as Alaska Native communities and trails. Alaska and Polar Regions Collections and Archives, Elmer E. Rasmuson Library, University of Alaska Fairbanks, Rare Book Collection, no. A0503.

Published in 1839, the Wrangell map (figure 7.5) illustrates the stage during which colonial cartographers relied exclusively on Indigenous knowledge, while also suggesting the limits of Russian hegemony in interior Alaska. The single feature alluding to a Russian presence is "Kupfer [Copper] Fort," located to the north of the mouth of the Chitina River. This was Mednovskaia Odinochka, a small trading post operated by one or two men that had been established by the Russian-American Company in 1821 (Znamenski 2003).

The map appeared in Wrangell's *Statistische und ethnographische Nachrichten über die Russischen Besitzungen an der Nordwestküste von Amerika* (Statistical and ethnographic reports regarding Russian possessions on the northwest coast of America) (Wrangell 1939). Exceptionally detailed, the map reflects some of the earliest first-hand information about the region predating the earliest English, French, and American surveys. Figure 7.5 shows only the eastern section of a map that also includes Cook Inlet and the Kuskokwim River.

Wrangell compiled information from hand-sketched maps, a diary made by the Russian explorer Afanasii Klimovskii (who explored the Copper River in 1819 and named Mount Wrangell), and information received from Dena'ina and Ahtna informants (Wrangell [1839] 1980). According to Wrangell, the "Galtsan," or Tanana River people, travelled ten days to Lake Knitiben (Butte Lake) to hunt "reindeer" (caribou), and the Dena'ina travelled to this lake to trade with the Tanana. He goes on to say that Upper Ahtna from the village of *Nataełde* ("roasted salmon place") and Ahtna from Tazlina Lake (identified as "Mantilbana" on the map) travelled to Lake Chluben to trade with the Dena'ina and hunt caribou (Wrangell [1839] 1980).

Because the Russians were so dependent on Native knowledge, they were also susceptible to misinformation provided by Native traders protecting their own interests. In his analysis of toponyms on the Wrangell map, Kari (1986) concluded that Dena'ina Athabaskans from Cook Inlet provided much of the information on the map. For example, the Upper Ahtna village of Batzulnetas, written as "Nutatlgat," is based on the Dena'ina pronunciation *Nutł Kaq*, and not the Ahtna, which is *Nataełde* (table 7.1). Kari also concluded that the Dena'ina

TABLE 7.1 Place names on the Wrangell map, 1839

Name on Map	Ahtna Place Name	Translation	Contemporary Wrangell Place Name
Atna	*Ahtna*	"beyond river"	Copper River
F. Suschitnoa[a]	*Sasutna'*	"sand river"	Susitna River
Kupfer Fort	*Tsedi Kulaende (possibly)*	"where copper exists"	"Copper Village"
Tschetschitno	*Tsedi Na'*	"copper river"	Chitina River
Nutatlga	*Nataełde*	"roasted salmon place"	Batzulnetas
S. Tatikniltunbenab[b]	*Titi'niłtaan Bene*	"game trail goes into water lake"	Stephan Lake
See Knituben	*Hwniidi Ben*	"upstream lake"	Butte Lake
See Kochobena	*Hwggandi Kacaagh Bene'*	"upland large area lake"	Deadman Lake
See Mantilbana	*Bendilbene'*	"lake flows lake"	Tazlina Lake
F. Taschlana	*Tezdlen Na'*	"swift current river"	Tazlina River
Tscheschlukina	*Tsiis Tl'edze' Na'*	"ocher paint river"	Chistochina River
Kohlschanen Villages	*Keltsaane*		Upper Tanana Villages

[a] FLUSS IS THE GERMAN WORD FOR "RIVER" AND IS ABBREVIATED ON THE MAP.
[b] SEE IS THE GERMAN WORD FOR "LAKE" AND IS SOMETIMES ABBREVIATED ON THE MAP.

may have deliberately provided misinformation to the Russians because the trail leading from Copper River to Athabascan ("Kohlschanen") villages that passes near Mount Wrangell ("Vulkan" on the map) is almost a mirror image of the actual trail around the base of Mounts Sanford and Drum (Kari 1986, 105; also see Kari and Fall 2003, 87). Ahtna elder Andy Brown said the trail went around the base of the two mountains, crossed over the upper Nadina and Dadina Rivers, the Chestaslina River, and ran into the upper Kotsina drainage before heading across the Chitina River to the village of Taral (Kari 1986). According to Wilson Justin (2014, 76), this trail belonged to the *Ałts'e'tnaey* and *Naltsiine* clans. The trail was later co-opted by the Americans and renamed the Millard Trail (see figure 7.12, Abercrombie's map of the Copper River Basin).

In 1867, Russia ceded Alaska to the United States through the signing of the Treaty of Cession, whereby the territory of Alaska became the property of the United States. Russia's legal claim to Alaska ultimately rested on the Doctrine of Discovery, a long-standing legal framework adopted by the colonial, Christian nations of Europe, according to which the nation that first "discovered" a land in the so-called New World "acquired title to the land and dominion over the original inhabitants exclusive of any other discovering nation" (Case 1984, 48). In 1823, the Doctrine of Discovery was formally recognized in a US Supreme Court decision, in which Chief Justice John Marshall argued that, upon discovery, European nations had assumed "ultimate dominion" over the lands of America, including the sole rights of alienation, and that the original inhabitants of these lands had lost "their rights to complete sovereignty, as independent nations," retaining only a right of "occupancy."[2] In essence, this meant that the Indigenous peoples of Alaska had no rights to their homelands except those granted by the United States government.

When the United States acquired Alaska, the Treaty of Cession conveyed to the United States dominion over the territory, and title to all public lands and vacant lands that were not individual property. The treaty provided that "uncivilized tribes," which included the Ahtna, would be subject to such laws and regulations as the United States might later adopt with respect to Indigenous land rights. In other words, the question of whether the Ahtna had Aboriginal title was left in limbo. In 1884 Congress passed the Organic Act, one of several statutes purporting to protect any land actually used or occupied by Alaska Natives (Case and Voluck 2012, 24). The unspoken implication was that Indigenous people in Alaska, unlike those in the contiguous United States, could not claim Aboriginal title to vast tracts of tribal property (Case and Voluck 2012, 24).

The US government was the first jurisdiction to acknowledge Aboriginal title, which is based on actual use and occupancy by Indigenous people. Under American law, Congress has the authority to convert Aboriginal title into a full fee title, in whole or in part, or to extinguish Aboriginal title either with or without monetary or other consideration. US government policy is to grant tribes title to the portion of the lands that they occupy and to extinguish Aboriginal title to the remainder of the lands by placing such lands in the public domain (Case and Voluck 2012). As a result, when Russia sold Alaska to the United States, Ahtna territory, along with most of Alaska, became public domain and open for settlement and development.

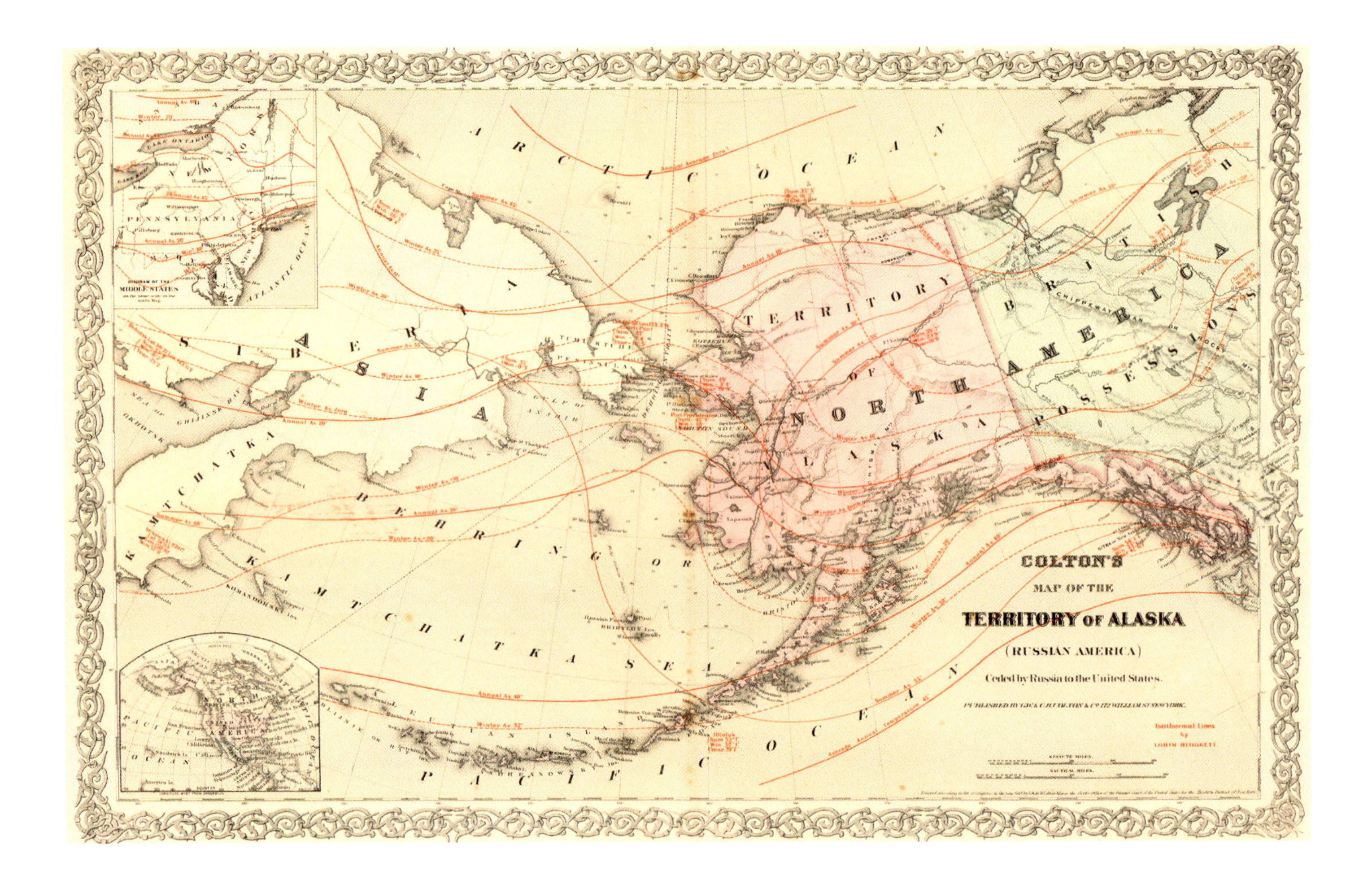

After the United State purchased Alaska, a number of maps were published showing the new acquisition. Colton's map (figure 7.6), published in 1868, is one example. An unusual feature of this map is the isothermal lines. The map shows that American cartographers had some knowledge of the Alaskan coast but knew very little about interior Alaska or the Copper River. None of the Indigenous toponyms that appear on Wrangell's map appear on Colton's map. What is left is the name "Atna or Copper River," "Mt. Wrangel," and "Mantilbana L.," along with the now long-abandoned "Mednovskaia Odinochka" (written as "Odinotenka" on the map), but little else. Interior Alaska and the Copper River basin appear as vacant land, truly *terra nullius*.

While Colton's map shows an apparently vacant land, William Healy Dall's map (figure 7.7) shows Ahtna territory encompassing a large swath of land—all of the Copper River drainage as far west as the upper Susitna River basin (an area roughly similar to that shown in figure 7.2). Colonial powers acquired new territory in order to obtain land and resources. To make use of these new assets they first had to be systematically located, inventoried, and mapped. Often these new lands were already inhabited, so the current residents had to be inventoried as well.

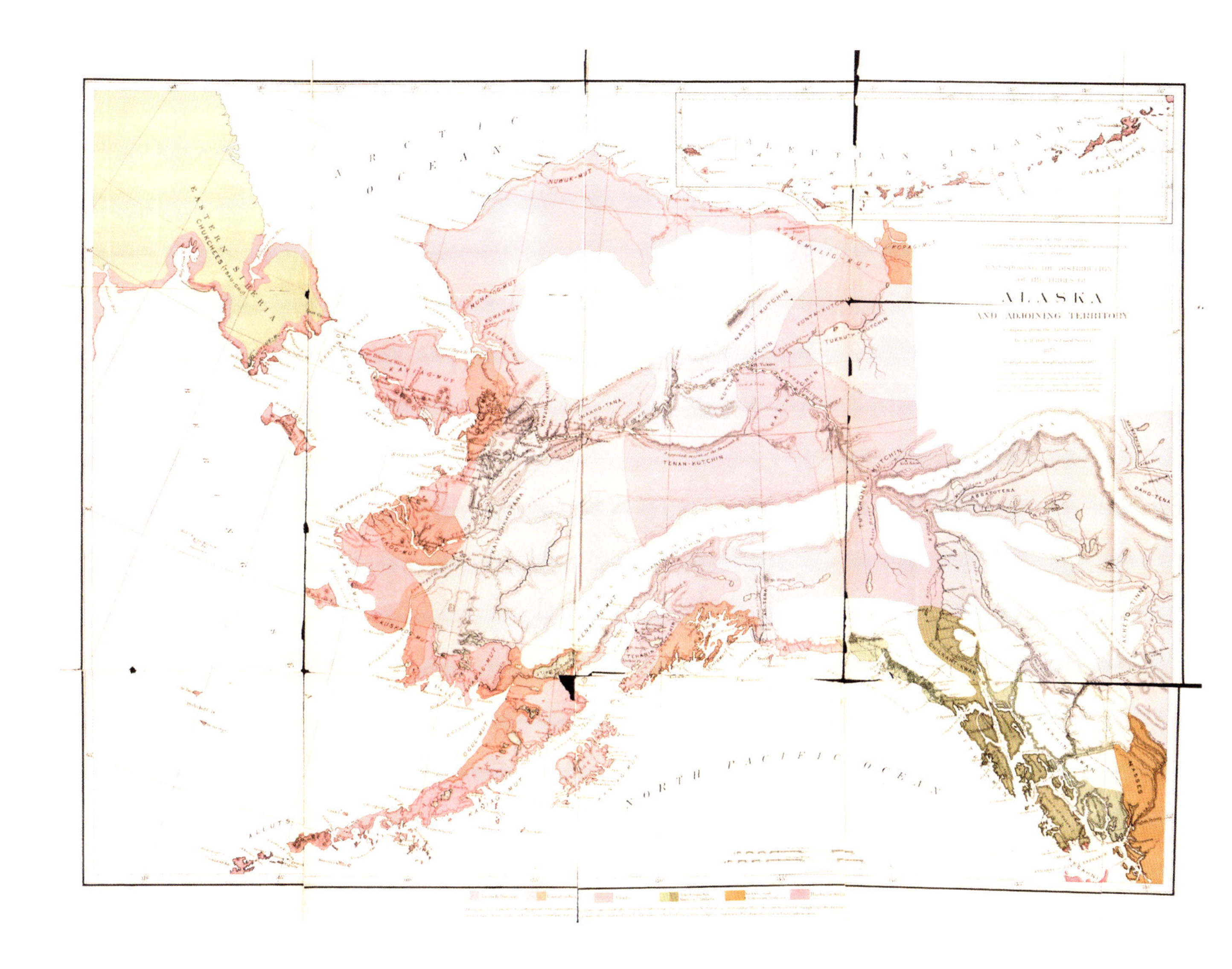

Dall was part of the American effort to inventory the mineral, animal, and human resources of Alaska. In 1871, he was appointed to the United States Coastal Survey, and later joined the USGS as a paleontologist. Dall's map resembles later maps produced by geologists, with swirls of colour indicating the location of different Indigenous peoples and the languages they spoke. The spelling "Ah-tena" was introduced by Dall, who erred in thinking this was "their own name for themselves" (Dall 1877, 34). In his short description, Dall (1877, 34) writes that the Ahtna are "known principally by report . . . and occupy the basin of the Atna or Copper River."

(FACING) FIGURE 7.6 "Colton's map of the territory of Alaska (Russian America) ceded by Russia to the United States." 1868. Produced by G. W. and C. B. Colton & Co., this is one of several early maps published to display the newly acquired territory of Alaska. The large blank areas on the map create the impression that the United States purchased a vast expanse of land that was largely uninhabited, thereby erasing the Indigenous presence. Norman B. Leventhal Map Center Collection, no. 06_01_011367.

(ABOVE) FIGURE 7.7 "Map showing the distribution of the tribes of Alaska and adjoining territories compiled from the latest authorities by W. H. Dall, U.S. Coast Survey." 1875. Dall's map represents the early stages of colonial administration, during which the colonial power begins to inventory the resources of the new territory, including the location of Indigenous groups. By 1875, the United States was embroiled in a war with Native Americans. It was therefore important to know something about the disposition of Indigenous groups in the new territory. University of Washington, University Libraries, Digital Collections, MAP179.

In 1881, as the Indian Wars in the continental United States were drawing to a close, the veteran Indian fighter Major General Nelson A. Miles was put in charge of the US Army's Department of the Columbia, which was responsible for operations in the Pacific Northwest, including Alaska. Fascinated with reports from Alaska, Miles sent Lieutenant Frederick Schwatka on an expedition to explore the Yukon River in the summer of 1883. Schwatka's success led Miles to determine a more ambitious goal of ascending the Copper River and crossing the Alaska Range into the Yukon River drainage. A new cartographic period for the Copper River was about to begin.

Miles first sent Lieutenant William Abercrombie to explore the Copper River, but Abercrombie turned back after advancing only fifty miles. So in the spring of 1885, Lieutenant Henry Allen and two hand-picked men began an expedition in which they travelled 1,500 miles, ascending the Copper River, crossing the Alaska Range, floating down the Tanana River to the Yukon, then crossing overland from the Yukon to Koyukuk River, floating down that river to the Yukon, and then out to St. Michael on the Bering Sea coast. The goal was to explore "uncharted" territory and report on the disposition of the Native people, including whether they posed a threat to future development of the territory. Allen's expedition is significant because he provided the first detailed information about the geography of the Copper River and much of interior Alaska. Allen also set the cartography of the Copper River; indeed, all his place names remain in use today. For example, after Allen, the Copper River was never again labelled on maps the "Ahtna or Copper River" but always the "Copper River."

Allen produced several maps, including a map of the Copper River basin published in 1887 (figure 7.8). The map represents an intermediate stage in the evolution of the cartographic tradition, as Allen begins the process of filling out the blank spaces on the map using both Indigenous and colonial toponyms. American hegemony is stamped on the region by the naming of all of the major peaks of the Wrangell Mountains after American personalities, but Allen also acknowledges the Ahtna presence by using Indigenous toponyms for all of the major tributaries.

Born in Kentucky, Allen attended West Point and was educated in various languages; he could read both French and German and was learning Russian so he could read the Russian literature on the Copper River (Twichell 1974). His interest in languages is reflected in the fact that he compiled a brief word list of the Ahtna language and recorded and retained Ahtna toponyms for most of the major tributaries of the Copper River.

Allen's success on the Copper River was based, in great part, on the Ahtna's willingness to guide him, and he was made well aware of territorial boundaries, observing that different leaders controlled various segments of the Copper River. Nicolai was the "autocrat" of the Chitina River and Taral, while two other chiefs, Conaquánta and Liebigstag, "held sway" over the river between Taral and the mouth of the Tazlina. Batzulnetas was the leader of the Tatlatans—or Ahtna who lived on the upper Copper River. According to Ahtna elder Andy Brown (Reckord 1983, 77), Chief Nicolai told Allen, "We have law in our village that you can't stay here. You've got to get your own place to stay. We got law here and it's the same all the way up the river." Nicolai then said

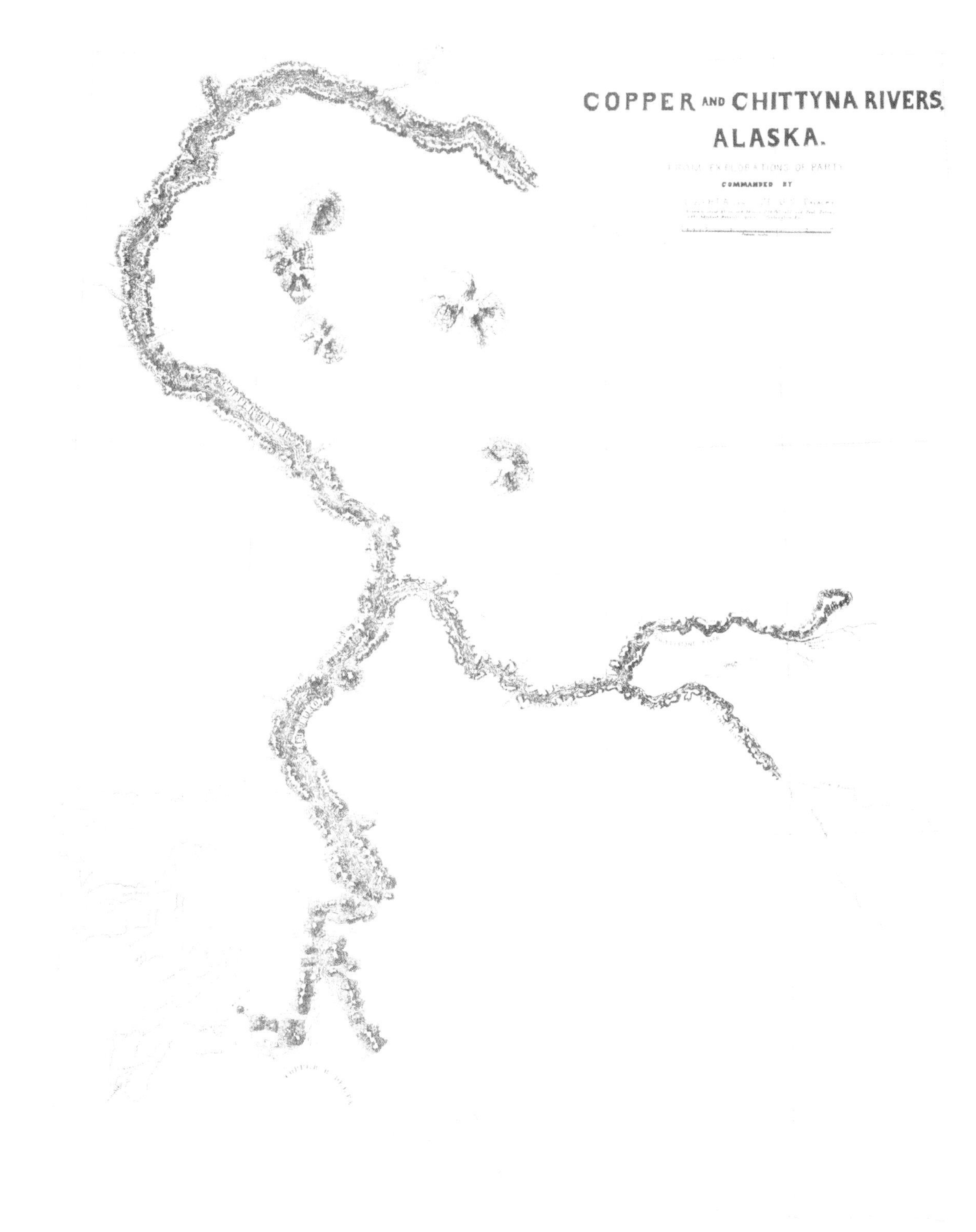

FIGURE 7.8 "Copper and Chittyna Rivers, Alaska, from the explorations of party commanded by Lieut. H. T. Allen." In 1887, Ahtna territory would shortly be discovered by the American public, in the wake of the Klondike stampede of 1898. Alaska and Polar Regions Collections and Archives, Elmer E. Rasmuson Library, University of Alaska Fairbanks, Rare Books and Maps Collection, A0737, folded map no. 2.

he would send a man so that nothing happened to Allen and the guide would tell other Ahtna, "They not Russians. Americans look like good people to us. Don't bother them." Then from the next chief other guides would be sent further up the river so that Nicolai's men could return home.

Allen (1887, 67) also remarked, "how great is the geographical knowledge of these primitive people." His guides provided information about trails, which enabled Allen to avoid costly detours, as well as names of all the principal tributaries of the Copper River, many of which Allen recorded. Over time these names have become altered so that *Kentsii Na'* ("spruce bark canoe river") became the Tonsina River, *Tl'atina'* ("rear water") became the Klutina River, *Tezdlen Na'* ("swift current river") became the Tazlina River, *C'el C'ena'* ("tearing river") became the Gulkana River, and *Ggax Kuna'* ("rabbit river") became the Gakona River. In the Ahtna language, *na'* is the word for river (Kari 2008). In addition to collecting Ahtna toponyms, Allen recorded the names of Ahtna leaders he met along the way. Instead of using the appropriate Ahtna place name, Allen often substituted the name of a leader, and for a number of years these names appeared on subsequent maps of the Copper River. The Ahtna called "Liebestag's village," *Bes Cene*, or "base of river bank" (no. 26 on figure 7.4), while "Conaquánta's village" is probably *Nic'akuni'aaden*, or "place that extends off from shore" (no. 35 on figure 7.4). Perhaps the most famous of these substitutions was Batzulnetas. This settlement is located at the confluence of Tanada Creek and the Copper River, and in the Ahtna language is called *Nataełde*, or "roasted salmon

(FACING) FIGURE 7.9 Mount Wrangell, known as *Uk'ełedi* ("the one with smoke on it"), is a massive shield volcano that rises 14,163 feet above the Copper River. East view; photograph by William E. Simeone, 2015. (BELOW) FIGURE 7.10 Mount Drum, or *Hwdaandi K'ełt'aeni* (downriver *K'ełt'aeni*), is a stratovolcano rising 12,010 feet above the Copper River. Off to the right is the smaller peak of Mount Zanetti, known to the Ahtna as *Kaghaxi* ("brown bear cub"). East view; photograph by William E. Simeone, 2015.

place" (no. 89 on figure 7.4). Allen called *Nataełde* Batzulnetas, using the name of the leader/shaman *Bets'ulnii Ta'* (Father of Someone Respects Him), who was actually the headman for the village at the mouth of the Slana River (Kari 1986). The name Batzulnetas stuck and is often used by Native people today, and it appeared on many subsequent maps of the river.

Allen's map represents a hybrid stage in the cartographic process by which explorers relied extensively on Native knowledge but also began to symbolically claim the land for the United States by naming the most dominant geographic features in the Copper River basin, the great phalanx of the Wrangell Mountains. The enormous shield volcano Mount Wrangell (14,163 feet) (figure 7.9) was already named after a Russian, but Allen named three other peaks after people prominent in his life: Mount Blackburn (16,390 feet), named after Joseph Clay Stiles Blackburn, a US congressman from Allen's home state of Kentucky; Mount Sanford (16,337 feet), after Allen's great-grandfather Reuben Sanford; and Mount Drum (12,010 feet) (figure 7.10), named for Adjutant General Richard Coulter Drum.[3]

In the Ahtna language, mountain ranges, such as the Wrangell Mountains, are referred to as *dghelaay*, "mountains," or "plural objects that are suspended." Mount Wrangell is called *K'ełt aeni*, but also *Uk'ełedi* "the one with smoke on it." Mount Drum is referred to as *Hwdaandi K'ełt'aeni*, or "downriver *K'ełt'aeni*," while Mount Sanford is *Hwniindi K'ełt'aeni*, or "upriver *K'ełt'aeni*." Mount Blackburn is *K'a'si Tlaadi*, "the one at cold headwaters" (Kari 2008).

In 1898, gold was discovered on the Klondike River in what is now the Yukon territory of Canada, resulting in a stampede that brought thousands of people north. The problem was access: How to reach the goldfields? Initially the stampeders followed a trail through Canada, but American objections to Canadian regulations created a desire for an all-American route. One route, pioneered by the Ahtna, led over the Valdez Glacier to Klutina Lake and then up the Copper River, through Mentasta Pass and on to the Tanana and Yukon Rivers.

Stampeders needed maps, and one result of the gold rush was the publication of maps that could be used to reach the goldfields. The Canadian geologist and cartographer Joseph B. Tyrrell produced one

FIGURE 7.11 "Copper River Alaska Route Map," 1898, by Joseph B. Tyrrell. This was one of many maps published to capitalize on the gold rush of 1898. Tyrrell's map is interesting for the detailed information it provides, compiled from the surveys of Allen, Schwatka, and Hayes, as well as other sources, while it also seems to issue an invitation for colonial development. Historical Map and Chart Collection, National Oceanic and Atmospheric Association, Office of Coast Survey, United States Department of Commerce, US Coast and Geodetic Survey, Library and Archives, Accession no. 440a.

such map titled "Copper River Alaska Route Map" (figure 7.11). As a travel guide, the map includes information about river conditions, the location of forage for horses, and hearsay evidence regarding prospective deposits of gold, copper, and iron. In the lower right, Tyrell lists travel distances from Alaganik (at the mouth of the Copper River) to specific Ahtna villages, including Liebigstag and "Conagunto" (that is, Conaquánta). There is also a note about where to find "Game etc.," as if to convey the impression that it would be easy to live off the land—when in fact, as Allen himself attests, he would probably have starved to death if it were not for the Ahtna (Allen 1887, 59–61).

In 1898, the disposition of Indigenous peoples was still an important consideration when one was travelling through unknown lands, so Tyrrell not only includes the location of Ahtna villages on his map but also adds a quotation from the explorer Charles W. Hayes (1892, 125), who explored the Copper River in 1891, reassuring the traveller that the Ahtna are a friendly people: "The Copper River Indians have an unenviable reputation for treachery and hostility to whites; but we saw nothing to justify it. They are greatly superior to the Yukon Natives physically, and have much more elaborate family and tribal organization." This comment appears near the center of the map, to the west and slightly south of the plot for "Liebigstags" village.

Nothing on the map, however, informs the user that the Copper River basin is Ahtna territory, or that the traveller should seek permission before crossing or using resources on that land. This omission is equally evident in Abercrombie's map (figure 7.12), which in its title claims to show "a proposed U.S. govt. mail road and shortest feasible all American Railroad route from Port Valdez via Copper Center." The implication of Abercrombie's map is that Americans have the right to build a road and railroad through Ahtna territory, including the usurpation of a traditional trail, that Abercrombie has labelled the Millard Trail. This trail is in fact the same trail that appears on Wrangell's map of 1839 (see figure 7.5).

However, Americans were well aware that the Ahtna claimed the Copper River basin and had, in the past, defended those claims with violence. More than once, American travellers encountered resistance when they did not ask permission to use the local resources. The prospector William E. Treloar (1898, 56) told of an encounter with an Ahtna *kaskae* or leader from Mentasta: "There was an Indian village a short ways above us and they had traps in the stream but were not catching many fish and when they saw us catching them it did not set very well with them. The old chief came down and stormed around and talked Indian to us" (Treloar 1898, 56). The chief then sent another Indian, who

> came down, one who had been out to Fortymile Post [on the upper Yukon River] and could speak a little English. He told us chief heap mad he say P-hat man (meaning white man) must not catch fish or else P-hat man leave quick. P-hat man catch all fish Indian man all die, so to pacify him we sent him a lot of fish. Before long the chief came down to our camp again and shook hands with us then he took up a fish and ran his hands across the back of its head and motioned that he wanted the head. Then he gave us to understand we could catch fish but we must give him the heads. We assented to this and he went away pleased. (Treloar 1898, 56)

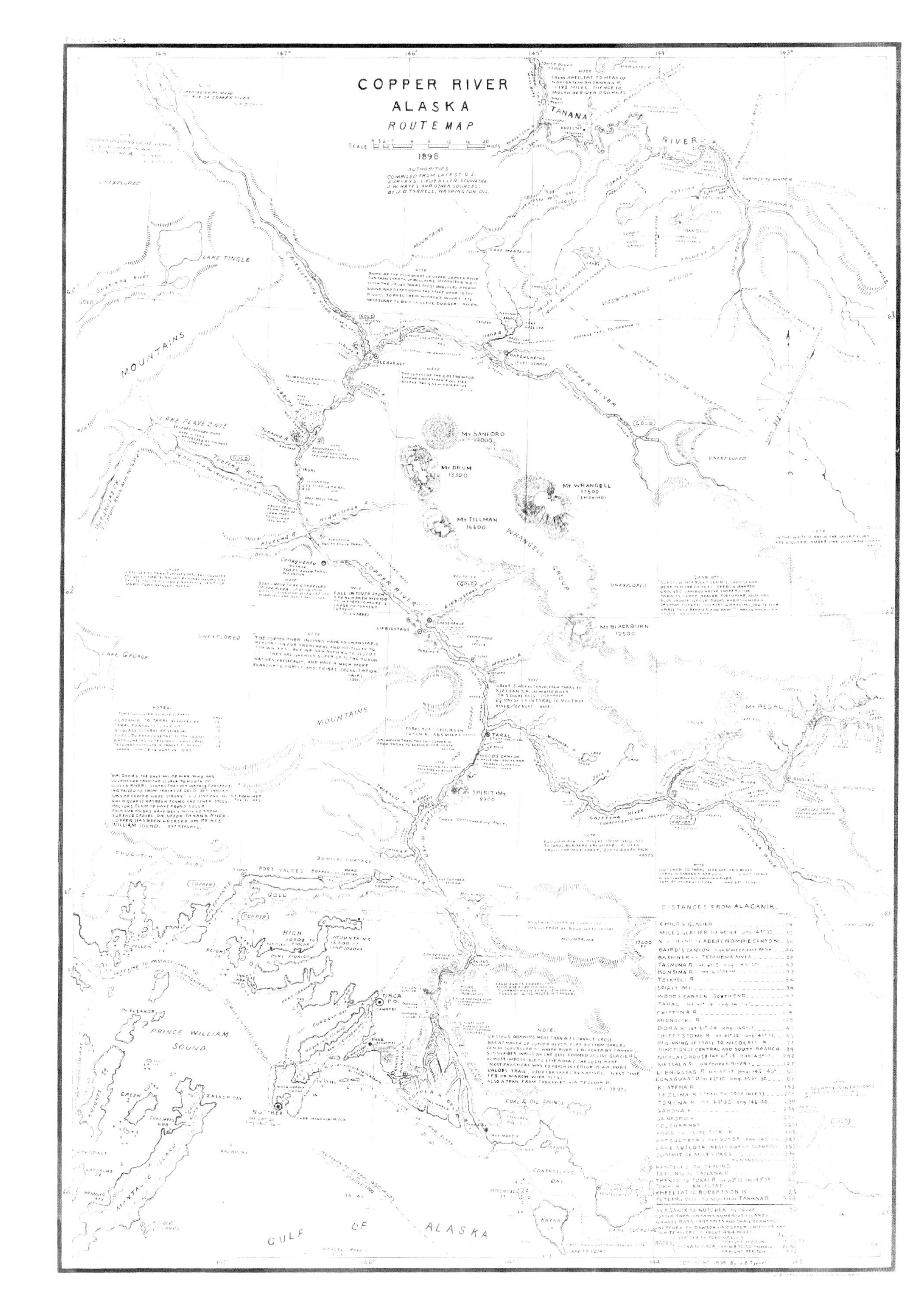

COPPER RIVER
ALASKA
ROUTE MAP
1898
MOUNTAINS
LAKE TINGLE
LAKE PLAVEZNIE
Mt SANFORD
19000
Mt DRUM
13300
Mt WRANGELL
17500
(SMOKING)
Mt TILLMAN
16600
WRANGELL GROUP
Mt BLACKBURN
12500
Mt REGAL
COPPER RIVER
TANANA
RIVER
CHITTYNA RIVER
SPIRIT Mt
TARAL
UNEXPLORED
MOUNTAINOUS REGION
PORT VALDES
PRINCE WILLIAM SOUND
ORCA P.O.
NUCHEK
GULF OF ALASKA
KAYAK
DISTANCES FROM ALAGANIK

"Birds Eye View of Copper River Valley" (figure 7.13) was included in a published pamphlet that touted the development and settlement in the Copper River Valley and included articles on the agricultural and mineral resources of the valley, investing in gold mining, and the availability of the "Free Lands in Alaska." Included with the publication was a fold-out map, printed on pink paper and titled "Birds Eye View of the Copper River Valley" (figure 7.13). The map is the epitome of colonial cartography, showing an accessible, bucolic land with military roads, telegraph lines and stations, and prospectors' trails, along with the new town of Copper Center. There are also locations of gold and copper. Three small dots identifying the locations of "Indian Villages" are the only evidence of an Ahtna presence.

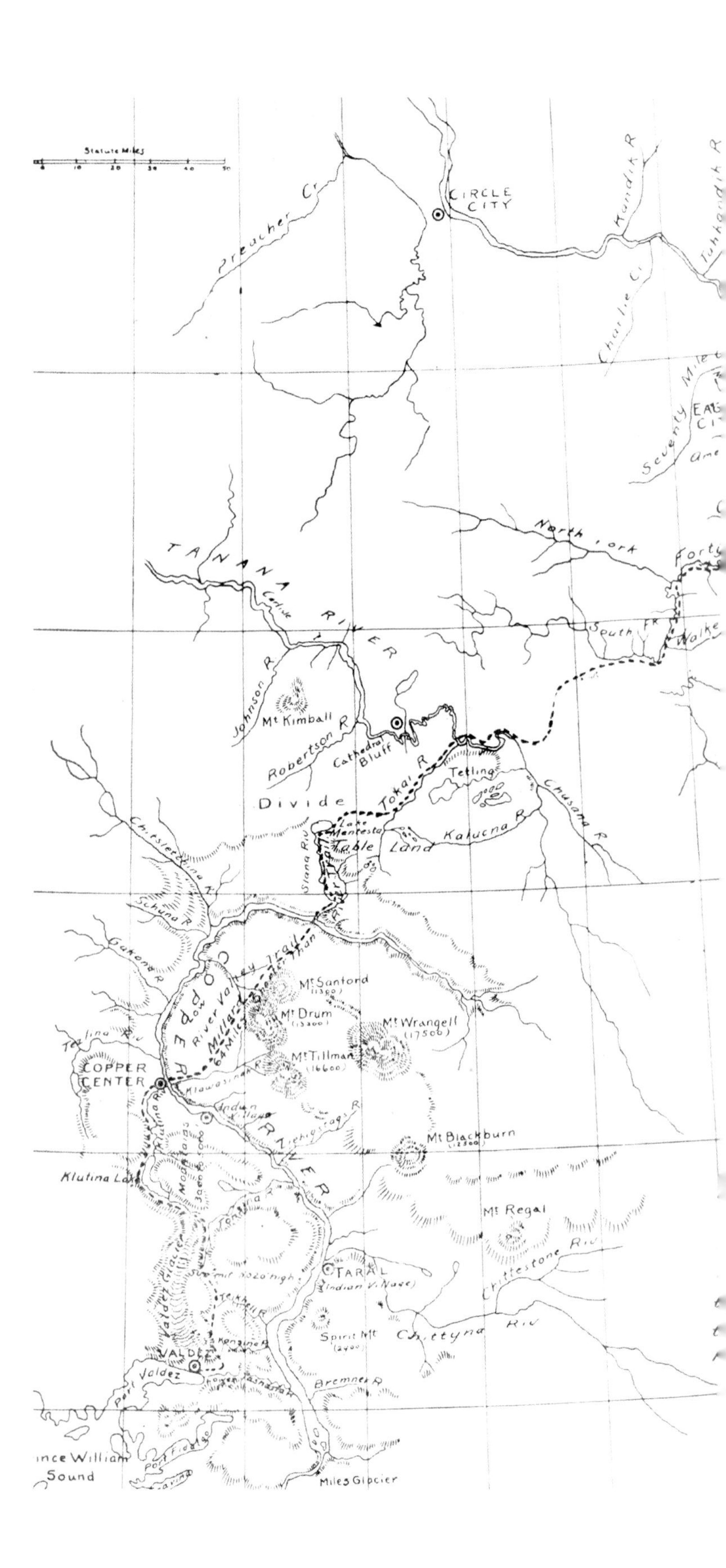

(LEFT) FIGURE 7.12 Abercrombie's map of the Copper River. 1898. With its emphasis on the construction of a government road and a railway route through traditional Ahtna territory, the map reveals how closely the US government was involved in promoting development, long before the question of Indigenous land title had received any serious consideration. Source: Copper River Mining, Trading and Development Company 1902, 51. Alaska and Polar Regions Collections and Archives, Elmer E. Rasmuson Library, University of Alaska Fairbanks, Rare Books and Maps Collection, no. A2345.

(RIGHT) FIGURE 7.13 "Birds Eye View of Copper River Valley." This map offers a bucolic view of the Copper River basin as a land of opportunity for miners, developers, and tourists. As in Abercrombie's map, the Ahtna have been reduced to a few dots on this map. Source: Copper River Mining, Trading and Development Company 1902, pocket map. Alaska and Polar Regions Collections and Archives, Elmer E. Rasmuson Library, University of Alaska Fairbanks, Rare Books and Maps Collection, no. A2345.

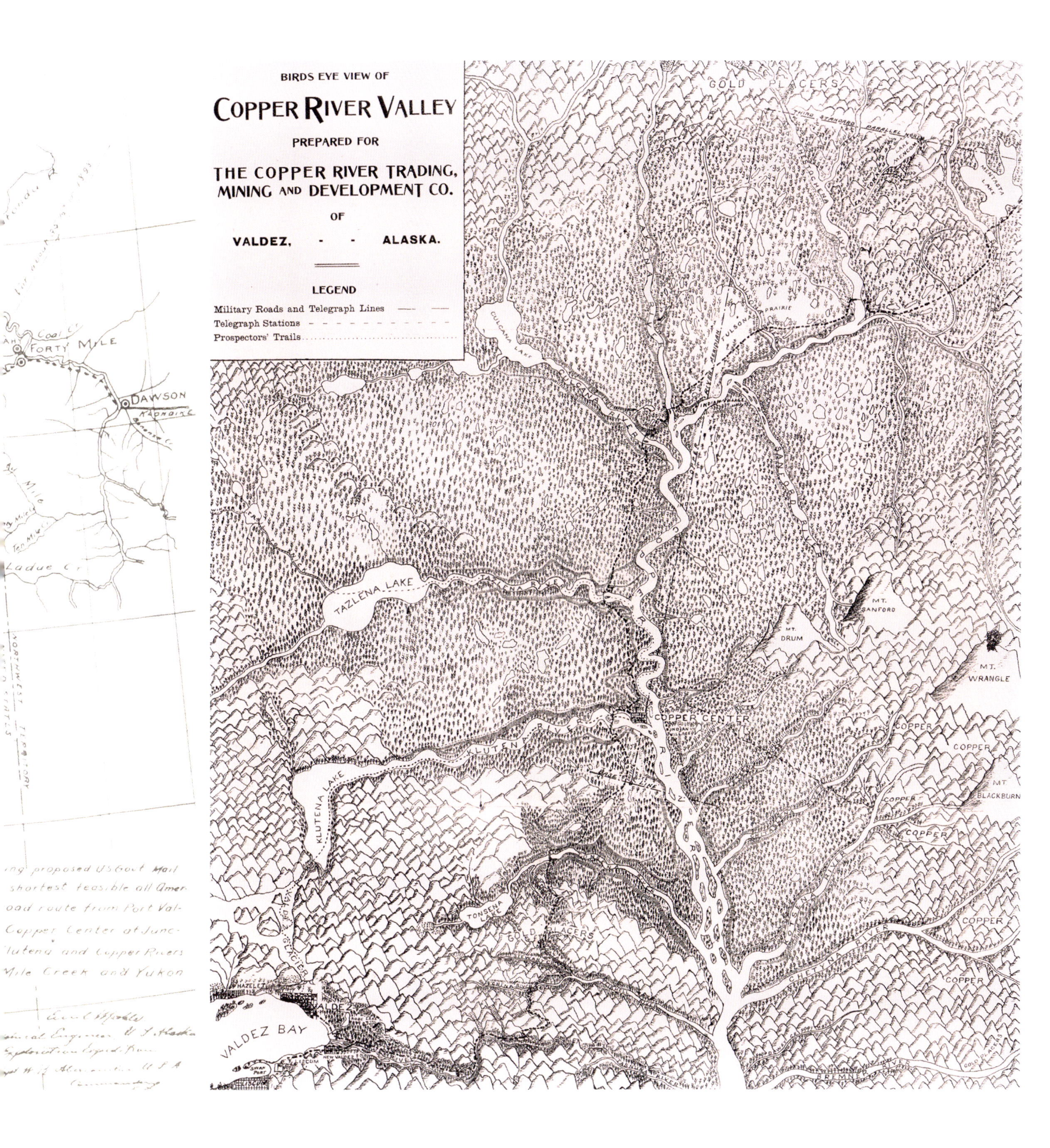
BIRDS EYE VIEW OF
COPPER RIVER VALLEY
PREPARED FOR
THE COPPER RIVER TRADING, MINING AND DEVELOPMENT CO.
OF
VALDEZ, - - ALASKA.
LEGEND
Military Roads and Telegraph Lines
Telegraph Stations
Prospectors' Trails
GOLD PLACERS
TAZLENA LAKE
KLUTENA LAKE
COPPER CENTER
MT. SANFORD
MT. DRUM
MT. WRANGLE
MT. BLACKBURN
COPPER
TONSENA LAKE
GOLD PLACERS
VALDEZ BAY
VALDEZ
HAZELET
CHETYNA RIVER
FORTY MILE
DAWSON
Ladue Cr.

FIGURE 7.14 Alaska Road Commission map. 1909. One of several sheets produced by the Alaska Road Commission, this map shows the route of the Richardson Highway and the Alaska Communications System line that bifurcated at Gulkana. One branch went to Fairbanks, the other to the town of Eagle, on the Yukon River. Telegraph stations were established at various intervals along the route, including Tonsina, Copper Center, Gulkana, Sourdough, Paxson, and Chistochina. Both Gulkana and Chistochina eventually became Ahtna villages after the Ahtna relinquished their traditional lifestyle under pressure from the American government to put their children in school. Historical Map and Chart Collection, National Oceanic and Atmospheric Association, Office of Coast Survey, United States Department of Commerce, Map 00-A-00-1909.

The desire for an all-American route to the Klondike resulted in the US Army constructing a pack trail between Valdez and Eagle in 1898 that was eventually upgraded and renamed the Richardson Highway, after a general in the US Army, Wilds P. Richardson. Congress also authorized construction of a telegraph line between Valdez and Eagle, and by 1904 the Alaska Communications System had stretched a cable and established "meteorological stations" between the two communities. Figure 7.14 is one of four sheets published in 1909 by the Alaska Road Commission showing trails and roads in Alaska. At this stage in the mapping process, all Ahtna toponyms have become anglicized or have disappeared altogether. For example, the Copper River is never again referred to as the "Atna or Copper River" but only as the "Copper River."

In the Euro-American imagination, the Copper River is famous for two things: copper and salmon. Copper can be found lying on the ground throughout certain parts of the upper Copper River drainage, and the Chitina basin has particularly rich deposits (Mendenhall and Schrader 1903, 16; Moffit and Maddren 1909, 47). Archaeologists have concluded that the Ahtna began using copper between 1,000 and 500 years ago (Cooper 2012; Workman 1977, 31). In 1797, the Russian explorer Demitri Tarkhanov (or Dmitrii Tarkhonov, in an alternative spelling) explored the Copper River looking for the source of copper (Grinev 1993, 57). Tarkhanov reached the Lower Ahtna village of Takekat, or *Hwt'aa Cae'e* (Fox Creek village, no. 6 in figure 7.4), located across from the mouth of the Chitina River. He was probably the first European to see the Chitina River, but he never learned the source of copper (Grinev 1997, 8; Kari 2005).[4] Allen (1887) may have been the first non-Native to obtain knowledge of a source of copper. In April of 1885, he visited Chief Nicolai upstream on one of the Chitina's main tributaries, the Nizina River (*Nizii Na'*), at its junction with Dan Creek, and subsequently reported that Nicolai had pointed out the locality of a copper deposit that was then above the snow line (Allen 1887, 158).

There is some question as to why Nicolai would reveal the source of copper to Allen when, according to most Russian sources the Ahtna violently resisted showing them (Grinev 1993, 1997). One reason, given by Ahtna elder Frank Billum (John Billum's brother), is that Nicolai felt well disposed toward Allen because he was a "nice guy" who wanted to know what Indians knew and wanted their help, in contrast to the Russians, who were "pretty bad guys" (Billum 1992; see also Pratt 1998, 85–95).

Another interpretation, provided by Ronald Simpson (2001, 106–107), imagines Nicolai showing Allen the source of the copper by pointing across the "Chettystone" River or *Tsedi Ts'ese'Na'* ("copper stone creek"). As he points, the white explorers turn silent: "It was as if they had found something holy." When Allen asks Nicolai to describe the place, Nicolai waves him off, although he senses that "he had just done something he might later regret" (Simpson 2001, 106–107). Nicolai reasons that Allen is merely the leader of a small expedition, not a prospector, and he wants only to know that the source of the copper exists, or so Nicolai hoped. Of course, that was not the end of it.

In July 1900, two prospectors discovered the first of several large copper deposits in the Kennicott Valley. Eventually a syndicate of Eastern financiers—known as the Alaska Syndicate, which included the Guggenheim brothers and the House

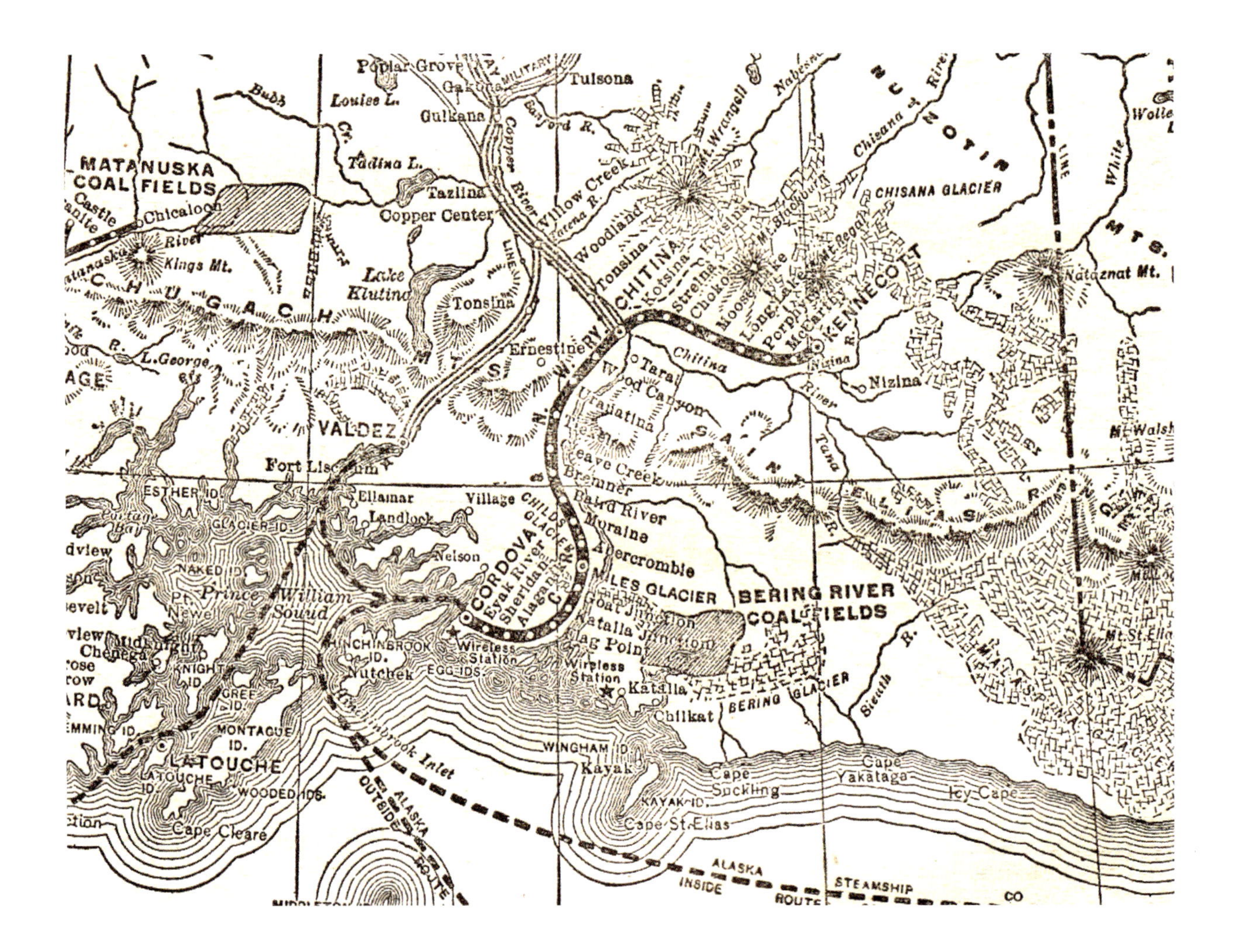

of Morgan—developed the Kennicott Valley prospects, investing in a mining operation and building the Copper River and Northwestern Railroad to transport the ore to tidewater (Bleakley n.d.). Construction of the railroad, the route of which is shown in figure 7.15, began in 1907 and was completed in 1911. After flourishing for roughly two decades, the mine ceased to be sufficiently productive, and, in 1935, it closed. By the end of 1938, the railroad had been abandoned as well. Like many colonial entrepreneurs, the Alaska Syndicate appropriated the land, developed it, and then abandoned both the mine and the railroad as soon as they were no longer profitable.

While copper was important to the Ahtna as a material and trade item, salmon were critical to their existence, and it was over salmon that Ahtna challenged American industry and government.

A commercial fishery began to exploit Copper River salmon runs in 1889, and by 1896 the Ahtna were protesting that the runs were depleted, and they were facing starvation (Moser 1899, 134). In 1915, commercial fishers began fishing in the Copper River and built a cannery at Abercrombie, located about 55 miles (just over 88 kilometres) north of Cordova. As a result, the commercial salmon harvest increased from an average of about 250,000 sockeye before 1915, to over 600,000 in 1915, and over 1.25

(FACING) FIGURE 7.15 The route of the Copper River and Northwestern Railroad (CRNR), a map produced in 1911 by the Alaska Steamship Company, a subsidiary of the Alaska Syndicate, for use as an advertisement. By the beginning of the twentieth century, large-scale, well-financed mining companies such as the Alaska Syndicate had entered Alaska. Millions of dollars were spent on building the CRNR, which served to haul ore from the Kennecott copper mine to the port of Cordova and to transport workers and supplies back to the mine. Tourists also rode the rails. A few of the place names along the rail route are derived from Ahtna place names—such as the Uranatina River, which is *Ighenetina* ("bend water") in Ahtna—but there is no doubt that this is American territory. "The Copper River & Northwestern Railway," www.frrandp.com.

(RIGHT) FIGURE 7.16 A. H. Miller's map of Ahtna villages and populations, 1918. This map is significant because it shows that the Ahtna had not disappeared from the Copper River country. By 1918, however, the Ahtna were struggling to adapt to the new order imposed by the Americans, which included not only the huge Kennecott copper mine, but a commercial fishery seemingly intent on taking all of the salmon out of the Copper River and leaving the Ahtna to starve. US Fish and Wildlife Service, Record Group 22, box 2, US National Archives and Records Administration, Washington.

million in 1919 (Gilbert 1921, 1). The Ahtna protested and eventually their complaint came to the attention of the Bureau of Education, the agency responsible for the welfare of Indigenous people in Alaska. Arthur Miller, an agent of the bureau working at Copper Center, drafted a formal petition.

Miller produced a map (figure 7.16) to present at a hearing in Seattle about the Copper River fishery in November 1918. In sharp contrast to other colonial maps of the region, this map emphasizes the presence of the Ahtna and was used to present their case to the government and commercial fishing industry. The map shows the locations of Ahtna villages and estimated populations as well as the location of the commercial fishery in Miles Lake, and the location of the cannery at Mile 55 on the Copper River and Northwestern Railroad. Eventually, commercial fishing within the Copper River was banned, saving the fishery from probable extinction. However, in banning in-river commercial fishing, the US government also outlawed any commercial enterprise by the Ahtna that would have allowed them to benefit from a naturally occurring resource in their own home territory. Instead, it became an issue of regulating the commercial fishery to protect the capital investments of the canners, who agreed to the conservation measures to protect their property (Taylor 2002, 366).

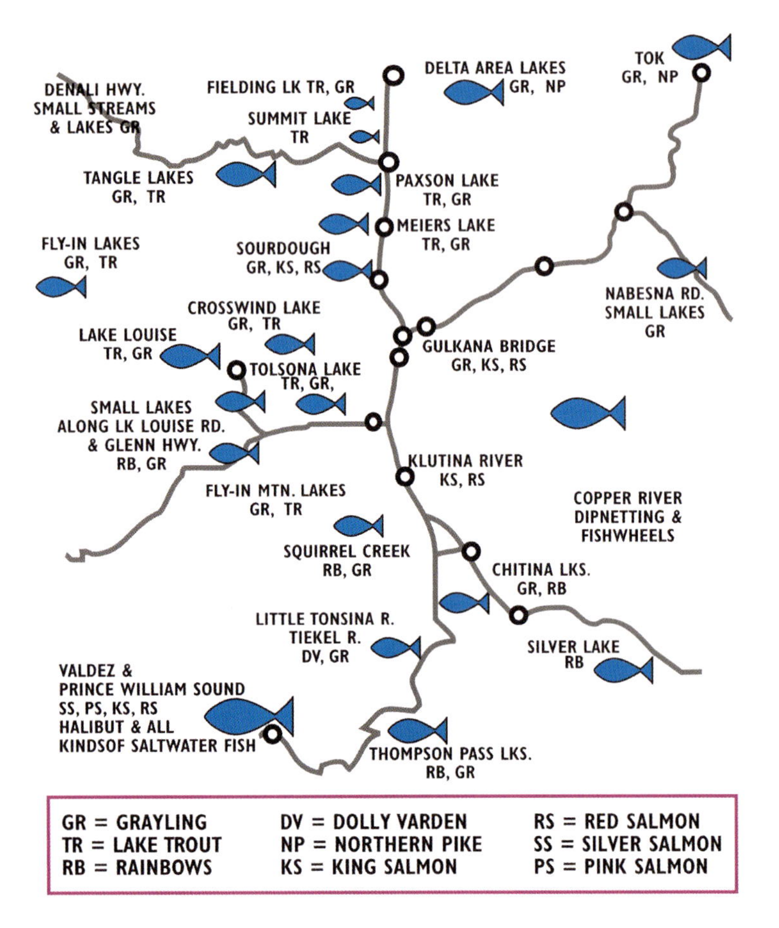

FIGURE 7.17 Recreational fishing in the Copper River basin. Published in 2000, this map shows the Copper basin as a recreational destination for sports fishermen. The black lines represent the Glenn, Richardson, and Edgerton Highways, the "Tok cutoff," and the Nabesna Road, which had been built for trucks carrying ore from the Nabesna Mine. Map courtesy of Bearfoot Travel Magazines.

During World War II, the road system in Alaska was improved, such that by the end of the war the Copper River and its rich salmon resource was accessible by road from the growing urban centres of Anchorage and Fairbanks. In effect, Ahtna territory became a recreational area for outsiders who wanted to fish or hunt. Figure 7.17 shows a map produced by the *Bearfoot* series of travel magazines showing recreational fishing locations within the Copper basin. Many of these locations were once traditional Ahtna fishing sites (see figure 7.4).

Between 1867 and 1959, when Alaska became a state, little was done to solve the issue of Indigenous land claims. When admitted into the union in 1959, the State of Alaska was authorized to select and obtain title to more than 103 million acres of public lands. These lands were regarded as essential to the economic viability of the state. Although the Statehood Act stipulated that Indigenous lands were exempt from selection, the state swiftly moved to expropriate lands still being used and occupied by Alaska Natives. Without informing the affected Native villages, and ignoring the blanket claims the Natives already had on file, the Bureau of Land Management, an arm of the US Department of the Interior, began to process the state's selections. Natives became alarmed and pressed for a settlement of their claims.

The Alaska Native Claims Settlement Act (ANCSA) of 1971 was a watershed in Alaska Native history. In exchange for relinquishing their land claims and hunting and fishing rights, Alaska Natives received close to a billion dollars and 40 million acres of land. Instead of creating reservations, the land was conveyed to Native corporations, whose stockholders are Alaska Native people. In his report, published in 1887, Allen (1887, 128) had estimated that Ahtna territory encompassed approximately 25,000 square miles. More recent research has expanded the area to about 41,000 square miles (de Laguna and McClellan 1981; Kari 2008). ANCSA entitled the Ahtna to 1.77 million acres, or 2,765 square miles—about 7 percent of their traditional territory. The remainder is owned by the State of Alaska, the federal government, and private landowners.

An essential fact of American colonialism is that Indigenous land was taken and then transformed into national land so that it could be settled and developed. Maps were an essential part of this process. The Indigenous presence was first eliminated and then relegated or confined to dots on the landscape. These dots represent the recalibration of land and life on the colonizers' terms without reference to Indigenous antecedents (Harris 2004, 179). As villages, the dots represent the triumph of civilization over savagery, of the American ideal of a settled existence. Erasing Alaska Native toponyms and introducing new place names further transforms the landscape from an alien, unknown space to a landscape familiar to the colonizers. Even when Ahtna place names were used, they were altered for convenience and their meanings were subsequently lost. A case in point is the Copper River itself. In the Ahtna language, the river now known as the Copper River is called *Atna* (beyond river) or *Ts'itu'* (major river or straight river), while the Chitina River is called "copper river" or *Tsedi Na'* (Kari 2008, 37, 44).

When tourists enter the Copper River basin today, they have no idea they are entering the Ahtna homeland. Most information provided to the casual tourist about the basin emphasizes the spectacular mountain scenery, Kennecott copper mine, and fishing. For example, the *Milepost*, which advertises itself as the "Bible of north country travel" and is probably the most widely used traveller's guide in Alaska, describes the Tok Cutoff as the "principal access route from the Alaska Highway west to Anchorage," and provides detailed information about the area, but makes no mention of the Ahtna.

Maps are not transparent openings to the areas they depict; rather, they comprise a particularly human way of looking at the world (Harley 1989). We are taught that maps are objective descriptions of "natural facts," that is, of the lay of the land, but they also reveal "political facts," that is, who has hegemony over the land. In short, maps are about who controls the narrative about land. The maps in this series demonstrate the development of the colonial narrative. When Russia ceded Alaska to the United States in 1867, interior Alaska appears as a blank space. Allen's map reveals the Ahtna presence, reflecting his charge to assess the disposition of the Ahtna toward the US government. Subsequent maps reflect the American interest in developing the riches of Alaska. No longer considered an impediment to development, the Ahtna have been erased from the maps.

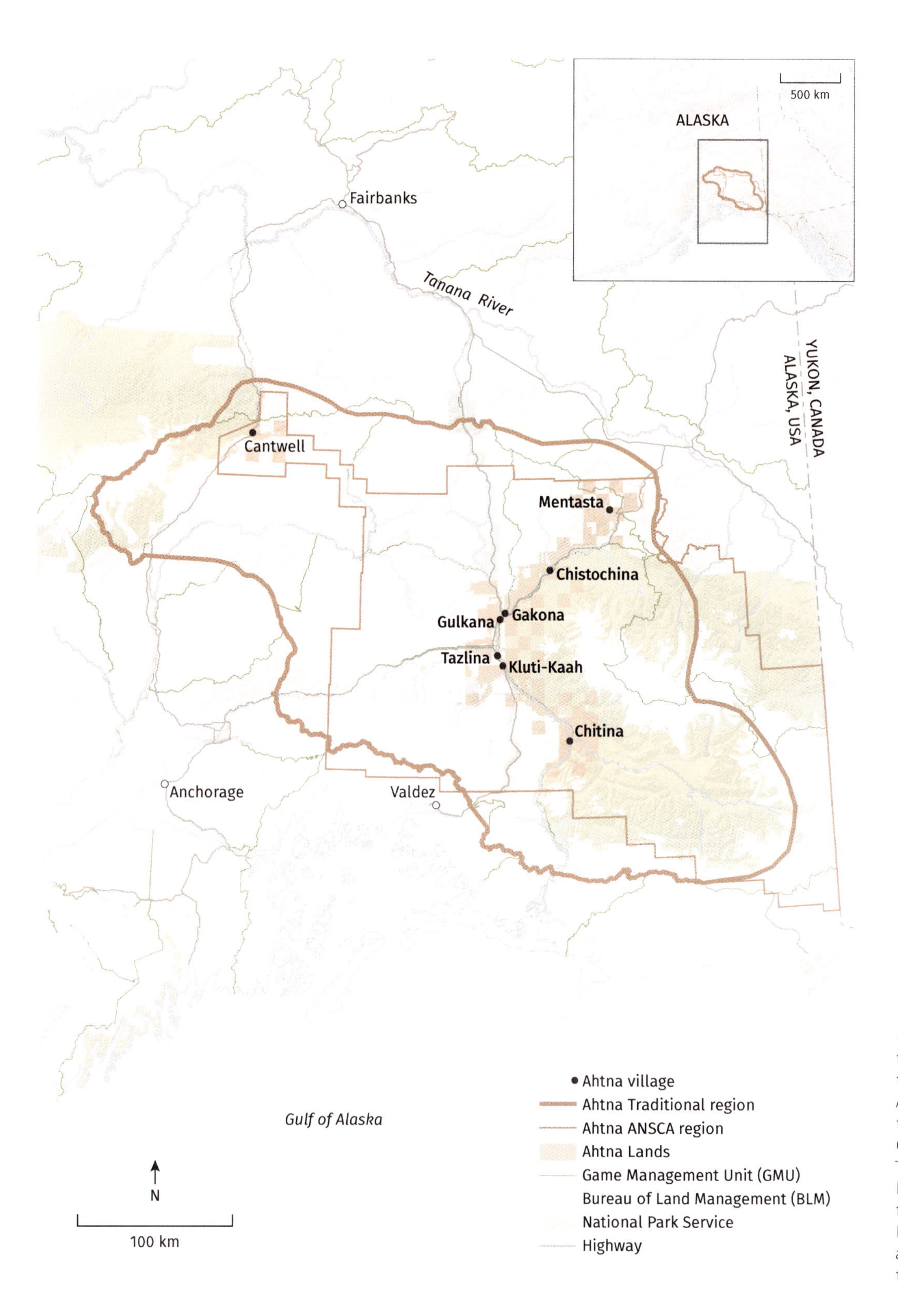

FIGURE 7.18 Ahtna traditional territory and the lands received by Ahtna communities under the 1971 Alaska Native Claims Settlement Act. This map was produced by Ahtna, Inc., and shows the current disposition of lands within the boundaries of Ahtna traditional territory. Ahtna, Inc.

While the Ahtna presence was erased, they have never been physically removed from their homeland. Eventually, the US government and the State of Alaska were forced to acknowledge the Ahtna presence and their land claim. Produced by the land department of Ahtna, Inc., the final map in this series shows the results of this acknowledgement (figure 7.18). Land received by Ahtna under ANCSA is depicted by pale red squares, federal land shown in green (Wrangell-St. Elias National Park and Preserve), and land managed by the Bureau of Land Management is shown in pale grey. Current Ahtna villages are located along the road system. But the map also shows the outline of the Ahtna homeland. Recently, Ahtna Inc., with support from the Bureau of Indian Affairs, has put this map on one of six informational signs developed to reverse the colonial narrative and inform the public of the Ahtna presence. Produced by Ahtna, Inc., the map is an assertion of Ahtna claims running counter to those of the State of Alaska or federal government. It is a declaration that Ahtna are still present and have persevered in place despite a century of colonial policies designed to erase them from their homeland.

Acknowledgements

I received assistance in writing this chapter from my father, William E. Simeone Sr., from my dear wife, Colleen Tyrrell, from Ken Pratt, who has an incredible eye for detail, and from Scott Heyes. I also want to acknowledge those elders who have tutored me over the years, as well as the work of Jim Kari, who has contributed so much to our knowledge of Ahtna history and culture. *Tsin'aen*—thank you all.

Notes

1 With regard to Ahtna territory, one map that would have been very valuable has unfortunately been lost. Judy Ferguson (2012, 67) reports that, in 1949, a Bureau of Indian Affairs teacher named Charles O'Brien asked Mr. John Billum Sr., an Ahtna elder from Chitina, to draw a map of Ahtna territory. Mr. Billum drew a line "from the mouth of the Bremner River near Cordova, up the Copper River, all the way to Cantwell over to McCarthy and to Kennicott." In 1951, the map, along with a land claim signed by Mr. Billum, was sent to Washington, DC, but the map has since disappeared.

2 *Johnson and Graham's Lessee v. William M'Intosh*, 21 US (8 Wheat.) 543 at 574. See also Wheaton (1916, 270–271). The case established that, as the sovereign power, the United States had the sole right to purchase land from Indigenous peoples, who were thus unable to convey it to anyone else.

3 Allen also mistakenly identified a fourth peak that he named Mount Tillman in honour of a teacher at the United States Military Academy.

4 According to James VanStone (1955, 118), a prospector named John Bremner, who spent the winter of 1883–1884 at Taral, was reported to have explored the Chitina River sometime between February and April 1885. He, too, was eager to locate copper sources in the area (Seton Karr 1887, 207). There is, however, some question as to whether Bremner actually did make a solo trip to the Chitina River (see Pratt 1998, 87–88).

References

Abercrombie, William R.

1900 A Military Reconnaissance of the Copper River Valley, 1898. In *Compilation of Narratives of the Exploration of Alaska*, pp. 563–590. Government Printing Office, Washington, DC.

Ainsworth, Cynthea L.

1999 *Chistochina Community History Project, 1996–1999*. National Park Service, Wrangell–St. Elias National Park and Preserve, Copper Center, Alaska. Manuscript in possession of author.

Allen, Henry T.

1887 Report of an Expedition to the Copper, Tananáa, and Kóoyukuk Rivers, in the Territory of Alaska, in the Year 1885, for the Purpose of Obtaining All Information Which Will Be Valuable and Important, Especially to the Military Branch of the Government. Government Printing Office, Washington, DC.

Berez, Andrea L.

2011 Directional Reference, Discourse, and Landscape in Ahtna. PhD dissertation, University of California, Santa Barbara.

Bleakley, Geoffrey T.

n.d. In the Shadow of Kennecott: A History of Mining in the Wrangell–St. Elias Mountain Region, 1898–1998. Unpublished manuscript, history files, Wrangell–St. Elias National Park and Preserve, National Park Service, Copper Center, Alaska.

Billum, Frank

1992 Taped interview. Mary E. Fogerty and Karen Shemet, interviewers; Mary E. Fogerty, transcriber. 24 June. Chitina, Alaska. Tapes 92AHT004 and 92AHT005. Bureau of Indian Affairs, ANCSA Office, Anchorage.

Boelhower, William

1988 Inventing America: A Model of Cartographic Semiosis. *Word and Image* 4(2): 475–496.

Case, David

1984 *Alaska Natives and American Laws*. Rev. ed. University of Alaska Press, Fairbanks.

Case, David, and D. Voluck

2012 *Alaska Natives and American Laws*. 3rd ed. University of Alaska Press, Fairbanks.

Cooper, H. Kory

2012 Innovation and Prestige Among Northern Hunter-Gatherers: Late Prehistoric Native Copper Use in Alaska and Yukon. *American Antiquity* 77(3): 565–590.

Copper River Mining, Trading and Development Company

1902 *A Guide for Alaska Miners, Settlers and Tourists*. Trade Register Print, Seattle.

Cruikshank, Julie

2005 *Do Glaciers Listen? Local Knowledge, Colonial Encounters, and Social Imagination*. University of British Columbia Press, Vancouver.

Dall, William H.

1877 *Tribes of the Extreme Northwest*. Government Printing Office, Washington, DC.

de Laguna, Frederica, and Catharine McClellan

1981 Ahtna. In *Handbook of North American Indians*, vol. 6, *Subarctic*, edited by June Helm, pp. 641–663. Smithsonian Institution Press, Washington, DC.

Ferguson, Judy

2012 *Windows on the Land*. Vol. 1, *Alaska Native Claims Trailblazers*. Voice of Alaska Press. Big Delta, Alaska.

Gilbert, C. H.

1921 Letter to Dr. H. M. Smith, Commissioner of Fisheries, 19 November. RG 22, Records of the US Fish and Wildlife Service, Reports and Related Records, 1869–1937. Records of Division of Alaska Fisheries, National Archives, Washington, DC.

Grinev, Andrei V.

1993 On the Banks of the Copper River: The Ahtna Indians and the Russians, 1783–1867. *Arctic Anthropology* 30(1): 54–66.

1997 The Forgotten Expedition of Dmitrii Tarkhonov on the Copper River. *Alaska History* 12(1): 1–17.

Hämäläinen, Pekka

2008 *The Comanche Empire*. Yale University Press, New Haven, Connecticut.

Harley, J. B.

1989 Deconstructing the Map. *Cartographica* 26(2): 1–20.

Harris, Cole

2004 How Did Colonialism Dispossess? Comments from the Edge of Empire. In *Annals of the Association of American Geographers* 94(1): 165–182.

Hayes, Charles W.

1892 An Expedition through the Yukon District. *National Geographic Magazine* 4: 117–162.

Innis, Harold A.

1950 *Empire and Communications*. Clarendon Press, Oxford.

Justin, Jack John

1991 Taped interview. Matt Ganley, interviewer; Lincoln B. Smith, transcriber. 1 November. Chistochina, Alaska. Interview #91-09. Ahtna, Inc. Land and Resources Department, Glennallen, Alaska. Transcript in possession of the author.

Justin, Wilson

2014 Boundaries of Upper Ahtna Territory. Appendix A in William Simeone, *Along the Ałts'e'tnaey-Nal'cine Trail: Historical Narratives, Historical Places*. Mount Sanford Tribal Consortium in collaboration with the National Park Service, Wrangell–St. Elias National Park and Preserve. Copper Center, Alaska.

Kari, James (editor)

1986 *Tatl'ahwt'aenn Nenn': The Headwaters People's Country. Narratives of the Upper Ahtna Athabaskans*. Translated by Katie John and James Kari. Alaska Native Language Center, University of Alaska Fairbanks.

1990 *Ahtna Athabaskan Dictionary.* Alaska Native Language Center, University of Alaska Fairbanks.

2008 *Ahtna Place Names Lists.* 2nd ed. Alaska Native Language Center, University of Alaska Fairbanks.

2010 *Ahtna Travel Narratives: A Demonstration of Shared Geographical Knowledge Among Alaska Athabascans.* Alaska Native Language Center, University of Alaska Fairbanks.

Kari, James, and James A. Fall (editors)

2003 *Shem Pete's Alaska: The Territory of the Upper Cook Inlet Dena'ina.* University of Alaska Press, Fairbanks.

McClellan, Catharine

1975 Feuding and Warfare Among Northwestern Athapaskans. In *Proceedings: Northern Athapaskan Conference, 1971*, vol. 1, edited by A. M. Clark, pp. 181–258. National Museums of Canada, Ottawa.

Medzini, Arnon

2012 The War of the Maps: The Political Use of Maps and Atlases to Shape National Consciousness—Israel Versus the Palestinian Authority. *European Journal of Geography* 3(1): 23–40.

Mendenhall, Walter C., and Frank C. Schrader

1903 *The Mineral Resources of the Mount Wrangell District, Alaska.* Geological Survey Professional Paper No. 15. Government Printing Office, Washington, DC.

Moffit, Fred H., and A. G. Maddren

1909 *The Mineral Resources of the Kotsina and Chitina Valleys, Copper River Basin.* US Geological Survey Bulletin No. 345, pp. 127–178. Government Printing Office, Washington. DC.

Moser, Jefferson F.

1899 Bulletin of the US Fish Commission, Volume XVIII for 1898. Government Printing Office, Washington, DC.

Pierce, Richard A.

1990 *Russian America: A Biographical Dictionary.* Alaska History No. 33. Limestone Press, Kingston, Ontario.

Pratt, Kenneth L.

1998 Copper, Trade, and Tradition Among the Lower Ahtna of the Chitina River Basin: The Nicolai Era, 1884–1900. *Arctic Anthropology* 35(2): 77–98.

Reckord, Holly

1983 *That's the Way We Live: Subsistence in the Wrangell–St. Elias National Park and Preserve.* Anthropology and Historic Preservation, Cooperative Park Studies Unit, Occasional Paper No. 34. University of Alaska, Fairbanks.

Rice, John

1900 A Story of Hardship and Suffering in Alaska. In *Compilation of Narratives of Explorations on Alaska*, pp. 686–713. Government Printing Office, Washington, DC.

Seton Karr, Heywood W.

1887 *Shores and Alps of Alaska.* Sampson Low, Marsten, Searle, and Rivington, London.

Simeone, William E., and Erica McCall Valentine

2007 *Ahtna Knowledge of Long-Term Changes in Salmon Runs in the Upper Copper River Drainage, Alaska.* Technical Paper No. 324. Alaska Department of Fish and Game, Division of Subsistence, Juneau.

Simeone, William E., Wilson Justin, Michelle Anderson, and Kathryn Martin

2019 The Ahtna Homeland. *Alaska Journal of Anthropology* 17(1–2): 121–138.

Simpson, Ronald N.

2001 *Legacy of the Chief.* Copper Rail Histories, Copper Center, Alaska.

Taylor, Joseph E.

2002 "Well-Thinking Men and Women": The Battle of the White Act and the Meaning of Conservation in the 1920s. *Pacific Historical Review* 71(3): 357–387.

Treloar, William

1898 *Journal of William Treloar.* Valdez Museum and Historical Archives Association, Valdez, Alaska.

Twichell, Heath, Jr.

1974 *Allen: The Biography of an Army Officer, 1859–1930.* Rutgers University Press, New Brunswick, New Jersey.

VanStone, James W.

1955 Exploring the Copper River Country. *Pacific Northwest Quarterly* 46(4): 115–123.

Wheaton, Henry

1916 *Elements of International Law.* 6th ed. Little, Brown and Company, Boston.

Workman, William

1977 Ahtna Archaeology: A Preliminary Statement. In *Problems in the Prehistory of the North American Subarctic: The Athapaskan Question*, edited by J. W. Helmer, S. VanDyke, and F. J. Kense, pp. 22–39. University of Calgary Archaeology Association, Calgary.

Wrangell, Ferdinand P. von

1980 (1839) *Russian America: Statistical and Ethnographic Information, with Additional Information by Karl Ernst von Baer.* Edited by Richard A. Pierce. Translated by Mary Sadouski. Limestone Press, Kingston, Ontario. First published in German as *Statistische und ethnographische Nachrichten über die Russischen Besitzungen an der Nordwestküste von Amerika* [Statistical and ethnographic reports regarding Russian possessions on the northwest coast of America].

Znamenski, Andrei A.

2003 *Through Orthodox Eyes: Russian Missionary Narratives of Travels to the Dena'ina and Ahtna, 1850s–1930s.* University of Alaska Press, Fairbanks.

FIGURE 8.1 *The Torngats That Come Knocking in the Night*, 1975, stonecut, 21½" × 29⅜". The print by Tivi Etok of Kangiqsualujjuaq recounts a story told during the time of Tivi's grandmother, when people lived in tents made of skins. The people would hear scratching sounds at night outside the tents. These noises were made by evil spirits and would continue most of the night. Private collection, Peter Jacobs.

SCOTT A. HEYES AND PETER JACOBS

8 Inuit Identity and the Land

Toward Distinctive Built Form in the Nunavik Homeland

Land-based activities and pursuits have long informed a powerful sense of Canadian Inuit identity. For Inuit, being "out on the land" (*maqainniq*) hunting, camping, and fishing is an essential part of Inuit culture and the sense of connectedness to place. It is on the land, far beyond the boundaries and hilltops of villages (*nunalik*) and hamlets, where Inuit often say that they feel most at home (see Dorais 1997; Heyes 2007). The land (*nuna*) is where their elders walked, and where their ancestors are buried and their memories are stored (Nuttall 1992). Specific points on the land are also associated with place names, forged and passed on by generations of Inuit (see Goehring 1990; Müller-Wille 1987). Embedded in these names are stories about hunting tragedies, legendary figures, the spirit world, and other significant events that reveal much about local history and world views (see Collignon 2006).

The form of shelter on the land has evolved as well, and over time semi-buried pit houses were replaced by sod and stone shelters, and in some locations tent structures were erected to house as many as thirty Inuit. The well-known igloo, built of ice blocks in the winter, is most commonly associated with Indigenous architecture of the highest quality. All of these housing forms were impermanent in keeping with the nomadic nature of Inuit life.

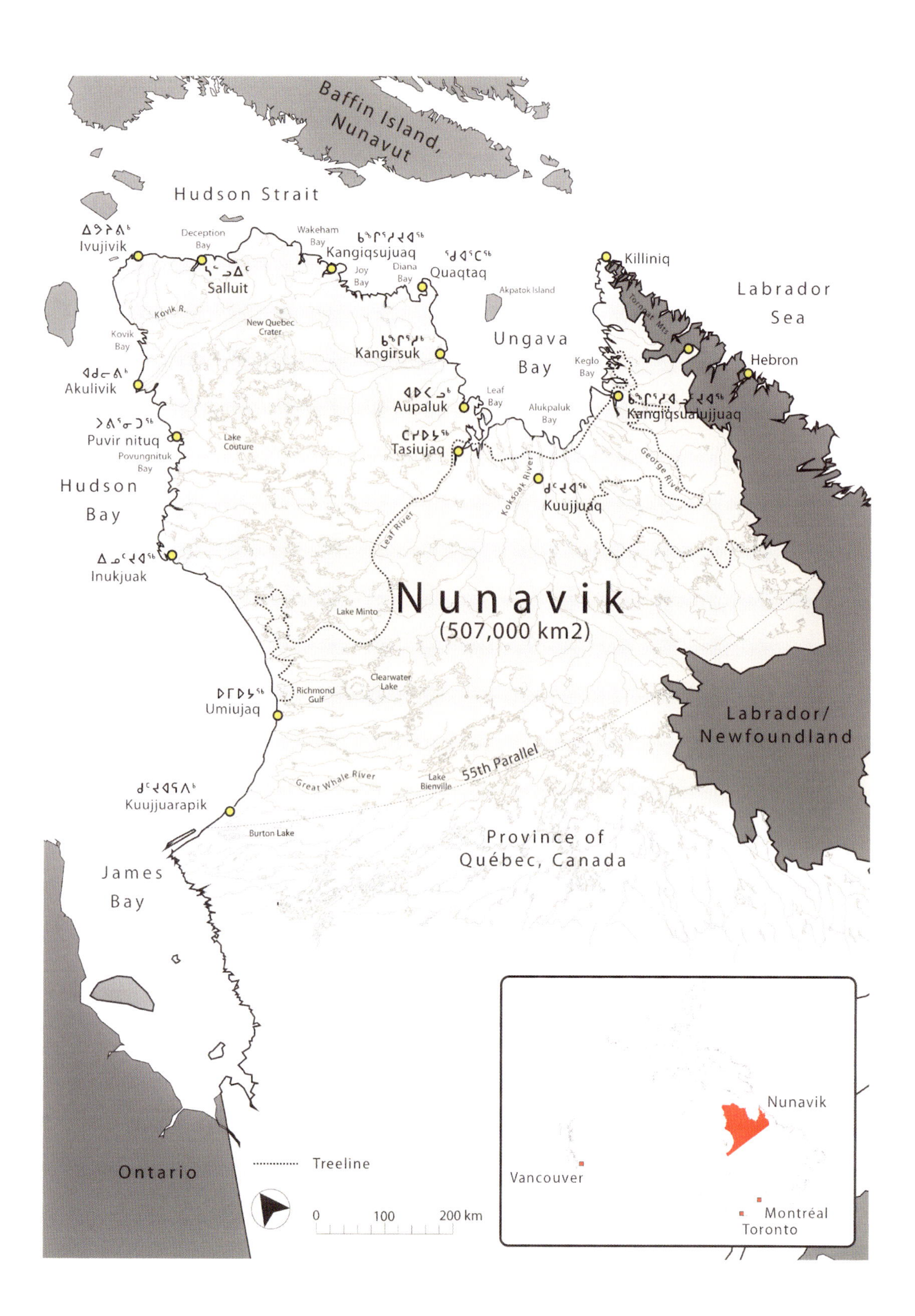

FIGURE 8.2 Nunavik, the remote land mass to the north of the 55th parallel in Québec, is home to some 10,800 Inuit. Although Nunavik is officially part of Québec, its people share political, cultural, and social values and aspirations with the circumpolar world. Of the fourteen Inuit communities, the largest is Kuujjuaq, which was the site of the former Hudson's Bay Company trading post called Fort Chimo. The village of Kangiqsualujjuaq is located on the eastern shore of Ungava Bay, at the mouth of the George River. Map created by Scott A. Heyes.

Yet, conditions in the Arctic are swiftly changing, affecting the ability of Inuit to venture over great distances, as was standard in previous times. These changes include a rapidly growing Inuit population, the fact that going "out on the land" is increasingly difficult due to the prohibitive costs of travel for large families, and the fact that many Inuit are working in the cash economy on a full-time basis. Given these constraints, in this chapter we consider the importance of villages themselves, the architectural forms that constitute these settlements, and their ability to support and maintain Inuit identity. Inuit are spending considerably more time indoors in village settings than ever before, and consequently are unable to connect as readily as did their elders with the identity derived from land-based activity.

Drawing on our own land- and village-based experiences in Nunavik (northern Québec) (figure 8.2) and the guidance of Inuit elders and friends, and given our interest in Indigenous spaces and place making, we discuss an initial set of culturally appropriate design principles that might assist those responsible for the making of spaces and architecture in Northern villages. Ethnographically, the ensuing discussion on Inuit place making and identity has been drawn from our respective engagement with built environment studies and projects in Nunavik.

Specifically, Scott Heyes has been undertaking place-based studies with thirty-four male and female Inuit hunters from Kangiqsualujjuaq since 2002, and findings from this larger study on Inuit perceptions of the environment (Heyes 2007; Heyes and Jacobs 2008) have informed a number of themes in this chapter. We also base our discussion on Peter Jacobs's knowledge and professional evaluation of the social and environmental impacts of built projects proposed throughout Nunavik (Jacobs 1986, 2001) during his tenure as chair of the Kativik Environmental Quality Commission (KEQC), a position he held from 1979 to 2017. The KEQC's mission is to ensure that development proposals respond to the needs of the community, respect the cultural and natural heritage of Nunavik, and are consistent with best professional practices (KEQC 2009, 5, 7).

Based on our collective experiences in Nunavik, working at both the community and regional scale, we argue in this chapter that Northern architecture, when responsive to Inuit culture and inspired by a variety of Arctic settings, can and does contribute to Inuit identity. We engage in this discussion while recognizing that "identity is a dynamic and creative process that is best expressed through the strategies developed to relate to one's physical, social, and spiritual environments" and that "these environments may change over time and space, and thus identity is never fixed" (Dorais 1997, 5).

Architectural Forms in Nunavik

Notwithstanding variations in natural landforms, orientation, and elevation, practically every Inuit village across the eastern Canadian Arctic resembles the others. Whether in the central Baffin Island region, along the Hudson Bay coast, or in northern Labrador, most villages feature free-standing, timber-clad dwellings called *illujuaq* (or *ilualuk*), the term for a modern house or Euro-Canadian house (Schneider 1985, 69). These are typically elevated dwellings that rest on adjustable supports designed to overcome heavy drifts of wind-blown snow and movements of the foundation caused by permafrost melt, while the space beneath the house also provides shelter for outdoor storage (Mactavish 2004, 40). The dwellings, which may be single- or two-storey, are often painted vibrant colours and are generally set out in neat rows and grids, much as in suburban housing developments in southern Canada (figure 8.3). Aside from the occasional caribou antler mounted above entranceways to celebrate a hunting excursion, few adornments or modifications are apparent.

FIGURE 8.3 Inuit villages are architecturally very similar all across the Arctic. The two-storey frame dwellings pictured here in the Nunavik community of Kangiqsualujjuaq became fixtures in Arctic villages from the 1980s onward. Photograph by Scott A. Heyes, 2003.

As Leo Zrudlo (2001) discussed in the late 1990s—and this is still the case today—the standard contemporary architecture of the North does not echo the cultural context, nor does it represent Inuit identity. The region's dwellings and community buildings are engineered to withstand harsh Arctic climates but lack features characteristic or emblematic of Inuit culture. Apart from the occasional municipal building that has been given individual treatment, there is little architectural variety apparent in the modern built form from village to village. (By "built form," or "built environment," we mean all forms of constructed environments in village settings, including dwellings, community buildings, shops and businesses, infrastructure, foot paths, and roads.) Housing forms are so uniform across the North that it remains difficult to distinguish villages from each other by observing the built form alone.

While contemporary architecture in Nunavik largely reflects the top-down imposition of low-cost, utilitarian styles originating in southern Canada, Inuit society has been subject to other government interventions and decisions, including the introduction of health, educational, governance, and justice systems modelled on English- and French-Canadian institutions. This ongoing incursion of southern assumptions, attitudes, and agendas was the impetus for the Nunavik-wide Parnasimautik consultation process undertaken in 2013, which sought to identify ways to both protect and strengthen Inuit identity, culture, and traditional livelihoods. The process enabled Inuit, young and old, to have their voices heard by government, while it also alerted policy makers to the need to develop decision-making practices that are more sensitive to Inuit priorities and protocols.

Historic Dwelling Types

When we discuss architecture and other built forms in contemporary Inuit communities, it is useful to reflect on traditional architectural practices that the Inuit and the Thule, their direct ancestors, developed. This is not for comparative purposes, nor to lament the loss of architectural forms that served Inuit and their forebears in the past, but to draw attention to the sheer ingenuity and variety of styles and techniques that they developed so as to survive and thrive in a harsh climate.

Focusing on the Nunavik homeland, we learn from archaeologists that the Thule constructed and lived in "permanent winter settlements that were composed of semi-subterranean dwellings, or pit houses" (Pinard 1993, 62; see also Kativik Regional Government 2005, 105–117). Archaeological excavations suggest that these dwellings, described and illustrated in figure 8.4, began to appear in the southern portions of the Ungava region of Nunavik between 1350 and 1500 AD. These dwellings were robust and made from locally available materials:

> These dwellings consist of relatively deep depressions lined with slabs [1] or boulders encircled by a raised rim [2]. The houses were covered with sod and skin roofs [3] supported by a framework [4] made of wood, upright rocks, and, in numerous instances, whale bones. Ribs and jawbones were most frequently used for this purpose. Although the dwellings vary in shape and size, most are oval and average about 4 × 5 metres in interior dimensions. The tunnels [5] are often more than 5 metres in length but rarely exceed 60 centimetres in height and width.
>
> The floor in the front part of the house was generally paved with flagstones while the rear part contained a raised sleeping platform. In many cases, the platform was also paved with flagstones and was erected on pillars, providing storage space beneath the sleeping area [6]. Other interior features include meat and blubber storage bins constructed of vertically placed flat stones and paved kitchen areas located on both sides of the tunnel opening. Entrance tunnels were lower than the dwelling floors and usually ended in a dipper pit that trapped cold air [7]. (Pinard 1993, 62)

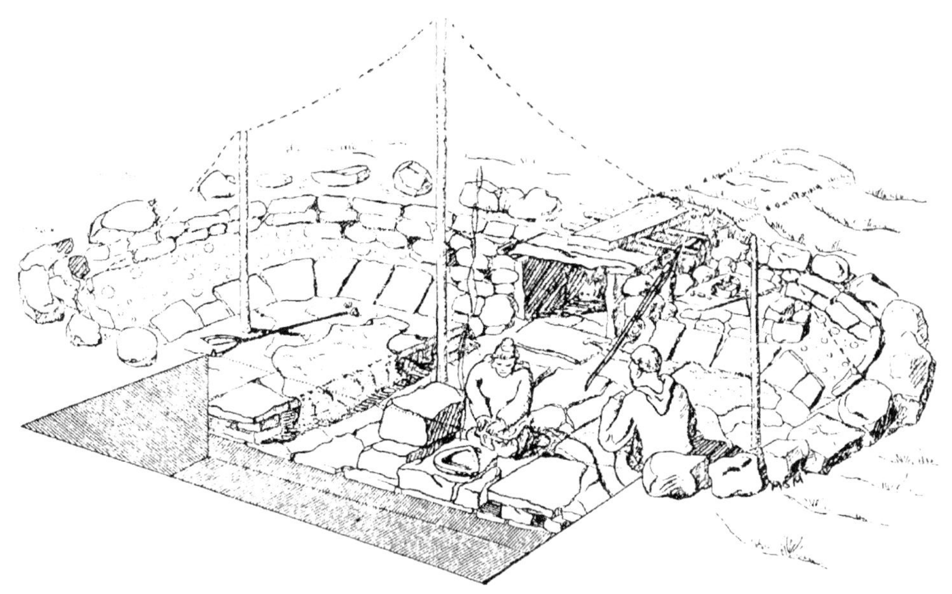

FIGURE 8.4 Artists' impressions of a Thule semi-subterranean dwelling made from a combination of sod, grass, whale bone, and wood. The modern-day Inuit descend from the Thule peoples, who appeared in Alaska around 1000 AD and moved eastward across the Canadian Arctic over the next several centuries. Sources: Maxwell 1985, 287 (left); Tassé 2000, 118 (below).

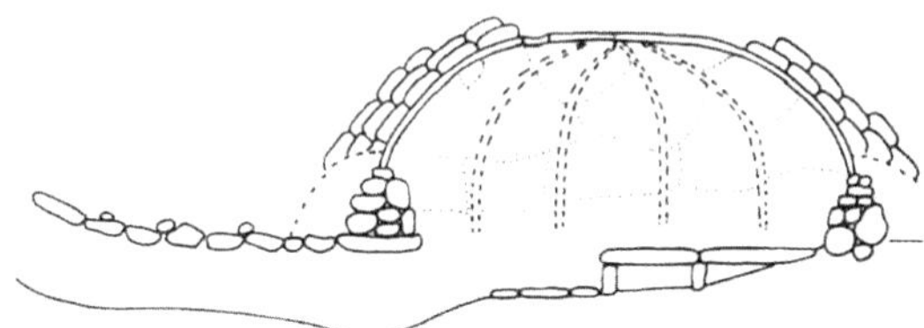

It is believed that "pit houses" remained in use in Nunavik up to three hundred years ago and were replaced by a dwelling known as *qarmat* (or *qarmak*), which was principally occupied during fall and spring. They were constructed from sod and stone and featured roofs made of seal-skin guts to allow light to penetrate below (Hantzsch 1932, 63). The dwellings were supported by wooden poles. Excavations of seventeen *qarmat* dwellings on an island near the eastern Ungava locality of Killiniq revealed that two dwellings had been constructed on top of "pit house" sites, and that there was evidence to suggest that some dwellings had been continually used until the 1930s (Pinard 1993, 64). It is likely that *qarmat* dwelling sites were relatively confined to favourable hunting sites across the Ungava Peninsula, for it was reported in the 1800s that the population of Inuit from the George River to Hebron (the localities that mark the triangular extent of the Ungava region and that are separated by over 350 miles of coastline) were fewer than thirteen families or seventy individuals (Turner 1894, 176). The robust construction and design consideration given to the making of *qarmat* dwellings suggest that Inuit of this region, and perhaps across Nunavik more broadly, remained close to their homes for a considerable portion of the year, especially where good hunting of land and marine mammals was available nearby.

The naturalist Bernard Hantzsch made observations of *qarmat* dwellings while based in Killiniq in 1906; he remarked that Inuit in this location had begun to transform the design of their *qarmat*, largely under the instruction of Moravian missionaries. This included changing the form to make them more "roomy and comfortable inside," as well as abandoning sod walls in favour of wooden panels (Hantzsch 1932, 63). Hantzsch made special mention of this change in dwelling construction and saw this as an impractical development, especially given the lack of wood supply in Killiniq:

> What is the use of a fine house, if you are cold in it! A small iron stove such as the Eskimos use occasionally, helps only if you have coal or wood, but that has become scarce even in the mission buildings. Let the old Eskimo houses be made somewhat roomier, brighter and healthier; let boards be used to sheathe them, and better ventilation be introduced, but desist from buildings which cannot be heated by oil lamps. (Hantzsch 1932, 63)

In Killiniq, as elsewhere across Nunavik (up to and during the period of first contact), with the onset of winter Inuit built and moved into snow houses variously referred to as *illu* ("dwelling; house, snow house or tent"; Schneider 1985, 69), *iglu* ("house"; Turner 1884), or *igluvigak* ("snow hut"; Turner 1884). In southeast Ungava, Turner (1887, 259) documented that snow house construction usually started in October, with the first snowfall. These shelters provided more security from inclement weather than stone, sod, and wooden buildings, and afforded warmth in the absence of fire (Hantzsch 1932, 63; McLean 1849, 145–146). Hantzsch noted that twenty-eight Inuit resided in a snow house "bee hive" at Killiniq, remarking that small structures could be built in under half an hour by two individuals. On the construction technique, he wrote:

> These remarkable buildings, well known to all Eskimo districts, are erected from quadrangular snow blocks of perhaps forty centimeters length and fifteen centimeters thickness, which are cut from well-frozen places with long, broad snow knives and are placed in layers in a helical-shaped wall. Usually they are supplied with a tunnel-shaped entrance-way, occasionally with adjoining rooms for dogs and tools, and when the house is to be used for any length of time, with a chimney and a gut window. (Hantzsch 1932, 84)

As well as being captivated by the ingenuity of Inuit architecture, Hantzsch appreciated the ambience created by snow houses (figure 8.5): "It must be a charming sight, when the hemispherical building on a dark winter's night reflects the rays of the dimly shining lights" (Hantzsch 1932, 84). The snow house building process and interior characteristics were also observed by John McLean at Fort Chimo (now Kuujjuaq), where he was based as the Hudson's Bay Company postmaster from 1837 to 1843:

> Blocks of snow are first cut out with some sharp instrument from the spot that is intended to form the floor of the dwelling, and raised on edge, inclining a little inward around the cavity. These blocks are generally about two feet in length, two feet in breadth, and eight inches thick, and are joined close together. In this manner the edifice is erected, contracting at each successive tier, until there only remains a small aperture at the top, which is filled by a slab of clear ice, that serves both as a keystone to the arch, and a window to light the dwelling. An embankment of snow is raised around the interior walls, and covered with skins, which answers the double purpose of beds and seats. The inside of the hut presents the figure of an arch or dome; the usual dimensions are ten or twelve feet in diameter, and about eight feet in height at the centre. Sometimes two or three families congregate under the same roof, having separate apartments communicating with the main building, that are used as bedrooms. The entrance to the igloo is effected through a winding covered passage, which stands open by day, but is closed up at night by placing slabs of ice at the angle of each bend, and thus the inmates are perfectly secured against the severest cold. (McLean 1849, 146)

A 2005 drawing by Inuit elder Johnny George Annanack describing igloo construction (figure 8.6) serves as a reminder that the knowledge and skills for building snow houses remains with Inuit today, even though snow houses are only occasionally built, such as for demonstration purposes, or for when hunters find themselves in blizzard conditions. Canvas tents are now used in lieu of snow houses during short trips on the land.

During the warmer months, Inuit lived in tents made of seal skins (figure 8.7). The technology and techniques surrounding the construction of a traditional Inuit tent, or *tupik* (also *itsaq* or *nuirtaq*; Schneider 1985, 106, 218), as well as their manner of use, were recorded in the journals and photographs of Smithsonian Institution naturalist Lucien Turner when he was based in Fort Chimo in the 1880s. He observed that during the summer the Inuit in the region lived in tents—sometimes housing as many as thirty individuals—with waterproof coverings made from the skins of bearded, ringed, and harp seals.

> The skins are then sewed side to side to another until reaching a length necessary to enclose an area of sufficient size to accommodate the number of persons to be sheltered within. . . . The tents vary in length from eight or ten feet to thirty feet in length and a breadth of six to ten feet. The supports are always of wood and vary in length. They are arranged as follows, beginning at the rear; three, two, two, two or three. The back three are two shorter and one longer poles; the longer is thrust behind while the shorter are the side slopes, the next two pairs are of the same length as the

(FACING) FIGURE 8.5 Building a snow house at Little Whale River, Québec, 1872. This house is representative of those that Inuit throughout the Nunavik region built each winter. Used with permission of the McCord Museum, Montréal (MP-0000.391.1). Photograph by James Laurence Cotter.

FIGURE 8.6 Snow house construction. This drawing, by elder Johnny George Annanack from Kangiqsualujjuaq, illustrates a story about a husband and wife who had no dogs and had to pull their sled long distances all by themselves. When they were tired, they would build a snow house in which to rest. As Annanack explains, the man is cutting blocks of snow using his *pana* (snow knife), and the woman is using her *ulu* (crescent-moon-shaped knife) to fill in gaps between the snow blocks. Source: Heyes 2007, 452 and 456.

> anterior pair of the posterior three. The front pair, or three, are like the rear ones except they are slightly longer [so] as to give a gentle slope from front to rear. One or two ridge poles are also added.
>
> It will be seen that the fully equipped tent has six sides, the two ends having two each and the two long sides. If the tent be small, the front ends with a pair of poles. The end is thus truncate or cut off. In either case the overlapping skin serves as a place of ingress and exit.
>
> The internal arrangement of the occupants and properties depends also upon certain social customs of those people. The head man of the tent occupies the space under the three rear poles of the tent. Those next in importance occupy the space to the right or left and those dependent are placed near the entrance. The fire is made without the tent if the weather be warm, but if chilly the place of making it is near the center or toward the front of the tent. Here all the cooking or the work goes on. The bedding consisting of skins, blankets or merely the bare earth is left where each person sleeps. (Turner 1887, 219–224)

These descriptions of sod houses, snow houses, and skin tents, which were made and used by Inuit until relatively recently, highlight the resourcefulness and innovative design skills of the Inuit. Their architecture was a product of their place, a product of accumulated knowledge and understandings of micro-climate and weather systems, and it took into consideration the materials available to them and the spatial configuration necessary to maintain good family cohesion.

Toward an Architecture of Identity

Insofar as Inuit villages lack architectural variety today and are largely indistinguishable on this basis, the cultural practices of each Inuit community go some way toward setting villages apart from one another. The identity of some communities is a product of forms of artwork and creative practices, hunting techniques, strength of Inuktitut language use, and/or adherence to traditional practices and knowledge.

A recognition of architecture's potential as a vehicle for contemplating changing Inuit identities has not yet occurred in Nunavik, on either a small or large scale. Aesthetically, the contemporary architecture in the region is rather bland, and it is questionable whether it truly contributes to the celebration and enrichment of Inuit culture. Yet Indigenous nations across the world—even in urban settings—are aspiring to generate built environments that reflect their cultural contexts, heritage, values, and aspirations (Grant et al. 2018; Krinsky 1996; Malnar and Vodvarka 2013; Memmott 2007; Stuart and Thompson-Fawcett 2010; Walker, Jojola, and Natcher 2013). Why, then, does the design manual created by the Gouvernement du Québec (2017), *Housing Construction in Nunavik: Guide to Good Practice*, omit mention of Inuit culture? Why should the first principles in any design-orientated manual for Nunavik centre on engineering standards rather than the human condition? Despite good design intentions, must everything in the North be built so austerely and speak so little about the Inuit people themselves? Indeed, de Botton (2006) suggests in the *Architecture of Happiness* that architecture should also respond to individual and collective memories and identities:

FIGURE 8.7 A group of Inuit beside a skin tent, Fort Chimo, Nunavik, 1896. Photographer: Albert Peter Low. Library and Archives Canada, Geological Survey of Canada Collection, C-005591 (item no. 4194005, MIKAN no. 3624421).

> We depend on our surroundings obliquely to embody the moods and ideas we respect and then to remind us of them. We look to our buildings to hold us, like a kind of psychological mould, to a helpful vision of ourselves. We arrange around us material forms which communicate to us what we need—but are at constant risk of forgetting we need—within. (de Botton 2006, 107)

Collignon (2005) argues that architecture should be responsive to and reflective of culture in Arctic contexts. Writing on the effects of building multi-roomed homes in favour of single-roomed dwellings, she observed that

> dwellers are confronted with a subdivided space that separates individuals. The proximity (visual, auditory, and physical) that was crucial in the shaping of both collective and individual identity has been lost. Interior walls are not only functional dividers, but structures imbued with Western morals of spatial division and specialization. These walls provide a spatial break inside the multigenerational dwelling unit, creating a space in which traditional nonverbal modes of communication are no longer effective. (Collignon 2005, 878)

The absence of architectural variety in Nunavik today and the design configuration of interior spaces are products of colonial and paternalistic practices. As Inuit elder Taamusi Qumaq recalled on the construction of the first buildings in his village of Puvirnituq, Nunavik, in 1958, "We Inuit had no say whosoever in how development was to proceed. We did not know. It was as if we were just 'watching' what was being done in our community" (Qumaq 1996, 67).

Indeed, there is an historical and land-tenure legacy behind village designs and built forms. As noted earlier, prior to the formation of centralized villages in the 1950s and 1960s, most Inuit lived in small hunting bands, usually frequenting hunting and fishing grounds close to rivers and coastlines. Inuit families maintained their identity, and distinguished themselves from one another, based on ancestral connections to certain regions and places. The way of describing one's affiliation with place also extends to the village level. Throughout the Arctic, people identify themselves by adding the suffix *-miut* to the name of the place that they are from or to which they belong. Thus, residents of Kuujjuaq (Big River, from *kuuk*, "flow" or "river," and *-juaq*, "big") would call themselves *Kuujjuamiut*. This naming convention cements Inuit to place and characterizes one's sense of belonging to community, family, and heritage. This form of identifying with place is an old practice. Lucien Turner paid special interest to Inuit forms of attachment to place when recording the customs and language of the Inuit of northern Québec and Labrador in the 1880s (Turner 1884). On naming conventions, he remarked,

> Locality has an important bearing on the character of an Innuit and unless those influences are carefully studied many important facts may not be clearly understood. The region of one's birth clings to him and designates him, wherever he may journey, as one from that place. That place may be excessively restricted, even a neck of land extending into the sea, yet the local designation of that point is sufficient to stamp each Innuit as one from that locality. While there are as many names for natural objects as there are objects, they may be included as a part of tract and he who is born on any part of that tract belongs by birthright to that tract or territory. (Turner 1887, 44)

FIGURE 8.8 The Hudson's Bay Company's Fort Chimo trading post, 1919. The first permanent villages established in the Arctic regions of northern Québec were designed to support and serve the employees of the fur trade. The colonial-style buildings that characterized Hudson's Bay Company trading posts were the first non-Inuit architectural forms introduced into Arctic settings. Some Inuit families moved to Fort Chimo on a semi-permanent basis as early as the late 1800s, usually living on the outskirts of the village in skin tents. Many modern-day villages in Nunavik grew up around these established posts. Used with permission of McCord Museum, Montréal (MP-1984.128.43). Photographer is unknown.

Inuit lived in skin or sod houses in summer and snow houses in winter. They would meet neighbouring bands only occasionally and usually for cultural, ceremonial, or trading purposes. The notion of congregating in one place for extended periods, as villages promote today, was a relatively foreign concept to Inuit. Indeed, some Inuit families had modified their traditional travel patterns to include spending more time at fur trading posts (figure 8.8) and mission sites when these were established from the 1800s; but, by and large, Inuit families lived away from other Inuit families for most of the year. It was not until the 1950s that the Canadian government (through what was then the Department of Indian and Northern Affairs) met with local Inuit bands to discuss the prospect of forming centralized communities (villages) along coastal fringes, predicated on the assumption that this would allow the government to provide better health and educational services and support for the sick and elderly.[1]

Centralized communities were generally established by mutual agreement. In some cases, this was highly desirable for Inuit, as the land was periodically starved of large game such as caribou. Villages provided a sense of food security during hard times, and support to those suffering from tuberculous, which impacted many Inuit during this era. Some of these villages were formed near existing Hudson's Bay Company trading posts, where some basic infrastructure had already been established and where Inuit were already used to congregating with other Inuit families, although not always permanently, in the newly formed villages.

Inuit bands moved away from their family-based hunting grounds gradually, taking up residence in villages as schools, churches, health clinics, and stores became operational, and once housing materials became available. These early forms of housing, now mostly removed, were often built by Inuit themselves out of materials supplied from the South, as well as from local materials where available. These forms of built heritage were progressively replaced during the 1980s and 1990s with standardized forms of houses that were designed and prefabricated in the South (Robson 1995). It is these extant buildings, created without the design or cultural input of Inuit, that form the basis of the comments and criticisms that follow.

Home Ownership and Dynamics

As of 2016, Nunavik was home to 10,880 people, 10,775 of whom (98 percent) are Inuit (Statistics Canada 2016). The urgent appeal to construct more houses centres on a serious shortage of available homes for Inuit residents, an object of daily conversation among Inuit families, who are frustrated by the lack of building progress in line with surging village populations.[2] While the need for shelter is perceived as a top priority, the desire to construct culturally appropriate forms of housing is neither the only nor the most frequently cited issue. This is understandable, for Inuit themselves have indicated in community forums that the lack of housing is contributing to poor family cohesion and a rise in serious mental and physical health issues (Kativik Regional Government and Makivik Corporation 2012, 357–366).[3] The housing crisis shows no signs of being rectified in the immediate future, even with hundreds of homes slated for construction across Nunavik in the coming construction seasons. According to Statistics Canada (2016), 49 percent of Nunavik Inuit live in crowded homes (defined as more than one person per room; the comparable figure for the non-Indigenous population was 7 percent), which amounts to a shortfall of approximately 1,200 homes (Kativik Regional Government and Makivik Corporation 2012, 370; Makivik Corporation et al. 2014, 102).

The housing crisis is compounded in Nunavik by a number of factors. Most Inuit do not have the means to become homeowners, so the vast majority rent from one of the 2,734 dwellings that are managed by the Kativik Regional Government (KRG), an Inuit authority that manages affairs such as health and education under the auspices of the Québec government (Gouvernement du Québec 2014, 17).[4] Private ownership of housing in Nunavik is almost non-existent (only 130 homes are privately owned by Inuit [Makivik Corporation et al. 2014, 103]) and, even then, many of these homeowners struggle to keep up with mortgage payments. Under rental arrangements, dwellings are leased to Inuit families and maintained by the KRG. The conditions of lease, however, generally restrict any modifications to dwellings. This has meant that since 1999, when the KRG first began management of the dwelling stocks, 99 percent of the Inuit population have effectively been unable to repurpose their homes to suit their respective family and cultural requirements. This means that almost all Nunavik Inuit have lived in similar types of homes for nearly two decades, and that the cultural issues they have confronted by living in these spaces is known to and shared by the entire population. The need to modify, extend, and rectify their homes to overcome the housing situation and the lack of cultural consideration afforded in the housing configuration is apparent to all. Many of the social issues in Arctic communities may well be a reaction to the living situations that have been imposed upon Inuit residents (Dawson 2008). As lessees, they do not have the authority or freedom to mould their physical surroundings to suit their cultural context. Rapoport (1969) argues that a house should be seen as a social unit of space, and the current housing

FIGURE 8.9 Inuit schoolteacher and carver Daniel Annanack making an artwork from caribou antler in his hunting shack. A portable heater warms this space during winter. Other than by the electrical extension cord, the shack is not connected to the main house. Photograph by Scott A. Heyes, 2007.

tenure arrangements in the Arctic do not serve this function. As he points out,

> Once the identity and character of a culture has been grasped, and some insight gained into its values, its choices among possible dwelling responses to both physical and cultural variables become much clearer. The specific characteristics of a culture—the accepted way of doing things, the socially unacceptable ways and the implicit ideals—need to be considered since they will affect housing and settlement form; this includes the subtleties as well as the more obvious or utilitarian features. It is often what a culture makes impossible by prohibiting it either explicitly or implicitly, rather than what it makes inevitable, which is significant. (Rapoport 1969, 47)

The personalization of Inuit homes has been restricted to the use of decor; the exterior forms and internal divisions of space are not able to be modified. For too long, Inuit have had to endure living in prefabricated dwellings and tight leasehold arrangements that are not congruent with their cultural beliefs and practices. Instead, they have had to revert to outdoor spaces and outbuildings to express many of their cultural habits. Hunting shacks (figure 8.9) at the rear of homes are places where Inuit land-based identity has an opportunity to flourish. These small buildings, often made from repurposed shipping containers and surplus building supplies left behind at the end of each building season by fly-in construction companies, are places full of life. It is in these spaces that Inuit clean fish, animals, and birds. It is where sculpture-making occurs, and where mechanical repairs on boats, sleds, and snowmobiles are carried out. It is within and around these peripheral spaces of the main dwelling where children watch their parents and elders go about their traditional practices.

These small shelters support important forms of knowledge transmission. They are quiet places for contemplation and discussion, for learning and becoming part of the Inuit community. With so many family members coming and going, the principal dwelling is often just too noisy and too distracting for many forms of traditional knowledge to be passed on.

The irony of the current housing situation is that, less than sixty years ago, Inuit lived freely on the land wherever they chose, making camp near productive hunting and fishing sites. The land is still free to pursue, of course. Outside village life, the land and its animals remain a communal resource to Inuit. Even today, a tree can be felled without permission, and a fish net set beside any river or lake. A trail can be blazed through any terrain, and a hunting cabin (providing it is situated outside municipal boundaries) can be erected on any site without planning approval or the need to follow municipal building regulations.

Toward an Architecture of Resistance

A groundswell of critical concern with normative housing solutions, including that associated with design and architecture, is occurring in settler nations across the world. This is being led by Indigenous groups and their allies. In Australia, Canada, Fiji, New Zealand, and the United States, the voice of Indigenous designers has started to be heard, leading to important changes in architectural and planning practices. For the first time, Indigenous world views and design practices are now being taught at design schools in these countries. Furthermore, many non-Indigenous designers have taken heed of the importance of recognizing that Indigenous people have maintained design practices for generations, and that Indigenous ways of configuring the environment are constantly evolving in tune with shifting identities and belief systems. The transition to teaching and internalizing Indigenous design values and beliefs takes time, however, and changing deeply entrenched design paradigms does not come without challenges.

Ryan Walker, Ted Jojola, and David Natcher (2013, 5) discuss this issue with respect to Indigenous planning, noting that for this practice to be truly reclaimed, a strong level of resistance must be mounted against current design paradigms, in tandem with a commitment to political change. As they argue, "Indigenous planning isn't just an armchair theoretical approach or a set of methods and practices, but a political strategy aimed at improving the lives and environments of Indigenous peoples. To do Indigenous planning requires a commitment to political, social, economic, and environmental change." They go on to point out that

> the central tenets of Indigenous planning are essentially community/kinship- and place-based. It is a form of planning whose roots and traditions are grounded in specific Indigenous peoples' experiences linked to specific places, lands, and resources. . . . To do Indigenous planning requires that it be done in/at the place *with* the people of that place. (Walker, Jojola, and Natcher 2013, 5)

In the Nunavik context, the plea for government agencies to engage directly with Inuit as equal partners in the design and layout of villages and urban forms (among other things) rings loudly and clearly. As mentioned earlier, the Parnasimautik consultation process undertaken by the Nunivak Inuit in 2013 focused on concerns surrounding Inuit autonomy in areas such as culture, identity, food, housing, health, justice, education, and employment.[5] A sense of urgency in reclaiming agency around various facets of Inuit life is apparent

in a quotation from one Inuit participant in the consultation process: “We are a unique people. We have to preserve our culture and identity. We have to improve our way of life not just by getting more things from the south, but by doing things on our own” (Makivik Corporation et al. 2014, 21). These words suggest that Nunavik Inuit will push back more and more against any structures and systems that have been designed and developed without reference to their culture.

In an Inuit homeland (Nunavik) that will always remain as such because of land-right treaty arrangements signed in the 1970s that guarantee the preservation of their land and use of resources, it is logical that Inuit would want to determine and manage their own living environment and affairs themselves. Inuit are increasingly taking control of their own affairs, and housing and village design are a natural part of this dynamic. The housing situation in Nunavik is still very much attached to the powers and control of southern Canadian government agencies, a system that is now recognized as increasingly untenable.

The rapidly expanding construction of family hunting cabins on the outskirts of Nunavik villages (figure 8.10), particularly in those villages nearer to the treeline, where building materials can be readily sourced (such as Kuujjuarapik, Tasiujaq, Kuujjuaq, and Kangiqsualujjuaq), is an effective form of architectural resistance toward community design and the housing situation in Nunavik. While, on the surface, it might appear that these cabins are situated at random, their placement on the landscape is quite deliberate, with consideration given to maximizing views and access to trails and to community infrastructure nearby. Most importantly, these

FIGURE 8.10 A cabin on the outskirts of Kangiqsualujjuaq made from local timbers and heated by a wood-burning stove. Photograph by Scott A. Heyes, 2008.

dwellings are designed and built by Inuit to suit their own purposes and circumstances. Clusters of these cabins are now part of the fabric of village life, replete with their own built character and form.

Family units, once separated in villages because the housing situation forced them to rent wherever a house was available, are now returning to build cabins close to each other. Inuit talk about the sense of peace and pride they derive from living in these cabins, and of how living outside of villages allows them to escape some of the social challenges and noise associated with village life. They are enjoying porches as part of their living quarters for the first time, as well as the luxury of living in spaces with high ceilings. Cabin living approximates to some extent what being on the land means to Inuit. This Inuit-based, home-grown design of cabins, and their deliberate siting in the landscape by Inuit, suggests that the houses and housing layouts in Nunavik from which Inuit have escaped do not fully or even adequately meet their cultural needs and desires. Locked into rental situations, they are unable to express themselves and their identity through built form. Cabin construction provides some relief, a way of returning to the land without actually being on it. The cabins are stamps of contemporary Inuit identity, providing Inuit the freedom to be Inuit.

The cabins (one- and two-storey buildings) we have visited are innovative, original, and ingeniously designed. They make use of locally sourced materials in resourceful and sustainable ways, and they highlight the enormous range of skills that Inuit have developed in engineering and constructing robust structures in a formidable climate. They are generally self-powered and self-heated, making use of solar aspect to draw as much light as possible into the cabin spaces. Below the treeline, the cabin builders have explained to us that they are deliberately situating their buildings within the woods, where it is possible to seek shelter from the wind (thereby saving electricity and heating) and as a way to be connected to mammals and birds. The builders have remarked on the prospect of hunting a ptarmigan from their window or observing an inquisitive black bear or rabbit. The point here is that cabin life is about being close to the land, somewhat the opposite of village living.

The cabins stand as reminders that Inuit villages would likely look very different than they do now, should there be an opportunity for them to have more autonomy in the planning and design of the built environment in the future. And while not everyone in villages agrees with the sprawl of cabins on the outskirts of town, it is important that future village planning take into consideration the meaning and intent of these cabins. They are marks of resistance and an affirmation of Inuit values such as living close to nature and supporting family units. They are a product of Inuit design values and innovation. They are constructed by and for Inuit in places where *they* want to build them. They are loved and make for healthy living spaces.[6] In many respects, they are also expressions of Inuit forms of art. In *Art as Experience*, Dewey (1934, 230) writes that "buildings, among all art objects, come the nearest to expressing the stability and endurance of existence. They are to mountains what music is to the sea. Because of its inherent power to endure, architecture records and celebrates more than any other art the generic features of our common human life." These statements would hardly describe the rental homes that most Inuit inhabit within existing Northern villages.

Envisioning New Built Environments in Nunavik

In supporting Inuit visions to generate new urban forms and dwellings that are based on their cultural practices and values, it is important to recognize, review, and understand the heritage value of residential building forms that have been built since Northern villages were developed. This means exploring ways to preserve buildings that were not necessarily culturally or climatically appropriate for Nunavik (figure 8.11). These buildings would stand as reference points on a pathway toward a renewal of Indigenous autonomy in design and planning that might represent the dynamic social, economic, political, and environmental changes that have occurred in the Arctic within the past sixty years. Remember that early villages changed from tents to clusters of buildings and then to urban sprawl in only a very few years.

Currently, there is virtually no form of management of the built form in Nunavik that pays specific attention to the issue of cultural heritage, although the *Plan Nunavik* document prepared by Inuit in 2012 did highlight the urgent need for a heritage program. The document proposed that historical buildings, including churches, be preserved for future generations, and that processes be developed to identify, document, present, and interpret Nunavik's natural, man-made, and cultural landscapes (Makivik Corporation et al. 2014, 23). The preservation of some buildings that mark different ways of thinking, being, and knowing in the Arctic context might serve to support the argument for constructing new Arctic villages and homes that are oriented toward Inuit cultural traditions and ways of being in the landscape.

So what might new forms of Inuit villages and dwellings look like in generations to come as Inuit resistance to southern planning and design systems increases? Taking into account the arguments presented earlier in this chapter with regard to buildings serving as forms that embody cultural identity and cultural values, we suggest that new dwellings and their collective patterns be based on the principles of participative, flexible, and sustainable planning and design. While these three principles are not exhaustive, they are, we believe, essential to achieving Inuit identity reflected in the built form of Northern communities and their dwellings throughout Nunavik.

PARTICIPATIVE PLANNING AND DESIGN

There is an urgent need for those most affected by their dwelling environments to be involved in their planning and design. There is ample evidence that, throughout Nunavik, the village environment will remain the locus of most social, economic, and political activity in the North when Inuit are not on the land, an activity that, while still cherished, occupies far less time than it has in the past. The form of the village and the form of the house is thus the principal container for community life, and as such must respond to the challenges discussed above.

A participative planning and design approach is likely to result in achieving an environment where Inuit feel more at home, forging identities and love and pride of place that arise from, and are connected to, the built form. A new built environment, envisaged by Inuit for Inuit, will ultimately form new ways of belonging to place. Ideally, the village form should be a product of the needs and desires of the people and would be based on design processes that are meaningful to Inuit. Adherence to such processes may lead to a transformation in the way that villages are conceived—resulting in villages built upon radically different processes than those used by designers and planners from the South. This should be embraced rather than resisted, even if it means that village forms are nested more within the landscape than being set out in formal arrangements. Rather than being regarded as separate to the broader landscape, villages may once again be regarded as part of the landscape, part of nature. The implementation of participatory planning and design practices is an important step toward decolonizing design practice, and the recognition that Inuit have a right to determine their own living conditions. The design process is just as important as other aspects of Inuit life that are now largely determined by Inuit, such as hunting and fishing quotas, which are now based on cultural needs.

FIGURE 8.11 "Nunavut, 1960." Most of the early forms of built heritage in the Arctic (some experimental) have been removed or repurposed to make way for more contemporary designs. Pictured here are three types of housing: a Styrofoam igloo, a prefabricated wooden house, and a canvas tent. Photograph by Rosemary Gilliat Eaton. Library and Archives Canada, Rosemary Gilliat Eaton fonds, Arctic travel series, e010835896 (item no. 4424960).

FLEXIBLE SPACE AND FLEXIBLE FUNCTIONS

The discrete allocation of specific functions to specific rooms is not necessarily consistent with the typical extended family in the North, nor does it correspond to the changing dynamic of shelters that frequently house three generations of a family and its extended household members at different times of the year and in different years altogether. It is not unusual to find children, parents, and grandparents talking, sleeping, watching television, and eating in the same space, frequently at the same time. This overlapping of functions can be explained, but only in part, through a lack of available housing units throughout the North; but more importantly, it reflects people coming and going at all times of the day and night, visiting with each other for a variety of reasons, in a social dynamic that forms and re-forms on an ongoing basis. Clearly, structural provision for flexible spaces is required to accommodate this social dynamic and these spaces must be conceived at the core of the dwelling, as much as it must be found in numerous sites throughout the village. As it stands, Inuit occupants can choose to use rooms as they please, but due to lease agreements, internal divisions and panels within the home cannot be modified or removed to suit inhabitants' cultural needs and family requirements.

Learning about cabin designs from local Inuit, it seems that making and building a cabin and deciding on its interior floor plan are akin to producing works of art where decisions are made iteratively. The arrangements and division of interior space, with cabins at least, seem to be determined as the building form comes together, rather than determined in advance. Families have their own needs and different living arrangements, and Inuit have indicated to us that the decision about interior forms needs to respect the specific requirements of each family.

SUSTAINABLE BUILT FORM STRATEGIES

The allocation of suitable land for housing and municipal buildings, as well as the infrastructure to support them, is constrained throughout Nunavik by relatively poor soil depth, steep slopes, and rocky terrain. Prime land close to the shores of rivers and bays is in relatively short supply, as are large stretches of flat land. In one community, Salluit, substantial pads of gravel were required to provide level housing sites on relatively steep slopes as no other sites were available in close proximity to the village. Water and waste are supplied and evacuated by truck, and most electrical energy is provided by diesel fuel. Building materials are shipped in from the South, and the unused or discarded waste from construction is frequently consigned to already overflowing waste sites. Much remains to be done in the realm of the collective built form if a reasonable degree of sustainability is to be achieved.

With the Nunavik Inuit population swiftly growing, and with this population trend expected to continue in the region, it is apparent that sustainable design approaches are in urgent need of implementation. Dealing with sustainability will require engaging with Inuit identity and place-based associations, and questioning the physical footprint currently occupied by constructed villages.

Conclusions

Achieving equitable and sustainable built forms responsive to the needs and values of Inuit throughout Nunavik is a challenge that can no longer be avoided. The strategies that are required must include the active participation, financial commitment, and cultural input of the Inuit population. Existing models of housing and other components of Northern villages lack the flexibility and creativity required to properly reflect the lifestyles and environment of the North, as do the sources of energy, materials, and the infrastructure required to provide water and remove waste. All require new and creative management strategies. The adoption of new design and planning processes—to initiate new Inuit ways of living and connections to place—effectively require the removal of decades of non-Inuit design thinking and practice. Indeed, design can shape, celebrate, and connect Inuit with their land more than ever before.

The cabin belts that may soon encircle the wooded Inuit villages of Nunavik are an arresting indication of new architectural developments. Inuit decide how they want to live, while, incidentally, paying no municipal or land tax. These cabins are marks on the landscape that highlight the lengths that Inuit will go to achieving a housing environment that reflects their values and identity.

With the shackles of current design practices removed, and imagining new building forms in Nunavik, it is likely that new forms of Inuit identity will emerge that are just as much associated with village life as with the land. Nunavik is on the cusp of a new planning and architectural regime, and all should lend their hand in support as Inuit forge ahead to create built environments that future generations will see as a natural extension of the land.

Acknowledgements

We thank our Inuit colleagues and friends for passing on their knowledge of the land to us and for welcoming us into their homes. Thank you to Rhonda Nichols for her research assistance on this project and to Christine Heyes LaBond for her comments. Thank you also to the anonymous reviewers for providing constructive feedback and comments in the preparation of this chapter.

Notes

1. The *Housing Construction in Nunavik* report (Gouvernement du Québec 2017, 11) states that the first housing trial in Nunavik occurred in the village of Puvirnituq, which resulted in seven private homes being constructed. It was soon realized that future homes would need to be larger and that better insulation materials were required. Inuit elder Taamusi Qumaq, reflecting on his time in Purvirnituq in an interview for *Tumivut* magazine (1996, 67), recalls that ten houses were first erected in Puvirnituq and that the families built them themselves. He noted that families insulated the sheet-metal-clad buildings with sod and grass to make them more liveable.
2. For a complete discussion of the ramifications of the housing crisis in Nunavik, see Makivik Corporation et al. (2014) and Gouvernement du Québec (2017).
3. The health issues related to overcrowding in the neighbouring region of Nunavut are discussed in Lauster and Tester (2010).
4. A few hundred additional units exist in Nunavik and are owned by various government and regional departments and agencies to house their employees; and there are slightly less than a hundred owner-occupied homes (Gouvernement du Québec 2014, 17).
5. The results of the consultation process were presented in a report the following year: see Makivik Corporation et al. (2014). The Parnasimautik consulations built on Plan Nunavik, an earlier policy statement outlining the Inuit vision for the future development of the region, with an emphasis on both cultural and environmental sustainability (Kativik Regional Government and Makivik Corporation 2012). Plan Nunavik was the Inuit response to Plan Nord, the Québec government's own vision of the Nunavik future.
6. We do not wish to suggest here that rental homes are not cherished by Inuit families. We recognize that families have been raised in these settings and memories have been built. Rather, we suggest that buildings designed and built by Inuit themselves are likely to afford a different type of connection to the built form. For a detailed study of the impact of Inuit housing on health, see Young and Mullins (1996).

References

Collignon, Béatrice

2005 Housing. In *Encyclopaedia of the Arctic*, vol. 2, edited by Mark Nuttall, pp. 877–878. Routledge, New York.

2006 *Knowing Places: The Inuinnait, Landscapes, and the Environment.* Canadian Circumpolar Institute. Edmonton.

Dawson, Peter

2008 Unfriendly Architecture: Using Observations of Inuit Spatial Behavior to Design Culturally Sustaining Houses in Arctic Canada. *Housing Studies* 23(1): 111–128.

de Botton, Alain

2006 *The Architecture of Happiness.* Penguin Books, London.

Dewey, John

1934 *Art as Experience.* Capricorn Books, New York.

Dorais, Louis-Jacques

1997 *Quaqtaq: Modernity and Identity in an Inuit Community.* University of Toronto Press, Toronto.

Goehring, Brian

1990 Inuit Place-Names and Man-Land Relationships, Pelly Bay, Northwest Territories. Master's thesis, Department of Geography, University of British Columbia, Vancouver.

Gouvernement du Québec

2014 *Housing in Nunavik: Information Document.* Société d'habitation du Québec, Québec City. http://www.habitation.gouv.qc.ca/fileadmin/internet/documents/English/logement__nunavik_2014.pdf.

2017 *Housing Construction in Nunavik: Guide to Good Practice.* Société d'habitation du Québec, Québec City. http://www.habitation.gouv.qc.ca/fileadmin/internet/documents/English/HousingConstructionInNunavik.pdf.

Grant, Elizabeth, Kelly Greenop, Albert L. Refiti, and Daniel J. Glenn (editors)

2018 *The Handbook of Contemporary Indigenous Architecture.* Springer, Singapore.

Hantzsch, Bernard

1932 Contributions to the Knowledge of Extreme North-Eastern Labrador. Translated by M. B. A. Anderson. *Canadian Field-Naturalist* 46: 56–64. Originally published in German, 1909.

Heyes, Scott A.

2007 Inuit Knowledge and Perceptions of the Land-Water Interface. PhD dissertation, Department of Geography, McGill University, Montréal.

Heyes, Scott A., and Peter Jacobs

2008 Losing Place: Diminishing Traditional Knowledge of the Arctic Coastal Landscape. In *Making Sense of Place: Exploring Concepts and Expressions of Place Through Different Lenses and Senses*, edited by Frank Vanclay, Matthew Higgins, and Adam Blackshaw, pp. 135–154. National Museum of Australia, Canberra.

Jacobs, Peter

1986 Sustaining Landscapes: Sustaining Societies. *Landscape and Urban Planning* 13: 349–358.

2001 The Landscape of Nunavik/The Territory of Nouveau-Québec. In *Aboriginal Autonomy and Development in Northern Quebec and Labrador*, edited by Colin Scott, pp. 63–77. University of British Columbia Press, Vancouver.

Kativik Environmental Quality Commission (KEQC)

2009 *Nunavik: A Homeland in Transition*. Kativik Environmental Quality Commission, Kuujjuaq, Québec.

Kativik Regional Government

2005 *Kuururjuaq Park Project: Status Report, September 2005*. Kativik Regional Government, Renewable Resources, Environmental and Land Use Planning Department, Parks Section. Kuujjuaq, Québec.

Kativik Regional Government and Makivik Corporation

2012 *Plan Nunavik: Past, Present, and Future*. Avataq Cultural Institute, Montréal.

Krinsky, Carol H.

1996 *Contemporary Native American Architecture: Cultural Regeneration and Creativity*. Oxford University Press, New York.

Lauster, Nathanael, and Frank Tester

2010 Culture as a Problem in Linking Material Inequality to Health: On Residential Crowding in the Arctic. *Health and Place* 16(3): 523–530.

Mactavish, Tracey

2004 Northern Detail. *On Site Review 11: Architecture in the Circumpolar Regions*, 40–41.

Makivik Corporation, Kativik Regional Government, Nunavik Regional Board of Health and Social Services, Kativik School Board, Nunavik Landholding Corporations Association, Avataq Cultural Institute, and Saputiit Youth Association

2014 *Parnasimautik Consultation Report*. Makivik Corporation, Montréal.

Malnar, Joy M., and Vodvarka, Frank

2013 *New Architecture on Indigenous Lands*. University of Minnesota Press, Minneapolis.

Maxwell, Moreau. S

1985 *Prehistory of the Eastern Arctic*. Academic Press, New York.

McLean, John

1849 *Notes of a Twenty-Five Years' Service in the Hudson's Bay Territory: Volume I*. Richard Bentley, London.

Memmott, Paul

2007 *Gunyah, Goondie & Wurley: The Aboriginal Architecture of Australia*. University of Queensland Press, Brisbane.

Müller-Wille, Ludger

1987 *Inuttitut Nunait Atingitta Katirsutauningit Nunavimmi (Kupaimmi, Kanatami): Gazetteer of Inuit Place Names in Nunavik (Quebec, Canada)*. Avataq Cultural Institute, Inukjuak, Québec.

Nuttall, Mark

1992 *Arctic Homeland: Kinship, Community and Development in Northwest Greenland*. University of Toronto Press, Toronto.

Pinard, Claude

1993 Thule Winter Houses. *Tumivut* 4: 62–64.

Qumaq, Taamusi

1996 The Autobiography of Taamusi Qumaq. *Tumivut* 8: 62–79.

Rapoport, Amos

1969 *House Form and Culture*. Prentice-Hall, Englewood Cliffs, New Jersey.

Robson, Robert

1995 Housing in the Northwest Territories: The Post-War Vision. *Urban History Review* 24(1): 3–20.

Schneider, Lucien

1985 *Ulirnaisigutiit: An Inuktitut-English Dictionary of Northern Quebec, Labrador and Eastern Arctic Dialects*. Translated by Dermot Ronan F. Collis. Les Presses de l'Université Laval, Québec City.

Statistics Canada

2016 *Inuit: Fact Sheet for Nunavik*. 29 March. http://www.statcan.gc.ca/pub/89-656-x/89-656-x2016016-eng.htm.

Stuart, Keriata, and Michelle Thompson-Fawcett (editors)

2010 *Tāone Tupu Ora: Indigenous Knowledge and Sustainable Urban Design*. New Zealand Centre for Sustainable Cities, University of Otago, Wellington.

Tassé, Gilles

2000 *L'archéologie au Québec: mots, techniques, objets*. Fides, Quebec.

Turner, Lucien M.

1884 Language of the "Koksoagmyut" Eskimo at Ft. Chimo, Ungava, Labrador Peninsula (1882–1884). 3 vols., Unpublished manuscript, BAE MS 2505-a. Records of the Bureau of American Ethnology, National Anthropological Archives, Smithsonian Institution, Washington, DC.

1887 Descriptive Catalogue of Ethnological Collections Made by Lucien M. Turner in Ungava and Labrador, Hudson Bay Territory, June 24, 1882 to October 1884, Part 1 on Innuit. Unpublished manuscript, Record Unit 7192, box 1 of 2 (3 folders), Lucien M. Turner Papers, circa 1882–1884, Smithsonian Institution Archives, Washington, DC.

1894 *Ethnology of the Ungava District, Hudson Bay Territory*. Smithsonian Institution Press, Washington, DC.

Walker, Ryan, Ted Jojola, and David Natcher (editors)

2013 *Reclaiming Indigenous Planning*. McGill-Queen's University Press, Montréal.

Young, T. Kue, and C. Joan Mullins

1996 The Impact of Housing on Health: An Ecologic Study from the Canadian Arctic. *Arctic Medical Research* 55(2): 52–61.

Zrudlo, Leo

2001 A Search for Cultural and Contextual Identity in Contemporary Arctic Architecture. *Polar Record* 37(200): 55–66.

PART THREE

KNOWING THE LAND

EVON PETER

PERSPECTIVE

Our identity, our sense of belonging, our understanding of being human, are all connected to our relationship with the land. And our relationship with these lands span millennia. Our grandfathers and grandmothers who came before us walked these same ridges, valleys, and trails. They fished the same lakes, streams, and rivers. They cherished memories carried in the pungent smell of the fall tundra, in wafts of spruce, cottonwood, and willow smoke. They ventured throughout these lands until their final rest. Our ancestors are literally part of this land. We are part of this land.

FACING *Nitsii Ddhah*, a major landmark located upriver from *Vashrąįį K'ǫǫ* (Arctic Village), in northeastern Alaska. Photograph by Evon Peter, 2016.

Evon Peter as a child during an ice-fishing trip for *shriijyaa* (grayling) upriver from *Vashrąįį K'ǫǫ*, ca. 1987. Photographer unknown. Courtesy of Evon Peter.

As a child, I had the opportunity to spend time living with my grandfather Steven Tsee Gho' Tsyatsal Peter Sr. in our village of *Vashrąįį K'ǫǫ* (Arctic Village in English) in the southern foothills of *Gwazhal* (the Brooks Range). My earliest memories are almost entirely of the outdoors: we spent little time inside, and the land was our playground. We would roam the shores of *Vashrąįį K'ǫǫ*, the creek our village was named after, up to *Vashrąįį Van*, the lake that feeds into the creek. Elders set fishnets in *Vashrąįį K'ǫǫ* to catch *łuk daagąįį* (whitefish), and us kids would use spears in the narrow channels to catch *iltin* (northern pike).

In the fall time, most families would move up onto *Dachan Lee* (Tree Line) campsites to hunt for *vadzaih* (caribou) and make dry meat for the long winter. The smells of wood fire, freshly fried meat, and campfire tea permeate memories of those days. Sometimes we would run down the mountain to the glacier creek to fish for *shriijaa* (grayling). On the land, we were free. On the land, we were nurtured.

When my grandfather was nearing his last days, he asked to return to his birthplace, over the mountain from *Vashrąįį K'ǫǫ*, to the shore of *Van K'ehdee*. He is there now. A long wood pole with a carved fish up top marks his final

resting place. When I can, I make the day-long trek over the mountain to visit him there in the summer. He was among the last of his generation, raised among families who followed a nomadic life, moving with the seasons, across our lands.

He spoke about the importance of our Gwich'in language. How the *Vaanoodlit* (white man) had enforced educational policies that were stripping the language from our young people. To him it was absurd, and he was sad to see it happening. When he was growing up on the land, our language was the only one he knew. He remembered seeing the first *Vaanoodlit* in our country and reflected on how much has changed since that time.

In our generation, we are tasked with the responsibility to revitalize the use of our language and ensure the knowledge it holds continued to be transferred down the generations. Our language is descriptive, full of poetry, humour, and meaning. The small drops of water that rest on a leaf following a rainfall are sometimes called *dil chųų gahtsii* ("water made for the lesser yellowlegs"). My grandfather's resting place is on the shore of *Van K'ehdee* ("lake on top of a lake"), named for shallow water surrounded by a deep crater filled with water.

Through our language we more fully understand the perspectives, world view, and knowledge our people had of the land and our environment. We can situate ourselves

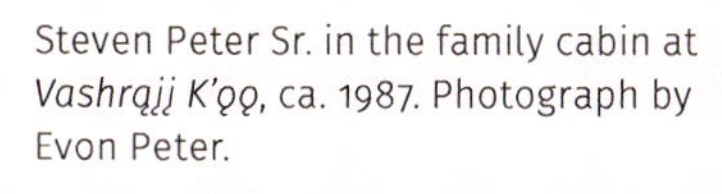

Steven Peter Sr. in the family cabin at *Vashrąįį K'ǫǫ*, ca. 1987. Photograph by Evon Peter.

geographically in places on the land, understand the hydrological connections among lakes, streams, and rivers, and reference geological attributes of hills, ridges, and mountains for navigation. Our ancestors were philosophers, historians, geologists, hydrologists, biologists, healers, and intellectuals. They crafted systematic methods for naming places and integrated them into stories to perpetuate the knowledge. We are the beneficiaries of this knowledge, and it is incumbent upon us to value it for what it is: thousands of years of lived experience compounded into stories, songs, history, names, and ceremonies—our world view.

We have only scratched the surface in recognizing the value that Indigenous knowledge, values, and perspectives have to offer more broadly, to the social and physical sciences, as well as to political and international relations. We are pressed for time to document and expand the understanding of our languages while the remaining first-language speakers are still with us. Expanding this knowledge will require commitment from learners and investment by institutions.

Still, the late Chief David Salmon of *Jałgiitsik* (Chalkyitsik) once shared with me that the land is also our teacher, as it was for our ancestors. As the drive to revitalize the Gwich'in language and cultural practices grows among the people, we understand that it is to the land that we must return for many important lessons. This is natural, as we are part of the land.

FIGURE 9.1 West view of a peak on *Iñgisugruich* (Jade Mountain), in northwest Alaska, August 1987. Not only was *Iñgisugruich* an important source of jade, but among the Iñupiat of the Kobuk River area, the mountain was also strongly associated with spiritual forces. Sanctions surrounding *Iñgisugruich* meant that only shamans could safely visit, and then only after lengthy ceremonies of purification. Photograph by Eric Loring. Bureau of Indian Affairs, ANCSA 14(h)(1) Collection, case file F-22292, Anchorage.

GARY HOLTON

9 Place-Naming Strategies in Inuit-Yupik and Dene Languages in Alaska

The two major language families in Alaska, Inuit-Yupik and Dene (or Athabascan), share a boundary that forms an arc nearly 2,000 kilometres long. Beginning from Cook Inlet, off the south coast of Alaska, the boundary extends north and then east, all the way to the Canadian border on the shore of the Beaufort Sea, with Inuit-Yupik languages spoken in coastal areas and Dene languages in the interior.[1] In Canada, Inuit languages are spoken all the way to Greenland, while Dene languages range across the north as far as Hudson Bay. Along this shared border in Alaska, many thousands of places have been named, and these names—and the place-naming strategies that underlie them—provide insight into Indigenous conceptualizations of the landscape. Inuit-Yupik place naming is grounded in human affordance; names are assigned based on people's relationship to the land. In contrast, Dene place naming is highly deterministic, based on a generative geographic directional system. There are, of course, plenty of exceptions that prove these rules, but, broadly speaking, these generalizations hold across the two language families.

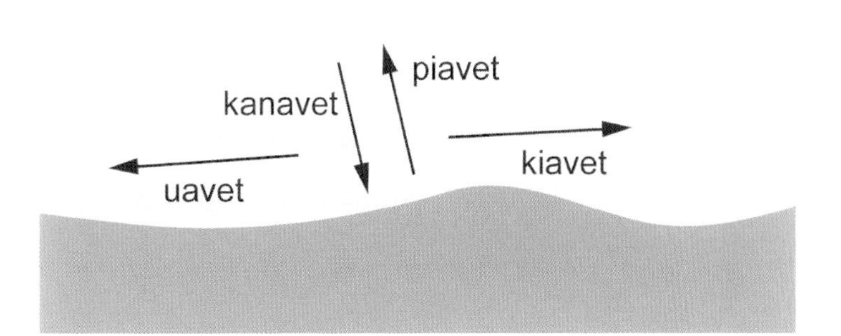

FIGURE 9.2 Coastal orientation roots in Central Alaskan Yup'ik (Inuit-Yupik).

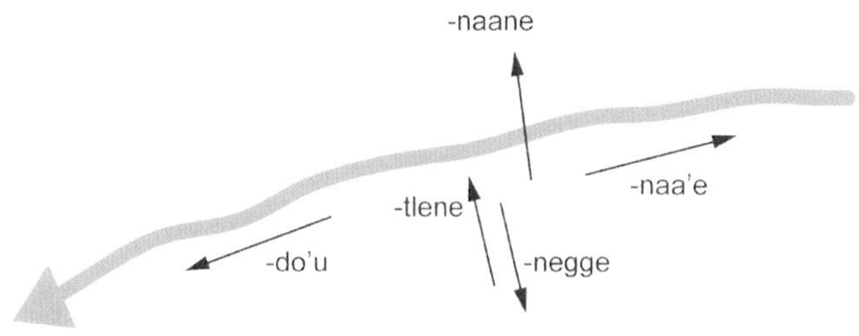

FIGURE 9.3 Riverine orientation roots in Koyukon (Dene).

Here I suggest that this difference in place-naming strategies can be explained partly in terms of differences in the way that the demonstrative systems of the two language families are extended to spatial reference. Both Inuit-Yupik and Dene languages include elaborate systems of words expressing spatial relations, allowing a much finer distinction than is possible with the proximal "this" and distal "that" in English. However, the function of the demonstrative system differs greatly in the two language families. In Inuit-Yupik languages, the demonstrative systems operate primarily on the local level and have limited application relative to the broader landscape. In Dene languages, however, the demonstrative systems are fundamental to the conceptualization of landscape, playing a key role in place-naming strategies.

To a certain extent this should not be surprising. Landscape is a semantic domain whose categorization is known to vary across languages. As Stephen Levinson (2008, 257) notes, "from a geological point of view," landscape is "mere deformation of a continuous surface, so that discrete units and categories must be the construction of the cognizer." In other words, concepts such as "mountain" are not universal in either denotation or connotation. Put another way, "different language groups/cultures have different ways of conceptualizing landscape, as evidenced by different terminology and ways of talking about and naming landscape features" (Mark, Turk, and Stea 2007, 16). Further evidence from specific languages can be found in the various case studies contained in the collection *Landscape in Language* (Mark et al. 2011). However, landscape categorization is not limited to feature terminology. Place names also provide insight into the categorization of landscape, and these names may also be deeply embedded within orientation systems. For example, a language employing a riverine orientation system embodies a very different approach to landscape than does a language employing a cardinal system based on compass directions, even though both are "absolute" systems in the sense described by Levinson (2003). In a riverine system, movement and location are contextualized within the parameters of upstream-downstream and landward–waterward. The valley system is "burned in" to a speaker's relationship to the land. In a cardinal system, by contrast, locations and movement can be described without any reference to the notion of valley.

In comparing Inuit-Yupik and Dene languages, the relevance of orientation systems is easily overlooked. On first glance, the two language families appear to have very similar orientation systems, both essentially riverine in nature (though coastal languages substitute upcoast-downcoast for upstream-downstream). The geographic dimension is based on either a riverine or a coastal template, consisting at its core of an orthogonal distinction between an upstream-downstream (or upcoast-downcoast) axis and a landward-waterward axis. The basic geographic template is superficially similar in the two language families. This can be illustrated by comparing the basic orientation roots in Central Alaskan Yup'ik (figure 9.2) and Koyukon, a Dene language (figure 9.3).[2]

These sorts of orientation systems are quite common in the world's languages, being found, for example, in various Austronesian languages (Adelaar 1997). However, of particular relevance here is the fact that these systems of orientation ultimately derive from larger systems of demonstratives, and the paths by which these larger demonstrative systems have come to be reduced to orientation systems differs significantly between Inuit-Yupik and Dene languages. In the remainder of this chapter, I first describe the demonstrative and orientation systems in Inuit-Yupik and Dene languages before turning to a comparison of different place-naming strategies.

Inuit-Yupik Orientation Systems

Inuit-Yupik languages are notable for their complex systems of demonstratives. The precise realization varies across individual Inuit-Yupik languages. It is most elaborated in Central Alaskan Yup'ik, which contrasts three dimensions corresponding to "directivity," roughly the distance from the deictic centre (origin); a dimension termed "indicability"; and a dimension termed "accessibility" (Jacobson 1984). Although the structure of the system varies greatly across individual languages, the forms correspond regularly, permitting the entire system to be reconstructed at the level of Proto-Inuit-Yupik (PIY) by application of the standard tools of the linguistic comparative method (see table 9.1). Although we think of orientation systems in modern languages as being based on relationship to water (river or coast), the PIY demonstrative system can be better described as an elevation-based system distinguishing up, down, and same level. To these basic elevations are added proximal (near the deictic centre) and distal (away from the deictic centre) terms, which are independent of elevation. Such elevation-based systems are not uncommon in the world's languages (Diessel 1999).

TABLE 9.1 Proto-Inuit-Yupik Demonstrative Roots

	restricted		**extended**		**obscured**	
	accessible	non-accessible	accessible	non-accessible	accessible	non-accessible
distal	*kiv-	*kiɣ-	*qav-	*qaɣ-	*qam-	*qakəm-
level	*iŋ-	*ik-	*av-	*aɣ-	*am-	*akəm-
down	*kan-/*kað-	*uɣ-	*un-	*unəɣ-	*cam-	*cakəm-
up	*piŋ-	*pik-	*pav-	*paɣ-	*pam-	*pakəm-

SOURCE: FORTESCUE, JACOBSON, AND KAPLAN 1994.

But the PIY demonstrative system adds two additional dimensions, those of indicability and accessibility. The dimension labelled "indicability" by Jacobson (1984) has to do with visibility and distinguishes among "restricted" (confined within a specific limit), "extended" (moving or unconfined), and "obscured" (blocked from view). The semantics of the dimension of accessibility are less consistent but nonetheless clearly defined for each accessible and non-accessible pair of terms. The precise semantics of the system need not concern us here. Rather, what is of interest is the way this system is realized in the individual Inuit-Yupik languages, and in particular how the system maps onto the landscape domain.

Not all of the original PIY demonstrative roots survive in modern languages, and the modern orientation systems make use of only a small subset of the larger demonstrative system. Moreover, the modern orientation systems are based not on the up-level-down elevation distinction found in the reconstruction PIY system, but rather on an orthogonal coordinate system. To derive the modern orientation systems from the original PIY demonstrative system, modern languages employ a subset of the original demonstratives and then reassign their semantics to form an orthogonal grid. Each modern Inuit-Yupik language achieves this in a slightly different way. Consider first the Inupiaq (North Slope dialect) demonstrative system, as shown in table 9.2. The table is laid out here to parallel the organization of the PIY demonstratives shown in table 9.1. Gaps indicate PIY demonstratives that lack a reflex in Inupiaq. The highlighted cells indicate terms that are used in the orientation system, to be discussed below.

Comparing the Inupiaq demonstratives with their PIY counterparts, two things are immediately evident. First, both the forms of the Inupiaq roots and their structural distribution are very much like those found in PIY. Only some minor sound changes have occurred, such as PIY *c > Inupiaq s. (Note that in the Inupiaq practical orthography, <g> represents [ɣ], so is unchanged from PIY.) Second, there are some gaps in the table, reflecting PIY demonstrative roots that have been lost in modern Inupiaq. In general, as one moves east across the Arctic, fewer of the original PIY demonstrative roots survive in modern languages. In Inupiaq these gaps lead to the partial collapse of the accessibility dimension with the restricted and extended terms.

The demonstrative system provides the basis for and coexists with an orientation system that contrasts the orthogonal dimensions of upcoast-downcoast versus waterward-landward. The full orientation system also includes terms deriving from winds, with the choice of wind term varying greatly by location (Fortescue 1988). However, if we ignore the wind terms for a moment, we can posit a kind of intermediate orientation system based only on the demonstrative system, as in table 9.3.

The Inupiaq orientation terms are precisely those that are shaded in table 9.2. Of the six restricted Inupiaq demonstrative roots shown in table 9.2, only four are employed in the orientation system. As in all Inuit-Yupik languages, the proximal term is not employed in the orientation system. The down and up terms *kan-* and *pik-* are used for the waterward-landward axis, that is, "down toward the coast" versus "up away from the coast." The accessibility distinction is irrelevant here since these terms have no counterpart in the accessibility parameter in modern Inupiaq. The single restricted level term *ik-* is used to mean “down the coast” or “to the left facing the water.” The accessible distal term *kiv-* is used to mean “up the coast” or “to the right facing the water.” This latter term retains as well its demonstrative sense of “inside,” which contrasts with the non-accessible form *kig-*, meaning “outside.” This results in homophony between the orientation system’s sense of *kiv-* meaning “down the coast” and the more localized sense of “inside.” This ambiguity is clearly the result of the original demonstrative system being extended for use as part of the orientation system.

A general rule for mapping the demonstrative system onto the orientation system is that wherever an accessible term exists it is the one employed in the orientation, and thus, like *kiv*, becomes polysemous between its larger orientation sense and its more localized demonstrative sense. The corresponding non-accessible term is not used, as in the orientation system, but maintains its demonstrative sense. In particular, none of the obscured non-accessible terms are employed in the orientation system, but they continue to be used as demonstratives: *qakim-* (“out there, not visible”); *akim-* (“over there across, not visible”); *sakim-* (“out there in the Arctic entry, not visible”); and *pakim* (“up there on the roof, not visible”).

Quite a different picture emerges in the neighbouring Central Alaskan Yup’ik language. Here, the PIY demonstrative system is preserved almost wholly intact, as shown in table 9.4. Unlike in the Inupiaq system, there are no gaps to facilitate choice of accessible or non-accessible terms for use in the orientation system.

TABLE 9.2 Alaskan Inupiaq Demonstrative Roots

	restricted		**extended**		**obscured**	
proximate	uv-		ma-		sam-	
	accessible	non-accessible	accessible	non-accessible	accessible	non-accessible
distal	kiv-	kig-	qav-	qag-	qam-	qakim-
level		ik-	av-	ag-	am-	akim-
down	kan-		un-		sam-	sakim-
up		pik-		pag-	pam-	pakim-

NOTE: SHADING INDICATES ROOTS USED IN THE ORIENTATION SYSTEM. SOURCE: MACLEAN 2014.

TABLE 9.3 Alaskan Inupiaq Orientation System (wind terms ignored)

	restricted	**extended**	**obscured**
upcoast	kiv-	qav-	qam-
downcoast	ik-	av-	am-
waterward	kan-	un-	sam-
landward	pik-	pag-	pam-

TABLE 9.4 Central Alaskan Yup’ik Demonstrative Adverbs (terminalis case)

	restricted		**extended**		**obscured**	
proximate	wavet		maavet			
	accessible	non-accessible	accessible	non-accessible	accessible	non-accessible
distal	kiavet	keggavet	qavavet	qagaavet	qamavet	qakmavet
level	yaavet	ikavet	avavet	agaavet	amavet	akmavet
down	kanavet	uavet	unavet	un’gavet	camavet	cakmavet
up	piavet	pikavet	pavavet	pagaavet	pamavet	pakmavet

NOTE: SHADING INDICATES ROOTS USED IN THE ORIENTATION SYSTEM. SOURCE: AFTER JACOBSON 2012.

TABLE 9.5 West Greenlandic Demonstrative Roots

	restricted		**extended**		**obscured**	
proximate	u-		ma-		(im-)	
	accessible	non-accessible	accessible	non-accessible	accessible	non-accessible
distal		kig-	qav-		qam-	
level		ik-	av-			
down	kan-				sam-	
up		pik-	pav-			

NOTE: SHADING INDICATES ROOTS USED IN THE ORIENTATION SYSTEM.

FIGURE 9.4 Yup'ik orientation system in a riverine system (restricted, terminalis case).

FIGURE 9.5 Greenlandic coastal orientation roots.

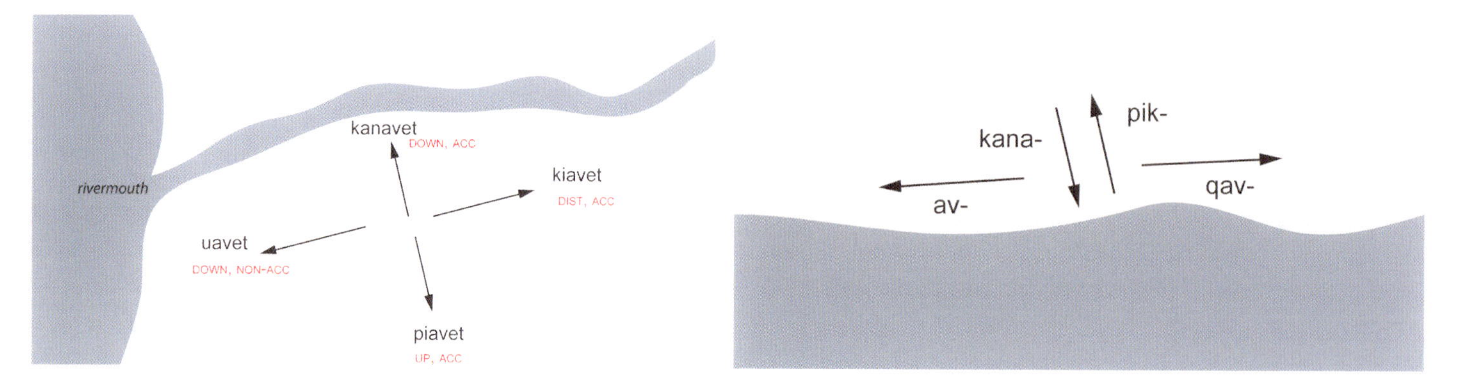

The Yup'ik demonstrative system does not make use of level demonstratives in the orientation system. Rather, both the accessible and non-accessible down terms are used. The accessible term *kana-* ("down there") is used for the direction toward water, while the non-accessible term *ua-* is used for the "downriver" direction. The term *kana-* ("toward water") is paired with the up accessible term *pia-* ("up there") to mean "away from water," while the downriver term *ua-* is paired with the distal accessible term *kia-* ("inside") to mean "upriver." This yields an orthogonal riverine directional, illustrated in figure 9.4 with restricted terms inflected for the terminalis case, expressing the meaning "toward."

The same Yup'ik orientation terms can also map onto a coastal system in which the downward non-accessible term denotes not "downriver" but rather "down the coast" or "to the right facing the water," and the distal accessible term denotes not "upriver" but rather "up the coast" or "to the left facing the water."

The Inupiaq and Yup'ik systems represent but two of the many ways in which the PIY demonstrative systems are realized in modern Inuit-Yupik languages and are extended to wider-scale orientation. A more extreme example of how demonstrative systems can be reanalyzed is found in West Greenlandic. As shown in table 9.5, the Greenlandic demonstrative system is greatly reduced from PIY.[3] In no dimension other than the proximal is an entire series of roots preserved.

The lack of terms in the extended and obscured domains has led to an orientation system in which this distinction is no longer made. Rather, the Greenlandic orientation system uses terms drawn from both the restricted and extended subsystems, and terms that may have originally belonged to different dimensions of the demonstrative paradigm (see figure 9.5). Thus, an originally accessible demonstrative, *kan* ("down [toward the coast]") is now opposed to an originally non-accessible demonstrative, *pik* ("up [away from the coast]"). The original non-accessible "down" demonstrative has been lost, as has the original accessible "up" demonstrative. With the accessibility dimension thus extinguished, the juxtaposition of *av* and *qav* is now unproblematic.

While the Greenlandic system is not directly relevant to the Alaskan languages considered here, it serves to illustrate the significant variation among the Inuit-Yupik languages in both the realization of the demonstrative system and the use of the demonstratives to form an orientation system. While the demonstrative terminology have their sources in

FIGURE 9.6 Yup'ik (left) and Inupiaq (right) directional terms compared.

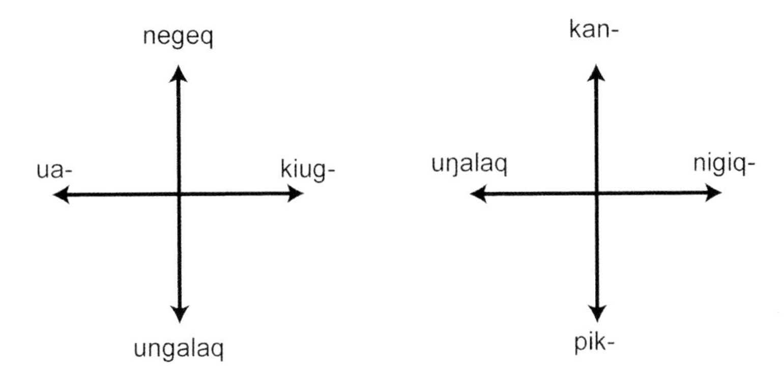

PIY, the individual demonstrative systems themselves function quite differently. These differences are greater still when we move to larger geographic scales beyond a single village. As one moves toward these larger scales, the undulations of the local coastline vary, and the need for less locally dependent terminology increases. The geographic integrity of the system is maintained by employing wind terms in lieu of some of the demonstrative roots. This strategy is found throughout the Inuit-Yupik languages, but the particular implementation varies greatly not only by language but also by geographic location within a given language (Fortescue 1988). This variation can be illustrated by comparing Yup'ik and Inupiaq (North Slope) directional terms (as in figure 9.6).

Both Yup'ik and Inupiaq employ reflexes of the wind terms PIY *nəɣəʀ and *uŋalaʀ. In Yup'ik, the wind terms *negeq* and *ungalaq* are paired with the upriver-downriver (or upcoast-downcoast) terms. In Inupiaq, the wind terms *nigiq* and *uŋalaq* are paired with the toward-away from coast terms.

The variation in the realization of Inuit-Yupik directional systems can be explained in terms of geography (Fortescue 1988, 2011). In Yup'ik, *negeq* is a north wind, hence orthogonal to the prevailing east-west trending rivers and their concomitant downstream-upstream terms. In North Slope Inupiaq, *nigiq* is an east wind, hence orthogonal to the toward-away from water direction. So the choice of the downstream–upstream axis in Yup'ik versus the toward-away from water axis in Inupiaq is readily explained. However, the ability of Inuit-Yupik languages to essentially pick and choose among demonstratives has significant consequences for the conceptualization of landscape. The reification of these orientation terms into an essentially cardinal directional system decouples the terms from the landscape, depriving them of their potential function as guides to the topography and sources for place naming.

In practice, Inuit-Yupik orientation terms may have very little to do with the wider landscape. In my own field work with speakers of Yup'ik, I have noted a great reluctance to use these orientation terms on any scale beyond the immediate vicinity. Travel along rivers is much more likely to be described either in terms of cardinal directions (e.g., *negeq*, or "north") or in terms of movement either with or against the current (e.g., *asgur-*, or "move against the current") than with the orientation system. So while the Yup'ik demonstrative and orientation systems may be extremely rich and complex, they have little practical relevance to the domain of landscape. Nor, as we shall see below, do they play major roles in place naming.

Dene Demonstrative Systems

A very different situation is found in Dene languages. The Proto-Dene demonstrative system is reconstructed in table 9.6. There are two paradigms corresponding to motion away (allative) and static (punctual). Modern Dene languages add additional dimensions of motion toward the deictic centre and static location in an area.

Rather than a three-way, elevation-based contrast between up/level/down, as in Inuit-Yupik, the Proto-Dene system contrasts the four basic demonstratives of upstream, downstream, landward, and waterward, forming a two-dimensional coordinate system (for an example, see figure 9.7). To these basic terms are added additional terms indicating "ahead into open country or water"; "across water"; "away in a non-specific direction"; "above vertically"; and "below vertically." The resulting system is thus three-dimensional and highly descriptive of the riverine valley that characterizes much of the Alaskan Dene landscape.

Another major difference between the Inuit-Yupik and Dene demonstrative systems is that the Proto-Dene system is realized homologously across the Alaskan Dene languages, augmented to varying degrees with prefixes specifying distance and suffixes specifying motion or area. That is, the ancient Proto-Dene system is robustly preserved in all modern languages. The system used in the Tanacross language (shown in table 9.7) is typical in that it includes a four-way distinction between allative (movement away from deictic centre), ablative (movement toward the deictic centre), punctual (static location at specific point), and areal (static location in general area). These four paradigms derive ultimately from suffixation patterns that have been historically obscured.

The forms shown in table 9.7 are stems and must be inflected in order to form a demonstrative word. As in other Dene languages, the demonstratives are preceded by a prefix indicating distance from the deictic centre. In Tanacross, these prefixes are *a-* (neutral), *da-* (proximal), *na-* (intermediate), *ja-* (distal), and *jaʔa* (distant).

As in Inuit-Yupik languages, this three-dimensional paradigm of demonstratives allows very precise orientation. However, unlike Inuit-Yupik, this extends across the entire language family, robustly attested in each of the Alaskan Dene languages.[4] Moreover, the system operates at all levels, being equally relevant when applied at the large-scale geographic domain, within a house, or locally on the human body (see table 9.8). This contrasts with Inuit-Yupik languages, in which the demonstrative system functions only at a very local scale, while the more generalized orientation system functions at larger scales relevant to the landscape domain. In Dene languages, the riverine-based system permeates all aspects of orientation, independent of scale.

To understand just how pervasive the Dene riverine orientation system is, consider the usage of the demonstrative system within a house. The extension of demonstratives within a house is based on a conventionalization in which the front door of the house is orientated facing the river. Thus, "upstream" within a house is the direction to the left or right of the door, depending on the direction of flow of the river.[5] The upstream-downstream and inland-waterward axes are reflected throughout Dene languages in both local (for examples, within the home) and regional spatial domains. The robustness of the riverine demonstrative system within the family underscores the importance of the riverine valley in Dene. As discussed in the following section, it also provides the motivation for place-naming strategies.

Place-Naming Strategies

Although the Inuit-Yupik and Dene orientation systems are superficially similar, they are reflected quite differently in the toponymic systems for the two language families. The Dene demonstrative roots define a streamscape based on the orthogonal dimensions of upstream-downstream and toward-away from water. This streamscape is used regularly to generate toponymic clusters based on shared landscape generic terms.[6] The core set of generics is composed of **kæq'* ("stream mouth"), **tł'at* ("stream headwaters"), **wən* ("lake"), and **naʔ/*niq'ə* ("stream") (where the asterisk indicates a reconstructed Proto-Dene form), as shown in figure 9.8.[7] These terms are not related to the demonstrative system, but they are determined by that system. That is, the riverine structure of the demonstratives delineates a linear valley template to which these landscape terms are assigned. As with the demonstrative system, reflexes of the Proto-Dene streamscape generic terms are robustly attested in all modern Alaskan Dene languages.

The system is generative in the sense that, for any given specific term, each member of the limited set of generic landscape terms can (and usually does) occur (Kari 2010b; Levinson 2003). As an example, consider the Tanacross word *ch'inchedl* ("nose ridge").

TABLE 9.6 Proto-Dene Demonstrative Roots

	allative	punctual
upstream	*niʔ	*ni'-d
downstream	*daʔ	*da'-d
landward	*nəɢ-ə	*nəχ
waterward	*tsənʔ	*tsį'-d
ahead	*nəs-ə	*nəs
across	*ɲa·nʔ	*ɲą'·-d
away	*ʔɑnʔ	*ʔą'·-d
above	*-ə	*-d
below	*dəɢ-ə	*deχ

SOURCE: LEER 1989.

TABLE 9.7 Tanacross (Dene) Demonstrative Roots

	allative		punctual	areal
upstream	-ndéʔe	-ndî·dz	-ndé·	-ndí·g
downstream	-ndá·ʔa	-ndâ·dz	-nda·	
inland	-ndeg	-ndêdz	-ndég	-ndóg
waterward	-tθέnʔ		-tθí·	-tθúg
ahead	-nεð			-noð
across	-ná·nʔ	-ndáz	-ná·n	-ndás
away	-ʔέnʔ	-ʔáz		-ʔóg
above	-deg	-dêdz	-dé·	-ndóg
below	-ʒégʔ	-ʒêz	-ʒé·	-ʒóg

NOTE: GAPS IN THE TABLE REFLECT FORMS NOT CURRENTLY ATTESTED, POSSIBLY OWING TO LANGUAGE ATTRITION. SOURCE: ARNOLD, THOMAN, AND HOLTON 2009.

TABLE 9.8 Examples of Tanacross Demonstratives at Various Scales

Example	Demonstrative
yandá'a Fairbanks ts'į tíhhaay ("I'm going down to Fairbanks")	distal, downstream, allative
dandee didhindah ("Sit down on the upstream side [of the table]")	proximal, upstream, punctual
nandôg shtthí' tah shá? xúntee ("I have lice in my hair")	intermediate, above, areal

FIGURE 9.7 Tanacross (Dene) demonstratives (distal, allative paradigm).

FIGURE 9.8 Proto-Dene streamscape generic terms.

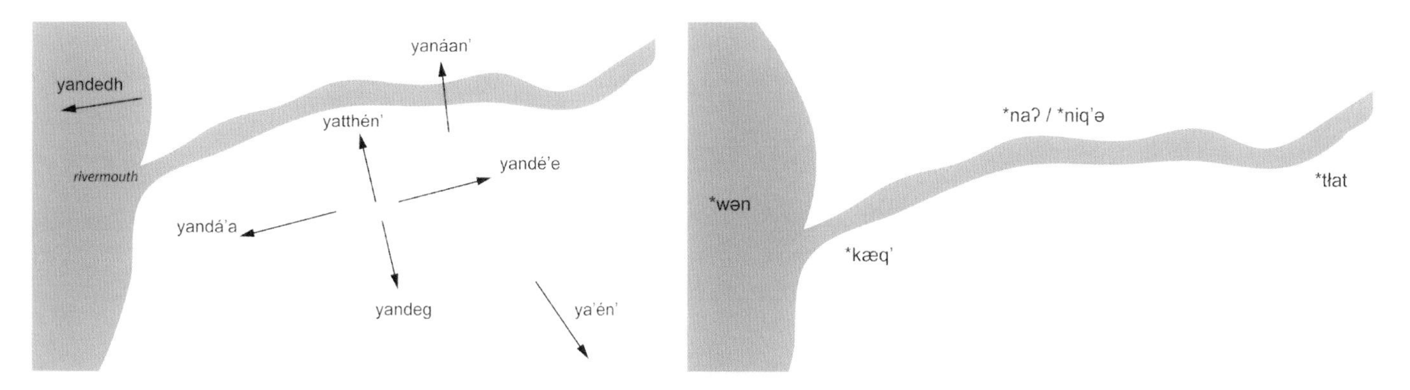

The word occurs as the name for a prominent ridge rising some five hundred metres to the north of the Tanana River. It is used as a specific term to generate a cluster of names in that locality, including *Ch'inchedl Ndiig* ("nose creek") (< **niq'ə*), a creek that drains the back side of *Ch'inchedl*; *Ch'inchedl Menn'* ("nose lake") (< **wən*), the lake from which the creek flows; *Ch'inchedl Tl'aa* ("nose headwaters") (< **tł'at*), the headwaters of the creek; and *Ch'inchedl Teyy'* ("nose hill"), a peak that rises above the headwaters. This last generic term *teyy'* ("hill") augments the basic streamscape system. Crucially, a given specific term may be repeated only if it is not used to generate name clusters. Thus, the Tanacross name *Ch'inchedl* is a singleton, that is, a unique name that is not repeated.

The singleton *Ch'inchedl* can be contrasted with the specific term *ch'endaag* ("mineral lick"). This latter term occurs in the name *Ch'endaag Menn'* ("mineral lick lake"), which is repeated fully five times. This is rather striking given that the territory in which the Tanacross language is spoken is among the smallest of any Dene language in Alaska, and the five places with the name "mineral lick lake" are located within ten to fifty kilometres of each other. However, none of these names participates in a larger generative naming pattern (figure 9.9).

That is, the specific term *ch'endaag* does not occur in any other derived forms—either referring to neighbouring or distant features. There is simply no "mineral lick mouth," "mineral lick creek," "mineral lick headwaters," and so on. This distinction between specific terms that generate name clusters and those that do not is clearly functional. Because the former are not repeated outside the cluster, these singleton specifics essentially denote a region or territory. Names for individual parts of the territory can be generated readily even by those unfamiliar with the territory by drawing the generative principles of the Dene naming system.

The generative capacity of the Dene naming system is so deeply entrenched as to seem almost deterministic. This is particularly true for the generic term **kæq'* ("mouth"). Once one knows the name of a particular river, the name of its mouth is easily ascertained. This is not simply a matter of specifying a location using a geographic term. Rather, if the mouth is named, its name is almost invariably based on **kæq'*; alternate names are simply not possible. These mouth names are often highly lexicalized and often borrowed into English with the generic term. Thus, at the mouth of the Kantishna River is located a village known in English as Crossjacket. The Lower Tanana name for the Kantishna River is *K'osr No,'* a binominal name composed of the specific *k'osr* ("polishing stone") and the generic *no'* (< **naʔ*). Thus, the village at its mouth must be *K'osr Chaget* (< **kæq'*), which is readily seen to be the etymological source of the English name. Examples like this abound across the Dene territory in Alaska (see table 9.9).

The generative capacity also has synchronic relevance. New names are rarely coined in Dene languages, as most of the country is already named, obviating the need for further appellations. However, where new names are coined, the riverine system provides the template. Thus, a new name near a mouth of a creek will almost invariably be named using the generic "mouth." There are exceptions to this rule, but these arise only when there is an overriding influence from a competing naming strategy. There is a single such example in the list of 2,436 Ahtna names: the name *Naghilden*, which denotes a location at the mouth of Canyon Creek. Rather than the generic *cae'e* ("mouth," it contains a generic *den* ("place, area") and means literally "waterfall place." In this single case, the prominence of a nearby hydrologic feature took precedence, but in the vast majority of cases the system exhibits a constrained productivity in which new names must follow the generative strategy.

FIGURE 9.9 Ray Sanford reviewing maps of Tanacross place names, noting locations of places named *Ch'endaag Menn'*. Photograph by Gary Holton, 2012.

TABLE 9.9 Some Common Village Names with Dene Etymologies Based on **kæq'*

English	**Dene name**	**Language**
Salcha	*Sołt Chaget*	Lower Tanana
Bearpaw	*Ch'edzaya' Chaget*	Lower Tanana
Chena	*Ch'eno' Khwdochaget*	Lower Tanana
Healy Lake	*Mendees Cheeg*	Tanacross
Ketchumstuck	*Saages Cheeg*	Tanacross
Holikachuk	*Holjichak'*	Holikachuk
Anvik	*Gitr'ingith Chagg*	Deg Xinag
Stony River	*K'qizaghetnu Hdakaq'*	Dena'ina
Chistochina	*Tsiis Tl'edze' Caegge*	Ahtna
Copper Center	*Tl'aticae'e*	Athna
Allakaket	*Aalaa Kkaakk'et*	Koyukon
Hughes	*Hut'odlee Kkaakk'et*	Koyukon
McGrath	*Tochak'*	Upper Kuskokwim

FIGURE 9.10 Dene elder and Lower Tanana speaker Percy Duyck (1929–2014) reviewing Nenana-area place names. Duyck and other Dene speakers make use of the riverine demonstrative system to identify and locate place names. Photograph by Gary Holton, 2011.

The use of generics in Inuit-Yupik languages is quite different. In particular, Inuit-Yupik place naming is not generative. To see just how different the Inuit-Yupik strategy is, it is worth comparing the use of the Inuit-Yupik generic **paðə* ("mouth") with Dene **kæq'ə*. As in Dene languages, the Inuit-Yupik generic "mouth" can be used in place names. For example, the Central Yup'ik name for the village of Stony River is *Teggalqum Kuigan Painga*, incorporating the Yup'ik word *pai* ("mouth") (< **paðə*). This village is located in a bilingual region bordering Yup'ik and Dena'ina (Dene) territory, so it also has a Dena'ina name, *K'qizaghetnu Hdakaq,'* which also incorporates the Dena'ina generic *kaq'* ("mouth") (< **kæq'ə*). Yet the name for Stony River is actually quite exceptional in this regard. Most Yup'ik names for villages located at river mouths do not in fact contain the generic "mouth." For example, Egegik, located at the mouth of the Egegik River, is known simply as *Igyagiiq*, a generic term meaning "throat" and referring metaphorically to "the area of a river a little ways back from the mouth" (Jacobson 2012, 279). This name contains no specific component; it is simply a landscape generic. In other words, it is descriptive but not generative.

The contrast between Inuit-Yupik and Dene extends to features beyond river mouths themselves. A large mountain above the Cheeneetnuk River, known locally as Swift River Mountain, is called in Deg Xinag (Dene) *Jonetno' Xidochagg Deloy Chux*, literally "big mountain at mouth of Jonetno" (*chagg* < **kæq'ə*). *Jonetno,'* literally "clear water creek," is the Deg Xinag name for the Cheeneetnuk River. But the Yup'ik name has nothing to do with either the creek or its mouth. Instead, this mountain is known in Yup'ik by the highly descriptive name

Kiturciigalnguq, meaning "place one cannot pass." Gusty Mikhail explains the name as follows: "That means 'we can't pass mountain.' You see the river is so crooked that that mountain when you go up, you go sometimes behind like that, sometimes it hit us. Sometimes sideways. You can't pass it. That's why they call him that way. You can't pass that mountain" (quoted in Kari 1980).

While the Deg Xinag language anchors the name generatively in the landscape via the generics "river," "mouth," and "mountain," the Yup'ik name forgoes landscape terminology in favour of a name based on human affordance. This difference is fundamental to understanding place-naming strategies in the two languages—a point to which we will return below.

Not only is the usage of the Inuit-Yupik and Dene "mouth" generic quite different, the terms also have fundamentally different semantics. Inuit-Yupik **paðə* has broad semantics referring to an "opening" or "entrance." This broad semantics is preserved in most of the languages of the family, including Yup'ik (Fortescue, Jacobson, and Kaplan 1994). Thus, Yup'ik *pai* (variant *paa*) can refer not only to the "mouth of river" but also to "opening of den, bottle," etc. or the "cockpit of kayak" (Jacobson 2012). In contrast, the Dene generic **kæq'* is restricted to the landscape domain, referring only to "river mouth." It is distinguished from roots such as *du* ("orifice" and *zaq'* ("mouth" [anatomical]). As I have argued previously, this Dene generic serves to delineate a prototypical Dene streamscape centred around a valley. The term **kæq'* is not just "river mouth" but, more properly, "mouth of a valley," as evidenced, for example, by the Lower Tanana name *Dradlaya Chaget*, which is located not at a river mouth, as the term *chaget* (< **kæq'*) might imply, but at the place where the river leaves a steep-walled valley and spills onto the Minto Flats (Holton 2011, 234) (figure 9.10).

The Dene examples given above reflect the fundamental importance of the riverine orientation system for Dene place naming. Although the grammar of demonstratives is extremely complex in both Dene and Inuit-Yupik languages, only in Dene is the demonstrative system so fully embedded within place names. This becomes especially apparent when place-naming strategies are compared quantitatively. In order to do this, we must consider comprehensive name inventories, since selective name lists could potentially skew the results. Within Alaskan Dene, the most comprehensive published place-name inventories are those for Ahtna (Kari 2008) and Lower Tanana (Kari et al. 2012), listing 2,208 and 1,064 names, respectively.[8] No study of similar scope has yet been published for Inuit-Yupik languages in Alaska; however, we are fortunate to have available a comprehensive list of 1,007 names for the Inuinnait of western Canada, which can be used as a proxy for Alaskan Inuit-Yupik languages (Collignon 2006). The Ahtna and Inuinnait territories are comparable in size, and the name inventories are similarly exhaustive.[9] The Ahtna name density is thus roughly twice that of the Inuinnait, but the two systems can nevertheless be compared without undue risk of sampling error.

As we expect given the claimed generative capacity of Dene naming, more than 60 percent of Ahtna names are binominal (or trinomial) and headed by one of twenty-two landscape generics. In contrast, only 21 percent of Inuinnait names are based on a landscape generic (see table 9.10). Moreover, nearly half of these names (94 of 207) are duplicates, so that the percentage of unique Inuinnait names based on

a landscape generic is more like 11 percent.
In fact, name duplication is much more prevalent in Inuinnait than in Dene. Fully 26 percent (257 of 1,007) of Inuinnait names are duplicates, compared to only 6 percent (155 of 2,436) of Ahtna names and just 4 percent (44 of 1,064) of Lower Tanana names. Even if we ignore name duplication, the percentage of landscape-based names in Ahtna is three times that in Inuinnait. However, this figure ignores grammatical structure of Dene binomial names. Inuinnait names based on landscape terms include many that are simply a landscape term or a landscape term modified by an adjectival suffix (post-base).

This is also true of the Yup'ik (Inuit-Yupik) names on Nunivak Island, one of the few sub-regions of Inuit-Yupik territory in Alaska for which comprehensive published name data are available.[10] A large number of Nunivak names consist only of a generic name with a modifying adjectival suffix. This includes twenty single-word names consisting of the generic root *kuik-* ("river") together with one or more derivational suffixes (see table 9.11).

Frequent use of generic names leads naturally to a high incidence of name repetition. The seven tokens of Nunivak *Kuigaar* is one example of such repetition. We also find on Nunivak Island five tokens of *Pengur* ("dune") (as well as fifteen more names derived from the same root); four tokens of *Penarrat* ("small cliffs") (as well as twenty other names derived from *penat* ["cliffs"]); and four tokens of *Qemirrlag* ("major hill/ridge") (as well as fourteen other terms based on the root *qemir* ["hill/ridge"]).

Names comprised solely of a landscape generic are impossible in Ahtna, and names based on adjectival modification of a landscape generic are extremely rare, comprising less than 2 per cent of the inventory. Such names tend to refer to major features, such as *Dghelaay Ce'e* for Denali, literally "big mountain." The more common generative pattern can be exemplified by the Ahtna names based on *yidateni* ("jaw trail"). The nine names in listed in table 9.12 make use of landscape generics referring to "canyon," "mountain," "river mouth," "hill," "creek," "headwaters," "lake," and "uplands." In addition, the specific term itself occurs as a name, *Yidateni*, denoting a convex landform. The landscape generics themselves do not occur as names.

The names shown in table 9.12 form what Kari (2008) has described as a place-name cluster built upon a single specific term. Examples of such clusters abound in Alaskan Dene languages. Within a cluster, names are generated by addition of one or more landscape generics. Crucially, the domain of application of the cluster is the river valley. All but one of the names in table 9.12 include generics referring to the riverine valley: "canyon," "creek," "river mouth," and "headwaters." The sole exception is *Yidateni Dghelaaye'*, which contains only the generic "mountain." This name refers to mountains on either side of the headwaters of *Yidateni Na.'*

The generative nature of Dene naming has important functional implications. The most striking feature of the system is its near predictive value. The major creek in the vicinity of *Yidateni* must almost obligatorily be named *Yidateni Na,'* and the pass located at the headwaters of *Yidateni Na'* is similarly known as *Yidateni Tl'aa.* Such statements must of course be qualified, for exceptions do exist, and the fact that such Ahtna names "make sense" in terms of the local geography should not be confused with a claim that those same names are predetermined. For example, where two lakes exist at the headwaters of the stream, it is not possible to know a priori which will be named with the generics "headwater lake." However, where both lakes are named, the typical pattern would be to distinguish them with the directional terms "upstream" and "downstream," as in the Ahtna names *Hwdaandi Taltsogh Bene,'* literally "downstream yellow-water lake," and *Hwniindi Taltsogh Bene,'* literally "upstream yellow-water lake." The overwhelming tendency toward deterministic naming practices in Dene languages is very real, both to observers and the speakers themselves. As Kari (2010a, xv; emphasis added) notes, "Ahtna geographic names are so informative and *learnable* that they facilitate the understanding and recognition of the landscape." Ahtna names index the landscape in a reciprocal fashion. On the one hand, the names literally describe the landscape, providing knowledge of places with which one is not familiar; on the other, the landscape imposes the names, providing a physio-geographic structure that facilitates memorization and usage of names. Knowledge of a small number of specific terms can be readily extended to a large geographic area using the generative naming system. The robustness of this system is further attested by the widespread agreement in linguistically cognate names across language boundaries (Kari 2010b).

The contrast with Inuinnait could not be more stark. There is no way to know in advance whether a particular river will be known as "big river" or "long river" or simply "river." Given this ambiguity, it is perhaps not surprising that knowledge of Inuinnait names is not considered a prerequisite for travelling or hunting on the land (Collignon 2006, 107). Rather,

TABLE 9.10 Examples of Inuinnait Names Based on Landscape Generic

Name	Literal
Kuunayuq	long river
Kuugaluk	big river
Kuugaaryuk	small river
Palliq	bay
Qikiqtahuk	small island
Tahialuk	(big) lake
Ikpik	slope

SOURCE: COLLIGNON 2006.

TABLE 9.11 Yup'ik Place Names Based on Generic *Kuik-* ("River") on Nunivak Island

Name	**Literal**
Kuicungar	dear little river
Kuigaar (7)	little river
Kuigaarag	two little rivers
Kuigaaremiut	village of little river
Kuiggavluar (2)	just a little river
Kuigglugar	poor old river
Kuigglugarmiut	village of poor-old-river
Kuigkaun	future river
Kugimiutuli	one who stays at the river
Kuigpii	its big river
Kuiguar (2)	imitation river
Kuileg	one with a river

NOTE: WHERE A NAME REFERS TO MORE THAN ONE PLACE, NUMBERS IN PARENTHESES INDICATE THE NUMBER OF DISTINCT PLACES WITH THAT NAME. SOURCE: DROZDA 1994.

TABLE 9.12 Ahtna Names Based on Specific Term *Yidateni*

Name	**Literal**
Yidateni Dyii	jaw trail canyon
Yidateni Dyii Dghelaaye'	jaw trail canyon mountain
Yidateni Caek'e	jaw trail mouth
Yidateni Caek'e Tes	jaw trail mouth hill
Yidateni Na'	jaw trail creek
Yidateni Tl'aa	jaw trail headwaters
Yidateni Tl'aa Bene'	jaw trail headwaters lake
Yidateni Dghelaaye'	jaw trail mountain
Yidateni Na' Ngge'	jaw trail creek uplands

SOURCE: KARI 2008, 27.

FIGURE 9.11 *Tr'edhdode*, a landmark situated in the pass between the *Dradlaya Nik'a* (Chatanika River) and *Tsogho Nik'a* (Beaver Creek) drainages. Photograph courtesy Chris Cannon, 2016.

Inuinnait names connect people to the landscape and serve to create a human dimension to it. Of course, the same could be said for Ahtna names. The difference is that where Inuinnait names are deliberately chosen, Ahtna names are largely imparted by the landscape itself; indeed, they are inseparable from it. That is not to say that naming is completely unconstrained in Inuinnait: one would presumably be unlikely to name a lake using the Inuinnait generic for "mountain." Nor is naming completely constrained in Ahtna: the choice of specific terms such as *yidateni* reflects speaker creativity. But these observations are secondary to the basic distinction in the role of landscape in Inuit-Yupik and Dene place naming.

Inuit names are much more likely to be based on human experience (Collignon's *uumajuit*), with no reference to landscape. One thus finds Inuinnait names such as *Alliakhaqhiurvik* ("place to search for material to make sledges") and *Ihurvik* ("place where hunters wait for game"). For this reason, Inuit names are also readily coined. This is true in Alaska among the Yup'ik just as much as with the Inuinnait. Although Yup'ik names are sometimes said to be of great antiquity, Fienup-Riordan (2011, xxix) cites numerous examples of recently coined whimsical names, noting that "some places were named simply to make us smile." Thus, the Yup'ik place *Kass'aq*, literally "white person," is so named simply because a white person lived there. Such recently coined whimsical names are almost entirely absent in Dene languages. Rather, Dene names are predominantly landscape-based (see figure 9.11), generated in clusters within the domain of the riverine valley.

Conclusions

The comparisons presented here lend some support to the hypothesis that Alaska's two major language families conceptualize the landscape in very different ways. Though both groups are nomadic hunter-gatherers sharing a common border across the Subarctic, their linguistic relationships to this landscape are quite different. The primary contribution of this chapter is to suggest a relationship between demonstrative systems and place-naming strategies. Although both Inuit-Yupik and Dene languages have extremely rich demonstrative systems, the Inuit-Yupik systems operate primarily at a local scale. At larger scales relevant to landscape, the systems have been reduced and altered in language-specific ways. There is no overarching Inuit-Yupik landscape demonstrative system.

In contrast, the Dene demonstrative system is preserved intact in all of the Alaskan Dene languages, giving special prominence to the linear valley. This valley system can be thought of as a semantic template, or "semplate"—that is, a semantic system that is reflected in more than one area of the grammar (Levinson and Burenhult 2009). The linear valley also serves as the organizing principle for generative place naming based on a shared specific term combined with a suite of landscape generics. The existence of the linear valley semplate provides evidence for a deep-rooted Dene conceptualization of the valley as central to the landscape. This concept is further reinforced by the reciprocal nature of Dene place naming, through which the landscape essentially names itself.

Place-naming strategies in Inuit-Yupik and Dene languages draw on different linguistic resources, rooted in the underlying differences in their demonstrative systems. As a result, Alaska's two major language families, which seem at first glance to have very similar demonstrative systems, approach the naming of the landscape in very different ways. Whether or not this difference in naming strategies reflects different ways of conceptualizing the landscape, or simply different linguistic designs, remains an outstanding question.

Of course, any conclusions drawn here are necessarily tentative, as they rely on disparate (and often incomplete) sources from a variety of languages. Inadequate documentation remains a major barrier to the analysis of the landscape domain in Alaska. Research on Indigenous toponymy requires exhaustive documentation in order to avoid sampling bias. Yet most place-name studies in Alaska have been opportunistic or guided by etic territorial boundaries. Place-name documentation driven by Indigenous communities tends to focus on single communities rather than entire language areas, and research driven by government agencies tends to impose artificial boundaries. More popular and widely distributed name lists are often redacted, resulting in what is only a subjective sampling of names for more prominent features. While these materials may be informative about the names they do contain, they do not admit a larger synthesis. For example, without comprehensive coverage one cannot extract information about name density or the relative frequency of certain naming strategies.

To date, comprehensive place-name lists have been published for just three Alaskan languages, and these only recently: Ahtna (Kari 2008), Lower Tanana (Kari et al. 2012), and Tlingit (Thornton 2012). Even the best reference dictionaries provide little information about the semantics of generic landscape terms. There is still much to learn, and ongoing documentation efforts must also be supplemented by experimental work.

Acknowledgements

This work was supported by National Science Foundation Alaska EPSCoR award 335863 and grant OPP-1203194. Thanks to James Kari, Robert Charlie, Dora Andrew-Ihrke, and Evelyn Yanez for their assistance with field work, and to Ken Pratt, Robert Drozda, and Lawrence Kaplan for helpful feedback on an earlier draft of this chapter. They are of course not responsible for any remaining errors contained herein.

Notes

1 Inuit and Yupik languages are the two branches of a language family traditionally known as "Eskimo"—a term no longer acceptable in Canada but still in use in Alaska. Likewise, in Canada, the term "Dene" has largely supplanted "Athabaskan" (the spelling generally preferred there), whereas in Alaska "Athabascan" remains the more common term. I use the terms Inuit-Yupik and Dene in place of Eskimo and Athabascan, respectively.

2 For the sake of consistency, I follow the conventional practice of using ethnonyms to refer to language. The language spoken by the Yup'ik people is more properly known as Yugtun. Similarly, the languages spoken by the Koyukon and Inuinnait peoples are more properly Denakk'e and Inuinnaqtun, respectively.

3 The values in table 9.5 reflect a more conservative stage of the language. In modern West Greenlandic, the distinction between restricted and extended demonstratives has been neutralized (Fortescue 1984, 259). However, this difference is not relevant to the argument made in this chapter.

4 Notably, the riverine system does not reconstruct to the higher-level branch of the larger Na-Dene family. Rather, the riverine system is an innovation within the Dene branch (Leer 1989, 602).

5 In practice, local river direction will also be conventionalized. Thus, in Tanacross village, houses are treated as if they were facing the river flowing from right to left as one looks out the door. This remains the case even though only one house is actually situated in this fashion today. Nonetheless, demonstrative terms are applied unambiguously within the house based on this conventionalization.

6 In both English and Dene languages, many place names are composed of a combination of a generic landscape term from a limited set (for example, "lake," "mountain," "river," etc.) plus a specific term which provides additional identification. Thus, in the English name "Big Lake," "lake" is the generic and "big" is the specific.

7 For the difference in distribution of reflexes of Proto-Dene **na* and **niq'e*, see Kari (1996).

8 The list published in 2008 includes 2,208 names; a revised and updated list available from the Alaska Native Language Archive includes a total of 2,436 names.

9 Kari (2008) estimates the size of the Ahtna territory as 50,000 square miles (13 million hectares). Inuinnait territory is roughly five times as large, at approximately 270,000 square miles, or 70 million hectares (Collignon, pers. comm.), and thus the same order of magnitude as Ahtna territory.

10 The variety of Yup'ik spoken on Nunivak Island is usually referred to as Cup'ig. Though the structure of the directional system in Cup'ig is similar to that found in other varieties of Central Alaskan Yup'ik, Cup'ig exhibits significant lexical and phonological differences, to the extent that some speakers consider Cup'ig to be a distinct language (Amos and Amos 2003, viii; Jacobson 2012, 42).

References

Adelaar, K. Alexander

1997 An Exploration of Directional Systems in West Indonesia and Madagascar. In *Referring to Space: Studies in Austronesian and Papuan Languages*, edited by Gunter Senft, pp. 53–82. Oxford University Press, Oxford.

Amos, Muriel M., and Howard T. Amos

2003 *Cup'ig Eskimo Dictionary.* Alaska Native Language Center, University of Alaska Fairbanks.

Arnold, Irene, Richard Thoman, and Gary Holton

2009 *Tanacross Learners' Dictionary: Dihtâad Xt'een Iin Anděg Dínahtlăa.'* Alaska Native Language Center, University of Alaska Fairbanks.

Collignon, Béatrice

2006 *Knowing Places: The Inuinnait, Landscapes, and the Environment.* Translated by L. W. Müller-Wille. Canadian Circumpolar Institute, Edmonton.

Diessel, Holger

1999 *Demonstratives: Form, Function, and Grammaticalization.* John Benjamins, Amsterdam.

Drozda, Robert M.

1994 *Qikertamteni Nunat Atrit Nuniwarmiuni: The Names of Places on Our Island Nunivak.* Bureau of Indian Affairs, ANCSA Office, Anchorage.

Fienup-Riordan, Ann (editor)

2011 *Qaluyaarmiuni Nunamtenek Qanemciput: Our Nelson Island Stories.* University of Washington Press, Seattle.

Fortescue, Michael D.

1984 *West Greenlandic.* Croom Helm, London.

1988 *Eskimo Orientation Systems.* Meddelelser om Grønland [Monographs on Greenland], Man and Society 11. Commission for Scientific Research in Greenland, Copenhagen.

2011 *Orientation Systems of the North Pacific Rim.* Meddelelser om Grønland [Monographs on Greenland] 352. Museum Tuscalanum Press, Copenhagen.

Fortescue, Michael D., Steven A. Jacobson, and Lawrence Kaplan

1994 *Comparative Eskimo Dictionary, with Aleut Cognates.* Research Paper No. 9. Alaska Native Language Center, University of Alaska Fairbanks.

Holton, Gary

2011 Differing Conceptualizations of the Same Landscape: The Athabaskan and Eskimo Language Boundary in Alaska. In *Landscape in Language*, edited by David M. Mark, Andrew G. Turk, Niclas Burenhult, and David Stea, pp. 225–237. John Benjamins, Amsterdam.

Jacobson, Steven A.

1984 Semantics and Morphology of Demonstratives in Central Yup'ik Eskimo. *Études/Inuit/Studies* 8 (Supplementary Issue): 185–192.

2012 *Yup'ik Eskimo Dictionary.* 2nd ed. Alaska Native Language Center, University of Alaska Fairbanks.

Kari, James

1980 Kuskokwim River Placenames by Gusty Mikhail [Item IK974K1979f]. Alaska Native Language Archive, University of Alaska Fairbanks.

1996 A Preliminary View of Hydronymic Districts in Northern Athabaskan Prehistory. *Names* 44(4): 253–271.

2008 *Athna Place Names Lists.* 2nd ed. Alaska Native Language Center, University of Alaska Fairbanks.

2010a *Ahtna Travel Narratives: A Demonstration of Shared Geographic Knowledge Among Alaska Athabascans.* Alaska Native Language Center, University of Alaska Fairbanks.

2010b The Concept of Geolinguistic Conservatism in Na-Dene Prehistory. In *The Dene-Yeniseian Connection*, edited by James Kari and Ben A. Potter, pp. 194–222. Anthropological Papers of the University of Alaska, new ser., Vol. 5(1–2). Department of Anthropology and Alaska Native Language Center, University of Alaska Fairbanks.

Kari, James, Gary Holton, Brett Parks, and Robert Charlie

2012 *Lower Tanana Athabaskan Place Names.* Alaska Native Language Center, University of Alaska Fairbanks.

Leer, Jeff

1989 Directional Systems in Athapaskan and Na-Dene. In *Athapaskan Linguistics: Current Perspectives on a Language Family*, edited by Eung-Do Cook and Keren D. Rice, pp. 575–622. Mouton de Gruyter, Berlin.

Levinson, Stephen C.

2003 *Space in Language and Cognition.* Cambridge University Press, Cambridge.

2008 Landscape, Seascape and the Ontology of Places on Rossel Island, Papua New Guinea. *Language Sciences* 30(3): 256–290.

Levinson, Stephen C., and Niclas Burenhult

2009 Semplates: A New Concept in Lexical Semantics? *Language* 85(1): 153–174.

MacLean, Edna Ahgeak

2014 *Iñupiatun Uqaluit Taniktun Sivunniuġutiŋit; North Slope Iñupiaq to English Dictionary.* University of Alaska Press, Fairbanks.

Mark, David M., Andrew G. Turk, Niclas Burenhult, and David Stea

2011 Introduction. In *Landscape in Language*, edited by David M. Mark, Andrew G. Turk, Niclas Burenhult, and David Stea, pp. 1–24. John Benjamins, Amsterdam.

Mark, David M., Andrew G. Turk, and David Stea

2007 Progress on Yindjibarndi Ethnophysiography. In *Proceedings of the 8th International Conference on Spatial Information Theory*, edited by Stephan Winter, Matt Duckham, Lars Kulik, and Benjamin Kuipers, pp. 1–19. Springer, Melbourne.

Thornton, Thomas, ed.

2012 *Haa Léelk'w Hás Aaní Saax'ú: Our Grandparents' Names on the Land.* University of Washington Press, Seattle.

FIGURE 10.1 Yup'ik women at a camp preparing fish to be hung to dry. The woman on the left is holding the handle of an *uluaq*, an arc-shaped knife traditionally used by women, primarily for skinning and cutting fish. Raised on the crossed poles are two sealskin *qayaqs*, both lying on their sides, with their keels facing the stream. The photograph, while undated, was in the possession of Dr. Joseph H. Romig, a physician and Moravian missionary who served villages in the vicinity of Bethel from 1896 to 1905. Joseph H. Romig Collection, acc. no. 90-0043-0-1933-1, Alaska and Polar Regions Collections and Archives, Elmer E. Rasmuson Library, University of Alaska Fairbanks.

LOUANN RANK

10 Watershed Ethnoecology in Yup'ik Place Names of the Yukon-Kuskokwim Delta

Here is this lake, which is the water source. And then during the spring, when the fish are returning upstream, fish traps are used; then, once the fish are plenty, the traps are removed and the fish continue upstream. Then, in the fall, they are used again when the fish are returning downstream, reversing what was done in the spring.
PETER WASKIE (IN PHILLIP, WASKIE, AND NAPOKA 1988)

Traditional Yup'ik place names in the Yukon-Kuskokwim Delta traced seasonal migrations of fish through local waterways, interpreting linear and spatial networks of resources within the tundra. These names remain as historical markers of Indigenous cultural settlement and land use. The immense watersheds of the Yukon River and the Kuskokwim River in southwest Alaska merge in the delta and have supported traditional Yup'ik fishing through time over thousands of square miles. Nearly half of the tundra surface area between the rivers is covered by water, in the form of rivers, shallow lakes, and meandering sloughs and streams. These arteries abound in fish, which were, and still are, central to Yup'ik diet and culture. Among the more important species are Pacific salmon (*Oncorhynchus* spp.), whitefish (*Coregonus* spp.), northern pike (*Esox lucius*), Alaska blackfish (*Dallia pectoralis*), and burbot (*Lota lota*), known locally as lushfish.

Yup'ik names for fish species vary by dialect area within the wider delta, but in the lower Kuskokwim area, the Yup'ik names for the five local species of salmon are *taryaqvak* (chinook/*Oncorhynchus tshawytscha*); *iqalluk* (chum/*O. keta*); *sayak* (sockeye/*O. nerka*); *amaqaayak* (pink/*O. gorbuscha*); and *qakiiyak* (coho/*O. kisutch*) (Coffing et al. 2001, 30). These five species arrive sequentially on the Kuskokwim River from late spring into the fall, in the order just listed, with the runs determining harvesting seasons. The principal non-salmon species include freshwater whitefish: *akakiik* (broad whitefish), *cavirrutnaq* (round whitefish), and *imarpinaq* (Bering cisco); *cuukvak* (northern pike); *can'giiq or imangaq* (Alaska blackfish); and *manignaq* (burbot/lushfish). Of these, local varieties of whitefish, as well as northern pike and burbot, can be harvested throughout the year while blackfish are harvested primarily during late fall and winter months of the year. In keeping with the species, the season, and the waterway, Yup'ik fishers have traditionally employed a variety of methods: gillnets, dipnets, weirs, *taluyaq* (traditional fish trap), and hook and line through the ice.

For those living along the lower Kuskokwim River, whitefish were especially crucial as a food source. Whitefish feed in lakes and small adjoining streams over the summer and then migrate in early fall into tributaries of the Kuskokwim to spawn. As anthropologist Darryl Maddox (1975, 210) observed, whitefish "are taken in the greatest numbers in set nets anchored at the mouths of creeks and sloughs or in eddies along either the main body of the river or a short distance up its tributaries and feeder streams." At the end of the spawning season, the fish move into deeper river waters for the winter, before migrating in the spring back into summer lakes.

Yup'ik oral history traces the enduring presence and movement of fish species between source lakes, streams, and rivers, naming waterways together with associated settlements and seasonal harvest sites to create an ethnoecological map for the region. In this Yup'ik landscape, certain harvest site toponyms share their names with proximate streams and lakes, a repetition that serves to mark pathways along which fish travel, as well as the linear watercourses significant to traditional fishing within watershed networks.

In the 1980s, researchers involved with a program established pursuant to section 14(h)(1) of the 1971 Alaska Native Claims Settlement Act interviewed Yup'ik elders from villages in the Yukon-Kuskokwim Delta, in the course of investigating sites of cultural and historical significance.[1] Although elders from communities along both the Yukon (*Kuigpak*) and Kuskokwim (*Kusquqvaq*) rivers contributed invaluable oral histories of local sites, this chapter focuses on information provided in 1982 and 1988 by elders residing in the lower Kuskokwim communities of Akiachak (*Akiacuaq*), Akiak (*Akiaq*), and Tuluksak (*Tuulkssaaq*). Contemporary residents of these communities are descendants of the families who settled, camped, and named the mosaic of sites along the inland lakes, streams, and rivers of the region. The elders whose comments are

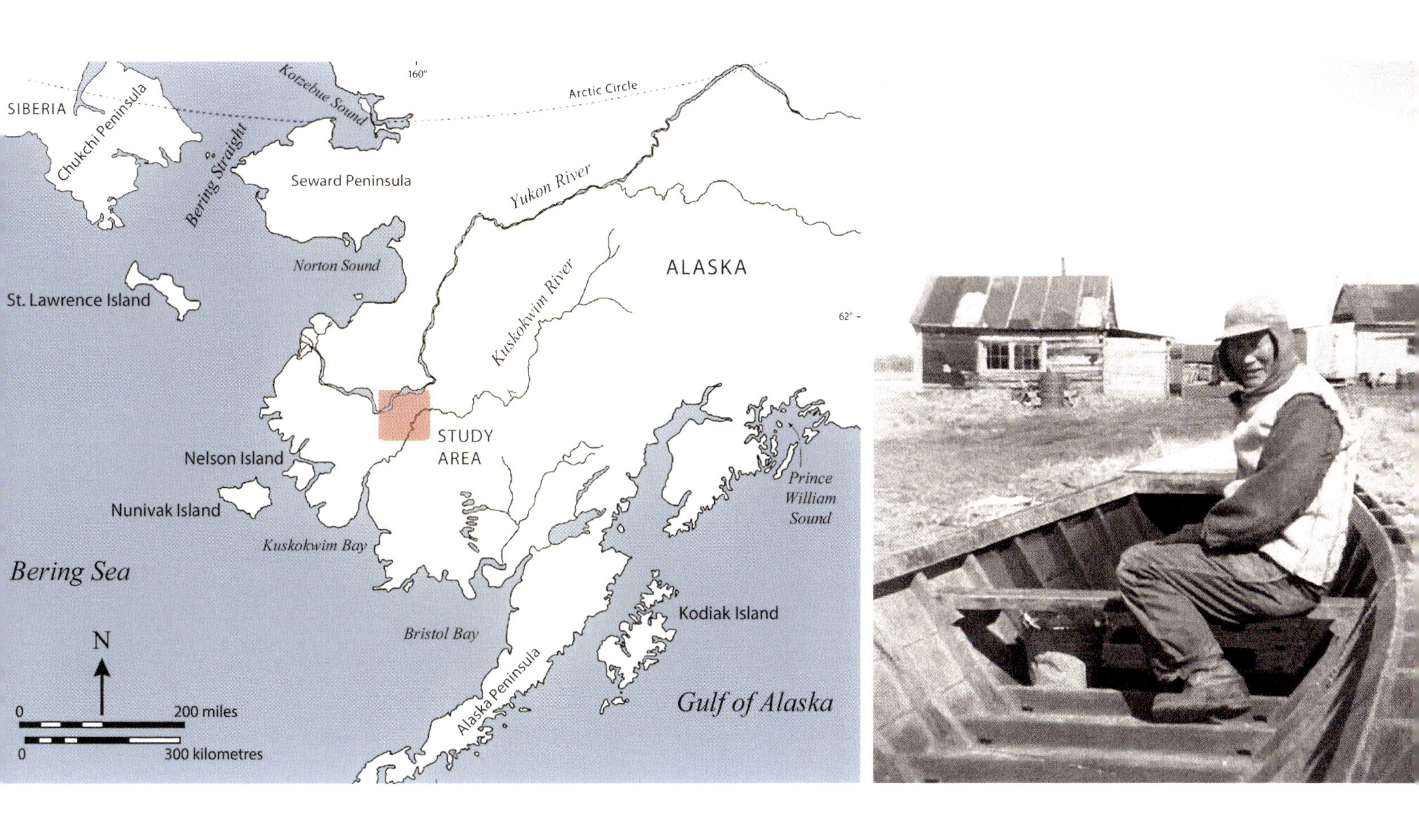

quoted below belonged to interrelated families that had lived in the area for many generations, and all seven were fluent speakers of one or more dialects of Central Alaskan Yup'ik. Together, they identified more than five hundred local place names, which were subsequently mapped onto an area of the Yukon-Kuskokwim Delta of approximately 12,905 square kilometers (4,983 square miles) (figure 10.2). One of them, Joshua Phillip (1912–2008) (figure 10.3), was responsible for the identification of over 350 place names.[2] He offered especially vivid accounts of how these sites were used, along with detailed descriptions of waterways and fish behaviour.

(LEFT) FIGURE 10.2 The study area (indicated by the shaded square) lies between the Yukon and Kuskokwim rivers in southwest Alaska. Map produced by Robert Drozda.

(RIGHT) FIGURE 10.3 Joshua (*Maqista*) Phillip at spring preparation time for wooden boats prior to summer fishing, ca. 1950s, Akiachak, Alaska. From the collection of Tom Kasayulie by permission of Willie Kasayulie (2017).

Landscape Names, Settlements, and the Seasonal Round

Indigenous place names are often rooted in the local landscape and its resources. In the area of the Yukon-Kuskokwim Delta, terms such as *qagatii* ("lake from which a river flows") and *painga* ("mouth") may be incorporated into proper names. For example, the source lake of a stream named *Keggiartuliar* is known as *Keggiartuliaraam Qagatii*, while *Quuyam Painga* ("*Quuyaq*'s mouth") is the name of a traditional seasonal camp located at the point where a stream called *Quuyaq* joins a larger river. As we will see from these and other examples below, such names are fundamentally relational, serving to designate hydrological networks. A similar emphasis on geographic relationships is also visible in names that identify routes or paths, as in *Kuigpagcaraq* ("the way to *Kuigpak* [the Yukon River]"), *Arviryaraq* ("the way to cross over" or "to take a shortcut"), *Kanaryaraq* ("a place or way to go down, usually to water"), and *Qipsaraq* ("the way with a sharp bend").[3]

The primary focus of the present discussion is that of Yup'ik toponyms and hydronyms that identify the natural resources or waterways available at specific sites. Examples of traditional place names identifying resources found at a site include:

Cavirrutnartuli: "one with an abundance of [round] whitefish"

Cimerlituli: "one with plenty of smelt or smelt-like fish"

Cuukvagtuli: "one with plenty of pike"

Qugtuliar: "one with plenty of firewood"

Qugyugtuli: "one with lots of whistling [tundra] swans"

Tayarungualek: "one that has false mare's tail [*Hippurus vulgaris*]"

In the context of a subsistence economy, the functional utility of such names is obvious.

Although Yup'ik knowledge and use of resources in the study area encompassed fur-bearing mammals, waterfowl and other bird species, and diverse flora, of particular interest in the present context is the subsistence round as it related to fish. Simply put, people established settlements and travelled to seasonal camps primarily according to where the fish were. As Joshua Phillip put it, "They did not stay in places where there are no food sources, our ancestors, for the fish was what kept them alive" (1988a, 3). Phillip also illustrated the depth of local knowledge about fish and their movements:

> There were people who camped in the fall, dipnetting whitefish [broad whitefish, Coregonus nasus]. That is the way the river was used. They would also build a weir and fence and set fish traps for whitefish at the upper end of the river. [. . .]
>
> The blackfish was the chief use from the rivers branching off. They would migrate out to the [Kuskokwim] river itself. They would remain in the deeper areas of the river during winter. Then, when the current becomes active, they'd return back upstream to release their eggs in the lake sources. . . .
>
> The lower river in the area behind *Akiacuarmiut* called *Makeggsaq* had many whitefish. The river has a large lake source. There were not only one [kind] of fish but several kinds which have been mentioned. The first fish that swam out are whitefish, then the pike, including lush (loche/burbot). Then at the end of the pike and the lushfish season, the blackfish migration strikes

FIGURE 10.4
Disturbance vegetation denotes the old village site of *Pugcenar*, on the *Elaayiq* river. View to the southeast, May 1988. Photograph by Matthew O'Leary. ANCSA 14(h)(1) Collection, case file AA-10208, Bureau of Indian Affairs, Anchorage.

> when the weather is starting to get cold. There were some little rivers that had fish all winter season. . . .
>
> They certainly knew the kinds of fish swimming in the rivers, our ancestors of the past. They were able to give descriptions of the fish in certain rivers. [. . .] They were very knowledgeable about where the fish come from. Some of the little rivers only had young pike fish with no blackfish. That is the way it is in our area up there. The many settlement sites are all located in places where there are fish. (Phillip 1988a, 1–3)

It is worth noting Phillip's reference to an area "behind *Akiacuarmiut*." As is well known, throughout Yup'ik-speaking areas groups of people commonly refer to themselves by the addition of the postbase *-miut* to the name of the place where they live. Thus, *Akiacuarmiut* literally means "the people of *Akiacuaq*," that is, Akiachak. Particularly at the local level, however, such collective terms often function as metonyms for the village or settlement itself, such that *Akiacuarmiut* becomes a place name, a fused identity that underscores the symbiotic relationship between people and place.

These village communities were fundamental to Yup'ik social organization. Fienup-Riordan (1984, 64) notes that Yup'ik family networks were rooted in "territorially centered village groups," in a pattern whereby "a single village group might gather at a central winter settlement, but ordinarily was scattered among a number of seasonal camps." Resource use areas extended out from settlements to include seasonal camps that were associated with specific extended families and individuals who used the site or sites and had become familiar with that locality. However, land was not owned in the Western sense: it was not regarded as personal property. As Joshua Phillip (1988a, 17) explained, "Traditionally, people were always moving and did not claim to have ownership to the land. They all survived from the land. [. . .] They all shared the land."

Yup'ik customary land use supported shared access; however, the established occupants of a site were recognized as holding certain rights of usage. As Phillip described, "it was the custom of the people to always notify the usual hunter in the area before someone decides to hunt there. We were told to notify the seasonal hunter in the area. Even though they didn't claim ownership of the land and allowed one another hunting rights, they were always careful not to hurt the other's feelings" (1988a, 19). These comments are consistent with patterns of Yup'ik land use and territoriality also found in the lower Yukon River area. As summarized by Robert Wolfe (1981, 242), "there are rightful occupants and users of a region of land and water, but no rightful owners. This idea approximates the concept of 'usufruct.'"

Collective Yup'ik knowledge of kinship ties remain culturally central, and narratives concerning traditional sites often include acknowledgment of the individuals who generally hunted and fished there. The hunting and fishing areas discussed here were used by families affiliated with the modern communities of Akiachak, Akiak, and Tuluksak. Each village's resource use area was loosely bounded according to the families who seasonally camped at named peripheral sites. Village camp areas overlapped between the Kuskokwim and Yukon rivers, and continued southeast of the Kuskokwim beyond Tuluksak.

The blend of ecological significance and social history attached to many Yup'ik place names is encapsulated in Joshua Phillip's description of an old settlement called *Pugcenar* (figure 10.4), located on the *Elaayiq* river about 32 kilometres (20 miles) north of the contemporary community of Akiachak. As he explained, the site had been occupied longer than anyone could remember and had been used by the ancestors of those who eventually became the Akiacuarmiut. These ancestors had once occupied a site named *Nunapiaq,* which was located "about one or two miles" upriver from the site that became Akichuaq. According to Phillip:

> *Pugcenar* is an old village site from time immemorial. Our ancestors probably didn't even know when it became inhabited. But I know that it is one of the original sites [. . .] the houses were no longer standing even before I was aware of my surroundings, but there are a lot of house pits. That was how that place was. But then as life continued, houses were once again built. Then after the residents all died off, another person reinhabited it. . . .
>
> Beginning from time immemorial, whenever a site was deserted, another person would come in and re-inhabit it, that's how it was since the past. They never settled just anywhere; they'd set up sites where fish were bountiful. That is how *Pugcenar* is. [. . .] It was a site which was occupied by the residents of *Nunapiaq,* who are now the *Akiacuaq* peoples today. If they had not moved they would have been the people of *Nunapiaq,* those residents of *Akiacuaq.* It was right above their village, close by. (Phillip 1988b, 1–2)

Phillip went on to comment on the origin of the site's name:

> The meaning they say [. . .] there is a lot of fish there, those ones, whitefish, and they are usually fat. When they cook those, they would skim the fat with a wooden spoon, skimming them. That is what is referred to as skimming (*pugciluteng)* the oil, doing like so (motioning with hands) that is why it is referred to as *Pugcenar.* They would cook the stomachs of the fish and when the oil rendered, then they would skim them with a wooden spoon, dipping out the fat and storing them carefully. [. . .] That is the meaning [of] *Pugcenar*; it was because of the fat fish. It is [. . .] the old village site of the residents of the Akiacuaq people, their ancestors. (Phillip 1988b, 4)[4]

Thus, embedded in the name *Pugcenar* is knowledge not only of the history of the site but also the preparation and use of whitefish, for which the site was named.

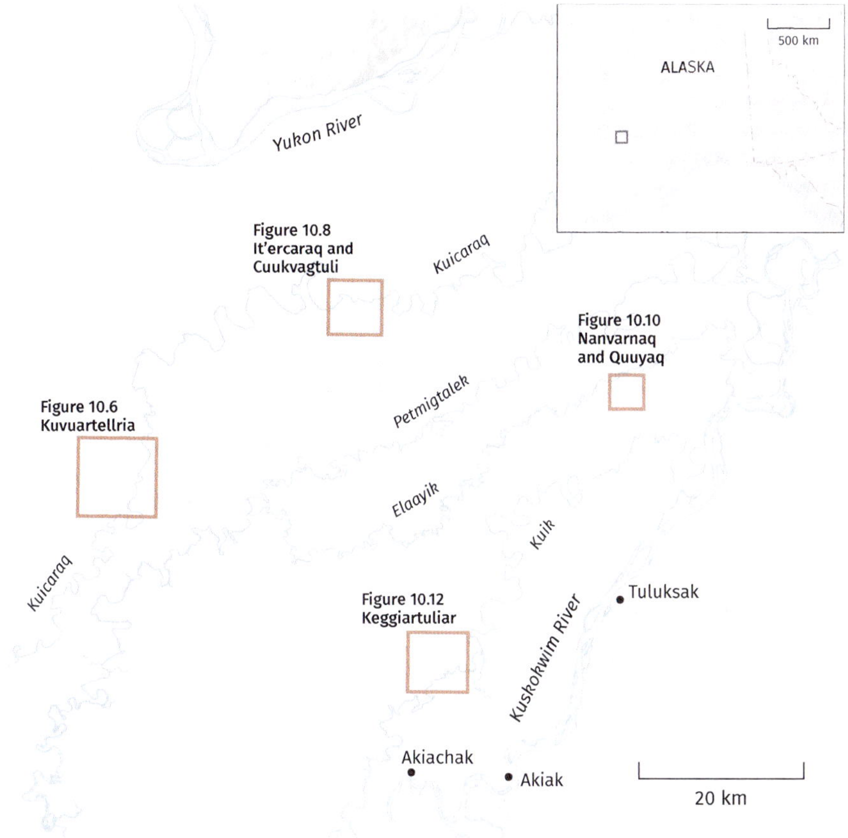

FIGURE 10.5 Source and stream networks. The distance from the community of Akiachak on the Kuskowim River northwest to the Yukon River is approximately 80 kilometres (50 miles). Map produced by Robert Drozda.

Source Lake and Stream Site Networks

"The mouths of every little river have old settlements," said Joshua Phillip (1988c, 6). Traditional settlements and seasonal camps in the Yukon-Kuskokwim Delta were indeed often located at the outlet, or *igyaraq* ("throat"), of a source lake, or at the *painga*, or mouth, or *painga* of a lake's stream emanating from the lake as it entered a larger stream or river.

As an analysis of place names in the lower Kuskokwim region located within the traditional resource use areas of Akiachak, Akiak, and Tuluksak reveals, an emergent conceptual pattern for certain fish harvest sites is evident across the study area. In this pattern, camps and settlements were often named in relation to their watercourse sources. Accordingly, Yup'ik hydronyms would trace a distinct pathway from a source along a stream to a site, with source lake, stream, and harvest sites mutually identified by a shared base name. Where a site is named along a stream emanating from a source lake, the source and site, and often the connecting stream, may have the same base name. A source lake may have *qagatii* or *qagan* ("lake from which a river flows") appended to the base name. This source, stream, and site naming pattern is visible at a number of fish harvesting network sites in the study area, of which six have been selected for discussion, situated in one of four localities on the *Kuicaraq*, the *Elaayiq*, and the *Kuik* rivers. These six harvest networks are described within the four localities: *Kuvuartellria*, *It'ercaraq* and *Cuukvagtuli*, *Nanvarnaq* and *Quuyaq*, and *Keggiartuliar*.

FIGURE 10.6 Location of the seasonal fish camp *Kuvuartellria* relative to the surrounding water system. Note the overland winter trail connecting the site to Akiachak, on the Kuskokwim River. Map produced by Robert Drozda, from USBIA MAP 88CAL12A, Marshall B-1.

KUVUARTELLRIA

The fish camp site named *Kuvuartellria* is located at the mouth of a stream also called *Kuvuartellria* ("one that suddenly poured out") that originates at a source lake known as *Kuvuartellriim Qagatii*. From the lake, the *Kuvuartellria* stream meanders southeast through a marsh before flowing into the *Kuicaraq* river (known in English as the Johnson River) at the site of the fish camp. Thus, the stream emanating from the source lake is called *Kuvuartellria*; the source lake is *Kuvuartellriim Qagatii*; and the seasonal camp named *Kuvuartellria* is at the mouth of the stream. Another stream, called *Kuvuartellriim Egmiumanra* ("*Kuvuartellria*'s feeder"), joins the lake at its upper end (figure 10.6). As Wassillie George Sr. (1924–1996), of Akiachak, explained: "*Kuvuartellria* has a *qagan*, a lake source, and stream ['river feeder'] running off. That one used to abound with blackfish. And all the fish traps would be full of the overnight catch" (George 1988b, 12).

In both spring and fall, residents of Akiachak would travel up to *Kuvuartellria* to fish, harvesting primarily Alaska blackfish but also whitefish. As George notes, fish traps were used for blackfish, and people would dipnet for whitefish. He remembered the site well:

> *Kuvuartellria* was my hunting place. That *Kuvuartellria* was a place to catch blackfish, fish, that is, like a supply of fish (or "food"). But now, I see, the beaver have made it less of a river. And sometimes that *Kuvuartellria* tends to produce *neqpiat* ("real fish"), little white fish. That's how . . . that's how that *Kuvuartellria* is.

FIGURE 10.7 Replica of a traditional Yup'ik *kuusqun*—a loosely woven grass basket used to store freshly harvested fish—made by students of Akiachak School, 2015. This basket is about 23 cm (9 in.) in diameter and 38 cm (15 in.) long. Photograph provided by Sophie Kasayulie with permission of Katie George, Akiachak (2017).

> ... And whenever we go up to *Kuvuartellria* by dog team or boat in the fall and spring, we go back and forth to that one. And blocking the river, we [would] dipnet, at *Kuicaraq*. Sometimes we would catch a few fish. Those much earlier used to catch fish there. And when they went fishing for blackfish from there, they would fill over 15 or 20 grass baskets full of blackfish from that *Kuvuartellria*. (1988b, 2)

George refers here to a type of basket called a *kuusqun*, woven of grass or reeds, that was traditionally used for storing and transporting freshly caught fish (figure 10.7). Joan Neck—an elder from the village of *Kassigluq*, situated inland between the Yukon and Kuskokwim rivers roughly 60 kilometres (37 miles) west of Akiachak—described the *kuusqun* as follows: "We made them different sizes, some bottoms were almost as big as a large tub. We fill the grass *kuusqun* with gutted white fish, big ones in separate *kuusqun*, little ones in another. And we made ones out of dried reeds, bigger than those grass ones. We fill these with dried salmon" (quoted in Monica Shelden, pers. comm., 2017).

George went on to describe seasonal travel between Akiachak and the *Kuvuartellria* fish camp:

> The people of *Kuvuartellria* go to spring camp there at its mouth [the mouth of the *Kuvuartellria* stream]. And it's a travel route to *Akiacuaq* from there. When they move from *Kuvuartellria* they use it as a trail. And they sled by way of its *qagan* in the winter. (1988b, 10)

As was generally the case with such camp sites, *Kuvuartellria* was occupied consistently over time by certain families, often interrelated, and their descendants. George Moses Sr. (1920–2005), of Akiachak, emphasized the importance of family connections:

> So that is *Kuvuartellria*. They used to call them *Kuvuartellriarmiut*. It was their fall camp, they would go fall camping there. And we, joining them, used to be there [. . .] because, I discovered, we were related to them through the children of my father's older sister, and through this one [. . .] whose habitation it is, the one to whom it was handed down. (Moses 1988a, 15–16)

As mentioned earlier, such extended family groups did not own these sites, in the Western sense of holding legal title to land. They did not claim sovereign power over these lands, but they did exercise certain rights of access and use, which were then transferred from one generation to the next.

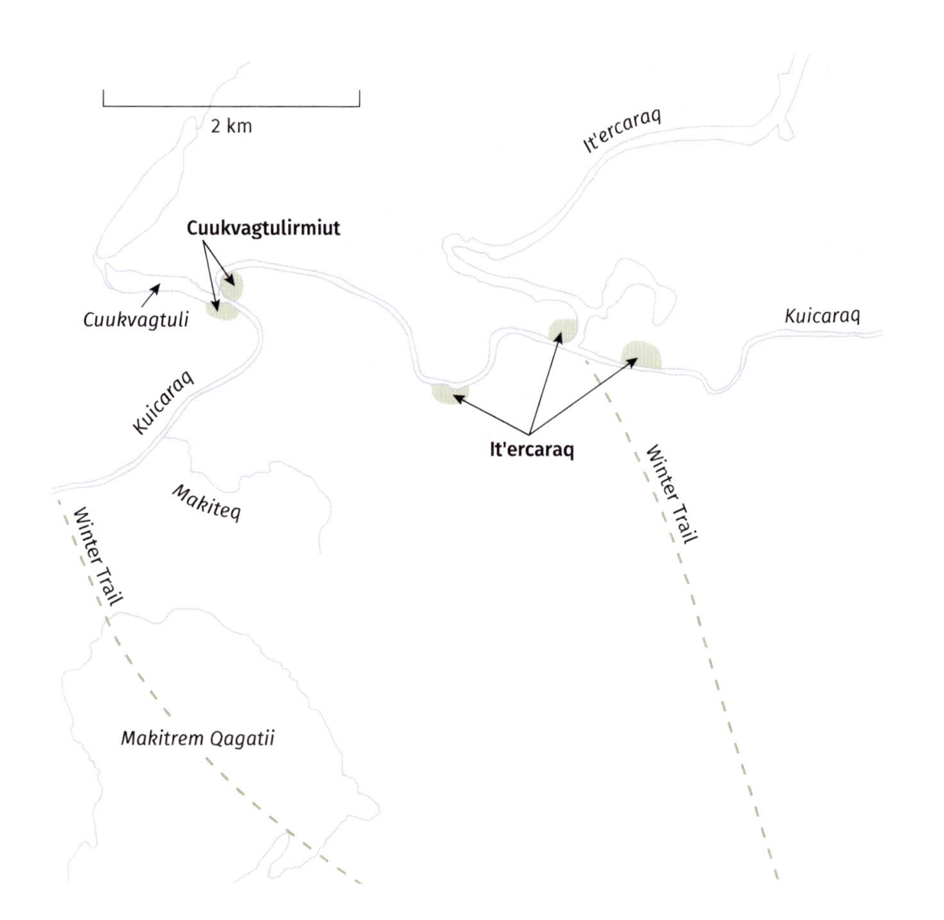

FIGURE 10.8 The *Kuicaraq* river flows to the southwest, so the two *Cuukvagtulirmiut* sites lie downriver from the those at the junction of the *Kuicaraq* and *It'ercaraq* rivers. Two overland trails lead to Akiachak. Map produced by Robert Drozda, from USBIA Map 88CAL12A, Russian Mission B-7.

(FACING) FIGURE 10.9 "Aug. 1896. Bethel. Fish trap." Established as a Moravian mission in 1885 on the Kuskokwim River, Bethel is approximately 30 km (19 mi.) downriver from Akiachak. Note that the funnel-shaped wicker entrance commonly inserted into the larger end of a fish trap is not pictured here. Joseph H. Romig Collection, accession no. 90-043-863a, Archives, Alaska and Polar Regions Department, University of Alaska Fairbanks.

IT'ERCARAQ AND *CUUKVAGTULI*

Further upriver on the *Kuicaraq* were three sites named *It'ercaraq*: one site located directly at the confluence of the *It'ercaraq* river and the *Kuicaraq*, with the other two on either side (figure 10.8). The word *it'ercaraq* means "place or way to put something in quickly or briefly."

Joshua Phillip (1982, 5) reported that his grandfather, *Ircalik*, was "the first in this land" at *It'ercaraq* and used the area all year round. Peter Nick (ca. 1917–2010), a resident of Russian Mission, located on the Yukon River roughly due north of Tuluksak, also remembered fishing at *It'ercaraq*:

> They call this river *It'ercaraq*. And mouth, mouth of *It'ercaraq*, used to be old, old village. And they call them *It'ercaraq* village. [. . .] I used to [travel], every year, back and forth, spring and fall time, by that winter trail. . . . In fall time, we used to put a fence in that creek. A lot of whitefish in there. With fish trap. Used to be this [. . .] round. Maybe 30 feet long. They made it by hand. Sticks. Sometimes boatload of whitefish. Nothing but whitefish, they come out in fall time. In October, they started [. . .] to run. [. . .] People long ago used to stay in a place where lot of fish. Lot of blackfish and whitefish. They stay in winter and summer, summer they can go for salmon. And hook whitefish. Even they dry those blackfish. Put through the sticks. Lots of them, bunch of them. [. . .] And [. . .] just dry them and put it away. Wintertime, they eat it with whitefish oil, seal oil. And some [. . .] make it blackfish from under the ice. On the little creeks. (Nick 1982, 1–2)

Writing at the end of the nineteenth century ethnologist Edward W. Nelson described the traditional Yup'ik *taluyaq*, or fish trap, of the sort to which Nick refers:

> On lower Yukon and Kuskokwim rivers wicker fish traps are set, with a brush and wicker-work fence connecting them with the shore. These fish traps form an elongated cone, with a funnel-shape entrance in the larger end. Each has two long poles at the sides of the mouth or broad end and another at the small end, by means of which it is raised or lowered. It is set at the outer end of the wicker-work fence [. . .] and held in place by poles driven in the river bottom with their ends projecting above the water. (Nelson [1899] 1983, 184)

Cuukvagtulirmiut is the name applied to two seasonal sites at the outlet of the lake called *Cuukvagtuli* ("one with plenty of pike fish"). In this example, the lake outlet also forms a confluence with the *Kuicaraq*.

Wassillie George, Sr., of Akiachak, knew both *It'ercaraq* and *Cuukvagtuli*:

> When I became old enough to remember, this is how we were: by dogs, by boats. There were no snowmobiles. We would travel around by dog team. We would relocate in the fall and in the spring. We used to be in the same site as our relatives from the Yukon, *Kuigpagmiut*, at the mouth of *It'ercaraq, It'ercaram Painga*. That is, those cross-cousins of mine. And so there were mud houses, perhaps five in number. [. . .] Then, we lived this way: in the fall, when I observed it once one fall, blockading the river, they dipped whitefish all night with dipnets. The boat was really full. Together, the relatives would feed on that supply of fish when they did that. (George 1988a, 2)
>
> . . . Downriver from *It'ercaraq*, that one that is a *kangiqucuk* ["a little bit of a lake source"] is called *Cuukvagtuliq*. That's what we call it. [. . .] This *It'ercaraq* is a former settlement of mine and my ancestors. (George 1988b, 7, 9)

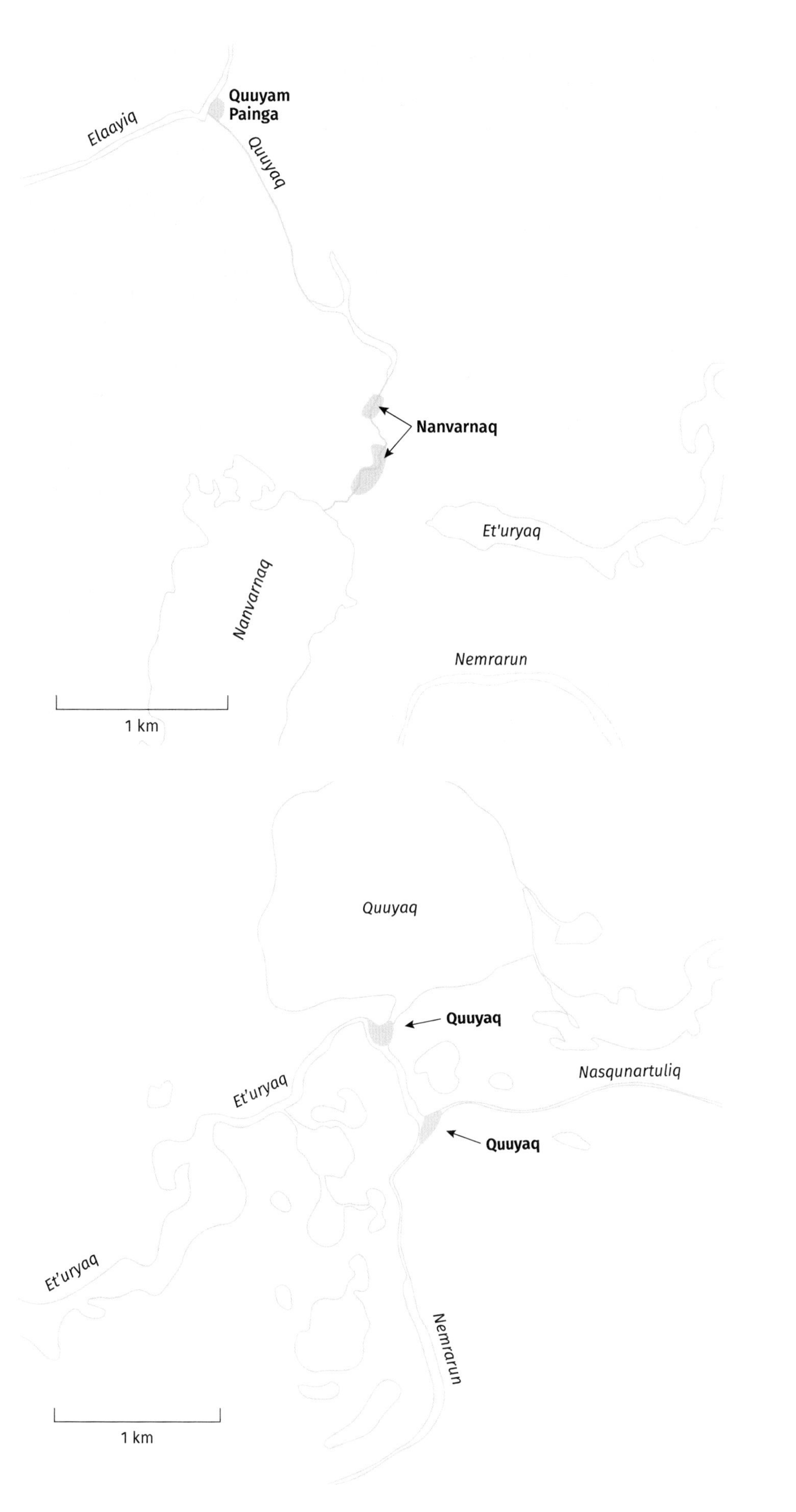

FIGURE 10.10 *Nanvarnaq* seasonal camps and old settlement sites. *Quuyam Painga*, also a seasonal camp, is located at the confluence of the *Quuyaq* and the *Elaayiq*. Adapted from AHP-CPSU site map for BLM AA-10336. Original map drawn by Ken Pratt and Sue Steinacher, 1982.

FIGURE 10.11 *Quuyaq* seasonal camps and old settlement sites, approximately 10 kilometres (6 miles) east of *Nanvarnaq* sites. Adapted from AHP-CPSU site map for BLM AA-10331 and AA-10332. Original map drawn by Ken Pratt and Sue Steinacher, 1982.

NANVARNAQ AND *QUUYAQ*

On the upper drainage of the *Elaayiq* river (location C in figure 10.5) are two large lakes, *Nanvarnaq* ("one like a big lake") and *Quuyaq* ("closed-in area"), with which a total of five named fish camp sites are associated (figures 10.10 and 10.11). Because of the close proximity of these sites, some residents reported having camped at either *Nanvarnaq* or *Quuyaq* at various times (Wise 1982, 1–2).[5] The remains of house pits were found in the 1980s at the settlement sites closest to each lake. Year-round settlement reportedly ended by the late 1800s, followed by seasonal camps at each location. The *Quuyaq* site at the confluence of the *Nemrarun* and the *Nasqunartuliq* streams (see figure 10.11) was used as a seasonal camp from the early 1900s. (Pratt 1983a, 1983b, 1983c).

Study interviewees for these harvest networks were from Tuluksak, some of whose residents continued to use *Nanvarnaq* and *Quuyaq* in the 1980s for spring and fall camps. *Et'uryaq*, the elongated lake between *Quuyaq* and *Nanvarnaq*, is translated as "a big deep one." On the 1952 USGS map (Russian Mission B-6), the stream named *Quuyaq* that flows from *Nanvarnaq* into the *Elaayiq* river does not appear to be physically connected to the lake of *Quuyaq,* but their shared name indicates such a connection formerly existed.

Edward Wise (ca. 1921–1999), a Tuluksak resident, described the sites of *Nanvarnaq* and *Quuyaq*. *Nanvarnaq*, he said, "was a spring camp":

> Younger generation, we just move in[to] a spring camp. In the fall I lived there, hunted. This is an old, old village . . . before I was born. [. . .] My dad used to stay there in the camp in fall and spring. [. . .] Sometimes we live here in *Quuyaq*. (1–2)

> . . . And then there's another lake to *Nanvarnaq*. [. . .] We use that long lake. [. . .] Summer and winter in here. I think from *Nanvarnaq*, they move here [*Quuyam Painga*] . . . because there's lots of fish in there. [. . .] Fishing, whitefish. They move from here [*Nanvarnaq*], sometimes they live in springtime . . . *Quuyaq*, yeah. (3, 5)

> . . . We call that little creek *Quuyaq* to *Nanvarnaq*. [. . .] Only when they move down there they stop at *Quuyam Painga* . . . they just stop there to get proper rest [. . .] There's no cabin. Just a camp. [. . .] Two, three days. 'Cause they had to row . . . by hand. They rest, *Quuyum Painga*. (Wise 1982, 13–14)

KEGGIARTULIAR

The old settlement site and seasonal camp of *Keggiartuliar* is several miles downstream from its named lake source (figure 10.12). A stream meanders southward from *Keggiartuliaraam Qagatii* to terminate at a lower lake, where the *Keggiartuliar* site is located at that lake's outlet into a stream named *Keggiartuliar*. Linking *Keggiartuliar*'s source lake and harvest site by name across miles of marsh and tundra reflects a thorough understanding of both the watershed and fish migrations. The knowledge required to name the *Keggiartuliar* network is more fully illustrated by the USGS map used in the field by ANCSA researchers to record place names, which shows the complexity of intervening streams and ponds in the area (figure 10.13).

Joshua Phillip called attention to the association of *Keggiartuliar* ("something to do with biting well, as with an animal or insect") with several interrelated families who had occupied the site for many generations:

> It is *Keggiartuliar*. An old settlement, a spring camp and a fall camp, and their ancestors used to stay over during the summer, because it was a good fishing site for whitefish, this area here. [. . .] They referred to them as the residents of *Keggiartuliar* [. . .] as the people of *Keggiartuliar*. [6]
>
> *Akiacuaq* already had had a school for some time when there were still houses still standing there, and it was still inhabited by people at that time, it was around 1929. Well, it was since a long time ago they talk about the residents of that village, *Keggiartuliar*. That river is a good fishing area. [The people of *Keggiartuliar*] were related. Their descendants, the people that lived there, are living down at *Akiacuaq*. (Phillip and Waskie 1988, 6, 10)

"The ancestors remained there," Phillip recalled. "There was always somebody there" (10).

The *Keggiartuliar* site is distinctive both for the distance that separates it from its source lake, *Keggiartuliaraam Qagatii*, and for the intricate network of streams that intervenes between the two. The shared name suggests that the people of *Keggiartuliar* had a close understanding of the migratory behaviour of fish and the paths along which they travel. A somewhat similar situation is visible at the *Kuvuartellria* harvest site, which is situated more than a mile from its source lake. The two are linked by a somewhat tenuously defined stream, also called *Kuvuartellria*, that makes its way through an expanse of marshy terrain.

In contrast, several of the sites—*Cuukvagtulirmiut*, *Nanvarnaq*, and *Quuyaq*—sit very near the outlet of their respective source lakes, with which they exhibit a simple pairing of names. In a few cases, camp sites share a name with the stream on which they are located, most often at its confluence with a larger river. Yet what stands out is the connection between a fishing camp and a source lake, as signalled by a shared name. The Yup'ik residents of the area recognized and named each harvest network holistically, not only according to where fish were available but as to how they got there.

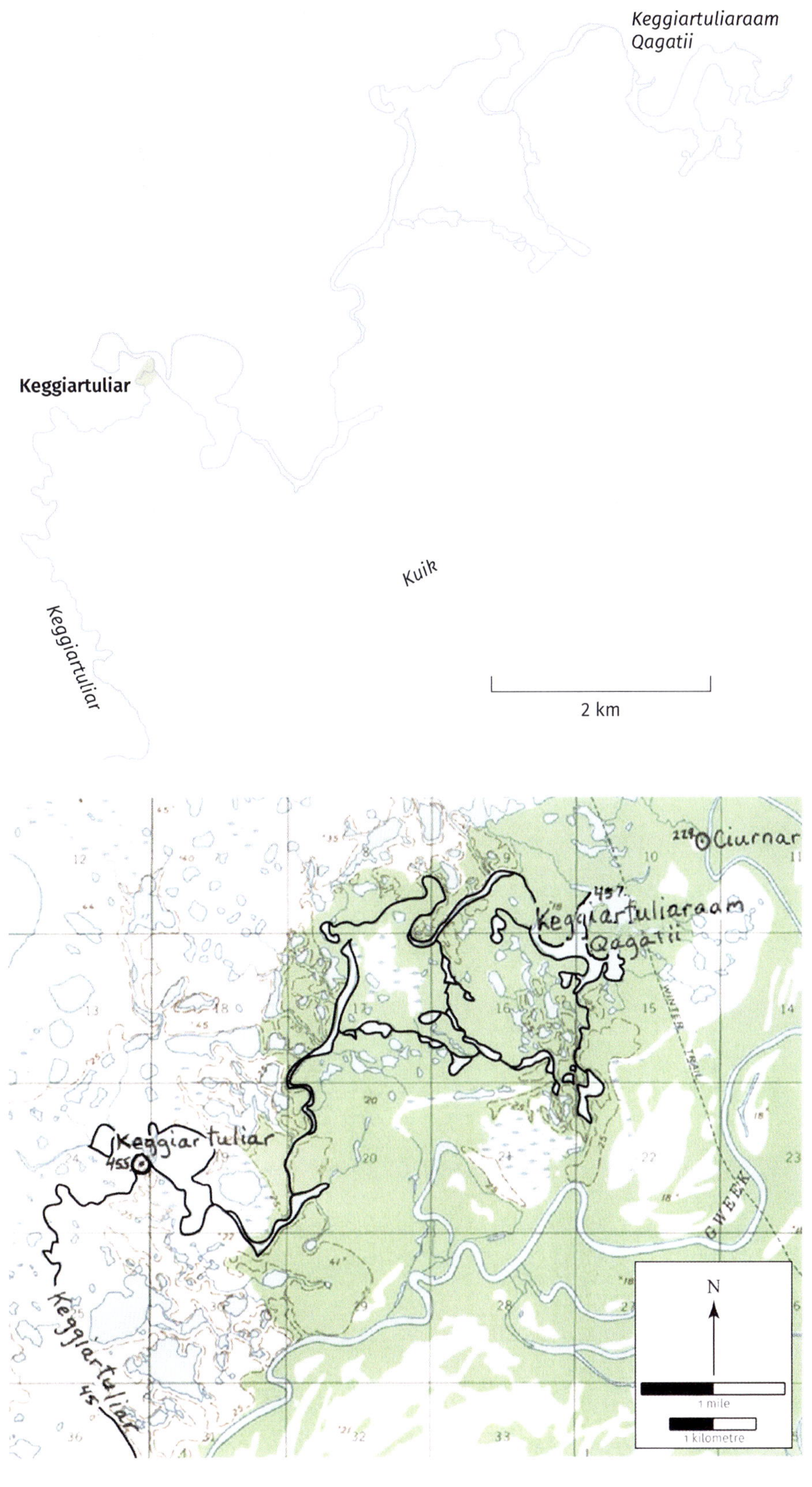

FIGURE 10.12 The old settlement and seasonal camp of *Keggiartuliar* is located at the outlet of a lake several miles from the named source lake, *Keggiartuliaraam Qagatii*. Map produced by Robert Drozda, from USBIA MAP88CAL12A, Russian Mission A-7.

FIGURE 10.13 The site of *Keggiartuliar* relative to its source lake and stream continuing southward. Place names were recorded by ANCSA researchers onto USGS map (1954) 1:63,360 Russian Mission A-7.

FIGURE 10.14 "Ougavig Natives. Nov. 1902. At Thanksgiving Time." Fish trap sections frame Yup'ik residents of the Moravian mission at *Uaravik* (or "Ougavig," as it was also spelled). The mission was established in 1892 at the pre-existing Yup'ik site, located approximately 100 kilometres (62 miles) upriver on the Kuskokwim from Akiachak. Although the Moravians abandoned the site in 1908, Yup'ik use and occupancy of *Uaravik* continued into the early 1920s. Joseph H. Romig Collection, accession no. 90-043-863a, Alaska and Polar Regions Collections and Archives, University of Alaska Fairbanks.

Conclusions

In Yup'ik communities, fishing was more than a subsistence strategy: it was integral to community life itself (as figure 10.14 suggests). The location of settlements and seasonal camp sites was grounded in an intimate understanding of local watersheds, as well as the fish present in them, and place names embodied this knowledge. A name might explicitly refer to fish resources: *Cuukvagtuli*, "place with plenty of pike," for example, or more indirectly signal significance, as with *Pugcenar,* whose name literally refers to the skimming of oil and implies "fat fish."

The Yup'ik place names discussed in this chapter illustrate the use of linguistic continuity to structurally describe dynamic ecological systems, an understanding of which was essential to subsistence strategies focused on the harvest of fish. Some names involved, such as "one that suddenly poured out" or "closed-in area," in and of themselves do not denote relationship, but rather illustrate connection through their repetition. Such patterns of naming broaden the capacity of language to interpret the landscape in terms of spatial configurations.

The historical and cultural context of Yup'ik place names is clearly integral to a more complete understanding of the communities' interactions with the landscape and its resources. An ethnoecological record exists in the names given to landforms, river drainage systems, and harvest practices, names whose origins and contextual meanings are ultimately reliant on collective memory embedded in shared oral history.

During the ANSCA 14(h)(1) interviews, elders of Akiachak, Akiak, and Tuluksak would often emphasize that specific individuals should be consulted for accurate knowledge of particular sites because of the long use of the sites by their families, and their consequent awareness of change over time. As George Moses Sr. observed of historical place names, "All of these, you know, after they have not been talked about all these years cannot be suddenly written down" (Moses 1988b, 16). Each place name has a long history. The names can be recorded, but, absent their particular cultural narratives, they have less meaning. As change continues over time, that meaning has come to reside largely in the knowledge of elders whose stories and landscape interpretations this chapter has endeavoured to capture.

Acknowledgements

This study builds on the work and insights of Robert Drozda, former manager of the ANCSA 14(h)(1) records in the Alaska and Polar Regions Department of the Elmer E. Rasmuson Library at the University of Alaska Fairbanks (UAF), whose detailed work on an impressive map of Yup'ik place names (compiled with Vernon Chimegalrea and other 1988 ANCSA field crew members) piqued my interest and made this research possible. This chapter owes its existence to the advice, perseverance, and map assistance of Kenneth Pratt, ANCSA program manager, Bureau of Indian Affairs, Anchorage. Dale Slaughter contributed final details for some of the maps. Rose Speranza, of Alaska and Polar Regions Collections and Archives at the Elmer E. Rasmuson Library, UAF assisted generously with photo research. Steven Street and Monica Shelden of the Cultural and Environmental Sciences Department of the Association of Village Council Presidents, Bethel, Alaska, assisted with *kuusqun* research, as did Sophie Kasayulie of Akiachak, who provided the photograph of a *kuusqun* shown in figure 10.7. I am forever grateful to Sophie and Willie Kasayulie for allowing the use of a photograph of Joshua Phillip from the collection of Tom Kasayulie. William Schneider, former curator of the Oral History Program at UAF, generously extended my research through support for travel, interviews, and map work carried out with elders of Akiachak, Akiak, and Tuluksak in 2004 as part of the Yupiit School District Project Jukebox. Early stages of the study for this chapter were supported financially by the UAF Center for Global Change and the International Arctic Research Center, as well as by the US National Science Foundation, through the Integrative Graduate Education and Research Training of the Resilience and Adaptation Program at UAF.

Notes

1 Under section 14(h)(1) of the Alaska Native Claims Settlement Act (ANCSA), passed by the US Congress in 1971, the Bureau of Indian Affairs was mandated to investigate late claims brought by Alaska Natives in connection with sites of cultural or historical significance and also burial sites (see Pratt 2009a). The program ultimately generated an irreplaceable collection of taped oral history interviews, translated transcripts, site investigation files, maps, and photographs (see O'Leary, Drozda, and Pratt 2009, 425–457). The interviews on which this chapter builds represent a total of more than ninety tape recordings within this collection.

2 A biography and photograph of Joshua Phillip, accompanied by excerpts from two 1988 ANCSA 14(h)(1) interviews, can be found at http://www.jukebox.uaf.edu/yupiit/akiachak/htm/interviews.htm, a page on the *Akiachak Then and Now* website, one of three schools featured on the Yupiit School District Project Jukebox website (http://www.jukebox.uaf.edu/yupiit/yupiit.htm).

3 Unless otherwise indicated, translations of Yup'ik words and place names are based on those originally provided by the late Irene Reed, who also supplied the orthographically correct spellings. A Yup'ik language specialist and former director of the Alaska Native Language Center (ANLC) at the University of Alaska Fairbanks, Reed was instrumental in developing the orthographic system that remains in use for Yup'ik today.

4 The original audio recording of Phillip's description of *Pugcenar*, accompanied by an English translation, is available on the *Pugcenar* Project Jukebox website at http://jukebox.uaf.edu/site7/interviews/4173.

5 Those for *Nanvarnaq* and *Quuyaq* were taken from ANCSA 14(h)(1) site survey forms AA-10335 (*Nanvarnaq*) and AA-10331 (*Quuyaq*) (Pratt 1983c, 9; 1983a, 9).

References

Coffing, Michael W., Louis Brown, Gretchen Jennings, and Charles J. Utermohle

2001 *The Subsistence Harvest and Use of Wild Resources in Akiachak, Alaska, 1998.* Technical Paper No. 258. Alaska Department of Fish and Game, Division of Subsistence, Juneau.

Conklin, Harold C.

1954 An Ethnoecological Approach to Shifting Agriculture. *Transactions of the New York Academy of Sciences* 17: 133–142.

Fienup-Riordan, Ann

1984 Regional Groups on the Yukon-Kuskokwim Delta. *Études/Inuit/Studies* 8 (supp.): 63–93.

George, Wassillie, Sr.

1988a Taped interview and transcript. Robert Drozda, interviewer; Vernon Chimegalrea, interpreter. Akiachak, Alaska. 30 August. Transcription/translation by Lucy Coolidge Daniels and Irene Reed. Tape 88CAL173. Bureau of Indian Affairs, ANCSA Office, Anchorage.

1988b Taped interview and transcript. Robert Drozda, interviewer; Vernon Chimegalrea, interpreter. Akiachak, Alaska. 1 September. Transcription/translation by Lucy Coolidge Daniels and Irene Reed. Tape 88CAL183. Bureau of Indian Affairs, ANCSA Office, Anchorage.

Henkelman, James W., and Kurt H. Vitt

1985 *Harmonious to Dwell: The History of the Alaska Moravian Church, 1885–1985.* Tundra Press, Moravian Seminary and Archives, Bethel, Alaska.

Maddox, Darryl M.

1975 On the Distribution of Kuskowagamiut Fishcamps: A Study in the Ecology of Adaptive Radiation. In *Maritime Adaptations of the Pacific*, edited by R. W. Casteel and G. I. Quimby, pp. 197–219. Mouton Publishers, Chicago.

Moses, George, Sr.

1988a Taped interview and transcript. Robert Drozda, interviewer; Vernon Chimegalrea, interpreter. Akiachak, Alaska. 23 August. Transcription/translation by Lucy Coolidge Daniels, Sophie Manutoli Shields and Irene Reed. Tape 88CAL161. Bureau of Indian Affairs, ANCSA Office, Anchorage.

1988b Taped interview and transcript. Robert Drozda, interviewer; Vernon Chimegalrea, interpreter. Akiachak, Alaska. 23 August. Transcription/translation by Lucy Coolidge Daniels, Sophie Manutoli Shields, and Irene Reed. Tape 88CAL162. Bureau of Indian Affairs, ANCSA Office, Anchorage.

Nelson, Edward W.

[1899] 1983 *The Eskimo About Bering Strait.* Bureau of American Ethnology, 18th Annual Report, Part 1, 1896–1897. Smithsonian Institution Press, Washington, DC.

Nick, Peter

1982 Taped interview. Alan Ziff and Nan Collins, interviewers. Transcription by Matthew O'Leary. *Itercaraq* (AA-10182), Alaska. 25 June. Tape 82RSM015. Bureau of Indian Affairs, ANCSA Office, Anchorage.

O'Leary, Matthew B., Robert M. Drozda, and Kenneth L. Pratt

2009 ANCSA Section 14(h)(1) Records. In *Chasing the Dark: Perspectives on Place, History and Alaska Native Land Claims,* edited by Kenneth L. Pratt, pp. 452–457. Bureau of Indian Affairs, ANCSA Office, Anchorage.

Phillip, Joshua

1982 Taped interview. Alan Ziff and Kate Rauch, interviewers; Anna Phillip, interpreter and translator. Conducted on sites *Urarraq* (AA-10183), *Itercaraq* (AA-10182), *Cupeggnartuli* (AA-10181) and *Ayakaucetalek* (AA-11474), Alaska. 16 July. Tape 82RSM025. Bureau of Indian Affairs, ANCSA Office, Anchorage.

1988a Taped interview and transcript. Robert Drozda, interviewer; Vernon Chimegalrea, interpreter. Tuluksak, Alaska. 29 June. Transcription/translation by Marie Meade and Irene Reed. Tape 88CAL046. Bureau of Indian Affairs, ANCSA Office, Anchorage.

1988b Taped interview and transcript. Robert Drozda, interviewer; Vernon Chimegalrea, interpreter and transcriber/translator. Tuluksak, Alaska. 1 July. Tape 88CAL048. Bureau of Indian Affairs, ANCSA Office, Anchorage.

1988c Taped interview and transcript. Robert Drozda, interviewer; Vernon Chimegalrea, interpreter. Transcription/translation by Marie Meade. Tuluksak, Alaska. 9 July. Tape 88CAL058. Bureau of Indian Affairs, ANCSA Office, Anchorage.

Phillip, Joshua, Peter Waskie, and Peter Napoka

1988 Taped interview and transcript. Robert Drozda, interviewer; Vernon Chimegalrea, interpreter and transcriber/translator. Tuluksak, Alaska. 27 May. Tape 88CAL004. Bureau of Indian Affairs, ANCSA Office, Anchorage.

Pratt, Kenneth L.

1983a ANCSA 14(h)(1) Site Survey Form for *Quuyaq*, AA-10331 (Calista Corporation). Bureau of Indian Affairs, ANCSA Office, Anchorage.

1983b ANCSA 14(h)(1) Site Survey Form for *Quuyaq*, AA-10332 (Calista Corporation). Bureau of Indian Affairs, ANCSA Office, Anchorage.

1983c ANCSA 14(h)(1) Site Survey Form for *Nanvarnaq*, AA-10335 (Calista Corporation). Bureau of Indian Affairs, ANCSA Office, Anchorage.

2009a A History of the ANCSA 14(h)(1) Program and Significant Reckoning Points, 1975–2008. In *Chasing the Dark: Perspectives on Place, History and Alaska Native Land Claims,* edited by Kenneth L. Pratt, pp. 2–43. Bureau of Indian Affairs, ANCSA Office, Anchorage.

2009b Nuniwarmiut Land Use, Settlement History and Socio-Territorial Organization, 1880–1960. PhD dissertation, Department of Anthropology, University of Alaska Fairbanks.

United States Bureau of Indian Affairs (USBIA)

1988 Composite field map of Yup'ik place names in the Yukon-Kuskokwim Delta. Map 88CAL12A, with associated place names list compiled by Robert Drozda and Vernon Chimegalrea. Bureau of Indian Affairs, ANCSA Office, Anchorage.

Wise, Edward

1982 Taped interview. Robert Drozda, interviewer; Anna Phillip, interpreter. Transcription (English only) by Robert Drozda. Tuluksak, Alaska. 14 August. Tape 82RSM037. Bureau of Indian Affairs, ANCSA Office, Anchorage.

Wolfe, Robert J.

1981 *Norton Sound/Yukon Delta Sociocultural Systems Baseline Analysis.* Technical Paper No. 72. Alaska Outer Continental Shelf Socioeconomic Studies Program, Bureau of Land Management, Anchorage.

FIGURE 11.1 One of many navigational markers on the landscape near the community of Arviat, on the western shore of Hudson Bay. This one marks the location of the mouth of the Maguse River. Photograph by Peter C. Dawson, 2007.

PETER C. DAWSON, COLLEEN HUGHES, DONALD BUTLER, AND KENNETH BUCK

11 Sentiment Analysis of Inuit Place Names from the Kivalliq Region of Nunavut

Landscape archaeology has emerged as a significant area of research within mainstream archaeology, yet recent debates indicate fundamental disagreement over key theoretical and methodological approaches. Calls for greater attention to human engagement with landscape accompanied the emergence of experiential approaches within the broader field of archaeology during the late 1970s and the 1980s (Gosden 1994; Tilley 1994). By adopting a phenomenological perspective, archaeologists are better able to consider landscapes as vast reservoirs of memories and experiences, not simply as physical spaces containing essential resources (Lyons et al. 2010; Whitridge 2004). While agreeing with the need to examine cultural landscapes from new perspectives, critics have nevertheless argued that phenomenological approaches lack a coherent methodology (Fleming 2006; Johnson 2012).

One approach that has gained traction among North American archaeologists interested in phenomenology has been the use of oral histories and place names gathered from descendant Indigenous communities (Lyons et al. 2010; Mason 2000; Thornton 1997). Within many Indigenous

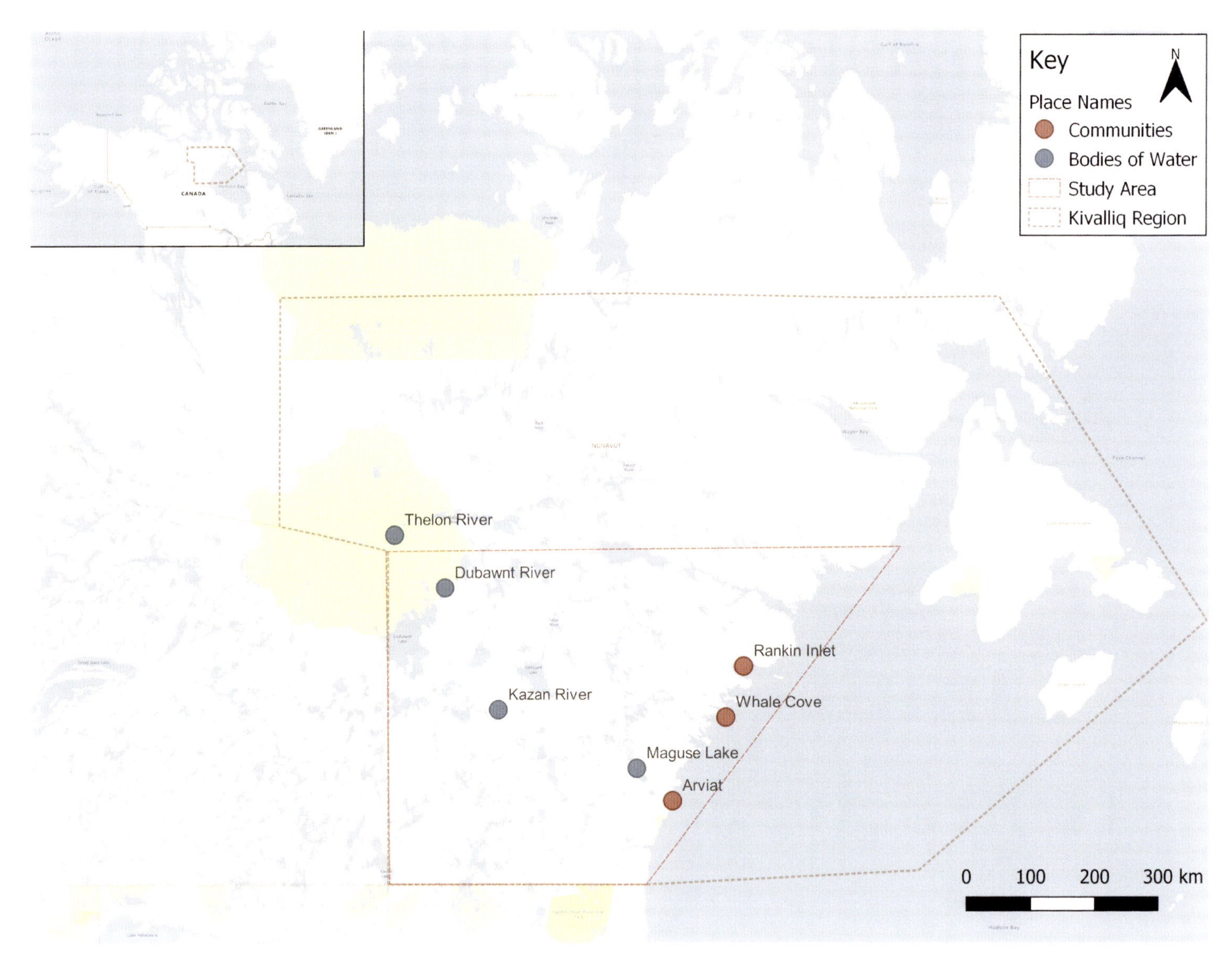

FIGURE 11.2 Western Nunavut, including the territory covered by the Kivalliq Region

societies, the act of naming places on the landscape serves to preserve the collective memories of a community by anchoring individuals, mythological beings, historic events, and stories to landforms such as lakes, ridges, hills, and mountains, among many other places. In short, place names chart the lived experiences, shared histories, values, and beliefs of these descendant communities (Basso 1996; Cruikshank 1981, 1990; Utok, Suluk, and Keith 1994). It should therefore come as no surprise that place names frequently evoke strong responses from Indigenous knowledge holders. Such responses can be positive, recalling pleasant memories or an amusing story, or negative, reminding someone of experiences involving tragedy and grief. These associations can also be largely neutral to the extent that they simply state facts or describe particular locations, such as an important river mouth. Measuring and mapping the sentiments expressed in place names allows one to visualize landscapes in an entirely different way—as a kind of synesthesia, in which the emotional connections people have to landscape are rendered visible (Dawson, Levy, and Lyons 2011).

In this chapter, we analyze 1,031 Inuit place names from the Kivalliq Region of Nunavut using sentiment analysis (figure 11.2). This method uses linguistic algorithms or natural language processing to track the "mood" of a community around a particular subject based on related Internet conversations. Sentiment analysis, also called opinion mining, works by measuring the co-occurrence of a word related to the subject of interest with another word of known polarity, such as "fantastic" (positive), "average" (neutral), or "terrible" (negative) (Feldman 2013; Kumar and Sebastian 2012b, 4). These coded sentiment lexicons are currently being used to examine the opinions of millions of Twitter users and bloggers (Mohammad Kiritchencko and Zhu 2013). Not surprisingly, sentiment analysis has been widely used on the Internet to evaluate the success of advertising campaigns, to discover which products appeal to particular demographics, and to gain insight into why individuals like or dislike certain product features (Feldman 2013; Kumar and Sebastian 2012a, 2012b).

This chapter explores the idea that sentiment analysis might also be useful for tracking people's opinions and feelings about different places on the landscapes they inhabit. Although researchers often assume that place names convey certain pieces of factual information, these names are not unlike the opinions mined in sentiment analysis in that they commonly evoke views or judgments about specific points on the land. For example, the narrows on a lake might be considered an "excellent" place for caribou hunting, while an area with poor ice conditions would be viewed as "dangerous." The same can be said of the historic events, individuals, and mythological stories that are often tied to specific locations. By way of illustration, places associated with malevolent supernatural beings, taboos, and malicious acts of violence are often judged to be negative. Conversely, places associated with pleasant memories, happy events, and successful harvesting activities are usually viewed in a more positive light.

We contend that greater attention to these affective associations may help archaeologists to develop a methodology for examining the subjective aspects of landscape in a way that addresses some of the criticisms levelled by those who are more closely aligned with empiricism and scientific realism (that is, the view that the world described by science is real regardless of how human beings perceive and interpret it). It is therefore appropriate that we begin our discussion with a brief overview of the issues concerning the philosophical tradition of phenomenology and its application in landscape archaeology before moving to our analysis of Inuit place names.

Phenomenology, Landscape, and the Search for a Methodology

Landscape archaeology took shape as a specific branch of archaeology during the 1960s and 1970s, at a time when so-called processual archaeology, with its characteristic support for scientific methods, held sway. As a field of study, landscape archaeology was initially couched firmly within paradigms of ecology and physical geography (Aston 1985; Hodder et al. 1995; Hodder 1987; Johnson 2012). Researchers explored how certain geographical features and the distribution of key resources influenced human interactions with the landscape in the distant past. Empirical data were sought to test ideas about why specific types of archaeological sites were located where they were. Armed with maps and aerial photographs, archaeologists used objective variables such as vegetation, elevation, geology, and hydrology to explain the locations of known archaeological sites, as well as to predict where additional sites might be found. Reconstructing and then mapping the spatial distributions of plant and animal communities, as well as the physical geography and hydrology of past landscapes, provided a powerful means of objectively exploring why people in the past chose to live where they did. With the rise of processual archaeology in the 1960s, archaeologists would expand on this idea by incorporating ecological concepts such as carrying capacity, habitat, and resource patches as a means of developing more robust, science-based interpretations of human-landscape interactions (Binford 1962, 1972; Trigger 2006, 396). In the eyes of many, this constituted a methodology for examining the relationship between landscape and people that was both rigorous and repeatable.

By the early 1980s, a few archaeologists were becoming increasingly concerned about the degree of "scientism" existing within archaeology. In response, symbolism, meaning, and human subjectivity became areas of interest in what became known as post-processual archaeology. The philosophical tradition of phenomenology provided an appealing alternative for the study of human-environment interactions. First introduced into British landscape archaeology by Christopher Tilley (1994) and Christopher Gosden (1994), phenomenological approaches represented a radical departure from those based on ecology in terms of both theory and method. The ideas of Martin Heidegger (1962, 1971) and of human geographers Denis Cosgrove and Stephen Daniels (1988) were inspirational to British post-processual archaeologists, including Julian Thomas (1999, 2008), Barbara Bender and Margot Winer (2001), and Mark Edmonds (1999, 2004).

Collectively, post-processual archaeologists critiqued objective and neutral views of space and time, in which Cartesian frameworks positioned landscapes as "objects" of study. Instead, they argued that perceptions of urban and rural landscapes were grounded in specific historical and cultural contexts and even in individual experiences. The notion that landscapes were subjectively constituted opened new avenues of research concerning the fundamental differences between "space" and "place." In the resulting body of work, "spaces" are understood as geographical locations, or sites on the physical landscape, whereas "places" are imbued with people's memories and lived experiences. Both Heidegger (1971) and Henri Lefebvre (2004) address the experiential dimension of space, whereby locations acquire meaning through the act of dwelling on the landscape. Through this process, often termed "place-making," individuals invest specific locations with both personal and collective significance through their daily practices of living (see Barrett 1994; Ingold 1993, 2000; Tilley 1994; see also Gieryn 2000).

Archaeologists have investigated the distinction between space and place in both archaeological and contemporary contexts (see, for example, Bender 1998; Bender, Hamilton, and Tilley 2007; Knapp and Ashmore 1999). Because places are so closely bound up with lived experiences, whether past or relatively recent, people and communities often harbour deep-seated emotional attachments to places on the landscape. This is why landscapes are so often contested and defended, especially in post-colonial contexts. From the standpoint of research, however, the phenomenological orientation poses the problem of how best to identify, analyze, and perhaps even measure the strength of the connections people feel to the landscapes they inhabit.

Developing a systematic methodology suitable to the phenomenology of landscape proved, however, to be challenging. As Matthew Johnson notes, some archaeologists initially looked to the romantic poet William Wordsworth, who drew inspiration from the surrounding landscape simply by walking through it and immersing himself in it (Johnson 2012, 273; see also Ljunge 2013, 140). Tim Ingold's anthropological studies of the cultural and historical reasons that people walk similarly explore the meanings derived from movement on foot through various landscapes (Ingold 2010; see also Ingold and Vergunst 2008). Others have examined the relationship between walking and storytelling among Indigenous peoples, including the Inuit (Aporta 2009), the Tłįchǫ Dene (Legat 2008), and Batek hunter-gatherers in Malaysia (Tuck-Po 2008). Yet, on a more general level, the subjective and time-bound nature of such perceptions of landscape, as well as the impossibility of reproducing any given experience of it, have led some to question the analytical rigour of such methods (Fleming 2006, 273–274). Contemporary studies have begun to utilize spatial technologies such as GPS to transform the ephemeral paths and patterns of human movement into graphic representations that are scalable, accurate, and georeferenced. Although the use of these and other digital tools, such as viewsheds and augmented reality, can be viewed as attempts to make the methodology of "phenomenological walking" more analytically robust, they can only do so much.

In another line of inquiry, anthropologists and archaeologists interested in how landscape is experienced in Indigenous cultures have focused attention on the knowledge bound up in place names and oral histories (Basso 1996; Chapin, Lamb, and Threlkeld 2005; Cruikshank 1981; Henshaw 2006; Keith 1997, 2004; Nuttall 1992; Stewart et al. 2000; Stewart, Keith, and Scottie 2004). Research into language and place names has revealed the intricate and multilayered relationships that exist between Indigenous peoples and the physical and cultural landscapes they inhabit, in both the past and the present (Bennett and Rowley 2004; Campbell 1997; Cruikshank 1990; Helleland 2006; Lyons et al. 2010; Müller-Wille and Weber Müller-Wille 1989–1991).

Our own work in the Inuit community of Arviat, on the western shore of Hudson Bay, reveals that place names are a rich source of information about how people living in the Kivalliq Region experience the coastal and inland landscapes. The people who inhabited and named these places are descendants of a group collectively known as the Caribou Inuit, a term first used by ethnographers of the Fifth Thule Expedition (1921–1924), given the group's reliance on barren-ground caribou as a primary resource. The Caribou Inuit comprise many rather loosely affiliated groups, such as the Paatlirmiut, Nuvurugmiut, Ahairmiut, Kivihiktormiut, Qainirmiut, Hauniqtuurmiut, and Harvaqtuurmiut (Arima 1984; Birket-Smith 1929; Burch 1978, 1986). Evidence of rich and varied lifeways can be found in numerous locations in the region. In figure 11.3, we see the outlines of tent rings, caches, and hunting blinds that have been excavated out of glacial till. These stone features are situated on an island in Maguse

FIGURE 11.3 The terrain on the island of Ikirahak, located in Maguse Lake. The long, narrow island contains several large archaeological sites. Maguse Lake, which is situated in the southeastern part of the Kivalliq Region, was an important fish harvesting location, as well as a caribou crossing spot. Photograph by Peter C. Dawson, 2007.

FIGURE 11.4 A kayak (*qajaq*) stand at Maguse Lake. Kayak stands, used to store kayak frames during the cold season, are numerous throughout the region. Photograph by Peter C. Dawson, 2007.

Lake called Ikirahak, the site of a major inland caribou crossing. Figure 11.4 shows *qajaq* (kayak) stands along the Maguse River, where the frames of these iconic watercraft would be placed when the *qajaq* was not in use.

Traditional place names are highly valued within the Arviat community for many reasons. On a practical level, they provide important information that allows knowledge holders to orient themselves on the landscape, thereby aiding in navigation and travel. For example, the name Matugijjat, meaning "steep hills, an obstacle for going around," describes a geographical feature that might make travelling through this area more challenging. Other names orient a person by referencing river flow or wind direction, such as Hannirut, which means "the island is facing north." Organizations like Rankin Inlet Search and Rescue recognize that such knowledge facilitates people's ability to safely navigate the land, and therefore actively advocate the teaching of place names and related information in schools.

As our conversations with Arviarmiut (that is, the people of Arviat) revealed, place names also mark the deep-seated personal and emotional connections that people have with places on the land. While some place names identify excellent harvesting and camping locations, others offer warnings about the presence of malevolent animals or supernatural beings or note significant events and associated individuals. If place names are intrinsically linked to landscape, then they represent a potentially rich data set for exploring the phenomenological dimensions of landscape. The challenge is finding a methodology with the potential to measure the strength and direction (positive or negative) of the connections that human beings have with the landscapes they inhabit.

Sentiment Analysis of Inuit Place Names

It is evident that the nature of Inuit place names and the functions they serve express a wide range of opinions or sentiments about the land and its relationship to individuals and their cultural values. For these reasons, many Inuit place names carry an *affect*—an underlying emotional valence that is manifested in a person's feelings about a place or an event. For example, a place name acquires a negative valence if the location it refers to provokes fear or disgust or is perhaps associated with physical and/or spiritual danger (see, for example, Burch 1971; Grønnow 2009; Kilabuk 2011). Similarly, a place name that provides needed information about where to collect water and food educes feelings of comfort and security. This suggests that the deeply seated emotional connections people have to the landscapes they inhabit are reflected in place names, albeit to varying degrees.

When Arviarmiut describe a particular place, one can usually determine fairly easily whether they have a largely positive or negative impression of it. However, such assessments become far more complicated when one is faced with hundreds or even thousands of place names and translations. What if computers could use algorithms to classify large numbers of place names as "positive," "negative," or "neutral"? Machines cannot understand natural language. However, by means of natural language processing algorithms, computers can be programmed to recognize key words within a given translation and then identify the emotional associations of a particular place. When these key words appear in a document, sentiment analysis algorithms assign a score that reflects the overall levels of positive and negative sentiment being expressed. More complex algorithms break down statements into a string of individual words and then use lexical libraries, or "bags of words," to assign a positive and negative polarity to a particular statement. Given the complexities and organic nature of human language, computational linguists assume that most sentiment analysis algorithms are about 80 percent accurate. Nevertheless, an increasing number of businesses are using sentiment analysis of microblogging sites such as Twitter as guidelines for understanding how people feel about their products or services.

In our study, we were interested in exploring whether sentiment analysis could be used to identify places that elicited positive or negative emotions from Arviarmiut knowledge holders. We began by compiling a large database of place names from the Kivalliq Region of Nunavut, entered into an Internet-based Web application called Arctic IQ. This online electronic atlas of Inuit place names was developed in 2013 by two of the authors of this chapter, Peter Dawson and Kenneth Buck, to compile, archive, and manage a large database of place names collected during the most recent International Polar Year (2007–2008). The place names, along with their translations, were solicited in collaboration with knowledge holders living in Arviat, a small community located on the western shore of Hudson Bay. Louis Angalik, Donald Uluadluak, and Mark Kalluak worked together with the authors to enter place name information directly into the electronic map sheets contained within the Arctic IQ website and database.

Participants in the Arctic IQ project met regularly at the Nunavut Department of Education Building in Arviat to discuss place names. Working together, they effectively pooled their collective knowledge to reach a consensus on each place name as well as its location and associated meaning. The advantage of this approach is that everyone has a seat at the table.

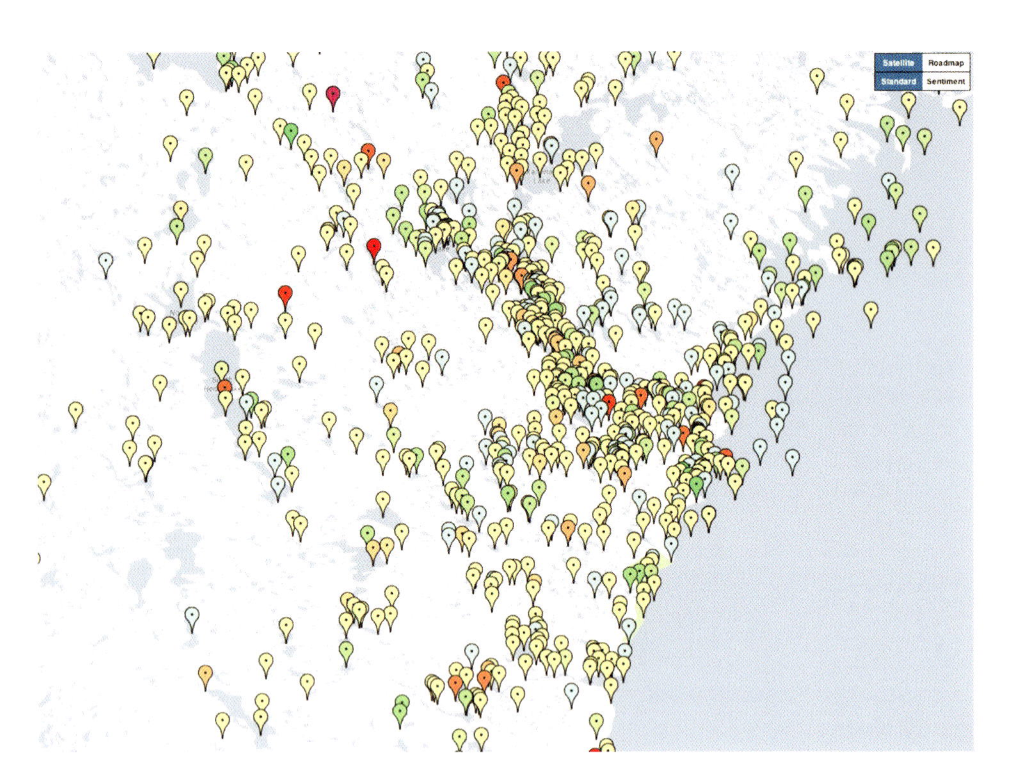

FIGURE 11.5 Place name markers from the area around Arviat displayed on the Arctic IQ website. The markers are colour-coded according to sentiment scores: red indicates most negative, and green indicates most positive. Clicking on the "sentiment" tab in the upper right-hand corner on the website (https://www.arcticiq.ca/place) automatically calculates sentiment scores for each place included in the database.

Knowledge keepers who feel they lack expertise in certain areas, for example, can still participate and contribute to the overall project. The challenge, of course, lies in assessing the reliability of the data that are collected (Brabham 2013). As with sites like Wikipedia, the basic assumption with Arctic IQ is that place names are deemed reliable when consensus on location, spelling, and meaning has been reached among the collaborators. Regardless, because errors are likely unavoidable, we consider the data contained within Arctic IQ as akin to "opinions" rather than hard facts. As opinions, they are informed by oral history and traditional knowledge, as well as by the lived experiences of their Inuit contributors. When considered in this way, it should be possible to explore the polarities of feelings and thoughts about landscape using a tool like sentiment analysis.

A natural language processing service called Lexalytics Semantria API was used to analyze the sentiments expressed by Inuit knowledge keepers relative to the 1,031 place names and their translated meanings contained in the Arctic IQ database. Each call generates a series of response fields for each place name:

Status: success/failure status indicating whether the request was processed
Language: language of the source text as detected
Type: sentiment polarity: "positive," "negative," or "neutral"
Score: sentiment strength (0.0 = neutral)

As an example, running place name translations through Semantria might generate negative scores of (–) 3.45724 and (–) 1.47295 for two place names, based on analysis of the words used to describe the place and its associations with events or history. In this instance, both scores are less than zero, indicating that each place name would be categorized as "negative," with the lower score conveying a stronger negative opinion. Once the sentiment scores had been calculated for the 1,031 place names, each place name marker on the Arctic IQ map sheet was colour-coded along a sliding scale, from red (highly negative) through yellow to blue (neutral) and finally green (highly positive) (figure 11.5).

Results of the Sentiment Analysis of the Arctic IQ Database

The resulting scores for Arviat place names range from highly positive (+) 0.7500000 to highly negative (–) 0.7500000. As there is no absolute way to measure the polarity of sentiment scores against a universal standard, we simply compared place name scores relative to other scores within the same data set. For our discussion, we have chosen to analyze five of the highest-scoring place names in each position on this "continuum of opinion." The names, translations, and sentiment scores are summarized in table 11.1 and discussed in the following section. The three columns in table 11.1 provide the place name, its description, and the sentiment analysis score. A theme is also listed below the place name description. The themes created by Semantria identify topics of discussion and are determined by analyzing the context of the entity (or entities) referred to in the place name description. For example, certain words, such as "bark," can have multiple meanings. As a noun, "bark" refers to the outer covering of a tree, while, as a verb, "bark" refers to the sound a dog makes. Semantria distinguishes between the two by determining the context in which the word is used. The result is then summarized as a particular theme, as in "dogs barking" or "tree covering."

EXPRESSIONS OF POSITIVE SENTIMENT

In table 11.1, the highest-scoring positive place name is Kalitaq (+) 0.7500000. The place name description focuses on the successful harvesting of fish by trawling/dragging nets or hooks using a kayak (*qayaq*). The context in which the entities are mentioned (fish, kayak, lake, hook) is that of a successful catch (theme), which explains the highly positive score.

The place name Ijiralik (+) 0.7000850, however, is not as clear-cut. The description indicates the association of this location with potentially malevolent shape-shifting spirits known as *ijirait* (singular, *ijiraq*), who are closely associated with caribou. These anthropomorphic beings possess the unusual characteristic of having their mouths and eyes placed sideways on their faces. In Inuit stories, *ijirait* are frequently associated with child abduction and are often referred to as the "spirts that hide people." The name Ijiralik can be applied to any place said to be inhabited by *ijirait*. Interviews with Arviarmiut knowledge holders identify at least two additional places called Ijiralik. One of these locations is described as an upright hill where two different incidents involving *ijiriat* were recounted. The first involved a sighting by Louis Angalik's older brother, while the second involved a man from the community of Whale Cove. Both locations scored negatively in the sentiment analysis. This raises a question: Why did one of these three Ijiralik locations earn such a positive score?

The answer seems to lie in the varying degrees of contextual information provided in each of the three place name descriptions. Simply describing the appearance of *Ijirait* and identifying them as "supernatural" did not provide enough contextual information for Semantria to arrive at a negative score. In contrast, the other two descriptions make specific reference to malevolent acts, providing more detailed contextual information. As the term "supernatural" alone can have both positive and negative connotations, it appears Semantria defaulted to the former when assigning a sentiment score.

In contrast, the place name description for Kakiakturyuak (+) 0.67954051 provides a great

TABLE 11.1 Highest-, Lowest-, and Neutral-Scoring Place Names

Positive Place Names	Description	SA Score
Kalitaq	Either trying to catch a fish with a hook or dragging a lake using a net. Kalitaq means "to drag something." Place for trawling for fish. An old name, so probably refers to using a kayak to trawl for fish. A man on a kayak might be hauling a successful catch of fish. Theme: successful catch (positive)	0.7500000
Ijiralik	Supernatural beings who have their mouths sideways *ijiraq* = "people" ("place" is *ijiralik*) Theme: supernatural (positive)	0.7000850
Kakiakturyuak	Clear water lake. Clear water or mineral water. Correct spelling for this lake. It means clear water or mineral water. Themes: mineral water (positive), water lake (neutral), correct spelling (neutral), clear water (positive), water (neutral).	0.67954051
Arviaraarjuk	Lovely little Arviat. A beautiful area for camping. Some graves in this area. Themes: little Arviat (positive), beautiful area (positive)	0.6750000
Inukku'naat	Stone markers put up by people going to Churchill. Popular location for moving inland from wintering, would spend spring/summer there. Access to good, freshwater. Themes: stone markers (neutral), popular location (positive), freshwater (positive)	0.6448403
Negative Place Names	**Description**	**SA Score**
Ihiqtulik	Big waterfall, place where there is smoke. Respelling of original name. A terrible little river. In the winter, it never stops steaming, so it is called a smoky place. There is also a waterfall there. Mouth of a river here. Always steaming in the wintertime. Terrible little river. Name refers to "a smoky place." There is a waterfall here as well, which ices over completely. Themes: smoky place (neutral), little river (negative)	– 0.7500000
Inuarvik	Place where a human was killed, probably over a woman. Really old name. Associated with a very old event. Name of the lake as well? Place of murder—place where someone was killed over a woman. / Someone was murdered here. Theme: none provided	– 0.7500000
Kuunga	A stinky place because there are so many ducks laying eggs. Theme: stinky place (negative), laying eggs (negative)	– 0.7500000
Paqllirjuaq	Big mouth of river. Theme: big mouth (negative)	– 0.7500000
Ikkriliuyat	A drop-off [in the land] close to the Kannakłik Kuuk, a sand bank that looks like a tipi. "Ikkriliuyat" refers to a First Nations camp, on account of the shape of the hillside: a sandy bank is located on this side of the river, and the way it is eroded makes it look like a tipi. Theme: sand bank (neutral), sandy bank (neutral)	– 0.6600000
Neutral Place Names	**Description**	**SA Score**
Aamalanna'juak	Two big hills in the area. Theme: big hills (neutral)	0
Hiulili'naaq	Pike can be found here. Theme: none provided	0
Imaujaaqtut	Looks like water and trees. Treed area looks like water from a distance. A wet area that looks like the sea. Themes: treed area (neutral), wet area (neutral)	0
Karngalanniarvi'naaq	Caribou used to migrate through this lake, from south to north. Theme: none provided	0
Murjungnirjuaq	Start of the river flow. Theme: river flow (neutral)	0

deal of contextual information. This is reflected in such themes as "mineral water" and "clear water." Consequently, the association of this location with clean drinking water is closely correlated with its highly positive sentiment score. The place name Arviaraarjuk (+) 0.6750000 expresses the themes of "Arviat" and "beautiful" in its use of Arviat as a metaphor for an ideal camping location. In this instance, the use of both themes is indicative of the highly positive opinion of this location. The final name, Inukku'naat (+) 0.6448403, refers to stone markers that served as navigational aids and as indicators for inland areas where fresh water was accessible during spring/summer movements from coastal to inland areas. In this instance, the themes of "popular location" and "fresh water" extracted from the translation explain why this place name earned such a positive score.

EXPRESSIONS OF NEGATIVE SENTIMENT

At the opposite end of the "continuum of opinion" defined by Semantria are names that express negative opinions about locations on the land. The first name in table 11.1 is Ihiqtulik (–) 0.7500000, which describes a river mouth where a waterfall is located. During the winter months, this location "never stops steaming" and is therefore described as a "smoky place." It is also referred to as a "terrible little river." The presence of the waterfall may have served as an obstacle to river travel. Likewise, the repeated references to steam fog suggest that it was often free of ice, which may have also made crossing the river mouth a challenge during the winter months. Taken together, these themes correlate with the highly negative score associated with this place name.

Strongly negative opinions were also expressed about places where human tragedies and disasters had taken place. The name Inuarvik (–) 0.7500000, for example, describes a location where a murder had taken place, perhaps owing to a conflict over a woman. The name Kuunga (–) 0.7500000 provides an example of a location that elicits strongly negative opinions because it is an unpleasant place to visit due to a persistent odour associated with a nearby duck nesting area. However, the negative score associated with the place name Paqllirjuaq (–) 0.7500000 explains why care needs to be taken when examining sources of the polarity in opinion calculated by natural language processing algorithms. The place is described as a large river mouth, but the phrasing "big mouth" has likely been taken out of context by Semantria here and linked to its derogatory meaning in the English language.

EXPRESSIONS OF NEUTRAL SENTIMENT

Table 11.1 also provides examples of place names from the middle of the "continuum of opinion," where sentiment scores of 0 indicate that they elicit opinions from local knowledge keepers that are neither positive nor negative. Examining the translations for Aamalanna'juak, Imaujaaqtut, and Murjungnirjuaq indicate that the names provide purely descriptive information about landscapes, such as the presence of hills, trees, and rivers. Likewise, Hiulili'naaq and Karngalanniarvi'naaq offer descriptive information about the locations and movements of resources such as fish and caribou (Aniksak and Suluk 1993).

Thus, at a basic level, the results shown in table 11.1 suggest that Semantria can distinguish between place names associated with cartographic and biogeographic knowledge versus those linked with more emotionally charged information associated with mythological stories, historical events, and lived experiences.

Examining the Spatial Distribution of Sentiment Scores

The colour-coding of place names by their sentiment scores allows the researcher to visualize how place name sentiments are distributed across the landscape and then search for meaningful patterns within the resulting distributions (figure 11.5). We were particularly interested in exploring whether factors like inland versus coastal positioning might produce detectable trends in sentiment polarity. By way of example, archaeologists believe that sometime during the eighteenth century coastal-dwelling Inuit groups on the western edge of Hudson Bay abandoned the relative economic security of sea mammal hunting and moved inland to hunt caribou—a resource that is far less reliable (Burch 1978, 1986, 1988; Friesen and Stewart 1994). This observation is supported by several well-documented famines that occurred in the area, following the disappearance of caribou herds (Fossett 2001, 192). If inland areas are more prone to food insecurity than coastal locations, then we might expect to see a directional trend toward place names expressing negative sentiment polarity as we move away from the coast.

Ethnohistoric accounts also indicate that tensions occurred sporadically among Inuit and First Nations groups in inland and coastal areas of southwestern Hudson Bay (but see Csonka [1994, 1995] for an opposing view). These tensions may have been heightened with the emergence of the fur trade, as well as the establishment of Fort Prince of Wales on the Churchill West Peninsula in 1717, as both Inuit and Chipewyan Dene entrepreneurs attempted to establish themselves as traders. Fossett (2001, 106) recounts one incident in which a party of Chipewyan attacked and killed several Inuit families near Knapps Bay (presently Arviat). Several place names contained in the Arctic IQ database describe skirmishes with Chipewyan at much smaller scales, all of which score negatively and appear confined to the southern portion of the Kivalliq Region. Consequently, if encounters with First Nations groups increased as Inuit moved south, then one might expect an associated trend toward named places expressing negative sentiment polarity in this area.

To explore the possibility that there might be directional trends in how opinions about places were distributed across the landscape, ArcGIS v.9.3 was used to produce an interpolation of the sentiment scores (Gillings 2012). This approach estimates values for points on a plane where no values are known on the basis of points for which values are available. In this case, interpolation offered a means to produce a simple visual representation of the extent to which the sentiment scores formed clustered or linear patterns across the landscape. Specifically, the method was used to produce an isopleth map displaying spatial variation in sentiment as a series of colour-coded zones or bands corresponding to a gradational scale of value ranges for these sentiment scores (Houlding 2000; Lu and Wong 2008). This map, in turn, provided a simple visual tool for exploring how opinions about places on the land vary based on personal experiences and local knowledge of these areas.

The isopleth map representing this interpolation surface (figure 11.6) reveals none of the directional trends hypothesized for the sentiment values within our data set. In other words, sentiment scores are not highly positive on the coast and then progressively lower and negative as one moves further inland to

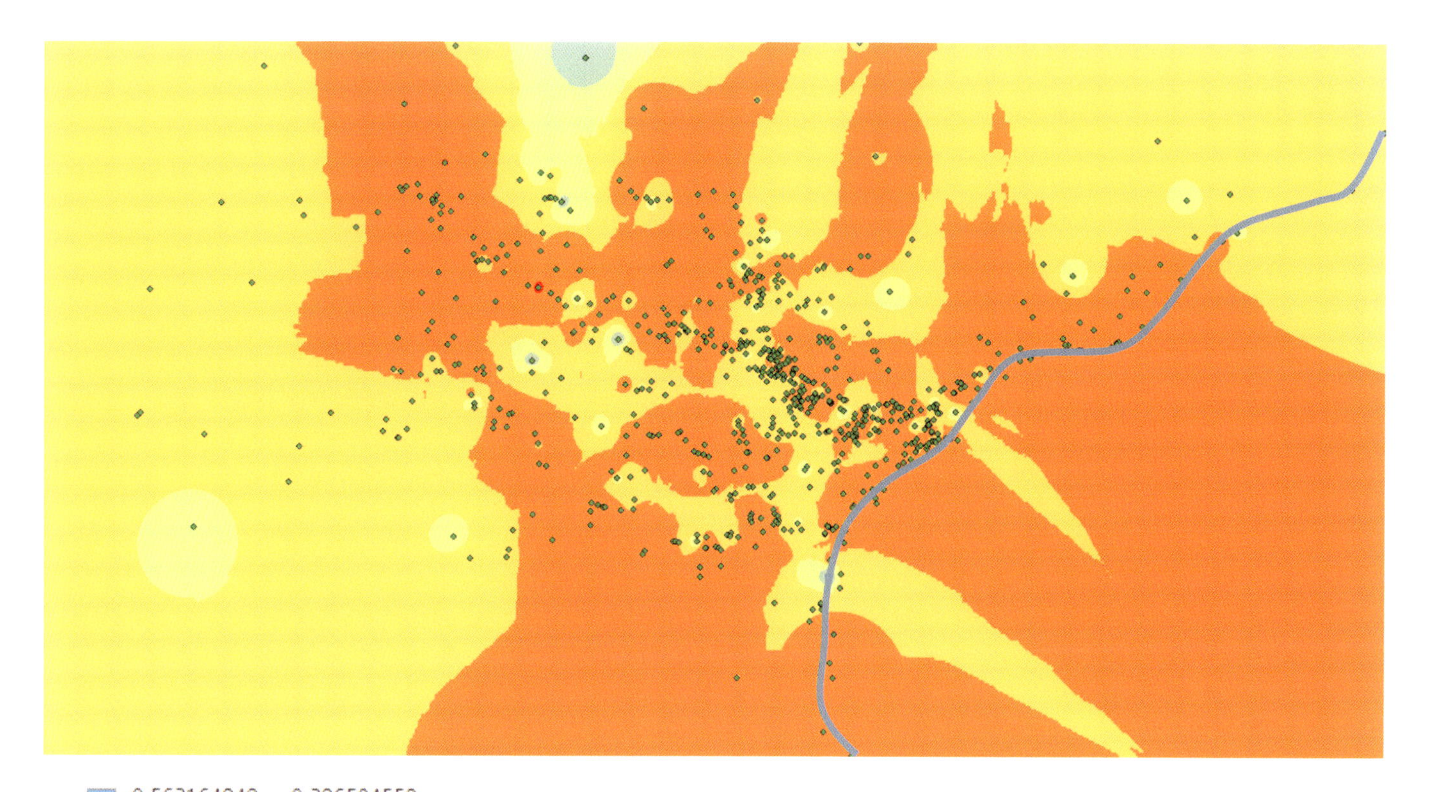

FIGURE 11.6 Interpolation of sentiment scores from the Arctic IQ database. The green patches indicate highly localized areas of negative sentiment. The blue line indicates approximate location of the coast of Hudson Bay.

the west, nor do they fall as one moves south toward the zone where the traditional territories of the Arviarmiut begin to overlap with areas also used by their Chipewyan Dene neighbours. Instead, low sentiment values are distributed in localized patches, as indicated in the small, isolated areas of negative sentiment represented by green and blue patches on the isopleth map. These patches do appear to be distributed in a roughly northeast–southwest axis within the study area, a pattern that is also echoed to some extent in the loosely northeast–southwest orientation of the red and orange bands that reflect high sentiment scores.

Still, there appears to be no large spatial scale process operating here based on the results of this analysis. Rather, the landscape of the Kivalliq Region appears to be a patchwork of highly localized areas associated with positive and negative experiences. For such distinct areas to have emerged, people must have experienced these places in similar ways and then shared these experiences across generations via oral traditions and place names. Experiences of notable events (for example, murders, conflicts) would have been also passed down through the generations with the associated emotional responses. Oral traditions are the verbal messages passed along

FIGURE 11.7 Luke Suluk stands beside a shaman's healing stone at Arvia'juaq National Historic Site, a location of great significance to Arviarmiut. Photograph by Peter C. Dawson, 2007.

from generation to generation and that extend well beyond the living memory of the group (Mason 2000, 240; Vansina 1985, 27). Oral histories are, in contrast, the experiences one has had within one's lifetime, and the maximum temporal scope of oral history must necessarily correspond with the age of the eldest community member (Mason 2000, 240). This is likely how the link between sentiment, landscape, and time is formed at such local levels.

When combined the interpolated ArcGIS scores, the results of the sentiment analysis provide the researcher with a visual representation of how people's opinions of places are spatially distributed across the landscape. By identifying areas that evoke either strongly positive or strongly negative opinions, researchers are better able to engage with local knowledge holders to discover why places are perceived in a certain way. For example, do the patches of negative sentiment identified in figure 11.6 represent areas that are more prone to localized resource failures? Are they areas that contain environmental or supernatural hazards or dangers? Are they associated with historic events or persons of significance? Or are they places where supernatural beings dwell, or where important stories or myths are anchored? We hope to explore each of these possibilities through future research.

The spatial distribution of sentiment scores across the Kivalliq landscape may also provide important insights into how heritage sites are valued from an Indigenous perspective. To illustrate, the shaman's healing stone (figure 11.7) is a site of great significance to many Arviarmiut. However, in the absence of oral histories and place names, its true meaning and value would be difficult to identify. It is therefore not surprising that heritage regulators in many provinces and territories assign value to archaeological sites based primarily on objective criteria such as age, function, and cultural affiliation. Heritage resources that fall within areas that provoke strong opinions from Indigenous knowledge keepers are likely valued for reasons that differ considerably from those emphasized by government regulators. Sentiment analysis could be used to create valuation criteria for heritage sites that take the polarity of Indigenous opinions into consideration.

Finally, we see sentiment analysis as having the potential to guide Indigenous consultation processes during proposed resource extraction and development activities. By identifying areas within a region that are likely to provoke positive or negative opinions from local stakeholders, industry representatives can work much more quickly to address community concerns.

Conclusions

Phenomenology in landscape archaeology represents a well-developed and sophisticated theoretical approach to understanding how people perceive the world around them. It is also an approach that requires a methodology that can yield something other than metaphorical interpretations of symbolism, meaning, experience, and identity.

While some researchers have abandoned their attempts to bridge the divide between phenomenology and technology through approaches like GIS, we propose that techniques currently being used to mine the vast amounts of data contained in social networking sites may bear fruit. Sentiment analysis, in particular, is emerging as an important area of research in computer science and computational linguistics. If place names are analyzed as "opinions" about places that are "informed" by lived experiences and cultural memories, our preliminary research shows that the different polarities of these opinions can be mined using sentiment analysis.

Our use of sentiment analysis to analyze 1,031 Inuit place names also suggests that even non-Indigenous lexical databases can identify positive and negative opinions expressed about certain places. This is not surprising, given that named places are strongly associated with deep-seated feelings derived from identity, memory, history, and mythology. Furthermore, the results of this preliminary analysis indicate that the expression of sentiment may be highly localized and structured in accordance with risk and uncertainty in the availability of key resources, historic events, and mythology, as well as geographic factors such as elevation. Our intention here is not to advocate the use of sentiment analysis as a means of "automating" the study of phenomenology in landscape archaeology. Rather, it is to explore the idea that the same techniques currently employed to "mine" the opinions of millions of Internet users might be profitably applied to toponymic research.

Clearly, there are many challenges that will have to be worked out. For example, a word that is considered "positive" in one situation may well be considered "negative" in another. The word "long" can be positive if we are describing the battery life of a smart phone, but negative if we are determining the time it takes to fully charge that smart phone. This can be further complicated when the data being analyzed have been translated from one language or cultural context into another. For example, the term "kill" has a negative association in most contexts, but a positive connotation when connected to Indigenous harvesting activities—as in a caribou kill site. This indicates that culturally sensitive lexical databases will need to be tailored to any future research.

In addition, phrases like "the book was great" and "the book was not great" indicate that even small changes in text can dramatically alter the polarity of the opinion being expressed. This could also be exacerbated when translating from a language like Inuktitut into English. Finally, most people express both positive and negative comments when reviewing a product or experience. For example, positive language could be used to describe the price of a hotel room, while the cleanliness and comfort of the room might be cast in a negative light. The same is often true for place names that describe locations where both positive and negative events have occurred.

While we fully acknowledge such caveats, the basic objective of this chapter has simply been to explore the possibility that sentiment analysis might provide new insights into how people perceive the landscapes they inhabit. Accordingly, it represents a new and novel approach to studying the phenomenology of landscape (see Eve 2012 and Hennessy et al. 2012 for examples of other new approaches). The next stage in such an analysis will necessarily involve the development of culturally sensitive lexical databases in Inuktitut. Regardless of these challenges, we believe that approaches like sentiment analysis demonstrate that technology does not have to be at odds with phenomenological approaches in landscape archaeology.

Acknowledgements

The authors would like to thank the community of Arviat for its support and hospitality over the years spanning this project. Special thanks to Donald Uluadluak, Mark Kalluak, Louis Angalik, Joe Karetak, and Luke Suluk for their generosity and for the knowledge they have shared. Thanks also to Shirley Tagalik, Natasha Lyons, and Nikki Oakden. Funding for this project was provided by the Social Sciences and Humanities Research Council of Canada, the Government of Nunavut, and the University of Calgary.

References

Aniksak, Margaret Uyauperk, and Luke Suluk

1993 *Sentry Island: An Ancient Land of Occupation*. Arviat Historical Society, Arviat, Nunavut.

Aporta, Claudio

2009 The Trail as Home: Inuit and Their Pan-Arctic Network of Routes. *Human Ecology* 3(2): 131–46.

Arima, Eugene Y.

1984 Caribou Eskimo. In *Handbook of North American Indians,* vol. 5, *Arctic*, edited by David Damas, pp. 447–462. Smithsonian Institution Press, Washington, D.C.

Aston, Mick

1985 *Interpreting the Landscape: Landscape Archaeology in Local Studies*. Batsford, London.

Barrett, John

1994 *Fragments from Antiquity: An Archaeology of Social Life in Britain, 2900–1200 BC*. Blackwell, Oxford.

Basso, Keith

1996 *Wisdom Sits in Places: Landscape, Language and the Western Apache*. University of New Mexico Press, Albuquerque.

Bender, Barbara

1998 *Stonehenge: Making Space*. Berg, Oxford.

Bender, Barbara, Sue Hamilton, and Christopher Tilley

2007 *Stone Worlds: Narratives and Reflexivity in Landscape Archaeology*. Left Coast Press, Walnut Creek, California.

Bender, Barbara, and Margot Winer

2001 *Contested Landscapes: Movement, Exile and Place*. Berg, Oxford.

Bennett, John, and Susan Rowley

2004 *Uqaluriat: An Oral History of Nunavut*. McGill-Queens University Press, Montréal.

Binford, Lewis R.

1962 Archaeology as Anthropology. *American Antiquity* 28: 217–225.

1972 *An Archaeological Perspective*. Seminar Press, New York.

Birket-Smith, Kaj

1929 *The Caribou Eskimos: Material and Social Life and Their Cultural Position*. Part 1, *Descriptive Part. Report of the Fifth Thule Expedition, 1921–24*, vol. 5. Gyldendalske Boghandel, Nordisk Forlag, Copenhagen.

Brabham, Darren

2013 *Crowdsourcing*. MIT Press, Cambridge, Massachusetts.

Burch, Ernest S., Jr.

1971 The Nonempirical Environment of the Arctic Alaskan Eskimos. *Southwestern Journal of Anthropology* 27(2): 148–165.

1978 Caribou Eskimo Origins: An Old Problem Reconsidered. *Arctic Anthropology* 15(1): 1–38.

1986 The Caribou Inuit. In *Native Peoples: The Canadian Experience*, edited by R. Bruce Morrison and C. Roderick Wilson, pp. 106–133. McClelland and Stewart, Toronto.

1988 Knud Rasmussen and the "Original" Inland Eskimos of Southern Keewatin. *Études/Inuit/Studies* 12: 81–100.

Campbell, Lyle

1997 *American Indian Languages: The Historical Linguistics of Native America*. Oxford Studies in Anthropological Linguistics Vol. 4. Oxford University Press, New York.

Chapin, Mac, Zachary Lamb, and Bill Threlkeld

2005 Mapping Indigenous Lands. *Annual Review of Anthropology* 34(1): 619–638.

Cosgrove, Denis, and Stephen Daniels

1988 *The Iconography of Landscape: Essays on the Symbolic Representation, Design, and Use of Past Environments*. Cambridge University Press, Cambridge.

Cruikshank, Julie

1981 Legend and Landscape: Convergence of Oral and Scientific Traditions in the Yukon Territory. *Arctic Anthropology* 18(2): 67–93.

1990 Getting the Words Right: Perspectives on Naming and Places in Athapaskan Oral History. *Arctic Anthropology* 27(1): 52–65.

Csonka, Yvon

1994 Intermédiaires au long cours: Les relations entre Inuit du Caribou et Inuit du Cuivre au début du XXe siècle. *Études/Inuit/Studies* 18(1–2): 21–48.

1995 *Les Ahiarmiut: Àl'écart des Inuit Caribous*. Editions Victor Attinger, Neuchatel, CH.

Dawson, Peter, Richard Levy, and Natasha Lyons

2011 Breaking the Fourth Wall: 3D Virtual Worlds as Tools for Knowledge Repatriation in Archaeology. *Journal of Social Archaeology* 11(3): 387–402.

Dorion, Henri

1987 Native Toponymy and Territorial Rights. *Acta Borealia: A Nordic Journal of Circumpolar Societies* 4(1–2): 119–126.

Edmonds, Mark

1999 *Ancestral Geographies of the Neolithic*. Routledge, London.

2004 *The Langdales: Landscape and Prehistory in a Lakeland Valley*. Tempus, Stroud, UK.

Eve, Stuart

2012 Augmenting Phenomenology: Using Augmented Reality to Aid Archaeological Phenomenology in the Landscape. *Journal of Archaeological Method and Theory* 19(4): 582–600.

Feldman, Ronen

2013 Techniques and Applications for Sentiment Analysis. *Communications of the ACM* 56(4): 82–89.

Fleming, Andrew

2006 Post-processual Landscape Archaeology: A Critique. *Cambridge Archaeological Journal* 16(3): 267–280.

Fossett, Renée

2001 *In Order to Live Untroubled: Inuit of the Central Arctic, 1550 to 1940.* University of Manitoba Press, Winnipeg.

Friesen, T. Max, and Andrew Stewart

1994 Protohistoric Settlement Patterns in the Interior District of Keewatin: Implications for Caribou Inuit Social Organization. In *Threads of Prehistory: Papers in Honour of William E. Taylor, Jr.*, edited by David Morrison and Jean-Luc Pilon, pp. 341–360. Canadian Museum of Civilization Paper 149, Ottawa.

Gieryn, Thomas F.

2000 A Space for Place in Sociology. *Annual Review of Sociology* 26: 463–496.

Gillings, Mark

2012 Landscape Phenomenology, GIS and the Role of Affordance. *Journal of Archaeological Method and Theory* 19(4): 601–611.

Gosden, Christopher

1994 *Social Being and Time.* Wiley-Blackwell, New York.

Grønnow, Bjarne

2009 Blessings and Horrors of the Interior: Ethnohistorical Studies of Inuit Perceptions Concerning the Inland Region of West Greenland. *Arctic Anthropology* 46(1–2): 191–201.

Heidegger, Martin

1962 *Being and Time.* SCM Press, London.

1971 Building, Dwelling, Thinking. In Martin Heidegger, *Poetry, Language, Thought*, pp. 141–160. Translated by Albert Hofstadter. Harper & Row, New York.

Helleland, Botolv

2006 The Social and Cultural Values of Geographical Names. In United Nations Group of Experts on Geographical Names, *Manual for the Standardization of Geographical Names*, pp. 121–128. United Nations, New York.

Hennessy, Kate, Ryan Wallace, Nicholas Jakobsen, and Charles Arnold

2012 Virtual Repatriation and the Application Programming Interface: From the Smithsonian Institution's MacFarlane Collection to "Inuvialuit Living History." In *Reconsidering Barnett Newman*, edited by Melissa Ho, pp. 12–21. Philadelphia Museum of Art, Philadelphia.

Henshaw, Anne

2006 Pausing along the Journey: Learning Landscapes, Environmental Change, and Toponymy amongst the Sikusilarmiut. *Arctic Anthropology* 43(1): 52–66.

Hodder, Ian

1987 *The Archaeology of Conceptual Meaning.* Cambridge University Press, Cambridge.

Hodder, Ian, Michael Shanks, Alexandra Alexandri, Victor Buchli, John Carman, Jonathan Last, and Gavin Lucas

1995 *Interpreting Archaeology: Finding Meaning in the Past.* Routledge, London.

Houlding, Simon

2000 *Practical Geostatistics: Modeling and Spatial Analysis.* Springer, New York.

Ingold, Tim

1993 The Temporality of Landscape. *World Archaeology* 25: 152–174.

2000 *The Perception of the Environment: Essays on Livelihood, Dwelling and Skill.* Routledge, London.

2010 Footprints Through the Weather-World: Walking, Breathing, Knowing. *Journal of the Royal Anthropological Institute* 16(s1): s121–s139.

Ingold, Tim, and Jo Lee Vergunst

2008 *Ways of Walking: Ethnography and Practice on Foot.* Ashgate, Aldershot, UK.

Johnson, Matthew H.

2012 Phenomenological Approaches in Landscape Archaeology. *Annual Review of Anthropology* 41(1): 269–284.

Keith, Darren

1997 *Arvia'juaq National Historic Site: Conservation and Presentation Report.* Arviat Historical Society, Arviat, Nunavut, and Parks Canada.

2004 Caribou, River and Ocean: Harvaqtuurmiut Landscape Organization and Orientation. *Études/Inuit/Studies* 28(2): 39–56.

Kilabuk, Elisha

2011 *The Qalupalik.* Inhabit Media, Iqaluit.

Knapp, A. Bernard, and Wendy Ashmore

1999 Archaeological Landscapes: Constructed, Conceptualized, Ideational. In *Archaeologies of Landscape: Contemporary Perspectives*, edited by Wendy Ashmore and A. Bernard Knapp, pp. 1–30. Blackwell, Oxford.

Kumar, Akshi, and Teeja Mary Sebastian

2012a Sentiment Analysis on Twitter. *International Journal of Computer Science Issues* 9(4): 372–379.

2012b Sentiment Analysis: A Perspective on Its Past, Present and Future. *International Journal of Intelligent Systems and Applications* 4(10): 1–14.

Lefebvre, Henri

2004 *Rythmanalysis: Space, Time, and Everyday Life.* Continuum, London.

Legat, Allice

2008 Walking Stories; Leaving Footprints. In *Ways of Walking: Ethnography and Practice on Foot*, edited by Tim Ingold and Jo Lee Vergunst, pp. 35–50. Ashgate, Aldershot, UK.

Levy, Richard, and Peter Dawson

2014 Interactive Worlds as Educational Tools for Understanding Arctic Life. In *Pastplay: Playing with Technology and History*, edited by Kevin Kee, pp. 66–86. University of Michigan Press, Ann Arbor.

Lyons, Natasha, Peter Dawson, Matthew Walls, Donald Ulluadluak, Louis Angalik, Mark Kalluak, Philip Kigusiutuak, Lukle Kiniski, Joe Keretak, and Luke Suluk
2010 Person, Place, Memory, Thing: How Inuit Elders Are Informing Archaeological Practice in the Canadian North. *Canadian Journal of Archaeology* 34: 1–31.

Lu, George Y., and David W. Wong
2008 An Adaptive Inverse-Distance Weighting Spatial Interpolation Technique. *Computers and Geosciences* 34: 1044–1055.

Ljunge, Magnus
2013 Beyond "the Phenomenological Walk": Perspectives on the Experience of Images. *Norwegian Archaeological Review* 46(2): 139–158.

Mason, Ronald J.
2000 Archaeology and Native North American Oral Traditions. *American Antiquity* 65(2): 239–266.

Mohammad, Saif, Svetlana Kiritchencko, and Xiaodan Zhu
2013 NRC-Canada: Building the State-of-the-Art in Sentiment Analysis of Tweets. In *Proceedings of the Seventh International Workshop on Semantic Evaluation Exercises (SemEval-2013)*. Atlanta, Georgia.

Müller-Wille, Ludger, and Linna Weber Müller-Wille
1989–1991 *Keewatin NUNA-TOP Survey of Inuit Geographical Names*. Archival and Electronic Data and Maps. Indigenous Names Surveys. Department of Geography, McGill University, Montréal.

Nuttall, Mark
1992 *Arctic Homeland: Kinship, Community, and Development in Northwest Greenland*. University of Toronto Press, Toronto.

Stewart, Andrew, T. Max Friesen, Darren Keith, and Lyle Henderson
2000 Archaeology and Oral History of Inuit Land Use on the Kazan River, Nunavut: A Feature-Based Approach. *Arctic* 53(3): 260–278.

Stewart, Andrew, Darren Keith, and Joan Scottie
2004 Caribou Crossings and Cultural Meanings: Placing Traditional Knowledge and Archaeology in Context in an Inuit Landscape. *Journal of Archaeological Method and Theory* 11(2): 183–211.

Thomas, Julian
1999 *Culture, Time, and Identity: An Interpretive Archaeology*. Routledge, London.
2008 Archaeology, Landscape and Dwelling. In *Handbook of Landscape Archaeology*, edited by B. David and J. Thomas, pp. 300–306. Left Coast Press, Walnut Creek, California.

Thornton, Thomas F.
1997 Anthropological Studies of Native American Place Naming. *American Indian Quarterly* 21(2): 209–228.

Tilley, Christopher
1994 *A Phenomenology of Landscape: Places, Paths and Monuments*. Routledge, London.

Trigger, Bruce
2006 *A History of Archaeological Thought*. Cambridge University Press, Cambridge.

Tuck-Po, Lye
2008 Before a Step Too Far: Walking with Batek Hunter-Gatherers in the Forests of Pahang, Malaysia. In *Ways of Walking: Ethnography and Practice on Foot*, edited by Tim Ingold and Jo Lee Vergunst, pp. 21–34. Ashgate, Aldershot, UK.

Utok, Tony, Luke Suluk, and Darren Keith
1994 Maguse River Place Names Project. Field Report, Parks Canada, Department of Canadian Heritage, Gatineau, Québec.

Vansina, Jan
1985 *Oral Tradition as History*. University of Wisconsin Press, Madison.

Whitridge, Peter
2004 Landscapes, Houses, Bodies, Things: "Place" and the Archaeology of Inuit Imaginaries. *Journal of Archaeological Method and Theory* 11(2): 213–250.

FIGURE 12.1 Ngeellqat, on the northern coast of Cape Chaplin in the area around the Senyavin Strait, 2015. Photograph by Igor Zagrebin.

MICHAEL A. CHLENOV

With an introduction by IGOR KRUPNIK

12 Indigenous Place Names in the Senyavin Strait Area, Chukotka

INTRODUCTION: THE HISTORICAL CONTEXT OF THE DOCUMENTATION OF INDIGENOUS PLACE NAMES IN THE SENYAVIN STRAIT AREA

A few words are warranted to explain the significance of Michael Chlenov's compilation of traditional Siberian Yupik and Chukchi place names in the Senyavin Strait area, along the Russian side of the Bering Strait. As Chlenov's partner in his fieldwork in the 1970s and 1980s, his co-author on several publications, and the editor of the Russian collection in which the original version of this chapter (Chlenov 2016) was published, I have watched his work unfold, from the first field recordings to the final analysis and publication.

Beyond his meticulous research, a number of factors speak to the value of Chlenov's contributions. One, of course, is the natural flow of time, which has led to the passing of the Indigenous knowledge holders with whom he worked thirty to forty years ago. That generation, with all of its accumulated heritage knowledge, is, unfortunately, gone.

Two more factors make Chlenov's work irreplaceable. The first is the *population displacement* that had occurred in the study area. At the time that the elders to whom he spoke grew up, in the 1920s and 1930s, the Senyavin Strait islands and nearby mainland hosted substantial local populations, both Yupik and Chukchi. In the 1910s, the islands had at least six permanent settlements and several seasonal hunting camps, in addition to which over a dozen hunting and herding camps existed on the mainland. In the 1950s, the Russian administration started its policy of "modernization" by closing smaller Indigenous villages and camps and moving their residents to larger permanent communities (Krupnik and Chlenov 2013, esp. chap. 10), a common strategy of control and governance in use across the circumpolar North. Aside from the town of Yanrakynnot (Yagrakenutaq, in the Yupik spelling), which lies on the western shore of the Senyavin Strait to the north of Arakamchechen Island and has about four hundred residents, the area is now officially listed as "uninhabited"—even though it continues to be used on a seasonal or short-term basis by Yupik and Chukchi sea mammal hunters and reindeer herders and to be visited by game wardens and tourist groups. Since no children have been born or raised in the area for several decades, young people have had no opportunity to absorb the rich local geography and cultural heritage in a family setting, in contrast to the generation with whom Chlenov worked in the 1970s and 1980s.

The other key factor is *language replacement*. Elders such as Vladimir Tagitutqaq and Yuri Virineut were born and raised in monolingual Siberian Yupik and Chukchi environments, respectively. Traditional knowledge was conveyed to them by their parents and other community members in their native languages, and they learned to speak Russian only as adults. Today, the situation is entirely different. Although Siberian Yupik and Chukchi continue to be spoken by elders, as well as by some herders and hunters now in their middle age, there is hardly a family in which children are raised in their ancestral language. With language replacement comes a monumental shift in knowledge, as most of the local geographic features are currently either known by their Russian or Russianized names or simply not identified at all.

It is thus extremely fortunate that Chlenov had the foresight to record these place names before they were completely forgotten. Local residents still retain an impressive body of traditional ecological knowledge and continue to use Indigenous terms and concepts to refer to the physical environment, sea ice, and wildlife species (Apalu 2013; Apalu et al. 2016; Kalyuzhina, Borovik, and Apalu 2016). Yet knowledge of the cultural and linguistic heritage of the region has begun to fade. Were it not for Chlenov's dedicated research, the original names for points on the physical landscape would have been forever lost, along with the history and knowledge embedded in them.

Igor Krupnik

Indigenous Place Names in the Senyavin Strait Area, Chukotka

MICHAEL A. CHLENOV

Translated by Katerina Wessels

On the Russian side of the Bering Strait lie the Providensky and Chukotsky Districts of the Chukotka Autonomous Okrug, which face the United States territory of Alaska, on the other side of the international dateline.[1] The history of Russia's northeastern frontier is very complex, and its historical upheavals are reflected in its place names, or toponyms. Unfortunately, notwithstanding a number of very valuable publications (notably Dobrieva et al. 2004; Leont'ev and Novikova 1989; Menovshchikov 1972), these place names had never been systematically recorded and analyzed. Consequently, many of them were lost, along with various other elements of Indigenous tradition that were not transmitted to younger generations of the Yupik and Chukchi peoples who live on the Chukotka Peninsula.

During my fieldwork in Chukotka in the 1970s and 1980s, I recorded the place names described in this chapter from Yupik and Chukchi elders, for whom Russian was not their native language.[2] They were engaged in traditional subsistence activities—marine mammal hunting and reindeer herding. The contributions of two people, Vladimir Tagitutqaq (1922–1999) and Yuri Virineut (1925–?), were especially generous and truly irreplaceable.

Tagitutqaq (figure 12.2) was born in the small Yupik community of Napakutaq, on southeastern Itygran Island, and then moved to the village of Siqlluk (Russian, Siklyuk), on the island's north coast, where he lived for twenty years. After the local

FIGURE 12.2 Vladimir Tagitutqaq at the old settlement of Siqlluk, near the Whale Bone Alley archaeological site, July 1981. Photograph by Sergei A. Bogoslovskiy.

FIGURE 12.3 Yuri Virineut (foreground) with Nikolai Panagirgin, our Chukchi translator, on Arakamchechen Island, July 1981. Photograph by Sergei A. Bogoslovskiy.

Soviet administration emptied the village in 1951, he was resettled on the mainland to the south of the island in the community of Chaplino (Ungaziq), on Cape Chaplin, which subsequently became known as Staroe Chaplino (Old Chaplino). He was moved again in 1959, together with the other residents of Chaplino, to a site further south named Novoe Chaplino (New Chaplino), where he lived in his retirement. Although he continued to visit the Senyavin Strait area with Chaplino hunting crews in the 1960s and early 1970s, he had not been there for any extended time, mostly staying in the village on the mainland at the fjord-like Tkachen Bay [Novoe Chaplino]. I met him there in 1981 during our survey of the so-called "Whale Bone Alley," an ancient archaeological site next to his former home village of Siqlluk (Arutyunov, Krupnik, and Chlenov 1982). By that time, Tagitutqaq was already recognized as the oldest living man to have been raised in the area. We spent a lot of time together visiting the Itygran and Arakamchechen Islands and the areas belonging to the Novoe Chaplino and Yanrakynnot village councils adjacent to the strait. Most of the Yupik toponyms he provided, which he remembered from the time of his youth, were recorded in 1981.

Yuri Virineut (figure 12.3), nicknamed "Tamara," lived quite a different life. He was born in the mainland Chukchi community of Yanrakynnot, also in the Senyavin Strait area but further to the north, into a family of reindeer herders. They had very few reindeer, however, so they moved from one place to another, combining reindeer herding with the hunting of marine mammals. Chukchi was Virineut's native language, and, when we met in 1981, he didn't speak Russian very well, although he understood it. In 1964, when he was already a a fairly elderly man by Chukchi standards, he and his family moved to Arakamchechen Island, to the south of Yanrakynnot, which was by then essentially uninhabited. There he became a monitor at the Arakamchechen walrus haulout site, the largest in Chukotka at the time. He also trapped for Arctic foxes during the winter.

The history of the walrus haulout site is related to the almost forgotten story of how the newly arriving Soviet authorities in the Senyavin Strait area fought with the shamans, whom the Russians deemed to be "class enemies" of the local Indigenous people. In the 1920s, a certain Chukchi shaman by the name of Akyr gained exclusive control over the haulout site and announced that he was its "owner." In 1929, by decree of a recently established local body of the Soviet administration then located in the Yupik village of Ungaziq, Akyr was forcibly removed from the haulout site and stripped of all his power (Arutyunov, Krupnik, and Chlenov 1982, 63; Krupnik and Chlenov 2013, 232–234). Virineut's wife, Zina, was none other than Akyr's granddaughter.

It is striking how differently these two men, who belonged to two different cultures, the maritime Yupik and the tundra-dwelling Chukchi, demonstrated deeply rooted features of their ethnic background in the way that they perceived the space around them. Tagitutqaq recited toponyms systematically, as if he was sailing along the shore. It was as if, for him, the area was a line with notable landmarks on it—so, as he said, "it would be easier to tell where you were, where you came from; that is why the names are given [this way]." His reference point was the shore, and he was at a distance from it, looking at it from the sea. For Virineut, the land was not a shoreline but a circular space, with he himself in the centre of it. When I asked him to name Chukchi place names on Arakamchechen Island, he started naming them in what seemed to me a completely chaotic order, jumping from the southern shore to the northeastern, then to the northwestern, not in any way following the actual position and order of these sites on a map. Only later did I understand that, in his mind, all of these sites were connected by radial lines, and he was standing in the center of an imaginary circle at their convergence.

In general, Indigenous place names along the Russian shore of the Bering Strait are exceptionally multilayered. One of my local acquaintances, Vladimir S. Lyashenko, director of Geroy Truda state farm in Uelen, characterized it very accurately when I talked to him in 1986. Lyashenko was not involved in the study of toponyms, but he happened to be living in that area and, among other matters, commented on place names:

> There are several place name systems in the area: the Yupik [system] is almost forgotten, maybe five to ten people remember it; the Chukchi [system] is very vibrant and is used among the Chukchi people; the local Russian [system], for tourists—First River, Second River, Death Valley, Naukan, Old Naukan, and such; and the Russian maritime [system], in which the word "Dezhnev" identifies many different points: Naukan, Dezhnevo Post, and, finally, the entire area. It is interesting that no one is familiar with the place name Cape Peek, which appears on all maps. (Lyashenko, pers. comm., 1986)

However, my main task was to record the “almost forgotten” Yupik place names, which, as I suspected, can very quickly disappear from the memory of local inhabitants and be replaced by something else. There were several very compelling reasons for undertaking this work. The first one was related to the geography of the area where we worked. When I speak of the “Senyavin Strait area,” I mean the southern coast of the Chukotka Peninsula from Mechigmen Bay as far south as the northern shore of Cape Chaplin (see figure 12.4), including Itygran and Arakamchechen Islands, as well as several smaller islands that surround them. Today, this area is used by Yupik and Chukchi people from Novoe Chaplino and Chukchi people from Yanrakynnot, as well as some of that community’s Yupik residents. Both communities are in the Providensky District of Chukotka.

It is possible that as recently as two, but definitely three, centuries ago the whole shoreline in this area was inhabited by Yupik people, but they may not have occupied it continuously. The coastal area thus formed part of the Siberian Yupik toponymic region. Over the course of the past few centuries, historical and cultural developments led to the ongoing assimilation of Yupik-speaking people by the Chukchi, with the coastal Yupik groups shifting to the Chukchi language and the emergence of a new coastal Chukchi community.

At the end of the eighteenth century, the date of our earliest linguistic records, the Yupik language was spoken in Uelen, the now Chukchi-speaking community on the Russian Arctic coast next to Cape Dezhnev, the easternmost point of Northern Asia facing the Bering Strait. Place names indicate that a Yupik substratum is omnipresent over the area from the shores of the Chukchi Sea all the way south to the Gulf of Anadyr, which is today exclusively a Chukchi region (Chlenov 2006; Krauss 2005, 164–170; Leont’ev and Novikova 1989, 21–23; Titova 1978). Linguistic evidence also suggests that speakers of Naukanski Yupik, who occupied a separate enclave on the promontory of rocky Cape Dezhnev, arrived on the Chukotka Peninsula at some later date than speakers of Central Siberian Yupik (Chlenov 1988; Krauss 2005). Until the appearance of coastal Chukchi in the area of the Bering Strait, Central Siberian Yupik occupied a Z-shaped area from Kolyuchin Bay, on the coast of the Chukchi Sea to the northwest of Uelen, down along the entire Russian coast of the Bering Strait south to Provideniya Bay and, finally, east to Sivuqaq Island, also known as St. Lawrence Island, in the Bering Sea (Krauss 2005, 174).

In other words, almost all the shore zone of the Chukotka Peninsula was occupied by speakers of the Chaplinski dialect of Central Siberian Yupik, who, in all likelihood, created the Yupik toponymical area on the peninsula. In the southwest they shared borders with speakers of the Sirenikski Yupik language, now extinct, and on the promontory of Cape Dezhnev they shared borders with speakers of Naukanski Yupik. In addition, according to Michael Krauss, in the northern Chukotka Peninsula, along the coast of the Chukchi Sea to the west of Kolyuchin Bay, was an area occupied by speakers of Iñupiaq, an Inuit language, who could have migrated from Point Hope (Tikiġaq), on the northwestern coast of Alaska facing the Chukchi Sea, in the seventeenth or early eighteenth century (Krauss 2005, 171–180). In the second half of the nineteenth century, however, speakers of Chaplinski Yupik were once and for all pushed out into the fjord area of southeast Chukotka Peninsula, which lies between Sireniki in the west and the Senyavin Strait islands in the east.

FIGURE 12.4 Study area, with inset maps indicated

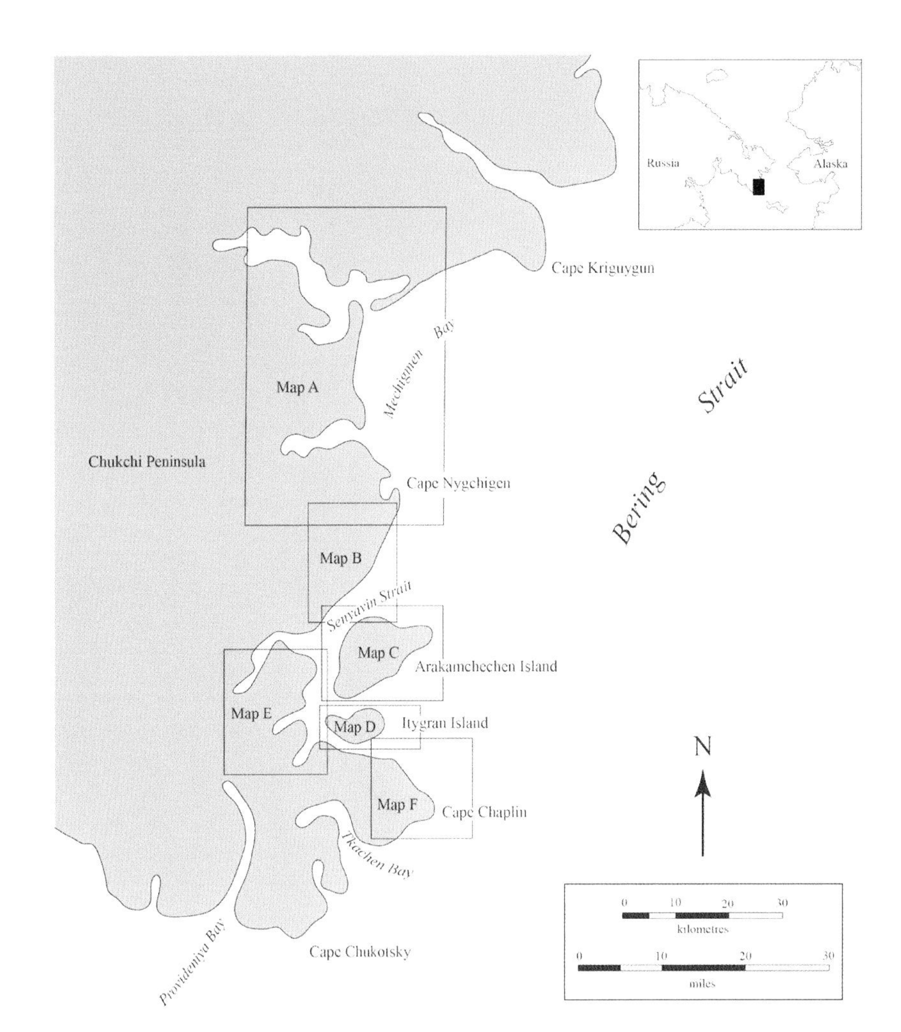

The region under consideration is thus divided into two sections. The southern section, which was until recently part of the Yupik toponymic area, includes Cape Chaplin and, moving north along the coast, Rumilet Bay, Inakhpak Bay, and part of Aboleshev Bay, as well as Itygran Island. The northern section is part of the Chukchi toponymic area; it includes Arakamchechen Island and, across from it on the mainland coast, Penkigney Bay (Qalareq) north to Mechigmen Bay. The southern shore of Arakamchechen, which up until the middle of the twentieth century was used by Chaplino Yupik, is a transition zone, in which Yupik place names survive alongside Chukchi place names, which are the more prevalent. Interaction between the Yupik and Chukchi cultural components in the area was quite intense. In the southern region, the Yupik component dominated (at least until recently), while the Chukchi component underwent Yupik adaptation. In the northern region, the reverse occurred: Yupik names were retained only for large and prominent places, such as Masiq (modern Mechigmen) and Nuqaq (modern Lorino) while all other Yupik place names underwent Chukchi adaptation or were simply replaced with Chukchi names.

Several details about place names on the Chukotka Peninsula are worth mentioning. Neither Yupik nor Chukchi peoples gave names to major geographical features of the sort that were of importance to Western sailors (mainly Russian, American, and British)—that is, seas, large islands, large straits, and gulfs. Among the local place names one will not find analogues to names like Chukotka, the Bering Sea, the Gulf of Anadyr, Alaska, or the Bering Strait. Presumably, it was always the case with respect to Indigenous cultures in and of themselves. Settlements, capes, visible or prominent rocks, large brooks, and natural landmarks or points of reference were almost always named, but there were other features, usually smaller but sometimes quite prominent, that were not named. Thus, for example, the two large islands in the Senyavin Strait, Arakamchechen and Itygran, did not traditionally have names in Chukchi or in Yupik but were instead known by reference to certain of their named features, such as settlements, natural landmarks, or notable capes.

What were taken to be Indigenous names for the islands as a whole began appearing on maps only after arrival of European sailors. The name Itygran was, for instance, borrowed from the name of the Estegraq locality on the western end of Siklyuk Bay, on the island's north shore, while Qigi, a name given to Arakamchechen Island, derived from the name of the island's easternmost cape. Similarly, St. Lawrence Island was named Sivuqaq after the name of the island's westernmost cape. Discrete names were given only to uninhabited islands where bird colonies were located, such as Nunangighhaq and Qiighhqaq. Most Yupik place names in the list below designate inhabited sites (communities), capes, rocks, brooks or creeks, lagoons, and natural points of reference, such as a coastal area between two capes, or between any other notable features, such as lakes or lagoons.

Another feature characteristic of Yupik place names in the Senyavin Strait area is the blurring of the line between place names and common nouns used as appellatives. Often a geographic feature is simply called by an appellative term. A good illustration is the name of a rather large lake on Cape Chaplin, which is called Naayvaq, the Yupik word for "lake." Yupik place names are generally formed from a base consisting of an appellative noun, but in rare cases the base is a personal name. For example, Akatam peghivigha, the name of a cliff on Itygran Island, derives from the name of a man named Akatak, who is said to have stored meat at a particular spot on the cliff to keep it safe from bears.

Starting in the mid-seventeenth century, Russian place names were layered on top of the complex bilingual pattern of Yupik and Chukchi place names. The first layer was laid down by Russian *promyshlenniki,* or fur traders, and Cossacks in the seventeenth and eighteenth centuries. Examples of place names in this layer include Cape Russkaya Koshka, at the mouth of Anadyr River, Cape Chukotskiy, and two capes called Serdtse-Kamen', one in Kresta Bay and the other on the coast of Chukchi Sea. The second, much more substantial layer consists of place names created by Russian seafarers in the eighteenth and nineteenth centuries. Among them, the most significant contribution was made by the 1826–1828 Russian exploratory expedition under the command of Fyodor P. Litke: "Senyavin Strait" was named after their sloop *Senyavin* (Litke 2014).

Starting in the second half of the nineteenth century, oceanographic exploration parties named numerous places, and twentieth-century topographical and geological parties continued the process, which remains ongoing. Some of the most recently created place names, such as Zvonkiy Ruchey ("resounding creek") or Mys Ostryy ("sharp cape"), simply mimic traditional toponymic styles. There are also many place names that were formed from personal names—such as Cape Mertens or Glasenap Bay. A special group is formed by Chukchi and, less often, Yupik, toponyms that were phonetically adapted to the Russian language.

English names assigned by English and American seafarers in the nineteenth and the early twentieth centuries are also part of the Chukotka toponymic "Babylon." These names, such as Khed' (Head) Bay and Estikhet (East Head), both an old village and a mountain, are mainly concentrated in the Provideniya Bay region.

Historical reconstruction of the distribution of Yupik languages on the Russian side of the Bering Sea suggests that the Yupik toponymic substrate in the region of the Senyavin Strait should be related specifically to Central Siberian Yupik. That proves to be true: most place names in the Senyavin Strait area can rather easily be etymologically explained on the basis of Central Siberian Yupik. However, several toponyms contain elements that appear to derive from other Yupik languages of the Bering Strait, namely, Old Sirenikski or Naukanski Yupik. These toponyms have Yupik bases that are not present in Central Siberian Yupik. The names Inghiluqaq, a cape on Itygran Island, and Inghisaget, a groups of mountains on Arakamchechen Island, can both be traced to the Proto-Eskimo root **iingghiq*, "mountain," which does not occur in modern Central Siberian Yupik (where mountain is *naayghaq*) but is present in other Yupik languages (for example, Naukanski *iingghiq* and Old Sirenikski *inggheX*) and in Inupiaq, an Inuit language, as *ighiq*. In this case, however, there is no reason to suspect a direct relationship to Naukanski Yupik or another Eskimo language. It is more reasonable to suppose that these two toponyms date to a time when the root **iingghiq* did exist in a local dialect of Central Siberian Yupik, now extinct.

The same can be said about Pagilleq, the name of a cape on the southern shore of Arakamchechen Island. The name can readily be traced to the Proto-Eskimo root **pagi-*, **pagu-*, "cormorant." While this root does not appear in either Central Siberian Yupik or Naukanski Yupik, it is present as *pagelleX* in Old Sirenikski and as *pagulluk* in Inupiaq. Other toponyms, such as Inqetuq, Qelengayen, Nashqaq, and Qeyuvaggpak, cannot be etymologically traced to Central Siberian Yupik either, although they can all be explained on the basis of the other two Yupik languages of Chukotka. It is significant, however, that the list below does not contain a single place name that can be etymologically derived from a base that occurs exclusively in Naukanski or Old Sirenikski or Inupiaq. This supports the conclusion that the toponymic substrate in the Senyavin Strait area is founded on roots and derivatives present in the Central Siberian Yupik spoken on the Chukotka Peninsula.

Acknowledgements

I thank Lyudmila Ainana (Aynganga) for her valuable assistance in collecting and analyzing the toponyms of the Senyavin Strait area and Igor Krupnik for bringing my work to the attention of volume editor Ken Pratt and assisting in various ways during the publication process. I am grateful as well to Katerina Wessels for her translation of the original Russian text and to Katerina Bogoslovskaya for sharing a number of the photographs taken in 1981 by the late Sergei A. Bogoslovskiy. I and Igor Krupnik both wish to extend our thanks to Igor Zagrebin for allowing us to include several of his beautiful landscape photographs in this chapter. Finally, I thank Dale Slaughter for redrawing my maps (originally prepared by Andrey Yashin) for publication in English.

Notes

1 An autonomous *okrug* is one of several administrative units in the Russian Federation. During the 1920s and 1930s, the Soviet government initiated the creation of what were then called "national *okrugs*," with the intention of granting some degree of autonomy to Indigenous peoples of the Russian North, while at the same time effectively cordoning off ethnic minorities. Historically, autonomous okrugs (the name was changed in 1977) have been part of larger federal units, most often *oblasts* (provinces). Today, Chukotka is a separate constituent unit of the Russian Federation. —Eds.

2 A large number of people were contacted in the course of this study, the genesis of which is tied to the fieldwork of the late Lyudmila Bogoslovskaya in the Chukotka area. The Senyavin Strait area falls under the administrative jurisdiction of two villages: the Yupik village of Novoe Chaplino (New Chaplino), which replaced the traditional village of Ungaziq in 1958, and the Chukchi village of Yanrakynnot. During the 1970s and 1980s, Novoe Chaplino was home to some 400 Yupik and Chukchi people, and Yanrakynnot housed about 350 people, primarily Chukchi. Both communities also had a substantial share of newcomers, primarily Russians but also people from other ethnic groups in the former Soviet Union. Our research team was in contact with practically all the older Yupik and Chukchi residents of Novoe Chaplino (about fifty to sixty persons), as well as with some three to five Chukchi and Yupik elders from Yanrakynnot. During our travels along the strait, we were normally accompanied by hunting crews from Novoe Chaplino and Sireniki. In the northern area of the strait, we spoke with Chukchi and Yupik (some of them Naukan) individuals both in Lorino (Lugren) and in the administrative center of Lavrentiya. So slightly less than a hundred persons were involved in the study of place names in the Senyavin Strait. But an estimate of the total number of Indigenous people we met and managed to communicate with during the twenty years of our fieldwork activities (1971–90)—that is, people from all of the tribes, including the Naukan, Sireniki, Central Siberian Yupik, and Chukchi individuals who lived along the Russian shore of the Bering Strait—would be somewhere in the range of 1,000 to 1,200 persons. Many people whom we met during that period still remembered life in old, abandoned settlements like Ungaziq and Naukan quite well, slightly less so in the case of Qiwaq, Avan, and Siqlluk—but no one could recall life in Chechen or Old Plover Bay in the late nineteenth to early twentieth centuries. The Yupik living in the village of Ungaziq, located at Cape Chaplin, were resettled not far from there in the Tkachen Bay area—so their hunters were able to continue using the old area. Much more tragic was the situation with the Naukan people, but because they live outside of the Senyavin Strait area, they are not discussed in this chapter.—Au.

References

Apalu, Arthur

2013 Ledovyi slovar' morskikh okhotnikov sela Yanrakynnot (chukotskii iazyk) [Sea ice dictionary of marine hunters of the community of Yanrakynnot (Chukchi language)]. In *Nashi l'dy, snega I vetry: Narodnye i nauchnye znaniia o ledovykh landshaftakh i climate Vostochnoi Chukotki* [Our ice, snow, and winds: Indigenous and academic knowledge on the icescapes and climate of Eastern Chukotka], edited by Lyudmila Bogoslovskaya and Igor Krupnik, pp. 125–137. Russian Heritage Institute, Moscow.

Apalu, Arthur, Alexander Borovik, Yurii Yatta, and Natalya Kalyuzhina

2016 Sovremennye chukotskie i eskimosskie nazvaniia ptits raiona proliva Senyavia i bukhty Tkachen [Modern Chukchi and Yupik names for birds in the Senayvin Strait region and Tkachen Bay]. In *Litsom k moryu: Pamiati Lyudmily Bogoslovskoy* [Those who face the sea: In memory of Lyudmila Bogoslovskaya], edited by Igor Krupnik, pp. 107–119. August Borg, Moscow.

Arutyunov, Sergei A., Igor I. Krupnik, and Michael A. Chlenov

1982 *Kitovaya alleia: Drevnosti ostrovov proliva Seniavina* (Whale Bone Alley: Antiquities of the Senyavin Strait Islands). Nauka Publishing House, Moscow.

Badten, Linda Womkon, Vera Oovi Kaneshiro, and Marie Oovi (compilers)

1987 *A Dictionary of the St. Lawrence Island / Siberian Yupik Eskimo Language*. 2nd prelim. ed. Edited by Steven A. Jacobson. Alaska Native Language Center, University of Alaska Fairbanks.

Badten, Linda Womkon, Vera Oovi Kaneshiro, Marie Oovi, and Christopher Koonooka (compilers)

2008 *St. Lawrence Island / Siberian Yupik Dictionary*. 2 vols. Edited by Steven A. Jacobson. Alaska Native Language Center, University of Alaska Fairbanks.

Chlenov, Michael A.

1988 Ekologicheskie factory etnicheskoi istorii Beringova proliva [Ecological Factors of Bering Strait Ethnic History]. In *Ekologiya amerikanskikh indeitsev i eskimosov* [Ecology of American Indians and Yupik Eskimos], edited by Valery Tishkov. pp. 64–75. Nauka Publishing House, Moscow.

2006 The "Uelenski Language" and Its Position Among Native Languages of the Chukchi Peninsula. *Alaska Journal of Anthropology* 4(1–2): 74–91.

2016 Eskimosskaya toponimika raiona proliva Senyavina (yugovostochnaya Chukotka) [Eskimo place names of the Senyavin Strait area, Eastern Chukotka]. In *Litsom k moryu: Pamiati Lyudmily Bogoslovskoy* [Those who face the sea: In memory of Lyudmila Bogoslovskaya], edited by Igor Krupnik, pp. 214–248. August Borg, Moscow.

Dobrieva, Elizaveta A., Evgenii V. Golovko, Steven A. Jacobson, and Michael E. Krauss (compilers)

2004 *Naukan Yupik Eskimo Dictionary*. Edited by Steven A. Jacobson. Alaska Native Language Center, University of Alaska, Fairbanks.

Kalyuzhina, Natalya, Alexander Borovik, and Arthur Apalu

2016 Mnogoletnie statsionarnye ledovye treshchiny u beregov yugovostochnoy Chukotki (Nablyudenia za traditsionnym ispolzovaniem ledovogo prostranstva) [Multi-year stationary ice leads along the shores of southeastern Chukotka: Observations on traditional use of icescapes]. In *Litsom k moryu: Pamiati Lyudmily Bogoslovskoy* [Those who face the sea: In memory of Lyudmila Bogoslovskaya], edited by Igor Krupnik, pp. 175–190. August Borg, Moscow.

Krauss, Michael E.

2004 Introduction to "Place Names (Toponyms)." In *Naukan Yupik Eskimo Dictionary*, compiled by Elizaveta A. Dobrieva, Evgenii V. Golovko, Steven A. Jacobson, and Michael E. Krauss, pp. 319–330. Edited by Steven A. Jacobson. Alaska Native Language Center, University of Alaska Fairbanks.

2005 Eskimo Languages in Asia, 1791 on, and the Wrangel Island–Point Hope Connection. *Études/Inuit/Studies* 29(1–2): 163–186.

Krupnik, Igor, and Michael A. Chlenov

2013 *Yupik Transitions: Change and Survival at Bering Strait, 1900–1960*. University of Alaska Press, Fairbanks.

Leont'ev, Vladilen V., and Klavdia A. Novikova

1989 *Toponimicheskii slovar' Severo-Vostoka SSSR* [Toponymic dictionary of the Northeast of the USSR]. Magadan Publishing House, Magadan.

Litke, Fyodor

2014 *Plavaniya kapitana flota Fedora Litke vokrug sveta i po Severnomu Ledovitomu okeanu* [Voyages of Navy Captain Fyodor Litke around the globe and in the Northern Polar Ocean]. Eksmo Publishing House, Moscow

Menovshchikov, Georgii A.

1972 *Mestnye nazvaniia na karte Chukotki. Kratkii toponimicheskii slovar'* [Local place names on the map of Chukotka: A brief toponymic dictionary]. Magadan Publishing House, Magadan.

1975 *Iazyk naukanskikh eskimosov* [The language of the Naukan Eskimo]. Nauka Publishing House, Leningrad.

Rubtsova, Ekaterina S.

1971 *Eskimossko-russkii slovar'* [Yupik-Russian dictionary]. Soviet Encyclopedia Publishers, Moscow.

Titova, Zinaida D. (editor and compiler)

1978 *Etnograficheskie materialy Severo-vostochnoi geogragicheskoi ekspeditsii, 1785–1797* [Ethnographic materials of the Northeastern Geographical Expedition, 1785–1795]. Magadan Publishing House, Magadan.

MAP A Mechigmen Bay

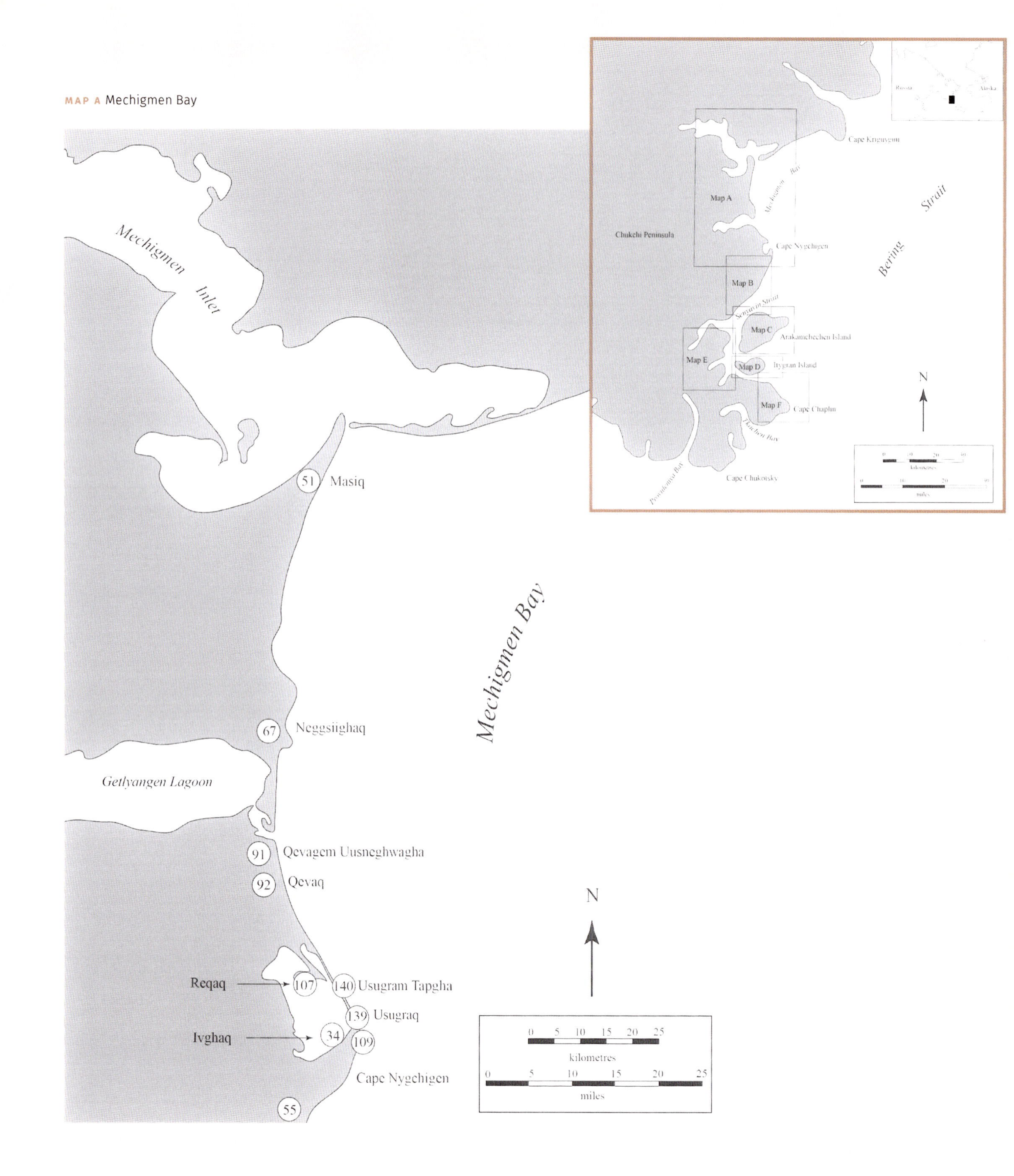

List of Place Names in the Senyavin Strait

The 160 place names in this list were recorded from 1977 to 1981. The sites to which they refer are marked by number on Maps A to F (covering the areas shown in figure 12.4). As noted earlier, Vladimir Tagitutqaq and Yuri Virineut were my primary sources of information, but other former residents of the Siqlluk community on Itygran Island also contributed their knowledge. Lyudmila I. Ainana—Yupik language specialist, public activist, and educator—was of great help in organizing and consolidating my field notes. In tracing etymologies, I drew on virtually all the existing academic dictionaries for Central Siberian Yupik languages (Badten, Kaneshiro, and Oovi 1987; Badten et al. 2008; Dobrieva et al. 2004; Menovshchikov 1975; Rubtsova 1971). Sources of particular value were the pioneering work of Georgii Menovshchikov (1972); the comprehensive *Toponimicheskii slovar' Severo-Vostoka SSSR* [Toponymic dictionary of the Northeast of the USSR], compiled by Vladilen V. Leont'ev and Klavdia A. Novikova (1989); and the toponymic section of the *Naukan Yupik Eskimo Dictionary* (Dobrieva et al. 2004), particularly the introduction to the section by Michael Krauss (2004).

Each place name in the list is followed by its spelling in the Cyrillic alphabet according to the orthography for Chaplinski Yupik adopted in Menovshchikov (1972) and Rubtsova (1971), as well as the orthography for Naukanski Yupik used by Krauss (2004). Entries include the most probable etymology of each name, along with any possible alternative derivations, and also list corresponding names in other Bering Strait languages. When available, information provided directly by Tagitutqaq is also included.

ABBREVIATIONS

CAY	Central Alaskan Yup'ik
Chuk.	Chukchi
CSY	Central Siberian Yupik
IN	Inupiaq/Iñupiaq
Intern.	International place name
NY	Naukanski Yupik
OS	Old Sirenikski Yupik
P-Esk.	Proto-Eskimo root
Rus.	Russian name
T.	Tagitutqaq

MAP B Senyavin Strait (northern part)

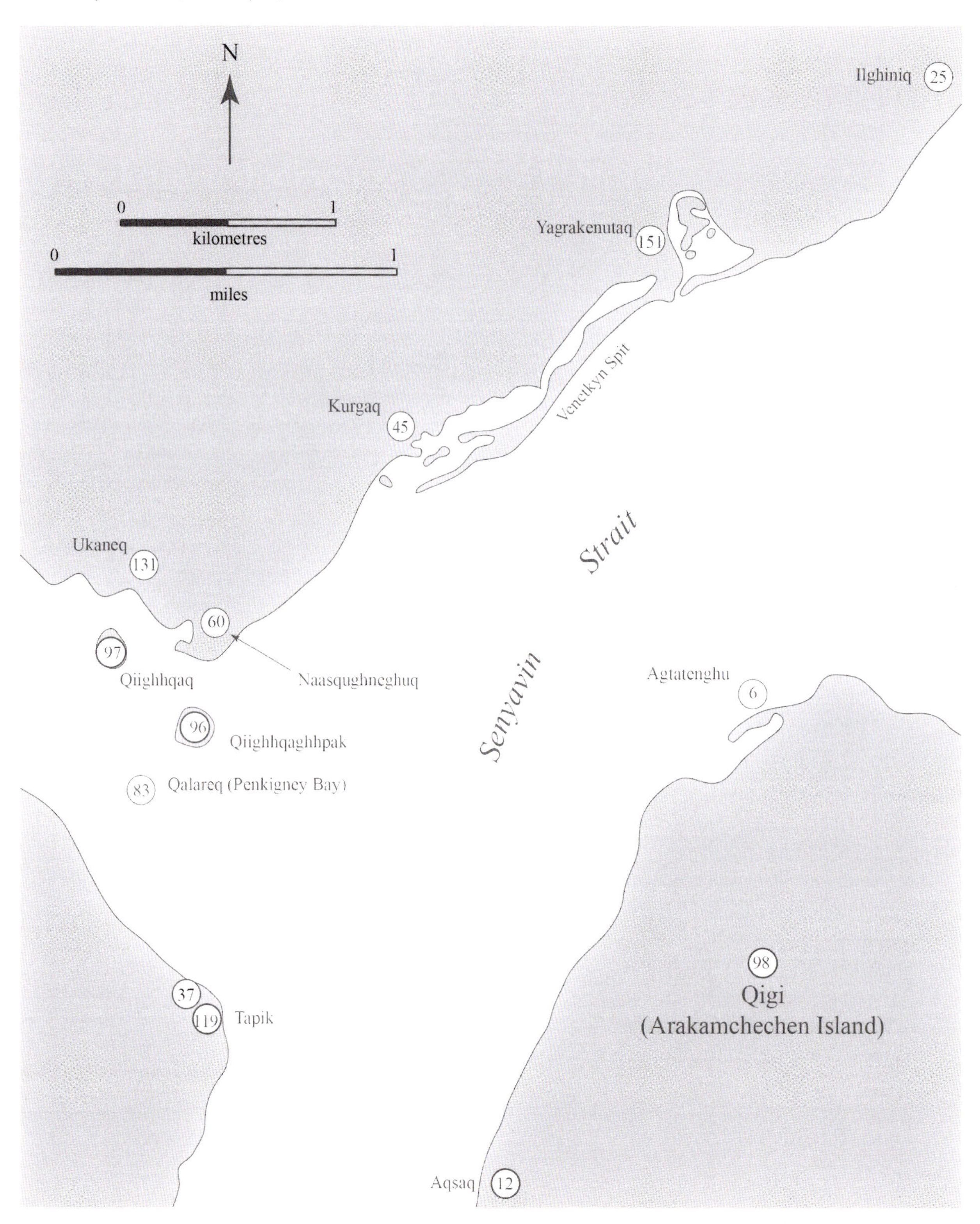

MAP C Arakamchechen Island

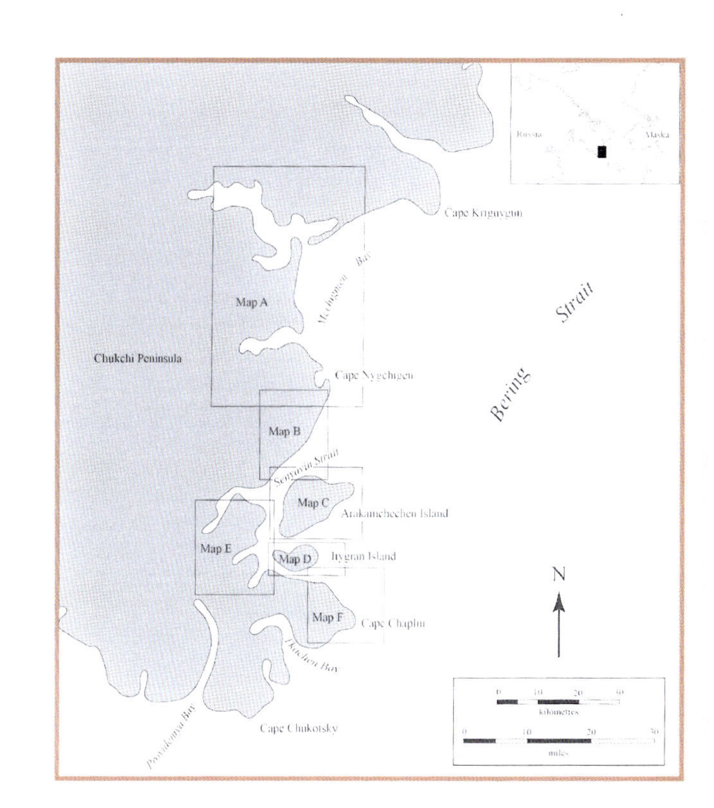

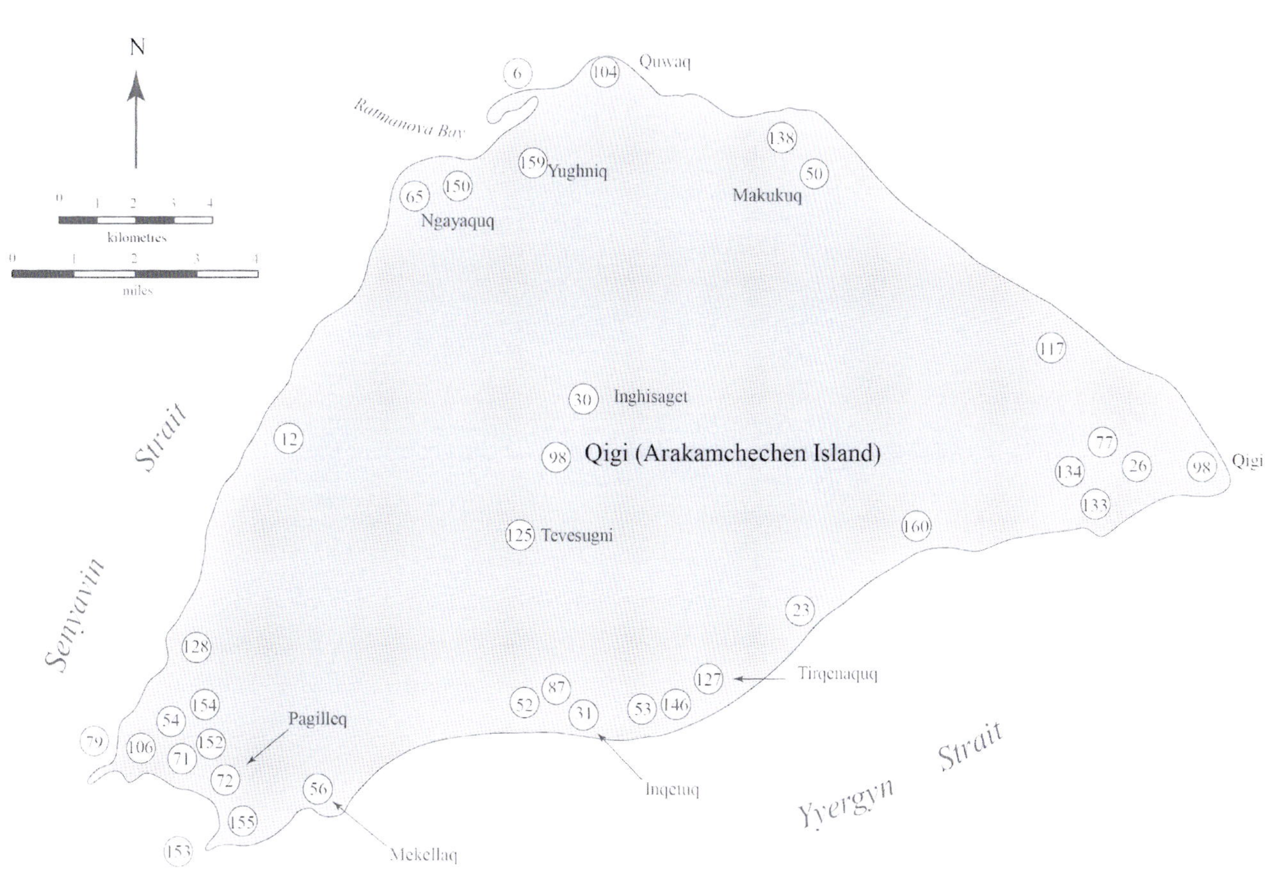

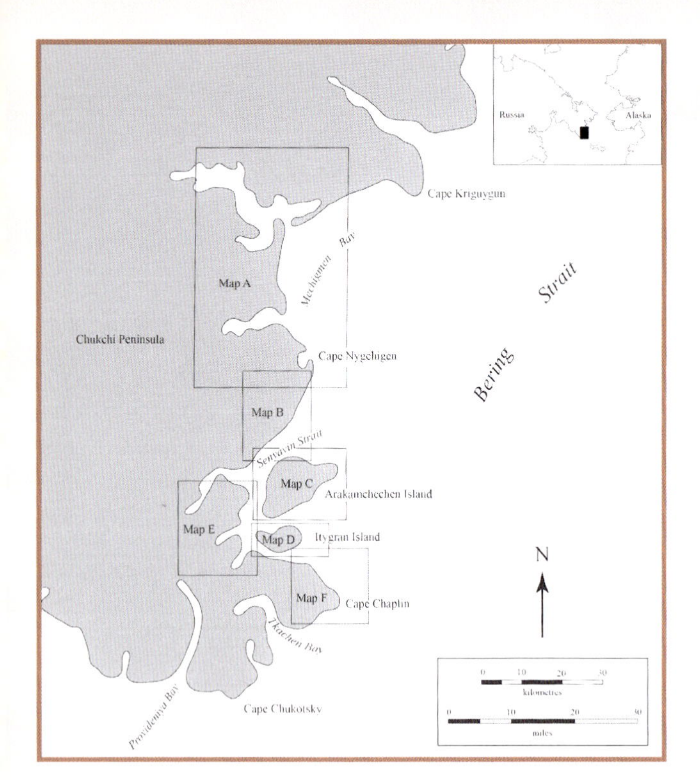

MAP D Itygran Island

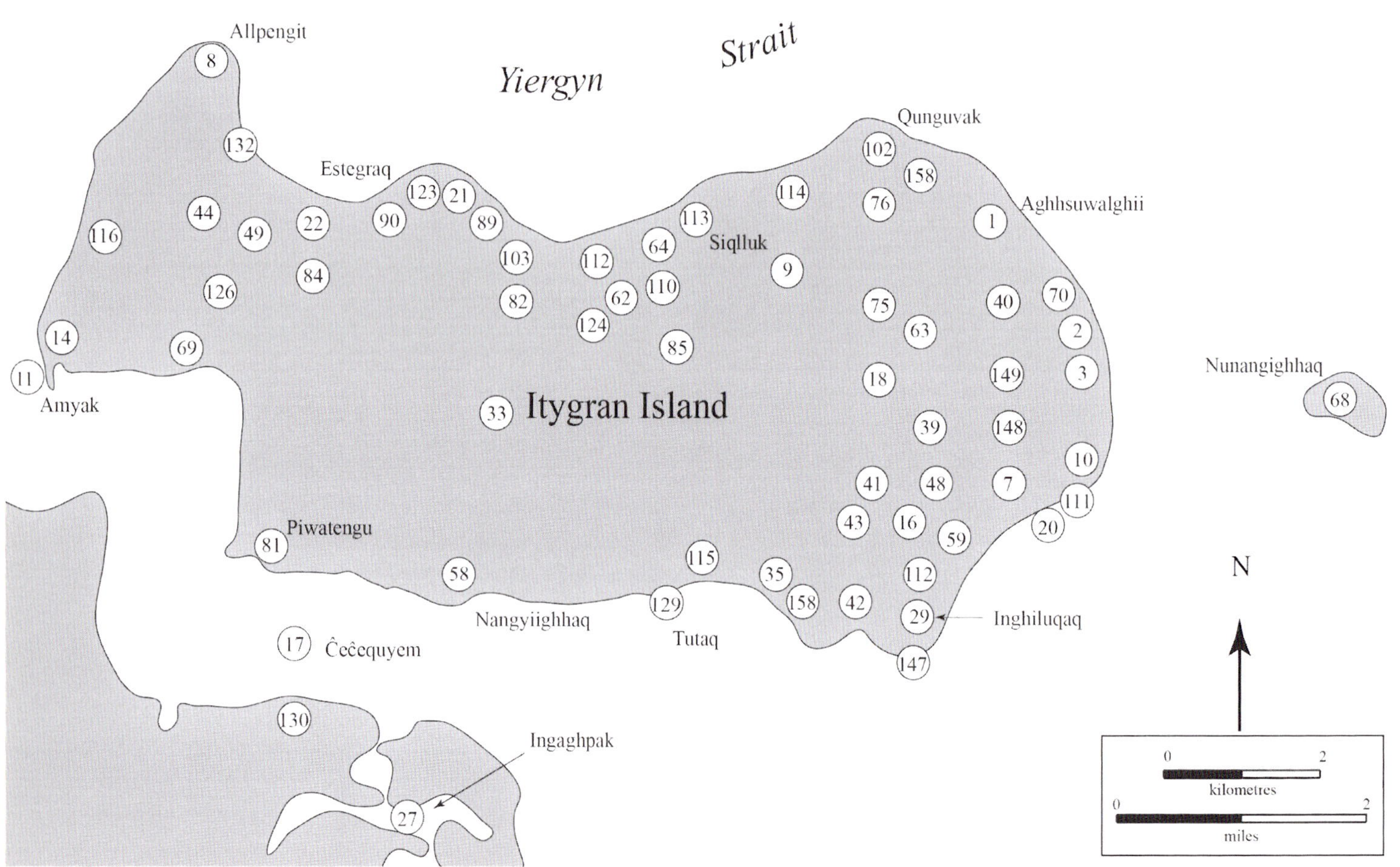

MAP E Senyavin Strait (southern part)

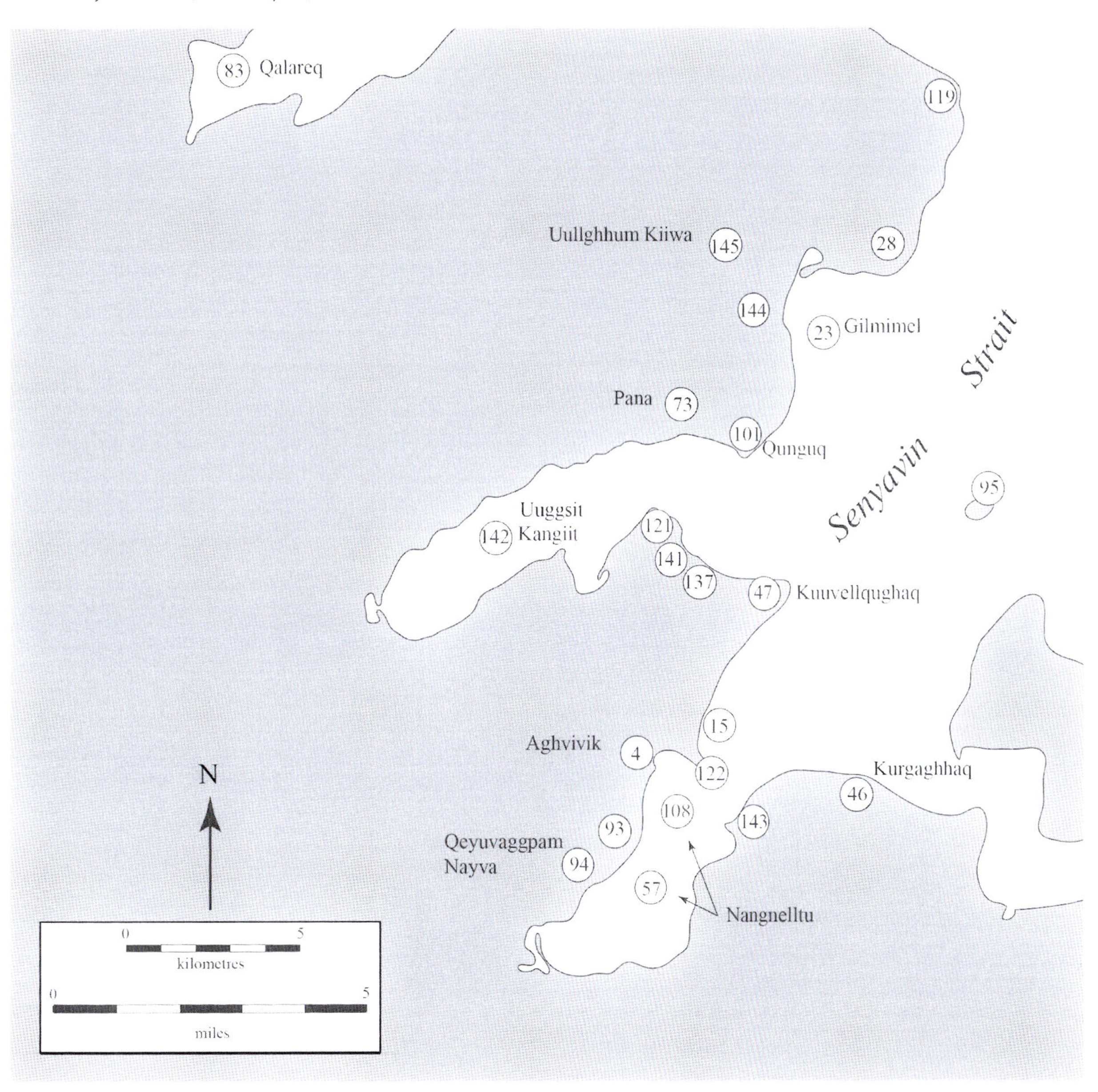

MAP F Cape Engelyukan to Cape Chaplin

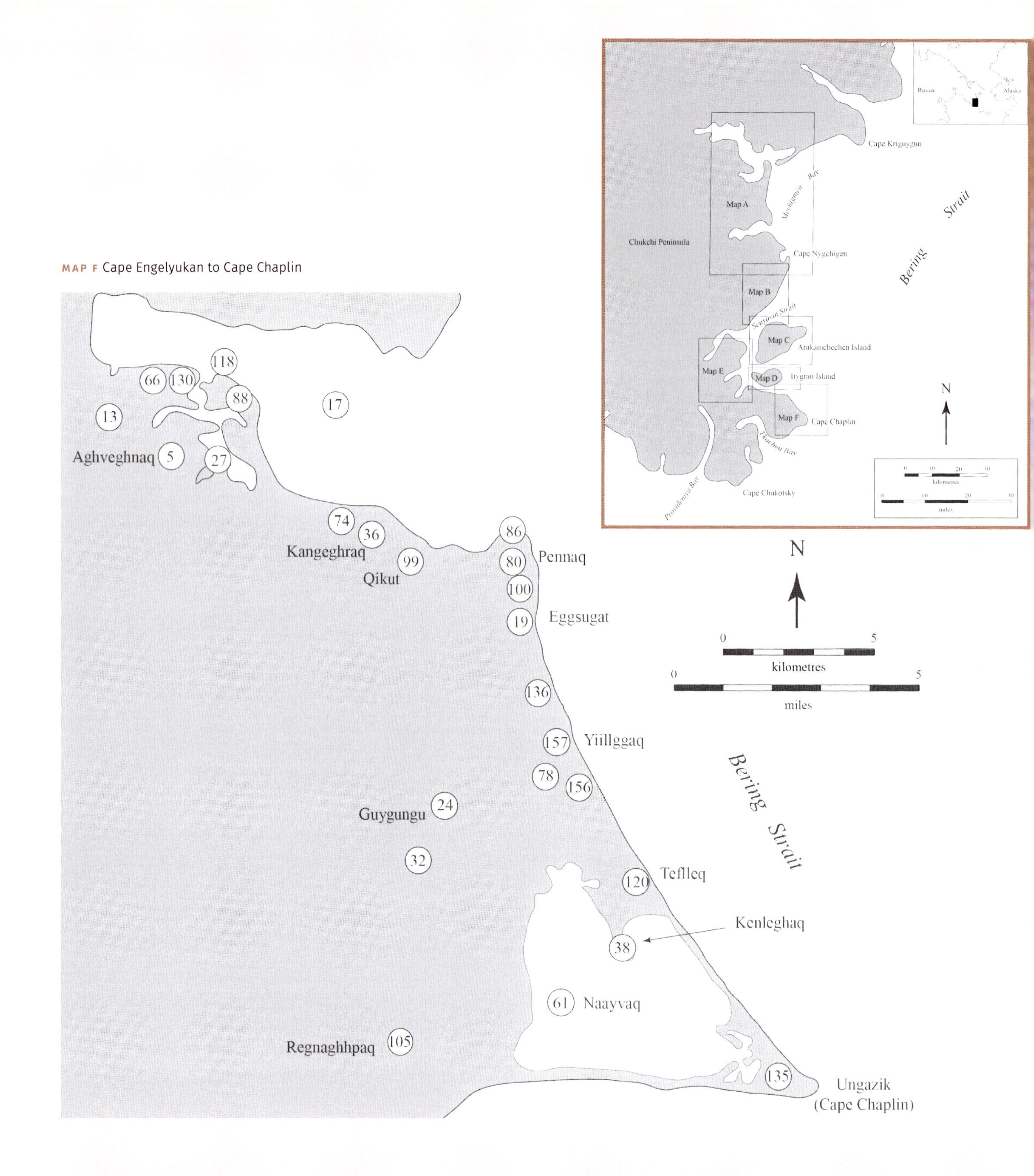

1 **Aghhsuwalghii (Ах'сюўалг'й)** – cliffs on the eastern shore of Itygran Island to the north of Napakutak. "Cliffs that appear white," from *aghhsugh*, "to be pale" (CSY). (Map D)

2 **Aghnaghaghham ana (Аг'наг'ах'ам ана)** – solitary rock in the water in front of Cape Nuvuk, on Itygran Island. "Maiden's feces," from *aghnaghaghhaq*, "maiden," and *anaq*, "feces, shit" (CSY). (Map D)

3 **Aghnam ana (Аг'нам ана)** – cliffs at Cape Nuvuk, on Itygran Island. "Female's feces" from *aghnaq*, "female," and *anaq*, "feces, shit" (CSY). (Map D)

4 **Aghvivik (Аг'вивик)** – seal rookery on the west shore of Rumilet Bay. "On the other shore," from *aghvighaquq*, "to come across, to cross over a water barrier"; *aghviqaq*, "the one that crossed over to the other side"; *aghvighvik*, "crossing"; *-vik* (CSY, NY, IN), *-veh* (OS) – locative suffix, indicating the location of an action. [T., "Doesn't have translation."] (Map E)

5 **Aghveghnaq (Аг'выг'нак')** – hill on the south side of Chechekuyum (Čečequyem) Strait, towering over Inakhpak Bay. "Convenient place for whale hunt," "good time for whale hunt," from *aghveq*, "whale" (CSY); *-naq* "something that causes V-ing," *-nak'*, *n"ak'* – suffix that references the time that is favorable for carrying out certain activity (CSY). [T., "Looks like a whale."] (Map F)

6 **Agtatenghu (Агтатынг'у)** – spit at the northern entrance to Ratmanov Bay, on Arakamchechen Island, also used to refer to Ratmanov Bay itself. "Moving a herd," from *agtatyk*, "to move a herd from one place to another" (Chuk.) Intern. – **Akhmatingu Spit**, **Ratmanov Bay**, named after naval officer Makar I. Ratmanov, a participant in the 1826–1829 Bering Sea expedition led by Fyodor Litke). (Maps B and C)

7 **Akatam peghivigha (Акатам пыг'ивиг'а)** – cliffs at the end of Esnaghhpaq Spit, on Itygran Island. "Temporary meat storage of Akatak," from *peghwaghaqa*, "to cover, to bury," *peghivighaq*, "temporary meat pit" (CSY). [T., "There is an indentation in the cliff; they say it was a temporary meat storage of ancient man named Akatak who hid meat there from bears."] (Map D)

8 **Allpengit (Алъпын'ит)** – cape located on the northwestern tip of Itygran Island. "Murre's," from *allpa*, "murre" (CSY), or, less likely, from *allpa-* "passage," literally, "their passage." Intern. – **Cape Skalisty**. (Map D)

9 **Amaghalek (Амаг'алык)** – mountain on northern Itygran Island, slightly to the east of centre. "Sitting on somebody's neck," from *amagh-*, "carry something on the shoulders" (CSY). [T., "Walrus cub on his mother."] (Map D)

10 **Amaghmelnguq (Амаг'мылн'ук')** – cape on the eastern promontory of Itygran Island. "Carrying on a neck," from *amagh-*, "to carry something on the shoulders, neck," *amaghaqaa*, "to lift and put somebody on one's neck" (CSY). Intern. – **Cape Amago Mel'got**. [T., "Overlapping one over another, as two boards nailed together."] (Map D)

11 **Amyak (Амьяк)** – cape on the southwestern promontory of Itygran Island. "Shell," from *amyak*, "scallop shell" (CSY), which the cape's terrain resembles. Intern. – **Cape Amyak**. [T., "It is called such because there are many shells. Siklyuk people used to travel to Amyak to hunt. They preferred to live in subterranean dwellings, and those who didn't have those lived under *baidaras*." (A *baidara* is an open skin-covered boat, similar to an umiak, used in sea hunting.)] (Map D)

12 **Aqsaq (Ак'сяк')** – western shore of Arakamchechen Island from Ngayaquq to Pagilleq. "(Island's) stomach," from *aqsa-*, "stomach" (CSY). (Maps B and C)

13 **Asagvek (Асягвык)** – mountains west of Kytlinay Bay, on the south side of Chechekuyum Strait. "Two women," from *asagvek*, "your two aunts," and *asak*, "father's sister" (CSY). [T., "There is Ugwinga Hill (see **Ugwinga**), but two wives, that is *asyagvyk*. The west hill has many children, that is, many hills on the western shore of Senyavin Strait, but the eastern [hill] has fewer children—these are small hills on Cape Chaplin."] (Map F)

14 **Awatghhutaghhaq (Аўатх'утах'ак')** – small rock overhang to the north of Cape Amyak, on Itygran Island. "It is possible to jump," from *awatghhutaqa*, "jump over," *-ghhaq* – diminutive suffix (CSY). [T., "Small rock, just a little bit taller than a human. That means that I can jump."] (Map D)

15 **Aywaan tekegha (Айўан тыкыг'а)** – spit at the northern entrance to Rumilet Bay. "Northern spit," from *aywaa*, "north," and *tekeghaq*, "spit, cape" (CSY). (Map E)

16 **Ayveghaghviggaq (Айвыг'аг'вихак')** – river on southeastern Itygran Island. "Place to harvest young walrus," from *ayveghaq*, "young walrus," *-vik* – locative suffix, *-ggaq* – diminutive suffix (CSY). [T., "Before a long time ago a walrus was killed there. That is why it was named so."] (Map D)

17 **Čečequyem (Чечек'уйым)** – strait between Itygran Island and northern shore of Cape Chaplin. **Ch'echen'k'uyym** – "cold frosty bay," from *ch'echen'*, "frost," and *k'uyym*, "bay, harbor" (Chuk.) (Leont'ev and Novikova 1989, 411). Siberian Yupik do not use the name Čečequyem, nor does the strait have a Yupik name. When necessary, they use the Russian name Chechekuyum. (Maps D and F)

18 **Eftughhtuk (ЫӀфтух'тук)** – river on eastern Itygran Island. "Making lots of noise," from *eftuq*, "rumble, barrage" (CSY). [T., "That is because in the spring it is very noisy. The waterfall forms."] (Map D)

19 **Eggsugat (ЫӀхсюгат)** – locality and former reindeer herders' camp on the northern shore of Cape Chaplin. Etymology is unclear; could be a Yupik name, "murky water," from *suughh-*, "murky" (CSY). (Map F)

20 **Esnaghhpaq (ЫӀснах'пак)** – a stretch of shore on eastern Itygran Island. "Large spit," from *esnaq*, "shore" (CSY). (Map D)

21 **Estegraghvaq (ЫӀстыграг'вак')** – the cape at the western end of Siklyuk Bay, off the north shore of Itygran Island. "Large Ystygraq [Estegraq]," "like Ystygraq" (CSY). Intern. – **Cape Tupoy**. See also **Qesiighyat**. (Map D)

22 **Estegraq (Ыстыграк’)** – locality and westernmost bay on the north shore of Itygran Island. "Femoral, muscular" from *estek*, "hip, muscle" (CSY). Intern. – **Stygrak Bay**. During Fyodor Litke's exploration of the Bering Strait, his sloop *Senyavin* approached Itygran Island from the northwest, so Estegraq ("Ytsygraq," in the standard transliteration of Ыстыграк’) was the very first place on the island that sailors saw. They asked their Chukchi guide for the name of the island, and, as neither the Chukchi nor the Yupik residents of the island had a name for it, he understandably gave them the Chukchi name of the bay and the locality, which they passed on to Litke. The name "Itygran" thus derives from Estegraq (that is, "Ytsygraq"), as does the name "Stygrak." (Map D)

23 **Gilmimel (Гилмимыль)** – (1) bay on the western side of Senyavin Strait. Chukchi name, "hot water," from *gyl*-, "hot," *mimyl*, "water" (Chuk.). See also **Ingapasungaq**, presumed CSY name. Intern. – **Gil'mimyl' Bay**. [T., "In the spring, [people] from Siklyuk fished in this bay; pink salmon come here."]. (2) river, hot spring, and locality on the southern shore of Arakamchechen Island. Intern. – **Pyl'mymlan River**, **Gylmylgyn River**. (Map E)

24 **Guygungu (Гуйгун’у)** – knoll and fort ruins at Cape Chaplin. "Fort" from *guygu*-, "house" (CSY). (Map F)

25 **Ilghiniq (Илг’иник’)** – locality and, in the past, a community on the western side of the Senyavin Strait to the north of Yanrakynnot. Etymology is unclear; possibly from *ilghi*-, "to hide" (CSY). Chuk. – **A'lyayonvyn**, "stinky place" (Leont'ev and Novikova 1989, 63). Rus. – **Alyaevo**. (Map B)

26 **Iluwaq (Илюўак’)** – part of a high knoll that borders Cape Kygynin from the west on Arakamchechen Island. "Similar to an interior part of a dwelling," from *ilu*-, "dwelling's interior," -*waq* – suffix signifying a resemblance (CSY). (Map C)

27 **Ingaghpak (Ин’аг’пак)** – bay and large hill on the southern side of Chechekuyum Strait, on the northern shore of Cape Chaplin. The site of a marine mammal hunting operation and supply facilities for the community of Novoe Chaplino, at Tkachen Bay. "Reclined hill," from *ingagh*-, "to lie on the side, to lie down to sleep" (CSY), -*pak* (CSY, NY) – augmentative suffix. Presumed etymology is "a place for overnighting or rest" or "a large hill that lies on a side." Rus. – **Inahpak**. Intern. – **Inakhpak, Inakhtak Mountain**, **Ch'echengkuyym Lagoon**. [T., "In the past, they came from Chaplino to hunt there."] (Maps D and F)

28 **Ingapasungaq (Ин’апасюн’ак’)** – cape at the northern entrance to Gil'mimyl' Bay. "Small hill that desired to be moved aside, that is lying separately from the other mountains," from *Ingapighhqaghaqa*, "to move," -*su-nga-q* – resultative suffix (CSY). Intern. – **Cape Krutoy**. (Map E)

29 **Inghiluqaq (Инг’илюк’ак’)** – cape at the southeastern end of Itygran Island. "Mountainous," from P-Esk. **iingghiq*, "mountain." This root does not occur in CSY but is present in all other Eskimo languages: *iingghiq* (NY), *inggheX* (OS), *ighiq* (IN). Intern. – **Cape Engelyukan**, **Cape Engelyukak**, **Cape Postels** (named after Aleksandr F. Postels, a participant in Fyodor Litke's Bering Strait expedition). (Map D)

30 **Inghisaget (Инг'исягыт)** – group of mountains in the central part of Arakamchechen Island. "Mountains," from P-Esk. **iingghiq*," mountain." [T., "There is no translation, just a name."] (Map C)

31 **Inqetuq (Инк'ытук')** – locality on the southern shore of Arakamchechen Island. Perhaps a Yupik adaptation of a Chukchi place name: compare Chukchi *enytkyn*, "cape, tip of a spit"; *i'nnysk'yn*, "hillock"; *i'nnun*, "hill." Possibly, if less likely, that it derives from P-Esk. **iingghiq*, "mountain," or from *ingki*, "rack, support" (NY). (Map C)

32 **Itghhit kiwa (Итх'ит киўа)** – river on Cape Chaplin. "River of intakes or entrances," from *iitghha*, "enter" (CSY). (Map F)

33 **Itygran (Итыгран)** – Russian and international place name of Itygran Island, in the area of Senyavin Strait; also spelled Ittygran and Yttygran. See **Estegraq**. (Map D)

34 **Ivghaq (Ивг'ак')** – bay, spit, and locality at the entrance to Gytkokuyym Lagoon. "Turning," from *ivgha-*, "enter into water" (CSY), *iivghaaq*, "turn" (NY), *ivghaq*, "place to turn" (Menovshchikov 1972, 95). Chuk. – **Gytkokuyym**. Intern. – **Cape Ikvyk**, **Gytgykuyym**, **Gytkokuyum Lagoon**. (Map A)

35 **Iwellqaq (Иўылъкъ'ак')** – mountain on the southern shore of Itygran Island. "Where a large tide is," from *iiw-*, "tide," *iiwaquq*, "tide is coming" (CSY). Intern. – **Ivyl'kak Mountain**. (Map D)

36 **Kangeghraq (Кан'ыг'рак')** – river that flows into Chechekuyum Strait to the west of Cape Mertens. Etymology is unclear. Possibly from *kangeq*, "skin under bird's feathers," perhaps related to *kangighaq*, "bay" (CSY). (Map F)

37 **Kavilut (Кавилют)** – mountain at Cape Tapik at the southern entrance to Penkigney Bay. "Red" from P-Esk. **kavi-*, CSY *kavilnguq*, NY *kavilghii*. Rus. –**Goryachie Klyuchi**. [T., "Only a temporary reindeer herding camp was here—they came here during calving. But a larger one was at Goryachie Klyuchi."] See also **Uullghhuk**. (Map B)

38 **Kenleghaq (Кынлыг'ак')** – cape on the shore of Naivak Lake. "Marginal," from *qenla*, "boundary, margin" (CSY). Intern. – **Cape Kogot**. [T., "It cannot be translated."] (Map F)

39 **Kiiggpak (Кӣхпак)** – river on eastern Itygran Island. "Large river," from *kiiwek*, "river," *-pak* – augmentative suffix (CSY). (Map D)

40 **Kiighaghhlleq (Кӣг'ах'лъык')** – hill next to Vostochnaya Mountain, on eastern Itygran Island. "Interval," from *kiigha-*, "distance between things" (CSY). [T., "Smallish hill near Nairakhpak, means "split rock."] (Map D)

41 **Kilgaquviggaq (Килгак'увихак')** – river on eastern Itygran Island, a tributary of the Kiiggpak River. "Small site for training," from *kiilgaaqu*, "long-distance running" (CSY). [T., "They ran there in the mornings to train."] (Map D)

42 **Kiwalighhaq (Киӯалих'ак')** – spit on the southern shore of Itygran Island that separates a lake from Chechekuyum Strait. "Site in the west," from *kiwalighneq*, *kigwani-*, "there, on the western side" (CSY). Apparently the name originated in Napakutak, where Tagitutqaq was born. Intern. – **Lake Kamalikakh**. [T., "Subterranean dwellings. No *nyn'lyu* [semi-dugout dwellings] there, only meat pits, simple depressions."] (Map D)

43 **Kiiweggpagek (Кӣӯыхпагык)** – river in the eastern part of Itygran Island. "Two large rivers," from *kiiwek*, "river" (dual), *-pa* – augmentative suffix (CSY). A place where two rivers merge and empty into a single channel. Intern. – **Napakutak River**. (Map D)

44 **Kumlungqaghhnaq (К'умлюн'к'ах'нак')** – hillock in the western part of Itygran Island. "Looks a lot like a thumb," from *qumlu*, "thumb," *-ngqaghhnaq*, suffix signifying a strong similarity (CSY). (Map D)

45 **Kurgaq (Кургак')** – locality to the south of Yanrakynnot, between the modern community of Yanrakynnot and the cape named Naasqughneghuq (CSY) (see **Naasqughneghuq**); in the past, it was a reindeer herders' camp and a small coastal community. Etymology unclear; possibly "joyful," from Chukchi *korgyl'yn*, "happy," or perhaps from Chukchi *kurgan*, "spider" (Leont'ev and Novikova 1989, 215). Chuk. – **Kurgan**. Rus. – **Naskonokytrykyr** (Map B)

46 **Kurgaghhaq (Кургах'ак')** – hill on the western end of southern shore of Chechekuyum Strait. "Little Kurgak" (see **Kurgaq**), *-ghhaq* – diminutive suffix (CSY). (Map E)

47 **Kuuvellqughaq (Кувылък'уг'ак')** – cape at the western exit from Rumilet Bay. "Continuously flooded," from *kuve-*, "pour, flood," *-llqughaq* – noun suffix (CSY).Rus. – **Mys Kuvilokuok**, **Mys Kuvylokuok**. Intern. – **Cape Kuvylokuok**, (Map E)

48 **Lliveghhtayaq (Лъивых'таяк')** – hillock on eastern Itygran Island where Napakutak cemetery was located. "Cemetery," from *illiveq*, "grave" (CSY). [T., "Small rocky hill, cemetery, where a naked corpse was put inside a ring of rocks."] (Map D)

49 **Makawaq (Макаўак')** – pass on the west end of Itygran Island, between Stygrak Bay, to the north, and the southern shore of the island. "Like a diaper," from *maka*, "flap of a child's *kukhlyanka* [upper garment made of fur, *kuspuk*], diaper," *-waq* – suffix signifying similarity (CSY). (Map D)

50 **Makukuq (Макукук')** – river on the north-eastern shore of Arakamchechen Island. Yupik adaptation of Chukchi place name **M"akok**, "little cauldron." Intern. – **Mokoku River**, **Zvonkiy Creek** (?). [T., "Simply 'Makukuk', it is untranslat-able."] (Map C)

51 **Masiq (Масик')** – locality and former community on the southern spit of Mechigmen Bay. Perhaps "warm," from *masigh-*, "to warm up around fire" (CSY). Chuk. – **Mesigmen**, **Machigmen**. Chukchi adaptation of P-Esk. **Masighmeng*, "from Masik," or *masighmii*, "in Masik" (see figure 12.5). Intern. – **Mechigmen**. (Map A)

52 **Mayngiatggergen (Майн'иатхыргын)** – locality on the southern shore of Arakamchechen Island. Yupik adaptation of Chukchi place name "large gorge," from Chukchi '*mayn'y-/meyn'y-*, "large," *eetyk*, "come down," *eetgyrgyn'*, *aatgyrgyn'*, "place to come down, gorge." Chuk. **Meyn'yaatgyrgyn**. [T., "There are rock pillars there. It seems like there were no dwellings."] (Map C)

53 **Mayngeguq (Майн'ыгук')** – locality and former reindeer herders' camp on the southern shore of Arakamchechen Island. Yupik adaptation of Chukchi place name "large rock," from Chukchi *mayn'y-/meyn'y-*, "large," *vykvyn*, "rock." Chuk. – **Meyn'ykvyn**. Rus. – **Meynyguk**, **Meynyruk**. (Map C)

54 **Mayngengay (Майн'ын'ай)** – mountain on the southwestern end of Arakamchechen Island. Yupik adaptation of Chukchi place name "large mountain," from Chukchi *mayn'y-/meyn'y-*, "large," *-n'ay/-n'ey*, "mountain." Chuk. – **Meyn'yn'ey**. Rus. – **Menyngan**. (Map C)

55 **Mayngeraq (Майн'ырак')** – locality on the western shore of Senyavin Strait between Yanrakynnot and Gytkokuyym Lagoon. Yupik adaptation from Chukchi place name **Mayn'yran**, "large house," from Chukchi *mayn'y-/meyn'y-*, "large," *–ran*, "dwelling." (Map A)

56 **Mekellaq (Мыкылъак')** – knoll on Yargem tekegha, a spit on Arakamchechen Island. "Little," from *meke-*, "little" (CSY). Chuk. – **Mykyl'an**. Intern. – **Cape Moklyak**. [T., "hump."] (Map C)

FIGURE 12.5 Dwelling ruins at the old village of Masiq, July 1981. The upright structural elements were made from the mandibles of bowhead whales. Photograph by Sergei A. Bogoslovskiy.

57 **Nangnelltu (Нан'ныльту)** – bay and southwestern entrance into the Senyavin Strait. Presumably "outermost, last" (that is, the last bay if one travels down the coast from the north), from *nangneq*, "end" (CSY). Etymology is unclear, but apparently an adaptation of the Chukchi place name **Rulmylen/Rulmylyt** (Menovshchikov 1972, 144). Intern. – **Rumilet** (Rumlet, Romulet, Rumulet, Ramulet, Rumilet, Roumilet). Also recorded was the Russian name, **Bukhta Ledyanaya**. Intern. – **Ledyanaya Bay**. (Map E)

58 **Nangyiighhaq (**Нан'йӥх'ак'**)** – cape on the southern shore of Itygran Island across from Inakhpak Bay. "Little brave man," from *nangyii-*, "brave" (CSY). (Map D)

59 **Napaqutaq (Напак'утак')** – locality and, until 1934, the site of an Indigenous community on southeastern Itygran Island. "Pillar-like," from *napaqaq* or *napaqutaq*, "post", *-taq* – repository suffix (CSY). Rus. – **Napakutak**. [T., "Old Napakutak [was located] above pillars of rock. Ayilin lived there. This is Napakutak proper, but during my time it was already called Inghiluqaq, and the place where we lived is called Siighwaq."] (See **Siighwaq**.) (Map D)

60 **Naasqughneghuq (Наск'уг'ныг'ук')** – cape at the northern entrance to Penkigney Bay. "This is a head," from *naasquq*, "head" (CSY). Chuk. – **Naskunukytrykyr**, from *-kytrykyr*, "cape." Rus. – **Naskonokytrykyr**. (Map B)

61 **Naayvaq (Нāйвак')** – lake on Cape Chaplin. "Lake," from *naayvaq*, "lake" (CSY). Chuk. – **Nayvan**. (Map F)

62 **Nashqaq (Нашк'ак')** – rockslide at Siklyuk, on northern Itygran Island. Etymology is unclear, but perhaps from *naarquaque*, "swan" (NY) or *narkaq*, "skin of reindeer's head" (NY) or *naasquq*, "head" (CSY). The phoneme *sh* does not exist in CSY. The sound *š* constitutes allophone of the phoneme *r* in the so-called feminine pronunciation. That is why one should discern a lexical element that is not etymologized directly from CSY in this particular place name and in several others on this list. (Map D)

63 **Nayghaghhpak (Найг'ах'пак)** – mountain in eastern Itygran Island. "Large mountain," from *naayghaq*, "mountain," *-pak* – augmentative suffix (CSY).Intern. – **Vostochnaya Mountain**. (Map D)

64 **Naayvaghhaq (Найвах'ак')** – lagoon at Siklyuk, on northern Itygran Island. "Small lake," from *nāyvaq*, "lake" (CSY). (Map D)

65 **Ngayaquq (Н'аяк'ук')** – cape at the southern entrance to Ratmanova Bay on northern Arakamchechen Island. Etymology is unclear. Phonetically the name resembles a Yupik toponym, but perhaps this is a Yupik adaptation of a Chukchi toponym, perhaps from *ngayagwell*, "herd"; looks like a borrowing from the Chukchi language. Chuk. – **N'ut'ekvyn**, "something that protects Earth.") Intern. – **Cape Nayakuk**. (Map C)

66 **Ngeellqat (Н'ылък'ат)** – hill and rock on the southern side of Chechekuyum Strait. "Cormorants," from *ngeellqat* (CSY). (See figure 12.1.) [T., "Because cormorants nest there."] (Map F)

FIGURE 12.6 Nunangighhaq, 2015. Photograph by Igor Zagrebin.

67 **Neggsiighaq (Ныхсӣг'ак')** – cape at the northern entrance to Getlyangen Lagoon in Mechigmen Bay. Etymology is unclear. A connection to *neghhsaq*, "seal" (CSY), is very unlikely. Chuk. – **Nygchigen**. Intern. – **Cape Khalyustkin**, **Nygchigey cabin**. (Map A)

68 **Nunangighhaq (Нунан'их'ак')** – small island in Bering Strait to the east of Itygran Island, the location of a bird rookery. "Small land," from *nuna*, "land" –*-ngighhaq* diminutive suffix (CSY). (See figure 12.6.) Chuk. – **Nunenen**. Rus. – **Ostrov Nuksagen**. Intern. – **Nuneangan**, **Nuneangan Island**. (Map D)

69 **Nuuvawalik (Нуваўалик)** – locality on the southern shore of Itygran Island, east of Cape Amyak. "Slobbered on," from *nuuvak*, "saliva" (CSY). [T., "There is no water there, [they] go in a whaleboat. River is very small."] (Map D)

70 **Nuvuk (Нувук)** – cape on the eastern shore of Itygran Island. "Final," from *nuvuk*, "cape, end" (CSY). Intern. – **Cape Navak**. (Map D)

71 **Pagilleghem tekegha (Пагилъыг'ым тыкыг'а)** – spit at the end of Cape Pygylyan, on southeastern Arakamchechen Island. "Spit Pygylyan," from Pagilleq, and *tekeghaq*, "spit, cape" (CSY). (Map C)

72 **Pagilleq (Пагилъык')** – cape on the southwestern end of Arakamchechen Island. "Cormorant," from P-Esk. **pagi-*, **pagu-*, "cormorant." This root is not present in either CSY or NY, but it appears in *pagelleX* (OS) and *pagulluk* (IN). It is less possible that the name derives from CSY *pagii-*, "remain, anticipate" (thus, "cape of anticipation"). Chuk. – **Pagelyan**. Intern. – **Cape Pygylyan**. (Map C)

73 **Pana (Пана)** – mountain on the northern shore of Aboleshev Bay. "Spear shaped," from *pana*, "spear" (CSY). [T., "Chaplino Yupik Tina and his family used to go there to collect plants and that is why it was called *panaghmiit*.."] (Map E)

74 **Pakfalltaq (Пакфалътак')** – hill and rock on the southern side of Chechekuyum Strait between Inakhpak Bay and Cape Mertens. "Where the southeastern wind blows," from *pakfalla*, "southeastern wind" (CSY). (Map F)

75 **Papeghaq (Папыг'ак')** – western spur of Nayghaghhpak Mountain, on Itygran Island. "Spur," from *papeghaq*, "hill adjacent to a mountain" (CSY). (Map D)

76 **Pawaghvik (Паўаг'вик)** – flat and overgrown with turf, the top of Konovak Mountain, on northeastern Itygran Island. [T., "From the word *pawaghluku*, which means to dry seal skin on a wooden stretching frame (*niillghhek*) on a frame. It got its name from many seal bones there."] (Map D)

77 **Payuggsaq (Паюхсяк')** – high hill on Cape Kygynin, on western Arakamchechen Island. "Observation point," from *payuggte-*, "to observe, to check" (CSY). (Map C)

78 **Pengut (Пын'ут)** – a range of hills on the northern shore of Cape Chaplin from Unyiramkyt to Tyflyak. "Hills," from *pengut*, "hills," "hillocks" (CSY). (Map F)

79 **Pennaghraq (Пынъаг'рак')** – cape on the shore of Glazenap Bay, on southwestern Arakamchechen Island. "Not a real rock," from *pennaq*, "rock, cliff," *-raq* – suffix that signifies something unreal (CSY). Intern. – **Cape Taylek**. (Map C)

80 **Pennaq (Пынъак')** – cape at the southeastern entrance to Chechekuyum Strait. "Rock, cliff," from *pennaq* (CSY).Intern. – **Cape Mertens**, named after naturalist Karl H. Mertens, who travelled with Fyodor Litke's expedition to the Bering Strait. (Map F)

81 **Piwatengu (Пиўатын'у)** – spit, cape on the southwestern shore of Itygran Island. "Send off to home," from *piwaghaquq*, "to go home" (CSY). Perhaps a Yupik adaptation of Chukchi place name Pygatyn, from *pygatyn*, "place where something will surface," "place for arranging an inflatable float, *pyg-pyg*" (Menovshchikov 1972, 139). Intern. – **Cape Ostryy**. (Map D)

82 **Pugneghem ullghhitaghviga (Пугныг'ым улъх'итаг'вига)** –northern spur of Itygran Mountain on the island of the same name. "As if balls of boiled reindeer fat are rolling," from *pugneq*, "ground reindeer fat and meat," *ulghhit*, "to roll" (CSY). [T., "As if boiled white fat is rolling, after the white marks on the slopes of a hill."] (Map D)

83 **Qalareq (К'алярык')** – a bay on the western side of Senyavin Strait. Etymology is unclear. Perhaps from P-Esk. **qala*, "fur seal," or Chuk. *kal'a*, "devil." Chuk. – **Kalyarakuyym**. Chuk. – **Pen'ken'ey**, "snowy mountain." Intern. – **Penkigney**, **Pinkigney**. [T., "Not a single Yupik would go hunting at Penkigney. Prior to collective farms, the reindeer herders were stationed there, and everyone kept reindeer.

The reindeer provided the herders with fat and other things, and in August, when reindeer skins are good, the reindeer herders would come to slaughter them, and Eskimo would visit them. I do not think that my father, Yama, had a reindeer herder with whom he traded regularly."] (Maps B and E)

84 **Qamughtughvik (К'амуг'туг'вик)** – a river that flows into Stygrak Bay, on western Itygran Island. "A place where there is a portage," from *qamuq-*, "to pull, drag (including something in a sled or on the ground)" (CSY). [T., "River where alder grows, from *qamughaqa*, which means to pull a seal by a rope, because a long time ago they had pulled a bearded seal from the southern shore across this river."] (Map D)

85 **Qavraatat (К'аврāтат)** – mountain, the highest peak on Itygran Island (454 metres). "Ravines," from *qavraatat*, "gorge, ravine" (CSY). Intern. – **Itygran Mountain**. (Map D)

86 **Qayam mayuqaghhfigha (К'аям маюк'ах'фиг'а)** – tip of Cape Mertens. "Lifting of kayak," from P-Esk. **qayaq-*, *mayughaquq*, "climb up, lift up," *mayughvik*, "a place of ascension," *mayuq*, "ascension" (CSY). [T., "Two people paddling in a kayak fought with each other, and then one ran to the shore and up the mountain and carried the kayak by himself."] (Map F)

87 **Qayovenliptaten (К'айовынлиптатын)** – river on southern Arakamchechen Island that flows into Yyergyn Strait between Mayngiatggergen and Inqetuq. A Chukchi place name that was has no Yupik adaptation. (Map C)

88 **Qelengayen, Qelengay (К'ылын'айын, К'ылын'ай)** – locality on the southern side of Chechekuyum Strait and the site of a marine mammal hunting base (see **Ingaghpak**) for the Senyavin Strait region. A Chukchi place name, from *k'ytl'ik*, "cannot, do not want to reach," *-n'ay/-n'ey*, "mountain." Chuk. – **K'ytlin'ay**. Rus. – **Kytlinay**. (Map F)

89 **Qesiighyat (К'ысӣг'ьят)** – Cape on the northern coast of Itygran Island, at the western end of Siklyuk Bay. "Covered with hoarfrost," from *qesiighaq*, "hoarfrost" (CSY). See also **Estegraghvaq**. (Map D)

90 **Qesiighyaghwaq (К'ысиг'ьяг'ӯак')** – small cape in Stygrak Bay, on northern Itygran Island. "Like Kysig'yat [Qesiighyat]" (CSY). (Map D)

91 **Qevagem uusneghwagha (К'ывагым усныг'ӯаг'а)** – hill in the Qevaq locality at the entrance to Getlyangen Lagoon, in Mechigmen Bay. "Kyvak [Qevaq] hillock," from *uusnevaghaq*, "small hillock" (CSY). (Map A)

92 **Qevaq (К'ывак')** – locality at the base of the southern spit at the entrance to Getlyangen Lagoon, in Mechigmen Bay. "Angry, mean," from P-Esk. **qeve-*, "angry," *qevute*, "to beat" (CSY), *qeveet*, "to be angry, to be ticked off" (NY). Perhaps a Yupik adaptation of a Chukchi place name **Kuvan**, "stone." Intern. – **Mount Kuvan**. (Map A)

93 **Qeyuvaggpak (К'ьювахпак)** – a low hillock on the western shore of Rumilet Bay. "A large green mountain" (NY), from *qeyuq*, "greenery, grass," *-pak* – augmentative suffix (CSY, NY). (Map E)

94 **Qeyuvaggpam nayva (К'ыювахпам найва)** – small lake near the Qeyuvaggpak hillock. "Kyyuvakhpak Lake," from *naayvaq*, "lake" (CSY). (Map E)

95 **Qiighhqaghhaq (К'ӣх'к'ах'ак')** – island in the Senyavin Strait between the southwestern end of Arakamchechen Island and an entrance into Aboleshev Bay. "A little island," from *qiighhqaq*, "an island," *-ghhaq* – diminutive suffix (CSY). Rus. – **Kynak**. (Map E)

96 **Qiighhqaghhpak (К'ӣх'к'ах'пак)** – island at the northern entrance to Penkigney Bay. "A large island," from *qiighhqaq*, "an island," *-pak* – augmentative suffix (CSY). Chuk. – **Ech'ynkinken**, "fatty." Intern. – **Achinkinkan**, **Orlov Island** (named after a participant in the Fyodor Litke expedition). (Map B)

97 **Qiighhqaq (К'ӣх'к'ак')** – island at the northern entrance to Penkigney Bay. From *qiighhqaq*, "an island" (CSY). Chuk. – **Mervykinken**, "skinny." Rus. – **Merkinkan**. (Map B)

98 **Qigi (К'иги)** – (1) an outermost eastern end of Arakamchechen Island. "Green, covered with greenery," from *qig-*, "green, to turn green" (CSY). Less possible connection with *qiighhqaq*, "island" (CSY). Perhaps a Yupik adaptation of a Chukchi place name, although there is no clear etymology for Chukchi **K'iginin'ytkyn**. Intern. – **Cape Kygynin**. (Map C) (2) Yupik name of the entire island of Arakamchechen, common in CSY since about the mid-twentieth century. Chuk. – **Ilir**, "island." Rus. – **Ostrov Arakamchechen**. Intern. – **Arakamchechen**. The participants in the expedition led by Fyodor Litke gave the island the last of these names. The name originated when expedition cartographers took a Chukchi phrase, which apparently was not very well understood, to be the name of the whole island. (Vladilen Leont'ev cites a Chukchi variation Y'r'ykamchech'yn, "deceptive place where one wanders" [Leont'ev and Novikova 1989, 72].) Despite its artificial origins, the place name Arakamchechen has become the most widely accepted name for this large island. (Maps B and C)

99 **Qikut (К'икут)** – rivers that flow from the south into Chechekuyum Strait between Inakhpak Bay and Cape Mertens. "Clay-like," from *qiku*, "grey clay, from which the oil lamps were made" (CSY). The western river is **Sivuli qiku (Сивули к'ику)**, "anterior Qiku"; the eastern river is **Kiwaliik Qiku (Киўалик К'ику)**, "aftermost Qiku." (Map F)

100 **Qilaget (К'илягыт)** – mountain on the northern shore of Cape Chaplin to the south of Cape Mertens. "Sky-like," from *qilak-*, *qilaget*, "skies" (CSY). Intern. – **Mount Kiyagat**. (Map F)

101 **Qunguq (К'ун'ук')** – cape at the northern entrance to Aboleshev Bay. "Burial," from **quŋuq*, "to bury, grave, cadaver" (CSY, NY, IN), *qungeX* (OS). Rus. – **Kunuk**. [T., "In the past, my father, Yama, went to this cape very often in September and October; he had a hunting cabin there—a semi-subterranean dwelling with wooden cover. There they hunted seals. In December they would return back to Napakutak on a sled."] (Map E)

FIGURE 12.7 Regnaghhpaq, 2015. Photograph by Igor Zagrebin.

102 **Qunguvak (К'ун'увак)** –northeastern cape on Itygran Island. "Large cemetery," from P-Esk. **quŋuR-*, "to bury," "grave, cadaver," *qungughaq*, "cemetery" (CSY). Intern. – **Cape Konovak**. [T., "A grave covered in rocks."] (Map D)

103 **Qupr(sh)uqellaq (К'упр(ш)ук'ылъяк')** – white rocks on the western end of Siklyuk Bay. "Tufted puffin," from *quprughaq*, "tufted puffin, horned puffin" (CSY). (Map D)

104 **Quwaq (К'уўак')** – northern end of Arakamchechen Island. Yupik adaptation of a Chukchi place name **K'ukven**, "wooded," from *quuk-*, "firewood" (CSY) and *-kven*, "rock" (Chuk.). Intern. – **Cape Kuguvan**, **Mount Kruglaya**. (Map C)

105 **Regnaghhpaq (Рыгнах'пак')** – butte and fort at Cape Chaplin. (See figure 12.7.) eEtymology is unclear, but possibly "large yearling reindeer," from Chukchi *rygna*, "yearling reindeer," and *-paq* – augmentative suffix (CSY). (Map F)

106 **Reperen (Рыпырын)** – cape at the entrance to Glazenap Bay, on the southwestern end of Arakamchechen Island. Yupik adaptation of a Chukchi place name, perhaps from Chukchi *rypattym*, "shoulder blade," "dwelling covered with whale shoulder blade." Intern. – **Cape Taylek**. (Map C)

107 **Reqaq (Рык'ак')** – Gytkokuyym Lagoon in Mechigmen Bay. Yupik adaptation of a Chukchi place name **Rekan**. Etymology is unclear; compare Chukchi *reken*, "reindeer that one can ride." (Map A)

108 **Rumilet Bay (Румилет)** – see **Nangnelltu**. (Map E)

109 **Sagayaq (Сягаяк')** – rocks at the southern base of Ivghaq Spit, at the entrance to Gytkokuyym Lagoon. "Expanded," from *saaq-*, "expanded, disordered" (CSY). Intern. – **Sapalon Spit**. (Map A)

110 **Saniighmelnguq (Сяни̅г'мылн'ук')** – hillock on northern Itygran Island. "Transversal," from *sanigh-*, "transverse" (CSY). (Map D)

111 **Siighwaq (Си̅г'ўак')** – a former Yupik camp on the eastern shore of Itygran Island, part of Napakutak. "A place where fog is clearing away," from *siigh-*, "to clear away (fog)" (CSY). [T., "That place, where we lived, is called Siighwaq. We all were called *siighwaghmiit napaqutaghmiit*."] (Map D)

112 **Singhaghhaq (Синг'ах'ак')** – spit on the northern shore of Itygran Island. "Little Singak" or "little shore," from P-Esk. **sin-*, "shore," *-ghhaq* – diminutive (CSY). The Whale Bone Alley site, is located on this spit, at **Siqlluk**. (Map D)

113 **Siqlluk (Сик'лъюк)** – bay, locality, and, until 1951, Yupik community on the northern shore of Itygran Island, sometimes used as an alternative name for the island itself. "Meat pit," from P-Esk. **siqlluk*, "meat pit, dwelling," *siqllugwaq*, "meat pit" (CSY). Chuk. – **Sya'alun**. Rus. – **Siklyuk**, **Seklyuk**. Inter. – **Seklyuk**. Whale Bone Alley, a famous cultural and historical site, is located at Siklyuk. [T., "All the area from Kunguvak to Napakakhpak. It [the name] originates from the word *sik'l"yuûak* because a lot of meat had been put on the rockslide. Hunters from Chaplino had recently put [it] there and then used sleds to transport it during winter."] (Map D)

114 **Siqlluwraq (Сик'лъуўрак')** – locality on the northern shore of Itygran Island to the east of Siklyuk. "Like Siklyuk," from **Siqlluk**, *-ra(q)* – suffix of similarity (CSY). (Map D)

115 **Sivughat (Сивуг'ат)** – (1) rocks on the southern shore of Itygran Island. "Foremost," from *sivu-*, "front, beginning" (CSY). (2) rock on the eastern shore of Itygran Island. Etymology is the same (CSY). (Map D)

116 **Sulghaq (Сулг'ак')** – locality on the western shore of Itygran Island. "Murky," from *sulghii-*, "murky"; possibly, but less likely, from *sullqu*, "grey ringed seal" (CSY). [T., "A shore on the western coast, place to hunt seals. Seals are there in the winter, rains comes upon it."] (Map D)

FIGURE 12.8 Ungiyeramken, 1981. Photograph by Igor Zagrebin.

117 **Suventatggergen (Сувынтатхыргын)** – isthmus between Yarvi Lake and the northeastern shore of Arakamchechen Island. Chukchi place name. (Map C)

118 **Talngighaq (Талн'иг'ак')** – hill on the southern side of Chechekuyum Strait. "Without a cover," from P-Esk. **tal-*, "to hide, conceal," *-ngigha* – suffix of negation (CSY). Perhaps Intern. – **Cape Topograficheskiy**. (Map F)

119 **Tapik (Тапик)** – cape at the southern entrance to Penkigney Bay. Etymology is unclear, but perhaps a Yupik adaptation of the Chukchi noun *tepk'en*, "spit." Rus. – **Iranki**, **Irankhi**. Also possibly from Russian *yarangi* (Leont'ev and Novikova 1989, 158). (Maps B and E)

120 **Teflleq (Тыфлъык')** – Yupik community on Peschanoe Lake that existed at the beginning of the twentieth century on the northern shore of Cape Chaplin. Etymology is unclear. Perhaps related to *tele-/*tefe-*, "to pass, go up," *tevaquq*, "to cross, pass" (CSY), then "large pass" (Menovshchikov 1972, 157). Rus. – **Tyflyak**. (Map F)

121 **Teghlawaquneq (Тыг'ляўак'унык')** – rocky cape on the southern shore of Aboleshev Bay. "Looks like a sitting owl," from *teghla*, "owl," *-waq* – suffix of similarity (CSY). Chuk. – **Taglyavakun**. (Map E)

122 **Tekeghat (Тыкыг'ат)** – two spits at the entrance of Rumilet Bay. "Spits," from *tekeghaq*, "spit, cape," pl. *tekeghat* (CSY). See **Aywaan tekegha**, **Uughhqan tekegha**. (Map E)

123 **Tengteghak (Тын'тыг'ак)** – small cape to the west of Siklyuk Bay, on northern Itygran Island. "Walrus nose," from *tengteghak*, "walrus nose" (CSY). (Map D)

124 **Tevek (Тывык)** – pass between two hills overlooking Siklyuk, on northern Itygran Island. *Tevek*, "pass" (CSY). (Map D)

125 **Tevesugni (Тывысюгни)** – pass on between the Menyngan and Afos mountains on Arakamchechen Island. "Looks like a pass," from *tevek*, "pass," *-sugni* – suffix of similarity (CSY). (Map C)

126 **Tevlighaq (Тывлиг'ак')** – pass between the northern and southern shores of western Itygran Island. "Small pass," from *teve-*, *teva-*, "to pass, go up," *tevaquq*, "to cross, pass," *-ghaq* – diminutive suffix (CSY). (Map D)

127 **Tirqenaquq (Тирк'ынак'ук')** – cape on the southern shore of Arakamchechen Island. "Creaky," from *teřqi*, "to creak" (CSY); perhaps also an adaptation of a Chukchi place name. The other Yupik name of this cape is **Uwaliq**. Intern. – **Cape Oleniy**. (Map C)

128 **Tuungliq (Тӯн'лик')** – spit on the western shore of Arakamchechen Island, several kilometres to the north of Pagilleq. "Next," from *tuungliq*, "next" (CSY). (Map C)

129 **Tutaq (Тутак')** – bay and river on the southern shore of Itygran Island. "Jounced against something," from *tutaqa*, "step on something, jounce against something" (CSY). Intern. – **Tugak Bay**. (Map D)

130 **Ugwinga (Угўин'а)** – mountain on the southern side of Chechekuyum Strait. "Her husband," from *ugwi*, "husband" (CSY). See also **Asagvek**. (Maps D and F)

131 **Ukaneq (Уканык')** – locality on the northern shore of Penkigney Bay. "Local," from *uka*, "here, local" (CSY). (Map B)

132 **Ukimaraguq (Укимарагук')** – rocks in Stygrak Bay, off northwestern Itygran Island. "Having holes," from *ukimalleq*, "hole" (CSY). [T., "There are some holes that are caves."] (Map D)

133 **Umiruu (Умирӯ)** – spit on the southeastern shore of Arakamchechen Island. Yupik adaptation of the Chukchi place name **Mumir"un**. Etymology is unclear. Intern. – **Cape Umiru**. (Map C)

134 **Umirum nayva (Умирум найва)** – lake on the southeastern shore of Arakamchechen Island. "Umirumskoe Lake," from *naayvaq*, "lake" (CSY). Chuk. – **Mumir"ugytkhyn**. Intern. – **Yarvi Lake**. (Map C)

135 **Ungaziq (Ун'азик')** – peninsula and former community at the eastern end of Cape Chaplin. "There lies," from *unga-*, "there, further" (CSY) (Krauss 2005, 169). Chuk. – **Un'iin**. Intern. – **Ungazik, Cape Chaplin, Staroe Chaplino**. (Map F)

136 **Ungiyeramken (Ун'ийырамкын), Ungiyeramka (Ун'ийырамка), Ungiyeramket (Ун'ийырамкыт)** – Yupik community on Peschanoe Lake that existed at the beginning of the twentieth century, on the northern shore of Cape Chaplin. (See figure 12.8.) "Ungazik people," from *Un'iin*, "Ungazik, Old Chaplino," *ramka*, "people" (Chuk.). Rus. – **Unyiramkyt, Uniyramkyt**. (Map F)

FIGURE 12.9 Yarga, July 1981. Photograph by Sergei A. Bogoslovskiy.

137 **Unuguteq (Унугутык’)** – river that flows into Aboleshev Bay between Kuuvellqughaq and Teghlawaquneq, two capes on the southern shore of Aboleshev Bay. “Place for overnight stop, overnight,” from *unuk*, “night” (CSY, NY, CY, IN). (Map E)

138 **Uqfigaqeggtaq (Ук’фигак’ыхтак’)** – cape on the northeastern shore of Arakamchechen Island. “Wooden, where good willow bushes with roots are,” from *ugfigaq*, “edible willow roots,” -*qeggtaq* – suffix indicating a stable characteristic (CSY). Chuk. – **M”akokykvyn**, “rock cauldron” (Menovshchikov 1972, 125). Intern. – **Cape Makokugvan**, **Makokuguan**. (Map C)

139 **Usugraq (Усюграк’)** – southern spit at the entrance to Gytkokuyym Lagoon, on the shore of Mechigmen Bay. “Looks like a penis,” from *usuk*, “penis” (CSY). Intern. – **Sapalon Spit**. (Map A)

140 **Usugram tapghha (Усюграм тапх’а)** – spit at the entrance to Gytkokuyym Lagoon, on the shore of Mechigmen Bay. “Usyugrakskaya spit,” from *tapghhaq*, “spit” (CSY). (Map A)

141 **Uuggsit (Ӯхсит)** – seal haulout on the southern shore of Aboleshev Bay, from *uuggsiq*, “dry spot,” *uuggsilghak*, “haulout of marine animals” (CSY). (Map E)

142 **Uuggsit kangiit** (Ӯхсит кан’йт) – bay on the western side of the Senyavin Strait. “Bay where a haulout is,” from *uuggsiq*, “dry spot,” *uuggsilghak*, “haulout of marine animals,” *kangiiq*, “bay, gulf” (CSY). Chuk. – **Kalilinvyn**. Rus. – **Bukhta Aboleshева**, **Aboleshева-buhta**, **Bahía Abolechef**, **Bukhta Kalalen**, **Bukhta Kalelen**, **Bukhta Kalyalen**. Intern. – **Aboleshev Bay**, named after M. N. Aboleshev, a naval officer who served with the Fyodor Litke expedition. Also known as Kalyalen Bay, an adaption of a Chukchi place name. [T., “People from Siklyuk hunted in this bay. A Siklyuk Eskimo named Akugyka hunted on the southern shore. They would depart from Napakutak in a *baidara* [a whaling boat] that would deliver them there and then go back, while they stayed to hunt seals from *baidarka*s [smaller *baidaras*] covered with walrus skins. Dogs pulled the *baidarka*s back.”] (Map E)

143 **Ughhqan tekegha (Ух’к’ан тыкыг’а)** – spit at the southern entrance to Rumilet Bay. “Southern spit,” from *uughqa*, “south,” *tekeghaq*, “spit, cape” (CSY). (Map E)

144 **Uullghhuk (Ӯлъх’ук)** – hot springs in the valley of Klyuchevaya River, which flows into Gal’mimyl’ Bay. “Hot springs,” from *uullghhuk*, “hot spring” (CSY). Chuk. – **Gilmimyl**. Intern. – **Senyavin Hot Springs**, **Chaplino Hot Springs**. [T., “There was a large reindeer herders’ camp at the hot springs. Nomads stayed there: Umrugvi and, before him, Yatylin, from Kurupka. Umrugvi was a local Yanrakynnot nomad.”] (Map E)

145 **Uullghhum kiiwa (Ӯлъх’ум кӣўа)** – river where the Senyavin Hot Springs are located. “River at hot springs,” from *uullghhuk*, “hot spring,” *kiiwa*, “river” (CSY). Intern. – **Klyuchevaya River**. (Map E)

146 **Uwaliq (Уўалик’)** – another name for cape **Tirqenaquq**, on southern Arakamchechen Island. “Eastern,” from *uwalighneq*, “east” (CSY). Intern. – **Cape Oleniy**. (Map C)

147 **Vuvelltu (Вувылъту)** – rock pillar near Cape Engelyukan (see **Inghiluqaq**), on southern Itygran Island. "Lemming," from *vuvelltu*, "lemming" (CSY). (Map D)

148 **Wesuggtan (Ӯысюхтан)** – river on eastern Itygran Island. Etymology is unclear. Perhaps from *suugh-*, "murky," then "murky river" (CSY). Possibly the name has a Chukchi origin. (Map D)

149 **Wingqurasiq (Ӯин'к'урасик')** – river on eastern Itygran Island that flows between Nayghaghhpak and Kiighaghhlleq mountains. "Unhurried," from *wiinqun-*, "not yet, thus far" (CSY). [T., "Doesn't freeze during winter: water is always under the ice."] (Map D)

150 **Wewtengay (Ӯыӯтын'ай)** – spit on the northwestern shore of Arakamchechen Island. Yupik adaptation of the Chukchi place name **Vyvtyn'ayen'ytkyn**, from *enytkyn*, "cape, spit," *n'ay-*, "mountain" (Chuk.). [T., "A little spit where people can take shelter from the north wind while they are at the western shore."] (Map C)

151 **Yagrakenutaq (Ягракынутак')** – community on the western side of Senyavin Strait. Yupik adaptation of the Chukchi place name **Yanrakynnot**, from Chukchi *yanra-*, "separately," *-kyn-*, "hard," *not-*, from *nytenum*, "earth" (Menovshchikov 1972, 174); that is, "a plot of land that lies separately." Rus. – **Yanrakinot**, **Yandrakinot**, **Yanrakennot**. (Map B)

152 **Yarga (Ярга)** – locality on the southwestern end of Arakamchechen Island (see figure 12.9). "Flat area," Yupik adaptation of a Chukchi place name, from Chukchi *ergyyikvik*, "valley." Chuk. – **Ergyn**. (Map C)

153 **Yargem kangigha (Яргым кан'иг'а)** – bay at the southwestern end of Arakamchechen Island. "Yarginskaya bay," from *kangighaq*, "gulf, bay" (CSY). Intern. – **Glazenap Harbor** (named after warrant officer B. Glazenap, participant in the Fyodor Litke expedition). (Map C)

154 **Yargem naayva (Яргым наайва)** – lake at the southwestern end of Arakamchechen Island. "Yarginskoe Lake," from *naayvaq*, "lake" (CSY). Intern. – **Gornoe Lake**. (Map C)

155 **Yargem tekegha (Яргым тыкыг'а)** – spit on the southwestern end of Arakamchechen Island. "Yarginskaya spit," from *tekeghaq*, "spit" (CSY). Intern. – **Cape Yyergyn**, **Cape Myergyn**. (Map C)

156 **Yiillggam naayva (Ййлъхам на̄йва)** – small lake on the northern shore of Cape Chaplin. "Iil'khakskoe lake," from *naayvaq*, "lake" (CSY). (Map F)

157 **Yiillggaq (Ййлъхак')** – locality on the northern shore of Cape Chaplin, adjacent to Cape Mertens. "Hidden," from *yillggani*, "unnoticed, hidden" (CSY). (Map F)

Yugaghhtaghhaq (Югах'тах'ак') – (1). *Kekur* (rock stack) on Konovak Mountain, on northeastern Itygran Island. "Small, looks like a human," from *yuuk*, "human," *yugaq*, "looks like a human" (CSY). [T., "A rock that looks like a human. One like that stands at the top of a hill; people pushed [it up] to become stronger."] (2). A group of tall, upright stones atop a cliff on a slope of Ivyl'kak Mountain, on the southern shore of Itygran Island. [T., "The rocks were once human beings. When one passes in a whaleboat, it looks like many people stretching upward."] (Map D)

158 **Yughniq (Юг'ник')** – river that flows into Ratmanov Bay, on northern Arakamchechen Island. Possible Yupik adaptation of the Chukchi name **Yugniveem River**, "river where edible plants grow," from *veem*, "river," *yun'i-*, "edible plants" (Chuk.). (Map C)

159 **Yughnivayam (Юг'ниваям)** – river that flows into Yyergyn Strait, on the southern shore of Arakamchechen Island. Yupik adaptation of a Chukchi place name, from *veem*, "river," *yun'i-*, "edible plants" (Chuk.). Chuk. – **Yugniveem**. Intern. – **Kamenistyy Creek**. (Map C)

Northern Animal Illustrations

The animals illustrated below by artist Emily Kearney-Williams were selected primarily on the basis of their connections to the topic or geography of individual chapters, although several were chosen in recognition of their somewhat iconic status as animals of the Arctic. In all cases, however, the animals illustrated are broadly distributed across the Arctic and have cultural importance to the region's Indigenous peoples.

Each of the animals illustrated is identified not only by its common name and scientific name but also by its name in one or more Indigenous languages. Scientific names are taken from the International Union for Conservation of Nature (IUCN) Red List of Threatened Species (https://www.iucnredlist.org/), version 2017-3.

Narwhal
Monodon monoceros
Northwest Greenlandic: *Qilaluqaq qernertaq*

Gray Wolf or Black Wolf
Canis lupus
Gwich'in: *Zhóh*
Central Alaskan Yup'ik: *Kegluneq*

Raven
Corvus corax
Central Alaskan Yup'ik: *Tulukaruk*
Iñupiaq: *Tulugaq*
Tanacross: *Taatsą́ą'*

Walrus
Odobenus rosmarus
Nunivak Cup'ig: *Kauxpax*
Central Alaskan Yup'ik: *Azveq*
Central Siberian Yupik: *Ayveq*
Iñupiaq: *Aiviq*

Muskox
Ovibos moschatus
Siglitun: *Umingmak*
Uummarmiutun: *Umiŋmak*

Red Salmon or Sockeye Salmon
Oncorhynchus nerka
Ahtna: *Łuk'ae*

Wolverine
Gulo gulo
Iñupiaq: *Qavvik*
Koyukon: *Nełtseel*

Brown Bear or Grizzly Bear
Ursus arctos
Gwich'in: *Shih*

Snowy Owl
Bubo scandiacus
Inuktitut: *Ukppik*

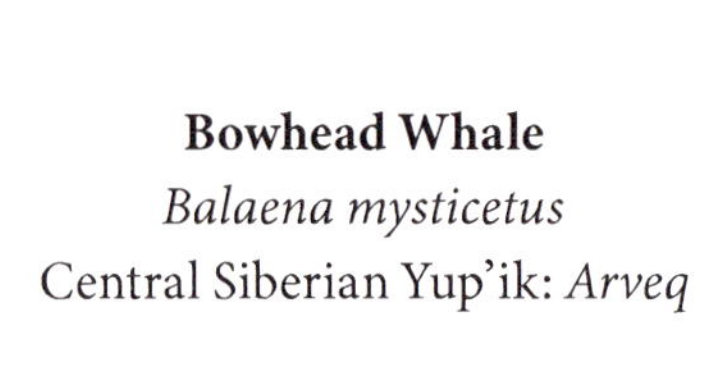

Bowhead Whale
Balaena mysticetus
Central Siberian Yup'ik: *Arveq*

Caribou
Rangifer tarandus
Inuinnaqtun: *Tuktu*
Inuktitut: *Tuttuk*

Lynx
Lynx canadensis
Lower Tanana: *Niduuy*
Iñupiaq: *Niutuiyiq*

Polar Bear
Ursus maritimus
Inuktitut: *Na'nuq*

Harbor Seal
Phoca vitulina
Tlingit: *Tsaa*

Red Fox
Vulpes vulpes
Central Alaskan Yup'ik: *Kaviaq*

Golden Eagle
Aquila chrysaetos
Iñupiaq: *Tiŋmiaqpak*
Upper Kuskokwim: *Yode*

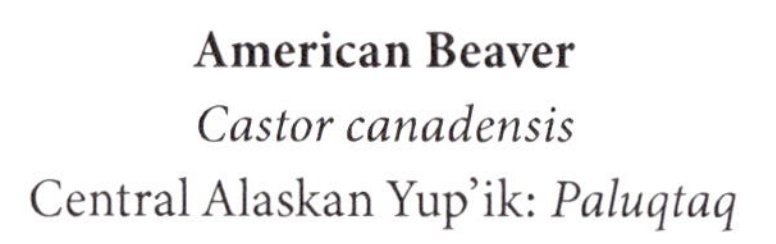

American Beaver
Castor canadensis
Central Alaskan Yup'ik: *Paluqtaq*

Black Bear
Ursus americanus
Inupiatun: *Iyyaġri*

Broad Whitefish
Coregonus nasus
Central Alaskan Yup'ik: *Akakiik, Qaurtuq*

Arctic Ground Squirrel
Urocitellus parryii
Central Alaskan Yup'ik: *Cikik*
Iñupiaq: *Siksrik*

FIGURE C.1 *Suluŋaaq* is a former Inupiaq village, originally occupied in the summer and fall during the caribou-hunting season. Situated on the westernmost tip of the Seward Peninsula, on a hilltop to the north of the modern village of Wales, the site features numerous stone structures and caches. *Suluŋaaq* was in use until the latter decades of the nineteenth century but was abandoned following the precipitous decline in the population of the Seward Peninsula caribou herd that began midway through the century. Photograph by Matt Ganley, September 2016.

Contributors

Vinnie Baron is a teacher at the local Ulluriaq School in Kangiqsualujjuaq, a village located on the east side of Ungava Bay, in Nunavik. She also serves on Makivik Corporation's board of directors, representing her community's and Nunavik's interests. She has a passion for going out on the land. She and her husband, Felix St-Aubin, have three wonderful children that they hope will practice their culture as they have been taught.

Hugh Brody is a writer, anthropologist, and filmmaker. He spent ten years immersed in the lives of Indigenous peoples of arctic and subarctic Canada. His books include *The People's Land, Maps and Dreams, Living Arctic,* and *The Other Side of Eden*. His films include *Nineteen-Nineteen,* starring Paul Scofield and Maria Schell; a series of documentaries made with peoples of the North; and *Tracks Across Sand,* a set of sixteen films made with the ‡Khomani San of the southern Kalahari. He holds the Canada Research Chair in Aboriginal Studies at the University of the Fraser Valley, in British Columbia, and is an honorary associate at the Scott Polar Research Institute at the University of Cambridge. He also is an honorary professor of anthropology at the University of Kent.

Kenneth Buck is a web designer and computer programmer who holds degrees in archaeology and computer science from the University of Calgary.

Anna Bunce was first introduced to Arctic berries during a trip to Iqaluit, on southern Baffin Island, where she was researching climate change adaptation and health as part of her master's degree in geography, which she earned at McGill University. She currently works as a First Nations relations advisor for the British Columbia government.

Donald Butler is a post-doctoral research fellow in the Laboratory for Sedimentary Archaeology, Department of Maritime Civilizations, at the University of Haifa, Israel. His research interests include multi-variate statistics and the multi-element and molecular analyses of soils at archaeological sites, including areas of the Canadian Arctic.

Michael A. Chlenov (PhD, Cultural Anthropology) started his professional career as a cultural anthropologist, historian and linguist in the early 1960s. He has conducted about 20 anthropological field studies in Indonesia, Yamal and the Bering Strait area of Siberia, Abkhazia and Daghestan in the Caucasus, Uzbekistan and Tajikistan in Central Asia. From 1965–1999 he was a fellow of the Moscow-based Institute of Ethnography of the Russian Academy of Sciences, and from 1994–2015 worked as a Dean at the Moscow-based State Jewish Academy. From 1998–2005 he worked as Deputy Director in the joint project between the Moscow State University and the Hebrew University in Jerusalem "Center for Jewish Studies and Jewish Civilization." He now serves as an alumni Professor at the Maimonides Academy in Moscow.

Aron L. Crowell is an Arctic anthropologist and Alaska Director of the Smithsonian Institution's Arctic Studies Center. His research and publications in cultural anthropology, archaeology, and oral history reflect collaborations with Indigenous communities of the North. He is the curator and project director for the exhibition *Living Our Cultures, Sharing Our Heritage: The First Peoples of Alaska*, at the Anchorage Museum, and leads ongoing community-based programs in Alaska Native heritage, languages, and arts. Crowell's doctorate in anthropology is from the University of California, Berkeley, and he is an affiliate professor of anthropology at the University of Alaska.

Peter C. Dawson is a professor in the Department of Anthropology and Archaeology at the University of Calgary and a research associate at the Arctic Institute of North America. His research interests include the digital preservation of tangible and intangible heritage at risk.

Martha Dowsley is an associate professor at Lakehead University, in Thunder Bay, Ontario. She has worked with northern Indigenous communities for the past ten years, examining human-environment relationships. A project on Inuit women's environmental relationships revealed the deep attachment to the land that is facilitated through berry harvesting. Dowsley hopes that the lessons learned from these women will help to encourage society at large to nurture the precious human-land connection.

Robert Drozda first developed an interest in Alaska Native oral history and place names in the early 1980s, when he began fieldwork associated with the US Bureau of Indian Affairs (BIA) ANCSA 14(h)(1) historical and cemetery sites project. His Alaska fieldwork spans the Yukon-Kuskokwim Rivers and Delta, Nunivak Island, northwest Alaska, and Agattu Island, at the far western end of the Aleutian chain. Working with the residents of Mekoryuk, on Nunivak Island, he developed the Nunivak Place Name Project and served as principal grant writer for Nunwarmiut Piciryarata Tamayalkuti (Nunivak Cultural Programs), most specifically in support of their Cup'ig language preservation and continuance projects.

Scott A. Heyes leads the Heritage Sustainability Team in cultural heritage at Rio Tinto in Perth, Western Australia. He also holds research associate positions at the Smithsonian Institution's Arctic Studies Center, in Washington, DC, and Monash University, Australia. He holds a PhD in Geography from McGill University.

Gary Holton is professor of linguistics at the University of Hawai'i at Mānoa and co-director of the Biocultural Initiative of the Pacific. His work focuses on the documentation of the Indigenous languages of Alaska and the Pacific, with an emphasis on spatial orientation and traditional knowledge systems.

Colleen Hughes holds a master's degree from the Department of Anthropology and Archaeology, University of Calgary. Her research interests include toponymy, digital heritage, and the archaeology of the Canadian Arctic.

Peter Jacobs is emeritus professor of landscape architecture at Université de Montréal. He served as chair of the Kativik Environmental Quality Commission, in northern Québec, for thirty-eight years and is the former chair of the Commission on Environmental Planning of the International Union for Conservation of Nature. He is a fellow of both the Canadian and the American Society of Landscape Architects and a member of the Royal Canadian Academy of the Arts. He is currently chair of the Montreal Heritage Council.

Emily Kearney-Williams is a science illustrator and fine artist who grew up on Tybee Island, off the coast of Georgia, to which she attributes her love of the ocean and the natural world. She studied science illustration at California State University, Monterey Bay, receiving her graduate certificate in 2017. She recently worked as a medical illustrator at St. George's University in Grenada, West Indies, in connection with the university's BioMedical Visualization Fellowship. She has used her art to help teach about environmental issues and Indigenous cultural history in the North and currently balances her time between medical illustration and studio art, in Half Moon Bay, California.

Igor Krupnik is Curator of Arctic and Northern Ethnology collections and Head of the Ethnology Division at the National Museum of Natural History, Smithsonian Institution in Washington, DC. His areas of expertise include ecological knowledge and cultural heritage of the people of the Arctic; impact of modern climate change on Arctic residents, their economies, and cultures; and interdisciplinary collaboration in Arctic research. He has worked for forty years with indigenous Arctic communities, primarily with the Siberian Yupik and Inupiat people in the Bering Strait Region on collaborative efforts in the documentation and sharing of cultural knowledge, and in opening archival and museum resources for people's use in education and heritage preservation. Krupnik has published and co-edited more than twenty books, collection volumes, catalogs, and community heritage sourcebooks, including many supporting the use of Arctic indigenous knowledge and languages.

Apay'u Moore is a Yup'ik artist from Bristol Bay, Alaska. Her work draws its inspiration primarily from her cultural values and from the wilderness. By focusing on this subject matter, she hopes to help people gain insight into the higher level of spiritual interconnectedness that her people have with the living world even in the face of cultural trauma and colonialism. She is best known for her whimsical salmon paintings that were inspired by the fight against the Pebble Mine prospect, which she staunchly opposes and believes is a prime example of the signs of cultural obliteration that Yup'ik elders have warned of for generations. She now lives in Aleknagik, Alaska, with her two children, with the goal of becoming more firmly rooted to the subsistence lifestyle that brings purpose to living in the present with gratitude and contentment.

Murielle Nagy is an anthropologist and archaeologist affiliated to the Archéologie des Amériques research centre (CNRS/Université Paris 1 Panthéon-Sorbonne). She received an MA in archaeology from Simon Fraser University and a PhD in anthropology from the University of Alberta. She has worked for

Indigenous, governmental, academic, and touristic organizations in the Yukon, Northwest Territories, Nunavut, Nunavik, Greenland, and Alaska. From 1990 to 2000, she led three oral history projects for the Inuvialuit Regional Corporation. At Université Laval, she was a postdoctoral researcher, an adjunct professor, and, from 2002 to 2017, the editor-in-chief of the journal *Études/Inuit/Studies*. She has written on Arctic archaeology; Inuvialuit oral history; intellectual property and ethics in Indigenous research; and missionary-explorer Émile Petitot.

Mark Nuttall is professor and Henry Marshall Tory Chair in the Department of Anthropology at the University of Alberta. With a focus on climate change, resource development, and human-environment relations, he has carried out extensive research in Greenland, Canada, Alaska, Finland, and Scotland. He also holds a visiting professorship at the University of Greenland and the Greenland Institute of Natural Resources. He is the author or editor of several books, including *Climate, Society and Subsurface Politics in Greenland: Under the Great Ice* (2017), *The Scramble for the Poles: The Geopolitics of the Arctic and Antarctic* (2016; co-authored with Klaus Dodds), and *Anthropology and Climate Change: From Actions to Transformations* (2016; co-edited with Susan Crate). He is the Arctic regional editor of *The Polar Journal*.

Evon Peter is a student and researcher of the Gwich'in language. From 2014 to 2020, he served as vice chancellor for Rural, Community and Native Education at the University of Alaska Fairbanks (UAF) and is currently senior scientist at the university's Center for Alaska Native Health Research. A UAF alumnus, Peter is Neets'ąįį Gwich'in from Vashrąįį K'ǫǫ (Arctic Village), Alaska, where he spent three years as the tribal chief. He is a member of the board of directors of the Gwich'in Council International, which represents the interests of the Gwich'in Nation in the Arctic Council forum. His work has focused on incorporating Indigenous knowledge and practices into healing, leadership development, and, most recently, Alaska Native language programs. He holds a bachelor's degree in Alaska Native studies and a master's in rural development.

Kenneth L. Pratt is an anthropologist and ethnohistorian employed by the US Bureau of Indian Affairs and has forty years of experience investigating Alaska Native land claims. His research interests include the ethnohistory of southwestern and western Alaska, Indigenous place names, oral history, intergroup relations and territoriality, and Russian America. He holds a PhD in anthropology from the University of Alaska Fairbanks, is a research associate of the Smithsonian Institution's Arctic Studies Center in Washington, DC, and serves as co-editor of the *Alaska Journal of Anthropology.*

Louann Rank worked with Yup'ik communities of the Yukon-Kuskokwim Delta over a period of eighteen years. She travelled for village outreach as an administrator with Bethel Community Services and then with a community health project for the Yukon-Kuskokwim Health Corporation. Later, she became an assistant professor in the Department of Alaska Native and Rural Development at the University of Alaska Fairbanks.

William E. ("Bill") Simeone has lived in Alaska for fifty years. During that time he has worked as a VISTA volunteer in the Yup'ik community of St. Michael, a lay worker for the Episcopal Church in the Dene community of Tanacross, a construction worker on the Trans-Alaska Pipeline, and a paralegal for Alaska Legal Services. After receiving his PhD in anthropology from McMaster University, he worked as a consulting anthropologist, as a subsistence resource specialist, and as regional supervisor for the Division of Subsistence, Alaska Department of Fish and Game. Simeone has worked with the Ahtna for over twenty years on concerns related to fish and game issues, while also documenting many facets of Ahtna culture and history.

Felix St-Aubin lives in his family's community of Kangiqsualujjuaq, in Nunavik, and is employed to assist with maintenance at the local Ulluriaq School. He learned about the land from his late grandfather, Willie Emudluk, and his friend Kenny Angnatuk. Both men were experienced hunters and knew the land well. He encourages younger generations to go out on the land camping more often to keep Inuit traditions going. He has taken up photography as a hobby.

Williams Stolz specializes in the study of forest foods. He completed his master's thesis at Lakehead University in 2018 on the social economy of blueberry foraging in the context of the boreal forest ecosystem of northwestern Ontario.

Katerina Solovjova Wessels was born in Moscow and graduated from the Moscow College of Architecture with a master's degree in the theory and history of architecture. She moved to Anchorage, Alaska, in 1990 and worked for twenty-six years with the National Park Service's Shared Beringian Heritage Program. Wessels also continued to conduct archival research on Russian-American history, which culminated in the publication of *The Fur Rush: Essays and Documents on the History of Alaska at the End of the Eighteenth Century* (2002), a monograph co-authored with Aleksandra Vovnyanko that focuses on the early period of the Russian presence in Alaska. Wessels is currently the Council Coordination Division supervisor for the Office of Subsistence Management, US Fish and Wildlife Service, Alaska Region.

Index

Page numbers in *italics* refer to illustrations.